Letters on Yoga — IV

Transformation of Human Nature
in the Integral Yoga

Sri Aurobindo

Letters on Yoga

Volume IV

Sri Aurobindo Ashram
Pondicherry

First edition 1958
Fourth edition (revised and enlarged) 2014
Third impression 2019

Rs. 565

ISBN 978-81-7058-962-4

© Sri Aurobindo Ashram Trust 1958, 2014
Published by Sri Aurobindo Ashram Publication Department
Pondicherry 605 002
Web https://www.sabda.in

Printed at Sri Aurobindo Ashram Press, Pondicherry
PRINTED IN INDIA

Publisher's Note

Letters on Yoga — IV contains letters written by Sri Aurobindo on the transformation of human nature, mental, vital and physical, through the practice of the Integral Yoga. It also includes letters on the difficulties encountered in the practice of this Yoga. This volume is the last of four volumes of *Letters on Yoga*, arranged by the editors as follows:

    I. Foundations of the Integral Yoga
   II. Practice of the Integral Yoga
  III. Experiences and Realisations in the Integral Yoga
  IV. Transformation of Human Nature in the Integral Yoga

The letters in these volumes have been selected from the large body of letters that Sri Aurobindo wrote to disciples and others between 1927 and 1950. Other letters from this period are published in *Letters on Poetry and Art*, *The Mother with Letters on the Mother* and *Letters on Himself and the Ashram*, volumes 27, 32 and 35 of THE COMPLETE WORKS OF SRI AUROBINDO. Letters written before 1927 are reproduced in *Autobiographical Notes and Other Writings of Historical Interest*, volume 36 of THE COMPLETE WORKS.

During Sri Aurobindo's lifetime, relatively few of his letters were published. Three small books of letters on Yoga were brought out in the 1930s. A more substantial collection came out between 1947 and 1951 in a four-volume series entitled *Letters of Sri Aurobindo* (including one volume of letters on poetry and literature). In 1958, many more letters were included in the two large tomes of *On Yoga — II*. A further expanded collection in three volumes entitled *Letters on Yoga* was published in 1970 as part of the Sri Aurobindo Birth Centenary Library. The present collection, also entitled *Letters on Yoga*, constitutes volumes 28 – 31 of THE COMPLETE WORKS. These volumes incorporate previously published letters and contain many new ones as well. About one-third of the letters in the present volume were not published in the Centenary Library.

This volume is arranged by subject in four parts:

1. Sadhana on the Level of the Mind
2. Sadhana on the Level of the Vital
3. Sadhana on the Physical, Subconscient and Inconscient Levels
4. Difficulties in the Practice of the Integral Yoga

The texts of all the letters have been checked against the available manuscripts, typescripts and printed versions.

CONTENTS

PART ONE
SADHANA ON THE LEVEL OF THE MIND

Section One
The Mind and Sadhana

The Mind and Other Levels of Being
The Mind and the Divine Consciousness	5
The Mind and the Supermind	5
The Mind and Intuition	6
The Mind and Inspiration	7
The Mind and the Psychic	7
The Mind and the Lower Nature	9

Intellect and the Intellectual
Limitations of the Intellect	11
The Intellect, the Pure Reason and Knowledge	14
Intellect, Intellectual and Intelligence	15
The Intellectual Man and the Emotional Man	18

Mental Difficulties and the Need of Quietude
The Activity of the Mind	20
Imaginations	21
Confusion	22
Worry	23
Hastiness	23
Slowness	24
Opposing Points of View	25
Silliness	25
Analysis and Dissection	25
The Need of Quietude	27

The Physical Mind and Sadhana
The Activity of the Physical Mind	30
The Unsteadiness of the Physical Mind	33

CONTENTS

The Obscurity of the Physical Mind	34
Other Problems of the Physical Mind	35
The Physical Mind and the Lower Vital	37
The Physical Mind and the Psychic	38
The Physical Mind and Peace and Silence	39

Thought and Knowledge

Thoughts Come from Outside	40
Control of One's Thoughts	43
Thoughts and Words	47
The Idea and What Lies Behind It	47
Thought and Knowledge	48
Knowledge and Ignorance	48
Knowledge and the Divine Consciousness	49
Mental Knowledge and Knowledge from Above	49
Knowledge and Mental Questions	50
Understanding and the Higher Light	52
Knowledge and the Psychic	53
Knowledge and Mental Silence	54
Knowledge, Experience and Realisation	56

Section Two
Cultivation of the Mind in Yoga

Mental Development and Sadhana

The Development of the Mind	59
Reading and Sadhana	60
Reading What Is Helpful to the Sadhana	62
Reading and Detachment	64
Reading Novels and Newspapers	65

The Place of Study in Sadhana

Study and Sadhana	69
Study and Mental Development	69
School Studies and Yoga	71
The Study of Languages	71
The Study of Philosophy	73

CONTENTS

The Study of Logic	74
The Study of Science	75

The Power of Expression and Yoga

Verbal Expression	76
Expression and Language	76
Spoken and Written Expression	77
Writing and Sadhana	77
Poetry and Sadhana	78

Speech and Yoga

Outer Speech and the Inner Life	80
Talking and Dispersion of the Consciousness	81
Talking and Fatigue	82
Useless, Unnecessary or Light Speech	83
Control of Speech	85
Criticising Others	87
Gossip	88
Speaking the Truth	89
Mauna or Keeping Silence	92
Other Aspects of Speech Control	94

PART TWO
SADHANA ON THE LEVEL OF THE VITAL

Section One
The Vital Being and Sadhana

The Nature of the Vital

Living in the Vital	101
The Irrationality of the Vital	103
The Deceptiveness of the Vital	104
A Good Instrument But a Bad Master	105
Purification of the Vital	107
Discipline of the Vital	107
Surrender of the Vital	109
Conversion of the Vital	110

CONTENTS

Liberation of the Vital	111
The Higher Vital Movement	111
The Emergence of the True Vital	111
Vital Sincerity, Aspiration, Consecration	113
Peace and Quiet in the Vital	114

The Vital and Other Levels of Being
The Spirit and the Vital	116
The Higher Consciousness and the Vital	116
The Intuition and the Vital	120
The Psychic and the Vital	120
The Mind and the Vital	123
The Physical and the Vital	127

Wrong Movements of the Vital
The Phrase "Wrong Movements"	129
Vital Reactions	129
Vital Suggestions	130
Vital Restlessness	132
Vital Dryness	134
Vital Resistance	136
Vital Dissatisfaction and Non-Cooperation	138
Vital Disturbance and Revolt	140
Rejection of Wrong Vital Movements	143
Return of Vital Movements after Rejection	145
Alternation of Good and Bad Vital Conditions	148

The Lower Vital Being
The Decisive Ordeal of This Yoga	150
The Lower Vital Not Reasonable	156
The Resistance of the Lower Vital	157
Rejecting Wrong Movements of the Lower Vital	158
Avoiding Premature Engagement with the Lower Vital	164
Ananda and the Lower Vital	165
Aspiration and Offering in the Lower Vital	168
Peace and Calm in the Lower Vital	169

CONTENTS

Section Two
Vital Temperament

Cheerfulness and Happiness
Cheerfulness	173
Humour and Seriousness	174
Happiness and Contentment	175

Sorrow and Suffering
Joy and Sorrow	177
Sorrow and Pain and Suffering	177
Melancholy	180

Depression and Despondency
Discouragement	182
Depression	183
Depression Often Comes from Outside	185
Dealing With Depression	186
Depression and the Gospel of Sorrow	189
Despair and Despondency	206

Sentimentalism, Sensitiveness, Instability, Laxity
Sentimentalism	210
Sensitiveness	210
Shyness	213
Indecision and Instability	213
Laxity	214

Section Three
Vital Defects

Ego and Its Forms
Ego and Egoism	217
Ego in Different Parts of the Being	221
The Vital Ego	222
Rajasic and Tamasic Ego (Ahankara)	225
Ego-centricity	228
The Egoism of the Instrument and the Magnified Ego	230

CONTENTS

Getting Rid of the Ego and of Egoism	232
Getting Rid of the Ego Altogether	236
Selfishness	238
Ambition	239
Vanity	240
Pride and Self-Esteem	241
Self-Respect, Amour-Propre, Superiority	243
Jealousy and Abhiman	244
Wounded Feeling	247
Ingratitude	250

Desire
The Nature of Desire	251
The Small Desires of the Vital Physical	256
Desire and Need	257
Demand and Desire	258
Getting Rid of Desire	260
Desire and Suppression (Nigraha)	264

Anger and Violence
The Nature of Anger	267
Anger Comes from Outside	271
Anger and the Psychic	274
Vindictiveness and Cruelty	276
Violence	276

Fear
Fear and Yoga	278

Section Four
Human Relations in Yoga

Human Relations and the Spiritual Life
Relations with Others in Yoga	283
Love for Others and Love for the Divine	290
Family Ties and Duties	291
Relations between Parents and Children	293
Old Relations	293

CONTENTS

Friendship and Affection	294
Vital Love	298
Vital Love and Psychic Love	301
Personal Relations in Yoga	302
Universal Love and Personal Relations	304
Relations between Men and Women in Yoga	306
Loneliness	310

Interactions with Others and the Practice of Yoga

Cultivating Equality and Goodwill	312
Indifference to What Others Think or Say	313
Overcoming Dependence	315
Overcoming Attachment	316
Helping Others	317
Receiving Help from Others	320
Concern for Others	320
Sympathy for Others	321
Mothering Others	321
Working with Others	322
Dispersion through Contact with Others	323
Mixing with Others	325
Vital Expansiveness	326
Vital Interchange	328
Talking, Letter-Writing and Vital Interchange	333
Talking or Thinking about Others	334
The Drawing of Vital Forces by Others	335
Limiting Contacts with Others	337
Inner Detachment Preferable to Outer Withdrawal	338
Qualified Utility of Retirement for Sadhana	339
Dangers of Complete Retirement	341
Relations in Ordinary Life	344

Problems in Human Relations

Hatred and Dislike	346
Quarrels and Clashes	347
Fault-Finding and Criticism	351
Benefiting from Criticism	352

CONTENTS

PART THREE
SADHANA ON THE PHYSICAL, SUBCONSCIENT AND INCONSCIENT LEVELS

Section One
Sadhana on the Level of the Physical

The Transformation of the Physical
- The Need to Transform the Physical — 359
- Coming Down into the Physical — 363
- The Bringing of Realisation into the Physical — 366
- The Physical Sadhana — 367

Levels of the Physical Being
- The Physical Consciousness — 372
- The Mental Physical and the Vital Physical — 375
- The Material Consciousness — 378
- The Body Consciousness — 379
- The Body — 379
- Care for the Body — 381
- Weakness of the Body — 381
- Forgetfulness of the Body — 383
- The Physical and the Mind — 383
- The Physical and the Vital — 384
- The Physical and the Psychic — 385
- The Ascent of the Being — 387

Difficulties of the Physical Nature
- The Real Difficulty — 388
- Obstruction and Obscuration — 389
- Inertia — 391
- Dealing with Inertia and Tamas — 395
- The Difficulty of Eliminating Inertia and Tamas — 397
- Physical Fatigue — 399
- Giddiness — 400
- Restlessness — 400
- Habitual Movements and Old Habits — 401
- Mechanical Movements — 405

CONTENTS

Externalisation	406
Feelings of Incapacity and Discouragement	408
Stupidity and Ignorance	412
Agnosticism	414
Fear of Death	415

Section Two
Food, Sleep, Dreams and Sex

Food

The Yogic Attitude towards Food	419
Attachment to Food	421
Greed for Food	422
Taste	424
Sensitivity to Smell	425
Hunger	426
Quantity of Food	427
Fasting	430
Types of Food	433
Intoxicants	435

Sleep

The Yogic Attitude towards Sleep and Food	437
The Need of Sleep and Rest	438
The Amount of Sleep Needed	440
The Real Rest which Restores	441
Getting Good Sleep	443
Sleep during the Day	444
Sleep and Sadhana	444
Loss of Consciousness during Sleep	445
Conscious Sleep	448
Concentration before and after Sleep	450
Hearing Music after Waking	452
The Waking Mind and Sleep	452
Depression in Sleep	452

Dreams

All Sleep Full of Dreams	455

CONTENTS

Different Kinds of Dreams   455
Subconscient Dreams   459
Vital Dreams   460
Symbolic Dreams on the Vital Plane   463
Formations in Vital Dreams   466
Unpleasant or Bad Vital Dreams   467
Mental Dreams   469
People Seen in Dreams   470
The Waking and Dream States   470
Dream-Experiences   471
Remembering Dreams   473
Understanding the Meaning of Dreams   475
The Meaning of Some Dreams   477

Sex
The Role of Sex in Nature   485
Sex a Movement of General Nature   486
Sex and Ananda   488
Sex and Love   490
Sex and the New European Mystics   493
Sex-Indulgence and the Integral Yoga   494
Subtle Forms of Sex-Indulgence   499
Transformation of the Sex-Energy: The Theory of Brahmacharya   504
Mastery of the Sex-Impulse through Detachment   508
Mastery through a Change in the Consciousness   512
Mastery through the Force of Purity   512
Mastery through the Working of the Higher Consciousness and Force   513
Rejection of the Sex-Impulse from the Various Parts of the Being   514
Sex and the Subconscient   520
Tamasic Inertia and the Sex-Impulse   522
Sex-Thoughts and Imaginations   522
Sexual Difficulties among Men   524
Sex-Dreams and Emissions   524

CONTENTS

Physical Causes of Sex-Dreams and Emissions	528
Worry, Depression and Sex-Dreams and Emissions	529
Masturbation	531
Sexual Difficulties among Women	534
Social Contact and Sex	538
Touch and Sex	540
Celibacy	542
Marriage	543
The Relationship of Man and Woman	545
Skin Diseases and Sex	545

Section Three
Illness, Doctors and Medicines

Illness and Health

Illness and Yoga	549
Illness Not the Result of the Force	552
The Lower Nature, the Hostile Forces and Illness	553
The Suggestion of Illness	555
Curative Auto-Suggestion: The Coué Method	559
Faith, Confidence and Cure	561
Parts of the Being and Illness	562
Accepting and Enjoying Illness	565
Depression and Illness	567
Fear and Illness	568
Inertia and Illness	570
Anger and Illness	571
Work and Illness	571
Sleep and Illness	572
Pain	572
Separation and Detachment from Pain	575

Doctors and Medicines

Cure by Yogic Force and by Medicines	578
The Role of Doctors	581
Medical Systems	582
The Right Use of Medicines	584

CONTENTS

Specific Illnesses, Ailments and Other Physical Problems
    Cancer   586
    Tuberculosis   586
    Fever   587
    Influenza   587
    Head Cold   587
    Weak Vision   588
    Glaucoma   588
    Stammering   588
    Menstrual Problems   589
    Constipation   589
    Sciatica   589
    Growing Taller   590
    Bearing the Heat   590

Section Four
The Subconscient and the Inconscient
and the Process of Yoga

The Subconscient and the Integral Yoga
    The Change of the Subconscient   595
    The Subconscient, the Inner Being and the
        Outer Being   596
    The Subconscient and the Physical Being   597
    Habits and the Subconscient   600
    The Environmental Consciousness and the
        Subconscient   601
    The Rising Up of Things from the Subconscient   603
    Dealing with the Subconscient   608
    Dealing with Memories from the Subconscient   610
    Clearing or Emptying the Subconscient   611
    Illumining the Subconscient   611
    Psycho-analysis and the Integral Yoga   612

The Inconscient and the Integral Yoga
    The Descent of the Sadhana into the Inconscient   617

CONTENTS

PART FOUR
DIFFICULTIES IN THE PRACTICE OF THE INTEGRAL YOGA

Section One
Difficulties of the Path

The Difficulties of Yoga
- Difficulties and the Aim of Life — 625
- Difficulties and the Integral Yoga — 627
- Why Difficulties Come — 635

The Difficulties of Human Nature
- Obstacles of Human Nature — 638
- The Dual Nature of the Human Being — 639
- The Good and the Evil Persona — 647
- Outward Circumstances and Personal Defects — 653

Imperfections and Periods of Arrest
- Imperfections and Progress towards Perfection — 655
- Periods of Difficulty and Arrest — 663

Resistances, Sufferings and Falls
- Resistances in Sadhana — 667
- Pain and Suffering — 670
- Dangers, Falls and Failures — 674

Section Two
Overcoming the Difficulties of Yoga

The Right Attitude towards Difficulties
- The Sunlit Path and the Path of Darkness — 681
- Optimism and Pessimism — 692
- Treating Difficulties as Opportunities — 692
- The Certitude of Victory — 694

Steps towards Overcoming Difficulties
- Ways of Dealing with Difficulties — 696
- Facing Circumstances — 697
- Recognising One's Weaknesses — 699

CONTENTS

Stating One's Difficulties	703
Detaching Oneself from Difficulties	705
Rejecting Wrong Movements	707

Vigilance, Resolution, Will and the Divine Help

The Need of Vigilance	709
The Need of Resolution	712
The Need of Aspiration	713
The Need of Will	715
Lack of Will	719
Will and the Divine Force or Power	720
Personal Effort and the Divine Force or Power	722
Letting the Force Work	724
The Divine Help	724
The Divine Protection	724

Time and Change of the Nature

Time Needed for Change	726
Freedom from the Past	730
The Past and the Future	732

Dealing with Depression and Despondency

Despondency over Difficulties	734
Dwelling on One's Weaknesses or Difficulties	739
Raising Up Difficulties	743
Struggling with Difficulties	744
The Absurdity of Suicide	747

Section Three
The Opposition of the Hostile Forces

The Hostile Forces and the Difficulties of Yoga

The Existence of the Hostile Forces	757
The Function of the Hostile Forces	758
Testing Oneself against the Hostile Forces	761
The Divine Force and the Adverse Force	762
The Forces of the Lower Nature and the Hostile Forces	763

CONTENTS

Vital Resistance, Physical Inertia and the
    Hostile Forces   767
The Hostile Forces and Universal Forces   768
The Hostile Forces and the Spiritual Consciousness   768

Attacks by the Hostile Forces
Attacks Not Uncommon   769
Attacks Often Follow a Progress   770
Positive and Negative Means of Attack   776
Attacks through Suggestions   776
Attacks through Others   780

Dealing with Hostile Attacks
Fear of Attacks   782
Thinking Too Much about Attacks   782
Discouragement about Attacks   784
Rejection of Attacks   787
Detachment   792
Dissolution   792
Steadiness and Persistence   793
Peace and Purity   793
Faith and Surrender   794
Psychic Openness   795
Reliance on the Power or Force   796
Reliance on the Mother   797

Accidents, Possession, Madness
Accidents   800
Possession by Vital Forces   801
Neurasthenia   802
Hysteria   804
Epilepsy   805
Madness   806

NOTE ON THE TEXTS   813

INDEX   823

Part One

Sadhana on the Level of the Mind

Section One

The Mind and Sadhana

Chapter One
The Mind and Other Levels of Being

The Mind and the Divine Consciousness

The ways of the Divine are not like those of the human mind or according to our patterns and it is impossible to judge them or to lay down for Him what He shall or shall not do, for the Divine knows better than we can know. If we admit the Divine at all, both true reason and bhakti seem to me to be at one in demanding implicit faith and surrender.

*

To understand divine movements one must enter into the divine consciousness; till then faith and surrender are the only right attitude. How can the mind judge what is beyond all its measures?

The Mind and the Supermind

The less pet ideas are petted and cherished, the better for the supramental Yoga. The mind is always building up ideas, some of which are wrong, some a mixture of truth and error, some true in their way, but true only in a certain field or in certain conditions or for some people, and it proceeds not only to make "pets" of them, but to try to impose them as universal and absolute truths or general standards which everybody must follow. The mind is a rigid instrument: it finds it difficult to adapt itself to the greater plasticity of the play of life or the freedom of the play of the Spirit. It wants to catch hold of either or both of these spontaneous powers and cut them into its own measures. It poses as the mediator and interpreter between life and the spirit; but it knows neither; it only knows itself and its own constructions out of life and its own deformations or half reflections of the truth of the Spirit. Only the supermind can be a true mediator and interpreter. But if you want the supramental

Light, you must not tie yourself to mental ideas, but draw back from them and observe them with an impartial equality in the silence of the spirit. When the supramental Light touches them, it will put them in their place and finally replace them by the true truth of things.

The Mind and Intuition

For the human thinking mind there are always many sides to everything and it decides according to its own bent or preference or its habitual ideas or some reason that presents itself to the intellect as the best. It gets the real truth only when something else puts a higher light into it — when the psychic or the intuition touches it and makes it feel or see.

*

It is very usual for intuitive suggestions to come like that and the mind to disregard them. It is because the mind is too accustomed to follow its own process and cannot recognise or have confidence in the intuition when it comes. The mind has to learn to look at these things when they come and give them value if experience confirms their truth.

*

Yes, the active mind in people with a very intellectual turn can be an obstacle to the deeper more silent spiritual movement. Afterwards when it is turned into the higher thought (intuitive or overmental) it becomes on the contrary a great force.

*

The intuitive perception or discrimination is self-sufficient — it does not need any reasoning or process of thought to justify it. The intellectual depends on data and steps, even if the steps are hurried over or the data rapidly seized and swallowed into the intelligence.

*

It [*the perception of an intuitivised mind*] is when, instead of seeing things as they appear to the external mind and senses, one begins to see things about them with a subtler physical mind and sense — e.g. seeing intuitively what is to be done, how to do it, what the object (even so-called inanimate objects) wants or needs, what is likely to happen next (or sometimes sure to happen), what forces are at play on the physical plane etc. etc. Even the body becomes intuitively conscious in this way, feels without being told by the mind what it has to do, what it has to avoid, what is near it or coming to it (though unseen) etc. etc.

*

The heart has its intuitions as well as the mind and these are as true as any mental perceptions. But neither all feelings nor all mental perceptions nor all rational conclusions can be true.

The Mind and Inspiration

There are different kinds of knowledge. One is inspiration, i.e. something that comes out of the Knowledge planes like a flash and opens up the mind to the Truth in a moment. That is inspiration. It easily takes the form of words as when a poet writes or a speaker speaks, as people say, from inspiration.

*

The pure inspiration and conception is something quite different [*from ordinary thought*] — it comes from deep within or from high above. This is the lower vital mind at work making formations. When the calmness is there all sorts of things may rise on the surface — they have not to be accepted, but simply looked at. In time the calmness will be so developed as to quell the vital and outer mind also and in that complete quietude the true perceptions will come.

The Mind and the Psychic

Most people begin with the power [*of Yoga*] working in the

mind — it is only when the mind and vital have been changed to some extent that the psychic is ready to come forward.

*

The chief obstacle in you is the mind. If you can quiet your mind and give the psychic being a chance, that will be your spiritual salvation. Your mind is inordinately active, too full of questionings, too shrewd, worldly and practical, too much given to doubt and self-defence. All that is very useful in worldly life, it helps to bring success, but it is not the way to succeed in Yoga. No doubt in Yoga, the critical rational mind (self-critical as well as critical of things outside you) is an element that has its value so long as the true inner discrimination does not come; but of itself it cannot carry you on the way, it will only make your progress slow and stumbling. There must be something in you that will open itself directly to the Truth and Light. The unregenerated vital being of man cannot do that because it demands of the higher Power that it shall satisfy the vital desires, demands, ambitions, vanity, pride, etc., before it will accept the Truth. The unillumined mind also cannot do it because it refuses to recognise the Truth unless the Truth first satisfies its own judgments, ideas, opinions, critical or conventional standards, — unless in a word the Truth consents to narrow itself into the moulds of the mind's own ignorance. It is the psychic being alone that turns to the Truth directly, feels it instinctively behind all appearances and in spite of all disguises, accepts it without any egoistic demand or condition, is ready to serve it without reserve or refusal. It is the psychic being also that can at once feel and reject all imitations of the Truth, all shows, all pretences.

*

In the West the physical mind is too dominant, so that the psychic does not so easily get a chance — except of course in exceptional people.

*

It is the thoughts of the outer mind that have to be refused, the suggestions and ideas that end by disturbing the sadhana. There are also a number of thoughts of all kinds that have no interest, but which the mind is accustomed to allow to come as a habit, mechanically, — these sometimes come up when one tries to be quiet. They must be allowed to pass away without attending to them until they run down and the mind becomes still; to struggle with them and try to stop them is no use, there must be only a quiet rejection. On the other hand if thoughts come up from within, from the psychic, thoughts of the Mother, of divine love and joy, perceptions of truth etc., these of course must be permitted, as they help to make the psychic active.

*

When it [*one's inner perception*] is at the heart, it is probable that the psychic or at least the psychic mental thought is replacing the ordinary mental. Yogic thought comes from two sources, the psychic behind the heart and the higher consciousness from above the head.

*

Your nature has always been very self-centred and the mind active — in such a nature it is easier for the higher mind to act than for the psychic.

The Mind and the Lower Nature

It is necessary first to found the higher consciousness in the mind and heart. To deal with the lower nature before that means to fall into the struggle and confusion and disorder of the vital, for it all comes up. With the mind and heart prepared, one can deal with the vital without all that superfluous trouble.

*

So long as the mind is not entirely transformed, that is, penetrated and changed by the spiritual consciousness, things from below can always run into it more or less and dim the vision of the higher levels. If you can keep the vision always, even though dimmed, it is already a great progress.

*

There is only one sadhana for all parts, not a separate mental sadhana, vital sadhana or physical sadhana — but the action of the sadhana is applied sometimes separately to each part; sometimes on the contrary the action is on the mental and vital together, or vital and physical together, or all three together. But it is the same sadhana always.

Chapter Two

Intellect and the Intellectual

Limitations of the Intellect

Intellect is part of Mind and an instrument of half-truth like the rest of the Mind.

*

Intellectual activities are not part of the inner being — the intellect is the outer mind.

*

Its [*the intellect's*] function is to reason from the perceptions of the mind and senses, to form conclusions and to put things in logical relation with each other. A well-trained intellect is a good preparation of the mind for greater knowledge, but it cannot itself give the Yogic knowledge or know the Divine — it can only have ideas about the Divine, but having ideas is not knowledge. In the course of the sadhana intellect has to be transformed into the higher mind which is itself a passage towards the true knowledge.

*

It is no use trying to decide the things of the Spirit by the power and in the light of the intellect. The intellect can only reason and infer and its reasonings are partial and its inferences vitiated by error. One has to awaken the divinations in the soul, the psychic being, and wait for a higher knowledge which comes from above.

It is not safe to listen to or be influenced by the mental of other sadhaks. The Yoga aims at union with the Divine which will bring a spiritual oneness with other sadhaks, but a oneness in the Divine, in the Truth, not in the ignorance of the mind and the vital.

*

It is not by intellect that one can progress in the Yoga, but by psychic and spiritual receptivity — as for knowledge and true understanding it grows in sadhana by the growth of the intuition, not of the physical intellect.

*

The intellect can be as great an obstacle as the vital when it chooses to prefer its own constructions to the Truth.

*

What you have said is perfectly right. To see the Truth does not depend on a big intellect or a small intellect. It depends on being in contact with the Truth and the mind silent or quiet to receive it. The biggest intellects can make errors of the worst kind and confuse Truth and falsehood, if they have not the contact with Truth or the direct experience.

*

The intellect of most men is extremely imperfect, ill trained, half developed — therefore in most the conclusions of the intellect are hasty, ill founded and erroneous or, if right, right more by chance than by merit or right working. The conclusions are formed without knowing the facts or the correct or sufficient data, merely by a rapid inference and the process by which it comes from the premises to the conclusion is usually illogical or faulty — the process being unsound by which the conclusion is arrived at, the conclusion also is likely to be fallacious. At the same time the intellect is usually arrogant and presumptuous, confidently asserting its imperfect conclusions as the truth and setting down as mistaken, stupid or foolish those who differ from them. Even when fully trained and developed, the intellect cannot arrive at absolute certitude or complete truth, but it can arrive at one aspect or side of it and make a reasonable or probable affirmation; but untrained, it is a quite insufficient instrument, at once hasty and peremptory and unsafe and unreliable.

*

Intellectual statements about these things do not lead very far, for the basis of true statement is a consciousness which sees things not as the mind sees them but with a direct inner view, and unless one enters into that consciousness itself, it is difficult really to understand the intellectual statement. It is by sadhana only that one can enter into that consciousness in which one sees the divine reality behind things.

*

The point is that people take no trouble to see whether their intellect is giving them right thoughts, right conclusions, right views on things and persons, right indications about their conduct or course of action. They have their idea and accept it as truth or follow it simply because it is *their* idea. Even when they recognise that they have made mistakes of the mind, they do not consider it of any importance nor do they try to be more careful mentally than before. In the vital field people know that they must not follow their desires or impulses without check or control, they know that they ought to have a conscience or a moral sense which discriminates what they can or should do and what they cannot or should not do; in the field of intellect no such care is taken. Men are supposed to follow their intellect, to have and assert their own ideas right or wrong without any control; the intellect, it is said, is man's highest instrument and he must think and act according to its ideas. But this is not true; the intellect needs an inner light to guide, check and control it quite as much as the vital. There is something above the intellect which one has to discover and the intellect should be only an intermediary for the action of that source of true Knowledge.

*

There is no reason why one should not receive through the thinking mind, as one receives through the vital, the emotional and the body. The thinking mind is as capable of receiving as these are, and, since it has to be transformed as well as the rest, it must be trained to receive, otherwise no transformation of it could take place.

It is the ordinary unenlightened activity of the intellect that is an obstacle to spiritual experience, just as the ordinary unregenerated activity of the vital or the obscure stupidly obstructive consciousness of the body is an obstacle. What the sadhak has to be specially warned against in the wrong processes of the intellect is, first, any mistaking of mental ideas and impressions or intellectual conclusions for realisation; secondly, the restless activity of the mere mind, *cañcalaṁ manaḥ*, which disturbs the spontaneous accuracy of psychic and spiritual experience and gives no room for the descent of the true illuminating knowledge or else deforms it as soon as it touches or even before it fully touches the human mental plane. There are also of course the usual vices of the intellect, — its leaning towards sterile doubt instead of luminous reception and calm enlightened discrimination; its arrogance claiming to judge things that are beyond it, unknown to it, too deep for it by standards drawn from its own limited experience; its attempts to explain the supraphysical by the physical or its demand for the proof of higher and occult things by the criterions proper to Matter and to mind in Matter; others also too many to enumerate here. Always it is substituting its own representations and constructions and opinions for the true knowledge. But if the intellect is surrendered, open, quiet, receptive, there is no reason why it should not be a means of reception of the light or an aid to the experience of spiritual states and to the fullness of an inner change.

The Intellect, the Pure Reason and Knowledge

The intellect is made up of imaginations, perceptions, inferences. The pure reason is quite another thing, but only a few are able to use it. As for knowledge, — in Yoga it comes first from the higher mind, but even that does not see the whole Truth, only sides of it.

*

Pure reason deals with things in themselves, ideas, concepts, the essential nature of things. It lives in the world of ideas. It is philosophic and metaphysical in its nature.

Intellect, Intellectual and Intelligence

All depends on the meaning you attach to words used — it is a matter of nomenclature. Ordinarily one says a man has intellect if he can think well — the nature and process and field of the thought do not matter. If you take intellect in that sense, then you can say that intellect has different strata and Ford belongs to one stratum of intellect, Einstein to another — Ford has a practical and executive business intellect, Einstein a scientific discovering and theorising intellect. But Ford too in his own field theorises, invents, discovers. Yet would you call Ford an intellectual or a man of intellect? I would prefer to use for the general faculty of mind the word intelligence. Ford has a great and forceful practical intelligence, keen, quick, successful, dynamic. He has a brain that can deal with thoughts also, but even there his drive is towards practicality. He believes in rebirth (metempsychosis), for instance, not for any philosophic reason, but because it explains life as a school of experience in which one gathers more and more experience and develops by it. Einstein has on the other hand a great discovering scientific intellect, not like Marconi a powerful practical inventive intelligence for the application of scientific discovery. All men have of course an "intellect" of a kind, all for instance can discuss and debate (for which you say rightly intellect is needed); but it is only when one rises to the realm of ideas and moves freely in it that you say, "This man has an intellect." Address an assembly of peasants, you will find if you give them scope that they can put to you points and questions which may often leave the parliamentary debater panting. But we are content to say that these peasants have much practical intelligence.

The power to discuss and debate is, as I say, a common human faculty — and habit. Perhaps it is here that man begins to diverge from the animal; for animals have much intelligence — many animals and even insects — even some rudimentary power of practical reasoning, but so far as we know, they don't meet and put their ideas about things side by side or sling them at each other in a debate,[1] as even the most ignorant human can do and very animatedly does. There too is the beginning of intellect — for the reasons you allege. Also for the reason that it is a common faculty of the race, it can be specialised, so much so that a man whom it is dangerous to cross in debate in the field of literature or of science or of philosophy may yet make a fool of himself and wallow contentedly in a quagmire of blunders and fallacies if he discusses politics or economy or, let us say, spirituality or Yoga. His only salvation is the blissful depth of his ignorance which prevents him from seeing what a mess he has made. Again a man may be a keen legal or political debater, — the two very commonly go together, — yet no intellectual. I admit that a man must have some logical intellect to debate well. But after all the object of debate is to win, to make your point and you may do that even if your point is false; success, not truth, is the aim of debate. So I admit what you say, but with reservations.

I agree also that labels are unsatisfactory — even when applied to less developed persons; what we really do is to pick out something prominent and label with that as if it were all the person. But classification is impossible without that and man's intellect is driven always to classify, fix distinctions, set apart with a label. The philosophers have pointed out that Science does that too rigidly and in doing so cuts falsely across the truth of Nature. But if we don't do that, we can't have any Science.

*

X asked me the question and I answered it on the basis of the current meaning of "intellect" and "intellectual". People in ordinary speech do not make any distinction between intellect and intelligence, though of course it is quite true that a man may have a good or even a fine intelligence without being an intellectual. But ordinarily all thinking is attributed to the "intellect"; an intellectual therefore is a man whose main business or activity it is to think about things — a philosopher, a poet, a

---

[1] Perhaps the crows do in the "Crow Parliament" sometimes?

scientist, a critic of art and literature or of life, are all classed together as intellectuals. A theorist on economy and politics is an intellectual, a politician or a financier is not, unless he theorises on his own subject or is a thinker on another.

Y's distinction is based on those I have made here, but these distinctions are not current in ordinary speech, except one or two and those even in a very imperfect way. If I go by these distinctions, then the intellectuals will no longer be called intellectuals but thinkers and creators — except a certain class of them. An intellectual or intellectual thinker will then be one who is a thinker by his reason or mainly by his reason — e.g. Bertrand Russell, Bernard Shaw, Wells etc. Tagore thinks by vision, imagination, feeling or by intuition, not by the reason — at least that is true of his writings. C. R. Das himself would not be an intellectual; in politics, literature and everything else he was an "intuitive" and "emotive" man. But, as I say, these would be distinctions not ordinarily current. In ordinary parlance Tagore, Das and everybody else of the kind would all be called intellectuals. The general mind does not make these subtle distinctions: it takes things in the mass, roughly and it is right in doing so, for otherwise it would lose itself altogether.

As for barristers etc., a man to succeed as a barrister must have legal knowledge and the power to apply it. It is not necessary that he should be a thinker even in his own subject or an intellectual. It is the same with all professional men — doctors, engineers etc. etc.: they may be intellectuals as well as successful in their profession, but they need not be.

P. S. Argument properly speaking needs some power of logical intellect; but it can be specialised in a certain line. The power of arguing does not by itself make a man an intellectual.

*

X's main grievance with respect to the intellectuals is that he is cut off from all discussion of mental things and mental stimulus and so his mental energies are becoming atrophied. But a man who has a mental life ought surely not to be dependent on others for it, since that life is found within — there ought to be springs

The Intellectual Man and the Emotional Man

within that flow by their own force.

If the intellectual [*man*] will always have a greater wideness and vastness [*than the emotional man*], how can we be sure that he will have an equal fervour, depth and sweetness with the emotional man?

It may be that *homo intellectualis* will remain wider and *homo psychicus* will remain deeper in heart.

*

Please do not confuse the higher knowledge and mental knowledge. The intellectual man will be able to give a wider and more orderly expression to what higher knowledge he gets than the *homo psychicus*; but it does not follow he will have more of it. He will have that only if he rises to an equal width and plasticity and comprehensiveness of the higher knowledge planes. In that case he will replace his mental by his above-mental capacity. But for many intellectuals, so-called, their intellectuality may be a stumbling block as they bind themselves with mental conceptions or stifle the psychic fire under the heavy weight of rational thought. On the other hand I have seen comparatively uneducated people expressing higher knowledge with an astonishing fullness and depth and accuracy which the stumbling movements of their brain could never have allowed one to suppose possible. Therefore why fix beforehand by the mind what will or will not be possible when the Above-mind reigns? What the mind conceives as "must be" need not be the measure of the "will be". Such and such a *homo intellectualis* may turn out to be a more fervent God-lover than the effervescent emotional man; such and such an emotionalist may receive and express a wider knowledge than his intellect or even the intellect of the intellectual man could have harboured or organised. Let us not bind the phenomena of the higher consciousness by the possibilities and probabilities of a lower plane.

*

An unintellectual mind cannot bring down the Knowledge? What then about Ramakrishna? Do you mean to say that the majority of the sadhaks here who have not learned logic and are ignorant of philosophy will never get Knowledge?

*

Ramakrishna was an uneducated, nonintellectual man, yet his expression of knowledge was so perfect that the biggest intellects bowed down before it.

Chapter Three

Mental Difficulties and the Need of Quietude

The Activity of the Mind

This [*restless thinking*] is what we call the activity of the mind, which always comes in the way of the concentration and tries to create doubt and dispersion of the energies. It can be got rid of in two ways, by rejecting it and pushing it out, till it remains as an outside force only — by bringing down the higher peace and light into the physical mind.

*

It is the Light or the Force which comes from beyond the mind that keeps the mind truly concentrated. Otherwise the mind is naturally restless, unfixed, constantly changing from one thing to another.

*

Then for the tumultuous activity of the mind which prevents your concentration. But that or else a more tiresome obstinate grinding mechanical activity is always the difficulty when one tries to concentrate and it takes a long time to get the better of it. That or the habit of sleep which prevents either the waking concentration or the conscious samadhi or the absorbed and all-excluding trance which are the three forms that Yogic concentration takes. But it is surely ignorance of Yoga, its processes and its difficulties that makes you feel desperate and pronounce yourself unfit for ever because of this quite ordinary obstacle. The insistence of the ordinary mind and its wrong reasonings, sentiments and judgments, the random activity of the thinking mind in concentration or its mechanical activity, the slowness of response to the veiled or the initial touch are the ordinary obstacles the mind imposes just as pride, ambition, vanity, sex, greed, grasping of things for one's own ego are the difficulties and obstacles offered by the vital. As the vital difficulties can be fought down and conquered, so can the mental. Only one has to see that these are the inevitable obstacles and neither cling to them nor be terrified or overwhelmed because they are there. One has to persevere till one can stand back from the mind as from the vital and feel the deeper and larger mental and vital Purushas within one which are capable of silence, capable of a straight receptivity of the true Word and Force as of the true silence. If the nature takes the way of fighting down the difficulties first, then the first half of the way is long and tedious and the complaint of the want of the response of the Divine arises. But really the Divine is there all the time, working behind the veil as well as waiting for the recognition of his response and for the response to the response to be possible.

*

If the thoughts are not regarded as one's own, it should become possible to look at them from a silent mind, detached and separate from the thoughts.

*

It is more difficult to separate oneself from the mind when it is active than from the body. It is quite possible however for one part of the mind to stand back and remember the Mother and receive her presence and the force while the other is busy with the work. Meanwhile what you are doing is the right way. Remember always that whatever the difficulties the Mother's love is with you and will lead you through.

Imaginations

The first necessity is not to allow yourself to be upset by this difficulty [*of a restless mind full of imaginations*]. It is one that often occurs, for these imaginations come easily to the human mind, but they can be got rid of in time, and even in a comparatively short time if one faces them with calm resolution, detachment and patience. It is simply a habit that has taken hold of the mind — it can be dissolved and cease to recur.

It will help if you can cease to regard them as creations of your own mind — they are not, they are foreign matter thrown on it from outside. The physical mind which they attack has to learn to see and feel them as something foreign and refuse to accept them. Then they will go. For that you will receive my help and the Mother's. Keep yourself inwardly confident and open, all will be done.

*

The mind does not record things as they are, but as they appear to it. It catches parts, omits others; afterwards the memory and imagination mix together and make a quite different representation of it.

Confusion

The mind has to be remoulded and changed, but in a definite way, becoming more and more full of the Light and Truth. In that way it will begin to take on a luminous consistency and become "stronger and stronger till it is dependable". A mere confused instability is not the right way. When the confusion comes, you should remain quiet, reject it and call in the Mother's light and force.

*

Who does not feel the confusion or ignorance somewhere in himself so long as the full light and the true force have not come? Your mistake is to be always thinking about the confusion and struggling with it, dwelling on it, magnifying it by thinking about it, treating it as if it were the only thing real and true. When you feel the force, turn to the force and let it act — it is that force and not you or your brooding and struggles that can get rid of the confusion and darkness. What is the use of examining whether your faith and confidence are of the "true" kind or not? To feel the force, be quiet, let it act is all that is needed.

*

If you can stand back from all this [*mental commotion*] and observe calmly and clearly and precisely, this confusion of voices ought to stop.[1] It is only a part of the mind that is like that. But you get absorbed by this part and then it looks as if it were the whole mind that is confused. If you stand back from it and observe it with your *real* mind, then this small part will lose its power to confuse.

Worry

It is simply the habit of the mind when troubles come to worry about them. You must train your mind to remain calm and equal when troubles come — to do the thing that has to be done and rely on the Divine Power.

Hastiness

In the mind there is always a certain haste to seize quickly at what is presented to it as the highest Truth. That is unavoidable, but the more one is still in mind, the less this will distort things.

*

The attempt of the mind and vital to seize on the experience is always one of the chief obstacles.

*

It [*impulsive action*] is not any weakness of the will or the result of passivity, but an overhaste of decision upon a mental impulse. That is the usual movement of the mind — and it is sometimes the fruit of a certain kind of sattwic zeal. But owing to the haste there is not sufficient time taken to see the opposite side, the defects of the decision taken, or the possible objection that

---

[1] *The correspondent kept hearing the voices of persons who shouted abuses at him.* — Ed.

might be made. Peace is the basis, but into it must come the action of a certain Light from above which shows each thing in its right proportions as a whole — for the mind at its best is incomplete and usually one-sided in its perceptions without the guidance of such a higher Light.

*

It is necessary to curb the mind's impatience a little. Knowledge is progressive — if it tries to leap up to the top at once, it may make a hasty construction which it will have afterwards to undo. The knowledge and experience must come by degrees and step by step.

Slowness

It is as you say and there is a certain element of inertia in it; the slowness of the mind and the nature to seize something new to it, the non-distinction between what is true and to be held and what is not true and not to be held, is due to a certain absence of quickness of movement in the being. But each human quality has its advantages and disadvantages. A quick mind is often unstable — it catches but does not keep; or it catches but only superficially and thinks it has got everything when it has got only a little and not enough. A slow mind that takes slowly but holds on to what it has got, can be slow but sure in its movement. The disadvantage of it is obstinacy, unwillingness to admit what it should receive, unwillingness to let go what is mistaken. Its advantage is steadiness, a firm hold when it gets the right thing. Therefore you should not mind if it takes long to absorb and hold the new consciousness — as a matter of fact, to hold takes long with everybody. Once you have got it well established, your nature is likely to hold it firmly. As for the lack of discrimination, that is only in the physical and lower vital mind — within you there is something that can discriminate, the psychic. The only thing is to get it out and keep it in front. When you had the psychic state or rather a touch of it from time to time, you saw things very clearly. When the psychic state fixes itself, that discrimination also will become a part of the nature.

Opposing Points of View

Don't accept and hug and dandle these [*conflicting*] ideas. Everybody has thoughts opposing each other — it is the very nature of mind — one has to draw back from all that and fix on the straight things alone that lead to the Divine. The rest one must treat as external rubbish.

*

Many things are bad only in the way people look at them. Things which you consider all right, other people call bad; what you think to be bad, others find quite natural.

*

As for facts each mind always arranges them in its own way. It is a well-known phenomenon which psychologists constantly emphasise that each mind arranges facts according to its own impressions, predilections, convenience and, while this may be partly done with a conscious twist, conscious omissions and additions, it is quite or as often and more often done without any wilful intentions and by a sort of subconscious selection in the mental hinterland. That is why no three witnesses of an incident can give the same account of it — unless of course they have talked it over together — each tells a different story.

Silliness

People are exceedingly silly — but I suppose they can't help themselves. The more I observe humanity, the more that forces itself upon me — the abysses of silliness of which its mind is capable.

Analysis and Dissection

What the Mother spoke of was not self-analysis nor dissection.

Analysis and dissection are mental things which can deal with the inanimate or make the live dead — they are not spiritual methods. What the Mother spoke of was not analysis, but a seeing of oneself and of all the living movements of the being and the nature, a vivid observation of the personalities and forces that move on the stage of our being, their motives, their impulses, their potentialities — an observation quite as interesting as the seeing and understanding of a drama or a novel — a living vision and perception of how things are done in us which brings also a living mastery over this inner universe. Such things become dry only when one deals with them with the analytic and ratiocinative mind, not when one deals with them thus seeingly and intuitively as a movement of life. If you had that observation (from the inner spiritual, not the outer intellectual and ethical viewpoint), then it would be comparatively easy for you to get out of your difficulties; for instance you would find at once where this irrational impulse to flee away came from and it would not have any hold upon you. Of course, all that can only be done to the best effect when you stand back from the play of your nature and become the Witness-Control or the Spectator-Actor-Manager. But that is what happens when you take this kind of self-seeing posture.

*

You stick to your intellectual-ethical version of the inner self-vision? Dry? policeman? criminal? Great Lord! If it were that, it would cease to be self-vision at all — for in the true self-vision there is no policemanship and no criminaldom at all. All that belongs to the intellectual-ethical virtue-and-sin dodge which is only a mental construction of practical value for the outward life but not a truth of real inner values. In the true self-vision we see only harmonies and disharmonies and set the wrong notes right and replace them by the true notes. But I say that for the sake of truth, not to persuade you to start the self-vision effort; for if you did with these ideas of it, you would inevitably start it on the policeman basis and get into trouble. Besides, evidently, you prefer in the Yoga to be the piano and not the pianist, which is all right but involves total self-giving and the intervention of the supreme musician and harmonist. May it be so.

I am glad to know that your vital has been frightened into acquiescence in self-giving — even if only by the imaginary horror of being obliged to become the policeman of yourself. But to explain why these contradictions existed in you one has to have recourse to this very business of harmonies and disharmonies and the inner knowledge. You were in fact a piano played on by several pianists at a time each with his own different musical piece to play! In plain words and without images, every man is full of these contradictions because he is one person, no doubt, but made up of different personalities — the perception of multiple personality is becoming well-known to psychologists now — who very commonly disagree with each other. So long as one does not aim at unity in a single dominant intention, like that of seeking and self-dedication to the Divine, they get on somehow together, alternating or quarrelling or muddling through or else one taking the lead and compelling the others to take a minor part — but once you try to unite them in one aim, then the trouble becomes evident. One element wanted the Divine from the first, another wanted music, literature, poetry, a third wanted life at its best, a fourth wanted life — well, not at its best. Finally there was another element which wanted life not at all, but was rather disgusted with it and wanted either a better (diviner) life or something better than life. It was this element evidently that created the *vairāgya* and in the struggle between that and the life-partisans, a black element stole in (not one of the personalities, but a formation, a dark intrusion from outside), which wanted to turn the whole thing into a drama or tragedy of despair — despair of life but despair of the Divine also. That has to be rejected, the rest changed and harmonised. That is the only true explanation of the whole difficulty in your nature.

The Need of Quietude

There is no possibility of doing this Yoga, if one cannot give himself to the Divine Power and trust to its workings. If one lives only in the mind and its questioning and ideas, it is not possible. The test of capacity is to be able to quiet the mind, to feel a greater Divine Power at work in one, the Power of the Mother, and to be able to trust to it and aid its workings by the rejection of all that contradicts them in the nature.

*

To quiet your mind means to stop thinking about the things that disturb you and let the peace and power manifest themselves and work. The "living inside" will come of itself in that case — that is to say, you will feel the inner peace and the consciousness that comes with it more and more as yourself and all else as something outer and superficial.

*

How can the mind find out or decide what is the right thing to do for your sadhana? The more it is active in that way, the more confusion there will be. In sadhana the mind has to be quiet, fixed in aspiration towards the Divine — the true experience and change will come in the quietude of the mind from within and from above.

*

It is also a mistake to take quietude for callousness. If you are no longer disturbed by what people say or do, then that is a great progress. If you have no abhiman against the Mother, that also is surely very desirable. Abhiman, disturbance etc. may be signs of life, but of a vital, not of the inner life. They must quiet down and give room for the inner life. At first the result may be a neutral quiet, but one has often to pass through that to arrive at a more positive new consciousness. When the mind thus falls quiet the thoughts of the past, all sorts of repetitive or mechanical thoughts begin to rise up — these come from the physical mind or the subconscient. One has to refuse them and let them pass away, aspiring for the complete mental quietude in which the new consciousness can reveal itself little by little. Remain firm and quiet with the right will in you and let the

Force do its work. That will may not bear recognisable fruit at once, but adhere to it and the fruit will come.

*

You should not belittle the inner quietness by calling it a foolish kind of quietness — quietness in itself, knowing or unknowing, is to be valued, for it means that even in the midst of confusion a basis has still been kept. The understanding is at present covered over by a remnant of the old ignorance and confusion, but if a fundamental quietude is maintained or remains of itself, that will make it easier for this recurrence to pass.

As for the thought of your mother, it is always a symbol in your consciousness of the old nature and the old life — that is why it gets force when the confusion comes.

Remain firm and the cloud will pass and the true consciousness reassert itself with more firmness and vigour.

*

Not to allow the mind to bubble up with all sorts of ideas and feelings etc. but to remain quiet and learn to think and feel only what is true and right.[2]

---

[2] *The correspondent asked Sri Aurobindo how to "meet things without any superficial and unnecessary reaction". — Ed.*

Chapter Four
The Physical Mind and Sadhana

The Activity of the Physical Mind

Activity of the physical mind is not a new thing that needs to take root. It has been there very well rooted since you began your human evolution in the primaeval forests.

*

What you have now seen and describe in your letter is the ordinary activity of the physical mind which is full of ordinary habitual and constantly recurrent thoughts and is always busy with external objects and activities. What used to trouble you before was the vital mind which is different, — for that is always occupied with emotions, passions, desires, reactions of all kinds to the contacts of life and the behaviour of others. The physical mind also can be responsive to these things but in a different way — its nature is less that of desire than of habitual activity, small common interests, pains and pleasures. If one tries to control or suppress it, it becomes more active.

To deal with this mind two things are necessary, (1) not so much to try to control or fight with or suppress it as to stand back from it: one looks at it and sees what it is but refuses to follow its thoughts or run about among the objects it pursues, remaining at the back of the mind quiet and separate; (2) to practise quietude and concentration in this separateness, until the habit of quiet takes hold of the physical mind and replaces the habit of these small activities. This of course takes time and can only come by practice. What you propose to do is therefore the right thing.

*

The mechanical movements are always more difficult to stop by the mental will, because they do not in the least depend upon reason or any mental justification but are founded upon association or else a mere mechanical memory and habit.

*

This mechanical putting out of the thoughts happens to everybody at all times and it is especially strong in the physical mind — one has not to be upset by it, but go on quietly drawing the mind in, for if one does that, the obstacle after a time will diminish and one can then remain inside with the greater part of the consciousness, even if there are some wandering thoughts. So long as there is interest in outward things this can only be done for short periods, — but if there is not any strong interest, then the habit becomes purely mechanical and it can be got over in a shorter time. Its entire disappearance comes only when there is a complete silence in the being, but even before complete disappearance, one can arrive at a point when, in spite of it, one can go inside at will and remain there.

*

This going out of the mind and this siege of thoughts is a difficulty which everybody has to meet for a time or often when he wants to concentrate within. You should not allow it to depress you or make you hopeless or lead you to think that there is some special disability in you from which others do not suffer. One has to keep one's poise, recognise it as an inherent difficulty of the nature of mind (physical mind), one which has to be overcome and will be overcome in time. In that way one feels the pressure of these obstacles less and gets over it sooner than if one gets distressed or upset by them or takes them for a sign of incapacity for the Yoga.

*

It is the usual fit and the same round of thoughts mechanically repeated that you always get in these fits. These thoughts have no light in them and no truth, for the physical mind which engenders this routine wheel of suggestions is shut up in surface appearances and knows nothing of deeper truth or the things of the spirit. There is plenty of "increment", but with this superficial part of the physical mind it is not likely or possible that you can see it. Your impression of the dwindling light is also an impression of this mind natural to it especially in its periods of darkness; for that matter when the periods of darkness come to any sadhak they always seem darker than before; that is the nature of the darkness, to give that impression always. It is also quite according to the rule of these reactions that it should have come immediately after a considerable progress in bhakti and the will to surrender in the inner being — for it comes from the spirit of darkness which attacks the sadhak whenever it can, and that spirit resents fiercely all progress made and hates the very idea of progress and its whole policy is to convince him by its attacks and suggestions that he has made none or that what progress he has made is after all null and inconclusive.

The laws of this world as it is are the laws of the Ignorance and the Divine in the world maintains them so long as there is the Ignorance — if He did not, the universe would crumble to pieces, *utsīdeyur ime lokāḥ*, as the Gita puts it. There are also, very naturally, conditions for getting out of the Ignorance into the Light. One of them is that the mind of the sadhak should cooperate with the Truth and that his will should cooperate with the Divine Power which, however slow its action may seem to the vital or to the physical mind, is uplifting the nature towards the Light. When that cooperation is complete, then the progress can be rapid enough; but the sadhak should not grudge the time and labour needed to make that cooperation fully possible to the blindness and weakness of human nature and effective.

All the call for faith, sincerity, surrender is only an invitation to make that cooperation more easily possible. If the physical mind ceases to judge all things including those that it does not know or are beyond it, like the deeper things of the spirit, then it becomes easier for it to receive the Light and know by illumination and experience the things that it does not yet know. If the mental and vital will place themselves in the Divine Hand without reservation, then it is easier for the Power to work and produce "tangible" effects. If there is resistance, then it is natural that it should take more time and the work should be done from within or as it might appear underground so as to prepare the nature and undermine the resistance. It seems to me that the demand for patience is not so terribly unreasonable.

*

It [*perfection of the physical mind*] can come only by farther development and the activity of another kind of knowledge communicating itself to the physical and taking up gradually the functions of the mind in all its parts.

The Unsteadiness of the Physical Mind

The unsteadiness you speak of is the nature of the human physical mind — almost everybody has it, for the physical mind goes after all sorts of outward things. To fix the consciousness within, to keep it concentrated on the Divine alone is a great difficulty for all, it is what makes sadhana a thing for which long time and a slow development of the consciousness is usually necessary, at first at any rate. So that need not discourage you. In your inner vital there is plenty of strong will and deep down in your psychic there is the true aspiration and love which come up when the psychic is active and will eventually possess the whole nature.

*

It is quite natural that the unsteadiness of the physical mind should interfere with the settling of full and constant quietude and faith — it always does with everybody, but that does not mean that this quietude and faith will not or cannot settle in the nature. All that I meant was that you should try to get a constant will for that quietude, so that when the restlessness or unsteadiness come across, your will to quiet might meet it or soon reappear and dispel the disturbance. That would make the elimination of the restlessness or impatience easier; but in any case the Mother's force is there working behind the variations of the surface consciousness and it will bring you through them.

The experiences you had were renewed glimpses of the

psychic working that is going on all the time even when there is no sign of it on the surface. The golden sword was the sword of Truth which will destroy the difficulties.

*

Of course it is difficult to be withdrawn inwardly, difficult especially for the physical mind and consciousness with which you are now in contact. But that is not peculiar to you, — as in the other things, it is a general difficulty of human nature. The instability of which you speak is also a usual characteristic of the external mind and vital. But you have the capacity to do it as recent experiences have shown; the capacity will grow, for as the psychic develops that develops and the inability or instability of the physical consciousness becomes less pressing.

*

Diabetes or any other physical illness cannot be a cause of absence of concentration. There is always a difficulty in the beginning to concentrate for more than a short time because it is contrary to the habits of the physical mind. Perseverance is necessary. At the same time there should be a call for the help of the Divine Power above the mind; for if one can open to that, the process can be more rapid.

The Obscurity of the Physical Mind

What you felt was the obscurity of the external physical mind and nature (the centre in the throat is the centre of this external mind). So long as that is there the external nature and action remain as they always were and there is no correspondence between it and the inner spiritual consciousness and experience. This cannot disappear by a single experience; a steady will to change is necessary.

*

It means that the outer physical mind has a certain obscurity in it which impedes the knowledge from coming out. This obscurity is universal in the external physical mind — you feel it more just now because it is in the physical consciousness that the opposition is now centred. It will pass as soon as the Force can descend through the mind and vital and act directly on the physical nature.

*

But that is a common experience — it is extraordinary how long it takes for the simple and right thing to do to dawn on the physical mind.[1]

*

It is the nature of the physical mind not to believe or accept anything that is supraphysical unless it is enlightened and compelled by the light to do it. Do not identify yourself with this mind, do not consider it as yourself but only as an obscure functioning of Nature. Call down the light into it until it is compelled to believe.

Other Problems of the Physical Mind

Yes, it [*the physical mind*] is closely connected with the brain functioning. All these things — irritation, grief, fear etc. etc. — can become entirely discharged of thought content and felt simply as a physical sensation in the cells, not accepted by the thought (even in the physical mind), not shared in by the emotional being — a wave brought from outside into the material body consciousness.

*

These small things of the physical mind [*such as being disturbed by the defects of others*] are such as everybody has and they will fall off when the truer wider consciousness comes out. You have the understanding in your mind, but these things persist because they really belong to the smaller vital part and when

---

[1] *The correspondent wrote that it took him a long time to figure out the best place to put the cot in his room. — Ed.*

that part widens, then they will no longer be able to recur. One can discourage them by keeping certain ideas in mind, such as that the things which vex you belong to the nature and can go only with the change of the nature, that one has to do the work well oneself but not be troubled by the defects of others in their work, that a quiet inner will for their doing right is more effective than getting vexed and disturbed by their lapses. But fundamentally it is by the widened consciousness in your mind and vital and physical that you will be quite freed from these small reactions. You have only to continue with the Mother's Force working in you and these things will smooth themselves out hereafter.

*

These small movements [*such as useless talking*] are the most difficult of all to change owing to their very smallness and the habit of frequent indulgence as natural and trifling everyday movements of life. The best thing to do is to mass the force and light and peace in the mind and higher vital until they can occupy the physical mind even — then through the physical mind, which usually supports more or less these movements, they can be worked on with more success.

*

It [*chasing sparrows out of a garden because they made it dirty*] was I suppose an idea that came through the physical mind, suggesting the following of a physical utility only and ignoring all other perceptions and motives. You must be on your guard against the ideas and suggestions of this physical mind and accept none without discrimination and subjection to a higher light.

*

The confusion and inertia of which you speak must be in the physical mind which has not yet the Light. It does not matter very much if you keep in touch with the consciousness of the Force working upon you; for such periods of inertia in one part or another, especially in the physical consciousness, come to everybody. If you keep and deepen the quietude and become continuously conscious of the Force, it will itself work these defective states and movements out of the being in time. All depends on that, increasing quietude, increasing consciousness of the Force at work in you.

*

One is either conscious of the power or peace or other force (light, ananda, knowledge, movements of the divine working) or, if not conscious of that, is aware of the results — either of these things is sufficient to show that one is open. To feel the grace descending and yet doubt whether it is not a vital imagination is a folly of the physical mind; a spiritual experience must be accepted as it is; if one questions at every moment whether an experience is an experience or Grace is grace or peace is peace or light is light, one will spend all the time in these useless and fantastic doubts instead of making a quiet and natural progress.

*

It is the physical mind that would like everything made easy.

The Physical Mind and the Lower Vital

Formerly the mental will and the higher vital and the psychic were active, so their consent was sufficient for the lower vital to be kept down or to be influenced. But now it is the physical mind that is active in you and the physical mind gives a value and therefore a power to the lower vital which it did not have before.

*

What you describe, the insistence of the physical mind and the insistence of the small desire vital, are indeed the two things that still obstruct the sadhana. The mind must give up its insistence on its own ideas and the vital the insistence on satisfying its desires for the full quietude to come and for the permanent opening of the inner experience to realise itself. We shall put our

Force persistently for the removal of these two difficulties till it is done.

*

No, there is a limit to the resistance [*of the physical mind and the lower vital*]. At any rate a time comes when the fundamental resistance is broken for good and there is only left a dealing with details which is not troublesome.

The Physical Mind and the Psychic

It [*the psychic*] can have a very great influence [*on the physical mind*] by giving it the right attitude and the right way of looking at things so that it supports the emotional being in its aspiration, love and surrender and itself gets interest, faith and insight in the inner truth of things instead of seeing only their outer aspects and following false inferences and appearances. It also helps it to get rid of the narrowness and doubt which are the chief defects of the physical mind.

*

When the physical mind is disturbed by the vital, it is not easily convinced because its reasoning is supplied to it by the vital which thinks according to its own desires and feelings — unless a great clarity from the psychic or from the thinking mind above comes to the rescue.

It is the psychic consciousness, not perfect but still well developed, that supports some of those whom you mention and makes it easy for them to go on in faith — but it is only after much vital difficulty that it developed in them, — and there is no reason why that should not happen speedily in you also.

*

The psychic if it gets hold of them [*the vital physical and the physical mind*] can change completely their will and outlook and orientation and open them to the true perception of things and right impulse. The mind and higher vital can help much towards that.

The Physical Mind and Peace and Silence

There is always a difficulty in keeping the physical mind within or silent, because it has been its nature to occupy itself with outward things and it finds a difficulty in accustoming itself to a contrary movement. You must not be depressed by that, but persist in the aspiration and will till it is done. The Mother's Force will be there to bring it about as soon as possible.

*

You have only to allow the consciousness to develop — at first there will be mistakes as well as true ideas, but when there is sufficient development and the Mother's force and knowledge directly working in you, things will become more and more right — not only so, but you will have the certitude. At present there is still too much of the old physical mind for perceptions to be always right. As the Peace and Force take direct and complete possession of the physical consciousness, this will change and the consciousness develop more surely and with a greater light.

*

To get rid of the random thoughts of the surface physical mind is not easy. It is sometimes done by a sudden miracle, as in my own case, but that is rare. Some get it done by a slow process of concentration, but that may take a very long time. It is easier to have a quiet mind with things that come in passing on the surface, as people pass in the street, and one is free to attend to them or not — that is to say, there develops a sort of double mind, one inner silent and concentrated when it pleases to be so, a quiet witness when it chooses to see thoughts and things, — the other meant for surface dynamism. It is probable in your case that this will come as soon as these descents of peace, intensity or Ananda get strong enough to occupy the whole system.

*

If the peace and silence continue to come down, they usually become so intense as to seize the physical mind also after a time.

Chapter Five
Thought and Knowledge

Thoughts Come from Outside

First of all, these thought-waves, thought-seeds or thought-forms or whatever they are, are of different values and come from different planes of consciousness. Even the same thought-substance can take higher or lower vibrations according to the plane of consciousness through which the thoughts come in (e.g., thinking mind, vital mind, physical mind, subconscient mind) or the power of consciousness which catches them and pushes them into one man or another. Moreover there is a stuff of mind in each man and the incoming thought uses that for shaping itself or translating itself (transcribing we usually call it), but the stuff is finer or coarser, stronger or weaker etc. etc. in one mind than in another. Also there is a mind-energy actual or potential in each which differs and this mind-energy in its recipience of the thought can be luminous or obscure, sattwic, rajasic or tamasic with consequences that vary in each case.

*

There is no difficulty about explaining [*how a thought rejected by one person gets picked up by another*]. You are as naive and ignorant as a newborn lamb. That is the way things come, only one does not notice. Thoughts, ideas, happy inventions etc. etc. are always wandering about (in thought waves or otherwise) seeking a mind that may embody them. One mind takes, looks, rejects — another takes, looks, accepts. Two different minds catch the same thought-form or thought-wave, but the mental activities being different make different results out of them. Or it comes to one and he does nothing, then it walks off, crying "O this unready animal!" and goes to another who promptly annexes it and it settles into expression with a joyous bubble of inspiration, illumination or enthusiasm of original discovery or creation and the recipient cries proudly, "I, I have done this." Ego, sir! ego! You are the recipient, the conditioning medium, if you like — nothing more.

*

That is the silliness of the mind. Why should it be impossible to fill up a vacancy?[1] It is easier for things to come into an empty space than into a full one. The error comes from thinking that your thoughts are your own and that you are their maker and if you don't create thoughts (i.e. think), there will be none. A little observation ought to show that you are not manufacturing your own thoughts, but rather thoughts occur in you. Thoughts are born, not made — like poets, according to the proverb. Of course, there is a sort of labour and effort when you try to produce or else to think on a certain subject, but that is a concentration for making thoughts come up, come in, come down, as the case may be, and fit themselves together. The idea that you are shaping the thoughts or fitting them together is an egoistic delusion. They are doing it themselves, or Nature is doing it for you, only under a certain compulsion; you have to beat her often in order to make her do it, and the beating is not always successful. But the mind or nature or mental energy — whatever you like to call it — does this in a certain way and carries on with a certain order of thoughts, haphazard intelligentialities (excuse the barbarism) or asininities, rigidly ordered or imperfectly ordered intellectualities, logical sequences and logical inconsequences, etc. etc. How the devil is an intuition to get in in the midst of that waltzing and colliding crowd? It does sometimes, — in some minds often intuitions do come in, — but immediately the ordinary thoughts surround it and eat it up alive, and then with some fragment of the murdered intuition shining through their non-intuitive stomachs they look up smiling at you and say, "I am an intuition, sir." But they are only intellect, intelligence or ordinary thought with part of

---

[1] *The correspondent said that his mind found it hard to believe that a vacancy in the mind could suddenly be filled with an intuition without one's thinking about it. — Ed.*

a dismembered and therefore misleading intuition inside them. Now in a vacant mind, vacant but not inert (that is important), intuitions have a chance of getting in alive and whole. But don't run away with the idea that all that comes into an empty mind, even a clear or luminous empty mind, will be intuitive. Anything, any blessed kind of idea, can come in. One has to be vigilant and examine the credentials of the visitor. In other words, the mental being must be there, silent but vigilant, impartial but discriminating. That is, however, when you are in search of truth. For poetry so much is not necessary. There it is only the poetic quality of the visitor that has to be scrutinised and that can be done after he has left his packet — by results.

*

What you perceive as suggestions or voices, are accepted and felt by people to be thoughts of their own mind. When one practises Yoga and observes the thoughts, one sees that they come from outside, from universal Nature, from the mental, vital or subtle physical worlds etc. The proper thing is then to stand back from these thoughts, voices or suggestions, to reject them or else control them, to make the mind free and quiet and open only to the divine light, force, knowledge and the presence of the Divine. Your mistake has been to allow free play to these thoughts, voices and suggestions instead of rejecting, silencing and controlling them. It is what you must now do. Aspire, get into contact with the Light and the true Force, reassert your will to reject these suggestions and voices. Do not take interest in these voices, keep the mind quiet.

*

All these thoughts and influences come really from outside, from universal Nature — they create formations in us or get habitual responses from the individual being. When they are rejected, they go back into the external universal Nature and if one becomes conscious, one can feel them coming from outside and trying to get a lodging inside again or reawaken the habitual response. One has to reject them persistently till no possibility of response remains any longer. This is hastened much if a certain inner calm, purity and silence can be established from which these things fall away without being able to touch it.

*

What you say is true. The power to open is there in your mind and vital and psychic being, but this recurrence of the external thoughts and feelings is making a strong obstruction and a persistent rejection is needed in order to get rid of it. There are some difficulties in the nature that fall away rapidly by the repeated touch of the inner Force, but those which are obstinately recurrent, especially in the physical field, need an equal persistence in the rejection before they will consent to fall away from the nature.

Control of One's Thoughts

To reject doubts means control of one's thoughts — very certainly so. But the control of one's thoughts is as necessary as the control of one's vital desires and passions or the control of the movements of one's body — for the Yoga, and not for the Yoga only. One cannot be a fully developed mental being even, if one has not a control of the thoughts, is not their observer, judge, master, — the mental Purusha, *manomaya puruṣa, sākṣī, anumantā, īśvara*. It is no more proper for the mental being to be the tennis ball of unruly and uncontrollable thoughts than to be a rudderless ship in the storm of the desires and passions or a slave of either the inertia or the impulses of the body. I know it is more difficult because man being primarily a creature of mental Prakriti identifies himself with the movements of his mind and cannot at once dissociate himself and stand free from the swirl and eddies of the mind whirlpool. It is comparatively easy for him to put a control on his body, at least a certain part of its movements: it is less easy but still very possible after a struggle to put a mental control on his vital impulsions and desires; but to sit, like the Tantrik Yogi on the river, above the whirlpool of his thoughts is less facile. Nevertheless it can be done; all developed mental men, those who get beyond the average, have in one way or other or at least at certain times and for certain purposes to separate the two parts of the mind, the active part which is a factory of thoughts and the quiet masterful part which is at once a Witness and a Will, observing them, judging, rejecting, eliminating, accepting, ordering corrections and changes, the Master in the House of Mind, capable of self-empire, *svārājya*.

The Yogi goes still farther; he is not only a master there, but even while in mind in a way, he gets out of it, as it were, and stands above or quite back from it and free. For him the image of the factory of thoughts is no longer quite valid; for he sees that thoughts come from outside, from the universal Mind or universal Nature, sometimes formed and distinct, sometimes unformed and then they are given shape somewhere in us. The principal business of our mind is either a response of acceptance or refusal to these thought-waves (as also vital waves, subtle physical energy waves) or this giving a personal-mental form to thought-stuff (or vital movements) from the environing Nature-Force. It was my great debt to Lele that he showed me this. "Sit in meditation," he said, "but do not think, look only at your mind; you will see thoughts *coming into it*; before they can enter throw them away from you till your mind is capable of entire silence." I had never heard before of thoughts coming visibly into the mind from outside, but I did not think of either questioning the truth or the possibility, I simply sat down and did it. In a moment my mind became silent as a windless air on a high mountain summit and then I saw a thought and then another thought coming in a concrete way from outside; I flung them away before they could enter and take hold of the brain and in three days I was free. From that moment, in principle, the mental being in me became a free Intelligence, a universal Mind, not limited to the narrow circle of personal thought or a labourer in a thought-factory, but a receiver of knowledge from all the hundred realms of being and free too to choose what it willed in this vast sight-empire and thought-empire.

I mention this only to emphasise that the possibilities of the mental being are not limited and that it can be the free Witness and Master in its own house. It is not to say that everybody can do it in the way I did and with the same rapidity of the decisive movement (for of course the later fullest development of this new untrammelled mental Power took time, many years); but a progressive freedom and mastery over one's mind is perfectly within the possibilities of anyone who has the faith and will to undertake it.

*

Assuredly, rejection means control of one's thoughts, and why should not one be master of one's own mind and thoughts and not only master of one's vital passions and bodily movements? If it is the right thing to control the body and not allow it to make a stupid, wrong or injurious movement, if it is the right thing to reject from the vital an ignorant passion or low desire, it must be equally the right thing to reject from the mind a thought that ought not to be there or that for good reasons one does not want to be there. As for possibility, I suppose when a thought that is manifestly stupid or false presents itself to the mind one can and usually does reject and throw it out and bid it not recur again. If one can do that with a given thought, it follows that one can do it with any thoughts that need for any reason to be excluded. If a scientist goes into his laboratory to work out a problem, he shuts out from his mind for the time being all thoughts of his wife, his family or his financial affairs, and if they come he repels them and says, "This is not your time." If he has resolved to carry out a line of investigation to the end or a method of invention and, if doubts assail him, he will certainly throw them aside and say, "I mean to see this through to the end and till I have reached the end, I have no intention of listening to you." At every step a man of any mental calibre has to exercise some power over his mind, otherwise he would be as much in a state of restless mental confusion or of mechanical incoherence as one who had no control over his impulses and desires.

*

To do anything by mental control is always difficult, when what is attempted runs contrary to the trend of human nature or of the personal nature. A strong will patiently and perseveringly turned towards its object can effect a change, but usually it takes a long time and the success at the beginning may be only partial and chequered by many failures.

To turn all actions automatically into worship cannot be done by thought control only; there must be a strong aspiration in the heart which will bring about some realisation or feeling of the presence of the One to whom worship is offered. The bhakta does not rely on his own effort alone, but on the grace and power of the Divine whom he adores.

*

What do you mean by control of the mind? Control of the thoughts or control of the passions and the sense impulses? The latter can be controlled by the mind (not abolished), if the will in the mind is strong enough. But this mental control is not Yoga.

Yogic control can come in one of two ways or by their combination. (1) To separate the witness Soul in you from the movements of the mental, vital and physical Prakriti to which these things belong, learn to look upon them and in the end to feel them as not yourself, not a part of the inner or true being but occurring on the surface, and to experience the inner being as the Purusha eternally calm, silent and immovable. This separation once done, learn by *abhyāsa* to give the effective command of the Purusha to the movements of the Prakriti to cease — refusing the sanction to all that you wish to eliminate. The process is long and laborious and the final perfection can only come by resolute and persevering practice. (2) To open yourself to the Divine Power and give up all into its hands, yourself only rejecting and refusing sanction to all that you feel to be false and contrary to truth and purity in you.

This is as an answer to your difficulty, but I cannot direct you or give you any Sadhana, which I give only to those who are called from within to my way of Yoga and not for any limited object like the one you have in view.

*

It is not so easy to do mental work and do sadhana at the same time, for it is with the mind that the sadhana is done. If one gets back from the mind as well as the body and lives in the inner Purusha consciousness, then it is possible.

*

Detach yourself from it [*the habitual movement of the mind*] — make your mind external to you, something that you can observe as you observe things occurring in the street. So long as you do not do that, it is difficult to be the mind's master.

*

The control over the thoughts and the power of seeing the image of the Mother and Sri Aurobindo in the head are a very good beginning. The heat in the head is not fever, but the result of the action of the Force in the mental centres working to overcome the mental resistance which there always is in the human mind — heaviness sometimes comes as a result of the pressure of the Force — it passes away of itself usually when the mind receives freely the Force.

Thoughts and Words

This is a wrong psychology. Thought is quite possible without words. Children have thoughts, animals too — thoughts can take another form than words. Thought perceptions come first — language comes to express the perceptions and itself leads to fresh thoughts.

*

They [*ideas in the universal Mind*] take word form in the mind when they enter into it — unless they come from beings, not as mere idea-forces.

The Idea and What Lies Behind It

There is a power in the idea — a force of which the idea is a shape. Again, behind the idea and force and word there is what is called the spirit, — a consciousness which generates the force.

*

The idea is not enough. It gives only a half-light — you must get to all the Truth that lies behind the idea and the object together. Being, consciousness, force, — that is the triple secret.

Thought and Knowledge

Thought is not the giver of Knowledge but the "mediator" between the Inconscient and the Superconscient. It compels the world born from the Inconscient to reach for a Knowledge other than the instinctive vital or merely empirical, for the Knowledge that itself exceeds thought; it calls for that superconscient Knowledge and prepares the consciousness here to receive it. It rises itself into the higher realms and even in disappearing into the supramental and Ananda levels is transformed into something that will bring down their powers into the silent Self which its cessation leaves behind it.

Knowledge and Ignorance

Knowledge is always better than ignorance. It makes things possible hereafter if not at the moment, while ignorance actively obstructs and misleads.

*

Who comes into the path of Yoga with full knowledge or even any knowledge? All are ignorant, it is only by Yoga itself that they get the knowledge.

*

Neither knowledge nor anything else is constant at first — and even when it is there one cannot expect it to be always active. That comes afterwards.

*

What is to be left out [*in expressing one's ideas*] is the ego. Limitation of knowledge will necessarily be there so long as there is not the fullest wideness from above; that does not matter.

*

Most people who have not knowledge are apt to be opinionated — they have their ideas and don't want them to be changed or their fixity disturbed.

Knowledge and the Divine Consciousness

Mental knowledge is of little use except sometimes as an introduction pointing towards the real knowledge which comes from a direct consciousness of things.

*

All consciousness comes from the one consciousness — knowledge is one aspect of the divine consciousness.

*

One must be conscious of all one's states and movements and the causes and influences that bring them about and conscious too of the Divine — the nearness, presence, power, peace, light, knowledge, love, Ananda of the Divine.

Mental Knowledge and Knowledge from Above

The knowledge of the mind and vital plane is no knowledge. Only from above can the true knowledge come.

*

No, these contacts with the violent vital forces do not bring knowledge — they rather stand in the way of true knowledge growing. The true knowledge comes from above, not from below. The knowledge from above is divine, the knowledge from below is not divine, it is a confusion full of darkness and disturbance. When the knowledge from above comes, then there is light and you will then be able to see what is the true vital movement and the real harmony of the mind, vital and body. Do not allow these stormy conditions to take hold of you.

*

Is getting knowledge from above and getting it by the mind in its own capacity the same thing? If the mind is capable, then there is no need of knowledge from above, it can do the getting of knowledge by its own greatness.

*

The mind in its higher part is aware of being one with the Divine, in all ways, in all things — having that supreme knowledge, it is not disturbed by its own ignorance and impotence in its lower instrumental parts; it looks on all that with a smile and remains happy and luminous with the light of the supreme knowledge.

The consciousness of union with the Divine is for the spiritual seeker the supreme knowledge.

Knowledge and Mental Questions

To answer your question [*about how the divine consciousness acts in life*] I would have to speak in the terms of a consciousness to which the mind has no key and at the same time try to explain its relations to the lower consciousness in which things are now happening. What is the use of doing this? The mind will either understand nothing or misunderstand or think it has understood when really it has understood nothing.

Or I would have to make up a mental answer to the question which would not be the real thing, but just something to keep the questioning mind quiet.

The true way to enter into these things is to still the mind and open to the consciousness from which things are done. Then you would first have a direct experience of the way the divine consciousness acts on different planes and secondly a light of

Thought and Knowledge

knowledge about the experience. This is the only true way — all the rest is only words and sterile mental logic.

*

A thousand questions can be asked about anything whatsoever, but to answer would require a volume, and even then the mind would understand nothing. It is only by a growth in the consciousness itself that you can get some direct perception of these things. But for that the mind must be quiet and a direct feeling and intuition take its place.

*

So long as the outer mind is not quiet, it is impossible for intuition to develop. So if you want to go on asking intellectual questions about what is beyond the intellect until the intuition develops in spite of this activity, you will have to go on for ever.

*

When you get the true intuitive plane, there will be no need for instructions or questions as to how to do sadhana. The sadhana will do itself under the light of the intuition.

*

Your mind is too active. If it were more quiet and less questioning and argumentative and restlessly wanting to find devices it seems to me that there would be more chance of knowledge coming down and of intuitive, non-intellectual consciousness developing within you.

*

Out of one thousand mental questions and answers there are only one or two here and there that are really of any dynamic assistance — while a single inner response or a little growth of consciousness will do what those thousand questions and answers could not do. The Yoga does not proceed by *upadeśa* but by inner influence. To state your condition, experiences etc. and open to the help is far more important than question-asking — especially the questions about why and how which your physical mind so persistently puts.

*

It is the physical mind that raises all these questions and cannot understand or give the right answer. The real knowledge and understanding can only come if you stop questioning with the small physical mind and allow a deeper and wider consciousness which is there within you to come out and grow. You would then get automatically the true answer and the true guidance. Your mistake is to attach so much importance to the external mind and its ideas and perceptions instead of concentrating on the growth of the inner consciousness.

*

Such [*mental*] questions should not be allowed to stop the flow [*of higher knowledge*]. Afterwards one can consider them and get the answer. The knowledge that comes is not necessarily complete or perfect in expression; but it must be allowed to come freely and amplifications or corrections can be made afterwards.

Understanding and the Higher Light

Get back to the true *feeling* of the Force and Peace — the understanding will grow with the growth of that feeling and experience. For with the Force and Peace comes always something of the Light and it is the Light illumining the mind that brings the understanding. So long as you try to understand with the unillumined mind, mistakes and non-understanding are inevitable.

*

Yes, that is the point. The ordinary mind governed by the vital desires and its own mental formations cannot understand — it must fall quiet and allow the Peace and Force to work so as to bring another consciousness with the true Light in it. When that is done, these questionings and their reactions will have no place.

*

Yes, it is that [*faith that the Mother will enlighten one's mind*] that is the real necessity. It is not possible for the mind to understand fully and rightly till it is filled with the higher Light; but it can feel and believe in the Divine and that the way of the Divine is sure, and this faith itself will bring the first true understanding.

*

What you say is quite true. No personal effort can get these things done; that is why we tell you always to keep yourself quiet and let the peace and the force work. As for understanding, it is your physical mind that wants to understand, but the physical mind is incapable of understanding these things by itself — for it has no knowledge of them and no means of knowledge. Its standards also are quite different from the standards of the true knowledge. All the physical mind can do is to be quiet and allow the light to come into it, accepting it, not interposing its own ideas — then it will progressively get the knowledge. It can't get it in this way; it must surrender.

*

If one has faith and openness, that is enough [*to get the understanding one needs to practise the Yoga*]. Besides there are two kinds of understanding — understanding by the intellect and understanding in the consciousness. It is good to have the former if it is accurate, but it is not indispensable. Understanding by the consciousness comes if there is faith and openness, though it may come only gradually and through steps of experience. But I have seen people without education or intellectuality understand in this way perfectly well the course of the Yoga in themselves, while intellectual men make big mistakes — e.g. take a neutral mental quietude for the spiritual peace and refuse to come out of it in order to go farther.

Knowledge and the Psychic

It is not a mental knowledge that is necessary, but a psychic perception or a direct perception in the consciousness. A mental knowledge can always be blinded by the tricks of the vital.

*

The one thing always is to let the Peace and Power work and not allow the mind to seek after things and get disturbed. All the values of the mind are constructions of ignorance — it is only when your psychic being comes forward that you have the true knowledge — for your psychic being knows.

Knowledge and Mental Silence

That [*incessant activity*] is always the difficulty with the mind. It must learn to be silent and let the knowledge come without trying to catch hold of it for its own play.

*

The turmoil of mental (intellectual) activity has also to be silenced like the vital activity of desire in order that the calm and peace may be complete. Knowledge has to come but from above. In this calm the ordinary mental activities like the ordinary vital activities become surface movements with which the silent inner self is not connected. It is the liberation necessary in order that the true knowledge and the true life activity may replace or transform the activities of the Ignorance.

*

The activity of mind is necessary so long as a higher activity cannot be reached; but if the spiritual consciousness becomes active with its direct power of perception, the mind must become more and more content and give place to spiritual perception, psychic intimations and discrimination, intuitions, a deeper knowledge from within, a higher knowledge from above.

*

The thinking mind has to learn how to be entirely silent. It is only then that true knowledge can come.

*

Of course [*a silent mind is the result of Yoga*]; the ordinary mind is never silent.

*

No, certainly not [*thinkers and philosophers do not have a silent mind*]. It is the active mind they have; only, of course, they concentrate, so the common incoherent mentalising stops and the thoughts that rise or enter and shape themselves are coherently restricted to the subject or activity in hand. But that is quite a different matter from the whole mind falling silent.

*

Ordinary human minds, Europeans especially, are accustomed to regard thought as indispensable and as the highest thing — so they are alarmed at silence. X when he was here asked for Yoga. I told him how to make his mind silent and it became silent. He immediately got frightened and said, "I am becoming a fool, I can't think", — so I took what I had given away from him. That is how the average mind regards silence.

*

Good; cessation of thought and other vibrations is the climax of the inner silence. When once one has got that, it is easier for the true knowledge to come from above in place of the mental thought.

*

It [*knowledge*] comes through the mind, so the mind can always modify its expression unless it is entirely and absolutely still.

*

When the personal mind is still, whatever mental action is needed is taken up and done by the Force itself which does all the necessary thinking and progressively transforms it by bringing down into it a higher and higher plane of perception and knowledge.

*

It is in the silence of the mind that the strongest and freest action can come, e.g. the writing of a book, poetry, inspired speech etc. When the mind is active it interferes with the inspiration, puts in its own small ideas which get mixed up with the inspiration or starts something from a lower level or simply stops the inspiration altogether by bubbling up with all sorts of mere mental suggestions. So also intuitions or action etc. can come more easily when the ordinary inferior movement of the mind is not there. It is also in the silence of the mind that it is easiest for knowledge to come from within or above, from the psychic or from the higher consciousness.

Knowledge, Experience and Realisation

Knowledge by thinking process would not be spiritual knowledge. True knowledge comes by spiritual realisation and experience. There are such realisations and experiences.

*

I was speaking of your experiences of the higher consciousness, of your seeing the Mother in all things — these are what are called spiritual realisations, spiritual knowledge. Realisations are the essence of knowledge — thoughts about them, expression of them in words are a lesser knowledge and if the thoughts are merely mental without experience or realisation, they are not regarded as *jñāna* in the spiritual sense at all.

*

It [*knowledge gained in Divine realisation*] is the conscious experience of the Truth, seen, felt, lived within and it is also a spiritual perception (more direct and concrete than the intellectual) of the true significance of things which may express itself in thought and speech, but is independent of them in itself.

*

Yes, it happens like that. A touch of realisation is enough to set the higher mind knowledge or the illumined mind knowledge flowing.

Section Two

Cultivation of the Mind in Yoga

Chapter One
Mental Development and Sadhana

The Development of the Mind

The development of the mind is a useful preliminary for the sadhak; it can also be pursued along with the sadhana on condition that it is not given too big a place and does not interfere with the one important thing, the sadhana itself.

*

To have a developed intellect is always helpful if one can enlighten it from above and turn it to divine use.

*

A well-developed intellect is one which is plastic, wide, free from rigidity and stiffness, — that can be of use.

*

It [*a developed mind*] may or may not [*help the sadhana*] — if it is too intellectually developed on certain rationalistic lines, it may hinder.

*

The tendency to inquire and know is in itself good, but it must be kept under control. What is needed for progress in sadhana is gained best by increase of consciousness and experience and of intuitive knowledge.

*

To be interested in outward things is not wrong in itself — it depends on the way in which one is interested. If it is done as part of the sadhana, looking on them from the true consciousness, then they become a means for the growth of the being. It is that

that matters, to get the true consciousness — and it is this that comes in you when you have the sense of the Peace and the working of the Force in it. There is no real reason for discontent or dissatisfaction with yourself — since progress is being made in spite of the resistance of the lower forces. The pressure which is translated by the heaviness in the stomach has to be got rid of — it is there that there is the chief resistance still. Peace within and a cheerful confidence and gladness without is what is wanted — then this kind of nervous pressure and disorder would cease.

*

It does not help for spiritual knowledge to be ignorant of the things of this world.

Reading and Sadhana

For one who wants to practise sadhana, sadhana must come first — reading and mental development can only be subordinate things.

*

I don't know that it [*mental development*] helps the sadhana and I don't quite understand what is meant by the phrase. What is a fact is that mental like physical work can be made a part of the sadhana, — not as a rival to the sadhana or as another activity with equal rights and less selfish and egoistic than seeking the Divine.

*

I have no objection to mental development. It is the idea that doing sadhana earnestly is egoistic and selfish, and reading is an unselfish noble pursuit that is absurd.

*

Reading can be only a momentary help to prepare the mind. But the real knowledge does not come by reading. Some preparation for the inner knowledge may be helpful — but the mind should not be too superficially active or seek to know only for curiosity's sake.

*

It [*reading*] does not take one inwards in any real sense — it only takes one from the more physical to the more mental part of the external consciousness.

*

If the power to meditate long is there, a sadhak will naturally do it and care little for reading — unless he has reached the stage when everything is part of the Yogic consciousness because that is permanent. Sadhana is the aim of a sadhak, not mental development. But if he has spare time, those who have the mental turn will naturally spend it in reading or study of some kind.

*

The attitude you describe is just what it should be — there is nothing wrong in it, — nor in your reading or letter-writing etc. There can be no objection to these activities in themselves, for the Yoga; only they must be done with the right attitude and spirit and as part of the sadhana — because the whole life has to become a sadhana, until it is able to become, the whole life, an embodiment of the *siddhi*.

*

If by passivity of the mind you mean laziness and inability to use it, then what Yoga makes that its basis? The mind has to be quieted and transformed, not made indolent and useless. Is there any old Yoga that makes it a rule not to allow those who practise it to study Sanskrit or philosophy? Did that prevent the Yogis from attaining mental quietude? Do you think that the Mother and myself never read anything and have to sit all day inactive in order to make our minds quiet? Are you not aware that the principle of this Yoga is to arrive at an inner silence in which all activities can take place without disturbing the inner silence?

*

When the passion for reading or study seizes hold of the mind, it is like that; one wants to spend all the time doing it. It is a force that wants to satisfy itself — like other forces — and takes hold of the consciousness for its purpose. One has to utilise these forces without letting them take hold; for this there must be the central being always in control of the forces of Nature that come to it, deciding for itself the choice of what it shall accept, how use, how arrange their action. Otherwise each Force catches hold of some part of the personality (the student, the social man, the erotic man, the fighter) and uses and drives the being instead of being controlled and used by it.

*

I do not think you should stop reading so long as the reading itself does not, as a passion, fall away from the mind; that happens when a higher order of consciousness and experiences begin within the being. Nor is it good to force yourself too much to do only the one work of painting. Such compulsion of the mind and vital tends usually either to be unsuccessful and make them more restless or else to create some kind of dullness and inertia.

For the work simply aspire for the Force to use you, put yourself inwardly in relation with the Mother when doing it and make it your aim to be the instrument for the expression of beauty without regard to personal fame or the praise and blame of others.

*

I don't think it would be advisable not to read at all. It is a relaxation of the tension of sadhana which can be at the same time useful to the mind. It is only when there is the spontaneous flow of sadhana all day without strain that reading is no longer needed.

Reading What Is Helpful to the Sadhana

Dhyana and work are both helpful for this Yoga to those who

can do both. Reading also can be made helpful.

*

Dedication to the Divine [*is the right attitude in reading*]. To read what will help the Yoga or what will be useful for the work or what will develop the capacities for the divine purpose. Not to read worthless stuff or for mere entertainment or for a dilettante intellectual curiosity which is of the nature of a mental dram-drinking. When one is established in the highest consciousness, one can read nothing or everything: it makes no difference — but that is still far off.

*

In the beginning of the sadhana you need nothing more than just what you say, "concentration with faith, devotion and sincerity" on a form of the Divine Being — you can add prayer or the name, if you like.

Reading good books can be of help in the early mental stage — they prepare the mind, put it in the right atmosphere — can even if one is very sensitive bring some glimpses of realisation on the mental plane. Afterwards the utility diminishes — you have to find the right knowledge and experience in yourself.

*

This [*inclination to meditate while reading books on spiritual life*] is quite a normal movement. In reading these books you get into touch with the Force behind them and it is this that pushes you into meditation and a corresponding experience.

*

It depends upon the nature of the things read, whether they are helpful to the growth of the being or not. No general rule can be made. It cannot be said that poetry or dramas ought or ought not to be read — it depends on the poem or the play — so with the rest.

*

It is quite permissible to do so [*read light literature at times for a change*] and may relieve. The one thing necessary is that you should be able to keep the consciousness behind free, as in this case.

*

What you can do is to read not for pastime but with the clear intention of furnishing your mind with knowledge.

*

Yes, reading can be done for the improvement of the mental instrument as part of the sadhana.

Reading and Detachment

You can remember at the beginning and offer your reading to the Divine and at the end again. There is a state of consciousness in which only a part of it is reading or doing the work and behind there is the consciousness of the Divine always.

*

A time must come when the reading as well as any other outward occupation does not interfere with the presence or activity of the higher consciousness.

*

The reading must learn to accommodate itself to the pressure [*of sadhana*] — that is, be done by the outer mind while the inner being remains in concentration.

*

That is good. Reading ought not to absorb the consciousness — there ought to be the larger part behind detached and conscious in a larger way.

*

The only way [*to separate oneself from mental activities such as reading*] is to separate the Prakriti and Purusha. When you feel something within watching all the mental activities but separate from them, just as you can watch things going on outside in the street, then that is the separation of Purusha from mental Prakriti.

*

That [*inability to understand what is read*] only means that you cannot separate yourself from your mental consciousness in its activity. Naturally, if you take your mental consciousness off the reading, you can't understand what is being read, for it is with the mental consciousness that one understands. You have not to make the mental consciousness separate from the reading, but yourself separate from the mental consciousness. You have to be the Witness watching it reading or writing or talking, just as you watch the body acting or moving.

*

What happens in reading such books [*as a book on zoology*] is that one comes into a very external consciousness which looks outward and not inward. When the reading is over the mind runs for a time in this external groove and then one has to remain quiet and call back or get back into the inward state to which the higher thoughts naturally come. This may take a little time.

*

The only harm in reading these things [*about procreation*] is that the vital makes it an excuse for sexual excitement. Otherwise there is no harm in reading for knowledge — the facts of existence have to be known, and we should learn them with a free and dispassionate mind. But such reading has to be avoided, if there is any vital reaction.

Reading Novels and Newspapers

Reading novels is always distracting if you are deep in sadhana. It is better to avoid it now.

*

If novels touch the lower vital or raise it, they ought not to be read by the sadhak. One can read them only if one can look at them from the literary point of view as a picture of human life and nature which one can observe, as the Yogi looks at life itself, without being involved in it or having any reaction.

*

I don't quite know about the novel. People bring in the relations of man and woman because it has been the habit for centuries to make every novel turn around that — except in the few which deal with history or adventure or similar things. In a novel based on spiritual philosophy should not the man and woman idea go into the background or disappear, the spiritual love not having anything based at all on sex, but on the relation between soul and soul?

*

It is not necessary to be in touch with the outside world in this way [*by reading newspapers*]; it may be useful under certain circumstances and for some purposes. It may act too as a hindrance. All depends upon the consciousness from which it is done.

The reading of books of a light character may act as a relaxation of the mental consciousness. In the early stages it is not always possible to keep the mind to an unbroken spiritual concentration and endeavour and it takes refuge in other occupations, feeling even instinctively drawn to those of a lighter character.

*

Obviously there are many things that apply to all equally and cannot be avoided in that way [*by saying that each one's way is different*]. The dictum that each has his own way is not true; each has his own way of following the common way and the "own way" may often be very defective. Of course it is true that natures are different and the approach whether to the sadhana or to other things. One can say generally that newspaper reading or novel reading is not helpful to the sadhana and is at best a concession to the vital which is not yet ready to be absorbed in the sadhana — unless and until one is able to read in the right way with a higher consciousness which is not only not "disturbed" by the reading or distracted by it from the concentrated Yoga-consciousness but is able to make the right use of what is read from the point of view of the inner consciousness and the inner life.

*

Merely following external rules cannot of course be sufficient. They are only an aid to the inner effort until the inner consciousness is thoroughly established. Usually much reading of newspapers in the ordinary way keeps one attached to the ordinary view and vision of things and interested in that — when one has the inner consciousness one can see things happening in the world with another eye of knowledge and then reading can be of some use, though even then most of what is published is empty and futile. But the mere not-reading by itself is not effective. Also if one has need of a distraction, reading newspapers serves the purpose.

*

Reasons given [*for reading newspapers*] of course prove nothing — they may be only excuses put forward by the mind for doing what the vital wants. The newspapers obviously carry with them a lowering atmosphere. It is a question of fact whether one can separate oneself sufficiently not to be pulled down by it. At the time of reading there is certainly a lower pitch of the consciousness in the frontal or outward parts. Only, if one has a consciousness behind which is not affected, then one can revert immediately after reading to the normal higher level.

*

It is not against the principle of Yogic life to know what is happening in the world — what is unyogic is to be attached to these things [*such as newspaper reading*] and not able to do without them or to think of them as a matter of main importance. The all-important thing must be the sadhana, the growth into a new consciousness and a new inner life. The rest must be done with detachment and without getting absorbed in them. The feeling must be such that if the Mother were to tell you never to see a newspaper at all, it would be no deprivation to you and you would not even feel the difference.

*

The inability to read books or papers is often felt when the consciousness is getting the tendency to go inside.

Chapter Two
The Place of Study in Sadhana

Study and Sadhana

Study cannot take the same or a greater importance than sadhana.

*

Study is of importance only if you study in the right way and with the turn for knowledge and mental discipline. What is the use of studying French if you go on always making the same mistakes and having the same inaccurate and slovenly hold of the language?

*

I have already said that you can spend the time in study as the sadhana is not active. If the sadhana were active then study could be done in the spare time, i.e. in times not given to work or meditation.

Study and Mental Development

A well-trained intellect and study are two different things — there are plenty of people who have read much but have not a well-trained intellect. Inertia can come to anybody, even to the most educated people.

*

Reading, learning about things, acquiring complete and accurate information, training oneself in logical thinking, considering dispassionately all sides of a question, rejecting hasty or wrong inferences and conclusions, learning to look at all things clearly and as a whole [*are what is meant by mental training*].

*

By training it to see, observe and understand in the right way [*one can have a well-developed intellect*]. Reading and study are only useful to acquire information and widen one's field of data. But that comes to nothing if one does not know how to discern and discriminate, judge, see what is within and behind things.

*

A man may have read much and yet be mentally undeveloped. It is by thinking, understanding, receiving mental influences from his intellectual superiors that a man's mind develops.

*

There is no such rule.[1] It is better if the mind is strong and developed, but scholarship does not necessarily create a strong and developed mind.

*

Intelligence does not depend on the amount one has read, it is a quality of the mind. Study only gives it material for its work as life also does. There are people who do not know how to read and write well who are more intelligent than many highly educated people and understand life and things better. On the other hand a good intelligence can improve itself by reading because it gets more material to work on and grows by exercise and by having a wider range to move in. But book knowledge by itself is not the real thing; it has to be used as a help to the intelligence, but it is often used only as a help to a loquacious stupidity or ignorance — ignorance because knowledge of facts is a poor thing if one cannot see their true significance.

*

You have either to train the memory by practising to remember — or if you cannot do that, try only to understand, read much and let the memory remember what it can. There are people who

---

[1] *The correspondent asked whether a scholar would progress rapidly in spiritual life if his mind was "developed, large and enlightened through education". — Ed.*

have a bad memory but they succeed in their studies in spite of it.

School Studies and Yoga

I see no objection to his going on with his studies, — whether they will be of any use to him for a life of sadhana will depend on the spirit in which he does them. The really important thing is to develop a state of consciousness in which one can live in the Divine and act from it on the physical world. A mental training and discipline, knowledge of men and things, culture, capacities of a useful kind are a preparation that the sadhak would be all the better for having, — even though they are not the one thing indispensable. Education in India gives very little of these things; but if one knows how to study without caring much for the form or for mere academic success, the life of the student can be used for the purpose.

*

At this age he is too young to give up study. It would be best for him to attend the school still; it will be worth while leaving it only if other and better arrangements could be made for his studies. Development of the mind is not a useless thing for one who wishes to follow this sadhana and it can very well go along with the Yoga.

*

There is no reason why X should not complete his studies or learn something which will make him useful in life. To be useless is not a qualification for Yoga.

The Study of Languages

Knowing languages is part of the equipment of the mind.

*

There is no harm in learning [*a new language*] — provided it is kept in its subordinate place and one is not too much lost in it.

*

Your objection was to learning languages and especially French as inimical to peace and silence because it meant activity. The mind, when it is not in meditation or in complete silence, is always active with something or another — with its own ideas or desires or with other people or with things or with talking etc. None of these is any less an activity than learning languages. Now you shift your ground and say it is because owing to their study they have no time for meditation that you object. That is absurd, for if people want to meditate, they will arrange their time of study for that; if they don't want to meditate, the reason must be something else than study and if they do not study they will simply go on thinking about "small things". Want of time is not the cause of their non-meditation and passion for study is not the cause.

*

One does not learn English or French as an aid to the sadhana; it is done for the development of the mind and as part of the activity given to the being. For that purpose learning French is as good as learning English and, if it is properly done, better. Nor is there any reason, if one has the capacity, to limit oneself to one language only.

*

It depends on what you want to do with the language. If it is only to read the literature, then to learn to read, pronounce and understand accurately is sufficient. If it is a complete mastery one wants, then conversation and writing have to be thoroughly learned in that language.

*

To read many books quickly gives freedom and ease and familiarity with the language. The other method [*to read a book carefully more than once*] is necessary for thoroughness and accuracy in detail.

The Study of Philosophy

I don't know that there is anything false in your philosophical reflections. Philosophy is of course a creation of the mind but its defect is not that it is false, but that a philosophical system is only a section of the Truth which the philosopher takes as a whole. If one does not shut oneself up like that but looks at all sides, there is no harm in philosophising.

*

It depends on the nature of the book [*whether it is harmful or useful*]. Philosophy makes the mind subtle in certain directions — or ought to do so. The only harm it can do is if the mind begins clinging to ideas instead of going forward to direct experience.

*

I do not know about this Commentary [*on the Taittiriya Upanishad*], but most commentaries on the Upanishads are written out of the reasoning and speculating intellect. They may be of use to people who are trying to find out intellectually the meaning of the Upanishads — but they can be of no help to you as a sadhak who are seeking experience; it is likely rather to confuse the mind by taking it off the true basis and throwing it out from the road of experience and spiritual receptivity into the tangle of intellectual debate.

*

Yes, that [*to read critically*] is the right way to read these things. These philosophies [*of the early Greeks*] are mostly mental intuitions mixed with much guessing (speculation), but behind, if one knows, one can catch some Truth to which they correspond.

*

Metaphysics deals with the ultimate cause of things and all that lies behind the world of phenomena. As regards mind and consciousness, it asks what they are, how they came into existence, what is their relation to Matter, Life etc. Psychology deals with mind and consciousness and tries to find out not so much their ultimate nature and relations as their actual workings and the rule and law of these workings.

The Study of Logic

It [*the study of logic*] is a theoretical training; you learn by it some rules of logical thinking. But the application depends on your own intelligence. In any sphere of knowledge or action a man may be a good theorist but a poor executant. A very good military theorist and critic if put in command of an army might very well lose all his battles, not being able to suit the theories rightly to the occasion. So a theoretical logician may bungle the problems of thought by want of insight, of quickness of mind or of plasticity in the use of his capacities. Besides, logic is not the whole of thinking; observation, intuition, sympathy, many-sidedness are more important.

*

I never heard that learning logic was necessary for good expression. So far as I know very few good writers ever bothered about learning that subject.

*

I am not aware that by learning logic one gets freed from physical things. A few intellectuals lead the mental life and are indifferent to physical needs to a great extent, but these are very few.

*

Common sense by the way is not logic (which is the least common-sense-like thing in the world), it is simply looking at things as they are without inflation or deflation — not imagining wild imaginations — or for that matter despairing "I know not why" despairs.

The Study of Science

I think some knowledge of science will be most useful to you — that field is quite a blank for most people here, and yet the greater part of modern thought and knowledge is influenced by it.

*

Yes, the scientific mind does not lead very far [*in spiritual life*]; it only multiplies experiences but brings neither the realisation, nor the knowledge.

Chapter Three
The Power of Expression and Yoga

Verbal Expression

It is the thinking mind that works out ideas, the externalising mental or physical mind that gives them form in words. Probably you have not developed this part sufficiently — the gift of verbal expression is besides comparatively rare. Most people are either clumsy in expression or if they write abundantly, it is without proper arrangement and style. But this is of no essential importance in sadhana — all that is needed is to convey clearly the perceptions and experiences of their sadhana.

*

The power of expression comes by getting into touch with the inner source from which these things come. A calm and silent mind is a great help for the free flow of the power, but it is not indispensable, nor will it of itself bring it.

*

Thought and expression always give one side of things; the thing is to see the whole but one can express only a part unless one writes a long essay. Most thinkers do not even see the whole, only sides and parts — that is why there is always conflict between philosophies and religions.

Expression and Language

The Knowledge from above or whatever comes down can express itself in any language.

*

When the knowledge comes strongly from above, it very often brings its own language and the defects of the instrument are overcome. There are people who knew very little but when the knowledge began to flow they wrote wonderfully — when it was not flowing, their language became incorrect and ordinary.

*

If you speak of the expression, the deeper things in these experiences cannot be expressed — except by a great spiritual poet and even then only imperfectly — they can only be realised and remembered.

*

What is expressed is always only a part of what is behind — which remains unexpressed and in the language of the manifestation inexpressible.

Spoken and Written Expression

The voice brings a vibration of force which it is more difficult to put in writing which is a more mechanic vehicle — although the written word can have a special power of its own.

Writing and Sadhana

Writing by itself on ordinary subjects has the externalising tendency unless one has got accustomed to write (whatever be the subject) with the inner consciousness detached and free from what the outer is doing.

*

Writing and reading absorb the mind and fill it with images and influences; if the images and influences are not of the right kind, they naturally turn away from the true consciousness. It is only if one has the true consciousness well established already, that one can read or write anything whatever without losing it or without any other harm.

*

The use of your writing is to keep you in touch with the inner source of inspiration and intuition, so as to wear thin the crude external crust in the consciousness and encourage the growth of the inner being.

Poetry and Sadhana

Of course when you are writing poems or composing you are in contact with your inner being, that is why you feel so different then. The whole art of Yoga is to get that contact and get from it into the inner being itself, for so one can enter directly into and remain in all that is great and luminous and beautiful. Then one can try to establish them in this troublesome and defective outer shell of oneself and in the outer world also.

*

It is obvious that poetry cannot be a substitute for sadhana; it can be an accompaniment only. If there is a feeling (of devotion, surrender etc.), it can express and confirm it; if there is an experience, it can express and strengthen the force of experience. As reading of books like the Upanishads or Gita or singing of devotional songs can help, especially at one stage or another, so this can help also. Also it opens a passage between the exterior consciousness and the inner mind or vital. But if one stops at that, then nothing much is gained. Sadhana must be the main thing and sadhana means the purification of the nature, the consecration of the being, the opening of the psychic and the inner mind and vital, the contact and presence of the Divine, the realisation of the Divine in all things, surrender, devotion, the widening of the consciousness into the cosmic Consciousness, the Self one in all, the psychic and the spiritual transformation of the nature. If these things are neglected and only poetry and mental development and social contacts occupy all the time, then that is not sadhana. Also the poetry must be written in the true spirit, not for fame or self-satisfaction, but as a means of contact with the Divine through aspiration or of the expression of one's own inner being, as it was written formerly by those who left behind them so much devotional and spiritual poetry in India; it does not help if it is written only in the spirit of the Western artist or *littérateur*. Even works or meditation cannot succeed unless they are done in the right spirit of consecration and spiritual aspiration gathering up the whole being and dominating all else. It is the lack of this gathering up of the whole life and nature and turning it towards the one aim, which is the defect in so many here, that lowers the atmosphere and stands in the way of what is being done by myself and the Mother.

Chapter Four
Speech and Yoga

Outer Speech and the Inner Life

Even those who have a strong inner life, take a long time before they can connect it with the outer speech and action. Outer speech belongs to the externalising mind — that is why it is so difficult to connect it with the inner life.

*

Talk is more external than writing, it depends more on the physical and its condition. Therefore in most cases it is more difficult to get it out of the clutch of the external mind.

*

In talking one has the tendency to come down into a lower and more external consciousness because talking comes from the external mind. But it is impossible to avoid it altogether. What you must do is to learn to get back at once to the inner consciousness — this so long as you are not able to speak always from the inner being or at least with the inner being supporting the action.

*

You have to learn not to allow the speaking to alter your condition or else to recover it as soon as the interruption is over.

*

In speaking there should be always a sort of instinctive defence — except with those who are free from the ordinary vital impulse.

*

To remain aloof from the talk is what you should always do. The detachment is the first necessary condition for being free.

Talking and Dispersion of the Consciousness

Talking cannot be always avoided. I don't think it matters much so long as there is not excessive dispersion of the consciousness.

*

There are some who have the flow of speech by nature and those who are very vital cannot do without it. But the latter case (not being able to do without it) is obviously a disability from the spiritual point of view. There are also certain stages in the sadhana when one has to go inward and silence is at that time very necessary while unnecessary speech becomes a dispersion of the energies or externalises the consciousness. It is especially this chat for chat's sake tendency that has to be overcome.

*

It is one thing to speak simply and easily with others, keeping the inner consciousness, and another to let oneself go in the vital stream of an externalised consciousness — it was that which I said I had told you not to do.

*

It [*a feeling of dispersion*] is of course because the consciousness is thrown out in these things [*light talk and laughter*] and one comes out of the inner poise and has difficulty in going back to it — especially as there is a sort of dispersion of the vital energy. If one attains to a condition in which one can do these things only with the surface of the consciousness, keeping inside and observing what is done on the surface, but not forgetting oneself in it, then the poise is not lost. But it is a little difficult to get at this duplication of oneself — one comes to it however in time especially if the inner peace and calm become very intense and durable.

*

X's talk is certainly not very helpful to his sadhana and I think he knows it — but he has not made any real attempt to control his tongue as yet. Talk — of the usual kind — does very easily disperse or bring down the inner condition because it usually comes out of the lower vital and the physical mind only and expresses that part of the consciousness — it has a tendency to externalise the being. That is of course why so many Yogis take refuge in silence.

Talking and Fatigue

Everyone who lives much inside tends to feel too much talking a fatiguing thing and quite shallow and unnecessary unless it is talk that comes from within. Of course if you make a practice of talking much, that will bring you outside, externalise you and then you will no longer find it fatiguing even if you talk for 18 hours out of the 24.

*

Talking has a very exhausting effect for the inner energies — unless the inner itself controls the talk.

*

That [*feeling of fatigue after talking*] happens very usually. Talking of an unnecessary character tires the inner being because the talk comes from the outer nature while the inner has to supply the energy which it feels squandered away.

*

Chat of that kind [*about others*] has indeed a very tiring effect when one is at all in the stream of true experience, because it dissipates the energy uselessly and makes the mind movement a thing of valueless shreds and patches instead of gathered and poised in itself so as to receive.

*

The headache and the fatigue is always a sign that the consciousness no longer wants this outward-going thought and speech and is even physically strained by it. But it is the subconscient habit that wants to continue. Mostly human speech and thought go on mechanically in certain grooves that always repeat themselves and it is not really the mind that controls or dictates them. That is why this habit can go on for some time even after the conscious mind has withdrawn its support and consent and resolved to do otherwise. But if one perseveres, this subconscious mechanical habit runs down like all machinery that is not kept wound up to go on again. Then one can form the opposite habit in the subconscient of admitting only what the inner being consents to think or speak.

*

It is the nervous envelope that is weak — it is this that you saw. The fact that you feel weak when talking with people shows that the origin of the whole trouble is a weakened nervous force. It is this that you have to get strong. You should avoid much talking with others — you can also take rest when you feel the symptoms very strong. But faith, quietude and openness to the higher force are the fundamental cure.

Useless, Unnecessary or Light Speech

There should be no useless talking or mere chat, still less anything untrue or prompted by egoism and desire. One can talk, but with silence within and quietude in the speech.

*

On the whole you are right. Useless conversation which lowers the consciousness or brings back something of a past consciousness is better avoided. Talking about sadhana also comes under the category when it is merely mental discussion of a superficial kind.

*

The depression came into you subconsciously because you had the discussion with X. When you discuss like that with people, you put something in them, but something also comes from them to you. So, as X was not in quite a good condition, though nothing like what he used to be in his depressions, you easily got a touch of it and as soon as the subconscious could find a habitual excuse it sent it up to the mind. You should always be on your guard against these automatic interchanges. A little care is sufficient — and no needless discussion.

*

It is true that to indulge in useless or harmful conversations is not good, but on the other hand it is not good to be too much shut up in oneself. Some company and going out of oneself is also necessary.

*

It is always helpful to limit a little unnecessary talking — it has always a tendency to bring the consciousness down and outwards.

*

You are right — to minimise speech is sure to be helpful both for right action and for inner sadhana.

*

It is something very external that takes pleasure in light talk, and it is only when the quietude and with it a certain spontaneous self-control is established in the lower vital nature that this tendency can be entirely conquered in those who have it — i.e. in most people.

All these things will be worked out in time. What is most important is to get down the quietude into all the being and with it the true force bringing the energy which you describe above.

*

There is always a chance of something light and unbalancing coming in when there is levity indulged in for its own sake.

The consciousness feels a little shaken in its seat, if not pulled out. Once the consciousness is well set inside, then the outward movement gets determined from within and there is no such trouble.

*

Yes; excessive hilarity and unnecessary chat do most undoubtedly dissipate the force. A great moderation is necessary in these things.

Control of Speech

Yes, it would be better to get full control of the speech — it is an important step towards going inward and developing a true inner and Yogic consciousness.

*

Yes. The speech must come from within and be controlled from within.

*

Yes, control of the speech is very necessary for the physical change.

*

To control speech is to stand back from the speech impulse and observe it, not to say whatever the impulse makes you say but only to speak what one really needs to say or chooses to say, not to speak in haste or anger or impatience or lightly, not to talk at random or say what is harmful. It does not necessarily mean to speak very little, though that is often helpful.

*

It [speech] can only be controlled if you separate yourself from the part that is speaking and are able to observe it. It is the external mind that speaks — one has to watch it from the inner witnessing mind and put a control.

*

Yes, of course, complete truth of speech is very important for the sadhak and a great help for bringing Truth into the consciousness. It is at the same time difficult to bring the speech under control; for people are accustomed to speak what comes to them and not to supervise and control what they say. There is something mechanical about speech and to bring it to the level of the highest part of the consciousness is never easy. That is one reason why to be sparing in speech is helpful. It helps to a more deliberate control and prevents the tongue from running away with one and doing whatever it likes.

To stand back means to become a witness of one's own mind and speech, to see them as something separate from oneself and not identify oneself with them. Watching them as a witness, separate from them, one gets to know what they are, how they act and then put a control over them, reject what one does not approve and think and speak only what one feels to be true. This cannot, of course, be done all at once. It takes time to establish this attitude of separateness, still more time to establish the control. But it can be done by practice and persistence.

*

It is obvious that things which are a long habit cannot go at once. Especially the speech is a thing which in most people is largely automatic and not under their control. It is the vigilance that establishes the control, so one must be on guard against the danger of which you speak, the slacking of the vigilance. Only the more it can be a quiet and unmixed, not an anxious vigilance, the better.

*

The habits of the physical or the vital-physical nature are always the most difficult to change, because their action is automatic and not governed by the mental will and it is therefore difficult for the mental will to control or transform them. You have to persevere and form the habit of control. If you can succeed in controlling the speech often, — it needs a constant vigilance, — you will finally find that the control extends itself and can in the long run always intervene. This must be done so long as that movement is not fully opened to the Mother's Light and Force, for if that happens the thing can be done more quickly and sometimes with a great rapidity. There is also the intervention of the psychic — if the psychic being is sufficiently awake and active to intervene each time you are going to speak at random and say "No", then the change becomes more easy.

*

The psychic self-control that is desirable in these surroundings and in the midst of discussion would mean among other things:

(1) Not to allow the impulse of speech to assert itself too much or say anything without reflection, but to speak always with a conscious control and only what is necessary and helpful.

(2) To avoid all debate, dispute or too animated discussion and simply say what has to be said and leave it there. There should also be no insistence that you are right and the others wrong, but what is said should only be thrown in as a contribution to the consideration of the truth of the matter. I notice that what you report X as having said in this discussion had its truth and what you said was also true, so that really there should have been no dispute.

(3) To keep the tone of speech and the wording very quiet and calm and uninsistent.

(4) Not to mind at all if others are heated and dispute, but remain quiet and undisturbed and yourself speak only what can help things to be smooth again.

(5) If there is gossip about others and harsh criticism (especially about sadhaks), not to join — for these things are helpful in no way and only lower the consciousness from its higher level.

(6) To avoid all that would hurt or wound others.

Criticising Others

The habit of criticism — mostly ignorant criticism of others — mixed with all sorts of imaginations, inferences, exaggerations, false interpretations, even gross inventions is one of the universal illnesses of the Asram. It is a disease of the vital aided by the physical mind which makes itself an instrument of the pleasure taken in this barren and harmful pursuit of the vital. Control of the speech, refusal of this disease and the itch of the vital is very necessary if inner experience has to have any true effect of transformation in the outer life.

*

It is also better to be more strict about not talking of others and criticising them with the ordinary mind — not only in the case of X or Y but all. It is necessary in order to develop a deeper consciousness and outlook on things that understands in silence the movements of Nature in oneself and others and is not moved or disturbed or superficially interested and drawn into an external movement.

Gossip

It [*gossiping*] can be and very often is [*a hindrance to sadhana*]. A gossiping spirit is always an obstacle.

*

The difficulty you experience exists because speech is a function which in the past has worked much more as an expression of the vital in man than of the mental will. Speech breaks out as the expression of the vital and its habits without caring to wait for the control of the mind; the tongue has been spoken of as the unruly member. In your case the difficulty has been increased by the habit of talk about others, — gossip, to which your vital was very partial, so much that it cannot even yet give up the pleasure in it. It is therefore this tendency that must cease in the vital itself. Not to be under the control of the impulse to speech, to be able to do without it as a necessity and to speak only when one sees that it is right to do so and only what one sees to be right to say, is a very necessary part of Yogic self-control.

It is only by perseverance and vigilance and a strong resolution that this can be done, but if the resolution is there, it can be done in a short time by the aid of the Force behind.

*

Truth is far above this false gossip and scandal. Care only for the Divine's opinion and not for that of men.

Speaking the Truth

It [*truthfulness*] means first truth-speaking, but beyond that to keep the speech in harmony with the deepest truth of which one is conscious.

*

It is very evident from this inward control which you feel enlightening and guiding you and the resolution of truth-speaking that it made you take, that your psychic being is awake within you.

The fault of character of which you speak is common and almost universal in human nature. The impulse to speak what is untrue or at least to exaggerate or understate or twist the truth so as to flatter one's own vanity, preferences, wishes or to get some advantage or secure something desired is very general. But one must learn to speak the truth alone if one is to succeed truly in changing the nature.

To become conscious of what is to be changed in the nature is the first step towards changing it. But one must observe these things without being despondent or thinking "it is hopeless" or "I cannot change". You do right to be confident that the change will come. For nothing is impossible in the nature if the psychic being is awake and leading you with the Mother's consciousness and force behind it and working in you. This is now happening. Be sure that all will be done.

*

Very obviously, you ought not to have said or written what was a lie, and you should avoid doing it in future.

The things that you imagined, would not have happened

and therefore there was not even any use in this untruth — but useless or not, untruth should be avoided.

*

In the first place, there is a great difference between uttering as truth what one believes or knows to be false and uttering as truth what one conscientiously believes to be true, but is not in fact true. The first is obviously going against the spirit of truth, the second does homage to it. The first is deliberate falsehood, the second is only error at worst or ignorance.

This is from the practical point of view of truth-speaking. From the point of view of the higher Truth, it must not be forgotten that each plane of consciousness has its own standard — what is truth to the mind, may be only partial truth to a higher consciousness, but it is through the partial truth that the mind has to go in order to reach the wider more perfect truth beyond. All that is necessary for it is to be open and plastic, to be ready to recognise the higher when it comes, not to cling to the lower because it is its own, not to allow the desires and passions of the vital to blind it to the Light or to twist and pervert things. When once the higher consciousness begins to act, the difficulty diminishes and there is a clear progress from truth to greater truth.

*

If you get the English original[1] from X, you will see that what is written is from the highest standpoint. If you want to be an instrument of the Truth, you must always speak the truth and not falsehood. But this does not mean that you must tell everything to everybody. To conceal the truth by silence or refusal to speak is permissible, because the truth may be misunderstood or misused by those who are not prepared for it or who are opposed to it

---

[1] *Sri Aurobindo is referring to the following statement of the Mother: "If we allow a falsehood, however small, to express itself through our mouth or our pen, how can we hope to become perfect messengers of Truth? A perfect servant of Truth should abstain even from the slightest inexactitude, exaggeration or deformation."* Words of the Mother — II *(Pondicherry: Sri Aurobindo Ashram, 2004),* Collected Works of the Mother *(second edition), vol. 14, p. 202. — Ed.*

— it may even be made a starting point for distortion or sheer falsehood. But to speak falsehood is another matter. Even in jest it should be avoided, because it tends to lower the consciousness. As for the last point, it is again from the highest standpoint — the truth as one knows it in the mind is not enough, for the mind's idea may be erroneous or insufficient — it is necessary to have the true knowledge in the true consciousness.

*

Why should it be lying [*to leave something unsaid*]? One is not bound to tell everything to everybody — it might often do more harm than good. One has only to say what is necessary. Of course what is said must be true and not false and there must never be any intention to deceive.

*

"As one likes" is never a formula that leads to truth; it implies enthroning the vital and its desire as the standard or following the mind's preferences — which even in any mental discipline is regarded as contrary to the very principle of the search for Truth.

*

Because one is dealing with dishonest people, that does not justify one in going down to their own level.

If you think that the prices are too high, or, simply, if you want them to be lower, you can say so and ask for a reduction, but it is not right to support your demand by a false statement.

No one is bound to speak the truth when it would be harmful or to speak whatever is in one's mind; it is always permissible to keep silence or evade a reply and not to say what one does not wish or think it right to tell. But to tell a lie is superfluous and not justifiable.

It is usually out of weakness (mind and vital) that people lie; those who are strong in nature do not need to lie. A sadhak has to be strong and not weak — straightforward when necessary, silent when necessary, but not a liar. Straightforwardness does not mean of course that one has to babble out everything to everybody — to keep things to oneself, not to tell what should not be told is very necessary; but falsehood is not the right way to conceal things that have not to be told, the right way is silence.

*

If it [*what one has said to someone*] is true, it should not be withdrawn [*even if the person is troubled by it*]. But the truth need be told only when it helps the person spoken to, otherwise silence is better.

*

It is not the fact that if a man is truthful (in the sense of not lying), all he says happens. For that he must know the Truth — be in touch with the truth of things, not merely speak the truth as his mind knows it.

*

Things said of sadhana — or any kind of real truth — always give more meaning with the growth of consciousness and experience. That is why when one rises in the level of consciousness the truth seen before in the mind becomes a new and vastly deeper thing always.

*

That [*talking about spiritual things when one is full of imperfections*] is not hypocrisy but a conflict between two parts of the nature. Hypocrisy comes in only when one preaches a thing one does not believe or deliberately pretends to be or aim at what one is not and has no intention of trying to become.

Mauna or Keeping Silence

That is not the way. Absolute silence and looseness of talk are two extremes; neither is good. I have seen many people practising *maunavrata*, but afterwards they are just as talkative as before. It is self-mastery you must get.

*

Mauna is seldom of much use. After it is over, the speech starts again as on the old lines. It is in speech itself that the speech must change.

*

It is no use giving up talking altogether — the proper course is to speak usefully to people but not to talk for the sake of talking.

*

There is not much utility in complete outer silence or absolute retirement. Unless one is very strong spiritually, these things often end by creating a moribund condition of the consciousness.

*

To remain in silence as much as possible is good for a time. But entire retirement is seldom found to be helpful — the lower movements may remain quiescent owing to want of stimulus from outside, but do not disappear. For that you must be able to get an inner quietude and a mastery over the outer movements which will resist any atmosphere.

*

The difficulty is that the things in the atmosphere come in even if one does not speak with people. There are always mind waves moving about. It is a mastery that has to be developed, beginning with a power of silence, exclusion, non-response.

*

It is really an inner silence that is needed — a something silent within that looks at outer talk and action but feels it as something superficial, not as itself and is quite indifferent and untouched by it. It can bring forces to support speech and action or it can stop them by withdrawal or it can let them go on and observe without being involved or moved.

*

If one keeps the inner silence even when among the friends, that is the real thing; the outer silence need only be relative until the time comes when speech itself is an expression out of the silence.

*

If the peace is very strong within, talking does not cloud it — because this peace is not mental or vital even when it pervades the mind and vital — or else it is a cloud that quickly passes without touching deeply. Usually however such talk [*about others*] disperses the consciousness and one can lose much. The only disadvantage of not talking is that it isolates too much, if it is absolute, but by not talking these things one loses nothing.

Other Aspects of Speech Control

In all things there must be a control over thought and speech also. But while rajasic violence is excluded, a calmly forceful severity of thought and speech where severity is needed is sometimes indispensable.

*

Yes, obviously, the power to say "No" is indispensable in life and still more so in sadhana. It is the power of rejection put into speech.

*

These [*heated*] discussions are perfectly useless, they only deflect the mind and open the gate to falsehood.

*

Harangues and exhortations touch only the surface of the mind. If the mind is in agreement it is pleased and stimulated, but that is all. If it is not in agreement the mind criticises or becomes impatient and turns aside. If the harangue is very forcible it may touch the vital sometimes and produce a momentary effect.

*

It is no use being moved by the talk of others; one who follows the path, must be strong enough to go on upon it untouched by the opinion of the outside world. And it is best not to speak of these things to the indifferent or the hostile.

*

Hastiness of speech and action — (in excess, because to a certain extent it exists in everybody) — is a matter of temperament. I do not suppose it is more in you than in many others here. Of course it has to be got rid of, but it is one of the lesser, not one of the major imperfections of nature with which the Yogic Force has to deal. It is the externalising mind that has to be disciplined so that it may not leap too soon to conclusions or rush immediately from thought to speech and action.

*

That (thinking over what was talked) is a physical mind habit which should in course of time wear out. The mind should be free to shut off immediately as soon as the talk is done.

Part Two

Sadhana on the Level of the Vital

Section One

The Vital Being and Sadhana

Chapter One

The Nature of the Vital

Living in the Vital

Man is a mental being and cannot come from the vital, although part of him may live on the vital plane or rather in connection with it. Most men in fact live much in the vital and therefore when they practise sadhana it is first on the vital plane that they find themselves, in dreams, experiences etc. When the supramental opens then something will descend from the supramental in each as he becomes ready and forms a supramental Purusha in him. What he is now, cannot limit what he will become.

*

That [*a routine of work and study*] is not living in the vital — these are physical and mental occupations merely. Living in the vital is a psychological condition.
 Most people live in their vital. That means that they live in their desires, sensations, emotional feelings, vital imaginations and see and experience and judge everything from that point of view. It is the vital that moves them, the mind being at its service, not its master. In Yoga also many people do sadhana from that plane and their experience is full of vital visions, formations, experiences of all kinds, but there is no mental clarity or order, neither do they rise above the mind. It is only the minority of men who live in the mind or in the psychic or try to live on the spiritual plane.

*

Of course most men live in their physical mind and vital, except a few saints and a rather larger number of intellectuals. That is why, as it is now discovered, humanity has made little progress in the last three thousand years, except in information and material equipment. A little less cruelty and brutality perhaps, more plasticity of the intellect in the elite, a quicker habit of change in forms, that is all.

*

A vital life, "a little higher than the animals" because of some play of mind, with death as its answer is all that human existence is as it is ordinarily envisaged. And yet there is an aspiration for something more; but the religions take hold of it and canalise it into something pointless for life and things remain as they are. Only a few indeed get beyond this limit.

The "after all" is indeed only an excuse.[1] Nobody can become more than human if he refuses to make a sacrifice of his ego — for "human" means a vital animal ego mentalised by a little outward thought and knowledge. So long as one is satisfied with remaining that, one will remain human "even here" or anywhere.

*

People are living now so much in the vital when they do not live in the intellect, and so unguardedly and without restraint, the old mental conventions and restraints being in a state of deliquescence, that catastrophes are likely to be common. The disappearance of conventions and the urge to a larger life are in themselves good things, but on condition that a greater control and a truer harmony are discovered. At present people are going about it in the wrong way — hence the perilous condition of Europe and of the world. Nor are these convulsed and insecure conditions a very favourable environment for the development of a spiritual life either. But it seems that it is in the midst of difficulties that it is destined to come.

*

The times now are both worse and better than in Wordsworth's — on one side there is a collapse into the worst parts of human

---

[1] *The correspondent wrote, "When people say — even here — 'After all we are human, we have not become gods', it seems to me only an excuse." — Ed.*

nature and a riot of the vital forces, on the other there is in compensation a greater seeking for something beyond and a seeking with more light and knowledge in it.

The Irrationality of the Vital

The vital started in its evolution with obedience to impulse and not reason — as for strategy, the only strategy it understands is some tactics by which it can compass its desires. It does not like the voice of knowledge and wisdom — but curiously enough by the necessity which has grown up in man of justifying action by reason, the vital mind has developed a strategy of its own which is to get the reason to find out reasons for justifying its own feelings and impulses. When the reason is too clear to lend itself to this game, the vital falls back on its native habit of shutting its ears and going on its course. In these attacks, the plea of unfitness, "Since you are not pleased with my impulses and I can't change them, that shows I am unfit, so I had better go", is the counter-strategy it adopts. But even if one counters that, the impulse itself is sufficient, coming strongly as it does from universal Nature, to restore to the vital for a short time its old blind irrational instinct to obey the push that has come.

*

The doubts of the sadhaks more often rise from the vital than from the true mental — when the vital goes wrong or is in trouble or depression, the doubts rise and repeat themselves in the same form and the same language, no matter how much the mind had been convinced by either patent proofs or intellectual answers. I have noticed that always. The vital is irrational (even when it uses the reason to justify itself) and it believes or disbelieves according to its feeling, not according to reason.

*

The opposition of the vital is never reasonable, even when it puts forward reasons. It acts from its nature and habit of desire, not from reason.

The Deceptiveness of the Vital

The vital always prefers to cover its movements from the Light.

*

The whole significance of your sentences was that you had made all the necessary resolutions, but you could not carry them out because the Force refused to support you. That is the usual trick of the vital mind when it wants to rid itself of the blame for difficulties or want of progress in the sadhana: "I am doing all I can, but the Force is not supporting me." It is no use your quoting other sentences, because you write now one thing, now another, shifting your ground for the sake of your argument. If logic could help you to get rid of this trickery of the vital mind, it would be worth while learning Logic.

*

As to what you ask about anything else being behind than what your mind was conscious of in its surface intention, there is more often than not something behind when the vital meddles in the matter — and it is a part of self-knowledge not to be misled by the mind's surface movements but to detect this something behind. For it is the habit of the vital to make a mask of the mind's arrangements about feelings and actions in order to conceal even from the self-observation of the doer the secret underlying motive or forces behind the speech, act or feelings.

*

It is indeed amazing that you should have lost yourself to an extravagant deception such as X has set on foot. It is simply the spirit of vital falsehood, dramatic and romantic, obscuring the reason and shutting out common sense and simple truth. To clear the vital, you must get out of it all compromise with falsehood — no matter how specious the reason it advances — and get the habit of simple straightforward psychic truth engraved in it so that nothing may have a chance to enter. If this lesson can be imprinted in that part of the vital which is capable of such compromises, some good will come out of this wrong movement. Put the Mother's notice henceforth at the door of your vital being, "No falsehood hereafter shall ever enter here", and station a sentry there to see that it is put into execution.

*

You have to develop discrimination so that it becomes impossible for the vital to deceive you.

*

If there is this unconsciousness, you have to learn to be conscious in all your actions, so that the vital movements will no longer be able to deceive you or take any cover. You must make a point of being perfectly sincere in looking at these vital movements and seeing them as they are.

If once you can open in the psychic being and keep it open, then from within yourself will come constantly a perception that will show you at each step the actual truth and keep you on your guard against any kind of deception. If you aspire constantly and allow the peace to grow and the Force to work in you, this opening will come.

A Good Instrument But a Bad Master

The human vital is almost always of that nature [*full of desires and fancies*], but that is no reason why one should accept it as an unchangeable fact and allow a restless vital to drive one as it likes. Even apart from Yoga, in ordinary life, only those are considered to have full manhood or are likely to succeed in their life, their ideals or their undertakings who take in hand this restless vital, concentrate and control it and subject it to discipline. It is by the use of the mental will that they discipline it, compelling it to do not what it wants but what the reason or the will sees to be right or desirable. In Yoga one uses the inner will and compels the vital to submit itself to tapasya so that it may become calm, strong, obedient — or else one calls down the calm from above obliging the vital to renounce desire and become quiet and receptive. The vital is a good instrument but a bad master. If you allow it to follow its likes and dislikes, its fancies, its desires, its bad habits, it becomes your master and peace and happiness are no longer possible. It becomes not your instrument or the instrument of the Divine Shakti, but of any force of the Ignorance or even any hostile force that is able to seize and use it.

*

Yes, that is the nature of the vital. It can make the absolute and enthusiastic surrender as well as cause all the trouble possible. Without the vital there is no life or force of action or manifestation; it is a necessary instrument of the spirit for life.

*

Vitality means life-force — wherever there is life, in plant or animal or man, there is life-force — without the vital there can be no life in matter and no living action. The vital is a necessary force and nothing can be done or created in the bodily existence, if the vital is not there as an instrument. Even sadhana needs that vital force.

But if the vital is unregenerate and enslaved to desire, passion and ego, then it is as harmful as it can otherwise be helpful. Even in ordinary life the vital has to be controlled by the mind and mental will, otherwise it brings disorder or disaster. When people speak of a vital man, they mean one under the domination of vital force not controlled by the mind or the spirit. The vital can be a good instrument, but it is a bad master.

The vital has not to be killed or destroyed, but purified and transformed by the psychic and spiritual control.

*

What has been put into the vital receptacle by life can be got out by reversing it, turning it towards the Divine and not towards yourself. You will then find that the vital is as excellent an instrument as it is a bad master.

*

If your will is strong and stiff, always, the vital however obstinate is bound to yield in the end and become your instrument and not your master.

Purification of the Vital

Purification of the vital is usually considered to be a condition for successful sadhana. One may have some experiences without it, but at least a complete detachment from the vital movements is necessary for a sustained realisation.

Discipline of the Vital

It is true that for the external vital an outer discipline is necessary for the purification, otherwise it remains restless and fanciful and at the mercy of its own impulses — so that no basis can be built there for a quiet and abiding higher consciousness to remain firmly. The attitude you have taken for the work is of course the best one and, applying it steadily, the progress you feel was bound to come and is sure to increase.

*

To live and act under control or according to a standard of what is right — not to allow the vital or the physical to do whatever they like and not to let the mind run about according to its fancy without truth or order [*is the meaning of discipline*]. Also to obey those who ought to be obeyed.

*

An overmastering impulse is not necessarily an inspiration of true guidance; in following always such impulses one is more likely to become a creature of random caprices. Inexhaustible energy is an excellent thing, but not an energy without discipline.

*

The will ought to have the same mastery over impulses as over the thoughts. Many people find it easier to control an impulse than to prevent a thought.

*

The vital is good when it is properly used — it is a necessary instrument for action. But ordinarily it is in its lower action an instrument of ego and desire — that is why it has not to be indulged, but rather put under strong discipline.

*

The vital has to be controlled and not allowed to do what it likes. It is not the vital that has to control you, it is you who have to control the vital.

*

Be careful about vital movements and formations — when you allow them, you are on a dangerous slope.

*

If you want the Divine and the inner life, the old vital moorings must be cut.

*

It is certainly the abrupt and decisive breaking that is the easiest and best way for these things — vital habits.

*

People are here to change what is wrong in their nature so that they may do an effective sadhana.

*

If you want to change, you must first resolutely get rid of the defects of your vital being, persevering steadily, however difficult it may be or however long it may take, calling in always the divine help and compelling yourself always to be entirely sincere.

As for fitness and unfitness, nobody is entirely fit for this Yoga; one has to become fit by aspiration, by *abhyāsa*, by sincerity and surrender. If you have always desired the spiritual life, it is the psychic part of you that desired it, but your vital has always come in the way. Establish a sincere will in the vital; do not allow personal desires and demands and selfishness and falsehood to mix in your sadhana; then alone the vital in you will become fit for the sadhana. Lately you seem to have made a more sincere endeavour; if you want it to succeed, the endeavour must become always purer and more steady and persistent. If you practise sincerely, you will get the help needed by you.

If you take the right attitude in your work, that itself will bring the help. The right attitude is to work for the sake of the Divine, as an offering, without demand for any reward, without selfish claims and desires, without self-assertion and arrogance, not quarrelling with your fellow workers, thinking it to be the Mother's work and not your own, and trying to feel her power behind the work. If you can do that, your nature will progress and change.

I write this much in answer to your letter because I find in it a beginning of vital sincerity which was not there before. The rest depends upon you. If you become vitally sincere, the help will be with you.

Surrender of the Vital

There is nothing definite that I can tell you. Mother finds no conscious opposition in your mind or will to surrender and transformation. But probably the difficulty lies in the vital (not mind) of the artist (the poet, painter etc. in you), because the vital of the artist is always accustomed to its independence, to follow its own way, to make and live in its own world and pursue the impulses of its nature. If that element changes, then probably surrender and transformation could be more rapid, but it is not always easy for it to change at once, it usually goes by a gradual and almost unobserved change.

*

It is not at all a fact that your nature is incapable of love and bhakti; on the contrary that is the right way for you. Meditation is all right, but it will be most profitable for you if it is directed towards the increase of love and devotion; the rest will come of itself afterwards.

Also, it is not true that your nature is incapable of surrender; you made a great progress in that direction. But the complete surrender of all parts, especially of the whole vital, is certainly difficult. It can only come with the development of the consciousness. Meanwhile, that it has not fully come, is no reason for despair or giving up.

You are taking too bleak a view of things, the usual result of your giving way to depression. You used to have this before and you got over it by persistence. Now also by persistence it will go. To make radical decisions under the influence of depression is not good. To brace yourself up and, however persistent the difficulties are, to stick it out, is always the best.

Be faithful and persevering, then, however long the way, you cannot fail to reach the goal.

Conversion of the Vital

It is not easy to compel the vital, though it can be done. It is easier by the constant pressure of the mind to persuade and convert it; but it is true that in this mental way of doing it the vital does often attach itself to the spiritual ideal for some gain of its own. The one effective way is to bring the light down always in the vital, exposing it to itself, so that it is obliged to see what is wrong with itself and in the end to wish sincerely for a change. The light can be brought upon it either from within from the psychic or from above through the mind into the vital nature. To call down this light and force from above the mind is one of the chief methods of the Yoga. But whatever way is used, it is always a work of persistent and patient spiritual labour. The vital *can* be converted suddenly, but even after a sudden conversion the effects of it have to be worked out, applied to every part of the vital until the effect is complete and that takes often a long time. As for the physical consciousness, that can only be converted by long spade work, as it were, — rapid changes in this or that point can be made; but the whole change means a long and persistent endeavour.

Liberation of the Vital

The liberation you are aspiring for is indeed extremely necessary for the sadhak, but it means the liberation of the whole vital part of the nature — not a thing that can be done easily or at once. The *mūla jalada* is not in you or in anyone, it is in the universal vital Nature. The aspiration must be constant, patient and persistent, in the end it will prevail. To call the higher calm and peace down into the system from above is the main thing — if you feel that coming down, it will be the beginning of the liberation.

*

You were getting the true consciousness down into the vital, but as the old difficulty rose again in the physical, there is again the vital attack. The sign of complete liberation will be when your vital can face this attack always without being upset or crying out, repelling its force by a calm rejecting force from within.

The Higher Vital Movement

The higher vital movement is more refined and large in motion than that of the ordinary vital. It stresses emotion rather than sensation and desire, but it is not free from demand and the desire of possession.

The Emergence of the True Vital

It is through a change in the vital that the deliverance from the blind vital energy must come — by the emergence of the true vital which is strong, wide, at peace, a willing instrument of the Divine and of the Divine alone.

*

The vital is an indispensable instrument — no creation or strong action is possible without it. It is simply a question of mastering it and of converting it into the true vital which is at once strong and calm and capable of great intensity and free from ego.

*

It is the nature of the unregenerated vital part on the surface to do like that [*express dissatisfaction, resist change*]. The true vital is different, calm and strong and a powerful instrument submitted to the Divine. But for that to come forward, it is necessary first to get this fixed poise above in the mind — when the consciousness is there and the mind calm, free and wide, then the true vital can come forward.

*

Why the Apollyon do you suppose that all vital things are impure? The vital has strength, ardour, enthusiasm, self-confidence, generosity, the victor spirit — a host of other very necessary things. The only difficulty is that they get mixed up with others that *are* impure. All the same they are there and much needed.

*

It [*the psychic life-energy*] means the life-energy which comes from within and is in consonance with the psychic being — it is the energy of the true vital being, but in the ordinary ignorant vital it is deformed into desire.

You have to quiet and purify the vital and let the true vital emerge.

Or you have to bring the psychic in front, and the psychic will purify and psychicise the vital and then you will have the true vital energy.

*

Certainly it is better if the vital is brought to the true movement — renouncing its wrong movements and asking only for growth of the self-realisation, psychic love and psychicisation of the nature. But it is possible to get rid from above of the more active forms of obstruction even with a neutral vital.

Vital Sincerity, Aspiration, Consecration

It [*vital sincerity*] is the one-pointed will in the vital to be transformed.

*

The vital can rise to the head in two ways — one to cloud the mind with the vital impulses, the other to aspire and join with the higher Consciousness. If you noticed the aspiration, it was evidently the latter movement.

*

It [*vital consecration*] is to offer all the vital nature and its movements to the Divine so that it may be purified and only the true movements in consonance with the Divine Will may be there and all egoistic desires and impulses disappear.

*

Consecration means offering and making sacred to the Mother so that the whole vital nature may belong to her and not to the lower nature.[2]

*

As for the offering of the actions to the Divine and the vital difficulty it raises, it is not possible to avoid the difficulty, — you have to go through and conquer it. For the moment you make this attempt, the vital arises with all its restless imperfections to oppose the change. However, there are three things you can do to alleviate and shorten the difficulty:
    1. Detach yourself from this vital-physical — observe it as something not yourself; reject it, refuse your consent to its claims and impulses, but quietly as the witness Purusha whose refusal

---

[2] *The correspondent asked the meaning of "vital consecration" and how one may offer the vital to the Mother. — Ed.*

of sanction must ultimately prevail. This ought not to be difficult for you, if you have already learned to live more and more in the impersonal Self.

2. When you are not in this impersonality, still use your mental will and its power of assent or refusal, — not with a painful struggle, but in the same way, quietly, denying the claims of desire, till these claims by loss of sanction and assent lose their force of return and become more and more faint and external.

3. If you become aware of the Divine above you or in your heart, call for help, for light and power from there to change the vital itself, and at the same time insist upon this vital till it itself learns to pray for the change.

Finally, the difficulty will be reduced to its smallest proportions the moment you can by the sincerity of your aspiration to the Divine and your surrender awaken the psychic being in you (the Purusha in the secret heart) so that it will come forward and remain in front and pour its influence on all the movements of the mind, the vital and the physical consciousness. The work of transformation will still have to be done, but from that moment it will no longer be so hard and painful.

Peace and Quiet in the Vital

What you have to aspire for and bring down in you is the peace of the Mother's consciousness. Peace, calm, equanimity in the emotional being and the rest of the vital especially — it is that which will purify the emotions and deliver the vital.

*

If you bring down the peace into your vital, it will be liberated — for even if wrong movements come, it will be able to reject them.

*

A quiet and even basis [*for sadhana*] means a condition of the sadhana in which there is no tossing about between eager bursts of experience and a depressed inert or half inert condition, but whether in progress or in difficulty there is always a quiet consciousness behind turned in confidence and faith towards the Divine.

*

This quietude is not tamas at all — it is a quiescence of the ordinary rajasic movements of the nature (desire, grief, attachment and other reactions), which is very necessary in order that peace may come. It is what we may call the quiet vital — and it is in the quiet mind and the quiet vital that the true spiritual consciousness can most easily come.

Chapter Two
The Vital and Other Levels of Being

The Spirit and the Vital

The Spirit itself if it wants to manifest in matter must use the vital. It is so that things are arranged.

The Higher Consciousness and the Vital

The two movements whose apparent contradiction confuses your mind, are the two ends of a single consciousness whose motions, now separated from each other, must join if the life-power is to have its more and more perfect action and fulfilment or the transformation for which we hope.

The vital being with the life-force in it is one of these ends; the other is a latent dynamic power of the higher consciousness through which the Divine Truth can act, take hold of the vital and its life-force and use it for a greater purpose here.

The life-force in the vital is the indispensable instrument for all action of the Divine Power on the material world and the physical nature. It is therefore only when this vital is transformed and made a pure and strong instrument of the Divine Shakti, that there can be a divine life. Then only can there be a successful transformation of the physical nature or a free perfected divine action on the external world; for with our present means any such action is impossible. That is why you feel that the vital movement gives all the energy one can need, that all things are possible by this energy and that you can get with it any experience you like, whether good or bad, of the ordinary or of the spiritual life, — and that also is why, when this energy comes, you feel power pervading the body-consciousness and its matter. As for the contact with the Mother in the vital and your sense of the fine, the magnificent experience it was, — that too is natural and right; for the vital, no less than the psychic and every other part of the being, has to feel the Divine Mother and give itself entirely to her.

But this must always be remembered that the vital being and the life-force in man are separated from the Divine Light and, so separated, they are an instrument for any power that can take hold of them, illumined or obscure, divine or undivine. Ordinarily, the vital energy serves the common obscure or half-conscious movements of the human mind and human life, its normal ideas, interests, passions and desires. But it is possible for the vital energy to increase beyond the ordinary limits and, if so increased, it can attain an impetus, an intensity, an excitation or sublimation of its force by which it can become, is almost bound to become an instrument either of divine powers, the powers of the gods, or of Asuric forces. Or, if there is no settled central control in the nature, its action can be a confused mixture of these opposites, or in an inconsequent oscillation serve now one and now the other. It is not enough then to have a great vital energy acting in you; it must be put in contact with the higher consciousness, it must be surrendered to the true control, it must be placed under the government of the Divine. That is why there is sometimes felt a contempt for the action of the vital force or a condemnation of it, because it has an insufficient light and control and is wedded to an ignorant undivine movement. That also is why there is the necessity of opening to inspiration and power from a higher source. The vital energy by itself leads nowhere, runs in chequered, often painful and ruinous circles, takes even to the precipice, because it has no right guidance; it must be connected with the dynamic power of the higher consciousness and with the Divine Force acting through it for a great and luminous purpose.

There are two movements necessary for this connection to be established. One is upward; the vital rises to join with the higher consciousness and steeps itself in the light and in the impulsion of a higher force: the other is downward; the vital remains silent, tranquillised, pure, empty of the ordinary movements, waiting, till the dynamic power from above descends into it, changes it to its true self and informs its movements with knowledge as well as power. That is why the sadhak feels sometimes that he is rising up into a happier and nobler consciousness, entering into a brighter domain and purer experience, but sometimes, on the contrary, feels the necessity of going back into the vital, doing sadhana there and bringing down into it the true consciousness. There is no real contradiction between these two movements; they are complementary and necessary to each other, the ascension enabling the divine descent, the descent fulfilling that for which the ascension aspires and which it makes inevitable.

When you rise with the vital from its lower reaches and join it to the psychic, then your vital being fills with the pure aspiration and devotion natural to the psychic; at the same time it gives to the feelings its own abundant energy, it makes them dynamic for the change of the whole nature down to the most physical and for the bringing down of the divine consciousness into earth matter. When it not only touches the psychic but fuses with the higher mind, it is able to come into contact with and obey a greater light and knowledge. Ordinarily, the vital is either moved by the human mind and governed by its more or less ignorant dictates, or takes violent hold of this mind and uses it for the satisfaction of its own passions, impulses or desires. Or it makes a mixture of these two movements; for the ordinary human mind is too ignorant for a better action or a perfect guidance. But when the vital is in contact with the higher mind, it is possible for it to be guided by a greater light and knowledge, by a higher intuition and inspiration, a truer discrimination and some revelations of the divine truth and the divine will. This obedience of the vital to the psychic and the higher mind is the beginning of the outgoing of the Yogic consciousness in its dynamic action upon life.

But this, too, is not sufficient for the divine life. To come into contact with the higher mind consciousness is not enough, it is only an indispensable stage. There must be a descent of the Divine Force from yet loftier and more powerful reaches. A transformation of the higher consciousness into a supramental light and power, a transformation of the vital and its life-force

The Vital and Other Levels of Being 119

into a pure, wide, calm, intense and powerful instrument of the Divine Energy, a transformation of the physical itself into a form of divine light, divine action, strength, beauty and joy are impossible without this descending Force from the now invisible summits. That is why in this Yoga the ascent to the Divine which it has in common with other paths of Yoga is not enough; there must be too a descent of the Divine to transform all the energies of the mind, life and body.

*

There is a stage in the transformation when the Power is pressing on the outer being, especially the vital, and bringing down the higher consciousness. But the natural movements of the vital (anger, restlessness and impatience) are frequently breaking out and disturbing the work. Do not be shaken by that but remain as separate as possible from these movements and let the Force work.

*

It [*a confused inner condition*] is because your sadhana has come down into the vital and in the vital there is not the Light or the higher consciousness. You must aspire for the Light and the true Consciousness to come down into the vital.

*

Your analysis [*of certain vital movements*] is perfectly accurate — with this clear knowledge of the mechanism of the whole thing it should be easier to get rid of these ignorant forces. It is true that they care nothing for truth or reason and appeal only to the blind feelings of the vital, but still the light of the true consciousness turned steadily on them ought to so much enlighten your own vital that it will no longer lend itself to the things that seek to disturb it and be ready to take its stand on the calm and happiness of surrender to the Divine.

*

Of course, it is true that the physical enjoyment is not the only enjoyment — the vital has its own way of enjoyment. The whole thing is to separate oneself from that and identify oneself with the psychic and spiritual being and through them receive the higher consciousness which will change the vital nature.

The Intuition and the Vital

The vital controlled and transformed by the Intuition has the spontaneous right sense of things instead of groping and getting things by the wrong end due to passion, desire etc.

The Psychic and the Vital

Your former sadhana was mostly on the vital plane. The experiences of the vital plane are very interesting to the sadhak but they are mixed, i.e. not all linked with the higher Truth. A greater, purer and firmer basis for the sadhana has to be established — the psychic basis. For that reason all the old experiences are stopped. The heart has to be made the centre and through bhakti and aspiration you have to bring forward the psychic being and enter into close touch with the Divine Shakti. If you can do this, your sadhana will begin again with a better result.

*

Obviously when there is that inability to control and over-eagerness, it must be a movement of a vital nature. The vital can take part in a movement but it must not be in control — it must be subordinated to the psychic.

*

They [*the vital and the psychic*] cannot be reconciled except by the submission of the vital to the psychic. Any other combination means either the submergence of the psychic by vital delusions or a confused and misleading mixture or the use of the psychic aspirations by the vital to justify things that are not spiritual.

*

It is the nature of the psychic pressure to change the former tendencies of the mind, vital and physical consciousness, and remove those that were of the nature of imperfections. This weakness in your outer vital and timidity before others and dependence on them and preoccupation with their opinion of you or their attitude towards you was one of the chief obstacles in your vital nature. If it is now going, it is because of the psychic pressure; for under it these things go slowly but surely.

*

The ordinary human emotions, good and bad, are all of them vital movements. It is only the psychic feelings that come from the deeper heart within which are not vital.

*

What he is having now are the true spiritual and psychic experiences — not those of the vital plane which most have at the beginning. The experiences of the vital plane (in which there is much imagination and fantasy) are useful for opening up the consciousness; but it is when they are replaced by the spiritual and psychic consciousness that there is the beginning of the true progress.

*

When the vital being has been touched by the psychic, mere vital pleasure has no longer any interest, and may also be felt as a disturbance and discomfort because of the lowering effect upon the consciousness.

*

The Ananda you describe is evidently that of the inner vital when it is full of the psychic influence and floods with it the external vital also. It is the true Ananda and there is nothing in it of the old vital nature. When the psychic thus uses the vital to express itself, this kind of intense ecstasy is the natural form it takes. This intensity and the old vital excitement are two quite different things and must not be confused together. Where there is the intensity with a pure and full satisfaction, contentment and gratitude leaving no room for claim, demand or depressing reaction, that is the true vital movement.

*

I think it needful at this stage of your sadhana to repeat my previous warning about not allowing any vital mixture. It is the crudity of the unregenerated vital that prevents the psychic from remaining always at the front. You have now seen clearly the two different consciousnesses, — according to what you have written in one of your letters, the psychic and the vital. To get rid of the old vital nature is now one of the most pressing needs of your sadhana. You are trying to get rid of the vital attachments and to turn entirely to the Mother. At this juncture you must be careful not to allow the movements of the old vital nature to enter into your relations with the Mother. Take this matter of your wish for more physical nearness to her or contact with her.[1] Take care not to allow this to gain on you or become a desire; for if you do, the vital will begin to play, to create demands and desires, to awaken in you jealousy and envy of others and other undesirable movements, and that would push your psychic being into the background and spoil the whole truth of your sadhana. There are some who have suffered much trouble and difficulty in their Yoga by making this mistake, and I think it therefore better to put you on your guard.

*

The vital may get psychicised or spiritualised, but the vital does not become the psychic or the spiritual part any more than the hand can become the head or the heart. You can put knowledge into the workings of the hand; so too you can put spirituality into the vital, but as the hand remains a hand even when it does the works of intelligence, so the vital remains the vital even when it becomes a pure instrument of the spirit.

---

[1] *The correspondent had asked to see the Mother for five minutes a day in order to have a short meditation with her. Sri Aurobindo replied that the Mother did not have time for this and had refused all who had made the same request. — Ed.*

The Mind and the Vital

It is evident that your sadhana has been up till now in the mind — that was why you found it easy to concentrate at the crown of the head because the centre there directly commands the whole mental range. The mind quieted and experiencing the effects of the sadhana quieted the vital disturbance, but did not clear and change the vital nature.

Now the sadhana seems to be descending into the vital to clear and change it. The first result is that the difficulty of the vital has shown itself — the ugly images and alarming dreams come from a hostile vital plane which is opposed to the sadhana. From there also comes the renewal of the agitation, the disinclination and resistance to the sadhana. This is not a going back to the old condition, but the result of a pressure of the Yoga-Force on the vital for change to which there is a resistance.

It is this descent of the sadhana to free the vital being that made you feel the necessity of concentrating in the region of the heart; for in the region of the heart is the psychic centre and below, behind the navel, is the vital centre. If these two can be awakened and occupied by the Yoga-Force, then the psychic or Soul-Power will command the whole vital range and purify the vital nature and tranquillise it and turn it towards the Divine. It will be best if you are able to concentrate at will in the heart-region and at the crown of the head, for that gives a more complete power of sadhana.

The other experiences you have are the beginning of the change in the vital, e.g. peace with yourself and those you thought had injured you, joy and freedom from all worldly cares and desires and ambitions. These came too with a quieted mind, but they can be fixed only when the vital is liberated and tranquillised.

Whatever difficulties or troubles arise, the one thing is to go on quietly with full faith in the Divine Power and the guidance, opening steadily and progressively the whole being to the workings of the sadhana till all becomes conscious and consenting to the needed change.

*

At present your experiences are on the mental plane, but that is the right movement. Many sadhaks are unable to advance because they open the vital plane before the mental and psychic are ready. After some beginning of true spiritual experiences on the mental plane there is a premature descent into the vital and great confusion and disturbance. This has to be guarded against. It is still worse if the vital desire-soul opens to experience before the mind has been touched by the things of the spirit.

Aspire always for the mind and psychic being to be filled with the true consciousness and experience and made ready. You must aspire especially for quietness, peace, a calm faith, an increasing steady wideness, for more and more knowledge, for a deep and intense but quiet devotion.

Do not be troubled by your surroundings and their opposition. These conditions are often imposed at first as a kind of ordeal. If you can remain tranquil and undisturbed and continue your sadhana without allowing yourself to be inwardly troubled under these circumstances, it will help to give you a much needed strength; for the path of Yoga is always beset with inner and outer difficulties and the sadhak must develop a quiet, firm and solid strength to meet them.

*

If you see more clearly any deficiencies of your vital nature and the necessity of a transformation, that itself is a sign of psychic growth. They should not be a cause of discouragement; for these are common defects of the human vital and by an increased psychic opening they will lose their hold and finally disappear.

As for the diminution of mental control over the vital movements, that often happens temporarily in the course of the Yoga. Mental control has to be replaced by a greater control from above and by the calm, purity and strong peace of the vital itself opened to the Divine Force and its government of the whole nature.

Do not allow yourself to be troubled or discouraged by any

difficulties, but quietly and simply open yourself to the Mother's force and allow it to change you.

*

It is not at all true that the Mother takes away the mental control — that is one of the many foolish misinterpretations that certain sadhaks make about the sadhana. What is true — and that is the cause of what you feel — is that when you try to control fully your habitual movements in the vital by the sadhana, instead of sometimes controlling them and sometimes indulging, then they make a violent resistance so that they seem to increase. The sadhak has to stand firm and refuse to be overborne or discouraged by this violence. In dream it is usually the case that even what one has thrown out from the waking state, comes up for a long time — that is because all these things remain still in the subconscient and it is the subconscient that creates a great part of people's dreams. Thus if one no longer has sexual desires in the waking state he can still have sex-dreams — and emissions — with a more or less frequent recurrence; he can still meet people in dreams whom he never sees or hears or thinks of in his waking hours, — and so on. All the more are such dreams likely to come when the waking mind is not free.

*

Once the vital being has come forward and shown its difficulty — there is nobody who has not one crucial difficulty or another there — it must be dealt with and conquered.

It must be dealt with not by the mind but directly by the supramental power.

Not peace and knowledge in the mind, but peace, faith, calm strength in the vital being itself (and especially in this part of it that is defective) is the thing to be established. To open yourself and allow all this to be brought down into it is the proper course.

The deficiency is not in the higher mind or mind proper; there is therefore no use in going back to establish mental peace. The difficulty is in that part of the vital being which is not sufficiently open and confident and not sufficiently strong and courageous and in the physical mind which lends its support to these things. To get the supramental light and calm and strength and intensity down there is what you need.

You may have all the mental knowledge in the world and yet be impotent to face vital difficulties. Courage, faith, sincerity towards the Light, rejection of opposite suggestions and adverse voices are there the true help. Then only can knowledge itself be at all effective.

Not mental control but some descent of a control from above the mind is the power demanded in the realisation. This control derived eventually from the supermind is a control by the Divine Power.

*

Your difficulty in getting rid of the aboriginal in your nature will remain so long as you try to change your vital part by the sole or main strength of your mind and mental will, calling in at most an indefinite and impersonal divine Power to aid you. It is an old difficulty which has never been radically solved in life itself because it has never been met in the true way. In many ways of Yoga it does not so supremely matter because the aim is not a transformed life but withdrawal from life. When that is the object of an endeavour, it may be sufficient to keep the vital down by a mental and moral compulsion, or else it may be stilled and kept lying in a kind of sleep and quiescence. There are some even who allow it to run and exhaust itself if it can while its possessor professes to be untouched and unconcerned by it; for it is only old Nature running on by a past impetus and will drop off with the fall of the body. When none of these solutions can be attained, the sadhaka sometimes simply leads a double inner life, divided between his spiritual experiences and his vital weaknesses to the end, making the most of his better part, making as little as may be of the outer being. But none of these methods will do for our purpose. If you want a true mastery and transformation of the vital movements, it can be done only on condition you allow your psychic being, the soul in you, to awake fully, to establish its rule and, opening all to the permanent touch of the divine Shakti, impose its own way of pure devotion, whole-hearted aspiration and complete uncompromising urge to all that is divine on the mind and heart and vital nature. There is no other way and it is no use hankering after a more comfortable path. *Nānyaḥ panthā vidyate'yanāya.*

*

For the mind to be quiet, the vital must be quiet, free of desires etc. or at any rate one must be able to control them so that they shall not interfere with the concentration.

*

What happens usually is that something touches the vital, often without one's knowing it, and brings up the old ordinary or external consciousness in such a way that the inner mind gets covered up and all the old thoughts and feelings return for a time. It is the physical mind that becomes active and gives its assent. If the whole mind remains quiet and detached observing the vital movement, but not giving its assent, then to reject it becomes more easy. This established quietude and detachment of the mind marks always a great step forward made in the sadhana.

*

The vital movements are always more difficult to deal with than the pure mental — but it comes with practice.

The Physical and the Vital

It is a great progress if you can now do that [*patiently go on trying, turned always to the Mother*]. The chief difficulty in the way of living in the light as well as the peace and force is the confused and turbid restlessness of man's vital nature. If that is quieted, the major difficulty is gone. There still remains the obstacle of the physical nature's non-understanding or inertia — but that is less troublesome — it is more of the nature of a quiet though sometimes obstinate obstruction than a disturbance. If the vital inquietude has been cured then certainly the physical obscurity or non-understanding will go.

*

The separate existence of the vital and physical comes to be known of itself usually in the progress of the Yoga. So long as one lives mainly in the surface consciousness one can only know them by their results — one can see that this or that is or must be a movement of the vital etc.; but the direct concrete experience comes only when one begins to live deeper down in the inner being.

Chapter Three

Wrong Movements of the Vital

The Phrase "Wrong Movements"

The phrase [*"wrong movements"*] covers pretty nearly everything that is hurtful to spiritual progress — movements of doubt, revolt, egoistic desire or ambition, sexual indulgence are the most common, but there are plenty of others.

*

It depends on what is meant by a wrong or unnecessary movement [*of the vital*]. Certain things have to fall off before the establishment [*of the higher consciousness*] can be *complete*. Others that are unnecessary have to be put aside if they are incompatible with the full sadhana or the growth of the inner consciousness, but can be continued if the consciousness established is such that doing or not doing makes no difference to it.

Vital Reactions

A vital reaction means a response of the vital to the touch or pressure of an idea, action, event, person or thing.

E.g. if someone speaks something you do not like and you get angry, that is a vital reaction. Or if a woman passes and you feel sexual desire, that is a vital reaction. Or if something unpleasant happens and you get a depression, that is a vital reaction. Most disturbances of the consciousness are due to vital reactions, though the mind may assist by wrong thoughts and judgments and misinterpretations. There can be good vital reactions as well as bad, but the term is usually applied to those that are undesirable and have to be surmounted by the sadhak.

The ideal condition is that of a calm, clear, strong vital free from the reactions of the vital ego and responding with true and high feelings only that are acceptable to the spiritual will and the psychic being.

Vital Suggestions

It would not be at all right to yield to these suggestions which are obviously those of a force that wants to make use of the unease and disappointment of the vital in order to drive you to break your sadhana. These are the usual suggestions that come to all under the stress of this vital condition: "I am not fit for this sadhana. I must go, I cannot stay here. The Mother does not love me. I have given up everything and got nothing. The struggle makes me too miserable; let me go." As a matter of fact there is no real foundation for these suggestions. Because an acute struggle has come, it would be absurd to conclude that you are unfit for the sadhana and to give it up after going so far. It is because you have asked the physical-vital to give up certain of its cherished attachments and habits that it is in this condition; unable to resist altogether, miserable at being deprived, it accepts these suggestions as an excuse for escape from the pressure you have put upon it. The acuteness of the struggle is due to the vehemence of the attack, but still more to this vital or a part of it responding to the suggestions; otherwise a less disturbing even if a slower movement would be quite possible. The Mother has in no way changed towards you nor is she disappointed with you — that is the suggestion drawn from your own state of mind and putting its wrong sense of disappointment and unfitness on to the Mother. She has no reason to change or be disappointed, as she has always been aware of the vital obstacles in you and still expected and expects you to overcome them. The call to change certain things that seem to be in the grain of character is proving difficult even for the best sadhaks, but the difficulty is no proof of incompetence. It is precisely this impulse to go that you must refuse to admit — for so long as these forces think they can bring it about, they will press as much as they can on this point. You must also open yourself more to the Mother's Force in that part and for that it is necessary to get rid of this suggestion about the Mother's disappointment or lack of love, for it is this which creates the reaction at the time of Pranam. Our help, support, love are there always as before — keep yourself open to them and with their aid drive out these suggestions.

*

The feelings and movements of the past always return at night in sleep. It is only when the consciousness that generated them is changed and cleared in the waking state, that afterwards one can clear them out of the sleep also.

You are listening too much to the suggestions of the outer consciousness, "not being able", etc. etc. Since you did begin to open a little for a time, it shows that you are able. You have to get back to that movement; for that you must persuade this outer vital not to go on repeating, "I am not able, my efforts cannot succeed, I am too crooked etc." — or if it goes on, you must not listen to it. You must affirm and concentrate on the possibility that was shown you and not on the supposed impossibility.

*

But how is it that any part of you gives any value to the suggestions? If no part gives any value then surely they must seem to you too laughable and contemptible to have any effect or power to make you revolt.

If you attach no value to the suggestions, then there may be the inertia still but not this.

*

The fact that your vital "goes out of the poise" and accepts them [*ego, demand and desire*] means that you keep yourself open to them. The sign that these things are no longer admitted is when the inner vital rejects them so that they become suggestions only and nothing else. There may arise a surge of suggestions or waves from the general nature, but they cannot get admission. It is only then that a will can be kept in which one is untouched by the general atmosphere.

*

It is not the mind, but the psychic being that made the suggestion through the mind. There is a part of the mind that is under the influence of the Truth and can be the channel of the psychic being's knowledge or feeling; there is another part that answers to the vital and expresses and supports the difficulties and oppositions in the nature. If the whole mind refuses to respond to the vital or accept or support its suggestions then much of the force of the vital attack disappears and one is more able to put a pressure on the vital and oblige it also to listen to the psychic and change.

What happened in your case was that the whole vital difficulty — the main one of the family — massed itself together and rose. When an attack like that is overcome, there is always a clearance of the inner atmosphere. It must not be allowed to gather force again — and for that the mind must always follow the psychic suggestion and refuse at once to harbour the opposite suggestions and at the same time keep itself open to the Mother, so that the Mother's Force may come down into it and occupy it and work there.

Vital Restlessness

I have no idea why he wants to change [*his work*]. If he wants to make himself some day fit for the spiritual life, the first thing to be avoided is vital restlessness. To do the work one has to do with a quiet mind, making an offering of it to the Divine and trying to get rid of egoism and vital desire, is the best way to prepare oneself.

*

The bitterness you feel is that of a restless and dissatisfied vital which did not get what it desired because it could not desire anything strongly and persistently. Otherwise it could have all the vital desires — marriage, friends, position etc. — but it could stick to nothing owing to a kind of weak restlessness. In the Yoga it has shown the same restless weakness, — otherwise it could by this time have attained something, and besides there was the sex-impulse which it would neither satisfy nor leave. You must know what you want and want it with your whole will — it is only so that there can be an end of this restlessness and failure.

*

As for the other thing it is the struggle between the mind and psychic which see the right thing to do and the restless vital. It is not something wrong in the head, on the contrary the head is getting more and more to see what is right; it is only that the vital restlessness is not dominated by the mind and wants to follow its own feeling. That happens to everybody so long as the vital is not properly under our control. Even in ordinary circumstances and in ordinary life the vital is always carrying away the being to do what the mind disapproves, but there it is felt to be something normal, especially as the vital very usually persuades the mind to find arguments and justify its mistakes. You have to persist until the understanding mind and psychic in you become normally stronger than this part of the vital that does not want to be quiet and concentrated or see things rightly. Then you will not be so much troubled by this disagreement between two parts of the being.

*

It is mostly when the sadhana condition is interrupted that the vital becomes agitated or impatient and restless. Instead of remaining quiet and waiting or calling down the real push from above, it begins to get vexed and restless and begins to ask questions: "Why this? why that?" These things do not mean that you are going astray — it means only that these defects are still not worked out, that is all. Also the old vital mental egoism rises up and if the answers do not please it, it becomes challenging, disputatious, insistent on its own point of view. These are old defects which are part of the external nature and therefore difficult to root out. You must learn to recognise them and get rid of them by a quiet rejection and disuse.

*

It is not true that you cannot or will never be put right. It is what appears to you when your lower vital is restless or else your physical mind comes uppermost. Only it is true that if you could keep yourself always in that part of you which is in contact, the thing would be done sooner and with much less difficulty and trouble.

*

If you reject the restlessness of the vital always, the whole being will be at peace and being at peace receive the divine Ananda. Only you must not let the Ananda go out in speech or action nor let it turn into outward vital joy. If you keep it silently within, it will work in you for the transformation.

Vital Dryness

The feeling of the desert comes because of the resistance of the vital which wants life to be governed by desire. If that is not allowed, it regards existence as a desert and puts that impression on the mind.

*

It is the resistance of the vital that takes the form of this dryness — a form of passive resistance, just as revolt or an excited activity of desire is its active form of resistance. But you should not be discouraged — these phases are normal and almost everybody has to face them. It is not really a sign of failure or inability, but a trying part of the process of change. Hold fast and aspire always for the love and the opening. The inner heart is there and that will receive an answer to the aspiration and one day quickly open the outer and make it also receive. To call to the Mother always is the main thing and with that to aspire and assent to the light when it comes, to reject and detach oneself from desire and any dark movement. But if one cannot do these other things successfully, then call and still call.

The Mother's force is there with you even when you do not feel it. Trust to it, remain quiet and persevere.

*

Wrong Movements of the Vital

Yes, dryness comes usually when the vital — here certainly the vital physical — dislikes a movement or condition or the refusal of its desires and starts non-cooperation. But sometimes it is a condition that has to be crossed through, e.g. the neutral or dry quietude which sometimes comes when the ordinary movements have been thrown out but nothing positive has yet come to take their place (e.g. peace, joy, a higher knowledge or force and action).

*

The ordinary freshness, energy, enthusiasm of the nature comes either from the vital, direct when it is satisfying its own instincts and impulses, indirect when it cooperates with or assents to the mental, physical or spiritual activities. If the vital resists, there is revolt and struggle. If the vital no longer insists on its own impulses and instincts but does not cooperate, there is either dryness or a neutral state. Dryness comes in when the vital is quiescent but passively unwilling, not interested, the neutral state when it neither assents nor is unwilling, — simply quiescent, passive. This however, the neutral state, can deepen into positive calm and peace by a greater influx from above which keeps the vital not only quiescent but at least passively acquiescent. With the active interest and consent of the vital the peace becomes a glad or joyful peace or a strong peace supporting and entering into action or active experience.

*

The dryness is usually only a passage of neutral quiet, — the vital withdrawing its stimulus gives to the neutrality a colour of dryness. To live in the peace is the natural condition of the Self and therefore the basis of the Yogic consciousness — it is possible when the peace has so deepened and generalised itself that even a vital attack cannot cover it up or penetrate it.

*

The slight dryness must have been the reaction caused in the physical vital by the "uninterest" in external things — because the physical vital depends very much on this external interest.

When it gets more accustomed to the silence, then the dryness disappears.

*

The feeling of loneliness, *udāsīnatā*, dryness and lack of *rasa* come very usually when the vital part is disappointed in its desires or tries to give them up but has not yet attained a quiet indifference towards them. It is necessary to replace this condition by the true quietude which will allow the psychic being to become again active and reopen the doors of inner experience, and we shall try to get this done.

*

I do not know that sadness has the power to cure [*dryness in the vital*]. I have myself followed the Gita's path of equanimity — but for some the psychic sadness may be necessary. But I think it is more an indication of a mistake than a cure.

Vital Resistance

The resistance and the contrary suggestions come from the vital nature which is in all men obscure and attached to ordinary ideas and aims and easily listens to such ideas and suggestions as those you mention. Faith and devotion come from the soul and it is only when the vital has entirely submitted to the soul that one can truly lead the spiritual life.

*

It is normal that when a special pressure is put on a vital movement, a resistance whether in the vital itself (here vital-physical) or in the subconscient should manifest itself. It is sometimes a real resistance, sometimes it is only the *pravṛtti* presenting itself for purification.

*

Why should you suppose it [*the effort of sadhana*] is vain? The purification of the vital takes a long time because until all the parts are free, none is quite free and because they use a multitude of movements which have to be changed or enlightened, — and moreover there is a great habit of persistence and resistance in the habitual movements of the nature. One therefore easily thinks that one has made no progress, — but all sincere and sustained effort of purification has its result and after a time the progress made will become evident.

*

You should not allow yourself to be invaded by this suggestion of not being fit or able to go through. The vital is the most difficult part of the being to change or control and even sadhaks who have advanced far have to struggle with it at times. But its more fundamental resistances can be overcome more quickly, and you have only to persevere in aspiration and opening to the Mother and this kind of denial will after a time come no more.

*

It is this idea that you are helpless because the vital consents to the wrong movement that comes in the way. You have to put your inner will and the Mother's light on the vital so that it shall change, not leave it to do what it likes. If one is to be "helpless" and ruled by any part of the instrumental being, how is change possible? The Mother's force or the psychic can act, but on condition that the assent of the being is there. If the vital is left to do what it likes, it will always go after its old habits; it has to be made to feel that it must change.

*

I suppose it is the nature of the vital which, when a thing is forbidden to it whether by the mind or by circumstances, runs after it more. But I suppose if you remain firm, this will pass.

*

When the vital takes hold of a thing it is often like that — it fixes it continually on the mind till it is either satisfied or the hold thrown off.

*

The one thing you have to avoid is losing patience; for that only prolongs the vital trouble. There is no reason for it. When the vital is to be changed (fundamentally) it always gives constant trouble like this until one can seat oneself fixedly in the calm of the inner consciousness and keep the vital movements quite on the surface.

*

It is always better to have peace. As for the vital, there is always something in it that resists and tries to retard, but if the inner being opens sufficiently and you can live in the inner being, peace can descend and establish itself there in such a way that the vital movements of the surface may be there but will not be able to break the inner peace.

Vital Dissatisfaction and Non-Cooperation

It is because the vital was very much under the grip of its desires and so, now that it is separately active, not controlled by mental will, it kicks and cries whenever its desires are not satisfied. That is an ordinary movement of the human vital when not dominated and kept in its place by the mental will.

*

It is an oscillation due to something in the resistant part (not the whole of it) being still dissatisfied at the call to change. When any vital element is disappointed, dissatisfied, called or compelled to change but not yet willing, it has the tendency to create non-response or non-cooperation of the vital, leaving the physical dull or insensible without the vital push. With the psychic pressure this remnant of resistance will pass.

*

There are two conditions in which it [*the vital*] becomes like that [*non-cooperative*]: (1) when its ordinary (ego) actions or motives of action are not allowed to it, (2) when one goes very much down into the physical, the vital sometimes or for a time becomes inert unless or until there is the Force from above.

*

The nervous being is under the influence of the vital forces; when they are denied or pushed out, it becomes depressed and wants to call them back — for it is accustomed to get the pleasure and strength of life from the vital movements and not from the spiritual or divine Force above.

*

The vital can be all right when things are going on swimmingly, but when difficulties become strong, it sinks and lies supine. Also if a bait is held out to the vital ego, then it can become enthusiastic and active.

*

It seems to be some tamas or inertia coming down on the system. It is sometimes like that when the vital gets dissatisfied with the conditions or with what has been attained and initiates a sort of non-cooperation or passive resistance, saying, "As I am not satisfied, I won't take interest in anything or help you to do anything."

It may be because I asked you to stop meditating and to wait. The vital does not like waiting. But I had to tell you that because of the burning of the centres, the disturbance of sleep and the rest — these must go before you can meditate in the right way and with success. If you meditate at all now, it should be only in calm and peace with a very quiet aspiration for the divine calm and peace to descend into you.

It is also perhaps due to your penchant for Nirvana. For the desire of Nirvana easily brings this kind of collapse of the energies. Nirvana is not the aim of my Yoga — but whether for Nirvana or for this Yoga, calm and peace in the whole being are the necessary foundation of all siddhi.

*

For the dissatisfaction of the vital, the only remedy is rejection and refusal to identify yourself with it. For the inertia the remedy is not to absorb yourself in thoughts about it, but to turn upwards and call the Light and Force to come into it.

Vital Disturbance and Revolt

The exacerbation of certain vital movements is a perfectly well-known phenomenon in Yoga and does not mean that one has degenerated, but only that one has come to close grips instead of to a pleasant nodding acquaintance with the basic instincts of the earthly vital nature. I have had myself the experience of this rising to a height, during a certain stage of the spiritual development, of things that before hardly existed and seemed quite absent in the pre-Yogic life. These things rise up like that because they are fighting for their existence — they are not really personal to you and the vehemence of their attack is not due to any "badness" in the personal nature. I dare say seven sadhaks out of ten have a similar experience. Afterwards when they cannot effect their object which is to drive the sadhak out of his sadhana, the whole thing sinks and there is no longer any vehement trouble. I repeat that the only serious thing about it is the depression created in you and the idea of inability in the Yoga that they take care to impress on the brain when they are at their work. If you can get rid of that, the violence of the vital attacks is only the phenomenon of a stage and does not in the end matter.

*

What you have noticed about the disturbances is true. There are now two consciousnesses in you, the new one that is growing and what is left of the old. The old has something in it which is a habit of the human vital, — the tendency to keep any touch of grief, anger, vexation etc. or any kind of emotional, vital or mental disturbance, to make much of it, to prolong it, not to wish to let it go, to return to it even when the cause of disturbance is past and could be forgotten, always to remember it and bring it up when it can. This is a common trait of human nature and a quite customary movement. The new consciousness on the contrary does not want these things and when they happen throws them off as quickly as possible. When the new consciousness is fully grown and established, then the disturbances will be altogether rejected. Even if the causes of them happen, there will be no response of grief, anger, vexation etc. in the nature.

*

The one thing necessary is to arrive at a fixed and definite choice in the mind which one can always oppose to the vital disturbance. Disturbance in the vital will always come so long as the full peace has not descended there, but with a fixed resolution in the mind kept always to the front the acuteness of the disturbance can disappear and the road become shorter.

*

Usually the vital tries to resist the call to change. That is what is meant by revolt or opposition. If the inner will insists and forbids revolt or opposition, the vital unwillingness may often take the form of depression and dejection accompanied by a resistance in the physical mind which supports the repetition of old ideas, habits, movements or actions which the body consciousness suffers from an apprehension or fear of the called for change, a drawing back from it or a dullness which does not receive the call.

It is these things you have to get rid of. But a sorrowful or despondent mood is not the proper condition for doing that. You have to stand back from the feeling of suffering, anguish and apprehension, reject it and look quietly at the resistance, affirming always to yourself your will to change and insisting that it shall be done and cannot fail to be done now or later with the divine help, because the divine help is there. It is then that the strength can come to you that will overcome the difficulties.

*

It was the dissatisfaction of the soul with the superficial vital life that brought you away from the outer world and it is the same dissatisfaction a hundred times increased and accompanied with an intense psychic sorrow that would come on you if you went away from the Yoga.

Your vital mind (which is the one which revolts and doubts) has strange misconceptions about the spiritual state. There is no grimness in being an instrument of the divine Will — it is the happiest and most joyous condition possible — it brings not only peace but an intense Ananda. Anyhow, the hold of the Yoga-force is increasing in spite of everything and you have only to go on for it to solve the struggle between the outer man and the inner Spirit.

*

This part of the vital [*which wants to revolt*] has no precise reasons to support itself with — it takes hold of any mood of disappointment or strong sense of difficulty. It is a factor in all human natures, — restless, desiring, eager, despondent, unstable. Stand back from it and do not allow it to govern or move you. There is a right part of the vital which must be used — ardent, sensitive to the higher things, capable of great love and devotion. Strengthen that and support it on the psychic and on the peace and wideness that comes from above.

*

Tell the vital that complaining and revolting only hampers you from getting what it wants — it is only when it is calm and confident that things can be done.

*

The outward revolt is the refusal of discipline and obedience — the inward revolt is of many kinds, it may take many forms, e.g. a revolt of the vital against the Mother, a revolt of the mind against the Truth, a rejection of the spiritual life, a demand to enthrone the ego as the Divine or to serve something that flatters the vital ego and supports its demands and call that the Divine, a response to vital suggestions of distrust, despair, self-destruction or departure — and many others.

*

The difficulty must have come from distrust and disobedience. For distrust and disobedience are like falsehood (they are themselves a falsity, based on false ideas and impulses), they interfere in the action of the Power, prevent it from being felt or from working fully and diminish the force of the Protection. Not only in your inward concentration, but in your outward acts and movements you must take the right attitude. If you do that and put everything under the Mother's guidance, you will find that difficulties begin to diminish or are much more easily got over and things become steadily smoother.

In your work and acts you must do the same as in your concentration. Open to the Mother, put them under her guidance, call in the peace, the supporting Power, the protection and, in order that they may work, reject all wrong influences that might come in their way by creating wrong, careless or unconscious movements.

Follow this principle and your whole being will become one, under one rule, in the peace and sheltering Power and Light.

Rejection of Wrong Vital Movements

It is quite true that rising into a higher consciousness than the ordinary human consciousness is the right way towards transformation. Merely to remain in the ordinary lower consciousness and try to reject from there the wrong movements can produce no permanent or complete result. But there are several points here which you must note or this perception may be accompanied by an error.

(1) As you have yourself subsequently seen, all the parts and personalities that constitute the being must share in the higher consciousness, otherwise the old movements under various pretexts will continue.

(2) You speak of rejecting the lower vital, but it is only the unregenerated lower vital movements that can be got rid of; you cannot get rid of the lower vital itself, for it is a necessary part of the manifested nature, like the higher vital or the mind. It has

to be changed in the power of the higher consciousness, not left to itself or dropped from you.

(3) If you do not so change it, if you simply remain content by living in the psychic or other higher consciousness internally then you raise the risk of doing like those who are satisfied to have experiences and some inner quietude or Ananda, but leave the external nature and surface active movements unchanged, either thinking them of no importance or justifying them under the plea that there is the psychic or spiritual consciousness behind them.

I asked you to look for the cause of the abatement of energy or zeal (*utsāha*), because it is evident that there must be some resistance somewhere, otherwise there would not be these constant headaches and this less intense condition. If the physical consciousness is open the headaches should disappear or at least diminish in frequency and force, and if the lower vital is all right, the intensity ought to continue.

*

But what do you want to do with all these obscure and useless vital movements that torment you, these wrong thoughts, suggestions, confusions, inabilities etc.? You seem to write as if you thought they must be kept and changed? But why kept and how changed? What would be the use? But precisely what you have got to do is to "shut them out", to reject, refuse to keep them, refuse to have them. It is precisely to see in another way, to see in the true way, that the Force is pressing on you. It would indeed be a great blessing if you could forget these other wrong things altogether. Again, why do you want to keep and change the "wrong things" as you yourself call them? If you have an illness, do you want to keep and change the pains, the sickness and all the rest of it? It is to throw out the illness that you want, for the body to forget it, not to keep any impression of it, to lose even the possibility of having it again, to live and feel in quite another way, the way of health. It is just the same here.

*

These wrong movements [*doubt, depression, sadness, hostility towards the Mother*] belong to the universal vital Nature, but the vital of man also shares in them, makes itself a centre and field of the play of these wrong forces: in that sense they are in you. But by constant rejection they are pushed out; you feel them no longer rising in you but coming from outside. The vital still admits them because it is not yet pure of the old habit of response. You have to persist till they are entirely foreign to your nature and no longer get admittance.

*

Keep your resolution firm in your mind. It is the vital that is invaded by something foreign from the outside (universal) Nature; it is not your own feeling. If you keep your resolution firm, the vital also will begin to throw out this foreign matter.

*

After each crisis there is something gained, if there has been a victory and rejection. The gain is to externalise the vital disturbance, so that even if it returns it will be felt so much an outside force that the observing consciousness (mental, higher vital) cannot be disturbed. If you keep that, it will be an immense advance.

Return of Vital Movements after Rejection

It was evidently not the action of something that is rooted still within, but an old movement returning from outside (from the universal Nature) to which something in the vital still responds by force of habit, force of accustomed recurrence. This is shown by the fact that you felt nothing at the time — only afterwards; also by the alternations of quiet and unrest after calling the Force, as if of something losing its hold and then trying to get it back and hold on still. Things thrown out always come back like that relying on the old habit of response in the stuff of the nature, — the old vibration. By throwing it out whenever it comes, in the end the part which responds begins to understand that it must not and is gradually or quickly liberated from the habit.

*

What comes back like that is the old vital movements which you used to have and which you have been throwing out. The vital gets disturbed and filled with these thoughts whenever something happens that hurts or displeases it strongly. To get rid of it one must have always a sense of complete reliance on the Mother, of surrender; that brings a calm which refuses to be moved by any outward happening or by what people do or say, a happiness which is not disturbed by any occurrence.

*

It must be that on that occasion the consciousness got lowered and some vital wave came in from the atmosphere resuscitating the old vibrations of the restless vital which had quieted down. You must separate yourself from them and get the poise of quietude again. They have no longer any real basis in mind or heart, they rely only on the force of repetition that comes up from the subconscient and once started try to keep these old ideas and feelings repeating themselves so as to prevent the consciousness from settling down into quietude. But the poise once obtained is there and has only been covered up and has got to be uncovered again from these cloudings. You must get the habit of keeping quiet somewhere in yourself when these attacks come, of keeping something within that refuses to say ditto to these suggestions or accept them as its own proper thoughts and feelings.

Anyhow the Force will be put to help you; receive it and all that will go.

*

It is very often when one thinks a particular resistance is finished and is no longer in the vital that it surges up again.

*

The only way to get rid of these vital movements is to do

persistently what he describes himself as doing with the invading forces — i.e. he must be always vigilant, try always at every moment to be conscious, always reject these things, refusing to take pleasure in them, call on the Mother, bring down the descent of the Light. If they return persistently he must not be discouraged; it is not possible to change the nature at once, it takes a long time. If, however, he can keep the psychic consciousness in the front, then it will be much easier and there will be much less difficulty and trouble in the change. That can be done by constant aspiration and *abhyāsa*.

*

The difficulty you have in your vital is not peculiar to you, but is in some degree and in one form or another a fairly general malady. Its constant return, the mechanical irrational return even when all the rest of the nature has rejected it, is due to the obstinacy of the material consciousness always repeating the old movement in the old groove at the least touch from the old habitual forces. It is a question of faith, patience and persistence. One must be more obstinate than the obstinate material nature and persevere until the light and truth can take permanent hold of the parts which are still responsive to the old movements. There can be no doubt that with this perseverance the Truth will in the end conquer.

It would make it easier if you could get rid of certain fixed ideas and of the habitual reaction of depression or despair when these recurrences come. For instance, you ought to throw away once for all this idea of X's malediction; it is a thing of the past and it is only the physical mind's memory of it that gives it some appearance of survival. The difficulties we are now meeting have nothing to do with X; they are part only of the necessity of conquest over the habits of the physical consciousness and he has nothing to do there and no influence of any kind whatever. Also dismiss any question about the "possibility" of conversion of your vital being; you should see rather that it is certain and not merely possible. This idea of identification with the dark Shakti is also another old notion which you ought to root out without cherishing any least trace of it. It has no meaning on the plane of the physical and vital physical consciousness where the whole work is now going on and to nourish any such ideas can only hamper your progress. Finally, when there are these recurrences, do not allow yourself to be depressed by them, but simply observe and stand back and call in the higher force with the full confidence that these are mechanical recurrences and in substance nothing more — however strong they may seem in appearance. The principle of mechanical repetition is very strong in the material nature, so strong that it makes one easily think that it is incurable. That however is only a trick of the forces of this material inconscience; it is by creating this impression that they try to endure. If, on the contrary, you remain firm, refuse to be depressed or discouraged and, even in the moment of attack, affirm the certainty of eventual victory, the victory itself will come much more easily and sooner.

*

All these things are there in human nature, habitual movements, which show their true nature only when the light of the higher consciousness is turned on them. Even after they have been rejected the possibility of a response to such suggestions from outside remains in the grain of the lower vital or vital physical or the subconscient till there is the full supramental enlightenment there.

Alternation of Good and Bad Vital Conditions

When one tries to change something in the vital, then, due to the nature's habit of persisting in a movement to which it has been accustomed, there is usually an alternation like this; the new condition persists for some days, then the old forces its way for some time to the surface. If one persists, the old movement begins to lose its force and die out and the new permanently replaces it.

*

At present I will only say that the alternations you feel are there between your psychic being and the mental and vital parts already submitted to it and the revolted vital parts full of the outcry of the vital ego stressing and increasing by brooding in them its own grievances and sufferings. That is a struggle which every sadhak has to go through with more or less acuteness; but the only way to escape from the suffering and struggle is for the mind to put itself wholly on the side of the soul and bring over the whole vital to the true attitude. It is absurd to think that we know nothing of these things; we know them very well but we know also that the solution lies not in the satisfaction of the revolted vital but in its submission and surrender to the soul within and to the Divine.

Chapter Four
The Lower Vital Being

The Decisive Ordeal of This Yoga

The cardinal defect, that which has been always standing in the way and is now isolated in an extreme prominence, is seated or at least is at present concentrated in the lower vital being. I mean that part of the vital-physical nature with its petty and obstinate egoism which actuates the external human personality, — that which supports its surface thoughts and dominates its habitual ways of feeling, character and action. I am not concerned here with the other parts of the being and I do not speak of anything in the higher mind, the psychic self or the higher and larger vital nature; for when the lower vital rises, these are pushed into the background, if not covered over for the time, by this lower vital being and this external personality. Whatever there may be in these higher parts, aspiration to the Truth, devotion or will to conquer the obstacles and the hostile forces, it cannot become integral, it cannot remain unmixed or unspoilt or continue to be effective so long as the lower vital and the external personality have not accepted the Light and consented to change.

It was inevitable that in the course of the sadhana these inferior parts of the nature should be brought forward in order that like the rest of the being they may make the crucial choice and either accept or refuse transformation. My whole work depends upon this movement; it is the decisive ordeal of this Yoga. For the physical consciousness and the material life cannot change if this does not change. Nothing that may have been done before, no inner illumination, experience, power or Ananda, is of any eventual value if this is not done. If the little external personality is to persist in retaining its obscure and limited, its petty and ignoble, its selfish and false and stupid human consciousness, this amounts to a flat negation of the work and the Sadhana. I have no intention of giving my sanction to a new edition of the old fiasco, a partial and transient spiritual opening within with no true and radical change in the law of the external nature. If, then, any sadhaka refuses in practice to admit this change, or if he refuses even to admit the necessity for any change of his lower vital being and his habitual external personality, I am entitled to conclude that, whatever his professions, he has not accepted either myself or my Yoga.

I am well aware that this change is not easy; the dynamic will towards it does not come at once and is difficult to fix and, even afterwards, the sadhaka often feels helpless against the force of habit. Knowing this, the Mother and myself have shown and are still showing sufficient patience in giving time for the true spirit to come up and form and act effectively in the external being of those around us. But if in anyone this part not only becomes obstinate, self-assertive or aggressive, but is supported and justified by the mind and will and tries to spread itself in the atmosphere, then it is a different and very serious matter.

The difficulty in the lower vital being is that it is still wedded to its old self and in revolt against the Light; it has not only not surrendered either to a greater Truth or to myself and the Mother, but it has up to now no such will and hardly any idea even of what true surrender is. When the lower vital assumes this attitude, it takes its stand upon a constant affirmation of the old personality and the past forms of the lower nature. Every time they are discouraged, it supports and brings them back and asserts its right to freedom — the freedom to affirm and follow its own crude and egoistic ideas, desires, fancies, impulses or convenience whenever it chooses. It claims, secretly or in so many words, the right to follow its nature, — its average unregenerate human nature, the right to be itself, — its natural, original, unchanged self with all the falsehood, ignorance and incoherence proper to this part of the being. And it claims or, if it does not claim in theory, it asserts in practice the right to express all this impure and inferior stuff in speech and act and behaviour. It defends, glosses over, paints in specious colours and tries to prolong indefinitely the past habitual ways of thinking, speaking and feeling and to eternise what is distorted and misformed in the character. This it does sometimes by open self-assertion and revolt, branding all that is done or said against it as error or oppression or injustice, sometimes behind a cover of self-deception or a mask of dissimulation, professing one thing and practising another. Often it tries to persuade itself and to convince others that these things are the only right reason and right way of acting for itself or for all or even that they are part of the true movement of the Yoga.

When this lower vital being is allowed to influence the action, as happens when the sadhaka in any way endorses its suggestions, its attitude, whether masked to himself or coming to the surface, dictates a considerable part of his speech and action and against it he makes no serious resistance. If he is frank with himself and straightforward to the Mother, he will begin to recognise the source and nature of the obstacle and will soon be on the direct road to correct and change it. But this, when under the adverse influence, he persistently refuses to be; he prefers to hide up these movements under any kind of concealment, denial, justification or excuse or other shelter.

In the nature the resistance takes certain characteristic forms which add to the confusion and to the difficulty of transformation. It is necessary to outline some of these forms because they are sufficiently common, in some in a less, in others in a greater degree, to demand a clear and strong exposure.

1. A certain vanity and arrogance and self-assertive rajasic vehemence which in this smaller vital being are, for those who have a pronounced strength in these parts, the deformation of the vital force and habit of leading and domination that certain qualities in the higher vital gave them. This is accompanied by an excessive *amour-propre* which creates the necessity of making a figure, maintaining by any means position and prestige, even of posturing before others, influencing, controlling or "helping" them, claiming the part of a superior sadhaka, one with greater knowledge and with occult powers. The larger vital being itself has to give up its powers and capacities to the Divine Shakti from whom they come and must use them only as the Mother's instrument and according to her directions; if it intervenes with

the claim of its ego and puts itself between her and the work or between her and other sadhakas, then whatever its natural power, it deviates from the true way, spoils the work, brings in adverse forces and wrong movements and does harm to those whom it imagines it is helping. When these things are transferred to the smallness of the lower vital nature and the external personality and take lower and pettier forms, they become still more false to the Truth, incongruous, grotesque, and at the same time can be viciously harmful, though in a smaller groove. There is no better way of calling in hostile forces into the general work or of vitiating and exposing to their influence one's own sadhana. On a smaller scale these defects of vanity, arrogance and rajasic violence are present in most human natures. They take other forms, but are then also a great obstacle to any true spiritual change.

2. Disobedience and indiscipline. This lower part of the being is always random, wayward, self-assertive and unwilling to accept the imposition on it of any order and discipline other than its own idea or impulse. Its defects even from the beginning stand in the way of the efforts of the higher vital to impose on the nature a truly regenerating tapasya. This habit of disobedience and disregard of discipline is so strong that it does not always need to be deliberate; the response to it seems to be immediate, irresistible and instinctive. Thus obedience to the Mother is repeatedly promised or professed, but the action done or the course followed is frequently the very opposite of the profession or promise. This constant indiscipline is a radical obstacle to the sadhana and the worst possible example to others.

3. Dissimulation and falsity of speech. This is an exceedingly injurious habit of the lower nature. Those who are not straightforward cannot profit by the Mother's help, for they themselves turn it away. Unless they change, they cannot hope for the descent of the supramental Light and Truth into the lower vital and physical nature; they remain stuck in their own self-created mud and cannot progress. Often it is not mere exaggeration or a false use of the imagination embroidering on the actual truth that is marked in the sadhaka, but also a positive denial and distortion as well as a falsifying concealment of facts. This

he does sometimes to cover up his disobedience or wrong or doubtful course of action, sometimes to keep up his position, at others to get his own way or indulge his preferred habits and desires. Very often, when one has this kind of vital habit, he clouds his own consciousness and does not altogether realise the falsity of what he is saying or doing; but in much that he says and does, it is quite impossible to extend to him even this inadequate excuse.

4. A dangerous habit of constant self-justification. When this becomes strong in the sadhaka, it is impossible to turn him in this part of his being to the right consciousness and action because at each step his whole preoccupation is to justify himself. His mind rushes at once to maintain his own idea, his own position or his own course of action. This he is ready to do by any kind of argument, sometimes the most clumsy and foolish or inconsistent with what he has been protesting the moment before, by any kind of misstatement or any kind of device. This is a common misuse, but none the less a misuse of the thinking mind; but it takes in him exaggerated proportions and so long as he keeps to it, it will be impossible for him to see or live the Truth.

Whatever the difficulties of the nature, however long and painful the process of dealing with them, they cannot stand to the end against the Truth, if there is or if there comes in these parts the true spirit, attitude and endeavour. But if a sadhaka continues out of self-esteem and self-will or out of tamasic inertia to shut his eyes or harden his heart against the Light, so long as he does that, no one can help him. The consent of all the being is necessary for the divine change, and it is the completeness and fullness of the consent that constitutes the integral surrender. But the consent of the lower vital must not be only a mental profession or a passing emotional adhesion; it must translate itself into an abiding attitude and a persistent and consistent action.

This Yoga can only be done to the end by those who are in total earnest about it and ready to abolish their little human ego and its demands in order to find themselves in the Divine. It cannot be done in a spirit of levity or laxity; the work is too high and difficult, the adverse powers in the lower Nature too ready to take advantage of the least sanction or the smallest opening, the aspiration and tapasya needed too constant and intense. It cannot be done if there is a petulant self-assertion of the ideas of the human mind or wilful indulgence of the demands and instincts and pretensions of the lowest part of the being, commonly justified under the name of human nature. It cannot be done if you insist on identifying these lowest things of the Ignorance with the divine Truth or even the lesser truth permissible on the way. It cannot be done if you cling to your past self and its old mental, vital and physical formations and habits; one has continually to leave behind his past selves and to see, act and live from an always higher and higher conscious level. It cannot be done if you insist on "freedom" for your human mind and vital ego. All the parts of the human being are entitled to express and satisfy themselves in their own way at their own risk and peril, if he so chooses, as long as he leads the ordinary life. But to enter into a path of Yoga whose whole object is to substitute for these human things the law and power of a greater Truth and the whole heart of whose method is surrender to the Divine Shakti, and yet to go on claiming this so-called freedom which is no more than a subjection to certain ignorant cosmic Forces, is to indulge in a blind contradiction and to claim the right to lead a double life.

Least of all can this Yoga be done if those who profess to be its sadhakas continue always to make themselves centres, instruments or spokesmen of the forces of the Ignorance which oppose, deny and ridicule its very principle and object. On one side there is the supramental realisation, the overshadowing and descending power of the supramental Divine, the light and force of a far greater Truth than any yet realised on the earth, something therefore beyond what the little human mind and its logic regard as the only permanent realities, something whose nature and way and process of development here it cannot conceive or perceive by its own inadequate instruments or judge by its puerile standards; in spite of all opposition this is pressing down for manifestation in the physical consciousness and the material life. On the other side is this lower vital nature with all its pretentious arrogance, ignorance, obscurity, dullness or incompetent turbulence, standing for its own prolongation, standing against the descent, refusing to believe in any real reality or real possibility of a supramental or suprahuman consciousness and creation or, still more absurd, demanding, if it exists at all, that it should conform to its own little standards, seizing greedily upon everything that seems to disprove it, denying the presence of the Divine — for it knows that without that presence the work is impossible, — affirming loudly its own thoughts, judgments, desires, instincts, and, if these are contradicted, avenging itself by casting abroad doubt, denial, disparaging criticism, revolt and disorder. These are the two things now in presence between which every one will have to choose.

For this opposition, this sterile obstruction and blockade against the descent of the divine Truth cannot last for ever. Every one must come down finally on one side or the other, on the side of the Truth or against it. The supramental realisation cannot coexist with the persistence of the lower Ignorance; it is incompatible with continued satisfaction in a double nature.

The Lower Vital Not Reasonable

The lower vital is not a part that listens to reason. There is no *why* to its action; it acts in a particular way because it has long been accustomed to act in that way, and it goes on even if the doing brings a painful reaction.

*

The lower vital is very slow in listening to reason — at least when reason is on the side of Truth; although it is very pleased to listen to the mind when the mind justifies the lower vital's wrong movements. In fact the lower vital moves on its own lines, not according to Truth or reason. It is only the insistence of a stronger Light that can enlighten it by changing it in its own substance of consciousness.

*

It is the lower vital energy that rushes to the brain and either confuses it and prevents mental self-control or else makes the mind its slave and uses reason to justify the passions.

*

It is the lower (physical) vital that acts like that [*expresses wrong thoughts and feelings*]. This part of Nature does not act according to reason, it has no understanding of things. It acts only according to desire, impulse and habit. The mind and the heart and the higher vital have understood and put themselves on the side of the Peace and Force that are acting to transform the nature. But this still responds to the old forces when they touch it. It is a question of getting down the Peace and Force and Light into this part, so that whenever the outside forces of the lower Nature touch they will find that force there and not the old response. It is a little difficult because of the long past habit, but it will come more and more as the Force descends into the body and pervades it in its descent.

The Resistance of the Lower Vital

In all it is the lower vital that is most full of ignorance and desire and therefore of falsehood.

*

There is very commonly a gulf between the higher parts and the lower vital even in ordinary life — in Yoga it is apt to get emphasised until the lower vital changes, but if we can judge from the majority of people here, that change is most extraordinarily difficult.

*

The struggle is always hard with the lower vital nature — because it has been indulged through so many lives and it is not easily made willing to change.

*

There is certainly a sincere will to change. This resistance of the lower vital is usual in everybody — it is the main difficulty in Yoga. If it were not there, the change would be easy. But once the steady mental will is there, it is a question of time and steady sadhana. With that the change is sure.

*

The resistance of the nerves persists because there is always a restlessness in the lower vital due to past errors and what they have left in the being until this part can be entirely opened to the peace and light and the presence of the Mother. It is towards this that your sadhana must be directed and you should not be discouraged if there is some resistance or even a strong resistance. That always happens; if the resistance is quietly and steadily rejected, then it can be overcome.

Rejecting Wrong Movements of the Lower Vital

The lower vital in most human beings is full of grave defects and of movements that respond to hostile forces. A constant psychic opening, a persistent rejection of these influences, a separation of oneself from all hostile suggestions and the inflow of the calm, light, peace, purity of the Mother's power would eventually free the system from the siege.

What is needed is to be quiet and more and more quiet, to look on these influences as something not yourself which has intruded, to separate yourself from it and deny it and to abide in a quiet confidence in the Divine Power. If your psychic being asks for the Divine and your mind is sincere and calls for liberation from the lower nature and from all hostile forces and if you can call the Mother's power into your heart and rely upon it more than on your own strength, this siege will in the end be driven away from you and strength and peace take its place.

*

It [*a troubled state of mind*] is because you entered on a wrong movement, taking the lower vital experiences for truth. You now find it difficult to get rid of them because of the hold you gave them. The two lines of forces are the line of these lower vital forces and the line of the true movement of forces resting on the psychic consciousness and opening the true mind, the true vital, the true physical consciousness to the action of the Higher Force. If you persist in rejecting the former and aspiring for the latter, the struggle will diminish after a time and the true path become more and more clear. Fidelity always and at every moment is what is required of you.

*

The condition [*for the change of the lower vital*] is that you must bring the sadhana into your physical consciousness and live for the sadhana and the Divine only. You must give up positively the bad habits that still persist and never resume those that have ceased or been interrupted. Inner experiences are helpful to the mind and higher vital for change, but for the lower vital and the outer being a sadhana of self-discipline is indispensable. The external actions and the spirit in them must change — your external thoughts and actions must be for the Divine only. There must be self-restraint, entire truthfulness, a constant thought of the Divine in all you do. This is the way for the change of the lower vital. By your constant self-dedication and self-discipline the Force will be brought down into the external being and the change made.

At present you have to go back, but this can very well be done outside. When it is done, then you will be truly ready for the complete spiritual life.

*

There can be only one "solution" of this kind of struggle, — to recognise these feelings for what they are, unregenerated movements of the old vital nature, and to reject these vital suggestions as suggestions of adverse forces that want to push you out of the straight path. If the mind of the sadhak supports these vital movements, if any part of his nature accepts and cherishes them, then, so long as he allows them to do so, he cannot get rid of the struggle.

All these suggestions are very familiar, and they are always the same both in expression and substance. The reactions too are always the same and their very nature is sufficient to show the source from which they come, — disappointment of unsatisfied desire, despondency, discontent, unhappiness, the sense of grievance and injustice, revolt, a fall to tamas and inertia (because the vital being refuses participation in the spiritual effort unless its egoistic demands are conceded), dryness, dullness, cessation of the sadhana. The same phrases even are repeated, — "no life in this existence", "suffocation", "limitation", "air-tight compartments"; and all this simply means that the lower vital nature — or some part of it — is in revolt and wants something else than the divine Truth and the tapasya that leads to the supramental change. It refuses to give up ego and desire and claim and demand or to accept a true self-giving and surrender, while yet it feels the pressure on it to transform itself into an instrument of the divine life. It is this pressure that it calls suffocation. The refusal to let it expand its desires and make a big place for itself it calls limitation of the being. The calm, purity, collected silence which are the basis of the tapasya for the supramental change, — this is what it stigmatises as "no life". Right rule and insistence on self-denial and self-mastery and restraint from claim and demand are what it calls air-tight compartments. And the worst suggestions and most dangerous deception come when this spirit of demand and desire is dissimulated in a spiritual garb and takes a form which makes it seem to the sadhak a part of the Yoga.

There is only one way of escape from this siege of the lower vital nature. It is the entire rejection of all egoistic vital demand, claim and desire and the replacement of the dissatisfied vital urge by the purity of psychic aspiration. Not the satisfaction of these vital clamours nor, either, an ascetic retirement is the true solution, but the surrender of the vital being to the Divine and a single-minded consecration to the supreme Truth into which desire and demand cannot enter. For the nature of the supreme Truth is Light and Ananda, and where desire and demand are there can be no Ananda.

It is not the vital demand but the psychic urge that alone can bring the nature towards the supramental transformation; for it alone can change the mental and vital and show them their own true movement. But constantly the vital demand is being taken for the psychic aspiration; and yet the difference is clear. In the psychic aspiration there are none of these reactions; there is no revolt, no justification of revolt: for the psychic aspires through inner union with the Divine and surrender. It does not question and challenge, but seeks to understand through unity with the Divine Will. It does not ask for small personal satisfactions, but finds its satisfaction in the growth of the Truth within the being; what it seeks and finds is not any indulgence of a vital and physical claim, but the true nearness which consists in the constant presence of the Divine in the heart and the rule of the Divine in all the nature. The cry of the psychic is always, "Let the Truth prevail, let Thy will be done and not mine." But the clamour of the vital is the very opposite: it calls to the Divine, "Let my will be Thine; obey my insistences, satisfy my desires, then only will I seek and accept Thee, for then only will I consent to see the Divine in Thee." It is hardly necessary to say which is the way to the Truth or which the right solution of any struggle in the nature.

The only creation for which there is any place here is the supramental, the bringing of the divine Truth down on the earth, not only into the mind and vital but into the body and into Matter. Our object is not to remove all "limitations" on the expansion of the ego or to give a free field and make unlimited room for the fulfilment of the ideas of the human mind or the desires of the ego-centred life-force. None of us are here to "do as we like", or to create a world in which we shall at last be able to do as we like; we are here to do what the Divine wills and to create a world in which the Divine Will can manifest its truth no longer deformed by human ignorance or perverted and mistranslated by vital desire. The work which the sadhak of the supramental Yoga has to do is not his own work for which he can lay down his own conditions, but the work of the Divine which he has to do according to the conditions laid down by the Divine. Our Yoga is not for our own sake but for the sake of the Divine. It is not our own personal manifestation that we are to seek, the manifestation of the individual ego freed from all bounds and from all bonds, but the manifestation of the Divine. Of that manifestation our own spiritual liberation, perfection, fullness is to be a result and a part, but not in any egoistic sense or for any ego-centred or self-seeking purpose. This liberation, perfection, fullness too must not be pursued for our own sake, but for the sake of the Divine. I emphasise this character of the creation because a constant forgetfulness of this simple and central truth, a conscious, half-conscious or wholly ignorant confusion about it has been at the root of most of the vital revolts that have spoiled many an individual sadhana here and disturbed the progress of the general inner work and the spiritual atmosphere.

The supramental creation, since it is to be a creation upon earth, must be not only an inner change but a physical and external manifestation also. And it is precisely for this part of the work, the most difficult of all, that surrender is most needful; for this reason, that it is the actual descent of the supramental Divine into Matter and the working of the Divine Presence and Power there that can alone make the physical and external change possible. Even the most powerful self-assertion of human will and endeavour is impotent to bring it about; as for egoistic insistence and vital revolt, they are, so long as they last, insuperable obstacles to the descent. Only a calm, pure and surrendered physical consciousness, full of the psychic aspiration, can be its field; this alone can make an effective opening of the material being to the Light and Power and the supramental change a thing actual and practicable. It is for this that we are here in the body, and it is for this that you and other sadhaks are in the Asram near us. But it is not by insistence on petty demands and satisfactions in the external field or on an outer nearness pleasing to the vital nature and its pride or desire that you can get the true relation with the Divine in this province. If you want the realisation there, it is the true nearness that you must seek, the descent and presence of the Mother in your physical consciousness, her constant inner touch in the physical being and its activities, her will and knowledge behind all its work and thought and movement and the ever present Ananda of that presence expelling all vital and physical separateness, craving and desire. If you have that, then you have all the nearness you can ask for and the rest you will gladly leave to the Mother's knowledge and will to decide. For with this in you there can be no feeling of being kept away, no sense of "gulf" and "distance", no complaint of a unity that is lacking or an empty dryness and denial of nearness.

A time comes when after a long preparation of the mind and vital being, it becomes necessary to open also the physical nature. But when that happens, very often the vital exaltation which can be very great when the experience is on its own plane, falls away and the obscure, obstructive physical and material consciousness appears in its unrelieved inertia. Inertia, tamas, stupidity, narrowness and limitation, an inability to progress, doubt, dullness, dryness, a constant forgetfulness of the spiritual experiences received are the characteristics of the unregenerated physical nature, when that is not pushed by the vital and is not supported either by the higher mental will and intelligence. This seems to be in part what has temporarily happened to you, but the way out is not to excite the physical by any vital revolt and outcry or to blame for your condition either circumstances or the Mother, — for that will only make things worse and increase the tamas, dryness, dullness, inertia, — but to recognise that there is here an element of the universal Nature reflected in yours which you must eliminate. And this can only be done by more and more surrender and aspiration and by so bringing in from beyond the vital and the mind the divine peace, light, power and presence. This is the only way towards the transformation and fulfilment of the physical nature.

I do not think after what I have written, I need add anything about the specific complaints that you make in your letter. Two things perhaps need to be made clear. First, the arrangements actually in existence about the work, about external demands, about correspondence and "seeing" people are the only feasible ones in the present circumstances if the heavy work the Mother has to do is to be at all physically possible. Next, it is precisely by action in silence that we can best do our work much more than by speech or writing, which can only be subordinate and secondary. For in this Yoga those will succeed best who know how to obey and follow the written and spoken word, but can also bear the silence and feel in it and receive (without listening to other voices or mistaking mental and vital suggestions and impulsions for the divine Truth and the divine Will) help, support and guidance.

Avoiding Premature Engagement with the Lower Vital

You cannot escape from these lower vital forces by being curious about them. This kind of curiosity only encourages and invites them and keeps them recurring. Their whole force is in their power of mechanical recurrence and, if you allow that, you will never get rid of them. Incoherence and confusion are the very nature of these forces and, if you encourage them, your whole nature will become a field of confusion and incoherence. The only way to know them and get rid of them is to be always above, in your true consciousness, in contact with the Mother's light and force. The light and force will then descend upon them, at once showing what they are and dissolving and eliminating them and changing that part of the nature. But first you must learn to keep always in contact with the Mother, always in the true consciousness, only then can these things be dealt with safely.

Do not go down into these lower unredeemed parts without the Mother's force with you. If you feel yourself down, remain quiet, call on the Mother and her force, but do not try to deal with it by your mind. But as far as possible resist the downward movement so long as the true consciousness is not settled in you.

*

It is certainly possible to draw forces from below. It may be the hidden divine forces from below that rise at your pull, and then this motion upward completes the motion and effort of the divine force from above, helping especially to bring it into the body. Or it may be the obscure forces from below that respond to the summons, and then this kind of drawing brings either tamas or disturbance — sometimes great masses of inertia or a formidable upheaval and disturbance.

The lower vital is a very obscure plane and it can be fully opened with advantage only when the other planes above it have been thrown wide to light and knowledge. One who concentrates on the lower vital without that higher preparation and without knowledge is likely to fall into many confusions. This does not mean that experiences of this plane may not come earlier or even at the beginning; they do come of themselves, but they must not be given too large a place.

*

In the lower vital all is a working of general forces which try to seize upon the individual and use him for their satisfaction; they are not his forces at all. In the mind or the higher vital it is much easier to establish some kind of control over the forces. That is the very reason why one should never put oneself into the control of these forces or make oneself a free crossways for their passage. It is only by opening to the Mother's force alone that a control can be established over these lower workings.

Ananda and the Lower Vital

It is indeed in the lower vital that there is the main difficulty for the spiritual change of human nature. If that were not there, the rest could be more easily dealt with and there would be no long resistance. The vital pleasure is not a true Ananda, but only a pleasant excitement which cannot abide — that pleasure and grief and pain are always near to each other and the consciousness passes easily from one to the other. One has to establish peace and quietude there, so that the true psychic and spiritual joy can take the place. It is the touch of the psychic that gives the soothing effect of which you speak.

*

Evidently, the condition into which you have fallen is due to an upsurging of suppressed elements in the lower vital nature. It has been compelled by the mind and the higher vital part in you to give up the little "joys and pleasures" to which it was habituated, but it — or at any rate the subconscient part of it which is often the most powerful — did that without entire conviction and probably with "reservations" and "safeguards" and in exchange for a promise of compensations, other and greater joys and pleasures to replace all it was losing. This is evident from what you write; your description of the nature of the depression, the return of what you call impure thoughts which are merely indices of the subconscient lower vital desire-complex, the doubt thrown upon the generosity of the Divine, the demand for compensation for losses, something like striking a bargain with the Divine, a *quid pro quo* pact, are all unmistakable. Latterly, there has been a combination of circumstances (X's turning inwards, Y's emigration etc.) which have rather suddenly increased the deprivation of its former outlets; this attack is its way of non-cooperation or protest. There is only one way to deal with it, — to cast the whole thing away — depression, demands, doubts, sex-thoughts, the whole undesirable baggage, — and have in its place the one true movement, the call for the true consciousness and the presence of the Divine.

It may be that behind this persistence of the lower vital demand for satisfaction there was something not quite clear — in the obscurer part of the physical mind — in your mental attitude towards the Yoga. You seem to regard this demand for the replacement of the old lower vital satisfactions by other joys and pleasures as something quite legitimate; but joys and pleasures are not the object of Yoga and a bargain or demand for a replacement of this kind can be no legitimate or healthy element in the sadhana. If it is there, it will surely impede the flow of spiritual experience. Ananda, yes; but Ananda and the spiritual happiness which precedes it (*adhyātma-sukham*) are something quite different from joys and pleasures. And even Ananda one cannot demand or make it a condition for pursuing the sadhana — it comes as a crown, a natural outcome and its precondition is the growth of the true consciousness, peace, calm, light, strength, the equanimity which resists all shocks and persists through success and failure. It is these things which must be the first objects of the sadhana, not any hedonistic experience even of the highest kind; for that must come of itself as a result of the Divine Presence.

I would rather like you to tell me what, *precisely*, you do in your hours of meditation, how you do it and what happens within you.

Meanwhile the first thing you must do is to throw out this perilous stuff of despondency and its accompaniments and recover a quiet and clear balance. A quiet mind and a quiet vital are the first conditions for success in sadhana.

*

To live within does not mean to give up reading and writing or other external activities; I shall try to explain to you what I meant. I had in fact started to do so when you had your last fit of despondency, but stopped when you recovered, thinking it was not after all necessary and supposing besides that the essential in what I was about to write must already be known to you. Now, however, that the despondency has returned and you put the question, I will this time try to explain the whole matter.

It is evident that you still cherish some misunderstanding about peace and joy and Ananda. (Peace by the way is not joy — for peace can be there even when joy is quiescent.) It is not a fact that one ought not to pray or aspire for peace or spiritual joy. Peace is the very basis of all the siddhi in the Yoga, and why should not one pray or aspire for foundation in the Yoga? Spiritual joy or a deep inner happiness (not disturbed even when there come superficial storms or perturbations) is a constant concomitant of contact or union with the Divine, and why should it be forbidden to pray or aspire for contact with the Divine and the joy that attends it? As for Ananda, I have already explained that I mean by Ananda something greater than peace or joy, something that, like Truth and Light, is the very nature of the supramental Divine. It can come by frequent inrushes or descents, partially or for a time even now, but it cannot remain in the system so long as the system has not been prepared for it. Meanwhile, peace and joy can be there permanently, but the condition of this permanence is that one should have the constant contact or indwelling of the Divine, and this comes naturally not to the outer mind or vital but to the inner soul or psychic being. Therefore one who wants his Yoga to be a path of peace or joy, must be prepared to dwell in his soul rather than in his outer mental and emotional nature.

I objected in a former letter not to aspiration but to a demand, to making peace, joy or Ananda a condition for following the Yoga. And it is undesirable because if you do so, then the vital, not the psychic, takes the lead. When the vital takes the lead, then unrest, despondency, unhappiness can always come, since these things are the very nature of the vital — the vital can never remain constantly in joy and peace, for it needs their opposites in order to have the sense of the drama of life. And yet when unrest and unhappiness come, the vital at once cries, "I am not given my due, what is the use of my doing this Yoga?" Or else it makes a gospel of its unhappiness and says, as you say in your letter, that the path to fulfilment must be a tragic road through the desert. And yet it is precisely this predominance of the vital in us that makes the necessity of passing through the desert. If the psychic were always there in front, the desert would be no longer a desert and the wilderness would blossom with the rose.

Apropos, if your despondency has lasted so long this time, is it not because something in the vital has been clinging to it, justifying it on one ground or another? That at least is what I have felt, every time we have tried to remove it.

Aspiration and Offering in the Lower Vital

Sometimes the aspiration is felt at the navel, but that is part of the larger vital. The lower vital is below. The lower vital aspires by offering all its small movements in the fire of purification, by calling for the light and power to descend into it and rid it of its little greeds, jealousies, resistances and revolts over small matters, angers, vanities, sexualities etc. to be replaced by the right movements governed by selflessness, purity, obedience to the urge of the Divine Force in all things.

*

It is evident that the lower vital has received the Divine Consciousness when even in the small movements of life there is an aspiration to the Divine, a reference as it were to the Divine Light for guidance or some feeling of offering to the Divine or guidance by the Divine. The lower vital commands the little details of emotion, impulse, sensation, action — it is these that, when converted, it offers to the Divine control for transformation.

Peace and Calm in the Lower Vital

The peacefulness in the lower abdomen is very good, for it means that the true consciousness is settling down in the lower vital — if the lower vital is liberated and peaceful, there is little ground for any perturbations to come.

*

It is what I meant when I spoke of something remaining calm even behind the surface disturbances. What happens is that some part of the being becomes quieted, enlightened and strong — say the mind or the mind and the higher vital. But perhaps the lower vital and the physical may be only temporarily influenced and quieted — in time the work begins on them to change permanently, and owing to some outer touch or the pressure of the hostile forces or the lower nature their possibilities of egoism or unrest rise up and have to be dealt with. The advantage is, as you have seen, that a part of the nature is there in which you can stand and deal with the still recalcitrant parts. One has to remain firm and persistently bring what has been gained down into the lower parts, till there is a permanent peace and freedom assured in the whole nature.

Section Two

Vital Temperament

Chapter One
Cheerfulness and Happiness

Cheerfulness

Cheerfulness is the salt of sadhana. It is a thousand times better than gloominess.

*

Be more cheerful and confident. Sex and Doubt and Co. are there, no doubt, but the Divine is there also inside you. Open your eyes and look and look till the veil is rent and you see Him — or Her.

*

The change noted by X evidently indicates a great progress in the vital and physical being. There is nothing spiritually wrong in being glad and cheerful, on the contrary it is the right thing. As for struggles and aspiration, struggles are really not indispensable to progress and there are many people who get so habituated to the struggling attitude that they have all the time struggles and very little else. That is not desirable. There is a sunlit path as well as a gloomy one and it is the better of the two — a path in which one goes forward in absolute reliance on the Mother, fearing nothing, sorrowing over nothing. Aspiration is needed but there can be a sunlit aspiration full of light and faith and confidence and joy. If difficulty comes, even that can be faced with a smile.

*

It is that cheerfulness that we want to be always there in you. It is the happiness of the psychic that has found its way and, whatever difficulties come, is sure that it will be led forward and reach the goal. When a sadhak has that constantly, we know that he has got over the worst difficulty and that he is now firmly on the safe path.

*

The cheerfulness [*of joking and hilarity*] is vital. I do not say that it should not be there, but there is a deeper cheerfulness, an inner *sukhahāsya* which is the spiritual condition of cheerfulness.

*

It is an inner joy and cheerfulness that helps, but this [*light joking*] is merely a vital bubbling on the surface. It is all right in ordinary life, but in Yoga it merely expends the vital force for nothing.

Humour and Seriousness

Sense of humour? It is the salt of existence. Without it the world would have got utterly out of balance — it is unbalanced enough already — and rushed to blazes long ago.

*

I am not aware that highly evolved personalities have no sense of humour or how the person can be said to be integrated when this sense is lacking; "looseness" applies only to a frivolous levity without any substance behind it. There is no law that wisdom should be something rigidly solemn and without a smile.

*

Whatever seriousness is necessary must come of itself from within. To be serious outwardly by rule is not needed.

*

Why on earth should people not be serious if they want? Life may be a joke, — though all do not find it so — but one can't be laughing at it all the time. The idea seems to be that one can't be serious unless one is either (1) in a rage, (2) discontented, (3) sad and miserable. But surely one can be serious when one is thinking or when one is looking at serious things or simply and purely when one is not laughing. And one can't be laughing 24 hours without stopping, — the muscles of the stomach would not stand it and even the American record makers might shy at such a test.

*

What you write about X is quite correct. It is not necessary to be always serious of face or silent in doing the Yoga, but it is necessary to take the Yoga seriously and silence and inward concentration have a large place. One can't be all the time throwing oneself outward if to go inside and meet the Divine there is one's aim. But that does not mean that one has to be grave and gloomy all the time or gloomy a big part of the time, and I don't suppose the sadhaks here are like that. It is X's rhetorical way of putting his difficulty — the difficulty of a vital that wants to throw itself always outward in action and emotion while another part is dissatisfied with the result and feels that its own movement is frustrated. There are two people in him, one wanting a life of vital expansion, the other an inner life. The first gets restless because the inner life is not a life of outward expansion; the other becomes miserable because its aim is not realised. Neither personality need be thrown away in this Yoga; but the outer vital one must allow the inner to establish itself, give it the first place and consent to be only an instrument of the soul and to obey the law of the inner life. This is what X's mind still refuses to understand; he thinks one must be either all gloomy and cold and grave or else bring the vital bubble and effervescence into the inner life. A quiet, happy and glad control of the vital by the inner being is a thing he is not able as yet to conceive.

Happiness and Contentment

Happiness in the ordinary sense is a sunlit state of the vital with or without cause. Contentment is less than happiness — joy of peace or being free from difficulty is rather a state of joyful śānti. Happiness ought not to be a state of self-satisfaction or inertia, and need not be, for one can combine happiness and aspiration. Of course there can be a state of happy inertia, but most people don't remain satisfied with that long, they begin to want something else. There are Yogins who are satisfied with a happy calm immobility, but that is because the happiness is a form of Ananda and in the immobility they feel the Self and its eternal calm and want nothing more.

Chapter Two
Sorrow and Suffering

Joy and Sorrow

Joy is a vital feeling, like its opposite, sorrow.

*

There is no real reason why delight should necessarily be followed by sorrow — except that it is the habit of the vital. But that habit can be overcome.

*

It is dangerous to have a heart insisting on its own vital emotions. Not to be the slave of vital joy or sorrow is a condition one has to pass through in order to arrive at true Anandam. If people are right [*that a heart indifferent to joy and sorrow is not desirable*] then there can never be any equality and we have even to say that equality is a bad thing. If so, then the whole of the Gita is a mass of nonsense.

*

There are vital joys that are innocent and need not be seriously put down — such as joy in art, poetry, literature. They have to be not put down, but put aside only when they interfere with sadhana.

Sorrow and Pain and Suffering

Sorrow and pain and suffering? The curious thing is that my Yoga does not approve of sorrow and suffering or of taking stumbles and difficulties too seriously, as the Tapaswis do or of viraha pangs as the Vaishnavas do or of vairagya as the Mayavadis do, yet the old ideas and forces bring these things into the Asram through the minds of the sadhaks and there they are. Well, well!

*

The thing in you which enjoys the suffering and wants it is part of the human vital — it is these things that we describe as the insincerity and perverse twist of the vital; it cries out against sorrow and trouble and accuses the Divine and life and everybody else of torturing it, but for the most part the sorrow and the trouble come and remain because the perverse something in the vital wants them! That element in the vital has to be got rid of altogether.

*

Yes, it is so [*that people themselves indirectly choose pain and misery by not turning to the Divine*]. Even there is something in the vital consciousness that would not feel at home if there were no suffering in life. It is the physical that fears and abhors suffering, but the vital takes it as part of the play of life.

*

It is the vital that enjoys the drama of life and takes a pleasure even in sorrow and suffering — it [*a movement of depression*] is not a revolt but an acceptance. Of course there are moods of revolt also in the vital in which it takes a pleasure. The part that does not like suffering and would be glad to get rid of it is the physical consciousness, but the vital pushes it always and so it cannot escape.

It is the rajaso-tamasic vital ego that is responsible both for revolt and for the acceptance of depression. Rajas predominating there is revolt, tamas predominating there is depression.

*

It is not the soul but the vital or rather something in it that takes pleasure in groaning and weeping and in fact in sorrow and suffering of all kinds.

*

The surface nature does not enjoy [*groaning and weeping*] — but something within enjoys the *līlā* of "laughter and tears", joy and grief, pleasure and pain, in a word the play of the ignorance.

In some people this comes up to a certain extent on the surface. Many, if you propose to them the removal of suffering from life, look askance at you and feel that it would be terribly boring to have nothing but joy and Ananda and peace — many even have said it.

*

The gloom and other difficulties come from a resistance of inertia in the lower vital and physical consciousness. What you have to do is to prepare the consciousness by getting rid of the inertia. A sattwic gladness and calm and confidence is the proper temperament for this Yoga; gloom, depression and weeping should not be indulged in, as they stand in the way of the opening, unless the tears are the psychic weeping of release or adoration or a moved love and bhakti. The progress made in controlling the sex and other rajasic movements of the lower vital is a good preparation, but not enough; by itself it is only the negative side, though indispensable. Aspire for a positive sattwic opening for strength, for light, for peace and do not worry or repine if the progress is slow at first, nor grudge the time and labour of preparation necessary before there can be a rapid advance in the Yoga.

*

You should not indulge this sense of grief — remain calm, confident, turned to the one Will in all circumstances; that is the way to secure that each step will be taken in the right measure and produce its best possible consequences. Regard henceforth the question of X and your relation with X as a minor and subordinate thing on the outer side of your sadhana. If you take it as a problem of the first importance it will become that and stand in your way again. Look at it as a question from the past that has been firmly settled and put in its place and turn to the central aim of your sadhana.

For the rest, apart from this circumstance, you need change nothing in the inward aim and concentration of your will and endeavour on the one thing to be done — the entire self-giving and self-dedication of your inner and outer being to the Divine alone. If you can adopt firmly the right inward attitude, it may even be easier than by an outward rule for your main guidance.

*

I hope you will be able to reject this *duḥkha*; it must be an attempt of something of the old consciousness to come back, — for a psychic sorrow would not burn. These things come from the subconscient, so for such a grief no particular reason would be necessary. It is the force of sorrow in itself that rises like that and lays a claim on the nature.

*

Tamasic indifference is one thing and the absence of sorrow is another. One has to observe what is wrong and do all that one can to set it right. Sadness in itself has no power to cure what is wrong; a firm quiet persistent will has the power.

*

It is clear that the force and peace are descending and working more and more to fix themselves in you.

The other feelings, the wanting to be sad, the fear of being happy, the suggestion of incapacity or unfitness are the usual movements of the vital formation which is not yourself and they come up to try and prevent the change in you. You have only to refuse to accept these suggestions and put yourself persistently on the side of the Truth in you which will make you free and happy, and all will be well.

Melancholy

It seems to me from what you have written that it is the old vital restlessness and indulgence in melancholy that has taken hold of you. It has no special cause, but takes hold of everything to feed itself; in itself it is only a habitual nervous weakness. The more one broods on it, the more it increases. There are three ways of combating it. One is to take interest and busy yourself in something else not yourself and to think of your condition as little as possible. Another is to separate yourself from this vital restlessness and melancholia as much as possible and face it, as you were doing, with an energetic and resolute refusal to accept it. The third is to habituate yourself to turn your mind upwards in a call for the Mother's peace. It is there above you waiting to come down if you make yourself open to it; if it came down, it would rid you permanently of all this suffering and trouble.

Chapter Three
Depression and Despondency

Discouragement

Not to get discouraged when there is no immediate result is very important — for then the force within sinks and when the force within sinks there is the *tapo-bhanga* of which the old Rishis were always complaining, for each time the tapas broke they had to start afresh till it was reconstructed.

*

Tell him that discouragement is the one thing that the sadhak should never indulge. One should go on steadily whether the pace is slow or hampered or swift and easy — one will always get to the goal in time. Difficulties and periods of darkness cannot be avoided — they have to be gone through with quietness and courage.

*

There is no reason to be discouraged. Three years is not too much for the preparation of the nature and it is usually through fluctuations that it gradually grows nearer to the point where a continuous progress becomes possible. One has to cleave firmly to the faith in the Mother's working behind all appearances and you will find that that will carry you through.

*

I do not quite know what is the drift of your questions. It sounds as if you had been allowing yourself to be influenced by a vague and confused atmosphere of discouragement and barren questioning which has caught many in the Asram. Otherwise there is no ground for any such feelings. Where you are? In the Mother's presence here and close to me. Where you are going? Towards union with the Divine through dedication and service. What you are doing here? Service and self-giving to the Divine. The rest depends, as the Mother writes to you, on the simplicity and fullness with which you give yourself and serve. If there is anything more special in your thoughts that has disturbed you, it is better to say clearly what it is. But do not listen to the thoughts spoken or silently suggested that are moving about the Asram and of which I have spoken, for these are a poison that will only bring discontent and depression.

Depression

The outer being does not care for the sadhana unless it gets something by it which is to it pleasant or gratifying or satisfying — depression therefore comes easy to it.

*

That is how the depression works in everybody. It takes hold of this or that excuse but really it comes for its own satisfaction and not for any particular reason.

*

All depression is bad as it lowers the consciousness, spends the energy, opens to adverse forces.

*

After you went from here it seems that the vital difficulties which you were emerging from here came back with your return to the atmosphere and that was the cause of the violent depression and ill-health that fell upon you. The depression again was the cause why everything went wrong and the arrangements made fell through or took a wrong turn. For depression prevents the Force from flowing through and calls in the adverse forces and gives them a chance to destroy the helpful formations that are made. All the trouble and difficulty you have had will disappear or be minimised if you shake off this tendency to depression altogether.

*

The vital may understand, but that is not enough, it must wholeheartedly call for the peace and transformation. There must be a large part of it unable to change its position and give up its moods or its way of receiving things; otherwise these depressions could not be so acute. There is no reason why you should not get the peace, but this must change.

*

One should certainly not overestimate one's progress, but not underestimate it either. I don't know whether dwelling on the defects and weaknesses is very wholesome. To know that they are there is one thing, to keep them always before the eye may be depressing and retard the progress.

*

There was nothing wrong in helping with the cooking. But if there were a wrong movement in that, it is not to be met by getting depression — for depression itself is a wrong or mistaken movement; and how can one mistake be corrected by another? The proper way to deal with a wrong movement is to look quietly at it and put the consciousness right at that point.

*

It [*vital joy*] is much better than vital depression at any rate. What is wanted is an inner peace and upon that a constant cheerfulness and gladness.

*

I am glad the cloud is lifting and hope to find it lifted altogether soon. It is the usual experience that if the humility and resignation are firmly founded in the heart, other things like trust come naturally afterwards. If once the psychic light and happiness which is born of these things is founded, it is not easy for other forces to cloud that state and not possible for them to destroy it. That is the common experience.

Depression Often Comes from Outside

Often waves of depression come from the general Nature — the mind finds out inner or external reasons for them when there are none. That may be the reason why the reasons are not clear. On the other hand it may be due to some part of the being getting discouraged or fatigued or unwilling to follow the movement either of work or of sadhana. If it is something in the vital being, it may hide itself so as not to be exposed or cleared; if a part of the physical, it may be simply dumb and obscure, unable to express itself. Finally, it may come up from the subconscient. These are various cases in which there is what seems a causeless depression. One has to see for oneself which it is.

*

Yes. The depression comes from without, not from within. But some part of the vital is too habituated to respond or at least passively accept or reflect and to take it as its own. If it were not for this, there would be little or no difficulty in throwing off the depression when it tries to come.

*

You seem to rely very much on X and his experiences and ideas about them. X's experience proves nothing because he is quite ignorant. His depression comes from outside and has its causes, only his vital mind does not record or understand the causes, but there is a response to them all the same. Because the vital mind has in the past always associated depression with these causes and that impression remains in the vital stuff, so it responds to the touch with the usual reaction taught to it by the vital mind. An ignorant and untrained mind like X's cannot be expected to realise the secret machinery of the movements of his own consciousness.

*

The vital mind is part of the mind. If mind (mental mind, vital mind, physical mind, subconscient mind) does not respond to outer things, depression is impossible. The self at one end, the stone at the other never get into depression. In between them, the true mind, true vital, true physical consciousness never get depression because they do not give the responses to things that create depression.

*

Naturally the deep depression and low vitality [*in another person*] try to get into you, or if the person pulls your vital force to restore hers or you yourself part with it for that purpose, you feel exhausted and empty afterwards. That is the natural result. One person may produce more of this result than another. Or if you are strong enough to resist in the mind and vital, the influence gets into the physical and produces some result there. According to the nature of the person approached, the result may be violent or intense or of a minor character. Also certain effects may not manifest at the time but only afterwards.

*

These cloudings are not rare and not personal to yourself — all get them, — very often they are formations thrown *from outside*. The important thing is not to get upset or distressed or take them to yourself or as your own, and to remain quiet till they pass.

*

Do not allow these depressing thoughts to find credit with you. If they come, look at them as not yours, as suggestions from outside. Remain as quiet as you can and let the Mother's Force work in you.

*

However or from wheresoever it came, the only thing to do with a depression is to throw it out.

Dealing With Depression

Naturally, if the vital is quiet and allows the mind to see things rightly, there will not be this depression.

*

Small desires and defects have not to be magnified or made a cause of worry or depression, but they have to be noted and quietly got rid of.

*

Be careful to reject always movements (like vexation, discontent etc.) that bring back confusion or depression. One cannot always help these movements coming, but one can reject them when they come; the more they are rejected, the more difficult it becomes for them to recur — or, if they recur, they hold only for a moment and then drop away. To entertain them means to give them a chance to cover the true consciousness once more.

*

It [*depression*] comes back if you give it a chance. Do not give it a chance. Do not give it a room to live in if it comes.

*

Depression should not be indulged, for all who do the Yoga have difficulties with their ego; but the higher consciousness will always prevail with a true aspiration.

*

Do not allow yourself to admit any movement of vital depression, still less a depressed condition. As for the external being, it is always, not only in you but in everyone, a difficult animal to handle. It has to be dealt with by patience and a quiet and cheerful perseverance; never get depressed by its resistance, for that only makes it sensitive and aggrieved and difficult, or else discouraged. Give it rather the encouragement of sunlight and a quiet pressure, and one day you will find it opening entirely to the Grace.

*

It is indeed good that the psychic intervened and prevented the mind taking the wrong direction. It is not possible that there should not be occasional stumbles, failures etc. in the work of self-purification and change; but to feel upset or remorseful over them is harmful rather than helpful; it easily brings depression and depression brings clouding of the mind and weakness. To observe calmly the wrong movement and its nature (here it was the tongue that was at fault and the tongue is always an easily erring member) and to set it right inwardly is always the best way. Calm, especially when the true spiritual calm of the self is there, is the thing that must always be preserved; for with that everything else can be done in time and with the least trouble.

*

Anutāp — remorse, repentance, is the natural movement of the vital mind when it sees it has done a mistake. It is certainly better than indifference. Its disadvantage is that it disturbs the vital stuff and sometimes leads to depression or discouragement. For that reason what is usually recommended to the sadhak is a quiet recognition of the mistake with a sincere aspiration and will that it should not be repeated or at least that the habit of making such mistakes should soon be eliminated. At a higher stage of development when the inner calm is established, one simply observes the defects of the nature as defects of a machinery that one has to put right and calls down the Light and Force for its rectification. In the beginning however the movement of repentance even helps provided it does not bring discouragement or depression.

*

This kind of dejection [*feeling that life is meaningless*] must be cast aside. Life always has a meaning whether in success or in difficulty so long as it is turned towards the Divine. Protection will be given, but depression must be put aside so that you may be able to receive and use the help and the force.

Depression and the Gospel of Sorrow[1]

I think the best thing I can write to you in the circumstances is to recommend to you X's aphorism, "Depression need not be depressing; rather it should be made a jumping-board for the leap to a higher and happier poise."

The rule in Yoga is not to let the depression depress you, to stand back from it, observe its cause and remove the cause; for the cause is always in oneself, perhaps a vital defect somewhere, a wrong movement indulged or a petty desire causing a recoil, sometimes by its satisfaction, sometimes by its disappointment. In Yoga a desire satisfied, a false movement given its head produces very often a worse recoil than disappointed desire.

What is needed for you is to live more deeply within, less in the outer vital and mental which is exposed to these touches. The inmost psychic being is not oppressed by them; it stands in its own closeness to the Divine and sees the small surface movements as surface things foreign to the true being.

*

It is regrettable that this attack [*of depression*] should recur. Perhaps it was a little my fault — you were or seemed to me going on so well that I was not on my guard against its possible recurrence. During the last two or three days the suggestion did come to me that there might be a turn of that kind, but I was so much in the joy of your music that I did not give it credence.

It is certainly not the answering of questions that will remove the underlying cause of this recurrence. Even if the answers satisfy, it could only be for a time. The same questionings would arise either in a mechanical reiteration — for it is not truly the reason from which they arise, it is a certain part of the vital consciousness affected by the surrounding atmosphere — or else presented from a shifted ground or a somewhat changed angle of vision. The difficulty can only disappear if you remain resolute

---

[1] *All the letters in this group were written to the same correspondent, a disciple who suffered from bouts of depression.*

that it shall disappear, — if you refuse to attach any value to the justifications which the mind is *made* to put forward for your "sadness" under this atmospheric influence and, as you did in certain other matters, stick fast to the resolution to make the Yogic change, to awake the psychic fully, not to follow the voices of the mind but to do rather what the Mother asks of you, persisting *however difficult it may be* or seem to be. It is so that the psychic can fully awaken and establish its influence — not on your higher vital where it is already awake and growing through your poetry and music and certain experiences so that whenever your higher vital is active you are in good condition, full of delight and creativeness and open to experience; but it is the influence on the lower vital, for it is there as I have already told you that your difficulties are and that this vital depression recurs.

*

It is quite unwarranted to say that you have been going in the wrong direction — going west when you thought you were going east. You were going towards the east, all right, but you were going as if with a chain on your ankles and the chain was a certain tension and stiffness in your endeavour. This is what was found to have been wrong in your way of meditation. Therefore there is no need to lament that you have been going in the wrong direction all the time — for that is not the case; what is needed is to profit by the discovery and get rid of the impediment.

The light which you saw seems to have got clouded by your indulging your vital more and more in the bitter pastime of sadness. That was quite natural, for that is the result sadness always does bring. It is the reason why I object to the gospel of sorrow and to any sadhana which makes sorrow one of its main planks (*abhimān*, revolt, *viraha*). For sorrow is not, as Spinoza pointed out, a passage to a greater perfection, a way to siddhi; it cannot be, for it confuses and weakens and distracts the mind, depresses the vital force, darkens the spirit. A relapse from joy and vital elasticity and Ananda to sorrow, self-distrust, despondency and weakness is a recoil from a greater to a lesser consciousness; —

Depression and Despondency

the habit of these moods shows a clinging of something in the vital to the smaller, obscurer, dark and distressed movement out of which it is the very aim of Yoga to rise.

It is incorrect to say that the wrong key with which you were trying to open the faery palace has been taken away from you and you are left with none at all. The true key has been given to you in the right kind or condition of meditation — a state of inner rest, not of straining, of quiet opening, not of eager or desperate pulling, a harmonious giving of oneself to the Divine Force for its working, and in that quietude a sense of the Force working and a restful confidence allowing it to act without any unquiet interference. Now that condition is the beginning of the psychic opening; there is of course much more that afterwards comes to complete it but this is the fundamental condition into which all the rest can most easily come. In this condition there may and will be call, prayer, aspiration. Intensity, concentration will come of themselves, not by a hard effort or tense strain on the nature. Rejection of wrong movements, frank confession of defects are not only not incompatible, but helpful to it; but this attitude makes the rejection, the confession easy, spontaneous, entirely complete and sincere and effective. That is the experience of all who have consented to take this attitude.

Now as to the tension and stiffness. I may say in passing that consciousness and receptivity are not the same thing; one may be receptive, yet externally unaware of how things are being done and of what is being done. But for such an external unconsciousness there must be a reason, — and in you it was the stiffness created by a tension and a straining which made the consciousness thus rigid and closed it up. Not that it closed you to the Force or that it took away the inner receptivity, but it did close you to the surface consciousness of what is being done. When that happens, the Force works, as I have repeatedly written, behind the veil; the results remain packed behind and come out afterwards, often slowly, little by little, until there is so much pressure that it breaks through somehow and forces open the external nature. There lies the difference between a mental and vital straining and pulling and a spontaneous psychic openness, and it is not at all the first time that we have spoken of the difference. It is not really a question of the right or the wrong key, but of putting the key in the lock in the right or the wrong way, whether because of some difficulty you try to force the lock turning the key this way and that with violence or confidently and quietly give it the right turn — and the door opens.

It is not that this pulling and straining and tension can do nothing; in the end they prevail for some result or another, but with difficulty, delay, struggle, strong upheavals of the Force breaking through in spite of all. Ramakrishna himself began by pulling and straining and got his result but at the cost of a tremendous and perilous upsetting; afterwards he took the quiet psychic way whenever he wanted a result and got it with ease and in a minimum time. You say that this way is too difficult for you but it is on the contrary the easiest and simplest and most direct way and anyone can do it, if he makes his mind and vital quiet. It is the other way of tension and strain and hard endeavour that is difficult and needs a great force of Tapasya. Take the psychic attitude; follow the straight sunlit path, with the Divine openly or secretly upbearing you — if secretly, he will yet show himself in good time, — do not insist on the hard, hampered, roundabout and difficult journey.

All this has been pointed out before: but you were not inclined to regard it as feasible or at least not ready to apply it in the field of meditation because your consciousness by tradition, owing to past lives and for other reasons, was clinging to former contrary conceptions. Something in you was harking back to one kind of Vaishnava sadhana, and that tended to bring in it its pain-giving feeling-elements of *abhimāna*, revolt, suffering, the Divine hiding himself ("always I seek, but never does he show himself") — the rarity of the unfolding and the *milana*. Something else in you was inclined to see as the only alternative some harsh, grim ascetic ideal, the blank featureless Brahman (and imagined that the supramental was that), something in the vital looked on the conquest of wrong movements as a hard desperate tapasya, not as a passage into the purity and joy of the Divine — even now some element in you seems to insist on regarding the psychic attitude as something extraordinary, difficult, inhuman and impossible! There were these and other old lingerings of the mind and the vital; you have to clear them out and look at the simplicity of the Truth with a straight and simple gaze.

The remedy we propose, the key we offer to you ought not to be so difficult to apply as you imagine. After all, it is only applying in "meditation" the way that has been so successful with you in your creative work. There is a way of creation by strain and tension, by beating of the brain, by hard and painful labour — often the passage clogged and nothing coming or else coming only in return for a sort of intellectual tapasya. There is the other way in which one remains quiet and opens oneself to a power that is there behind and waits for inspiration; the force pours in and with it the inspiration, the illumination, the Ananda, — all is done by an inner Power. The flood passes, but one remains quiet for the next flood and at its time surely it comes. Here too all is not perfect at once; but progress comes by ever new waves of the same Power. Not then a strain of mental activity, but a restful opening to the Force that is there all the time above and around you, so that it may flow freely and do its work in peace and illumination and Ananda. The way has been shown to you, you yourself have had from time to time the true condition; only you must learn how to continue in it or recover it and you must allow the Force to do its work in its own way. It may take some time to take entire hold of it, get the other habit out and make this normal; but you must not start by deciding that it is impossible! It is eminently possible and it is the door of definitive entrance. The difficulty, the struggle were only the period of preparation necessary to get rid of or to exhaust the obstruction in the consciousness which was a thorn-hedge round the faery palace.

*

I find it rather surprising that you should regard what the Mother said to you or what I wrote as a recommendation to relax aspiration or postpone the idea of any kind of siddhi till the Greek

Kalends! It was not so intended in the least — nor do I think either of us said or wrote anything which could justly bear such an interpretation. I said expressly that in the way of meditating of which we spoke, aspiration, prayer, concentration, intensity were a natural part of it; this way was put before you because our experience has been that those who take it go quicker and develop their sadhana, once they get fixed in it, much more easily as well as smoothly than by a distressed, doubtful and anxious straining with revulsions of despondency and turning away from hope and endeavour. We spoke of a steady opening to the Divine with a flow of the force doing its work in the adhar, a poised opening with a quiet mind and heart full of trust and the sunlight of confidence; where do you find that we said a helpless waiting must be your programme?

As for light-heartedness and insouciance, the Mother never spoke of insouciance — a light don't-care attitude is the last thing she would recommend to anybody. She spoke of cheerfulness, and if she used the word light-hearted it was not in the sense of anything lightly or frivolously gay and careless — although a deeper and finer gaiety can have its place as one element of the Yogic character. What she meant was a glad equanimity even in the face of difficulties and there is nothing in that contrary to Yogic teaching or to her own practice. The vital nature on the surface (the depths of the true vital are different) is attached on the one side to a superficial mirth and enjoyment, on the other to sorrow and despair and gloom and tragedy, — for these are for it the cherished lights and shades of life; but a bright or wide and free peace or an *ānandamaya* intensity or, best, a fusing of both in one is the true poise of both the soul and the mind — and of the true vital also — in Yoga. It is perfectly possible for a quite human sadhak to get to such a poise, it is not necessary to be divine before one can attain it. All this is nothing new and original; I have been saying it ever since I began speaking at all about Yoga and I cannot see anything in it resembling a gospel of helpless waiting or of light careless insouciance or anything contrary to our own practice. I do not think that we have either of us become relentlessly grim and solemn or lacking in humour or that the Mother has lost her smile! I am afraid you are looking at her and things as through a glass darkly and seeing them in too sombre colours. As for instance what you say about the music, — she came up straight to me from it and spoke at once about your music and the presence of Krishna there, and she was in a very different mood from what you describe.

*

Do not allow yourself to be overborne by the dejection; it can only be an incident in the ups and downs of the sadhana, and, as an incident, it should be made as short as possible. Remember that you have chosen a method of proceeding in the sadhana in which dejection ought to have no place. If you have a growing faith that all that is happening has somehow to happen and that God knows what is best for you, — that is already a great thing; if you add to it the will to keep your face always turned towards the goal and the confidence that you are being led towards it even through difficulties and apparent denials, there could be no better mental foundation for sadhana. And if not only the mind, but the vital and physical consciousness can be imbued with this faith, dejection will become either impossible or so evidently an outer thing thrown from outside and not belonging to the consciousness that it will not be able to keep its hold at all. A faith of that kind is a very helpful first step towards the reversal of consciousness which makes one see the inner truth of things rather than their outward phenomenal appearance.

As for the causes of the dejection, there were causes, partly general in the shape of a resistance to a great descending force which was not personal to you at all, and, so far as there was a response to it in you, it was not from your conscious being, otherwise you would not have had it in this way, but from the part in us which keeps things for a long time that have been suppressed or rejected by the conscious will. It is the conscious will that matters, for it is that that prevails in the end, the will of the Purusha and not the more blind and obstinate parts of Prakriti. Keep the conscious will all right and it will carry on to the goal, — just as the resistance in universal Nature will yield in the end before the Divine Descent.

*

The depression of the vital you feel is a continuation of the old feeling in the struggle, but you must reject it and make of it a diminishing movement. The past in Yoga is no guide to the future. For what happened in the past was due to temporary and not permanent causes and to eliminate them is the very purpose of the sadhana.

*

There is no doubt about the beauty of the poems you have written but if sometimes — not by any means always — our sweetest songs spring from saddest feelings, there is a quite different rule both for life and for Yoga. For the life in its progress, for the soul in its ascendance, grief and suffering should be only an incident on the way and the vision look always and steadily to a joy and a glory beyond it — let the gloom pass and look beyond it towards Light.

*

The difficulty you feel or any sadhak feels about sadhana is not really a question of meditation versus bhakti versus works, it is a difficulty of the attitude to be taken, the approach or whatever you like to call it. Yours seems to be characterised on one side by a tremendous effort in the mind, on the other by a gloomy certitude in the vital which seems to watch and mutter under its breath if not aloud, "Yes, yes, go ahead, my fine fellow, but — কিছুই কখনও হয়নি, কিছুই হচ্ছেনা, কিছুই হবেনা",[2] and at the end of the meditation, "What did I tell you, কিছুই হলনা".[3] A vital so ready to despair that even after a "glorious" flood of poetry, it uses the occasion to preach the gospel of despair. I have passed through most of the difficulties of the sadhak, but I cannot recollect to have looked on delight of poetical creation or concentration in

---

[2] *Nothing has ever happened, nothing is happening, nothing will happen.* — Ed.
[3] *Nothing happened.* — Ed.

it as something undivine and a cause for despair. This seems to me excessive.

*

I have always told you that you ought not to stop your poetry and similar activities. It is a mistake to do so out of asceticism or with the idea of tapasya. One can stop these things when they drop of themselves, because one is in full experience and so interested in one's inner life that one has no energy to spare for the rest. Even then, there is no rule for giving up; for there is no reason why the poetry etc. should not be a part of sadhana. The love of applause, of fame, the ego feeling have to be given up, but that can be done without giving up the activity itself. Your vital needs some activity, most vitals do, and to deprive it of its outlet, an outlet that can be helpful and is not harmful, makes it sulking, indifferent and despondent or else inclined to revolt at any moment and throw up the sponge. Without the assent of the vital it is difficult to do sadhana — it non-cooperates, or it watches with a grim even if silent dissatisfaction ready to express at any moment doubt and denial; or it makes a furious effort and then falls back saying, "I have got nothing." The mind by itself cannot do much; it must have support from the vital; for that the vital must be in a cheerful and acquiescent state. It has the joy of creation and there is nothing spiritually wrong in creative action. Why deny your vital this joy of outflow?

I had already hinted to you that to be able to wait for the Divine Grace (not in a tamasic spirit, but with a sattwic reliance) was the best course for you. Prayer, yes — but not prayer insisting on immediate fulfilment — but prayer that is itself a communion of the mind and the heart with the Divine and can have the joy and satisfaction of itself, trusting for fulfilment by the Divine in His own time. Meditation? Yes, but your meditation has got into a wrong Asana, that of an eager and vehement wrestling followed by a bitter despair. It is no use getting on with it like that; it is better to drop it till you get a new Asana. (I am referring to the old Rishis who established an Asana, a place and a fixed position, where they would sit till they got siddhi — but if the Asana got successfully disturbed by wrong forces (Asuras, Apsaras etc.), they left it and sought for a new one.) Moreover, your meditation is lacking in quietude, you meditate with a striving mind — but it is in the quiet mind that the experience comes, as all Yogis agree — the still water that reflects rightly the sun. Your vital besides is afraid of quietude and emptiness, and that is because, probably, the strife and effort in you make what comes of them something neutral or desert, while they should be a restful quietude and an emptiness giving the sense of peace, purity or release, the cup made empty so that the soma-rasa of the spirit may be poured in it. That is why I would like you to desist from these too strenuous efforts and go on quietly, praying and meditating if you like but tranquilly without strain and too vehement striving, letting the prayer and meditation (not too much of the latter) prepare the mind and heart till things begin to flow into them in a spontaneous current when all is ready.

*

Accustomed as I am to the misunderstanding or misreporting of the Mother's statements, I found that this about her having said that transformation is easy carries the habit to the extreme limit. Needless to say, she did not and could not say anything of the kind and it is astonishing that you should believe she could say anything so absurd and false. I must remind you that I have always insisted on the difficulty of the sadhana. I have never said that to overcome doubt is easy; I have said on the contrary that it was difficult because it was the nature of something in the human physical mind to cling to doubt for its own sake. I have never said that to overcome grief, depression, gloom and suffering was easy; I have said that it was difficult because something in the human vital clings to it and almost needs it as part of the drama of life. So also I have never said that sex, anger, jealousy etc. were easy to overcome; I have said it was difficult because they were ingrained in the human vital, and even if thrown out were always being brought back into it either by its own habit or by the invasion of the general Nature and the resurgence of its own old response. These things I have repeated hundreds of times. Your idea that my difficulties were different from those of human nature is a mental construction or inference without any real basis. If I am ignorant of human difficulties and therefore intolerant of them, how is it that I am so patient with them as you cannot deny that I am? Why for years and years do I go on patiently arguing about your doubts, spending so much of my time, always trying to throw light on your difficulties, to show how things stand, to give reasons for a knowledge gained by living and *indiscutable* experience? Am I writing these letters every night because I have no understanding and no sympathy with you in your doubts and difficulties? Why do I wait patiently for years for sadhaks to get over their sex difficulties? Why do I tolerate and help and write soothing and encouraging letters to these women who break out and hunger-strike and threaten suicide once a fortnight? Why do we bear all this trouble and *tracas* and *fracas* and resistance and obloquy and harsh criticism from the sadhaks, why were we so patient with men like X and Y and others, if we had no understanding and no sympathy with the difficulties of human nature? It is because I press always on faith and discourage doubt as a means of approach to the spiritual realisation. What spiritual guide with a respect for truth can do otherwise? And if I encourage and support doubt, the only result will be that doubt will last for ever and no assured realisation be possible — just as if I encourage and support sex or any other contrary movement, it will last for ever — even without that they last quite long enough by their own force and motion. All that I can do for them is to tolerate and be patient and give time enough for their transformation or removal. Surely when you look at all this fairly, you will see that you have made a very incorrect inference.

As to the statement about drama and something liking to suffer, nobody doubts that your external consciousness dislikes its suffering. The physical mind and consciousness of man hates its own suffering and if left to itself dislikes also to see others suffer. But if you will try to fathom the significance of your own admission of liking drama or of the turn towards drama — from which very few human beings escape — and if you go deep enough, you will find that there is something in the vital which likes suffering and clings to it for the sake of the drama; it is something below the surface, not on the surface, but it is strong, almost universal in human nature and difficult to eradicate unless one recognises it and gets inwardly away from it. The mind and the physical of man do not like suffering for if they did it would not be suffering any longer, but this thing in the vital wants it in order to give a spice to life. It is the reason why constant depressions can go on returning and returning even though the mind longs to get rid of them, because this in the vital responds, goes on repeating the same movement like a gramophone as soon as it is set going and insists on turning the whole round of the often repeated record. It does not really depend on the reasons which the vital gives for starting off the round, these are often of the most trivial character and wholly insufficient to justify it. It is only by a strong will to detach oneself, not to justify, to reject root and branch that one can in the end get rid of this most troublesome and dangerous streak in human nature. When therefore we speak of the vital comedy, the vital drama, we are speaking from a psychological knowledge which does not end with the surface of things and looks at these hidden movements. It is impossible to deal with things for the purposes of Yoga if we confine ourselves to the surface consciousness only.

*

I cannot candidly say that the Mother and I approve of the idea of your going to Calcutta for a fortnight for relief from your sufferings: if we ever sanction such a movement, it is against our own seeing of things because no choice is left to us owing to circumstances or the state of mind of the sadhak. We have never found that such absences do any spiritual good: they usually relax or lower the consciousness or renew old movements that must go. It is much better to face the difficulty however sticky it is till the conquest is there.

It is a pity that this movement of depression has come back with its painful and irrational circle. It must be thrown away for good: these movements go round in a circular repetitionary way characteristic of these things. It is lent force by the reasonings of the physical mind which are specious but of no value. It is not true of spiritual things that experience must come within a certain number of years or not at all. There are some who begin to succeed after a few years, some who take longer, succeeding only in work but not in meditation or activity of the inner consciousness, but finally the veiled inner preparation of so many years has prevailed and they begin to get the psychic change, the inner opening of head and heart, the descents, the growth through frequent though not uninterrupted experience. This has happened even to those who are troubled by these circular movements and have been again and again on the point of rushing away in despair. There is nothing more futile than to despair in the spiritual path and throw up the game: it is to break a working which would have led one to the realisation asked for if one had persevered.

*

Thirst for the Divine is one thing and depression is quite another, nor is depression a necessary consequence of the thirst being unsatisfied; that may lead to a more ardent thirst or to a fixed resolution and persistent effort or to a more and more yearning call or to a psychic sorrow which is not at all identical with depression and despair. Depression is a clouded grey state in its nature and it is more difficult for light to come through clouds and greyness than through a clear atmosphere. That depression obstructs the inner light is a matter of general experience. The Gita says expressly, "Yoga should be practised persistently with a heart free from depression" — *anirviṇṇacetasā*. Bunyan in *The Pilgrim's Progress* symbolises it as the Slough of Despond, one of the perils of the way that has to be overcome. It is no doubt impossible to escape from attacks of depression, almost all sadhaks go through these attacks, but the principle is that one should react against them and not allow them by any kind of mental encouragement or acceptance of their suggestions to persist or grow chronic.

It is hardly a fact that sorrow is *necessary* in order to make the soul seek the Divine. It is the call of the soul within for the Divine that makes it turn, and that may come under any circumstances — in full prosperity and enjoyment, at the height of outward conquest and victory without any sorrow or disappointment but by a sudden or growing enlightenment, by a flash of light in the midst of sensuous passion as in Bilwamangal, by the perception that there is something greater and truer than this outward life lived in ego and ignorance. None of these turns need be accompanied by sorrow and depression. Often one turns saying, "Life is all very well and interesting enough as a game, but it is only a game, the spiritual reality is greater than the life of the mind and senses." In whatever way it comes, it is the call of the Divine or the soul's call to the Divine that matters, the attraction of it as something far greater than the things that usually hold the nature. Certainly if one is satisfied with life, entranced by it so that it shuts out the sense of the soul within or hampers the attraction to the Divine, then a period of vairagya, sorrow, depression, a painful breaking of the vital ties may be necessary and many go through that. But once the turn made, it should be to the one direction and a perpetual vairagya is not needed. Nor when we speak of cheerfulness as the best condition, do we mean a cheerful following of the vital life, but a cheerful following of the path to the Divine which is not impossible if the mind and heart take the right view and posture. At any rate if positive cheerfulness is not possible in one's case, still one should not acquiesce in or mentally support a constant depression and sadness. That is not at all indispensable for keeping turned to the Divine.

In speaking of the Buddhist and his nine years of the wall and other instances the Mother was only disproving the view that not having succeeded in seven or eight years meant unfitness and debarred all hope for the future. The man of the wall stands among the greatest names in Japanese Buddhism and his long sterility did not mean incapacity or spiritual unfitness. But apart from that there are many who have gone on persisting for long periods and finally prevailed. It is a common, not an uncommon experience.

*

This movement [*of restlessness, sadness, gloom*] is one that always tries to come when you have a birthday or a darshan and is obviously a suggestion of forces that want to disturb you and give you a bad birthday or bad darshan. You must get rid of the idea that it is in any way helpful for sadhana, e.g. makes you remember the Divine etc. — if it does it makes you remember the Divine in the wrong way and in addition brings up the weakness, also depression, self-distrust etc. etc. À *quoi bon* cheerfulness? It puts you in the right condition for the psychic to work and without knowing it you grow in just the right perceptions and right feelings for the spiritual attitude. This growth I have been observing in you for a fairly long time now and it is in the cheerful states that it is the most active. Japa, thinking of the Divine is all right, but it must be on this basis and in company with work and mental activity, for then the instrument is in a healthy condition. But if you become restlessly eager to do nothing but japa and think of nothing but the Divine and of the "progress" you have or have not made (Ramana Maharshi says you should never think of "progress", it is according to him a movement of the ego), then all the fat is in the fire — because the system is not yet ready for a Herculean effort and it begins to get upset and think it is unfit and will never be fit. So be a good cheerful worker and offer your bhakti to the Divine in all ways you can but rely on him to work out things in you.

*

I don't remember saying anything on this subject [*of pain and suffering*],[4] except that disappointed vital desire must bring

---

[4] *The correspondent suggested that pain and suffering are sometimes necessary in spiritual life and may even enrich it. After the "deep suffering" experienced in the process of mental doubt and questioning, he had felt a sense of gain. "Through deep pain," he wrote, "one often feels a sense of fulfilment." — Ed.*

about suffering. Pain and suffering are necessary results of the Ignorance in which we live; men grow by all kinds of experience, pain and suffering as well as their opposites, joy and happiness and ecstasy. One can get strength from them if one meets them in the right way. Many take a joy in pain and suffering when associated with struggle or endeavour or adventure, but that is more because of the exhilaration and excitement of the struggle than because of suffering for its own sake. There is, however, something in the vital which takes joy in the whole of life, its dark as well as its bright sides. There is also something perverse in the vital which takes a kind of dramatic pleasure in its own misery and tragedy, even in degradation or in illness. I don't think mere doubt can bring any gain; mental questioning can bring gains if it is in pursuit of truth, but questioning just for the sake of sceptical questioning or in a pure spirit of contradiction can only bring, when it is directed against the truths of the spirit, either error or a lasting incertitude. If I am always questioning the Light when it comes and refusing its offer of truth, the Light cannot stay in me, cannot settle; eventually, finding no welcome and no foundation in the mind, it will retire. One has to push forward into the Light, not be always falling back into the darkness and hugging the darkness in the delusion that that is the real light. Whatever fulfilment one may feel in pain or in doubt belongs to the Ignorance; the real fulfilment is in the divine joy and the divine Truth and its certitude and it is that for which the Yogin strives. In the strife he may have to pass through doubt, not by his own choice or will, but because there is still imperfection in his knowledge.

*

If you accept Krishnaprem's insistence that this and no other must be your path, it is this that you have to attain and realise; any exclusive other-worldliness cannot be your way. I believe that you are quite capable of attaining this and realising the Divine and I have never been able to share your constantly recurring doubts about your capacity or the despair that arises in you so violently when there are these attacks, nor is their persistent recurrence a valid ground for believing that they can never be overcome. Such a persistent recurrence has been a feature in the sadhana of many who have finally emerged and reached the goal; even the sadhana of very great Yogis has not been exempt from such violent and constant recurrences; they have sometimes been special objects of such persistent assaults, as I have indeed indicated in *Savitri* in more places than one — and that was indeed founded on my own experience. In the nature of these recurrences there is usually a constant return of the same adverse experiences, the same adverse resistance, thoughts destructive of all belief and faith and confidence in the future of the sadhana, frustrating doubts of what one has known as the truth, voices of despondency and despair, urgings to abandonment of the Yoga or to suicide or else other disastrous counsels of *déchéance*. The course taken by the attacks is not indeed the same for all, but still they have strong family resemblance. One can eventually overcome if one begins to realise the nature and source of these assaults and acquires the faculty of observing them, bearing, without being involved or absorbed into their gulf, finally becoming the witness of their phenomena and understanding them and refusing the mind's sanction even when the vital is still tossed in the whirl or the most outward physical mind still reflects the adverse suggestions. In the end these attacks lose their power and fall away from the nature; the recurrence becomes feeble or has no power to last: even, if the detachment is strong enough, they can be cut out very soon or at once. The strongest attitude to take is to regard these things as what they really are, incursions of dark forces from outside taking advantage of certain openings in the physical mind or the vital part, but not a real part of oneself or spontaneous creation in one's own nature. To create a confusion and darkness in the physical mind and throw into it or awake in it mistaken ideas, dark thoughts, false impressions is a favourite method of these assailants, and if they can get the support of this mind from over-confidence in its own correctness or the natural rightness of its impressions and inferences, then they can have a field day until the true mind reasserts itself and blows the clouds away. Another device of theirs is to awake some hurt or rankling sense of grievance in the lower vital parts and keep them hurt or rankling as long as possible. In that case one has to discover these openings in one's nature and learn to close them permanently to such attacks or else to throw out intruders at once or as soon as possible. The recurrence is no proof of a fundamental incapacity; if one takes the right inner attitude, it can and will be overcome. The idea of suicide ought never to be accepted; there is no real ground for it and in any case it cannot be a remedy or a real escape: at most it can only be postponement of difficulties and the necessity for their solution under no better circumstances in another life. One must have faith in the Master of our life and works, even if for a long time he conceals himself, and then in his own right time he will reveal his Presence.

I have tried to dispel all the misconceptions, explain things as they are and meet all the points at issue. It is not that you really cannot make progress or have not made any progress; on the contrary, you yourself have admitted that you have made a good advance in many directions and there is no reason why, if you persevere, the rest should not come. You have always believed in the Guruvada: I would ask you then to put your faith in the Guru and the guidance and rely on the Ishwara for the fulfilment, to have faith in my abiding love and affection, in the affection and divine goodwill and loving kindness of the Mother, stand firm against all attacks and go forward perseveringly towards the spiritual goal and the all-fulfilling and all-satisfying touch of the All-Blissful, the Ishwara.

Despair and Despondency

Despair and despondency are always wrong. If you make a mistake, quietly observe it and correct the tendency next time. Even if the mistake recurs often, you have only to persevere quietly — remembering that nature cannot be changed in a day.

*

These feelings of despair and exaggerated sense of self-depreciation and helplessness are suggestions of a hostile Force and should never be admitted. The defects of which you speak are common to all human nature and the external being of every sadhak is full of them; to become aware of them is necessary for the transformation, but it must be done with a quiet mind and with the faith and surrender to the Divine and assured aspiration to the higher consciousness which are proper to the psychic being. The transformation of the external being is the most difficult part of the Yoga and it demands faith, patience, quietude and firm determination. It is in that spirit that you have to throw these depressions aside and go steadily on with the Yoga.

*

You are "alternately getting" these things [*the impulse to aspire and then to despair*], because you allow the vital despondency to lay hold on you. If you consistently rejected it, it would not be able to recur like this. When the difficulties come, you should call back the faith; that is the use of faith, to carry you through the difficulties and help to dissipate them.

*

Why allow yourself to be overpowered like that? These fits of despair are quite irrational — there is no true reason why you should feel so despondent. Our solicitude and help are there always — in spite of these attacks your spiritual capacity is constantly increasing — only remain firm, the victory of the Truth in you is then inevitable. I will do all to change your consciousness — only open yourself. Keep yourself open as much as you can in quietude — that is the *only* condition I ask of you.

*

I did not receive any letter from you so recently as a fortnight or three weeks ago. If you feel in a pitiable condition, it is certainly not because you have incurred our displeasure. I have said that we are always with you and it is true, but to feel it you must draw back from your vital and be able to concentrate in your inner being. If you do that faithfully and sincerely, after a time you will feel the connection and the support.

The meaning of the phrase you speak of is this, that usually the vital tries to resist the call to change. That is what is meant by revolt or opposition. If the inner will insists and forbids revolt or opposition, the vital unwillingness may often take the form of depression and dejection, accompanied by a resistance in the physical mind which supports the repetition of old ideas, habits, movements or actions while the body consciousness suffers from an apprehension or fear of the called-for change, a drawing back from it or a dullness which does not receive the call.

It is these things you have to get rid of. But a sorrowful or despondent mood is not the proper condition for doing that. You have to stand back from the feeling of suffering, anguish and apprehension, reject it and look quietly at the resistance, affirming always to yourself your will to change and insisting that it shall be done and cannot fail to be done now or later with the divine help, because the divine help is there. It is then that the strength can come to you that will overcome the difficulties.

*

The weakness in yourself of which you speak is there, as the persistency of these movements [*of despondency*] shows, but it is not in the heart — your heart is all right — but in the lower vital nature. All your weaknesses are there; the rest of your being is quite strong enough for the spiritual life. But this inadequacy of the lower vital is not peculiar to you, it is present in almost every human being. This tendency to irrational sadness and despondency and these imaginations, fears and perverse reasonings — always repeating, if you will take careful notice, the same movements, ideas and feelings and even the same language and phrases like a machine — is a characteristic working of the lower vital nature. The only way to get rid of it is to meet it with a fixed resolution of the higher vital and the mind and psychic being to combat, reject and master it. As you were determined to master the sex impulse and the desire of the palate, so you must determine to master this "irrational knot" of despondency in the lower vital nature. If you indulge it and regard it as a natural part of yourself with good causes for existence or if you busy yourself finding this or that justification for it when it comes, there is no reason why it should let go its unpleasant grip upon you. Be firm and courageous here, as you have learnt to be with other movements of your lower vital; you will then, I think, find less difficulty in your meditation and your general sadhana.

*

It is surely better to seek to right yourself than to let yourself float in the stream of vital despondency and weakness. What do you expect the Mother to answer to such prayers [*for death*]? It is not the soul's demand or need, but an outcry of vital weakness. X did not pray for death, but for light and progress out of his lower consciousness towards the Truth. Ramana Maharshi, whatever his objections to birth in this world, did not pray or seek for death, but for elevation to a height of consciousness for which there is neither birth nor death: he is certainly not so ignorant as to believe that the mere death of the body brings by itself a release; if he were, he would not have taken the trouble to go through so prolonged and intense a tapasya. If a way out is wanted, that is the only way out and there is no other.

*

The outer reasons [*for despondency*] are created by the mind and it is the mind that responds or does not respond to them. Nothing outward can affect unless the mind (vital mind usually) represents them to itself in a particular way and makes its own response.

*

If the mind does not respond to any suggested reasons for despondency, that is indeed a great liberation.

Chapter Four
Sentimentalism, Sensitiveness, Instability, Laxity

Sentimentalism

It is not a question of feeling sorrow or joy or any other emotion, everybody does that who has not overcome the ordinary Nature. That is not sentimental but emotional. Sentimentalism comes in when you take a pleasure either in indulging or in displaying the feelings or when you have them for no reason or without sufficient reason.

*

It is a sentimental part of the vital nature that quarrels with people and refuses to speak to them and it is the same part in a reaction against that mood that wants to speak and get the pleasure of the relation. So long as there is either of these movements, the other also is possible. It is only when you get rid of this sentimentalism and turn all your purified feelings towards the Divine, that these fluctuations disappear and a calm goodwill to all takes their place.

Sensitiveness

It [*sensitiveness*] is a matter of temperament. Some are psychically and vitally sensitive and responsive to all that comes from anywhere; others are solid of nerve and walled against invasion. It is not at all a question of strength or weakness. The first have a greater sense of life and answer to life; they suffer more from life and get more from it. It is the difference between the Greek and the Roman. Even without egoism the difference remains because it is of the temperament. In Yoga the first type are more able to feel everything directly and know everything in detail by close experience; it is their great advantage. The others have to use the mind to know and their grasp is less intimate.

*

It [*vital sensitiveness*] is neither good nor bad. It comes like that in the course of the development. Some are incapable of consciously or visibly opening to others because they are insensitive. On the other hand to be too open is troublesome.

*

There can be no transformation of the being in an insensitive consciousness.

*

Most sensitiveness is the result or sign of ego.

*

It was indeed a microscopically small cause for so strong an upsetting, but really it is the whole difficulty of this raw and unreasonable sensitiveness which cropped up with this very infinitesimally small excuse — and that sensitiveness is one of the most persistent obstacles of many sadhaks here. There are two remedies for it — the psychic's confidence in the Mother and the surrender that goes with it, i.e. "whatever she wills is best for me", and the vastness which you feel now, — it is the wideness of the true self, of the true mental, vital, physical being also, from which such things fall off like dust, for they are of no importance to it whatever.

It is the one thing to do, to get permanently into the wideness, peace and silence and let the ego dissolve in it and the attachments fall away.

*

The portion below the navel is the lower vital, — in your case it has become very sensitive to the condition of the same part in others or perhaps even to their general condition — so that it gives a sort of reflection or an appropriate reaction to that. It is a phase in the development that must be overpassed, because the lower vital must get a perfect peace in it and even if it feels the condition of others do it as an act of perception or knowledge without any reaction or reflection.

*

One has not to cure oneself of one's sensitiveness, but only acquire the power to rise to a higher consciousness taking such disenchantments as a sort of jumping-board. One way is not to expect even square dealings from others, no matter who the others are. And besides, it is good to have such experiences of the real nature of some people to which a generous nature is often blind, for that helps the growth of one's consciousness. The blow you wince at seems to you so hard because it is a blow the world of your mental formation has sustained. Such a world often becomes a part of our being. The result is that a blow dealt to it gives almost physical pain. The great compensation is that it makes you live more and more in the real world in contradistinction to the world of your imagination which is what you would like the real world to be. But the real world is not all that could be desired, you know, and that is why it has to be acted upon and transformed by the Divine Consciousness. But for that, knowledge of the reality, however unpalatable, is almost the first requisite. This knowledge often enough is best brought home to us through blows and bleedings. True, idealistic people, sensitive people, refined natures smart under such disillusionments more than do others who are somewhat thick-skinned, but that is no reason why fine feelings should be deprecated and the keen edge of fine susceptibilities be blunted. The thing is to learn to detach oneself from any such experience and learn to look at such perversions of others from a higher altitude from where one can regard these manifestations in the proper perspective — the impersonal one. Then our difficulties really and literally become opportunities. For knowledge, when it goes to the root of our troubles, has in itself a marvellous healing-power as it were. As soon as you touch the quick of the trouble, as soon as you, diving down and down, get at what really ails you, the pain disappears as though by a miracle. Unflinching courage to reach true Knowledge is therefore of the very essence of Yoga. No lasting superstructure can be erected except on a solid basis of true Knowledge. The feet must be sure of their ground before the head can hope to kiss the skies.

Shyness

As for shyness, there are two kinds: one is egoistic, being ashamed of expressing the Truth or showing allegiance to it in ways which would not be understood by others — the other is a certain reserve, an unwillingness to expose one's deeper feelings to the gaze of others, the wish to keep sacred and secret the relations of love with the Divine — that is a psychic feeling.

Indecision and Instability

The first [*case*] is vital indecision — the other is vital instability.[1] Those who can't choose, have the vital indecision and it is usually due to a too active physical mind, seeing too many things or too many sides at a time. The other rises from a lack of control and too much impulse.

*

It [*failure in whatever one tries to do*] usually comes from a certain instability in the lower vital which does not give a consistent support to the Will, but is restless and fluctuates from one interest to another. It does not mean an incapacity for success — usually one who has that could succeed in many directions, but the fluctuation prevents sustained success in any. It is a defect that has to be got over and can be got over.

*

The failure [*in studies and in sadhana*] is due not to want of capacity but to want of steadiness — a restlessness in the vital

---

[1] *The correspondent wrote: "There are people who cannot come to a definite decision when the situation demands it. There are others who are constantly changing their decisions. Are both of these cases of vital indecision?" — Ed.*

and a sort of ardent hastiness that lacks in care of detail and in perseverance. What you need is the inner silence and the solid strength and force that can act through this inner silence, making the vital its instrument but not allowing it to condition the action by its defects.

*

There are some who are solid and tenacious in their vital, it is they who can be steady — others are more mercurial and easily moved by impulses, it is these who are sometimes enthusiastic, sometimes drop into fatigue. It is a matter of temperament. On the other hand the mercurial people are often capable of a quicker ardour, so that they can progress fast if they want in their own way. In any case the remedy for all that is to find one's true self above mind and vital and so not bound by temperament.

Laxity

The rigidity was in the obstinacy with which your mind and vital clung to their own ideas and vital habits and did not want to change. But the result was rather laxity, a general looseness which did not want to tune the nature to the spiritual endeavour, but let all sorts of things wander over its strings at their pleasure. Plasticity of the consciousness is necessary, but plasticity to the true touch of the Power, not to any ordinary touch of the forces in Nature. To tune all to the Higher should be your aim — then there will be the full poetry of the spirit not in writing only but in life.

Section Three

Vital Defects

Chapter One
Ego and Its Forms

Ego and Egoism

I suppose the ego came there [*into human activity*] first as a means of the outer consciousness individualising itself in the flux of Nature and, secondly, as an incentive for tamasic animal man to act and get something done. Otherwise he might merely have contented himself with food and sleep and done nothing else. With that incentive of ego (possession, vanity, ambition, eagerness for power etc. etc.) he began doing all sorts of things he might never otherwise have done. But now that he has to go higher, this ego comes badly in the way.

*

Yes, ego is the reason of the difficulty in everybody.

*

But that [*pride of the ego*] is the case with all human beings. All the action is shot through with ego, acts, feelings, thoughts, everything, big or small, good or bad. Even humility and what is called altruism is with most people only a form of ego. It does not depend on having something to be proud of.

*

It is so with everybody. Human nature is shot through in all its stuff with the threads of the ego. Even when one tries to get away from it, it is in front or walks behind all the thoughts and actions like one's shadow. To see that is the first step — to discern the falsity and absurdity of the ego movements is the second — to discourage and refuse it at every step is the third — but it goes entirely only when one sees, experiences and lives the One in everything and equally everywhere.

*

The human being is naturally egoistic and ego-centred — all he does, thinks, feels has the stamp of the ego on it and it cannot be otherwise until he learns to make not the ego but the Divine the centre of his existence and thinks, acts, feels only for the Divine — or until he enters into the higher or divine consciousness or the divine consciousness into him — for in the divine consciousness there is no ego.

*

All human beings are full of ego. If you want to change, you must be very quiet and always aspire for a higher consciousness to come down into you in which there is not the ego. When it comes down, the real change will come. But you must be quiet within, not worried and restless — you must open confidently to the Mother's Force and let it work in you.

*

The human consciousness is permeated in all its past ideas with this substance of egoism. It is only by a constant quiet vigilance and increasing consciousness that it can be got out — for if it is not allowed to play openly, it conceals itself and takes subtle and disguised forms.

*

It is the ego that is showing itself in its true character. Formerly, it was associating with the sadhana because it either got something of what it desired or had great expectations. Now that these things are held back and the demand for the true attitude is made on it, it resists or non-cooperates, saying, "No value in such a sadhana." In all the sadhaks here, the ego (in its physical or vital physical roots) is proving to be the stumbling block. No transformation is possible unless it changes.

*

Obviously, unless the object is Nirvana, the small ego has to be attended to — not indulged, but transformed out of existence.

*

Yes, that is right — to remember constantly and live in the peace and calmness so that the Force may work and the Light may come. The small things of daily life must go on in the surface consciousness, not filling too large a place in it, until the Force and Light have taken possession and can lay direct hold of these also. It is the ego that gives them too big a place — the ego must be discouraged. "Not for myself, but for the Divine" should grow to be the law of the whole consciousness and thought and action. It cannot be done thoroughly all at once, but that must become the insistent note in the mind as soon as possible.

*

I meant [by *"thinking of the Divine"*] the giving up of the preoccupation with your ego and its rights and claims and ideas of unfair treatment and all the rest and to think more of the Divine and the seeking for the Divine for which you came here and make that your chief preoccupation. It is not in meditation alone, but in life and thought and act and feeling that that has to be done.

*

Human nature has always been egoistic in its basis and so it brings in the ego motive into the work for the Divine also. That can only be overcome slowly, for what is ingrained in the human vital nature and has been active through hundreds of lives cannot disappear at once. To be conscious and to have the steady will to change and make the inner motive of bhakti and self-giving prevail over the outer motives is the one thing necessary.

*

If you are becoming so conscious of the ego and the animal which fill so large a place in every human being, it is really a progress, because to be conscious is the first step. But along with it you must have an aspiration and a confident faith in the Divine Power and Grace and in the divine element within you, psychic and spiritual, that through these the nature will be transformed and the ego replaced by the true person and the animal by the true vital and physical being become fit instruments of the Divine Mother.

*

Yes, these experiences [*of the smallness of the egoistic person*] always come when one is opening into the wideness of the cosmic consciousness and your conclusions are correct. The self-importance of the ego has to dissolve — the importance of life or the progress of the being can come only from its being a vehicle of the Divine's play, evolution, realisation and that is independent of the vastness of Space and Time.

*

The right attitude is to see that as a separate being, as an ego, one has no importance whatever and the insistence on one's own desires, pride, position etc. is an ignorance, but one matters only as a spirit, as a portion of the Divine, not more than others, but as all souls matter to the Soul of all.

*

Impersonality in itself is not the Divine. All these mistakes can be and are made by many who claim to be in an impersonalised consciousness. A force may be impersonal but may be also a wrong force. Many think they are impersonal and free from ego because they are obeying a force or something bigger than their own personality — but that force or that something may be quite other than the Divine and it may hold them by something in their personality and ego.

*

It [*the degree of sensitivity*] depends on the nature of the ego. Some egoists are hard-skinned and not sensitive at all; others are hyper-sensitive.

Ego in Different Parts of the Being

It [*the ego*] rises because it is its nature to do so; it wants to keep hold of the being which it considers its property and field of expression.

*

Your ego does come up from time to time without your seeing that it is the ego. It comes up not in your higher parts but in your physical mind and consciousness and you think that because your higher parts are clear this also is clear.

*

Ego, whatever its basis, can reproduce itself in different parts of the being, e.g. a vital ego, a mental ego, but fundamentally it is one.

*

The mind and the vital are much more full of ego than the body — in the body the ego is obscure and instinctive only. There is no reason why ego should not be conquered in the end — although it is difficult — even in the external nature.

*

The fight with the ego is part of the fight with the physical nature, for it is the superficial ego in the physical consciousness, irrational and instinctive, that refuses to go.

*

No, it need not.[1] It is so thought because the old Yogas did not care about the liberation of the body and other instruments, and thought only of the separation of the soul from the Prakriti. If you do not liberate the Prakriti, ego and other forms of bondage will naturally remain so long as there is any action of Prakriti.

---

[1] *The correspondent asked whether egoism remains, at least in the physical being, as long as the body remains. — Ed.*

The Vital Ego

The earth-consciousness does not want to change, so it rejects what comes down to it from above — it has always done so. It is only if those who have taken this Yoga open themselves and are willing to change their lower nature that this unwillingness can disappear.

What stands in the way of course is always the vital ego with its ignorance and the pride of its ignorance and the physical consciousness with its inertia which resents and resists any call to change and its indolence which does not like to take the trouble — it finds it more comfortable to go on its own way repeating always the same old movements and, at best, expecting everything to be done for it in some way at some time.

The first thing is to have the right inner attitude — you have that; the rest is the will to transform oneself and the vigilance to perceive and reject all that belongs to the ego and the tamasic persistence of the lower nature. Finally, to keep oneself always open to the Mother in every part of the being so that the process of transformation may find no hindrance.

*

Yes, even in ordinary life there must be a control over the vital and the ego — otherwise life would be impossible. Even many animals, those who live in groups, have their strict rules imposing a control on the play of the ego and those who disobey will have a bad time of it. The Europeans especially understand this and even though they are full of ego, yet when there is a question of team work or group life, they are adepts at keeping it in leash, even if it growls inside; it is the secret of their success. But in Yoga life of course it is a question not of controlling ego but of getting rid of it and rising to a higher principle, so demand is much more strongly and insistently discouraged.

*

It is much better to tell [*any feelings of dissatisfaction*]. But you are not alone in these feelings — two-thirds of the Asram have them in more or less vehemence — it is the unregenerate vital ego which is just the thing that stands most in the way of the transformation — other things are comparatively mild obstacles compared with this part of the being. It is much better that the Mother refused consideration to this part of you — consideration would have been a much more dangerous test than refusal.

*

Yes, it [*a false sense of importance*] is a thing which comes to many; exaggerated and made a principal part of the vital attitude, it has been the cause of failure and departure of several who consider themselves great sadhaks — they made it an excuse for indulging and magnifying the vital ego. Since you see that it is ridiculous, you should have no difficulty in getting rid of it. The only truth in it is that each one who opens himself in such a way that the Force can get through to his material so as to change it, will by that be contributing to the victory of the Force — but it applies to everybody, not to any one individual.

*

Yes, the talk about "advanced" sadhaks is a thing I have always discouraged — but people go on because that appeals to the vital ego.

*

I have already told you the nature of the difficulty that has arisen in you, that it is nothing but the revolt of your vital mind and vital ego and I have pointed out to you the only way in which it can be overcome. You had by an effort supported by a special concentration from us arrived at a first psychic opening in your mind and heart which enabled you even to throw out for a time the sexual obsession from your vital consciousness. But, as often happens, soon after all that is obscure, egoistic, self-centred in the vital being rose up in revolt and created a confused farrago of desires, demands, disappointments, grievances, misapprehensions,[2] false reasonings and especially a wrong attitude of claim and demand which was the entire contradiction of the psychic and spiritual attitude and wholly inconsistent with the right conditions of sadhana. It is this of which your recent letters were full. The forces that use this kind of vital condition for the breaking of a sadhak's spiritual chances became active and turned all into a drive to go away. Your only chance is to refuse to listen to all these ideas and suggestions and adopt resolutely an attitude of complete self-giving and the refusal of all feelings of desire, claim and ego and all justifications of these feelings by the vital mind which is full of a false view of things and therefore cannot be trusted even when its reasonings seem to be plausible.

Others before you have entered into this whirl of the vital mind and ego and have gone on justifying it and indulging it. The only result was a constant repetition of vital crises sometimes ending in departure and the failure of the sadhana; others by a repeated reaction of their psychic being finally succeeded in emerging out of the chaos. But we have found that to comply with the claims, demands, clamours, ultimatums of the vital mind in this condition is the worst way to meet the difficulty. It only increases the demands, revolts, outbursts of ego and makes the recurrence or continuance of the vital crises endless. You must get out of your head the idea that you have a right to demand this or that from the Mother because she is accepted by you as the Divine and that she is bound to satisfy you and any refusal is an offence and an outrage. The Mother acts and decides in all freedom according to her vision and judgment and she cannot be expected to act according to the desires, opinions or demands of the sadhaks nor can they judge by their minds her reasons or motives, for these do not belong to the ordinary consciousness in which the mind moves. For her to obey the dictates of the sadhaks or their claims and desires would be to make her work meaningless and a failure. Apart from that, the

---

[2] Your present attitude to your poetry and painting is one of these misapprehensions of the vital mind and ego and is a mistake calculated to injure your sadhana.

basis of this Yoga is self-giving and surrender of the sadhak to the Divine, his acceptance of guidance by a higher consciousness than his own. A reversal of the position, an imposition of the will of the lower consciousness on the Divine or the Guru is not admissible; yet the position you have taken in your letters of demand amounts to that and nothing else. This attitude must cease if you want to get out of your difficulty.

I have tried to make the position clear to you. It is for you to accept or not to accept what I have said; but it is the only way possible for the sadhana.

*

Once the universality [*of the consciousness*] is established, there is no longer a secure fortress in the nature for the vital egoism — the walls of it having been broken down. They [*vital forces*] may still attack from outside, but it now lies in the power of the sadhak to prevent their making a settled formation in him any longer.

Rajasic and Tamasic Ego (Ahankara)

What you speak of as your nature, the distrust etc., is not the nature but only a particular turn or habit that has got into it like a crease in a dress. It can be smoothed out of the nature. Of course it has to be smoothed out, for just as the rajasic ahankara which exalts itself unduly is not good for the sadhana, creating pride, vanity and delusion, so this opposite thing, called often tamasic ahankara, is not good, for it creates diffidence, despondency and in some people inertia.

*

The tamasic ego is that which accepts and supports despondency, weakness, inertia, self-depreciation, unwillingness to act, unwillingness to know or be open, fatigue, indolence, do-nothingness. Contrary to the rajasic it says, "I am so weak, so obscure, so miserable, so oppressed and ill-used — there is no hope for me, no success, I am denied everything, I am unsupported — how can I do this, how can I do that, I have no power for it, no capacity, I am helpless; let me die; let me lie still and moan," etc. etc. Of course not all that at once or in every case; but I am giving the general character of the thing.

*

All that [*self-depreciation and depression*] is the usual play of the vital and the ego. It is the vital that can find satisfaction neither in talking with others nor in solitude — it has lost the old satisfaction in talks, but it cannot reconcile itself either to giving up the old attachment — it still feels a tie to it and so cannot get the joy of solitude.

It is the ego that is self-important and makes much of itself, but depression, self-depreciation and the feeling that others do not like or appreciate your company is also a working of the ego. The first is rajasic ego, the second tamasic ego. To be occupied always with oneself and the action of others on oneself is ego. One who is free from ego does not trouble about these things. In Yoga one must be unattached and indifferent to these things, concerned only with Sadhana and the Divine and towards others the attitude must be one of quiet goodwill without any demand or expectation. If one can't arrive at this yet, one must always endeavour to arrive at that and not feed the lower vital movement by brooding on these other things.

To depend on letters from me for getting free from depression will only create a habit of depression, demand for a tonic in the shape of a letter, then again depression, tonic and revival and the circle will go on. It is only by a resolute will to get rid of the vital and the ego through their reactions that you can keep yourself open to the Mother. Success may take time, but the steady will and aspiration must be there.

*

In spite of the outbreak of temper and violence with regard to the boy I do not think it can be said that you have not changed at all or made any progress. There are three obstacles that one has to overcome in the vital and they are very difficult to overcome, lust (sexual desire), wrath and rajasic ego. I think you have progressed much in all three. Even in regard to anger, the outbreaks are surely less common, less overpowering and long-continued than they were before. It has been so much in your vital nature that you have to be on your guard against fits like these coming back; you have also to overcome excitement and violence of speech; but if you persevere without being discouraged, the freedom will come. Rajasic ego is the ground of the others. I think your idea about X is good for this purpose. If you can accustom yourself to do as scrupulously work not attractive to you as you do what attracts you and to do it in accordance with the ideas and standards of another, not insisting on your own, that should be an excellent discipline for the rajasic ego and bring into the vital a greater power of self-giving and peace.

*

Do you mean to say that you never had any rajasic element in you? There is not a human being who has not got it in him so long as he is not divinised in his vital. What were all the vital suggestions coming to you so insistently always except appeals to the rajasic ego? When you threw out sex, jealousy, vanity, etc. what were you throwing out but the rajasic ego? What was the demand at the pranam or the disturbance caused there but a movement of the rajasic ego? Some of these things you threw out successfully — others still kept a response.

*

So long as you had fully the attitude of surrender, the rajasic ego could only take the form of suggestions from outside, uprisings from the subconscient. It was suppressed in the vital. When the inertia rose and the energy of will receded, it began to try to come in again.

*

These [*feelings of hopelessness*] are the feelings of the tamasic ego — the reaction to a disappointment in the rajasic ego. Mingled with the true attitude and experience or running concurrently along with it was a demand of the vital, "What I am having now, I must always have, otherwise I can't do sadhana; if I ever lose that, I shall die" — whereas the proper attitude is, "Even if I lose it for a time, it will be because something in me has to be changed in order that the Mother's consciousness may be fulfilled in me not only in the self but in every part." The lower forces attacked at this weak point, made demands through the vital and brought about a state of inertia in which what you had clung to seemed to be lost, went back behind the veil. So came the tamasic reaction of the ego, "What is the use of living, I prefer to die." Obviously it is not the whole of you that says it, it is a part in the disappointed vital and tamasic physical. It is not enough that the active demands should be broken and removed; for this also is a passive way of demand, "I can't have my demands; very well, I abdicate, don't want to exist." That must disappear.

*

Tamas and tamasic ego are implied in each other. When one yields to tamas, one indulges the tamasic ego.

Ego-centricity

The ego-centric man feels and values things as they affect him. "Does this please me or displease, give me gladness or pain, flatter my pride, vanity, ambition or hurt it, satisfy my desires or thwart them?" etc. The unegoistic man does not look at things like that. He looks to see what things are in themselves and would be even if he were not there, what is their meaning, how they fit into the scheme of things — or else he feels calm and equal, refers everything to the Divine, or if he is a man of action how they will serve the work that has to be done or the life of the world or the cause he serves etc. etc. There can be many points of view which are not ego-centric.

*

It is true about living and doing all for oneself, but that is the nature of man, he is centred in his ego, ego-centric, and does all for his ego; even his love and liking is mostly based on ego. All that has to be changed and all has to be centred in the Divine, done for the Divine Mother. It is the work of the sadhana to get that done. The silence, the growth of the psychic and all else is meant to bring about that — but it cannot be done all at once. When the consciousness is ready, then the psychic love, the impulse for self-giving begins to open out in the heart and the change is made — more and more till there is the complete self-giving.

*

But in what way do they [*internal and external things*] belong to the Divine, so long as the ego appropriates and uses them for its own purposes? Self-giving in fact means a change from ego-centricity to God-centricity; also such a giving as would lead to a change of the whole base of the consciousness.

*

Your nature like that of almost everybody has been largely ego-centric and the first stages of the sadhana are with almost everybody ego-centric. The main idea in it is always one's own sadhana, one's own endeavour, one's own development, perfection, siddhi. It is inevitable for most, for without that personal endeavour there would not be sufficient will or push to bring about the first necessary changes. But none of these things — development, perfection or siddhi — can really come in any degree of completeness or unmixed finality until this ego-centric attitude changes into the God-centric, until it becomes the development, perfection, siddhi of the Divine Consciousness, its will and its instrumentation in this body — and that can only be when these things become secondary, and bhakti for the Divine, love for the Divine, oneness with the Divine in consciousness, will, heart and body, become the sole aim — the rest is then only the fulfilment of the Divine Will by the Divine Power. This attitude is never difficult for the psychic, it is its natural position and feeling, and whenever your psychic was in front, you had it in your central consciousness. But there were the outer mind, vital and physical that brought in their mixture of desire and ego and there could be no effective liberation in life and action till these were liberated. The thinking mind and higher vital can accept without too much difficulty, but the difficulty is with the lower vital and physical and especially with the most external parts of them; for these are entirely creatures of habit, recurring movement, an obstinate repetition of the same movement always. This habit is so blind and obstinate and persistent as to seem almost invincible, especially when it is used at a juncture like this by the Forces of Ignorance as their last refuge or point of attack. But the apparent invincibility is not true. The most ego-centric can change and do change by the psychic principle becoming established in the external nature. That it can be done only by the Divine Grace and Power is true (that is true of all spiritual change) — but with the full consent of the being. As it was done in the inner being, so it can be done in the outer; give the adhesion of your full will and faith and, whatever the difficulty, it will be done.

*

Obviously one must not get egoistic about it [*one's sadhana*], but withdrawal from the outer or lower consciousness into the inner is not in itself an egoistic movement. If it were so, all sadhana would be egoism and to be always social and on the surface would be the only thing!

The Egoism of the Instrument and the Magnified Ego

The form of ego has to be dissolved,[3] it has not to be replaced by a bigger ego or another kind of ego. It has to be replaced by the true being which feels itself, even though individual, yet one with all and one with the Divine.

*

---

[3] *The correspondent asked whether the ego has to be transformed or dissolved. — Ed.*

The egoism of the instrument can be as dangerous or more dangerous to spiritual progress than the egoism of the doer. The ego-sense is contrary to spiritual realisation, so how can any kind of ego be a thing to be encouraged? As for the magnified ego, it is one of the most perilous obstacles to release and perfection. There should be no big I, not even a small one.

What is meant by the magnified ego is that when the limits of the ordinary mind and vital are broken, one feels a far vaster and more powerful consciousness and unlimited possibilities, but if one ties all that to the tail of one's own ego, then one becomes a thousand times more egoistic than the ordinary man. The greatness of the Divine becomes an excuse and a support for one's own greatness and the big I swells itself to fill not only the earth but the heavens. That magnification of the ego is a thing to be guarded against with a watchful care.

*

What you say about the ahankara of the instrument is true — it is one of the most sticky of the ego's self-deceptions and there are few who can detect it soon or get easily clear of it. I think I can congratulate you on your becoming aware of it at so early a stage. There are some who do not discover it even after ten or twenty years of sadhana.

*

Yes — these [*pride, a sense of superiority, the desire to show one's worth*] are small signs or little forms of the ego of the instrument — not very serious, but often rather sticky. There is a bigger kind of egoism which is not so common which can rise into a kind of megalomania: "I, I am *the* instrument — how great an instrument I am — through me all will be done", — there are three or four who have had that in a distressingly acute form, secretly or openly; often it ends by their going away to do great things outside — great things which somehow do not get done.

*

The Divine is there in all men, so the Divine and the ego do live together. But the Divine is veiled by the ego and manifests in proportion as the ego *first submits itself*, then recedes and disappears. There can be no complete possession by the Divine without disappearance of the ego. Any man can be an instrument of the Divine — the thing is to be a perfectly conscious instrument.

*

Well, it can hardly be that you alone are a chosen instrument. All who arrive at the realisation in this Yoga will be instruments — it is part of the realisation that the sadhak should turn himself into an instrument of the Divine Mother.

Getting Rid of the Ego and of Egoism

What you say [*about the need to purify oneself of ego*] is perfectly correct — I am glad you are becoming so lucid and clearsighted, the result surely of a psychic change. Ego is a very curious thing and in nothing more than in its way of hiding itself and pretending it is not the ego. It can always hide even behind an aspiration to serve the Mother. The only way of getting rid of it is to chase it out of all its veils and corners.

You are right also in thinking that this is really the most important part of your Yoga. The Rajayogis are right in putting purification in front of everything and a preliminary to successful meditation — as I was also right in putting it in front along with concentration in the *Synthesis*. You have only to look around you to see that experiences and even realisations cannot bring one to the goal if this is not done — at any moment they can fall owing to the vital still being impure and full of ego.

*

Yes, that [*the elimination of egoism*] is the first requisite of a true foundation in the sadhana. It is because people do not realise this and are satisfied with experiences, keeping the vital ego, not insisting on an egoless higher consciousness, that there is so much difficulty.

*

Obviously all that must go — it is the old vital egoism of the human being always preoccupied with itself, so that the being cannot give itself simply and unquestioningly to the adoration of the Divine.

*

Yes — it is from looking at things from the ego point of view that there comes all the confusion and trouble and ignorance. One has to think of the Divine, be still and let the divine consciousness come in and replace the egoistic human — then all that disappears.

*

All attachment and ego must disappear. No temptation of power, for power is given only to do the Divine's work and the power itself is the Divine's. No attachment to work, for the work is not the ego's, but the Divine's. No attachment or insistence on the fruits, for that too belongs to the Divine and will come when mind and circumstances are ready. It is the same with sadhana. Only one thing is to be the aim, to be in union and contact with the Divine through love and surrender, — the rest will come out of that, whatever is needed for the manifestation.

*

If the ego is gone and the full surrender is there, then there should be no obstacles [*to following the sunlit path of sadhana*]. If however the rajas of the vital is only quiescent, then its quiescence may bring up the tamas in its place, and that would be the obstacle.

*

Only calm in the vital is hardly sufficient [*to have psychic experiences*]. There must be something throwing out the ego from the vital.

*

Of course, they [*the ego and the vital*] always resist a pressure to get rid of them — and if one fixes a given time, they are all the more resistant in the hope of creating disappointment and discouragement by the failure to do it in the given time.

*

You cannot expect to drive the ego out of the movements in a short time. What is necessary is to see it quietly without being discouraged by its presence, and by a steady persistent action work it out of the system.

*

It is not possible to get rid of the ego-movements all at once. They have to be worked out of the nature by a constant consciousness and rejection. Even when the central ego has gone, the habitual movements stick for a long time.

*

These things [*little expressions of egoism*] either fade slowly out by constant rejection or else they drop off when the higher consciousness gets steadily down into the lower vital and, as it were, swallows it up. A sudden extinction is perhaps possible — at least there are reported cases of it — but usually they linger and go slowly, losing gradually force as if worn out.

*

For the ego, however insistent it may be, one has to keep one's eye on it and say no to all its suggestions so that each position it takes up proves to be a fruitless move. Treated in that way, it becomes ready for the moment when the psychic has only to give a slight push for it to fall away in each field of its activity from its loosened roots. Persevere steadily in the present movement and it cannot fail to be effective.

*

Ego is not so easy to get rid of. It remains not only in spite of work, but in spite of knowledge or bhakti. The disappearance of ego means complete *mukti*. But even the Yogi who feels his separate being swallowed up in cosmic consciousness or some kind of transcendental consciousness, yet when it comes to outward action and reaction finds the superficial ego still there. That is why the ascetic has a horror of action and says that without ego it can't be done. It can, but fully only when even these outermost things are finally taken up by the higher Consciousness entirely.

*

If you think there is no ego or desire in you, only pure devotion, that shows a great unconsciousness. To be free from ego and desire is a condition which needs a high siddhi in Yoga — even many Yogis of a great spiritual attainment are not free from it. For a sadhak at your stage of development to think he is free from ego and desire is to blind himself and prevent the clear perception of one's own nature movements which is necessary for progress towards spiritual perfection.

The Mother does not need to have your writings before her in order to see what is in you.

If your writings show ego and desire, and they certainly do, it is because they are there without your perceiving it and express themselves without your intending it. What the surface mind thinks and intends is one thing and what is behind the thoughts and actions is another thing. A man's surface mind shapes its own idea of oneself and one's nature in an entire self-ignorance. The first thing one has to do to get rid of this ignorance is to draw back from the surface mind and get into contact with the psychic which does not allow such delusions and shows one clearly the truth about one's movements.

*

Even if there is no consciousness of ego in the higher parts where oneness of all things has been realised, it does not follow that in the lower parts ego has been abolished. It can on the contrary become very strong and the actions can be very egoistic even while the mind is thinking "I have no ego."

*

Of course, such suggestions [*that one can be an instrument to help someone else on the path of Yoga*] are meant to wake the ego. I suppose they persist because they still have a hope of waking the ego. Even when one is quite free, all kinds of suggestions can come. One either takes no notice of them or else gives a glance to see whether there is any fragment of ego still lurking somewhere.

Getting Rid of the Ego Altogether

But what is this ego of which you speak? Everybody has the ego and it is impossible to get rid of it altogether except by two things — the opening of the psychic within and the descent of a wider ego-free consciousness from above. The psychic being opening does not get rid of the ego at once but purifies it and offers it and all the movements to the Divine, so that one becomes unegoistic through self-giving and surrender. At the same time the nature opens above and the wider ego-free consciousness comes down and ego disappears and by the power of the psychic you know your own true being which is a portion of the Mother. This is what has to happen, but it cannot happen in so short a time. Do not be always thinking of the vital movements and the ego — you have seen them and know that they are, it is enough. Concentrate rather in the heart on the opening there; concentrate persistently and aspire persistently and do not mind if it takes time. Call in any way, even if you cannot call yet deeply — then the deeper call will come.

*

It is possible [*to diminish the ego by the action of the Force*] if your consciousness associates itself with the action; then at least one can get rid of its major action and leave only minor traces. To get rid of the ego altogether however comes usually only by the descent of Consciousness from above and its occupation of the whole being aided of course by the rule of the psychic in the nature.

*

I think you still give an exaggerated importance and attention to the ego and other elements that are interwoven in the nature of humanity and cannot be entirely got rid of except by the coming of a new consciousness which replaces them by higher movements. If one rejects centrally and with all sincerity the ego and rajas, their roots get loosened and sattwa can prevail in the nature, but the expulsion of all ego and rajas cannot be done by the will and its effort. After a certain stage of preparation therefore one must stress more on the positive side of the sadhana than on the negative side of rejection, — though this of course must remain to help the other. Still what is important is to develop the psychic within and bring down the higher consciousness from above. The psychic as it grows and manifests detects immediately all wrong movements or elements and at the same time supplies almost automatically the true element or movement which will replace them — this psychic process is much easier and more effective than that of a severe tapasya of purification. The higher consciousness in descending brings peace and purity into all the inner parts; the inner being separates itself from the imperfect outer consciousness and at the same time the peace that comes carries in it a power which can throw out what contradicts the peace and purity. Ego can then slowly or swiftly but surely disappear — rajas and tamas change into their divine substitutes.

*

It is rather a wider than a higher consciousness that is necessary for the liberation from the ego. Going high is necessary of course, but by itself it is not sufficient.

*

Without persistent rejection it [*liberation from movements of the ego*] cannot be done. Going up into the self liberates the higher parts but the ego remains in the lower parts. The most effective force for this liberation is the psychic control along with steady rejection.

*

The sense of ego can disappear into that of the Self or the Purusha but that of itself does not bring about the disappearance of the old ego reactions in the Prakriti. The Purusha has to get rid of these by a process of constant rejection and remoulding. The remoulding consists in throwing everything into a consecration to the Mother and doing all for her without regard to oneself, one's desires, opinions, vital reactions as if they were the things to be fulfilled. This is most easily done if the psychic being becomes quite awake.

*

Without the liberation of the psychic and the realisation of the true Self the ego cannot go, both are necessary. If there is no consciousness of the Self how can the ego disappear? The psychic can be liberated by love and devotion, but I was speaking of a case in which it is not so liberated, and the realisation of the Self seems more easy — a case like yours.

Selfishness

To go away and suffer the consequences is not a solution. As for the rest, the selfishness of the ego is not a reason for not calling down the higher (divine) consciousness of which the peace and the force are as it were the front or the basis. How can you get rid of the selfish ego unless you call down that higher consciousness to which the ego is not a necessity?

In the evolution of the lower consciousness here ego and selfishness were a necessity. So long as the higher consciousness above ordinary mind does not descend, ego remains a necessity even in aspiring towards the Divine or towards Mukti, even if it becomes a sattwic ego. It is only in the higher consciousness that ego can dissolve, either by ascending there or by its descent into the consciousness below.

*

Why is it selfishness [*to be concentrated on the Divine*]? Selfishness is to live for oneself and not for something greater than the self. To be concentrated on the Divine at all times is to get out of the personal self and its aims into something greater and serve the aims of that greater Existence. It is no more selfishness than to live for others always would be selfishness.

*

As to egoism and selfishness, one can be generous and yet egoistic — one can be generous with vanity, pride etc. in the generosity; one can even be egoistic in self-sacrifice.

Ambition

Ambition is always a force of the vital.

*

A kind of siddhi or siddhis can come [*even if there is ambition in the nature*] — siddhis of power etc. There are Yogins who have great powers and also a big ego. Of course there can be no liberation without overcoming ambition and ego.

*

Suggestions of ambition etc. are always born in the vital mind or, as it might be called, the mind of the vital and from there they rush up to the thinking mind and claim its assent and the sanction of the mental will. When the thinking mind gets clouded by the uprush, it gets carried away and gives its assent. The thinking mind (reason) has always to remain unmoved above and judge what is right without being caught and carried away by the vital.

*

Ambition and vanity are things so natural to the human consciousness — they have even their use in ordinary life — that it is quite natural that at first they should enter into the sadhana also and linger even when they are rejected. But they have to be pushed out, before one is far on the path — otherwise they are very dangerous attendants and can pervert both aspiration and siddhi.

Vanity

It [*vanity*] is one of the things most difficult to get rid of. Even when the mind is unmoved, something in the vital or physical or perhaps even some little bit on the surface at once starts vibrating.

*

It is possible that X has experiences for he has probably some mental force and through that can build up mental realisations of what he reads, but he lives in the vital and whatever he experiences or receives the vital takes it and makes it a hundred times bigger in its construction than it really is. His claims *are* preposterous. It is evident that, like most people, he has no idea what the supramental is or he would never talk like that. People who live in the vital and have much vanity (there have been several examples here too) easily get the idea that they have attained everything, are without ego, all they receive is from the Divine (even when a magnified ego is driving them) etc. etc., for the vital ego is eager to arrive, to be big, to be siddha, and it persuades itself very easily that it is all these things. Let him however go on his own way; it is no use disturbing his self-content, as probably it is the only kind of self-expression he can do.

*

When vanity is there on a big scale, it usually works like that. The man feels the energy in all he does and mistakes the energy for high accomplishment. It is a common error. The high accomplishment is in only one or two fields.

*

It is vanity, but it is not humbug,[4] unless he does not believe in it. If he does not believe in it, it is humbug, but it is not vanity.

---

[4] *A doctor went about claiming that he could cure people because the Mother's Force worked through him. The correspondent asked, "Is not all this humbug?" — Ed.*

Pride and Self-Esteem

Pride is only one form of ego — there are ten thousand others. Every action of man is full of ego — the good ones as well as the bad, his humility as much as his pride, his virtues as much as his vices.

To get the ego out of the human nature is not so simple as that. If one is free from ego, does nothing with reference to himself or for his own sake but only for the Divine and all his thoughts and feelings are for the Divine, then he is Jivanmukta and a Siddha Yogi.

*

For many sadhaks there is a first stage governed by the mind or higher vital in which they go on very well, because in the mind and higher vital there are elements that are strong enough to control the rest while the first experiences or first progress is made. But a time comes when the sadhak has to deal with the lower parts of the being, *then* all the vital difficulties arise. If the early progress or experiences have engendered pride or ego or if there is a serious flaw somewhere, then they are unable to deal with these so long as the ego is not removed or broken or the flaw mended. X developed a pride of self-righteousness that stood in his way altogether; he has also the flaw of a narrow obstinate mind that sticks to its own ideas as if they alone were right — the instances you give of his conduct are illustrations of this defect. That is why here he quarrels with everyone thinking that he is right and they are very bad and mischievous, cannot see his own faults and mistakes and when he is not heard by the Mother or myself feels hurt and offended because we do not support his saintliness and righteousness against the wicked who oppress him. He is a good and clever worker but he cannot progress in sadhana so long as he keeps this stiffness and ego.

*

But that [*inability to recognise one's defects*] is a very common human weakness, although it ought not to exist in a sadhak whose progress depends largely on his recognising what has to be changed in him. Not that the recognition by itself is sufficient, but it is a necessary element. It is of course a kind of pride or vanity which considers this necessary for strength and standing. Not only will they not recognise it before others but they hide their defects from themselves or even if obliged to look at it with one eye look away from it with the other. Or they weave a veil of words and excuses and justifications trying to make it something other than it really is. X's saying [*"I would die if I had to admit my faults."*] is very characteristic of him — that has been his main stumbling block in the path of Yoga.

*

It is little use our trying to convey to you *our* will (in words), because what your vital seeks after is a sanction for your own will and its way of action, — and it is little use our trying to give you light, because your mind follows always its own light. Any attempt to correct from us you have always rejected as our error, our misunderstanding of you, an attempt to give you kicks, as you express it. In such a case we can only be silent, try to help your sadhana silently as much as you will allow and for the rest leave you to learn by experience as far as you may become willing to do so. You have capacities and Yogic stuff, but along with them goes a very strong self-esteem and a self-righteous spirit which stand in the way of perfection and constitute a very serious obstacle. So long as a sadhak has that, the attempt of the Truth to manifest in him will always be baffled by his changing it into mental and vital constructions which distort it, turn it into ineffective half-truth or even make truth itself a source of error.

I would not have written even so much if you had not pressed so persistently for an answer. I hope you will not take it as misunderstanding or merely another "kick". If you do not want criticism or correction from us, you should at least develop better the power of self-criticism and self-correction in yourself without which no perfection is possible.

*

The egoism in yourself of which you speak belongs to the relation of one human being with another and is common to almost all men and women; it is extremely difficult to get rid of, but if one sees it clearly and determines not to have it, then it can first be brought under control and then dismissed from the nature. But the egoism which made people go away from here through pride in their sadhana and attachment to the supposed greatness of their experiences is another kind and far more dangerous spiritually. You do not have it and I do not think you are in danger of ever having it.

Self-Respect, Amour-Propre, Superiority

Self-respect and a sense of superiority are two very different things. Self-respect is not necessarily a sign of egoism any more than its absence is a sign of liberation from egoism. Self-respect means observing a certain standard of conduct which is proper to the level of manhood to which I belong — e.g. I cannot make a false statement out of self-respect though it would be advantageous to do it and most people under the circumstances would make it. Amour-propre is different and belongs to the sattwic type of ego. When one is not free from ego, then amour-propre (as well as self-respect — for that can be with ego or without ego) is a necessary support for the maintenance of the personality at its proper level.

*

Amour-propre does not mean conceit. It means at its best the feeling not to make mistakes and to do as well as possible — at its worst it means to try to appear well and without mistakes or faults to others and not to like faults being pointed out.

*

Ideas of superiority and inferiority are not of much use or validity. Each one is himself with his own possibilities to which there need be no limit except that of will and development and time. Each nature has its own lines and own things that are more developed or less developed, but the standard should be set by what he in himself aims to be. Comparison with others brings in a wrong standard of values.

Jealousy and Abhiman

This is a very common disease with the sadhaks — making comparisons with feelings of jealousy and envy — in some it leads to revolt and self-assertion, in others to self-depreciation and depression. Naturally, these feelings are quite out of place and the judgments created are out of focus. Each sadhak has his own movement, his own relation with the Divine, his own place in the work or the general sadhana and to compare with others immediately brings in a wrong standard. It is on the truth of his own inner movement that he has to take his base — swadharma.

*

Jealousy should not be there if there is no ground for it, for then it is absurd and meaningless — but also when there is reason for it according to common standards, it should not be there, for it is a sentiment lacking in nobility and quite unyogic.

As for getting rid of *lobha*, certainly the Mother's full help will be with you.

*

It is jealousy of course.[5] Fame and success always create a great amount of jealousy and ill-will anywhere but most in countries where there has been a suppressed public life and solidarity does not exist.

*

This jealousy (which is a very common affliction of the vital) will go like the rest. If you have the aspiration to get rid of it, it

---

[5] *An Indian philosopher was invited to Europe to deliver several lectures and was received well everywhere. When he returned to India, he found that the number of his critics had greatly increased. He wrote to ask Sri Aurobindo the reason. — Ed.*

can only come by force of habit, and with the psychic growing in you and the Mother's force acting, the power of the habit is sure to diminish and fade away. Do not be discouraged by its occasional return, but reject it so that it may be unable to stay long and will be obliged to retire. Very soon then it will cease to come at all.

*

All that [*vanity, jealousy, the sense of not being loved*] of course is not love, but self-love. Jealousy is only an ugly form of self-love. That is what people do not understand — they even think that demands and jealousy and wounded vanity are signs of love or at least natural attendants of it.

*

The sooner you get rid of that [*abhiman*] the better. Anyone who indulges abhiman puts himself under the influence of the hostile forces. Abhiman has nothing to do with true love; it is like jealousy a part of the vital egoism.

*

The feeling of jealousy and abhiman was of course a survival from the past movements of the nature. It is so that these things go out if they are rejected; they lose their force, can stay less and less, can affect less and less the consciousness, — finally, they are able to touch no longer and so come no longer.

*

It is of course the old reaction — jealousy is certainly there, or you would not feel this violent sorrow. That it subsists still in the recesses and rises with such vehemence shows how deeply rooted this movement was in your physical consciousness. You have not been able to root it out, because when it comes you associate yourself entirely with it and abandon yourself to its outcries and violence. You must have the strength to stand back from it in that part of your nature which is free — only then will you be able to push it away from you; and it is only if it is pushed away from you each time it rises that it will consent to disappear and return no more. As for our support and help it is there, but you must remain conscious of it — and you must not allow any wrong ideas like those of this morning to diminish the sense of unity and contact with the Mother.

*

I do not see why you make such a big difference between the quarrels and jealousy over other women and quarrels and jealousy over other attractions not of a sexual character. They both spring from the same primary impulse, the possessive instinct which is at the base of ordinary vital love. In the latter case, as often sexual jealousy is not possible, the mind supports itself on other motives which seem to it quite reasonable and justifiable — it may not be conscious that it is being pushed by the vital, but the quarrels and the vivacity of the disagreement are there all the same. Whether you had or had not both forms of it, is not very material and does not make things better or worse. It is the getting rid of the instinct itself that matters, whether from the psychological point of view or from that of a spiritual change.

The one thing that is of any importance is the fact that the old personality which you were throwing out has reasserted itself for the moment, as you yourself see. It has confused your mind, otherwise you would not ask the question whether it is there still and how that agrees with my description of your aspiration and glimpse of turning entirely to the Mother as true and real. Of course, they were true and real and sincere and they are still there even if for a moment clouded over. You know well enough by this time that the whole being is not one block so that if one part changes, all changes miraculously at the same time. Something of the old things may be there submerged and rise up again if the pressure and fixed resolution to get rid of them slackens. I do not know to what you refer when you speak of the statement that "Light and Darkness, truth and falsehood cannot dwell together", but certainly it can only mean that in the spiritual endeavour one cannot allow them to dwell together, — the Light, the Truth must be kept, the Darkness, the falsehood or error pushed out altogether. It certainly did not mean that in the human being there can be either only all light or only all darkness and whoever has any weakness in him has no light and no sincere aspiration and no truth in his nature. If that were so, Yoga would be impossible. All the sadhaks in this Asram would be convicted of insincerity and of having no true sadhana — for who is there in whom there is no obscurity and no movement of ignorance?

If you have fallen down from the consciousness you had, it is because instead of dismissing the dispute with X as a moment's movement, you begin to brood on it and prolong the wrong turn it gave. It is no use persisting in the feelings that it created in you. You have only to do what I have been trying to tell you. Draw back from them and, having seen what was lingering in the nature, dismiss them quietly and turn back again to the true consciousness, opening yourself to receive once more the Truth that is creating you anew and let it come down into all your nature.

Wounded Feeling

Your letter of the morning came entirely from the disturbed and wounded vital; that was why I was in no hurry to answer. I do not know why you are so ready to believe that myself or the Mother act from ordinary movements of anger, vexation or displeasure; there was nothing of the kind in what I wrote. You had been repeatedly falling from your attained level of a higher consciousness and, in spite of our suggestions to you to see what was pulling you down, your only reply was that you could see nothing. We knew perfectly well that it was part of the vital which did not want to change and, not wanting to change, was hiding itself from the mind and the mind itself did not seem very willing to see, — so we thought it necessary when you gave us a chance by what you wrote — first about X and secondly about the thoughts of the past — to indicate plainly and strongly the nature of the obstacle — on one side your old sentiment persisting in the *viparīta* form of anger, resentment and wounded feeling, on the other the vital's habit of self-esteem, censorious judgment of others, a sense of superiority in sadhana or in other respects, a wish to appear well before others and before yourself also. This especially has a blinding influence and prevents the clear examination of oneself and the perception of the obstacles that are interfering with the spiritual progress. Even if the mind aspires to know and change, a habit of that kind acting concealed in the vital is quite enough to stand in the way and prevent both the knowledge and the change. I was therefore careful to speak plainly of vanity and self-righteousness — so that this part of the vital might not try not to see. The Mother speaks or writes much more pointedly and sharply to those whom she wishes to push rapidly on the way because they are capable of it and they do not resent or suffer but are glad of the pressure and the plainness because they know by experience that it helps them to see their obstacles and change. If you wish to progress rapidly, you must get rid of this vital reaction of *abhimāna*, suffering, wounded feeling, seeking for arguments of self-justification, outcry against the touch that is intended to liberate, — for so long as you have these, it is difficult for us to deal openly and firmly with the obstacles created by the vital nature.

In regard to the difference between you and X, the Mother's warning to you against the undesirability of too much talk, loose chat and gossip, social self-dispersion was entirely meant and stands; when you indulge in these things, you throw yourself out into a very small and ignorant consciousness in which your vital defects get free play and this is likely to bring you out of what you have developed in your inner consciousness. That was why we said that if you felt a reaction against these things when you went to X's, it was a sign of (psychic) sensitiveness coming into you — into your vital and nervous being — and we meant that it was all for the good. But in dealing with others, in withdrawing from these things you should not allow any sense of superiority to creep in or force on them by your manner or spirit a sense of disapproval or condemnation or pressure on them to change. It is for your personal inward need that you draw back from these things, that is all. As for them what they do in these matters, right or wrong, is their affair — and ours; we will deal with them according to what we see as necessary and possible for them at the moment and for that purpose we can not only deal quite differently with different people, allowing for one what we forbid for another, but we may deal differently with the same person at different times, allowing or even encouraging today what we shall forbid tomorrow. X's case is quite different from yours, for there is no resemblance in your natures. I told you that or something like it long ago and I emphasised in my letter to X that what might be the rule for myself or Y was not to be applied or going to be applied to his case. To deal otherwise would be to create difficulties in his sadhana and not to make it easier for him or swifter. I have also told him quite clearly in my letter that the attempt at meeting and mixing with others — which in the ordinary human life is attempted by sociableness and other contacts — has to be realised in Yoga on another plane of consciousness and without the lower mixture — for a higher unity with all on a spiritual and psychic basis. But the way, the time, the order of movements by which this is done, need not be the same for everybody. If he attempted to force himself it would lead to gloom, despondency and an artificial movement which would not be the true way to success. A human soul and nature cannot be dealt with by a set of mental rules applicable to everybody in the same way; if it were so, there would be no need of a Guru, each could set his chart of Yogic rules before him like the rules of Sandow's exercise and follow them till he became the perfect siddha!

I have said so much in order to let you understand why we do not deal in the same way with X as with you or another. The tendency to take what I lay down for one and apply it without discrimination to another is responsible for much misunderstanding. A general statement too, true in itself, cannot be applied to everyone alike or applied now and immediately without consideration of condition or circumstance or person or time. I may say generally that to bring down the supermind is my aim in the Yoga or that to do that one has first to rise out of mind into overmind, but if on the strength of that, anybody and everybody began trying to pull down the supermind or force his way immediately out of mind into overmind, the result would be disaster.

Therefore concern yourself with your own progress and follow there the lead the Mother gives you. Leave X or others to do the same; the Mother is there to guide and help them according to their need and their nature. It does not in the least matter if the way she follows with him seems different or the opposite of that which she takes with you. That is the right one for him as this is the right one for you.

You have now begun to see the difficulties that are still there in your vital; keep to that clear perception, let it grow clearer and more precise. Concentrate on what you have to do and do not let yourself be distracted this way and that by irrelevant preoccupations or any other influence.

Ingratitude

Your surprise at your cousin X's behaviour shows that you do not yet know what kind of thing is the average human nature. Did you never hear of the answer of Vidyasagar when he was told that a certain man was abusing him: "Why does he abuse me? I never did him a good turn (*upakāra*)." The unregenerate vital is not grateful for a benefit, it resents being under an obligation. So long as the benefit continues, it is effusive and says sweet things, as soon as it expects nothing more it turns round and bites the hand that fed it. Sometimes it does that even before, when it thinks it can do it without the benefactor knowing the origin of the slander, fault-finding or abuse. In all these dealings of your uncles and cousins with you there is nothing unusual, nothing, as you think, peculiar to you. Most have this kind of experience, few escape it altogether. Of course, people with a developed psychic element are by nature grateful and do not behave in this way.

Chapter Two
Desire

The Nature of Desire

Most men are, like animals, driven by the forces of Nature: whatever desires come, they fulfil them, whatever emotions come they allow them to play, whatever physical wants they have, they try to satisfy. We say then that the activities and feelings of men are controlled by their Prakriti, and mostly by the vital and physical nature. The body is the instrument of the Prakriti or Nature — it obeys its own nature or it obeys the vital forces of desire, passion, etc.

But man has also a mind and, as he develops, he learns to control his vital and physical nature by his reason and by his will. This control is very partial: for the reason is often deluded by vital desires and the ignorance of the physical and it puts itself on their side and tries to justify by its ideas, reasonings or arguments their mistakes and wrong movements. Even if the reason keeps free and tells the vital or the body, "Do not do this", yet the vital and the body often follow their own movement in spite of the prohibition — man's mental will is not strong enough to compel them.

When people do sadhana, there is a higher Nature that works within, the psychic and spiritual, and they have to put their nature under the influence of the psychic being and the higher spiritual self or of the Divine. Not only the vital and the body but the mind also has to learn the Divine Truth and obey the divine rule. But because of the lower nature and its continued hold on them, they are unable at first and for a long time to prevent their nature from following the old ways — even when they know or are told from within what to do or what not to do. It is only by persistent sadhana, by getting into the higher spiritual consciousness and spiritual nature that this difficulty can be overcome; but even for the strongest and best sadhaks it takes a long time.

*

All the ordinary vital movements are foreign to the true being and come from outside; they do not belong to the soul nor do they originate in it but are waves from the general Nature, Prakriti.

The desires come from outside, enter the subconscious vital and rise to the surface. It is only when they rise to the surface and the mind becomes aware of them, that we become conscious of the desire. It seems to us to be our own because we feel it thus rising from the vital into the mind and do not know that it came from outside. What belongs to the vital, to the being, what makes it responsible is not the desire itself, but the habit of responding to the waves or the currents of suggestion that come into it from the universal Prakriti.

*

It should be quite clear to you what the two opposite things are, the two things with which every sadhak is faced. One is the vehemence of earthly egoistic desire which brings only confusion and suffering and the other is the peace, force, joy, light of understanding which is the divine in you and which we are striving to establish in you. When you put yourself on the right side, things become easy; when you hesitate and are divided, there is a double state; when something in you receives and clings to the desires, then all goes wrong. You *must* learn to put always the weight of your choice on the right side. Certainly I shall do all to get the wrong will changed and the right one put in its place — whatever is the resistance or difficulty, that I shall do always.

*

It is again the old vain imagination prompted by an uprising of the dissatisfied desires of the vital nature. Evidently the old wrong attitude of desire must have been waiting for its opportunity and it gave the opportunity also for the old vital to rise and indulge in its accustomed movements. It is also evident that it was the pressure of the desire coming up from below that removed the Ananda. The psychic Ananda and the desires of the complaining and clamouring vital cannot go together; if desire comes up, the Ananda is obliged to draw back — unless you reject the desire in time and refuse to make any compromise with it. Especially when the Mother was giving you wideness and peace and intense Ananda, it was irrational in the extreme to give room to an external desire and sacrifice all that for its sake.

*

Saturate your mind and vital with the Truth and remain calm and still. It is from unsatisfied desire that all suffering arises; take your stand on a calm free from desire. When that has come, all else of the Divine Truth, Love and Ananda can come and stand securely upon it.

*

All belongs to the Divine — there must be no ego or desire — only the Divine and its Light, Knowledge, Power, Ananda, action. But all this must come from above — not from the mixed lower cosmic forces.

*

It is the vital which (in everybody and not in you only) is restless, full of desires, always falling into dejection and disappointment and sorrow. The only way to escape from it is to get rid of desires — to have no will or desire other than the will of the Divine.

*

That is the nature of the vital and its desires[1] — vital desire and its enjoyment and dissatisfactions and uneasinesses almost always go together.

*

---

[1] *The correspondent wrote that when he had tried to fulfil a vital desire, it led to a condition of unquietness and misery. — Ed.*

If you are anxious for them [*material possessions*], that means that you have desire and are bound. Ananda is one thing and vital enjoyment is another. One can have the *rasa* of a beautiful thing, for instance a picture, without wanting or needing to possess it or turn it to one's own purpose. Where that want comes in, there is vital desire. The sign of freedom from attachment is that one has no craving and can do without things without feeling anything for that or disappointment at their loss or absence or hankering or wish to have them. If one has, one takes the *rasa* in a free unattached way — if one does not get or loses them, it makes not the slightest difference. The true Ananda is the Ananda of the Divine and when one has the Yogic consciousness, it is the Divine one sees everywhere and has the Ananda of that, but there is no attachment to objects as objects.

It is not necessary to be a Sannyasi to have this inner freedom; it is only necessary to be sincere. There are many who say, "I have no attachment", but it is a self-deception. Therefore one must examine oneself very closely and strictly and see what is left of desire or attachment and reject it. This is difficult for the ordinary consciousness and never wholly achieved by it, even if things are outwardly given up; it is easy if the higher consciousness is there in all the parts of the being, provided one opens all one's movements to its Light.

*

About the attachment to things, the physical rejection of them is not the best way to get rid of it. Accept what is given you, ask for what is needed and think no more of it — attaching no importance, using them when you have, not troubled if you have not. That is the best way of getting rid of the attachment.

*

Kāmanā bāsanā have no part in Yoga, they cannot be its help (*sahāya*), they can only be hindrances. So long as desire and ego remain, there can be no surrender to the Divine, no fulfilment in the Yoga. They are movements of the vital and cannot be anything else.

Egoless strength is strength which does not act for selfish motives or for the desires of the vital or to carry out the ideas of one's own mind, but exists only for the service of the Divine and as an instrument of the Divine.

*

The seat of desire is not so much in the emotional as in the lower vital — but the desires rise up from there into the emotional part and even into the thinking mind.

*

It is always the habit of the vital being to find out things by which it persuades the mind and justifies its desires; and circumstances usually shape themselves to justify it still farther. For what we have within us creates the circumstances outside us. What matters is that you should take inwardly a different position in the future.

*

When you clutch at anything and try to make it your own with an egoistic sense of possession, then however beautiful and wonderful it may be, it loses its value and becomes ordinary.

*

It is often the experience that when one gives up the insistence of desire for a thing, then the thing itself comes. The right attitude is to wait on the Divine Will and seek that only — desire always creates perturbation and even its fulfilment does not satisfy. Aspiration is a different thing. The oscillation between the two conditions you speak of, is the sign of a struggle in the physical consciousness — it must end by the Peace and Power fixing itself there, then the other will disappear.

*

The desire for the Divine or of bhakti for the Divine is the one desire which can free one from all the others — at the core it is not a desire, but an aspiration, a soul need, the breath of existence of the inmost being, and as such it cannot be counted among desires.

The Small Desires of the Vital Physical

It is the vital physical that receives these suggestions and obeys these desires. What you have to do is to get the consciousness down into the whole of the vital proper — so that not only the mind but the vital itself will reject these desires. In that case the vital-physical desires will lose half their force.

*

If the peace and power that were acting on the head and in the chest have come down into the stomach and below, that would indicate that they are no longer acting on the mind and emotional being only, but fully on the vital also — that is a great progress.

The desires you refer to are those of the vital-physical in the subtle physical consciousness — impulse to talk, essential hunger, thirst, etc. Peace and quietude full in the vital-physical and subtle physical and down even in the lowest levels are necessary for the whole change to be made. The heat of which you speak is that of this subtle principle of vital-physical desire which exists for its own sake, not for the real needs of the body — that is why physical satisfaction does not diminish it.

*

These habits of the physical vital are almost automatic in their action and it takes either a very strong will or a persistent effort of self-discipline to get out this automatic, almost reflex action. You should not therefore be discouraged by the difficulty, but go on with the necessary perseverance of the will to press it out of existence.

*

It is the small habits of the lower vital being which gather all their strength to resist eviction and try to occupy the consciousness. When they come you must learn to detach your inner consciousness from them entirely so that even when they strongly come they will not be able to occupy the consciousness or get any assent.

*

The vital in the physical easily slips back to its old small habits if it gets a chance. It is there that they stick. They go entirely only when that part gets equanimity and a simple natural freedom from all desires.

*

You have done rightly about the things. These small desires obstruct greatly the change in the outer consciousness and the being must be free from them if the transformation is not to be hampered there.

Desire and Need

It would certainly be very easy if all that one had to do were to follow one's desires; but to be governed by one's desires is not Yoga.

Need and want are not the same thing. The fact that they [*the sadhaks*] could go on without it [*a lemon each day*] for so long shows that it was not a need.

*

Desire is a psychological movement, and it can attach itself to a "true need" as well as to things that are not true needs. One must approach even true needs without desire. If one does not get them, one must feel nothing.

*

The *necessities* of a sadhak should be as few as possible; for there are only a very few things that are real necessities in life. The rest are either utilities or things decorative to life or luxuries. These a Yogi has a right to possess or enjoy only on one of two conditions —

(1) if he uses them during his sadhana solely to train himself in possessing things without attachment or desire and learn to use them rightly, in harmony with the Divine Will, with a proper handling, a just organisation, arrangement and measure — or,

(2) if he has already attained a true freedom from desire and attachment and is not in the least moved or affected in any way by loss or withholding or deprival. If he has any greed, desire, demand, claim for possession or enjoyment, any anxiety, grief, anger or vexation when denied or deprived, he is not free in spirit and his use of the things he possesses is contrary to the spirit of sadhana. Even if he is free in spirit, he will not be fit for possession if he has not learned to use things not for himself, but for the Divine Will, as an instrument, with the right knowledge and action in the use for the proper equipment of a life lived not for oneself but for and in the Divine.

*

It should not be difficult for the man devoted to the spiritual aim [*to depend on the Divine for material things*] — for he is always expected to rely on the Divine even in his ordinary life in the world — such dependence being part of his mental atmosphere and the constitution of his vital nature.

Demand and Desire

If to you X says that her suffering and ill-health are due to your behaviour, to Y she has said it is all due to the bad room she has got! In fact it is due to her vital cherishing desires and getting disappointed because they are not fulfilled. If one cherishes desires, there is bound to be disappointment and suffering, especially if at the same time one does Yoga and takes up the spiritual life. For such desires, demand for vital affection and love from men and demand for physical comforts are not consistent with the spirit of Yoga in which one must turn one's heart to the Divine and be vitally pure and in physical things must be content with what one gets and equal-minded in all conditions. You were quite right in telling her that these outer demands should be given up altogether.

*

To yield to depression when things go wrong is the worst way of meeting the difficulty. There must be some desire or demand within you, conscious or subconscious, that gets excited and revolts against its not being satisfied. The best way is to be conscious of it, face it calmly and steadily throw it out.

If the lower vital (not the mind only) could permanently make up its mind that all desire and demand are contrary to the Truth and no longer call for them, these things would lose very soon their force of return.

*

It is not a demand to ask for things that one finds helpful, but it becomes a demand if there enters into it a feeling of claim, resentment when it is not conceded or other vital reactions. Be on your guard against any invasion by these reactions; the vital can only be conquered and changed and the physical opened up on a basis of faith and surrender and the psychic response overpowering all others.

*

Demand and desire are only two different aspects of the same thing — nor is it necessary that a feeling should be agitated or restless to be a desire; it can be, on the contrary, quietly fixed and persistent or persistently recurrent. Demand or desire comes from the mental or the vital and a psychic or spiritual need is a different thing. The psychic does not demand or desire; it aspires; it does not make conditions for its surrender or withdraw if its aspiration is not immediately satisfied — for the psychic has complete trust in the Divine or in the guru and can wait for the right time or the hour of the divine grace. The psychic has an insistence of its own, but it puts its pressure not on the Divine, but on the nature, placing a finger of light on all the defects there that stand in the way of the realisation, sifting out all that is mixed, ignorant or imperfect in the experience or in the movements of the Yoga and never satisfied with itself or with the nature till it has got it perfectly open to the Divine, free from all forms of ego, surrendered, simple and right in the attitude and all the movements. This is what has to be established entirely in the mind and vital and in the physical consciousness before supramentalisation of the whole nature is possible. Otherwise what one gets is more or less brilliant, half luminous, half cloudy illuminations and experiences on the mental and vital and physical planes, half truth, half error or at the best true only for those planes and inspired either from some larger mind or larger vital or at the best from the mental reaches above the human that intervene between the intellect and the Overmind. These can be very stimulating and satisfying up to a certain point and are good for those who want some spiritual realisation on these planes; but the supramental realisation is something much more difficult and exacting in its conditions and the most difficult of all is to bring it down on to the physical level.

Getting Rid of Desire

The satisfaction of the vital desires is a normal feature of the ordinary life, only it must be controlled and regulated by the mental will, so that one may not be enslaved to the desires. It is only if one turns to the spiritual life that one has to get rid of vital desires.

*

It is not Yoga to give free play to the natural instincts and desires. Yoga demands mastery over the nature, not subjection to the nature.

*

Is there any time in the "straight path" for satisfying desires? If desire is not mastered, how can there be any straight walking on the straight path?

*

You do not seem to have a correct idea of the nature of vital desire. Vital desire grows by being indulged, it does not become satisfied. If your desire were indulged, it would begin to grow more and more and ask for more and more. That has been our constant experience with the sadhaks and it confirms what has always been known about desire. Desire and envy have to be thrown out of the consciousness — there is no other way to deal with them.

*

That [indulging desire] is a mistake many have made because the vital wanted to make it.[2] Whether ascetic or non-ascetic, the Yogi, the sadhak must become free from vital desire and spiritually master of the movements of his nature — and for that he must be free from ego and desire and duality. I have always made that quite clear — that indulgence of desire is no more part of this Yoga than it is of Sannyasa. One must be able to use and handle physical things and physical life, but from the spiritual consciousness, not from the level of the vital ego.

*

It is the old vital nature that feels its human worldly desires will not be satisfied and feels like this. All that has not to be indulged but rejected and swept aside. In its place must come the wideness in which there is a self-existent peace and satisfaction and into that peace and wideness must come the Mother's greater peace, force, light, knowledge, Ananda.

*

The vital always wants the things of ordinary life, sex, rich food, enjoyments of all kinds; it does not get full satisfaction out of them, but it feels dissatisfied without them. The only way to get rid of it is to reject desire of these things from the vital itself and to have only the aspiration for the Divine in all parts of the being.

*

---

[2] *The correspondent observed that because Sri Aurobindo had condemned asceticism, many took it as a sanction to continue fulfilling their desires. — Ed.*

Everything which it hankers after is desirable to the vital — but the desire has to be rejected. "I won't desire" is quite the right thing to say, even if "I don't desire" cannot yet be said by the vital. Still there is something in the being that can even say "I don't desire" and refuse to recognise the vital desire as part of the true being. It is that consciousness which the peace and power bring that has to be recognised as the true "I" and made permanent in front.

*

It is difficult to get rid of desires *altogether* all at once — if the right ones have the upper hand, that already makes the ultimate victory sure. Therefore don't allow that to trouble you. A progressive change is the way these things work out — and if the progress has begun, then there can be a fundamental sense of certitude about the outcome of the sadhana and a quiet view upon what has to be done because it is sure to be done.

*

Desire always takes a long time to get rid of entirely. But, if you can once get it out of the nature and realise it as a force coming from outside and putting its claws into the vital and physical, it will be easier to get rid of the invader. You are too accustomed to feel it as part of yourself or planted in you — that makes it more difficult for you to deal with its movements and dismiss its ancient control over you.

You should not rely on anything else alone, however helpful it may seem, but chiefly, primarily, fundamentally on the Mother's Force. The Sun and the Light may be a help, and will be if it is the true Light and the true Sun, but cannot take the place of the Mother's Force.

*

It is good. No one can easily get rid of desires. What has first to be done is to exteriorise them, to push them out on the surface and get the inner parts quiet and clear. Afterwards they can be thrown out and replaced by the true thing, a happy and luminous will one with the Divine's.

*

It is because both your mind and vital have become sincere that the attack is strong and seems to you abnormal. Before as you were yielding from time to time, the part that wants was not acutely insistent and, when it pressed, it was not so acutely felt by the rest of the vital nature. It is your mental, psychic and higher vital beings that now stand completely apart from it. It is your physical vital that still keeps the desire and is pushed from time to time by opposite forces to make the desire active. It was also this desire that created the physical disturbance from which you suffered a few days ago. You must get rid of this desire of the lower vital altogether.

*

The fear is again that of the physical consciousness or of the vital element in it — it is afraid if it gives up desire that it will lose everything — or everything *it* wants — and gain nothing in exchange or at least nothing *it* wants. It does not realise that it will get something far greater and more powerful and happy in place of this troubled desire and its doubtful and precarious fruits — for it has been accustomed to think of desire as the only possible motive of life. It does not know that the divine Force is there waiting to descend with its light and peace and joy bringing much greater things and a happier life. When this part can be enlightened and persuaded to want wholeheartedly the change, then a great difficulty, indeed the central difficulty will have gone.

*

There was and is the opening before you of a new stage in your spiritual development. For it to realise itself you must progress first in two directions. The first we have already pressed on you — the surmounting of these vital temptations and desires which linked you to the lower movements and invited the pressure of a hostile Force on your lower vital and your body and the complete surrender of life and body to the One alone. The other is the descent of a full calm and strength and equanimity into these parts so that you may conquer life and its difficulties and do your work for the Divine. This calm and strength had often descended into your mind and higher vital, but these other parts were still open to much weakness and attachment and a self-indulgent movement. That must go if one wants to become a hero and master of spiritual action. In your life at Bogra these things were too much sheltered and allowed to remain; at Shillong you have a chance to be by yourself with the Divine Force and look life in the face from the soul's inner strength and become master of circumstances. Outer difficulties or inconveniences you should not allow to alarm or depress you. Inner difficulties should also be met with detachment, calm equality, the unshakable will to conquer.

For the rest, you have rightly said, "I must preserve my equanimity and have faith in Divine Guidance when falsehood" — or any trouble or difficulty — "confronts me." The defect that opened the way to the bodily and other troubles was the faltering in your resolution to conquer the vital and follow the straight and high path and the consequent violent despair and depression it brought in its wake. Let those disappear altogether and do not allow them to rise in that way again. The path of spiritual calm and strength and the consecration of all your forces to the Divine is the one safe way for you and that you must now consistently follow.

Desire and Suppression (Nigraha)

The rejection of desire is essentially the rejection of the element of craving, putting that out from the consciousness itself as a foreign element not belonging to the true self and the inner nature. But refusal to indulge the suggestions of desire is also a part of the rejection; to abstain from the action suggested, if it is not the right action, must be included in the Yogic discipline. It is only when this is done in the wrong way, by a mental ascetic principle or a hard moral rule, that it can be called suppression.

The difference between suppression and an inward essential rejection is the difference between mental or moral control and a spiritual purification.

When one lives in the true consciousness one feels the desires outside oneself, entering from outside, from the universal lower Prakriti, into the mind and the vital parts. In the ordinary human condition this is not felt; men become aware of the desire only when it is there, when it has come inside and found a lodging or a habitual harbourage and so they think it is their own and a part of themselves. The first condition for getting rid of desire is, therefore, to become conscious with the true consciousness; for then it becomes much easier to dismiss it than when one has to struggle with it as if it were a constituent part of oneself to be thrown out from the being. It is easier to cast off an accretion than to excise what is felt as a parcel of our substance.

When the psychic being is in front, then also to get rid of desire becomes easy; for the psychic being has in itself no desires, it has only aspirations and a seeking and love for the Divine and all things that are or tend towards the Divine. The constant prominence of the psychic being tends of itself to bring out the true consciousness and set right almost automatically the movements of the nature.

*

It is true that the mere suppression or holding down of desire is not enough, not by itself truly effective, but that does not mean that desires are to be indulged; it means that desires have not merely to be suppressed, but to be rejected from the nature. In place of desire there must be a single-minded aspiration towards the Divine.

As for love, the love must be turned singly towards the Divine. What men call by that name is a vital interchange for mutual satisfaction of desire, vital impulse or physical pleasure. There must be nothing of this interchange between sadhaks; for to seek for it or indulge this kind of impulse only leads away from the sadhana.

*

Your theory is a mistaken one. The free expression of a passion may relieve the vital for a time, but at the same time it gives it a right to return always. It is not reduced at all. Suppression with inner indulgence in subtle forms is not a cure, but expression in outer indulgence is still less a cure. It is perfectly possible to go on without manifestation if one is resolute to arrive at a complete control, the control being not a mere suppression but an inner and outer rejection.

*

Not necessarily suppression [*is indicated by the refusal to feed a desire*], if the refusal of food is accompanied by detachment in the major part of the being. The difference between suppression (*nigraha*) and self-control (*saṁyama*) is that one says, "I cannot help desiring but I will not satisfy my desire", while the other says, "I refuse the desire as well as the satisfaction of the desire".

*

Nigraha means holding down the movement, but a movement merely held down is only suspended — it is better to reject and dismiss, detaching yourself from it.

Chapter Three

Anger and Violence

The Nature of Anger

Yes, anger is a harmful and wasteful force, harmful both to the person himself and to the one on whom it is thrown. You are right in saying that it must be got rid of. Anger immediately opens the door to hostile forces; it is as if you were calling them.

*

It [*a violent outburst of anger*] is obviously a surprise attack that took you off your guard. But you must throw off the tendency to anger with yourself also as well as the other tendency to sudden anger with others — for all anger only disturbs the consciousness and makes it difficult to keep the quiet poise. The whole thing has to be thrown out and the consciousness has to recover and be as if it had not happened.

*

These things, hard forms of speech, anger etc., are habits formed by the vital-physical consciousness and, as they are supported by the subconscient, very difficult to change. If one can conquer or change them by force of will or mental or spiritual control, so much the better. But if one cannot do this at once, one must not be upset or think oneself unfit. It is easier for most to realise the Divine or enter into the psychic consciousness than to change this part of the nature; but once the psychic consciousness governs or the higher consciousness descends then it is much easier for these to go. You must not therefore be discouraged by these recurrences or persistences, but try always to stand back in an inner quietude and if they come let them pass away like a cloud across the light. In time these things will be finally dealt with by the Force.

*

It [*an outburst of anger*] is really simply the recurrence of an old habit of the nature. Look at it and see how trifling is the occasion of the rising of this anger and its outburst — it becomes more and more causeless and the absurdity of such movements reveals itself. It would not really be difficult to get rid of it if when it comes you looked at it calmly — for it is perfectly possible to stand back in one part of the being observing in a detached equanimity even while the anger rises on the surface, as if it were someone else in your being who had the anger. The difficulty is that you get alarmed, grieved and upset and that makes it easier for the thing to get hold of your mind which it should not do.

Help we are giving you — stand back so as to be able to feel it and not the obsession of these surface movements.

*

When you have such thoughts, it makes a formation of force which falls on the man against whom you are angry. If he is not on his guard or if he is sensitive in any way, it may become effective upon him. That is why such thoughts should be avoided altogether.

*

The reason why quietness is not yet fixed and anger returns is that you allow your physical mind to become active. In regard to the sadhana it begins to think there is this defect in you and that defect and therefore the sadhana does not become immediately effective and perfect. This makes the vital nervous or despondent and in the despondency a state of irritation arises. At the same time this mind becomes active as it has now with regard to X or begins to judge and criticise and this too leads to nervousness and irritation. These things belong to the old mind you are trying to leave and therefore stand in the way of concentration and quietude. They should be stopped at their root by rejecting the suggestions of the physical mind as soon as they begin. A new consciousness is coming based upon inner silence and quietude. You must wait quietly for that to develop. True knowledge, true perceptions of people and things will come in that new silent consciousness. The mind's view of people and things must necessarily be either limited and defective or erroneous — to go on judging by it is now a waste of time. Wait for the new consciousness to develop and show you all in a new and true light. Then the tendency to anger which arises from this mind and is a violent impatience directed against things the mind and vital do not like, would have no ground to rise at all — or if it rose without cause could be more easily rejected. Rely for the sadhana on the Mother's grace and her Force, yourself remembering always to keep only two things, quietude and confidence. For things and people, leave them to the Mother also; as you have difficulties in your nature, so they have too; but to deal with them needs insight, sympathy, patience.

*

It is indeed a very good sign that the anger when it comes is brief and subdued and no longer expressed in the outward — for that is one very marked stage always of the rejection of something not wanted by the nature. It comes still but it has no longer the old force, duration, intensity, completeness. The externalised condition is often used to show or test the progress made in the outer nature itself, for when one is entirely within these outward movements remain quiescent, so the extent to which they are changed cannot be so easily measured. But of course it is the going inward that most helps to deliver the nature.

*

If the anger did not come, it must be because the vital force of the attack is diminishing and it must be more in the physical mind and the external (physical) vital that it acts. You have a great strength for action; as for the inner growth and action of the sadhana you have a strength there too of the psychic and the vital, — it is only the external being that finds these difficulties in its way and is momentarily overcome or affected by them. Things always come in the way when one wants to progress in the sadhana, but in the end if one is sincere in one's aspiration these troubles help to prepare the victory of the soul over all that opposes.

The inner will prevails sometimes, sometimes it does not prevail for the time being. That is quite normal. It depends on certain conditions which the physical mind does not see. As one grows in knowledge, one becomes aware of these unseen conditions and understands better what happens.

The fire is always the fire of purification — it is very red when it is acting on the vital; when the vital no longer covers the psychic, then the rose colour of the psychic comes out more and more.

The house you saw is the new building of the nature, especially in the vital, which is being prepared by the sadhana.

*

Because anger etc. once used to come, it does not follow that they cannot die down in a short time, so his incredulity is not justifiable. This is just the way that these things do go. They come vehemently and resist the force used to eject them, but if they are still rejected or if there is a change in the consciousness, they lose their force and the consciousness quietly rejects them when they come.

*

It is rather perilous to think of anything like that — "Now it [anger] is finished" — it is better to wait some time and see. The hostiles have a habit of trying their strength when they hear anything like that; they want to show you that it is not so.

*

But is it true that even anger which is of the lower vital and therefore close to the body, invariably produces these effects?[1] Of course the psychologist can't know that another man is angry

---

[1] *Physical effects such as flushing of the face, flaring of the nostrils, clenched teeth and "ebullition" in the chest. The correspondent had read a book on psychology in which the author suggested that one cannot "fancy" the state of rage without such visible signs of anger. — Ed.*

unless he shows physical signs of it, but also he can't know what a man is thinking unless the man speaks or writes — does it follow that the state of thought cannot be "fancied" without its sign in speaking or writing? A Japanese who is accustomed to control all his "emotions" and give no sign (if he is angry the first sign you will have of it is a knife in your stomach from a calm or smiling assailant) will have none of these things when he is angry — not even the "ebullition" in the chest, — in its place there will be a settled fire that will burn till his anger achieves itself in action.

*

It is your angers that have resulted in these pains. Get rid of the bad temper and the stomach will be more at ease.

*

For some sex is more difficult [*to conquer than anger*], for some greed.

*

It [*the equivalent of anger in the higher nature*] is a *rudra* power of severity and indignation (in the deepest sense of the word) against what should not be — the warrior force of Mahakali in combating the Asura.

*

Yes, certainly. Infinite peace, universal love can remove anger — if they are complete and stable.

Anger Comes from Outside

The fact that the anger comes with such force is itself enough to show that it is not in you that it is, but that it comes from outside. It is a rush of force from the universal Nature that tries to take possession of the individual being and make that being act according to the will of this outside force and not according to the will of the soul within. These things come in the course of the sadhana because the sadhak is liberating himself from the lower nature and trying to turn towards the Mother and live in her divine consciousness and the higher nature. The forces of the lower nature do not want that and so they make these rushes in order to recover their rule. It is necessary when that comes to remain quiet within remembering the Mother or calling her and reject the anger or whatever else comes, whenever it comes or however often it comes. If that is done, then these forces begin to lose their power to invade. It is easier if one clearly feels them to be outside forces and foreign to oneself; but even if you cannot feel that yet when they enter, still the mind must keep that idea and refuse to accept them as any longer a part of the nature. The idea of the Mother being severe was of course a suggestion that came with the invading force so as to help it to enter. Such suggestions come to many sadhaks (though not so many as before) at Pranam and is the cause to them of much disturbance. Such suggestions must be firmly rejected at once.

*

I think you have always had an idea that to give expression to an impulse or a movement is the best way or even the only way to get rid of it. But that is a mistaken idea. If you give expression to anger, you prolong or confirm the habit of the recurrence of anger; you do not diminish or get rid of the habit. The very first step towards weakening the power of anger in the nature and afterwards getting rid of it altogether, is to refuse all expression to it in act or speech. Afterwards one can go on with more likelihood of success to throw it out from the thought and feeling also. And so with all other wrong movements.

All these movements come from outside, from the universal lower nature, or are suggested or thrown upon you by adverse forces — adverse to your spiritual progress. Your method of taking them as your own is again a wrong method; for by doing that you increase their power to recur and take hold of you. If you take them as your own, that gives them a kind of right to be there. If you feel them as *not* your own, then they have no right, and the will can develop more power to send them away. What you must always have and feel as yours, is this will, the power to refuse assent, to refuse admission to a wrong movement. Or if it comes in, the power to send it away, without expressing it.

If you find it difficult to reject in the sense of throwing away, what you have to do is to refuse assent. As for instance, as regards voices or suggestions, not to listen to them, not to believe what they want you to believe, not to do what they want or push you to do.

Of course the best way will be if you can keep the contact more with the Mother and her Light and Force and receive and accept and follow only what comes from that higher force. Secondly, to keep the mind quiet, not to allow it to be too active, going from one thing to another. That brings the confusion.

*

Anger comes from the vital nature or if it has been driven out from there rises back into it from the subconscient or from the environmental Nature.

*

It [*rejection*] is the way to get rid of these things [*anger and sex desire*] — when rejected they either sink into the subconscient or pass out into the surrounding (environmental) consciousness through which one is connected with the universal forces. They may try to rise up from the subconscient or come in again from outside; but if one always rejects them, calling in the aid of the Mother and does not allow them to take hold, their force of recurrence dies away and finally they come no more. Sometimes a very decisive rejection gets rid of them at a stroke once for all.

*

These things [*anger, desire etc.*] can only be got rid of if you do not accept them. When they come, you must stand back from them in your mind, look at them and say, "I don't want this." If it comes in spite of your not wanting and refusing them, then it shows it is not your own movement, but something thrown upon you by the outside Nature. If you can once see that and feel them as not yours, then by degrees you can get free of anger, desire and other things that trouble you.

*

In fact all these ignorant vital movements originate from outside in the ignorant universal Nature; the human being forms in his superficial parts of being, mental, vital, physical, a habit of certain responses to these waves from outside. It is these responses that he takes as his own character (anger, desire, sex etc.) and thinks he cannot be otherwise. But that is not so; he can change. There is another consciousness deeper within him, his true inner being, which is his real self, but is covered over by the superficial nature. This the ordinary man does not know, but the Yogi becomes aware of it as he progresses in his sadhana. As the consciousness of this inner being increases by sadhana, the surface nature and its responses are pushed out and can be got rid of altogether. But the ignorant universal Nature does not want to let go and throws the old movements on the sadhak and tries to get them inside him again; owing to a habit the superficial nature gives the old responses. If one can get the firm knowledge that these things are from outside and not a real part of oneself, then it is easier for the sadhak to repel such returns, or if they lay hold, he can get rid of them sooner. That is why I say repeatedly that these things rise not in yourself, but from outside.

Anger and the Psychic

If the will is strong enough, it [*anger*] can be held in check — but usually it is only if the psychic being becomes entirely awake and governs the vital that the tendency to anger can entirely disappear.

*

When it is the psychic that rules all the movements of the being, then it [*anger*] completely disappears and when the equanimity of the higher consciousness takes complete possession of the lower vital. Till then one can establish a control, diminish and reduce it to a touch that has no outward effect or a wave that passes without self-expression.

*

That [*inner detachment*] is the right thing that must happen always when anger or anything else rises. The psychic reply must become habitual pointing out that anger is neither right nor helpful and then the being must draw back from these outward things and take its stand in its inner self, detach from all these things and people. It is this detachment that is the first thing that must be gained by the sadhak — he must cease to live in these outward things and live in his inner being. The more that is done the more there is a release and peacefulness. Afterwards when one is secure in this inner being, the right thing to do, the right way to deal with men and things will begin to come.

*

It is true that anger and strife are in the nature of the human vital and do not go easily; but what is important is to have the will to change and the clear perception that these things must go. If that will and perception are there, then in the end they will go. The most important help to it is, here also, for the psychic being to grow within — for that brings a certain kindliness, patience, charity towards all and one no longer regards everything from the point of view of one's own ego and its pain or pleasure, likings and dislikings. The second help is the growth of the inner peace which outward things cannot trouble. With the peace comes a calm wideness in which one perceives all as one self, all beings as the children of the Mother and the Mother dwelling in oneself and in all. It is that towards which your sadhana will move, for these are the things which come with the growth of the psychic and spiritual consciousness. Then these troubled reactions to outward things will no longer come.

*

It is indeed when the quietude comes down from above or comes out from the psychic that the vital becomes full of peace or of kindliness and goodwill. It is therefore that the inner psychic quietude first and afterwards the peace from above must occupy the whole being. Otherwise such things as anger in the vital can be controlled but it is difficult to get rid of them altogether without this occupation by the inner quietude and higher peace. That you should depend on the Mother for the sadhana is the best attitude, for it is indeed her Force that does the sadhana in you.

*

It is not at all unnatural that the anger brought back peace and harmony:[2] for this anger was a form of loyalty to the Divine and that put you into touch with your psychic consciousness again. Sri Ramakrishna was quite right about anger. The hostile powers are proof against gentleness and sweetness and non-resistance and soul-force, but a current of righteous anger often sends them flying.

Vindictiveness and Cruelty

Vindictiveness, with or without a real cause for it, is even worse than anger because it is more cold and deliberate in its action and less of an impulse. One should be generous in nature and free from all rancour.

*

You must get rid of it [*cruelty*]. Cruelty and falsehood are the two things that separate most from the Divine.

Violence

An inner psychic or spiritual change is not brought about by violence. It is not a change of conduct that has to be done in the

---

[2] *The correspondent wrote that he grew angry when he read some false statements about Sri Aurobindo made by a journalist and that his anger relieved him of a slight depression. He was reminded of a remark made by Sri Ramakrishna: "The ripus (passions) too can help in the spiritual life provided you know the secret of the game: for instance, anger may help you if you turn it against all who are hostile to the Divine." — Ed.*

sadhak, but a change of soul and spirit governing the mind and vital and body instead of the mind and vital governing. Violence is the drastic contradiction of that; it makes mental egoism and vital passion and fury or else cruelty the rulers. Violence in ordinary Nature does not justify violence in a spiritual work.

*

The *Essays on the Gita* explain the ordinary karmayoga as developed in the Gita, in which the work done is the ordinary work of human life with only an inward change. There too the violence to be used is not a personal violence done from egoistic motives, but part of the ordered system of social life. Nothing can spiritually justify individual violence done in anger or passion or from any vital motive. In our Yoga our object is to rise higher than the ordinary life of man and in it violence has to be left aside altogether.

*

All vital violence in speech or action is rajasic and unyogic. One must be master of oneself and controlled in speech and act.

*

You must not accept everything; you should reject all suggestions of uncontrolled desire or anger. *You must not allow any wrong force to get hold of your body and use it.* It is not safe to accept these things and you should be very careful to reject them always.

It is necessary that there should be control and organisation, and these cannot come and get fixed if you accept *uncontrolled desires, violent anger, confusion* or *extreme restlessness of mind*, for all these are things that disorganise and destroy control.

Chapter Four

Fear

Fear and Yoga

If you want to do Yoga, you must get rid of fear. Yoga and fear do not go together.

*

There is no fear in the higher Nature. Fear is a creation of the vital plane, an instinct of the ignorance, a sense of danger with a violent vital reaction that replaces and usually prevents or distorts the intelligence of things. It might almost be considered as an invention of the hostile forces.

*

Yes, fear creates imaginary terrors — even if there is real danger, fear does not help; it clouds the intelligence, takes away presence of mind and prevents one seeing the right thing to do.

Let the Force at work increase, till it clears out the mixed consciousness altogether.

*

It is true that what one fears has the tendency to come until one is able to look it in the face and overcome one's shrinking. One must learn to take one's foundation on the Divine and overcome the fear, relying on the help to carry one through all things even unpleasant and adverse. There is a Force that works even through them for the seeker and carries him towards his goal.

*

You can write to her that to get rid of fear is the first necessity. Yoga can only be done on a basis of faith and confidence in the Divine.

At the same time one must be on guard against undesirable

movements or phenomena in the sadhana. The motion of her head is not a result of the descent of Force, or a sign that it is too much for her, but a wrong movement of the body which she must check and get rid of altogether.

The colours are only a sign that the inner vision is open; if it develops things of a more definite kind will appear.

*

Write to her again that if she wants to do sadhana, she must get rid of fear altogether; fear opens the door to the adverse forces. She should not listen to people who try to put fear in her. If ugly forms or sounds are seen and heard, one has not to fear but reject them and call in the Mother's protection. If she feels calmness in the meditation, that is the necessary basis — with that basis one can safely practise the Yoga. It is not indispensable that the mind should be entirely *blank* — it is sufficient that it is quiet with a fundamental silence which is not disturbed even if thoughts pass across it.

*

You should throw away fear as well as anger and go quietly on your way putting your confidence in the Mother.

*

It is a mistake to think that by fearing or being unhappy you can progress. Fear is always a feeling to be rejected, because what you fear is just the thing that is likely to come to you: fear attracts the object of fear. Unhappiness weakens the strength and lays one more open to the causes of unhappiness.

One can be quiet, happy, cheerful without being all that in a light or shallow way — and the happiness need not bring any vital reaction. All that you need to do is to be observant and vigilant, — watchful so that you may not give assent to wrong movements or the return of the old feelings, darkness, confusion etc. Not fear, but vigilance. If you remain vigilant, then with the increase of the Force upholding you, a power of self-control will come, a power to see and reject the wrong turn or the wrong reaction when it comes. Fear and unhappiness will not give you that. It is only by this vigilance accompanied by an opening to the supporting and guiding Force that it will come. What you describe as a capacity to choose the right and the feeling of strength or power that can stop the wrong movement and take the right one as soon as it recognises them, is just this control and vigilance. It is by this control and vigilance supported by the Force that you can prevent the love and devotion too from being mixed with or replaced by selfish desires and impurities. The more you open, the more this power will increase in you.

Certainly, if talking about old things or excessive speaking brings the wrong reactions at night, it is better to abstain from such talk or speech. Here also control is the thing you have to develop.

*

By bringing down strength and calm into the lower vital (region below the navel) [*fear can be eliminated*]. Also by will and imposing calm on the system when the fear arises. It can be done in either way or both together.

*

Fear is of course a vital and physical thing. Many people who have shown great courage, were not physically or even vitally brave; yet by force of mind they pushed themselves into all sorts of battle and danger. Henry IV of France, a great fighter and victor, was an example. Just because his body consciousness was in a panic, he forced it to go where the danger was thickest.

Section Four

Human Relations in Yoga

Chapter One

Human Relations and the Spiritual Life

Relations with Others in Yoga

The true unity with others, in the sadhana, is founded in the unity in the Divine Consciousness, not in the vital movement.

*

It is not because of your nature or evil destiny that the vital cannot find the satisfaction it expected from relations with others. These relations can never give a full or permanent satisfaction; if they did, there would be no reason why the human being would ever seek the Divine. He would remain satisfied in the ordinary earth life. It is only when the Divine is found and the consciousness lifted up into the true consciousness that the true relations with others can come.

*

Relations which are part of the ordinary vital nature in human life are of no value in the spiritual life — they rather interfere with the progress; for the mind and vital also should be wholly turned towards the Divine. Moreover, the purpose of sadhana is to enter into a spiritual consciousness and base everything on a new spiritual basis which can only be done when one has entered into complete unity with the Divine. Meanwhile one has to have a calm goodwill for all, but relations of a vital kind do not help — for they keep the consciousness down on a vital basis and prevent its rising to a higher level.

*

Until the vital has been purified, illumined and wholly offered to the Divine, there is always a vital mixture in these relations

— a mixture of the movements of the lower nature.

*

These movements [*of egoism*] are part of man's ignorant vital nature. The love which human beings feel for one another is also usually an egoistic vital love and these other movements, claim, demand, jealousy, abhiman, anger etc., are its common accompaniments. There is no place for them in Yoga — nor in true love, psychic or divine. In Yoga all love should be turned towards the Divine and to human or other beings only as vessels of the Divine — abhiman and the rest should have no place in it.

*

I have always said that the vital is indispensable for the divine or spiritual action — without it there can be no complete expression, no realisation in life — hardly even any realisation in sadhana. When I speak of the vital mixture or of the obstructions, revolts etc. of the vital, it is the unregenerated outer vital full of desire and ego and the lower passions of which I speak. I could say the same against the mind and the physical when they obstruct or oppose, but precisely because the vital is so powerful and indispensable, its obstruction, opposition or refusal of cooperation is more strikingly effective and its wrong mixtures are more dangerous to the sadhana. That is why I have always insisted on the dangers of the unregenerated vital and the necessity of mastery and purification there. It is not because I hold, like the Sannyasis, the vital and its life power to be a thing to be condemned and rejected in its very nature.

Affection, love, tenderness are in their nature psychic, — the vital has them because the psychic is trying to express itself through the vital. It is through the emotional being that the psychic most easily expresses, for it stands just behind it in the heart centre. But it wants these things to be pure. Not that it rejects the outward expression through the vital and the physical, but as the psychic being is the form of the soul, it naturally feels the attraction of soul to soul, the nearness of soul to soul, the union of soul with soul are the things that are to it most abiding and concrete. Mind, vital, body are means of expression and very precious means of expression, but the inner life is for the soul the first thing, the deepest reality, and these have to be subordinated to it and conditioned by it, its expression, its instruments and channel. I do not think that in my emphasis on the inner things, on the psychic and spiritual, I am saying anything new, strange or unintelligible. These things have always been stressed from the beginning and the more the human being is evolved, the more they take on importance. I do not see how Yoga can be possible without this premier stress on the inner life, on the soul and the spirit. The emphasis on the mastery of the vital, its subordination and subjection to the spiritual and the psychic is also nothing new, strange or exorbitant. It has been insisted on always for any kind of spiritual life; even the Yogas which seek most to use the vital, like certain forms of Vaishnavism, yet insist on the purification and the total offering of it to the Divine — and the relations with the Divine are an inner realisation, the soul offering itself through the emotional being. The soul or psychic being is not something unheard of or incomprehensible.

*

Absence of love and fellow-feeling is not necessary for nearness to the Divine; on the contrary, a sense of closeness and oneness with others is a part of the divine consciousness into which the sadhak enters by nearness to the Divine and the feeling of oneness with the Divine. An entire rejection of all relations is indeed the final aim of the Mayavadin, and in the ascetic Yoga an entire loss of all relations of friendship and affection and attachment to the world and its living beings would be regarded as a promising sign of advance towards liberation, Moksha; but even there, I think, a feeling of oneness and unattached spiritual sympathy for all is at least a penultimate stage, like the compassion of the Buddhist, before the turning to Moksha or Nirvana. In this Yoga the feeling of unity with others, love, universal joy and Ananda are an essential part of the liberation and perfection which are the aim of the sadhana.

On the other hand, human society, human friendship, love, affection, fellow-feeling are mostly and usually — not entirely or in all cases — founded on a vital basis and are ego-held at their centre. It is because of the pleasure of being loved, the pleasure of enlarging the ego by contact, mutual penetration of spirit, with another, the exhilaration of the vital interchange which feeds their personality that men usually love — and there are also other and still more selfish motives that mix with this essential movement. There are of course higher spiritual, psychic, mental, vital elements that come in or can come in; but the whole thing is very mixed, even at its best. This is the reason why at a certain stage with or without apparent reason the world and life and human society and relations and philanthropy (which is as ego-ridden as the rest) begin to pall. There is sometimes an ostensible reason — a disappointment of the surface vital, the withdrawal of affection by others, the perception that those loved or men generally are not what one thought them to be and a host of other causes; but often the cause is a secret disappointment of some part of the inner being, not translated or not well translated into the mind, because it expected from these things something which they cannot give. It is the case with many who turn or are pushed to the spiritual life. For some it takes the form of a *vairāgya* which drives them towards ascetic indifference and gives the urge towards Moksha. For us, what we hold to be necessary is that the mixture should disappear and that the consciousness should be established on a purer level (not only spiritual and psychic but a purer and higher mental, vital, physical consciousness) in which there is not this mixture. There one would feel the true Ananda of oneness and love and sympathy and fellowship, spiritual and self-existent in its basis but expressing itself through the other parts of the nature. If that is to happen, there must obviously be a change; the old form of these movements must drop off and leave room for a new and higher self to disclose its own way of expression and realisation of itself and of the Divine through these things — that is the inner truth of the matter.

I take it therefore that the condition you describe is a period of transition and change, negative in its beginning, as these movements often are at first, so as to create a vacant space for the new positive to appear and live in it and fill it. But the vital, not having a long continued or at all sufficient or complete experience of what is to fill the vacancy, feels only the loss and regrets it even while another part of the being, another part even of the vital, is ready to let go what is disappearing and does not yearn to keep it. If it were not for this movement of the vital (which in your case has been very strong and large and avid of life), the disappearance of these things would, at least after the first sense of void, bring only a feeling of peace, relief and a still expectation of greater things. What is intended in the first place to fill the void was indicated in the peace and joy which came to you as the touch of Shiva — naturally, this would not be all but a beginning, a basis for a new self, a new consciousness, an activity of a greater nature; as I told you, it is a deep spiritual calm and peace that is the only stable foundation for a lasting Bhakti and Ananda. In that new consciousness there would be a new basis for relations with others; for an ascetic dryness or isolated loneliness cannot be your spiritual destiny since it is not consonant with your Swabhava which is made for joy, largeness, expansion, a comprehensive movement of the life-force. Therefore do not be discouraged; wait upon the purifying movement of Shiva.

*

There is no taboo in the Yoga on any feeling that is true and pure, but all the feelings undergo the stress of a pressure from the spiritual consciousness and whatever there is that is mixed, impure, egoistic or the feeling itself if it is fundamentally self-regarding, either disappears or, if it remains, becomes an obstacle to the progress. In the ascetic Yoga all human feelings are regarded as illusory and have to disappear — "the knots of the heart are cut" — so as to leave only the one supreme aspiration. In this Yoga the emotional being has not to be got rid of, but to undergo a transformation; the shortest way of transformation is to turn all the being to the Divine. But when that is done, then it is found that what is pure and true in any human relation survives, but with a rich and subtle change, or else new relations are established that come straight from the Divine. If, however, something resists the change, then it is quite possible that there may be an oscillation between blank indifference or vairagya and the indulgence of the untransformed feeling — the human vital on one side, the disillusioned Vairagi on the other side. Some even have to pass through this vairagya in order to reach the possibility of a divinised emotional nature, but that is not the normal movement of this Yoga.

As for being self-centred, it is obviously not the right thing for Yoga to be centred in the ego and revolving round it; one has to be centred in the Divine with all the movements turning round that centre — until they can all be in the Divine. One has naturally to think much of one's own nature and its change, but that is inevitable for the sadhana — to prevent its turning into a self-centred condition, the aspiration to the Divine, vision of the Divine everywhere, the surrender to the Divine have to be made the main objective of the sadhana.

*

The idea that all sadhaks must be aloof from each other and at daggers drawn is itself a preconceived idea that must be abandoned. Harmony and not strife is the law of Yogic living. This preconceived idea arises perhaps from the old notion of Nirvana as the aim; but Nirvana is not the aim here. The aim here is fulfilment of the Divine in life and for that union and solidarity are indispensable. I find it difficult to see in the mind's eye X developing an aversion for you and it would not be easy for you to develop an aversion for X; so these nightmares of the vital imagination ought not to emerge. Aversion and quarrelling are unyogic, not Yogic tendencies; the fact that this Asram is full of quarrels only shows that it is still an Asram of very imperfect sadhaks, not yet an Asram of Yogis — it does not at all mean that aversion and quarrelling are the dharma of the spiritual seeker.

The ideal of the Yoga is that all should be centred in and around the Divine and the life of the sadhaks must be founded on that firm foundation, their personal relations also should have the Divine for their centre. Moreover, all relations should pass from the vital to the spiritual basis with the vital only as a form and instrument of the spiritual; — this means that from whatever relations they have with each other all jealousy, strife, hatred, aversion, rancour and other evil vital feelings should be abandoned, for they can be no part of the spiritual life. So also all egoistic love and attachment will have to disappear — the love that loves only for the ego's sake and as soon as the ego is hurt and dissatisfied ceases to love or even cherishes rancour and hate. There must be a real living and lasting unity behind the love. It is understood of course that such things as sexual impurity must disappear also.

That is the ideal, but as for the way of attainment, it may differ for different people. One way is that in which one leaves everything else to follow the Divine alone. This does not mean an aversion for anybody any more than it means aversion for the world and life. It only means absorption in one's central aim, with the idea that once that is attained it will be easy to found all relations on the true basis, to become truly united with others in the heart and the spirit and the life, united in the spiritual truth and in the Divine. The other way is to go forward from where one is, seeking the Divine centrally and subordinating all else to that, but not putting everything else aside, rather seeking to transform gradually and progressively whatever is capable of such transformation. All the things that are not wanted in the relation, — impurity, jealousy, anger, egoistic demand, — drop away as the inner being grows purer and is replaced by the unity of soul with soul and the binding together of the social life in the hoop of the Divine. Your eagerness to bring your friends into the Yoga was perhaps in reality due to a recognition somewhere in the being that this was the safest way to preserve the relation, to found it on the common search for the Divine. If quarrels intervene and there is strife, it is because the old ego-basis stuck still and brought in old reactions not of a Yogic character; but for that the Yoga is not to blame.

It is not that one cannot have relations with people outside the circle of the sadhaks, but there too if the spiritual life grows within, it must necessarily affect the relation and spiritualise it on the sadhak's side. And there must be no such attachment as would make the relation an obstacle or a rival to the Divine. Attachment to family etc. often is like that and, if so, it falls away from the sadhana. That is an exigence which, I think, should not be considered excessive. All that however can be progressively done; a severing of existing relations is necessary for some; it is not so for all. A transformation, however gradual, is indispensable, — severance where severance is the right thing to do.

P.S. I must repeat also that each case differs — one rule for all is not practical or practicable. What is needed by each for his spiritual progress is the one consideration to be held in view.

Love for Others and Love for the Divine

The love of the sadhak should be for the Divine. It is only when he has that fully that he can love others in the right way.

*

Yes. First, one should enter into union with the Divine, and learn to live in the true light, true consciousness, true force. Yogic relations with others should come only when one lives in the Divine — then it will be safe and then there can be no influence [*from others*], for the only influence will be that of the Divine.

*

It cannot be said that it [*one's affinity for certain persons*] is either bad or good in a general way. It depends on the person, the effects and many other things. As a general rule, all these affinities have to be surrendered to the Divine along with the rest of the old nature — so that only what is in harmony with the Divine Truth can be kept and transformed for its work in you. All relations with others must be relations in the Divine and not of the old personal nature.

*

It is not necessary to have love for everybody just now. If you have a general goodwill, that is enough.

*

It is as the love of the Divine grows that the other things cease to trouble the mind.

*

There is a love in which the emotion is turned towards the Divine in an increasing receptivity and growing union. What it receives from the Divine it pours out on others, but freely without demanding a return. If you are capable of that, then that is the highest and most satisfying way to love.[1]

Family Ties and Duties

What you write about the family ties is perfectly correct. It creates an unnecessary interchange and comes in the way of a complete turning to the Divine. Relations after taking up Yoga should be less and less based on a physical origin or the habits of the physical consciousness and more and more on the basis of sadhana — of sadhak with sadhaks, of others as souls travelling the same path or children of the Mother than in the ordinary way or with the old viewpoint.

*

When one enters the spiritual life, the family ties which belong to the ordinary nature fall away — one becomes indifferent to the old things. This indifference is a release. There need be no harshness in it at all. To remain tied to the old physical affections would mean to remain tied to the ordinary nature and that would prevent the spiritual progress.

*

---

[1] *The next day the correspondent asked, "What must one do to have this love?" Sri Aurobindo replied, "First you must want it in a continuous way." — Ed.*

Human physical relations are necessarily temporary — the soul has to go away and prepare itself for other lives through which it will move eventually nearer to the Divine. Regard it so and open yourself to the peace from above; turn yourself towards that which is Eternal and Divine.

*

You ought to be able to see, after receiving today's telegram, that the cause of the unrest is in yourself and not in the outward circumstances. It is your vital attachment to family ties and the ordinary social ideas and feelings that has risen in you and creates the difficulty. If you want to practise Yoga, you must be able to live in the world, so long as you are there, with a mind set upon the Divine and not bound by the environment. One who does this, can help those around him a hundred times more than one who is bound and attached to the world.

*

The question about the family duties can be answered in this way — the family duties exist so long as one is in the ordinary consciousness of the grahasthan; if the call to a spiritual life comes, whether one keeps to them or not depends partly upon the way of Yoga one follows, partly on one's own spiritual necessity. There are many who pursue inwardly the spiritual life and keep the family duties, not as social duties but as a field for the practice of karmayoga, others abandon everything to follow the spiritual call or line and they are justified if that is necessary for the Yoga they practise or if that is the imperative demand of the soul within them.

*

There is no harm in devoting yourself to occupations which will help the sadhana. The earning of money and family affairs have only to be looked after if the circumstances are such as to compel it. They should then be done in a spirit of entire detachment, dealing with them so as to develop in oneself the consciousness described in the Gita.

Relations between Parents and Children

There are many kinds of truth and in the Shastra you will find all kinds, some seeming in conflict with others. Service to parents is part of family and social duty. It has nothing to do in itself with Yoga. Yoga is truth not of family or society, but of spiritual life, and in spiritual life the seeking for the Divine takes precedence of everything.

If we ask you to remain still with your father and mother, it is not from the point of view of Truth, but of charity. Four of their children have already left them to come to the Asram; it would be too hard a blow if you also left them now. As you have remained with them so long, you might remain a little longer. Even while in the family, you can prepare yourself for the spiritual life, by remembering the Divine in all you do and by doing it as a sacrifice for the sake of the Divine.

*

It [*a child's debt to his parents*] is a law of human society, not a law of Karma. The child did not ask the father to bring him into the world — and if the father has done it for his own pleasure, it is the least he can do to bring up the child. All these are social relations (and it is not at all a one-sided debt of the child to the father, either), but whatever they are, they cease once one takes to the spiritual life. For the spiritual life does not at all rest on the external physical relations; it is the Divine alone with whom one has then to do.

*

The attachment to parents belongs to the ordinary physical nature — it has nothing to do with Divine Love.

Old Relations

We are sorry to hear that she is suffering from such serious difficulties and certainly we are prepared to give her what inner help we can. It is not, however, any force from us that has worked to separate her from her old supporters and friends. It is, evidently, one result of some change and progress in her consciousness which has disturbed the old relation between her internal nature and her external surroundings and power of action upon them. To try to go back to the old relation does not usually succeed; the only safe course is to progress still farther and arrive at a new consciousness and new power which will enable her to establish a fresh relation with her external environment. If one keeps courage and always looks forward, relying on the Force behind which supports, there are no troubles, no difficulties, no apparent disasters even which cannot be passed through safely and eventually overcome.

*

Yes. The inner being turned to the Divine naturally draws away from old vital relations and outer movements and contacts till it can bring a new consciousness into the external being.

*

The movement [*of rejection*] of which you speak is not psychic but emotive. It is a vital emotive force that you put out and waste. It is also harmful because, while on the one side you try to reject a past vital relation or tie with these people, you by this movement re-establish in another way a vital relation with them. If there was anything wrong in your first movement, this is quite a false way of remedying the defect.

Certainly, it would be better to reject without any violent feeling against any person, because the violence is a sign of a certain weakness in the vital which must be corrected — not for any other reason. The rejection should be quiet, firm, self-assured, decisive; it will then be more radical and effective.

Friendship and Affection

All are not indifferent in this Asram to each other, nor is friendship or affection excluded from the Yoga. Friendship with the Divine is a recognised relation in the sadhana. Friendships between the sadhaks exist and are encouraged by the Mother. Only we seek to found them on a surer basis than that on which the bulk of human friendships are insecurely founded. It is precisely because we hold friendship, brotherhood, love to be sacred things that we want this change — because we do not want to see them broken at every moment by the movements of the ego, soiled and spoiled and destroyed by the passions, jealousies, treacheries to which the vital is prone — it is to make them truly sacred and secure that we want them rooted in the soul, founded on the rock of the Divine. Our Yoga is not an ascetic Yoga: it aims at purity, but not at a cold austerity. Friendship and love are indispensable notes in the harmony to which we aspire. It is not a vain dream, for we have seen that even in imperfect conditions when a little of the indispensable element is there at the very root the thing is possible. It is difficult and the old obstacles still cling obstinately. But no victory can be won without a fixed fidelity to the aim and a long effort. There is no other way than to persevere.

*

In Yoga friendship can remain, but attachment has to fall away or any such engrossing affection as would keep one tied to the ordinary life and consciousness — human relations must take quite a small and secondary place and not interfere with the turn to the Divine.

*

As to the question about affections etc. I answered X long ago that in Yoga all attachments have to be given up so that there may be no rival to the Divine, but love and affection can be there — only as a new basis of consciousness has to be reached love and affection have to be rebased on that deeper and higher consciousness, not allowed to remain in their old form or on their old level — all the life must be centred round the Divine. It is so in this Yoga at least. There are others in which a man must become aloof from all things, but that is when one is bound towards Nirvana.

*

Human affection is obviously unreliable because it is so much bound up with selfishness and desire; it is a flame of the ego sometimes turbid and misty, sometimes more clear and brightly coloured — sometimes tamasic based on instinct and habit, sometimes rajasic and fed by passion or the cry for vital interchange, sometimes more sattwic and trying to be or look to itself disinterested. But fundamentally it depends on a personal need or a return of some kind inward or outward and when the need is not satisfied or the return ceases or is not given, it most often diminishes or dies or exists only as a tepid or troubled remnant of habit from the past or else turns for satisfaction elsewhere. The more intense it is, the more it is apt to be troubled by tumults, clashes, quarrels, egoistic disturbances of all kinds, selfishness, exactions, lapses even to rage and hatred, ruptures. It is not that these affections cannot last — tamasic instinctive affections last because of habit in spite of everything dividing the persons, e.g. certain family affections; rajasic affections can last sometimes in spite of all disturbances and incompatibilities and furious ruptures because one has a vital need of the other and clings because of that or because both have that need and are constantly separating to return and returning to separate, or proceeding from quarrel to reconciliation and from reconciliation to quarrel; sattwic affections last very often from duty to the ideal or with some other support though they may lose their keenness or intensity or brightness. But the true reliability is there only when the psychic element in human affection becomes strong enough to colour or dominate the rest. For that reason friendship is or rather can oftenest be the most durable of the human affections because there there is less interference of the vital and even though a flame of the ego it can be a quiet and pure fire giving always its warmth and light. Nevertheless reliable friendship is almost always with a very few; to have a horde of loving, unselfishly faithful friends is a phenomenon so rare that it can be safely taken as an illusion. In any case human affection whatever its value has its place, because through it the psychic being gets the emotional experiences it needs until it is ready to prefer the true to the apparent, the perfect to the imperfect, the divine to the human. As the consciousness has to rise to a higher level, so the activities of the heart also have to rise to that higher level and change their basis and character. Yoga is the founding of all the life and consciousness in the Divine, so also love and affection must be rooted in the Divine and a spiritual and psychic oneness in the Divine must be their foundation — to reach the Divine first leaving other things aside or to seek the Divine alone is the straight road towards that change. That means no attachment — it need not mean turning affection into disaffection or chill indifference. But X seems to want to take his vital emotions just as they are — *tels quels* — into the Divine — let him try and don't bother him with criticisms and lectures; if it can't be done, he will have to find it out himself. Or perhaps he wants to clap on the Divine to the rest as a crowning ornament, shikhara, of his pyramid of love and affections.

*

It [*ordinary affection*] is the vital seeking to pour itself out with the implicit idea of getting a return, an interchange. The consciousness of oneness is something behind all life and all forms of affection come no doubt from it, but not consciously, and they get changed, mixed, perverted when the vital takes up the action of the force of Love of whose true or divine nature it is unconscious.

*

But that is the nature of human vital affection, it is all selfishness disguised as love. Sometimes when there is a strong vital passion, need or tie, then the person is ready to do anything to retain the affection of the other. But it is only when the psychic is able to get into the movement that there is real unselfish affection or at least some element of it.

*

It is meant [*by not retaining vital relations*] that you should have the relation of sadhaks with each other, one of goodwill and friendly feeling, but not any special relation of a vital character.

If there is anyone you cannot meet without such a vital relation coming up, then only it is not advisable to meet him or her.

*

What you write is quite correct — each sadhak must have the direct inner contact with the Mother and rely on her for the spiritual help and progress. But there may be psychic or spiritual friendships which may be helpful in another way and especially in certain difficult stages before the inner contact with the Mother is consciously established.

Vital Love

It is not helpful to make so much of the past and give it such a primary value. Whatever may be the glamour of a vital love, once it falls away and one gets to a higher level, it should be seen to have been not the great thing one imagined. To keep the exaggerated estimate of it is to hold the consciousness back from the full *essor* towards the greater thing with which that cannot for a moment compare. If one keeps a fervour like that for an inferior past, it must make it more difficult to develop the entire person for a higher future. It is indeed not the Mother's wish that X or you either should look back in a spirit of enthusiastic appreciation to the old vital love. It was indeed "so little" in any true estimate of things. It is not at all a question of comparison or of exalting the vital passion of one at the expense of that of the other. It is the whole thing that must dwindle in its proportions and recede into the shadowy constructions of the past which have no longer any importance.

*

It is the ordinary nature of vital love not to last or, if it tries to last, not to satisfy, because it is a passion which Nature has thrown in in order to serve a temporary purpose; it is good enough therefore for a temporary purpose and its normal tendency is to wane when it has sufficiently served Nature's purpose. In mankind, as man is a more complex being, she calls in the aid of imagination and idealism to help her push, gives a sense of ardour, of beauty and fire and glory, but all that wanes after a time. It cannot last, because it is all a borrowed light and power, borrowed in the sense of being a reflection caught from something beyond and not native to the reflecting vital medium which imagination uses for the purpose. Moreover nothing lasts in the mind and vital, all is in a flux there. The one thing that endures is the soul, the spirit. Therefore love can last or satisfy only if it bases itself on the soul and spirit, if it has its roots there. But that means living no longer in the vital but in the soul and spirit.

The difficulty of the vital giving up is because the vital is not governed by reason or knowledge, but by instinct and impulse and the desire of pleasure. It draws back because it is disappointed, because it realises that the disappointment will always repeat itself, but it does not realise that the whole thing is in itself a glamour or, if it does, it repines that it should be so. Where the vairagya is sattwic, born not of disappointment but of the sense of greater and truer things to be attained, this difficulty does not arise. However the vital can learn by experience, can learn so much as to turn away from its regret of the beauty of the will-o'-the-wisp. Its vairagya can become sattwic and decisive.

*

There is nothing unusual in your feelings towards X. It is the way that vital love usually takes when there is no strong psychic force to correct and uphold it. After the first vital glow is over, the incompatibility of the two egos begins to show itself and there is more and more strain in the relations — for one or both the demands of the other become intolerable to the vital part, there is constant irritation and the claim is felt as a burden and a yoke. Naturally in a life of sadhana there is no room for vital relations — they are a stumbling block preventing the wholesale turning of the nature towards the Divine.

*

The phenomenon of which you speak is normal to human nature. People are drawn together or one is drawn to another by a certain feeling of affinity, of agreement or of attraction between some part of one's own nature and some part of the other's nature. At first this only is felt; one sees all that is good or pleasant to one in the other's nature and even attributes, perhaps, qualities to him that are not there or not so much there as one thinks. But with closer acquaintance other parts of the nature are felt with which one is not in affinity — perhaps there is a clash of ideas or opposition of feelings or conflict of two egos. If there is a strong love or friendship of a lasting character, then one may overcome these difficulties of contact and arrive at a harmonising or accommodation; but very often this is not there or the disagreement is so acute as to counteract the tendency of accommodation or else the ego gets so hurt as to recoil. Then it is quite possible for one to begin to see too much and exaggerate the faults of the other or to attribute things to him of a bad or unpleasant character that are not there. The whole view can change, the good feeling change into ill-feeling, alienation, even enmity or antipathy. This is always happening in human life. The opposite also happens, but less easily — i.e. the change from ill-feeling to good feeling, from opposition to harmony. But of course ill-opinion or ill-feeling towards a person need not arise from this cause alone. It happens from many causes, instinctive dislike, jealousy, conflicting interests, etc.

One must try to look calmly on others, not overstress either virtues or defects, without ill-feeling or misunderstanding or injustice, with a calm mind and vision.

*

There is the selfishness which is always a part if not the whole of human love — and it is the reaction of the demand and desire it brings that creates the opposite feeling. It is when this selfish element is rejected that one can feel the true psychic or divine love.

*

Love does not consist in demands and desires — demand and desire spring from ego. Love exists for its own sake and does not offer itself on conditions. These feelings do not spring from the psychic and it is only by the psychic prevailing in you that the true consciousness can become free and full in the nature and all these repinings and unhappinesses disappear.

*

The love in the vital or other parts is the true thing, good for the spiritual life, only when in the vital love is changed into a form of the psychic love and becomes an instrument for the transformation of the soul's love, no longer for the desires of the ego which men call love.

Vital Love and Psychic Love

Ordinary human love is vital, emotional and physical and always egoistic — a form of self-love. The psychic element is very small except in a few.

*

Human love is mainly vital, when it is not vital and physical together. It is also sometimes psychic + vital. But the Love with a dominant psychic element is rare.

*

It is difficult to define its [*psychic love's*] limits or to recognise it. For even when there is the psychic love for another person, it gets in the human being so mixed up with the vital that it is the commonest thing to justify a vital love by claiming for it a psychic character. One could say that psychic love is distinguished by an essential purity and selflessness — but the vital can put on a very brilliant imitation of that character, when it likes.

*

It depends on what you mean by psychic "love". One can have a psychic feeling for all beings; it does not depend on sex nor has it anything sexual in it.

*

There is a fundamental psychic feeling which is the same for all; but there can also be a special psychic feeling for one or another.

*

It [*psychic love*] is sometimes turned to the human person, but it never gets its true satisfaction till it turns to the Divine.

*

Men are necessarily separated by the individualisation of their nature and can only establish contacts there. In the psychic being one gets the sense of oneness by psychic sympathy, but not any unification, for the psychic is the individual soul and must unify itself with the Divine before it can through the Divine unify with others. In spiritual realisation there are two quite opposite forms — one in which one withdraws from all outer things including all material beings in the world to merge in the Divine and one in which one feels the Self or the Divine in all and through that realisation attains to a universal oneness.

*

Certainly, as the psychic attitude develops it is bound to have an effect not only on oneself but on the relations with others.

Personal Relations in Yoga

Personal relation is not a part of the Yoga. When one has the union with the Divine, then only can there be a true spiritual relation with others.

*

A personal relation is formed when there is an exclusive mutual looking to each other. The rule about personal relations in this Yoga is this: (1) All personal relations to disappear in the single relation between the sadhaka and the Divine; (2) All personal (psychic-spiritual) relations to proceed from the Divine Mother, determined by her, and to be part of the single relation with the Divine Mother. In so far as it keeps to this double rule and admits no physical indulgence or vital deformation or mixture, a personal relation can be there. But since as yet the Supramental has not taken possession but is only descending and there is still struggle in the vital and physical levels, there must be a great carefulness such as would not be necessary if the supramental transformation were already there. Both have to be in direct relation with the Mother and in a total dependence on her and to see that that remains and that nothing diminishes its totality or cuts across it in the least degree.

*

I don't think it is much use writing about personal relations in the true spiritual life (which does not yet exist here). None would understand it except as a form of words. Only three points —

(1) Its very base would have to be spiritual and psychic and *not* vital. The vital would be there but as an instrument only.

(2) It would be a relation flowing from the higher Truth, not continued from the lower Ignorance.

(3) It would not be impersonal in the sense of being colourless, but whatever colours were there would not be the egoistic and muddy colours of the present relations.

*

The Yoga cannot be done if equality is not established. Personal relations must be founded on the relation with the Divine in himself and the Divine in all and they must not be "ties" to pull one down and keep bound to the lower nature but part of the higher unity.

*

The natural feeling of one sadhak to another should be kindliness and good feeling to all and the friendliness which is natural or ought to be so between all who follow the same spiritual aim, but personal attachment is supposed to be overcome, as all attachments of the vital must be. Personal relations *can* exist if they are founded on the spiritual consciousness or help towards it, but nothing that holds one back or turns one away from the Divine. I have not opposed any sadhak having a friendly relation with another. But if it is based on ego, on vital desires and impulses or, if these come strongly in, then obviously there is something there that makes it undesirable. In this case, you have written very frankly that your intimacy with X would be of that character on your side. So I could not but acquiesce in your feeling that it would be better not to go to his room or resume the old close contact.

P. S. In what I have written of the relation of sadhaks, I mean of course the relation on the way. I leave aside the spiritual or psychic love for all which can come afterwards and be the radiation of the union with the Divine.

*

Our experience is that it is only when both are in the true consciousness centred round the Divine that there is some chance of a true meeting in the Divine. Otherwise, with the personal relation that forms there comes in either disappointment and alienation or else reactions that are not pure.

Universal Love and Personal Relations

One can talk to all, unless one has a reason for not doing so. The oneness with all is an internal realisation, but it does not necessarily impose the same dealing with all. It is the old story of *hāthi brahman* and *māhout brahman*. There is the fundamental realisation and there are the disparities of the Lila — both have to be taken into account.

*

No, that by itself [*expressing one's affection to all*] is not the wideness needed — the spiritual wideness brings the sense of being one being with all, of containing all in oneself, as it were, and with that comes a kind of universal love which is spiritual, free and pure, but which one is not moved to show to everybody by outward signs, but which has its effect. The personal relation can be only with some, not with all.

*

That was exactly what X tried to do — to express the love in connection with this or that person. But universal love is not personal — it has to be held within as a condition of the consciousness which will have its effects according to the Divine Will or be used by that Will if necessary, but to run about expressing it for one's personal satisfaction or the satisfaction of others is only to spoil and lose it.

*

The *dynamic* Love cannot go out equally to all — that would create a chaotic disturbance because of the unpreparedness of the majority. It is only the static immutable universal Love that can apply equally to all — that which comes in a still wideness of the heart which corresponds with the still wideness of the mind in which there is the equanimity and infinite peace.

*

So long as the whole consciousness is not clear of doubtful stuff and the realisation of oneness confirmed in the supreme purity, the expression of the all-love is not advisable. It is by holding it in oneself that it becomes a real part of the nature, established and purified by joining with it the other realisations still to come. At present it is only a first touch and to dissipate it by expression would be very imprudent. The sex and vital might easily become active — I have known cases of very good Yogis in whom the *viśvaprema* became the *viśvakāma*, all-love becoming all-lust. This has happened with many both in Europe and the East. Even apart from that it is always best to solidify and to confirm rather than to throw out and disperse. When the sadhana has progressed and the knowledge from above comes to enlighten and guide the love, then it will be another matter. My insistence on rejection of all untransformed vital movements is based on experience, mine and others' and that of past Yogas like the Vaishnava movement of Chaitanya (not to speak of the old Buddhist Sahaja dharma) which ended in much corruption. A wide movement such as that of all-love can only take place when the ground of Nature has been solidly prepared for it. I have no objection to your mixing with others, but only under a continual guard and control by a vigilant mind and will.

Relations between Men and Women in Yoga

As for turning all to the Divine, that is a counsel of perfection for those who don't care to carry any luggage. But otherwise friendship between man and man or man and woman or woman and woman is not forbidden provided it is the true thing and sex does not come in and also provided it does not turn one away from the goal. If the central aim is strong, that is sufficient. When I spoke of personal relation I certainly did not mean pure indifference, for indifference does not create a relation: it tends to non-relation altogether. Emotional friendship need not be an obstacle.

*

The only relation permissible between a sadhak and sadhika here is the same as between a sadhak and sadhak or between a sadhika and sadhika — a friendly relation between followers of the same path of Yoga and children of the Mother.

*

In a general way the only method for succeeding in having between a man and a woman the free and natural Yogic relations that should exist between a sadhak and a sadhika in this Yoga is to be able to meet each other without thinking at all that one is a man and another a woman — both are simply human beings, both sadhaks, both striving to serve the Divine and seeking the Divine alone and none else. Have that fully in yourself and no difficulty is likely to come.

*

Even in the world there have been relations between man and woman in which sex could not intervene — purely psychic relations. The consciousness of sex difference would be there no doubt, but without coming in as a source of desire or disturbance into the relation. But naturally it needs a certain psychic development before that is possible.

*

It is certainly easier to have friendship between man and man or between woman and woman than between man and woman, because there the sexual intrusion is normally absent. In a friendship between man and woman the sexual turn can at any moment come in in a subtle or a direct way and produce perturbations. But there is no impossibility of friendship between man and woman pure of this element; such friendships can exist and have always existed. All that is needed is that the lower vital should not look in at the back door or be permitted to enter. There is often a harmony between a masculine and a feminine nature, an attraction or an affinity which rests on something other than any open or covert lower vital (sexual) basis — it depends sometimes predominantly on the mental or on the psychic or on the higher vital, sometimes on a mixture of these for its substance. In such cases friendship is natural and there is little chance of other elements coming in to pull it downwards or break it.

It is also a mistake to think that the vital alone has warmth and the psychic is something frigid without any flame in it. A clear limpid goodwill is a very good and desirable thing — one has only to consider what a changed place the Asram would be if all had it for each other. But that is not what is meant by psychic love. Love is love and not merely goodwill. Psychic love can have a warmth and a flame as intense and more intense than the vital, only it is a pure fire, not dependent on the satisfaction of ego-desire or on the eating up of the fuel it embraces. It is a white flame, not a red one; but white heat is not inferior to the red variety in its ardour. It is true that the psychic love does not usually get its full play in human relations and human nature, it finds the fullness of its fire and ecstasy more easily when it is lifted towards the Divine. In the human relation the psychic love gets mixed up with other elements which seek at once to use it and overshadow it. It gets an outlet for its own full intensities only at rare moments. Otherwise it comes in only as an element, but even so it contributes all the higher things in a love that is predominantly vital — all the finer sweetness, tenderness, fidelity, self-giving, self-sacrifice, reachings of soul to soul, idealising sublimations that lift up human love beyond itself come from the psychic. If it could dominate and govern and transmute the other elements, mental, vital, physical, of human love, then love could be on the earth some reflection or preparation of the real thing, an integral union of the soul and its instruments in a dual life. But even some imperfect appearance of that is rare.

Here we do not talk of psychic love between sadhaks, for the reason that that comes usually to be employed as a cover and excuse for things that are not at all psychic and have no place in the spiritual life. Our view is that the normal thing is in Yoga for the entire flame of the nature to turn towards the Divine and the rest must wait for the true basis; to build higher things on the sand and mire of the ordinary consciousness is not safe. That does not necessarily exclude friendships or comradeships, but these must be subordinate altogether to the central fire. If anyone makes meanwhile the relation with the Divine his one absorbing aim, that is quite natural and gives the full force to the sadhana. Psychic love finds itself wholly when it is the radiation of the diviner consciousness for which we are seeking; till then it is difficult for it to put out its undimmed integral self and figure.

P. S. Mind, vital, physical are properly instruments for the soul and spirit; when they work for themselves then they produce ignorant and imperfect things — if they can be made into conscious instruments of the psychic and the spirit, then they get their own diviner fulfilment; that is the idea contained in what we call transformation in this Yoga.

*

To avoid X is not the way to get rid of these feelings [*of possessiveness and jealousy*]. The Mother allowed the relation between you because you had need of help and there was a need also of psychic and spiritual comradeship in the work, a support to each other among its difficulties. That something vital got into the relationship and caused the disturbances of jealousy, sense of possession etc. is true; but the remedy is not to break off but to let it grow into the true thing. It is difficult to get rid of the vital mixture all at once, because these movements had created in you a habit of recurrence supported by forces that wanted to break your sadhana. These forces have now lost a great deal of their power, — but the movement itself still recurs and from force of habit your nature responds and gets troubled. Do not be discouraged by this recurrence; it happens with everyone. Keep your psychic perception and quietly stand back from the jealousy and sense of possession when it occurs, not accepting it as a thing right or natural, but not desponding either because of its recurrence. In time the growth of the psychic in you will help you to turn the relation into the true thing altogether.

*

The first thing you have to do is to make up your mind what you want. If you want to have a free mind and vital to pursue your sadhana, you must get rid of the attachment for X left from the past; if you once do so entirely, you can either mix with him or not meet him without any reaction or inconvenience. Till then both the impulse or need of seeing him and the recoil from it carry too much of the savour of the old relation to be effective.

*

For a sadhak the suitable partner does not exist — and any "partner" would create a barrier between him and the Divine. A companion, not of the same sex, is a different matter.

*

It [*mixing with women*] is not so harmful for a woman as mixing freely with men under the vital impulse — but all mixing on the vital plane has its dangers. What you should do in mixing with women is not to give yourself vitally, to remain within yourself, but to mix with them outwardly in a quiet way — forming no vital relation with any.

*

The first [*question*] was about a complementary soul and marriage. The answer is easy to give; the way of the spiritual life lies for you in one direction and marriage lies in quite another and opposite. All talk about a complementary soul is a camouflage with which the mind tries to cover the sentimental, sensational and physical wants of the lower vital nature. It is that vital nature in you which puts the question and would like an answer reconciling its desires and demands with the call of the true soul in you. But it must not expect a sanction for any such incongruous reconciliation from here. The way of the supramental Yoga is clear; it lies not through any concession to these things, — not, in your case, through the satisfaction, under a spiritual cover if possible, of its craving for the comforts and gratifications of a domestic and conjugal life and the enjoyment of the ordinary emotional desires and physical passions, but through the purification and transformation of the forces which these movements pervert and misuse. Not these human and animal demands, but the divine Ananda which is above and beyond them and which the indulgence of these degraded forms would prevent from descending, is the great thing that the aspiration of the vital being must demand in the sadhaka.

*

If that [*contempt*] is your feeling about women the sooner you get rid of it the better — for it is very silly. As for shyness etc., it should be got rid of, but do not replace it by familiarity or overintimacy.

Loneliness

The inner loneliness can only be cured by the inner experience of union with the Divine; no human association can fill the void. In the same way, for the spiritual life the harmony with others must be founded not on mental and vital affinities, but on the divine consciousness and the union with the Divine. When one finds the Divine and finds others in the Divine, then the real harmony comes. Meanwhile what there can be is the goodwill and unity founded on the feeling of a common divine goal and the sense of being all children of the Mother. Real harmony can come only on a psychic or a spiritual basis.

*

To be alone with the Divine is the highest of all privileged states for the sadhak, for it is that in which inwardly he comes nearest to the Divine and can make all existence a communion in the chamber of the heart as well as in the temple of the universe. Moreover that is the beginning and base of the real oneness with all, for it establishes that oneness in its true base, on the Divine, for it is in the Divine that he meets and unites with all and no longer in a precarious interchange of the mental and vital ego. So do not fear loneliness but put your trust in the Mother and go forward on the Path in her strength and Grace.

Chapter Two

Interactions with Others and the Practice of Yoga

Cultivating Equality and Goodwill

The inequality of feelings towards others, liking and disliking, is ingrained in the nature of the human vital. This is because some harmonise with one's own vital temperament, others do not; also there is the vital ego which gets displeased when it is hurt or when things do not go or people do not act according to its preferences or its idea of what they should do. In the self above there is a spiritual calm and equality, a goodwill to all or at a certain stage a quiet indifference to all except the Divine; in the psychic there is an equal kindness or love to all fundamentally, but there may be special relations with one — but the vital is always unequal and full of likes and dislikes. By the sadhana the vital must be quieted down; it must receive from the self above its quiet goodwill and equality to all things and from the psychic its general kindness or love. This will come, but it may take time to come. You must get rid of all inner as well as all outer movements of anger, impatience or dislike. If things go wrong or are done wrongly, you will simply say, "The Mother knows" and go on quietly doing or getting things done as well as you can without friction. At a later period we will show you how to use the Mother's force so that things may go better, but first you must get your inner poise in a quiet vital, for only so can the Force be used with its full possible success.

*

There are two attitudes that a sadhak can have — either a quiet equality to all regardless of their friendliness or hostility or a general goodwill.

*

I would ask you not to let resentment or anything else rise or dictate your conduct. Put these things aside and see that peace within and the seeking of the Divine are the one thing important — these clashes being only spurts of the ego. Turn yourself in the one direction, but for the rest keep a quiet goodwill to all.

*

You must certainly give up all personal feelings of that kind [*resentment, ill will*]. Also you must not think if people differ from you and express their difference of opinion freely that that arises from personal hostility. In all things keep *samatā* and, if there are differences, try to see the other's point of view as well as yours.

*

As for the inconveniences, you should take them as a training in samata. To be able to bear inconveniences is one of the most elementary necessities if one wants to enter into the true spirit of Yoga.

*

The proper thing is to see all with an unmoved calm, both the "good" and "bad", but as a movement of Nature on the surface. But to do this truly without error or egoism or wrong reactions needs a consciousness and knowledge that is not personal and limited.

*

If you want to have knowledge or see all as brothers or have peace, you must think less of yourself, your desires, feelings, people's treatment of you, and think more of the Divine — living for the Divine, not for yourself.

Indifference to What Others Think or Say

It is not what others think of you that matters, but what you are yourself.

*

When you are doing sadhana, you have not to care what others want or think or say, but only for what is right and what the Divine wants of you.

*

It is no use listening to what people say or to suggestions. Both are things by which one must learn not to be affected. A certain samata in these matters is needed in order to get the true poise. The one thing that matters is realisation of the Divine.

*

So long as you go on listening to what people say or listening to your own wrong imaginations or insisting on your desires, how do you hope to get peace? Nobody ever got peace in that way.

*

To become entirely indifferent to the good and bad opinion of others, especially those who are or were near, and stand on the Truth alone is very difficult; some reaction of the old nature can easily come across; but if one remains calm and firm within, these surface reactions quickly disappear and their rejection helps the remnants of the old nature to disappear.

*

If you look closely, you will see that all these things — the rudeness of one, the anger of another — are exceedingly slight things which should be received with indifference. Do not allow them to trouble you so much. The one thing of supreme importance is your sadhana and your spiritual growth. Let nothing touch or disturb that.

*

It is not good to allow yourself to be upset so much by what others say or do — whether it be X or anybody else. There is a quietude and happiness which you can find by living in yourself in contact with the Divine which you will never get from outside.

*

I cannot quite say how far X is responsible — it is certainly always possible to get a lowering of consciousness from someone who is always gossiping or talking of her fears and difficulties. As for being kind, there is nothing harmful in kindness itself, but there is no reason why you should allow another to invade you with things you don't want to feel or hear. There is a measure in all things — and besides one should keep oneself inwardly free and not admit that the vital movements of others should be a cause of difficulties — one has enough to do combating one's own.

*

Such reproaches (the stone etc.) are quite usual from those who do not understand against the sadhak when he remains firm in his path against the ordinary human vital demands upon him. But that should not perturb you. It is better to be a stone on the road to the Divine than soft and weak clay in the muddy paths of the ordinary vital human nature.

Overcoming Dependence

What you say about your dependence on others is true, because this dependence is accompanied by a demand on those others, the desire that they should always be occupied with you alone, think, feel and act according to your own ideas, feelings and desires. This is not possible and so this dependence brings disappointment and, if the feelings are excessive, despair.

But for this demand the remedy for this dependence, which is the character of many especially among women, would be to depend not on others but on the Divine. But here too the demand comes and spoils the dependence. A dependence without demand is what is needed, then the Divine Power comes in and at every moment guides, helps and sustains the being. When the sadhana was going on in you, you had periods when you had this right attitude and could get glimpses of the true happiness and dedication. But the physical mind became active and with it there began the period of obscuration and trouble. The physical mind must become quiet and the heart open and the psychic become again active. It is for this you should aspire always and in time it will come.

It was not the Mother's intention in putting you with X that you should depend on him alone, but that with his help you should come to depend on the Mother. Owing to your weakness and his, it turned out otherwise.

*

If you wish to be free from people's expectations and the sense of obligation, it is indeed best not to take from anybody; for the sense of claim will otherwise be there. Not that it will be entirely absent even if you take nothing, but you will not be bound any longer.

Overcoming Attachment

All attachment is a hindrance to sadhana. Goodwill you should have for all, psychic kindness for all, but no vital attachment.

*

Yes, certainly, there should be no attachment [*to another person*]. The emotional feeling is safe only when it is governed by the psychic — for the psychic love is essentially a permanent soul-sympathy which is not attached but self-existent and self-content pouring itself out but asking for nothing.

The safest course in sadhana is to turn all to the Divine and to leave any other relation till all relations can be founded in the Divine; but that is not easy for everybody — only a few seem able to do it.

*

Yes, that is the bother of these attachments — the reason why the Yogis were so down on them — the Vedantists especially with their insistence on the breaking of the heart-knots. They must have known from their own difficulties in the matter.

*

If you expect a return for your kindness, you are bound to be disappointed. It is only those who give love or kindness for its own sake without expecting a return who escape from this experience. A relation also can be established on a sure basis only when it is free from attachment or when it is predominantly psychic on both sides.

*

When one deals with people there can be always a projection of consciousness to them or a reception of them into the consciousness, but that does not amount to an attachment — something more is needed, a grip of the vital on the person or a grip of the person on one's vital etc.

Helping Others

To concentrate most on one's own spiritual growth and experience is the first necessity of the sadhak — to be too eager to help others draws away from the inner work. There is also likely to be an overzeal and haste which clouds the discrimination and makes what help is given less effective than it should be. To grow in the spirit is the greatest help one can give to others, for then something flows out naturally to those around that helps them.

*

It [*trying to help someone through words*] is a relative and partial help, of course, but it is sometimes useful. A radical help can only come from within through the action of the Divine Force and the assent of the being. It must be said of course that it is not everyone that thinks he is helping who is really doing it; also if the help is accompanied with the exercising of an "influence", that influence may be of a mixed character and harm as well as help if the instrument is not pure.

*

Yes, it is always so with human conduct — men want to help

each other with a motive behind or a feeling which proceeds from the ego.

*

The idea of helping others is a subtle form of the ego. It is only the Divine Force that can help. One can be its instrument, but you should first learn to be a fit and egoless instrument.

*

The idea of helping others is a delusion of the ego. It is only when the Mother commissions and gives the force that one can help and even then only within limits.

*

The attempt to help people and clear things for others was an ego impulse. It magnified the ego and brought boasting, imagination, vital flattery. To clear yourself was the first necessity — afterwards to work not by one's own initiative, but in obedience to the will of the Mother, without ego.

*

As for helping [*others*], you can only be sure of that if you yourself have an assured basis, with the psychic being always prominent, full of faith and joy and strength, — then others can gather strength and faith and joy from such a one by speech or contact. But to arrive at that you must, as I have been telling you, open yourself to the Light and Force that come from myself and the Mother and *to no other influence.*

*

This "helping others" is a perilous business — it brings the "guru" ego or else you very uncertainly rid others of their difficulties and very certainly get them yourself. "Why do you have all these disciples?" said a sage to some Maratha saint (I have forgotten the names); "to have disciples means to add all their difficulties to your own." "Helping others" has the same disadvantage.

*

Interactions with Others and the Practice of Yoga 319

Of course it is the disadvantage of helping others that one comes into contact with their consciousness and their difficulties and also gets more externalised.

*

In "helping" one often gets part of the other's inconvenience and many Yogis refuse to take disciples because they will have to assume others' burdens as well as their own. There are also other dangers — growth of ego etc.

*

The bearing of others' difficulties would, I fear, be a heavy burden for anybody and I doubt the efficacy of the method. What one can do much more usefully is, if one has strength to give out of one's strength to the other, if one has peace to shed the peace on the other etc. This one can do without losing one's strength or peace — if it is done in the right way.

*

There are two possible attitudes in the matter [*of helping others*] and each has something to be said for it. There is much to be said for X's attitude [*of reserve*] — first, because until one's own siddhi is complete, the help one gives is always a little doubtful and imperfect and, secondly, there is the danger so often emphasised by experienced Yogis of taking on oneself the difficulties of those one helps. But all the same to wait for perfection is not always possible.

*

These things [*mixing with outsiders etc.*] (most of them, to take a walk or write a letter home are different) can be described as not safe. If one has the strong spiritual condition secure in its basis one can do them without invasion from outside or a stumble; if one has the divine protection and can remain in it wherever he goes because the psychic being is in front and the vital obedient, then also one will not suffer. But otherwise in so acting one is opened to the influences that hang around these outside people, one enters by sympathy with them into the movement of other forces than those of the spiritual life — and then it is quite possible that there may be untoward results as with X and Y and others too, in the physical, or in the vital, wherever there is most weakness.

*

To give oneself to an outsider is to go out from the atmosphere of sadhana and give oneself to the outer world forces.

One can have a psychic feeling of love for someone, a universal love for all creatures, but one has to give oneself only to the Divine.

*

To want unwaveringly the welfare of another both in the head and the heart, is the best help one can give.

*

It [*a sense of harmony and delight and love*] is in you and when it is like that it spreads out in the atmosphere — but naturally only those can share who are open and sensitive to the influence. Still everyone who has peace or love in him becomes an added influence for its increase in the atmosphere.

Receiving Help from Others

All change must come from within with the felt or the secret support of the Divine Power; it is only by one's own inner opening to that that one can receive help, not by mental, vital or physical contact with others.

Concern for Others

Whatever or whomever you have handed over to the Divine, you should not be any longer attached or anxious about him or it but leave all to the Divine to do for the best.

*

Interactions with Others and the Practice of Yoga

If your husband is in a perilous period of his life and suffering from ill-health and you feel for him, the best thing for him is still that you should tranquillise yourself and call the Divine to his help to pass through. Even in the ordinary life disquietude and depression create an unhelpful atmosphere for one who is ill or in difficulties. Once you are a sadhak, then whether for yourself or to help others for whom you still feel, the true spiritual attitude of reliance on the Divine Will and call for the help from above is always the best and most effective course.

*

It is very good that the condition you speak of has settled itself — that is a great progress. As for the prayers, the fact of praying and the attitude it brings, especially unselfish prayer for others, itself opens you to the higher Power, even if there is no corresponding result in the person prayed for. Nothing can be positively said about that, for the result must necessarily depend on the persons, whether they are open or receptive or something in them can respond to any Force the prayer brings down.

Sympathy for Others

By the sympathy you get into contact and receive what is in the other — or also you may give or let go or have drawn from you part of your force which goes to the other. It is the vital sympathy which has this effect; a calm spiritual or psychic goodwill does not bring these reactions.

*

Yes, it is dangerous [*to sympathise with someone who has gone wrong*], because it puts one in touch with the adverse Force that upset him and that Force at once tries to touch you and make its suggestions and contaminate by a sort of contagion or infection.

Mothering Others

You need not trouble yourself much about X's ideas or attach importance to them. The only truth about it is that a vital vital mixture does very easily get into the movements even of the sadhana, if one is not careful. The one safeguard against that is to turn all towards the Divine and draw all from the Divine, getting rid of attachment, ego and desire. In one's relations with other sadhaks there should be neither stiffness and hardness nor attachment and sentimental leanings.

As for the motherly feeling — it has to be transformed like everything else. The danger of all these relations when they are untransformed is that they may minister in a subtle way to the ego. To avoid that, one has to make oneself an instrument merely, but without even the ego of the instrument, and to be conscious of the source, not insisting on the action or any relation, but simply allowing it to be useful whenever one can clearly feel that it is intended. Also one must be careful that no force comes through one except the right forces, those which are in harmony with the higher consciousness and help. If one does always in that spirit and with that care, then even if mistakes are made, it does not matter — the growing consciousness will set them right and progress towards a more perfect working.

*

The real failing of the motherlike ambition — at least as it manifests in many — is that it conceals an ego movement, the desire to play a big part, to have people depending on one, to have the motherly reputation etc. etc. Most human altruism has really this ego basis. If one gets rid of that, then the will to help can take its true place as a movement of pure sympathy and psychic feeling.

Working with Others

Work is always best done in silence except so far as it is necessary to speak for the work itself. Conversation is best kept for leisure hours. So nobody should object to your silence during work.

For the rest what you should do is to keep your right attitude towards the others and not allow yourself to be upset, irritated or displeased by anything they may say or do — in other words keep the *samatā* and universal goodwill proper to a sadhak of Yoga. If you do that and still others get upset or displeased, you must not mind as you will not be responsible for their wrong reaction.

*

I have read your letter and I understand now what it is that you find trying — but they do not seem to us such serious things as to be rightly felt as a cause of disturbance. They are the kind of inconveniences that one always has when people live and work together. It arises from a misunderstanding between two minds or two wills, each pulling his own way and feeling hurt or vexed if the other does not follow. This can only be cured by a change of consciousness — for when one goes into a deeper consciousness, first, one sees the cause of these things and is not troubled; one acquires an understanding, patience and tolerance that makes one free from vexation and other reactions. If both or all grow in consciousness, then there arises a mutual understanding of each other's view-points which makes it easier to bring in harmony and smooth working. It is this that should be sought by the change within — to create the same harmony from outside by exterior means is not so easy, as the human mind is stiff in its perceptions and the human vital insistent on its own way of action. Let this be your main will — to grow yourself within and let the clearer and deeper consciousness come and have a good will for the same change to come in others so that clarity and harmony may come in the place of friction and misunderstanding.

Dispersion through Contact with Others

Dispersion and sadhana are two things that cannot go together. In sadhana one has to have a control over the mind and all its actions; in dispersion one is on the contrary controlled and run away with by the mind and unable to keep it to its subject. If the mind is to be always dispersed, then you can't concentrate on reading either or any other occupation, you will be fit for nothing except perhaps talking, mixing, flirting with women and similar occupations.

*

You are mistaken in thinking that the sadhana of X, Y and Z does not suffer by the dispersion of their minds in all directions. They would have been far farther on the path if they did a concentrated Yoga — even Y who has an enormous receptivity and is eager for progress might have gone thrice as far as he has done. Moreover, your nature is intense in all it does and it was therefore quite its natural path to take the straight way. Naturally, when once the higher consciousness is settled and both the vital and physical sufficiently ready for the sadhana to go on of itself, strict tapasya will no longer be necessary. But till then we consider it very useful and helpful and in many cases indispensable. But we do not insist on it when the nature is not willing. I see too that those who get into the direct line (there are not as yet very many), get of themselves the tendency to give up these mind-dispersing interests and occupations and throw themselves fully into the sadhana.

*

Yes, certainly, dispersion is an inner fact. But certain outer things help the dispersion of the consciousness and if anybody like X says that he is not dispersed when he is wandering about with a companion like Y, I would say he is either not telling the truth or he is deceiving himself. If one is always in the inner consciousness, then one can be not dispersed even when doing outward things — or if one is conscious of the Divine at all times and in all one does, then also can one read newspapers or do much correspondence without dispersion. But even then though there is not dispersion, yet there is less intensity of consciousness when reading a newspaper or writing a letter than when one is not putting part of oneself into quite external things. It is only when the consciousness is quite *siddha* that there is not even this difference. That does not mean one should not do external things at all, for then one gets no training in joining the two consciousnesses. But one must recognise that certain things do disperse the consciousness or lower it or externalise it more than others. Especially one should not deceive or pretend to oneself that one is not dispersed by them when one is. As for the people who want to draw others to the Yoga, I should say that if they draw themselves nearer to the inner goal that would be a much more fruitful activity. And in the end it would "draw" much more people and in a better way than the writing of many letters.

*

To be too sensitive and upset by any contact is excessive; but to have too many contacts and be always dispersing oneself prevents the sadhana from growing and solidifying in the inner being, since one is always being pulled out into the ordinary outer consciousness.

Mixing with Others

It is true that mixing with others too closely tends to lower the condition, if they are not themselves in the right attitude and live very much in the vital. In all contacts what you have to do is to remain within, keep a detached attitude and not allow yourself to be troubled by the difficulties that arise in work or the movements of people, but keep yourself the true movement. Do not be caught by the desire to "help" others — do and speak yourself the right thing from the inner poise and leave the help to come to them from the Divine. Nobody can really help — only the Divine Grace.

*

It might not be prudent to mix freely and too often. Enough to relieve any tension of the sadhana, but not so much as to dissipate its intensity.

*

Aloofness is very necessary at certain stages of the sadhana, —

but it cannot be maintained all through. One must be able to mix with others and act on them.

*

It is right to mix a little with the others — it helps to keep the balance.

*

You are quite right. Not to mix with others deprives of the test which contact with them imposes on the consciousness and the chance to progress in these respects. Mixing is unprofitable from the spiritual point of view when it is only to indulge the vital, chat, interchange vital movements etc.; but abstention from all mixing and contact is also not desirable. It is only when the consciousness truly needs a full retirement that such retirement can be made and even then it may be full, but not absolute. For in the absolute retirement one lives a purely subjective life and the opportunity for extending the spiritual progress to the outer life and testing it thoroughly is not there.

It is good that you got quickly the right attitude to what had happened; that indicates a good progress in the consciousness.

*

To be able to remain back [*while conversing with others*], entering only superficially without being involved is really the first step towards the secret of mixing with others without lowering the inner consciousness.

Vital Expansiveness

That [*mixing with people, laughing and joking with them*] is a kind of vital expansiveness, it is not vital strength — this expansiveness is also expensive. For when there is this mixing, the vitally strong get strength from it but the vitally weak expend what strength they have and become weaker.

*

I think no rule can be laid down applicable to all. There are some who have the expansive tendency of the vital, others who have the concentrative. The latter are absorbed in their own intensity of endeavour and certainly they gather from that a great force for progress and are saved the expense and loss of energy which frequently comes to the more communicative and also make themselves less open to reactions from others (though this cannot be altogether avoided). The others need to communicate what is in them and cannot wait for the full fullness before they use what they have. Even they may need to give out as well as to take in in order to progress. The only thing is that they must balance the two tendencies, concentrating to receive from above as much or more than they open sideways to distribute.

*

X has a very strong and expansive vital, so it is quite natural that if he likes anybody he can produce this kind of effect on him by meeting. But I do not know that he is conscious of what he gives or receives; it is more likely a spontaneous action. He is not accustomed to give only though, for a strong expansive vital as opposed to a strong self-contained one needs to receive as well as to give.

*

As for living a free outer life it cannot be said that that is good for everybody at every stage any more than living a retired life is good for everybody or at every stage. The disadvantage of a free jolly outward social life without restrictions is that one becomes entirely or mostly externalised and that all sorts of vital interchanges are part of it which can hamper the inner growth or the total self-consecration to the Divine. The disadvantage of too complete a retirement is that it makes the person one-sided and shut up in himself, subjective, without the stabilising contact with earth and consequently with the danger of morbidity and self-delusion. A middle path with the rule of living more and more within, standing back from outward things but not throwing them aside, looking at them with a new consciousness, a new view and acting on them from this inner consciousness is the best way. But there is need for some at some stages to minimise outward contacts without abolishing them during part of the process of this shifting of the consciousness. No absolute rule can be laid down in this matter.

Vital Interchange

Whenever one mixes with others, things are passing from one to the other. If I talk with a number of people, I bring away with me in my atmosphere many forces that were around them; they may affect me or not, but they remain for a time at least. If in that time I speak with another man, he may receive them from me. It is like a man carrying germs with him from a person he has visited; he may not fall ill himself (or he may), but, even if he does not, he can pass them on to another man he visits afterwards — who falls ill. It is the same thing here in the supraphysical parts.

*

There is always an interchange of vital forces going on between people. If you sit near one who is weak and depressed and needs vital force, you may have your forces pulled from you by his or her need and yourself feel depressed or weak or empty.

*

Small energies of that kind [*vital influences*] are always coming out from people and, if there is a connection, they can flow into another person sitting near. One has to live in one's own consciousness and reject all such interchanges, accepting only what comes from the Mother.

*

If someone throws something on you, you should throw it away and not keep it. It is like mud thrown on the body — immediately one washes it off.

*

You have to find that out [*which people are bad influences*] for yourself. There are people you mix with who have doubts, suggestions, depressions, jealousies, dissatisfactions with the Mother's action. They can easily throw that on you without intending it. These influences are all around in the atmosphere. It is not sufficient to avoid this or that person. You have to learn to be on your guard and self-contained.

*

When one is with another for some time, talking etc., there is always some vital interchange unless one rejects what comes from the other, instinctively or deliberately. If one is impressionable, there may be a strong influence or impression from the other. Then if one goes to another person, it is possible to pass it on to that other; that is a thing which is constantly happening. But these things happen automatically — without the knowledge of the transmitter. When one is conscious, one can prevent it happening.

*

No, people are not conscious of these things, only a few are.[1] The vital exchange is there, but they are not aware of it — because they live in the external mind (physical) and these things go on behind. Even if they feel more energetic after an interchange or depressed or tired, they would not attribute it to the talk or contact, because the interchange is unconscious, their external mind in which they live not being aware of it.

*

I don't suppose people are at all aware of this occult commerce [*of vital energies*]. Some like Daudet may observe the expenditure or throwing out of forces, but not the pulling or the effect on others. The idea of mental interchange is familiar though only of the superficial kind, not the silent action of mind on

---

[1] *The correspondent wrote that while talking with others he was often conscious of an exchange of vital energies. Sometimes he felt that energy was emptying out of him, sometimes that it was entering in. — Ed.*

mind which is always going on, but the vital impacts are known only to a few occultists. If one becomes very conscious one can become aware of the forces acting in and from all around, e.g. forces of joy or depression or anger.

*

The utility [*of knowing the effects of a vital interchange with someone*] depends upon the development of an inner power based upon peace which will act upon these things and prevent them. So long as one is unconscious, one undergoes the action in the Ignorance and there is no possibility of going out of the circle because there is no knowledge. The consciousness comes with a growing inner development in the being which makes the peace, the liberation a necessity — with that one opens to a higher Force of a new consciousness which puts an end to the vital interchange and creates a new poise for the vital as well as the mental life. If one stops with the increased sensitivity and does not go farther, then of course there is no proper use of it. There are some people like X and Y who got so absorbed in the "occult" knowledge that they stopped there going round and round in it and making all sorts of blunders because the spiritual light was not there. One has not to stop there, but go on and beyond to the spiritual consciousness and the greater light, strength and poise it brings.

*

The consciousness of these things [*such as the forces one feels coming from others*] is intended for knowledge — a psycho-occult knowledge, necessary for the fullness of consciousness and experience. It is not intended that what is felt should be allowed to become an influence, whether a good one or a bad one.

*

There must necessarily be a difference between the vital energy of a cultured and well-educated man and of one who is rough and ignorant. If nothing else, a greater refinement and subtlety in the vital substance and therefore in the energy is there. Drinking

Interactions with Others and the Practice of Yoga 331

if excessive affects the substance and quality of the energy — but probably a moderate drinking and smoking would have a less perceptible effect. I don't think people in ordinary life notice clearly, but they have often a general impression which they cannot explain or particularise.

*

It is mainly an inner guard that you must keep. At the same time, if you feel unease in crowds it is better to avoid them — except in case of music if you feel secure there. A crowd of people engaged in purely social interchange is necessarily on a lower level of consciousness in which undesirable forces may move, if there is anyone there open to them, and one who is in a stage of consciousness opening to higher things but not yet fixed in steady and self-supporting calm is safer away from it.

In sadhana one is supposed to keep outward forces at a distance or at least not to allow them to invade one. If one faces a difficulty in the right spirit and overcomes it, naturally one progresses, but that is a different thing from letting alien forces or influences enter into the conscious being. No one need invite that, — they are only too ready to do it without being invited. One can look at and become conscious of all forces, even the worst, darkest and most hostile, provided one remains on guard and refuses all credence or support to their suggestions and rejects all claim of theirs to a place in the consciousness and nature. But all cannot do that in the earlier stages.

*

It is not necessary to be so careful as all that.[2] Ordinary vital interchanges are of a slight character. Nobody can take away another's vital, for the very good reason that if that happened, the person from whom it was taken would die. It is possible of course for one person to drain another's vital forces so as to leave him limp or weak or dry, but it is only the vampire kind

---

[2] *The correspondent had been warned about someone who could "take away one's vital when he talks". If that is possible, he said, then one must be very careful in one's exchange with others. — Ed.*

that do that. It is possible also for one to give out too much of one's vital forces so as to weaken oneself or exhaust of energy, a thing which should not be done, — it is only those who know how to draw or can draw freely from the universal vital Force and replenish their life energies that can give out freely. All of course draw to some extent, otherwise they would not remain alive, for expenditure of vital energy is always going on and one has to replace it; but for most the capacity for drawing is limited and the capacity for giving without exhaustion is also limited.

But the ordinary movements of interchange are harmless provided they are kept within moderate limits. What creates a difficulty in the sadhana is that one may easily draw in undesirable influences or pass them on to others. It is the reason why at certain stages a limitation of talk, intercourse etc. is often advisable. But the true remedy is to become inwardly conscious, to know and be able to repel any undesirable incursion or influence, to be able when speaking, mixing etc. to keep a defence round one and allow to pass in only what one can accept and nothing else. Also to measure what one can give out safely and what one cannot. When one has the consciousness and the practice, this working becomes almost automatic.

*

As for what you say about the stimulus of vital interchange, it is true of the vital life. Men are constantly spending their vital energy and need to renew it; one way to do it is by pulling from others in a vital interchange. This however is not necessary if one knows how to draw from the universal Nature or from the Divine, i.e. from above. Moreover when the psychic is active — there is always more lost than gained by the vital interchange.

*

I suppose it depends upon the person [*whether contact with him is harmful*] and upon your reactions to him. If he gives sex vibrations or is an appropriator of vital energy, then opening to him may not be good. But in the ordinary superficial interchange one need not lose anything or what is lost is so little and so automatically repaired that it does not matter.

*

It is not that you have to speak to no one — that is not possible. But you must keep your body free and pure and reject all vital interchanges with men — do not speak too much or freely; do not allow yourself too much freedom or laughter, be simple and quiet and straight in all your actions and behaviour. Touch no sadhak and let none touch you. Above all, turn to the Divine only and form no relations or attachments with others.

*

It [*intimate vital contact with another person*] gives a temporary pleasure, but that does not last and it is certainly not profitable. After a time the vital interchange can no longer satisfy and the vital itself gets tired of it and turns away elsewhere. Of course for the spiritual aim it is a great interference.

*

A human vital interchange cannot be a true support for the sadhana and is, on the contrary, sure to impair and distort it, leading to self-deception in the consciousness and a wrong turn of the emotional being and vital nature.

Talking, Letter-Writing and Vital Interchange

It is quite possible for one person to get depressed by talking with another. Talking means a vital interchange, so that can always happen. Whether they have observed rightly in a particular case is another matter.

*

The disturbance in talking to people comes of course because they throw their own vibrations upon you and revive your old movements. Once the true consciousness is well fixed in your physical being, that effect need no longer happen.

*

To discuss with others, especially when they are in a bad state, is always a mistake. It is very easy for the disturbance in them to fall upon you while you speak even without your noticing it; it is afterwards that you feel it. That is why I told you to ignore X and what he says when he is in a bad state.

*

Every letter means an interchange with the person who writes it — for something is there behind the words, something of his person or of the forces he has put out or had around him while writing. Our thoughts and feelings are also forces and can have effects upon others. One has to grow conscious of the movement of these forces and then one can control one's own mental and vital formations and cease to be affected by those of others.

Talking or Thinking about Others

Talking about somebody may very well have an effect on him; it often does, for it can be an effective formulation of a thought or feeling which, so embodied, will reach him. But I don't suppose mere mechanical thoughts or ill-formed imaginations would do that — at any rate it must be rare and need exceptional conditions or a play of forces in which a trifle counts.

*

Yes, one's bad thoughts and good thoughts can have a bad or a good effect on others, though they have not always because they are not strong enough — but still that is the tendency. It is therefore always said by those who have this knowledge that we should abstain from bad thoughts of others for this reason. It is true that both kinds of thought come equally to the mind in its ordinary state; but if the mind and mental will are well developed, one can establish a control over one's thoughts as well as over one's acts and prevent the bad ones from having their play. But this mental control is not enough for the sadhak. He must attain to a quiet mind and in the silence of the mind receive only the Divine thought-forces or other divine Forces and be their field and instrument.

To silence the mind it is not enough to throw back each thought as it comes, that can only be a subordinate movement. One must get back from all thought and be separate from it, a silent consciousness observing the thoughts if they come, but not oneself thinking or identified with the thoughts. Thoughts must be felt as outside things altogether. It is then easier to reject thoughts or let them pass without their disturbing the quietude of the mind.

Not to be disturbed by either joy or grief, pleasure or displeasure by what people say or do or by any outward things is called in Yoga a state of *samatā*, equality to all things. It is of immense importance in sadhana to be able to reach this state. It helps the mental quietude and silence as well as the vital to come. It means indeed that the vital itself and the vital mind are already falling silent and becoming quiet. The thinking mind is sure to follow.

The Drawing of Vital Forces by Others

When people mix together there is generally some interchange of vital forces which is quite involuntary. X himself suffers from physical weakness and he complains of his vital forces being drawn out of him without knowing why it happens. Vampirising is a special phenomenon — a person who lives upon the vital of others and flourishes vitally at their expense.

*

The tired feeling which the people felt after seeing this X is a sign of vampirism, but very often there is no such feeling but there is an after-effect on the whole. The nerves get gradually wrong — what is called the nervous envelope becomes weak or in one way or another the vitality becomes weak or gets into an abnormal condition — excitable and unstable. There are many such ways in which the effect shows itself. Sex-vampirism is a different matter — in sex interchange the normal thing is to give and take, but the sex-vampire eats up the other's vital and gives nothing or very little.

*

There is always a drawing of vital forces from one to another in all human social mixture; it takes place automatically. Lovemaking is one of the most powerful ways of each drawing up the other's vital force, — or of one drawing the other's, which also often happens in a one-sided way to the great detriment of the "other". In the passage come many things good and bad, elation, feelings of strength, fullness, support or weakness and depletion, infiltration of good and bad qualities, interchange of psychological moods, states and movements, ideas helpful and harmful, depression, exhaustion — the whole gamut. In the ordinary consciousness one is not aware of these things; the effects come into the surface being, but the cause and process remain unknown and unnoticed because the interchange is subtle and covert, it takes place through what is called the subconscient, but is rather a behind-consciousness covered by the surface waking mind. When one gets into a certain Yogic consciousness, one becomes very much aware of this covert movement, very sensitive to all this interchange and action and reaction; but one has this advantage that one can consciously build a wall against them, reject, refuse, accept what helps, throw out or throw back what injures or hinders. Illnesses can also pass in this way from one to another, even those which are not medically regarded as contagious or infectious; one can even by will draw another's illness into oneself as did Antigonus of Macedon accepting death in this way in order to save his son Demetrius. This fact of vital interchange, which seems strange and unfamiliar to you, becomes quite intelligible if one realises that ideas, feelings etc. are not abstract things but in their way quite concrete, not confining their movements to the individual's mind or body but moving out very much like the "waves" of science and communicating themselves to anyone who can serve as a receiver. Just as people are not conscious of the material waves, so it is and still more with these mental or vital waves; but if the subtle mind and senses become active on the surface — and that is what takes place in Yoga — then the consciousness becomes aware in its reception of them and records accurately and automatically their vibrations.

*

It is quite possible that X pulls [*vital energy*] unconsciously, as he is vitally weak and people who are vitally weak do unconsciously and automatically pull on others.

Limiting Contacts with Others

It is certainly a great help to be able to limit one's contacts provided it is not carried too far. I must note however that even with limited contacts undesirable waves can get in — it is a measure of precaution but does not make you absolutely safe. On the other hand complete withdrawal carries one to another extreme and has its own dangers. The complete safety from "stuff" distracting, disturbing, externalising etc., can only come from a growth of the consciousness within. In the interim absorption and limitation of contacts like that can be a helpful measure if used in a judicious way.

*

One has to go inside into the inner being and one can minimise contacts, *if necessary*, not as an absolute rule — provided there is a real living in the inner being and sufficient contact with outside things not to lose one's hold of practical realities. But if there is an isolation which brings depression, inertia, unhappiness, gloom or else morbidity of any kind, then it is evident that the retirement is not wholesome.

*

The avoiding of contacts does not by itself bring the fundamental immunity, it is only a change of that part of the consciousness that can do it. But it may be advisable to minimise the contacts that strongly bring the trouble so long as the change is not there. It is not certain that a long retirement brings about the change of the subconscient, — the long retirement of the Sannyasin is part preparation of a retirement from life altogether — it is different in our Yoga which wants to change, but not reject life.

*

It is true that one has to try to keep the inner condition under all circumstances, even the most adverse; but that does not mean that one has to accept, unnecessarily, unfavourable conditions when there is no good reason for their being allowed to go on. Especially, the nervous system and the physical cannot bear an excessive strain as well as the mind and higher vital; your fatigue came from the strain of living in one consciousness and at the same time exposing yourself too much to prolonged contacts from the ordinary consciousness. A certain amount of self-defence is necessary — so that the consciousness may not be pulled down or out constantly into the ordinary atmosphere or the physical strained by being forced into activities that have become foreign to you. Those who practise Yoga often seek refuge in solitude from these difficulties; that is unnecessary here, but all the same you need not submit to being put under this kind of useless strain always.

Inner Detachment Preferable to Outer Withdrawal

Inner withdrawal is always much better than physical withdrawal.

*

I say that all that [*no vital relations with anyone*] is magnificent, if you can do it. But can't you see that it is the inward change that is wanted — the inward plunge? These dramatic outward breaks lead only to new joinings. Neither you nor she can keep it up. If there comes a strong ingoing movement, then it is another matter. That of itself would make it possible to readjust the relations or to withdraw if necessary. But splashings about on the surface — will it lead to anything? It does not look like it.

*

It is not a physical retirement that is needed, but an inner detachment from the mental formations and vital desires. To find the real self above and within and live in that, not in the mind's conceptions or the vital's reactions. These must be observed and looked at not as one's own but as movements of a surface ignorant nature.

Qualified Utility of Retirement for Sadhana

You can see whether such a retirement suits you or not. It is not the same for all. Most cannot stand retirement.

There is no harm in that kind of seclusion [*to find a deeper contact with the Mother*] and it can help provided you maintain the inner peace and a simple quietude turned towards the Mother.

*

We have no objection to your doing this [*withdrawing from social contacts*] for a week, as you propose; I understand that it is not a retirement, but a cessation of social visits. My objection to retirement is that so many have "gone morbid" by it or gone astray into zones of false vital experiences; secondly, that absolute retirement is not necessary for the spiritual life. It is different however for people like X who are to the manner born or at least perfectly trained. A "restriction of publicity" is quite another matter. Also to be capable of solitude and to have the Ananda of solitude can always be helpful to sadhana, and a power of inner solitude is natural to the Yogi.

We will give our help and hope you will succeed — at least, you will have established a precedent for withdrawing whenever you want in the future.

*

Retirement is not necessary for passing from one plane to another. It is needed only in rare cases and with certain temperaments for a time.

*

The impulse to retire comes from some push to concentrate within — but the cause of the push varies in different cases. There are certain cases in which there was a desire to isolate oneself from the Mother's influence (Pranam, meditation etc.) and follow one's own fancies, e.g. X, Y, also perhaps with a sense of superiority = "no need of these things for so great a Yogi as I". In other cases there was a marked desire for isolation, but that was where the brain was already upset (Z) or a wrong influence at work (A). But others have simply desired concentration or wished not to spend themselves in externalisation (B, C in their periods of retirement). So all cannot come under one sentence.

*

How are you going to find the right external relations by withdrawing altogether from external relations? And how do you propose to be *thoroughly* transformed and unified by living only in the internal life, without any test of the transformation and unity by external contact and the ordeals of the external work and life? Thoroughness includes external work and relations and not a retired inner life only.

It is only by the vital ego giving up its demands and claims and the reactions these produce when not satisfied, that the transformation and unification can come, and there is no other way.

*

You must make up your mind what you want. There is no harm in drawing back from all vital and physical relations and wanting only the true relation — that is in fact what happens to everybody who wants the true relation — the only thing kept is the universal goodwill (not vital affection) to all. But if you swing about from one mood to another — then of course they will not understand and have some ground to say that they are perplexed by your variations. This matter of touching and caressing is one on which you ought to take a firm and unvarying stand. If you don't want it, you should repel it always with the utmost firmness, otherwise there will necessarily be clash and disturbance. All depends upon your inner will and establishing a unity of will in yourself turned exclusively towards the Divine.

I think I have told you that an *entire* physical retirement is seldom healthy, although a comparative retirement is often helpful. But the main thing is the *inner* detachment and complete turning to the Divine.

Dangers of Complete Retirement

To live in the self is of course the proper object of withdrawal and to live in the self brings the higher experiences which must obviously be helpful and not harmful. What I wrote was only to explain what I meant by the danger of too complete retirement and why it turned out to be harmful to X, Y and others. There are some like Z who derived unmixed profit from it. It altogether depends on one's temperament and on one's attitude and aim and inner poise during the silence.

*

Retirement in the sense of all meditation without work is not suitable to this sadhana — it is one-sided and those who resort to it, unless they are very strong, often lose their balance.

*

To have no contact with people and shut oneself entirely is not healthy. But one can for a time diminish outward contacts so as to concentrate.

*

I doubt whether an entire retirement is very healthy except for certain people who have a contemplative nature coupled with a very sound and solid nervous system and firm balance of the mind — but a restriction of intercourse so as to go more in oneself and limit or select the contacts often has a good effect.

*

Yes, it is better [*not to talk with others except when necessary*] if you want to do sadhana seriously — but if your vital cannot do without these things, it is no use forcing it. Entire retirement is not good — it makes people morbid and they plunge into a world of imaginations without any check from life and actuality. But to avoid useless talk and unhelpful social interchange is good, if the vital can be made to acquiesce in an applied and serious sadhana.

*

Not speaking or contacting when one is in the intensity of the peace is one thing — that can be done. Remaining isolated at other times as a rule of life does not seem to me necessary — it is safe only for those who can live entirely within without losing their hold on outer reality. If one has always a solid poise of peace one can do that or a clear mind balanced and discriminating along with constant experiences which it is able to put in the right place. But some get absorbed in inner experiences which they get lost in and get passionately attached to and this inner life becomes for them the sole reality without the outer to poise it and keep it under check and test — there lies a danger. Again if one remains isolated without the support of a settled inner poise and constant experience over which one has a discriminating control, then in periods of emptiness the vital can arise bringing struggles, difficulties, unrest, suggestions of all kinds, a troubled and turbid state — rather than spend the time in that, as some do, it is better to mix with others or do some work or otherwise externalise oneself in a healthy way.

*

People will certainly regard it [*maintaining absolute silence*] as unnatural and there will be a lot of hubbub for a time. As to the dangers, the one real danger in these retirements (apart from

Interactions with Others and the Practice of Yoga 343

the pride) is the becoming a prey of subjective influences and imaginations and losing the hold of reality which work and contact with others help to keep up. Of course one can lose that even while keeping contact as happened to X and others. But I suppose you have a sufficiently cool and critical head to avoid that danger.

*

And if some find that retirement is the best way of giving oneself to the Higher, to the Divine by avoiding as much as possible occasions for the bubbling up of the lower, why not? The aim they have come for is that and why blame or look with distrust and suspicion on the means they find best or daub it with disparaging adjectives to discredit it — grim, inhuman and the rest? It is your vital that shrinks from it and your vital mind that supplies these epithets which express only your shrinking and not what the retirement really is. For it is the vital or the social part of it that shrinks from solitude; the thinking mind does not but rather courts it. The poet seeks solitude with himself or with Nature to listen to his inspiration; the thinker plunges into solitude to meditate on things and commune with a deeper knowledge; the scientist shuts himself up in his laboratory to pore by experiment into the secrets of Nature; these retirements are not grim and inhuman. Neither is the retirement of the sadhak into the exclusive concentration of which he feels the need; it is a means to an end, to the end on which his whole heart is set. As for the Yogin or bhakta who has already begun to have the fundamental experience, he is not in a grim and inhuman solitude. The Divine and all the world are there in the being of the one, the supreme Beloved or his Ananda is there in the heart of the other.

I say this as against your depreciation of retirement founded on ignorance of what it really is; but I do not, as I have often said, recommend a total seclusion, for I hold that to be a dangerous expedient which may lead to morbidity and much error. Nor do I impose retirement on anyone as a method or approve of it unless the person himself seeks it, feels its necessity, has the joy of it and the personal proof that it helps to the spiritual experience. It is not to be imposed on anyone as a principle, for that is the mental way of doing things, the way of the ordinary mind — it is as a need that it has to be accepted, when it is felt as a need, not as a general law or rule.

Relations in Ordinary Life

The best way to prepare oneself for the spiritual life when one has to live in the ordinary occupations and surroundings is to cultivate an entire equality and detachment and the *samatā* of the Gita with the faith that the Divine is there and the Divine Will at work in all things even though at present under the conditions of a world of Ignorance. Beyond this are the Light and Ananda towards which life is working, but the best way for their advent and foundation in the individual being and nature is to grow in this spiritual equality. That would also solve your difficulty about things unpleasant and disagreeable. All unpleasantness should be faced with this spirit of *samatā*.

*

When one is living in the world, one cannot do as in an Asram — one has to mix with others and keep up outwardly at least ordinary relations with others. The important thing is to keep the inner consciousness open to the Divine and grow in it. As one does that, more or less rapidly according to the inner intensity of the sadhana, the attitude towards others will change. All will be seen more and more in the Divine and the feeling, action, etc. will more and more be determined, not by the old external reactions, but by the growing consciousness within you.

*

The difficulty which you experience from relatives and others is always one that intervenes as an obstacle when one has to practise the sadhana in ordinary or unfavourable surroundings. The only way to escape from it is to be able to live in oneself in one's inner being — which becomes possible when the responsiveness and luminosity of which you speak in your letter increase and become normal, for then you are constantly aware of your inner being and even live in it — the outer becomes an instrument, a means of communication and action in the outer world. It is then possible to make the relations with people outside free from tie or necessary reaction — one can determine from within one's own reaction or absence of reaction; there is a fundamental liberation from the external nexuses, — of course, if one wills it to be so.

*

The life of *saṁsāra* is in its nature a field of unrest — to go through it in the right way one has to offer one's life and actions to the Divine and pray for the peace of the Divine within. When the mind becomes quiet, one can feel the Divine Mother supporting the life and put everything into her hands.

*

In her condition the one thing by which she can enter into the sadhana is to remember the Divine always, taking her difficulties as ordeals to be passed through, to pray constantly and seek the Divine help and protection and ask for the opening of her heart and consciousness to the supporting Divine Presence.

Chapter Three
Problems in Human Relations

Hatred and Dislike

That is quite right.[1] Only those who sympathise can help — surely also one should be able to see the faults of others without hatred. Hatred injures both parties, it helps none.

*

It is this feeling of dislike that must have been the ground for the attack to come in. All feelings of dislike for other sadhaks should be absolutely rejected. Each has his own nature, his own difficulties and has to struggle out of them with the Divine Help. Defects and limitations in them should not be made a ground for dislike.

*

These things [*reasons for disliking someone*] are not sufficient to justify dislike. These dislikes come from some vital feeling and these reasons put forward by the mind are excuses, not the real cause. This collaboration between the mind and the vital, the vital throwing up the wrong movement, the mind justifying it, is one of the chief difficulties in the way of getting rid of the vital deviations.

*

All antagonism to other sadhaks or dislike of them should go. There should be a calm goodwill and charity to all, but no inner mixing or interchange. Liking and disliking always means interchange of influences.

*

---

[1] *The correspondent said that he preferred to encourage a fellow sadhak for his good points rather than to hate him for his defects. — Ed.*

You can disapprove [*of what people say*], but there should be no feeling of dislike or disgust for the people.

*

The disgust should be for what is said, but not against those who say it.

*

Yes. One should not do to others what one cannot bear from others.

*

The position you took finally about what happened today is the right one — to make the effort for one's own perfection and not to be disturbed by any mistake in others but reply by a silent will for their perfection also is always the right attitude.

Quarrels and Clashes

Quarrels and clashes are a proof of absence of the Yogic poise and those who seriously want to do Yoga must learn to grow out of these things. It is easy enough not to clash when there is no cause for strife or dispute or quarrel; it is when there is cause and the other side is impossible and unreasonable that one gets the opportunity of rising above one's vital nature.

*

Well, I have said already that quarrels, cuttings are not a part of sadhana; the clashes and friction that you speak of are, just as in the outside world, rubbings of the vital ego. Antagonisms, antipathies, dislikes, quarrellings can no more be proclaimed as part of sadhana than sex impulses or acts can be part of sadhana. Harmony, goodwill, forbearance, equanimity are necessary ideals in the relation of sadhak with sadhak. One is not bound to mix, but if one keeps to oneself, it should be for reasons of sadhana, not out of other motives, — moreover it should be without any sense of superiority or contempt for others. The cases of friction you speak of seem to me to arise from ordinary motives of discord and they are certainly not the results of any spiritual Force working to heal the dangers of social or vital attraction by the blessings (!) of personal discord. If somebody finds that association with another for any reason raises undesirable vital feelings in him or her, he or she can certainly withdraw from that association as a matter of prudence until he or she gets over the weakness. But ostentation of avoidance, public cuttings etc. are not included in the necessity and betray feelings that equally ought to be overcome. There is a great confusion of thought about these things — for the vital gets in the way and disturbs the right view of things. It is only what is done sincerely with a sound spiritual motive that is proper to Yoga. The rest cannot be claimed as the working of a spiritual force mysteriously advancing its ends by ways contrary to its own nature.

*

Yes — self-justification [*in a quarrel*] keeps the thing going because it gives a mental support. Self-justification is always a sign of ego and ignorance. When one has a wider consciousness, one knows that each one has his own way of looking at things and finds in that way his own justification, so that both parties in a quarrel believe themselves to be in the right. It is only when one looks from above in a consciousness clear of ego that one sees all sides of a thing and also their real truth.

*

These results [*unhappiness, dullness, obscurity*] are not a punishment, they are a natural result of yielding to egoism. All quarrels proceed from egoism which pushes its own opinion and affirms its own importance, considering that it is right and everybody else wrong and thus creates anger and sense of injury etc. These things must not be indulged, but rejected at once.

*

You must remember that anger creates an atmosphere which

spreads and gets hold of those around. If you give free vent to your anger, that spirit catches hold of others who are open to it like X and makes them also angry and violent. X's conduct has been serious, but the best way is to show your superiority to him by mastering your own anger. Going outside won't cure this weakness of yours. You must conquer it here in yourself — otherwise it will go wherever you go and create trouble for you.

*

As to X and Y, I entirely disapprove of Y's action. Violence and blows are out of place in the Yoga. It is not by these means or by any physical or external impulsion or pressure that sadhana can be enforced but only by a psychic or other inner influence. On the other hand X ought to be less undisciplined and to put a curb on his temper which seems to be much too fiery; but he must do it himself by his own will, recognising that self-control and self-mastery are necessary even in the ordinary life and still more necessary — quite indispensable — in Yoga.

*

X's vision of Y and the spirit among you which it expresses belong to the old quarrelling egoistic movement that spoilt your sadhana. It does not matter whether the vision has some foundation or none. Neither he nor anyone else need trouble about Y and his defects which are not your concern. If you start this kind of thing again, you are likely to fall back into the same blunders and lose your sadhana.

Obviously, if Y indulges the passions of which you speak, it is not surprising that his illnesses continue; they must be the physical expression of his vital disturbances. But on the other hand, Z too must understand that he is not to indulge his former obscure arrogance which made him pose as a spiritual head leading people to me. He should understand that there is only one Power at work and neither Z nor Y nor anybody else matters. Let each one open himself to the working of that Power in him and let there be no attempt at forming a body of sadhakas with somebody leading or intervening between the one Power and the sadhakas. In that way there will be no room for rivalry or collision between opposing vital egoisms.

*

I am afraid that when vital passion disturbs the atmosphere, people very easily lose right perception and the sense of the thing that ought to be done, even those who are only or should be only onlookers. In this case everybody seems to have done and said or thought what ought not to have been thought and said and done. For you, however, looking at it from your standpoint only, the best thing is not to brood on these things, but to turn away from the memory of them altogether; for brooding on them only prolongs the inner consequences of a mistaken, disturbing and painful movement. There is no need that you should apologise for anything; what we should advise is to bury the past episode and its mistakes and return to normal undisturbing relations. Fix yourself more in an inner life and its opening to your soul's future.

*

It is better not to involve oneself in the dispute and to leave the combatants to throw their brahmastras at each other, oneself safe in a calm and judicious indifference. It is also the attitude most helpful to the sadhana. Of opinions and discussions there is no end and it is much better to remain inside and advance towards another light than the mind's — though there is more fire of a smoky kind than light in these discussions.

*

It is not always possible in life and work to avoid friction and collision; but it can be minimised or deprived of its worst developments if one has a large understanding of the men around one with whom one has to deal and acts in that spirit. If on the other hand one sticks to one's own position, done without regard for the standpoint of others, that creates resistance and friction.

Fault-Finding and Criticism

There is no harm in seeing and observing [*the behaviour of others*] if it is done with sympathy and impartiality — it is the tendency unnecessarily to criticise, find fault, condemn others (often quite wrongly) which creates a bad atmosphere both for oneself and others. And why this harshness and cocksure condemnation? Has not each man his own faults — why should he be so eager to find fault with others and condemn them? Sometimes one has to judge but it should not be done hastily or in a censorious spirit.

*

Men are always more able to criticise sharply the work of others and tell them how to do things or what not to do than skilful to avoid the same mistakes themselves. Often indeed one sees easily in others faults which are there in oneself but which one fails to see. These and other defects such as the last you mention are common to human nature and few escape them. The human mind is not really conscious of itself — that is why in Yoga one has always to look and see what is in oneself and become more and more conscious.

*

In ordinary life people always judge wrongly because they judge by mental standards and generally by conventional standards. The human mind is an instrument not of truth but of ignorance and error.

*

Do not dwell much on the defects of others. It is not helpful. Keep always quiet and peace in the attitude.

*

It is the petty ego in each that likes to discover and talk about the (real or unreal) defects of others — and it does not matter whether they are real or unreal. The ego has no right to judge them, because it has not the right view or the right spirit. It is only the calm, disinterested, dispassionate, all-compassionate and all-loving Spirit that can judge and see rightly the strength and the weakness in each being.

*

Yes, all that is true. The lower vital takes a mean and petty pleasure in picking out the faults of others and thereby one hampers both one's own progress and that of the subject of the criticism.

*

If you find fault with anybody, that fault is likely to increase in that person and to come also into you.

*

It is true that the habit of gossip and fault-finding with others does interfere because it brings down the consciousness from a higher to a lower level. But I do not think a retirement such as you propose is the way to cure it. It would only be suspended and the tendency come up again when you resumed free intercourse with others. It is on its field itself that it has to be first observed, then cured by detachment from it and rejection of it when it comes. A partial retirement may sometimes be helpful for concentration, — but not for these things; there the only cure is what I suggest or else the descent of a higher consciousness to replace the present imperfect nature.

Benefiting from Criticism

Even sometimes a malignant (not fair or well-intentioned) criticism can be helpful by some aspect of it, if one can look at it without being affected by the unfairness.

*

Naturally, praise and blame may have that effect[2] (the human

---

[2] *The correspondent remarked that praise may lead to pride and vanity, just as blame may lead to resentment and revolt. — Ed.*

nature is more sensitive to these than to almost anything else, more even than to real benefit or injury), unless either equanimity has been established or else there is so entire a confidence and happy dependence upon someone that both praise and blame are helpful to the nature. There are some men who even without Yoga have so balanced a mind that they take and adjudge praise and blame calmly for what they are worth, but that is extremely rare.

Part Three

Sadhana on the Physical, Subconscient and Inconscient Levels

Section One

Sadhana on the Level of the Physical

Chapter One

The Transformation of the Physical

The Need to Transform the Physical

The law of the physical is inertia, dullness, obstruction to whatever is new or not yet established.

*

Apart from the individual difficulty there is a general difficulty in the physical earth-nature. Physical nature is slow and inert and unwilling to change; its tendency is to be still and take long periods of time for a little progress. It is very difficult for even the strongest mental or vital or even psychic will to overcome this inertia. It is only by bringing down constantly the consciousness and force and light from above that it can be done. Therefore there must be a constant will and aspiration for that and for the change and it must be a steady and patient will not tired out even by the utmost resistance of the physical nature.

*

It is because your consciousness in the course of the sadhana has come into contact with the lower physical nature and sees it as it is in itself when it is not kept down or controlled either by the mind, the psychic or the spiritual force. This nature is in itself full of low and obscure desires, it is the most animal part of the human being. One has to come into contact with it so as to know what is there and transform it. Most sadhaks of the old type are satisfied with rising into the spiritual or psychic realms and leave this part to itself — but by that it remains unchanged, even if mostly quiescent, and no complete transformation is possible. You have only to remain quiet and undisturbed and let the higher Force work to change this obscure physical nature.

*

There is nothing to be discouraged about. The fact is that after being so long in the mental and vital plane you have become aware of the physical consciousness, and the physical consciousness in everybody is like that. It is inert, conservative, does not want to move, to change — it clings to its habits (what people call their character) or its habits (habitual movements) cling to it and repeat themselves like clockwork in a persistent mechanical way. When you have cleared your vital somewhat, things go down and stick there. You see, if you have become self-conscious, you put pressure, perhaps, but the physical responds very slowly, hardly at first seems to move at all. The remedy? Aspiration steady and unchanging, patient work, wakening the psychic in the physical, calling down the light and force into these obscure parts. The light brings the consciousness of what is there; the force has to follow and work on them till they change or disappear.

*

What you have been doing is to penetrate more into the physical consciousness where the peace and light of the higher consciousness have to be brought down. This often brings at first some relaxation of the intensity of experience, dispersion or recurrence of old movements which had been pushed out from the other levels, but one must not be discouraged by that. The remedy is to be more insistent on bringing down the higher forces (peace etc.) into this field.

*

This negation [of *deeper peace etc.*] is the very nature of the physical resistance and the physical resistance is the whole base of the denial of the Divine in the world. All in the physical is persistent, obstinate, with a massive force of negation and inertia — if it were not so, sadhana would be extremely cursory. You have to face this character of the physical resistance and conquer it however often it may rise. It is the price of the transformation of the earth-consciousness.

*

The Transformation of the Physical

It is the nature of the physical mind to be obstinate. Physical nature exists by constant repetition of the same thing — only a constant presentation of different forms of itself. This obstinate recurrence is therefore part of its nature when it is in activity; otherwise it remains in a dull inertia. When therefore we want to get rid of the old movements of physical nature, they resist by this kind of obstinate recurrence. One has to be very persistent in rejection to get rid of it.

There are two aspects of physical Nature as of all Nature — the individual and the universal. All things come into one from the universal Nature — but the individual physical keeps some of them and rejects others, and to those it keeps it gives a personal form. So these things can be said to be both inside it and coming outside from within or created by it because it gives a special form and also outside and coming in from outside. But when one wants to get rid of them, one first throws out all that is within into the surrounding Nature — from there the universal Nature tries to bring them back or bring in new and similar things of its own to replace them. One has then constantly to reject this invasion. By constant rejection, the force of recurrence finally dwindles and the individual becomes free and able to bring the higher consciousness and its movements into the physical being.

*

The difference [*between the physical consciousness of those who are doing sadhana and those who are not*] lies in the fact that those who are doing sadhana live on the physical plane in order to transform it — under the pressure of a Force created by the sadhana which urges towards that and must continue till it is achieved. Those who do not do sadhana live on the physical plane not to transform it but to continue it as it is — there is no such Force or pressure or necessity or urge. Those who are not sadhaks but have their minds turned to the higher consciousness are preparing for sadhana and will one day do it — whatever that sadhana may be.

The prevalence of the physical difficulties when one comes

down into the physical is the same phenomenon as the prevalence of the vital difficulties when one is on the vital plane. Transformation implies facing the difficulties and changing or overcoming what arises in each part of the being so that that part may respond to what is higher, but the full change of the whole can only come by the ascent to the Above and the descent from Above. The first step of that (usually though not always) is the realisation of the Self above and the full descent of the higher peace into all the being down to the most physical.

*

For your sadhana it is necessary first to establish the entire openness of the physical being and stabilise in it the descent of calm, strength, purity and joy with the feeling of the presence and working of the Mother's Force in you. It is only on that assured basis that one can become an entirely effective instrument for the work. Once that is done, there is still the dynamic transformation of the instrumental being to achieve and that depends on a descent of a higher and higher power of consciousness into the mind, vital and body — by "higher" being meant nearer and nearer to the supramental Light and Force. But that can only be done on the basis of which I have spoken and with the psychic being constantly in front and acting as an intermediary between the instrumental mind, vital and body and these higher planes of Being. So this basic stabilisation must first be completed.

*

It [*purification of the physical nature*] is rather a necessity of the work itself for the supramental descent. The effect in a particular person will still depend on the person himself though there will be much greater and quicker possibilities than now.

*

It is not possible to bring down the whole power or experience of a higher plane into the physical consciousness; it is only an influence that comes down to help in the transformation. When the transformation has taken place, the physical will be more capable.

Coming Down into the Physical

I have said that it [*your consciousness*] has come down into direct contact with the external physical nature which is always full of the lower movements and when that happens you see them as they are when they are not under the control of the mind and psychic. Everybody has to come into this direct contact — otherwise there can be no transformation of this part of the being.

*

It is always the effect of the physical consciousness being uppermost (so long as it is not entirely changed) that one feels like this — like an ordinary man or worse, altogether in the outer consciousness, the inner consciousness veiled, the action of Yoga power apparently suspended. This happens in the earlier stages also, but it is not quite complete usually then because something of the mind and vital is active in the physical still or, even if the interruption of sadhana is complete, it does not last long and so one does not so much notice it. But when from the mental and vital stage of the Yoga one comes down into the physical, this condition which is native to the physical consciousness fully manifests and is persistent for long periods. It happens because one has to come down and deal with this part directly by entering into it, — for if that is not done, there can be no complete change of the nature. What has to be done is to understand that it is a stage and to persist in the faith that it will be overcome. If this is done, then it will be easier for the Force, working behind the veil at first, then in front to bring out the Yoga consciousness into this outer physical shell and make it luminous and responsive. If one keeps steadily the faith and quietude, then this can be more quickly done — if the faith gets eclipsed or the quietude disturbed by the long difficulty, then it takes longer but even then it will be done; for, though not felt, the Force is there at work. It can only be prevented if one breaks away or throws up the sadhana, because one becomes too impatient of the difficulty to go through with it. That is the one thing that should never be done.

*

After receiving your account of your present condition which I understand perfectly well, my advice to you remains the same, to stick on and still stick on persistently until the dawn comes, which it surely will if you resist the temptation to run away into some outer darkness which it would have much more difficulty in reaching. The details you give do not at all convince me that X was right in thinking that your sadhana was not at all in the line of my Yoga or that you are right in concluding that you are not meant for this line. On the contrary, these are things which come almost inevitably in one degree or another at a certain critical stage through which almost everyone has to pass and which usually lasts for an uncomfortably long time but which need not be at all conclusive or definitive. Usually, if one persists, it is the period of darkest night before the dawn which comes to every or almost every spiritual aspirant. It is due to a plunge one has to take into the sheer physical consciousness unsupported by any true mental light or by any vital joy in life, for these usually withdraw behind the veil, though they are not, as they seem to be, permanently lost. It is a period when doubt, denial, dryness, greyness and all kindred things come up with a great force and often reign completely for a time. It is after this stage has been successfully crossed that the true light begins to come, the light which is not of the mind but of the spirit. The spiritual light no doubt comes to some to a certain extent, and to a few to a considerable extent, in the earlier stages, though that is not the case with all — for some have to wait till they can clear out the obstructing stuff in the mind, vital and physical consciousness, and until then they get only a touch now and then. But even at the best this earlier spiritual light is never complete until the darkness of the physical consciousness has been faced and overcome. It is not by one's own fault that one falls into this state, it can come when one is trying one's best to advance. It does not really indicate any radical disability in the nature but certainly it is a hard ordeal and one has to stick very firmly to pass through it. It is difficult to explain these things because the psychological necessity is difficult for the ordinary human reason to understand or to accept. I will try to have a shot at it, but it may take some days.[1] Meanwhile, as you have asked what is my advice I send you this brief answer.

*

The greater difficulty [*in freeing oneself from vital desire*] is because the sadhana is now taking place directly on the physical plane, where the force of a habit or habitual movement once formed is very great. When the sadhana is taking place on the mental or vital plane, it is more easy to control or change, because the mind and vital are more plastic than the physical. But on the other hand if something is definitely gained on the physical plane, there is a more lasting and complete fulfilment than when it is on the mental or vital alone.

*

The resistance is becoming more of a physical character. That is to be expected, for it is the ordinary course that it is pushed down from the vital into the physical — moreover in the general sadhana now it is in the material and subconscient that the struggle is mainly going on. The part above the neck, like the neck itself, belongs to the externalising mind or physical mental. Your difficulties are likely to cease only when you bring down the peace and wideness into the whole body or at any rate feel its effects there. If the whole mind admits the higher consciousness, that will be a definite step towards this.

*

In dealing with the physical and subconscient the working is always slower than when it acts on the mind and vital because

---

[1] *No subsequent letter of explanation has been found.* — Ed.

the resistance of physical stuff is always heavier and less intelligent and adaptable; but as a compensation the work done in the being by this slower movement is in the end more complete, solid and durable.

*

You feel as you do only because you are largely identified with the part that has to undergo change and so you feel the difficulty, even the impossibility of changing. But although the difficulty is there, the impossibility does not exist. Even this identification may be helpful, for so the change can be radical by a direct action in the part itself, instead of an indirect influence upon it through the mind or higher vital. Rest and restore your physical forces, open so that the Mother's Force may fully work on you, the trouble pass away and a new and stronger movement commence.

The Bringing of Realisation into the Physical

Yes, certainly, that is what I am insisting on — the bringing of realisation into this inert physical part which has made itself prominent. When any part of the being becomes prominent like this showing all its defects and limitations — here inertia or incapacity (*apravṛtti*), obscurity or forgetfulness (*aprakāśa*), it is in order to get set right, — it has come up for a first or preliminary transformation. Peace and light in the mind, love and sympathy in the heart, calm and power in the vital, a settled receptivity and response (*prakāśa*, *pravṛtti*) in the physical are the necessary change.

*

When I explained [*in the preceding letter*] about the physical inertia, I meant that it was this which had been preventing the elimination of the old movements all along and enabled them to return when they had been pushed out — for it is in the material half-conscious or subconscient that there is the bedrock of the resistance. When this comes up and shows itself in its separate existence, not sustained by the mind and vital, acting by the power of its own inertia and not covered by the sanction of the mind or the vital, only repeating the old movements by force of old habit — it is then possible to meet the resistance at its root instead of cutting off the flowers and fruits and branches when they appear.

It is precisely this lothness to do anything that must be got rid of — for it is simply an acquiescence in the force of the inertia. If you can do nothing else, the old methods of violence to yourself etc. will obviously be unfruitful — you should call on the Divine Peace and Force to descend and deal with it and open yourself to the action. If this obstructing physical is made to admit and respond to that, then the key of the solution will be there.

*

The realisation in the mind of the One brings or ought to bring a certain freedom in the mind, but it is possible for the vital and the body under its impulse to go on having the ordinary movements — for they depend only partially on the mind for their action. They can even carry it away, *haranti prasabhaṁ manaḥ*, or they can act in spite of the mind's reasoning and disapprobation. "I see the better and approve it, I follow the worse" as the Roman poet puts it — in the language of the Gita, *anicchannapi balād iva niyojitaḥ*. It is necessary therefore that the realisation with its peace and force of purity should come down concretely into the vital and physical itself so that when the vital movements try to rise they are met by it and unable to remain because of its automatic pressure.

The Physical Sadhana

The physical sadhana is to bring down the higher light and power and peace and Ananda into the body consciousness, to get rid of the inertia of the physical, the doubts, limitations, external tendency of the physical mind, the defective energies of the vital physical (nerves) and bring in instead the true consciousness there so that the physical may be a perfect instrument for the Divine Will. The food and care for the body is only to get it into good condition, afterwards it would not be necessary to attend to such things.

*

I understand that you have arrived at a prolonged lull or period of emptiness in your sadhana. This often happens especially when one is thrown out into the physical and external consciousness. The nervous and physical parts then become prominent and seem to become the standard of the being with that disappearance of the Yoga consciousness and the sensitiveness to small and outward things which you describe. A stage like this however may very well be an interval before a fresh progress. What you have to do is to insist on making time for meditation — at any time of the day when you are least likely to be disturbed — and through the meditation getting back the touch. There may be some difficulty because the physical consciousness is uppermost, but a persistent aspiration will bring it back. When once you again feel the connection reestablished between the inner being and the outer, call down the peace and light and power into the latter so as to build up a basis for a constant consciousness in the most external mind and being which will accompany you in work and action as much as in meditation and solitude.

*

Don't get disturbed. Remain quiet and let the Force work.

It is the most physical consciousness of which you have become aware; it is like that in almost everyone: when one gets fully or exclusively into it, one feels it to be like that of an animal, either obscure and restless or inert and stupid and in either condition not open to the Divine. It is only by bringing the Force and higher consciousness into it that it can fundamentally alter. When these things show themselves, do not be upset by their emergence, but understand that they are there to be changed.

Here as elsewhere, quiet is the first thing needed, to keep the consciousness quiet, not allow it to get agitated and in turmoil.

Then in the quiet to call for the Force to clear up all this obscurity and change it.

*

It is of course the physical consciousness that always came in with this ignorance, and the physical consciousness *is* stupid and obscure — even in men whose thinking minds are wise or at least intelligent. It is only by the Light from above that it can be illumined. It is always in the Peace and Power, which bring more and more that light, that you must take refuge.

*

"At the mercy of the external sounds and external bodily sensations", "no control to drop the ordinary consciousness at will", "the whole tendency of the being away from Yoga" — all that is unmistakably applicable to the physical mind and the physical consciousness when they isolate themselves, as it were, and take up the whole front, pushing the rest into the background. When a part of the being is brought forward to be worked upon for change, this kind of all-occupying emergence, the dominant activity of that part as if it alone existed, very usually happens — and unfortunately it is always what has to be changed, the undesirable conditions, the difficulties of that part which rise first and obstinately hold the field and recur. In the physical it is inertia, obscurity, inability that come up and the obstinacy of these things. The only thing to do in this unpleasant phase is to be more obstinate than the physical inertia and to persist in a fixed endeavour — steady persistency without any restless struggle — to get a wide and permanent opening made even in this solid rock of obstruction.

*

It is just in the physical consciousness that it is difficult to keep the fire burning — the physical can easily follow a constant routine, but not easily maintain a constant living endeavour. Nevertheless it can after a time be made ready to do so. All help will be given you.

*

You have entirely put yourself out in the external physical consciousness which is refusing to open itself on the plea of inability and by saying that all spiritual and inner things are unreal, only what is outward is real. That is what it always does, if you listen to it. But the plea of inability is untrue — and the other is also untrue. The inner, the spiritual, is perfectly true and real to you when you open yourself to it — as real as the physical or outward.

*

When you get the touch, concentrate on opening to it; do not accept the opposite suggestions of the physical consciousness. The whole difficulty comes from your identifying yourself with your external, physical consciousness which is only a small outward part of your self. You have to learn to live in the rest of your being, more real, more inward which is open to the Truth; you will then feel your physical consciousness as something external which can be worked upon through the true consciousness and changed by the Force.

*

It is very good that all should have gone like that and the true consciousness affirmed its control in the physical. These things are indeed attacks intended to prevent the control being established in the physical being as it was in the inner parts. Wherever the physical consciousness opens, the Force can sweep out all that could trouble. Sometimes it takes a little time to overcome the resistance, but finally all disappears before it.

*

Persevere quietly and let nothing discourage you. If the quietness and cheerfulness are not constant yet, that is to be expected; it is always like that at first when there is the working in the physical consciousness and its obstructions. If you persevere, they will become more and more frequent and last for a longer time, until you have a basis of peace and happiness and whatever disturbances come on the surface will no longer be able to penetrate or shake this basis or even cover it over except perhaps for a moment.

The constant changing of the mood is also common enough because the physical vital is being worked upon at the same time and this changeability is a character of the physical-vital nature. Let not that discourage you, — as soon as the basis is more fixed this will diminish and the vital become more settled and even.

*

The physical consciousness has to become balanced, filled with the light and force from above, conscious and responsive. That cannot be done in a day — so go on steadily and dismiss both discouragement and impatience.

*

It [*the use of violence to change the physical*] was done by some people, but I don't believe in its usefulness. No doubt the physical is an obstinate obstacle, but it must be enlightened, persuaded, pressed even to change, but not oppressed or violently driven. People use violence with the mind, vital, body because they are in a hurry, but my own observation has always been that it leads to more reactions and hindrances and not to a genuinely sound advance.

Chapter Two

Levels of the Physical Being

The Physical Consciousness

A certain inertia, tendency to sleep, indolence, unwillingness or inability to be strong for work or spiritual effort for long at a time, is in the nature of the human physical consciousness. When one goes down into the physical for its change (that has been the general condition here for a long time), this tends to increase. Even sometimes when the pressure of the sadhana on the physical increases or when one has to go much inside, this temporarily increases — the body either needing more rest or turning the inward movement into a tendency to sleep or be at rest. You need not, however, be anxious about that. After a time this rights itself; the physical consciousness gets the true peace and calm in the cells and feels at rest even in full work or in the most concentrated condition and this tendency of inertia goes out of the nature.

*

There are many [*defects of the physical consciousness*] — but mainly obscurity, inertia, tamas, a passive acceptance of the play of wrong forces, inability to change, attachment to habits, lack of plasticity, forgetfulness, loss of experiences or realisations gained, unwillingness to accept the Light or to follow it, incapacity (through tamas or through attachment or through passive reaction to accustomed forces) to do what it admits to be the Right and the Best.

*

There is always some tendency to looseness, forgetfulness and inattention in the physical consciousness. One has to be very vigilant and careful to prevent this tendency having its way.

*

These are the usual suggestions of the Ignorance in the physical consciousness — everybody in that condition says the same thing, "All the rest are so nicely off, I only am not progressing and there is no hope for me" etc. These things should not be listened to at all.

*

It is an inertia of the physical consciousness which allows these desires to come and does not react against the suggestions; it is that also which responds to the pains and suggestion of illness. But you must not accept the suggestion that you *cannot* react and be free, — the physical consciousness itself cannot as yet, but the will can if it is called on to act and made accustomed to act always. Not the struggling will, but a quiet will insisting on the quietude of the mind and vital and insisting on the rejection of these adverse things. That would soon prove sufficient to hold the ground for the Peace and Force to act and they would do the rest.

*

It is no doubt as you say,[1] but that is always the difficulty of the physical consciousness until it has been enlightened from within. It is the peace you feel — the peace that is taking little by little hold of the inner being — that has to deepen and strengthen itself till it can take hold of the physical also. When it can do that, the externalised physical consciousness will feel it no longer alien to itself. The Peace will enable the Force and Light to enter also into the physical and the true understanding will come there too and remove the sense of distance and difference. That is how the Yoga force always works in principle — but the more the quietude, the more rapidly and surely it will work.

*

It is the last reaction of the physical consciousness [*feeling dull,*

---

[1] *The correspondent wrote that although she wanted to get rid of her desires, confusions and wrong movements, the outward, physical part of her being wanted to hold on to them. — Ed.*

weak, confused] that must be got rid of — in its place there must be at such times peace constant so that you do not get restless or feel troubled. It is not possible to be always in the best condition of consciousness or sadhana — there are times when the physical needs to be merely quiet, the aspiration becomes quiescent, there is no sense of the Divine, no forward movement. Properly taken, these periods become periods of rest and assimilation but for that the consciousness must learn to be quiet, not to be troubled or thrown back into a bad or uneasy condition — it must remain at repose until the movement is resumed in a quiet peace. Or at least the greater part of the consciousness must feel like that — not even in these periods dull, weak or confused. This feeling seems to be gaining on you, but the physical consciousness or at least a part of it is still uneasy during such intervals. It must go on receiving more of the light and peace till this can no longer happen.

*

There comes for many a stage in the opening of the consciousness when the entrance of any wrong thought or feeling or movement brings an ache or uneasiness or other sign in the body — this is because these movements are becoming foreign to the consciousness, even the physical, and so produce a discomfort.

*

Sometimes when these forces cannot have a success in attacking the vital directly because the psychic rejects the attack, they try to fall on the physical consciousness and the body (the emptiness, headache, disturbance in the chest were that) so as to weaken, if possible, the resistance to their pressure. At such times you must be as quiet as possible and call the Mother. After a time the attacks will not come or will not last.

*

The legs, knees, feet — these indicate the physical consciousness — it was therefore into the obscure layers of the physical consciousness that you went down.

The Mental Physical and the Vital Physical

And how is it possible to perfect the mind and vital unless the physical is prepared? — for there is such a thing as the mental and vital physical, and mind and vital cannot be said to be perfectly prepared until these are ready.

*

The small things go with difficulty because they belong to the vital physical and the things of the physical consciousness are obstinate owing to the great subjection of the physical to the force of habit. All the same the Will can act on them so as to dismiss them either rapidly or by a slow pressure.

*

There is always the conflict between the consciousness that is coming into you and the ignorant consciousness that was there before. The new consciousness is gaining ground always but still against much resistance especially in the vital physical (which is indicated in the stomach attacks). But there is only one way to go and that is to insist always on the Power and Peace which are more and more felt to be always there and more and more dissociate yourself from the other condition. It is on that basis that the right understanding can come.

*

It is something in the vital part of the physical consciousness which has not yet understood — it feels the pressure to change, yet it is drawn outward to people or things in the old way, but is dissatisfied because the growth of the new consciousness behind prevents it taking pleasure in them, so that it remains restless, not understanding anything. What it has got to learn is that it must fall quiet and open to a new consciousness from above and within. This part of the being is obscure, — not sufficiently mentalised to understand things, it acts from instinct, impulse and habit only. When its old instincts, impulses and habits are checked, it does not know what to do or what is demanded of it. But after a certain amount of pressure from the mind and will it can be got to consent to a change of its ways.

The other thing, the habit of concentrating on one thing and forgetting everything else, is a turn of the vital — it is a faculty that has a value because it can give great intensity to the nature and to any endeavour made by the nature. Only it has to be turned in the right direction and used by the mind and the psychic being for a whole-hearted concentration and devotion to the Mother.

*

The attack comes evidently always on the vital physical and the physical — it is these parts that have to be cleared entirely — desires and dissatisfactions in the vital physical and the pain, unconsciousness and dullness in the physical. Do not yield to the idea of being helpless to repel or ignore when they come — even the pains can be rejected — you have to get the knack of bringing down the Force at once to drive them out.

*

The physical disturbance and weakness are simply the attack falling back on the physical system from the vital and producing there the corresponding movements — all of a nervous character — nervous restlessness, nervous pain and palpitation and trouble, nervous weakness of the body.

Take the lesson from what has happened, but now put away these thoughts and open yourself quietly to recover the true movement.

*

It [*the coming of disturbances*] is not the result of any pressure from above. If there were nothing coming from above, there would be no peace and clarity and the disturbances would still come and come more often.

The cravings once belonged to the vital physical, but when there is a sufficient force of peace in the being, then they go out and the vital physical is free and under the influence of the quietude. The forces of disturbance do not belong any longer to the personality, but although they have gone out, they wait in the atmosphere and, if they get a chance, try to come back and resume hold of the exterior being so as either to break or, if they can no longer do that, cover up the inner peace. Because the physical vital has been accustomed to respond to them for a time willingly, now unwillingly, they are still able to make it answer to their vibrations. The peace and clarity must acquire such a force that they will remain even if these forces come back — then there will be the phenomenon of the inner peace remaining undisturbed in the inner being even while the outer is superficially disturbed. This is a well-marked stage in the progress. Afterwards a force can be brought down strong enough to fill the outer being also with so strong a peace and clarity that the disturbances can no longer enter there. One may feel them still sometimes in the atmosphere but is no longer touched by them at all.

*

As for the vital physical readmitting the forces of disturbance, it is not always because it wants; it may happen also because in spite of itself certain impacts or suggestions revive the old vibrations and the habit of responding has been so strong in it that it responds *in spite of itself*, and for a time it is unable to recover its balance. This happens in all parts of the being, but it is especially true of the physical parts — physical mind yielding to habitual thoughts, physical vital yielding to habitual desires and impulsions etc., body yielding to habitual sensations, illnesses etc. etc. Often sadhaks write, "But I don't want these things, even my vital and body feel uncomfortable and wish them away, then why do they come?" It is because of this long established habit of response which is too strong for the yet too quiescent and passive will (if it can be called will) of rejection in the part affected. It is especially true of the physical parts because a passive quiescence, a habit of being driven by forces is their very nature, unless they are controlled from above or made to share in the idea and will of the higher parts.

The Material Consciousness

I do not see why you doubt the fulfilment in your material consciousness. If there is faith, quietude, openness in the rest of the being, the material is bound to open also. Tamas, inertia, ignorance, stupidity, littleness, obstruction to the true movement are universal characteristics of the material consciousness, so long as it is not enlightened, regenerated and transformed from above, — they are not peculiar to yours. Therefore, there is here no sufficient reason or justification for the doubt you describe.

When the Supramental comes down fully into the material consciousness, it will create the right conditions there. The oneness will be created, the constant presence and sense of contact will be felt in the material and there will be all the actual physical contact that is needed. The sadness you speak of is not psychic — for "painful longing" belongs to the vital, not to the psychic. The psychic never feels a sadness from disappointed desire, because that is not in its nature; the sorrow it sometimes feels is when it sees the Divine rejected or the mental, vital, physical in man or in nature turning away from the Truth to follow perversion, darkness or ignorance. However, with the reign of the Supramental even the vital external nature is bound to change and therefore there will be no chance of any feelings of this character.

*

You should not allow yourself to be discouraged by any persistence of the movements of the lower nature. There are some that tend always to persist and return until the whole physical nature is changed by the transformation of the most material consciousness; till then their pressure recurs — sometimes with a revival of their force, sometimes more dully — as a mechanical habit. Take from them all life-power by refusing any mental or vital assent; then the mechanical habit will become powerless to influence the thoughts and acts and will finally cease.

The Body Consciousness

The sense of being only the body belongs to the physical consciousness while the confusion came from the vital. The confusion must disappear because it makes a turmoil in the consciousness and stands in the way of the Force acting on the surface. The obstacle of the body consciousness is tedious, but it does not prevent the Force from growing and can be worn out by the action of the Force in time. It is a question of the Force, Peace, Light entering *into* the body and giving it the sense of not being only a body but the receptacle of a higher consciousness.

*

It is indeed the body consciousness that is still offering difficulties — but when the restlessness and confusion come, you must immediately offer it up and call for the opening of the part that resists. In this way it is possible to establish a condition in which as soon as the difficulty is there, the counteracting Force also comes. Then no long continued difficulty will be possible.

*

The flesh has a consciousness as well as the mind — all the consciousness is connected together so if the mind is freed, there is no reason why there should not be an effect on the physical also.

The Body

Man is not a body alone — the body is only a small part of his being.

*

One should not attach too much importance to the life of the body. The body is only an incident in the progress of the soul. Evolution of the soul is the objective of Karmic existence. When one has realised the soul, knowledge and enlightenment come and all the problems are solved. But before that, one should try to get peace, calm and light.

*

The body is always the most difficult part of the being because of its obscurity much more than of any bad will in it. But it could respond more and more as the Light grows.

*

The body itself must become more conscious so that it will make the right movements and avoid the wrong ones.

*

I mean [*by "the coming of consciousness into the body"*] the higher consciousness. The consciousness that is always there in the body is tamasic and obscure and the greater part of it is subconscient. If it opens then there will be an increasing union with the higher consciousness and it will be able to share the experiences and the developments in the mind and vital.

*

It depends on whether it [*the body*] is in tune with the vital or not. The nature of the body is tamasic — it is the vital which makes it move and uses it as an instrument: If the vital is enlightened then the Divine Force can act through it on the body.

*

It [*how the body receives the higher dynamism*] depends on the condition of the body or rather of the physical and the most material consciousness. In one condition it is tamasic, inert, unopen and cannot bear or cannot receive or cannot contain the force; in another rajas predominates and tries to seize on the dynamism, but wastes and spills and loses it; in another there is receptivity, harmony, balance and the result is a harmonious action without strain or effort.

*

I suppose the heat and thirst may be due to some struggle in the body, not altogether physical. I think it must be some contrary pressure on the body which the body is trying to throw off. I do not consider your condition of dissatisfaction and difficulties as inner but as outer. It is an outer mass of old movements pressing on the physical consciousness and trying to keep its place by memory and recurrent habit. The physical consciousness has to push it out more and more till it is no longer felt as within it, but seen for what it really is, an outer Nature of the ignorance which had usurped the consciousness and prevented the psychic being from manifesting.

*

The physical troubles that belong to the constitution of the body are usually the last things to disappear. When the true consciousness fixes itself in the body as elsewhere, then they can be reduced and dispelled by the same process as that which removes the wrong habits of the mind and vital.

Care for the Body

No need to despise the physical being — it is part of the intended manifestation.

*

The body is meant to be an instrument of the Divine and a means of sadhana and a temple for the Mother's presence. It has to be purified, not despised and cast away — without it there can be no manifestation here.

*

To care too much for the body is bad in sadhana, but to neglect it or overstrain it is also bad — for it is a necessary instrument and must be kept in good condition.

Weakness of the Body

You must keep your body in good condition. It is the necessary instrument and channel and if it gets weak or unfit, that hampers the expression or dynamism of the mind and the spirit.

*

The weakness of the body has to be cured, not disregarded. It can only be cured by bringing in strength from above, not by *merely* forcing the body.

*

If your body is aching after the work, it may be that you are doing too much for your physical strength and straining the body. When you work, the Force comes down in you, takes the form of vital energy and supports your body so that it does not *at the time* feel the strain; but when you stop, the body goes back to its normal condition and feels the effects — it has not yet been sufficiently opened to keep the Force. You must see whether this effect (of pain) continues; if it passes away, it is all right; otherwise you must take care and not overstrain yourself by doing too much.

*

Overstraining [*in work*] only increases the inertia — the mental and vital will may force the body, but the body feels more and more strained and finally asserts itself. It is only if the body itself feels a will and force to work that one can do that.

*

The first rule [*for overcoming weakness of the body*] is — there must be sufficient sleep and rest, not in excess but not too little.

The body must be trained to work, but not strained beyond its utmost capacity.

The outer means without the inner is not effective. Up to a certain point by a *progressive* training the body may be made more capable of work. But the important thing is to bring down the force for work and the rasa of work in the body. The body will then do what is asked of it without grudging or feeling fatigue.

Even so, even when the force and rasa are there, one must keep one's sense of measure.

Work is a means of self-dedication to the Divine, but it must be done with the necessary inner consciousness in which the lower vital and physical must also share.

A lazy body is certainly not a proper instrument for Yoga, it must stop being lazy. But a fatigued and unwilling body also cannot receive properly or be a good instrument. The proper thing is to avoid either extreme.

*

A strong mind and body and life-force are needed in the sadhana. Especially steps should be taken to throw out tamas and bring strength and force into the frame of the nature.

Forgetfulness of the Body

It [*living in the mind or the vital*] is more, I think, forgetting the body than non-identification with it. In an intense mentalisation or an intense vital activity the body takes a second place and becomes more outward and the same may happen to a certain extent more constantly to a man who lives in his mind or his vital and is identified more closely with that. But still it is the mental in the body, the vital in the body. There is no release, no getting entirely separate as in the spiritual liberation.

*

Yes, it is not possible for the human mind to live entirely in itself to such a degree as to ignore the body altogether — a real or complete liberation or non-identification is not possible without the spiritual release. All that is possible to the mind is a constant absorption in itself and an ignoring or forgetfulness as much as possible of the body. That one finds often in people who live a retired mental life (scholars, thinkers etc.) without the need to trouble themselves about their livelihood, family etc.

The Physical and the Mind

The physical consciousness has its own reactions — separate from those of the mind.

*

No, it is not necessary to lose the mental control; it is best to replace it gradually by the psychic or spiritual. But it happens to many that they lose it before the other is ready or while it is still imperfect and then the Nature-forces act in the physical consciousness which is sometimes held by the descending Peace or Power from above, sometimes by the ordinary Nature-forces. This alternation happens at one stage at least to almost everybody until the higher state prevails.

This over-sensitive brooding on past blows to the vital is an unhealthy sensitiveness. What is past ought not to have a hold like that but be allowed to fade out.

*

Probably in '33 you were doing more tapasya and putting a strong control on yourself? At any rate that was the state at one time. Afterwards when you came down from the mental-vital level, you let yourself go for a time, removing much of the control, hence now you find a difficulty in reestablishing it, — due to the habit of automatic repetition which is a characteristic of the physical nature. You have now to get the control in a different way by the reestablishment of the peace and building the higher consciousness upon it, the spiritual control replacing that of mental tapasya.

The Physical and the Vital

The physical depends on the vital at every step — it could not do anything without the help of the vital — so it is quite natural that it should receive its suggestions.

*

The physical world is only a last field in which not only the physical forces but those of other worlds also throw themselves for realisation. Whatever happens here has already been prepared or foreshadowed in the vital; it does not happen exactly as represented in the vital, but with a change suitable for the material world.

The Physical and the Psychic

All that is very good — it is the psychic condition that is increasing. The peace and spontaneous knowledge are in the psychic being and from there they spread to mind and vital and physical. It is in the outer physical consciousness that the difficulty still tries to persist and brings the restlessness sometimes into the physical mind, sometimes into the nerves, sometimes in the shape of bodily trouble into the body. But all these things can and must go. Even the illnesses can go entirely with the growth of peace and power in the nerves and physical cells — stomach pains, weakness of the eyes and everything else.

*

The narrowness etc. of which you complain are normal to the physical nature. It is the same thing acting in a different way which makes X rebellious to advice and full of irritation and bad temper when her mistakes are shown to her. The physical nature of almost everybody is like that, intolerant, easily irritated, lacking in patience when dealing with others. But this physical nature can be replaced and changed by the psychic nature and you have had the experience of what this psychic nature is and how it acts. You know therefore what change has to come in you and you know also that this new nature is already there in you preparing to come out. Have the faith therefore that it is sure to come — and when the physical comes and covers with the old movements try to remember that and remind the physical mind that it is only by this change in yourself and all that things can change. What is needed now is all should make this psychic change their main object, each for himself. If some develop it, then it will spread more rapidly among the rest. It is so only that the present state of the physical consciousness in the Asram full of ego and strife can become what it should be.

*

What has happened is that the psychic in you which had formerly been constantly in action in the mind and vital was for a time clouded or covered over by the ignorance of the physical consciousness. It is the psychic that connected you with the Mother and turned all the movements of your being towards her or drew them from her or made them united with and dependent on her. It had so done with all your mental and vital being and its movements and it had guarded you against all wrong mental and vital suggestions and attacks, showing you what was true and what was false. Now it is this psychic being which has manifested again in your physical consciousness also. You have only to live in that and your whole being will be turned towards the Mother, remain in union with her and be protected from doubt and error and false suggestion — and you can once more progress as you did before towards the full realisation of the sadhana.

*

The habit of return of these feelings belongs to the physical consciousness and in his physical consciousness the human being is always weak and unable to get rid of or resist its habitual movements. There are three things that help him to do so (apart from his mental will which is not always strong enough to do it). There is first the psychic being; for a few days your psychic was extremely active and pushing these movements away whenever they tried to come or throwing them out soon when they got in. This activity of the psychic will return and eventually come down into the physical consciousness itself; then there will be very little difficulty. The second is the inner consciousness always awake. At present that is difficult, because to keep the inner consciousness awake at all times can only come by a deepening of yourself so that the veil between the outer and inner which lifts only in concentration may cease to exist even when one is in the ordinary unconcentrated condition. It is for this deepening that the strong tendency to go inside comes upon you. Lastly, the Mother's force always there and receiving also a response at once from the physical consciousness. These three things together can do anything. It takes time to make them all three constantly active together, but that is sure to come and with them these inner difficulties will disappear.

*

You cannot so long as you have a body live without the physical consciousness, but you can live more centrally in the psychic and other parts and by them transform the physical.

The Ascent of the Being

The being is here on the physical plane although in touch with the mental and vital. The being that is the individual consciousness has to ascend and become conscious of all the planes (vital, mental and those above the mental) until it reaches the Divine Oneness which is above all the planes and from which they emerge.

Chapter Three
Difficulties of the Physical Nature

The Real Difficulty

It is no doubt quite true that if you could settle the true relation [*with the Mother*] in the psychic centre — the inner heart — and all the rest could be under its influence and take part in it, the fundamental difficulty would disappear; and that is what must happen. But the real difficulty is in the physical and external being — and it is this that the physical being is a creature of habit, of formed character, that is to say of a mass of accustomed movements. As your nature has been full of rajasic egoism, not only in this but in many past lives, it is the habit of this rajas and of the accustomed movements connected with it that the physical knows and to them it almost automatically responds; it is these movements that always easily took hold of you, mixed in the sadhana, even in the higher experience sometimes and cherished the revolt against the Mother because always her force was pressing for their removal; it was this pressure that they resented and felt as an absence of love. The mind in you is able to separate itself from these things and recognise (when not too much clouded) their true character, the higher vital also has another aim and aspiration; but the physical, especially the more material parts of it are still responding mechanically to the old movements which are wearing out indeed under the pressure, but are still strong enough to possess a great part of the consciousness when they come. One feels the power, the compulsory force of this mechanical physical response and gets the impression of their inevitability and the impossibility of ever getting free. This automatic compulsory character of the obstruction is the whole power of the difficulty in the material nature.

(1) The first thing is to reject the idea of helplessness, of impossibility of a successful reaction. The central will must

assert itself, not violently in a constant struggle, for that brings reaction, fatigue and inertia, but with a quiet pressure and insistence.

(2) The mind must learn (even the physical external mind) never to say yes to the suggestions and impulsions of the old movement or admit any justification for them however plausible or seemingly "true". However violently they return and insist, they must feel that they will never get any essential assent or sanction. You have almost reached that point, but it must be made more entire.

(3) There must be something in the vital itself that insists on its true aspiration and refuses even the vital consent or any vital pleasure in the wrong movements. If they come, they must feel their own fallen, ignorant, merely material brute character. This point you seem to be reaching, but it must be absolute.

(4) Lastly the physical, the material itself — to insist on the Light, the true will there also. For that, do not indulge the desires, the wrong impulses, the wrong brute feelings that come. Do not admit the idea that you cannot refuse. Throw them out each time they come, out of the body into the environmental consciousness till they can finally be pushed away from there also. For it is these that now separate you in the physical consciousness from the Mother.

Obstruction and Obscuration

The difficulty of the physical nature comes inevitably in the course of the development of the sadhana. Its obstruction, its inertia, its absence of aspiration or movement have to show themselves before they can be got rid of — otherwise it will always remain undetected, hampering even the best sadhana and preventing its completeness. This coming up of the physical nature lasts longer or less according to the circumstances, but there is none who does not go through it. What is necessary is not to get troubled or anxious or impatient, for that only makes it last more, but to put entire confidence in the Mother and quietly persist in faith, patience and steady will for the complete change. It is so that the Mother's force can best work in the being.

*

The sense of helplessness, of impossibility of removal [*of obscurity*] is like the obscurity itself a characteristic of the physical consciousness which is inert and mechanical and accustomed to be moved inertly by whatever forces take hold of it. But this sense of helplessness or impossibility is unreal and not to yield to it, not to accept it, to remove it is quite possible and very necessary for overcoming this physical obstacle which would otherwise greatly delay the progress.

*

It [*the nature of the obstruction of the physical consciousness*] depends on the weak points of the individual and the stage of his progress. In a general way, the obstruction creates an inertia which impedes the working of the higher Powers. In the early stage it can obstruct progress altogether. Afterwards it works to slow it down or else impede it by intervals of stationary inertia. The main difficulty of the physical consciousness is that it is incapable, before it is transformed, of maintaining any tension of tapasya — it wants periods of assimilation, sinking back into the ordinary consciousness to rest, — also there is a constant forgetfulness of what has been done etc.

*

What you felt in your chest was the attempt of the old Ignorance to bring back the vital restlessness, depression, confusion, through the physical attack — for it is on the obscuration of the physical that they now depend for stopping the Light and Force from coming and for obscuring their working and creating disturbance and destroying the quietude. Reject it as you did this time — whenever it tries to come.

*

What you say — especially the idea of being only body — proves that it is now really in the physical obscurity and obstruction that the difficulty lies and the vital resistance even if it recurs is no longer the central obstacle. Do not be discouraged by this physical unconsciousness — keep the quietude and it will be worked out of the system.

*

Do not be discouraged. To go on calling is always the right thing. The struggle to surmount the physical obscurity and inertia is sometimes very tedious and baffling, but if one persists the liberation from it comes — and it will surely come.

*

The physical obstruction is less boisterous [*than the vital resistance*], but I have not found it less obstinate or less troublesome.

Inertia

Inertia is a tremendous force — one of the biggest world-forces.

*

Inertia is the very character of the physical consciousness left to itself — it is accustomed to be passive to forces and to be their instrument or give a mechanical response to them.

*

Inertia is mental, vital, physical, subconscient. Physical inertia can produce mental inertia, mental inertia can produce physical inertia, vital inertia almost always makes the physical lifeless and lustreless and dull, and that is inertia. Vital inertia can also infect the mind, unless the mind is very strong and clear. I have always said that the physical consciousness is the main seat and source of inertia.

*

The hold of inertia always increases when the working comes down into the physical and subconscient. Before that the inertia is overpowered though not eradicated by the action in mind and vital — afterwards it comes up in its natural force and has to be met in its own field.

*

The physical's tendency to inertia is very great; even after the habit of living in the higher consciousness is there, some part may feel the pressure of the inertia — generally the outermost or most material parts. The inertia usually rises up from the subconscient. It does not abolish the higher consciousness in the physical, but dulls its action or else brings it down from a higher to a lower level, e.g. from the intuition to the higher mind or from the higher to the lower ranges of overmind. For some time it resists the completeness of the siddhi. It is only when the most material and the subconscient and the environmental consciousness are quite liberated that this retarding or lowering effect of the primal Inertia is entirely overcome.

*

What you describe — dullness, uneasiness, weakness, feeling old and worn out or ill, are the reactions that come when the inertia of the physical Nature is resisting the Light — the others about sense of feeling, dignity, self-respect (of the ego) are the reactions of the vital. Both must be refused acceptance. There is only one aim to be followed, the increase of the Peace, Light, Power and the growth of a new consciousness in the being. With that new consciousness the true knowledge, understanding, strength, feeling will come, creating harmony instead of revolt and struggle and union with the Divine consciousness and will.

*

Dullness and dispersion are the two sides of the physical's resistance to the peace and concentrated power. They correspond to the inertia and the chaotic activity of physical Nature, that aspect of it which makes some scientists now say that all is brought about by chance and there is no certitude of things but only probability.

*

It [*weakness of will*] is a first result of coming down into the physical consciousness or of the physical consciousness coming up prominently — formerly you were much in the mind and vital. The physical consciousness is full of inertia — it wants not to move but to be moved by whatever forces and that is its habit. This inertia has to be cured by putting it into contact with the right forces from above. That is why I asked you to aspire for the higher wideness, purity and peace, so that that may occupy the physical and the true Force work instead of these invading ideas and impulses.

*

It [*weakness of will*] is due to the influence of the physical consciousness. The physical consciousness or at least the more material parts of it are, as I have told you, in their nature inert — obeying whatever force they are habituated to obey, but not acting on their own initiative. When there is a strong influence of the physical inertia or when one is down in this part of the consciousness the mind feels like the material Nature that action of will is impossible. Mind and vital nature are on the contrary all for will and initiative and so when one is in mind or vital or acting under their influence will feels itself always ready to be active.

*

When the mental will acquiesces in the inertia, becomes passive to it, as we say — then one remains in the passive condition and there is no push against it until it of itself passes away. If the mental will or even the vital will or some dynamic part of the nature remains untouched and can react, then there is the effort to throw it off which may shorten the interim period.

*

Passivity must not lead to inactivity — otherwise it will encourage inertia in the being. It is only an inner passivity to what comes from above that is needed — inert passivity is the wrong kind of passivity.

*

If it is an inert tamasic passivity subject to any influence and unable to react, then it is subjection to Nature. If it is a sattwic passivity of the Witness observing and understanding the movements of Nature, then it is an intermediate condition, often necessary for knowledge. If it is a luminous passivity open to the Divine, shut to all other influences, then it is not subjection to Nature but surrender to the Divine.

*

It is the neutrality of the physical consciousness which says, "I move only when I am moved. Move me who can."

*

The period of no-effort is usually when the physical consciousness is uppermost — for the nature of that is inertia, to be moved by the higher forces or to be moved by the lower forces or any forces, but not to move itself. One must still use one's effort if one can, but the great thing is to be able to call down the Force from above into the physical — otherwise to remain perfectly quiet and, undisturbed, expect its coming.

*

Silence need not bring lassitude; there is all possible strength in silence. But it is possible that in your trend towards silence there is a tendency to draw back the energy from the body consciousness. That would bring physical inertia.

*

If the calm and silence are perfectly established in the physical, then if inertia comes it is itself something quiet and unaggressive, not bringing such disturbances. But to get rid of inertia altogether a strong dynamic calm is needed.

*

If the physical being has felt and assimilated the silence and peace, then inertia ought not to rise up.

*

There is always more chance of inertia at night because of the large part taken by the subconscient in sleep — but, apart from that, there should be a reaction (internal) against the rising of inertia. A quietness in the cells of the body, even a sense of immobility (so that the body seems to be moved rather than to move) is a different thing and easily distinguishable from the inertia. The downflow of peace usually brings much of the static Brahman into the consciousness down to the physical, so that one feels the Upanishadic "unmoving it moves".

*

The inertia itself is not a dynamic principle. The nature of inertia is *apravṛtti* — the action of the mechanical mind is a *pravṛtti*, though a tamasic obscure *pravṛtti*.

*

The rain has the effect of stressing the tamas of the vital physical consciousness and bringing out its greyer notes. Physical tamas by its laxity gives more opportunities for the play of sex etc.

*

Everything [*in the surrounding atmosphere*] can be responded to. Inertia also can spread waves of itself like other things.

Dealing with Inertia and Tamas

From what you describe it looks as if you had come down into the physical consciousness and were feeling the inertia that belongs to it. When that happens, the one way out is to open there so that the light and force may come down into the physical and replace the inertia. We shall try to get that done.

*

When one is covered by the physical inertia one may often feel as if the former experiences had never existed or were not real. But certainly your aspirations and experiences were real enough.

You have to fight out this difficulty until you have got through to the Light.

*

It is, I suppose, the full Inertia that has come upon you. Now you have to get the true Energy down into it.

*

It must be the tamas of the physical that has enveloped the inner consciousness. The one way to get out of it is to remain very quiet inwardly and call down persistently the Force from above.

*

It [*a condition of great inertia*] means that you are in full grips with the subconscient physical. However heavy and tedious the resistance you have to persevere till you have got the Peace, Knowledge, Force down there in place of the inertia.

*

I do not know that I can add anything more to what I have already written. It is only by a more constant dynamic force descending into an unalterable equality and peace that the physical nature's normal tendency can be eradicated.

The normal tendency of the physical nature is to be inert and in its inertia to respond only to the ordinary vital forces, not to the higher forces. If one has a perfect equality and peace then one can be unaffected by the spreading of the inertia and bring down into it gradually or quickly the same peace with a force of the higher consciousness which can alter it. When that is there there can be no longer the difficulty and fluctuations with a preponderance of inertia such as you are now having.

*

The first means [*of changing inertia into peace*] is not to get upset when it comes or when it stays. The second is to detach yourself, not only yourself above but yourself below and not identify. The third is to reject everything that is raised by the inertia and not regard it as your own or accept it at all.

If you can do these things then there will be something in you that remains perfectly quiet even in the pits of inertia. Through that quiet part you can bring down peace, force, even light and knowledge into the inertia itself.

*

When the mind and the vital take hold of the physical and make it an instrument, then there is no inertia. But here the physical consciousness has been dealt with. If it could have received the peace of the self into itself without covering it over with inertia, then it would have been all right. But the vital has intervened somehow with its demand and dissatisfaction, so there has been this obstruction and inability to progress. This thing often happens in the sadhana and one must have the power either to reject it dynamically or else to remain detached until it has exhausted itself. Then the true movement begins again.

*

Inertia or anything else must be felt as separate, not part of one's real self which is one with the Divine.

The Difficulty of Eliminating Inertia and Tamas

You cannot expect a persistent inertia like that to disappear in three days because you make some kind of a beginning of effort to resist it.

*

The inertia of the physical consciousness is always a difficult thing to eliminate — it is that, more even than any vital resistance, which keeps all the movements of the ignorance recurring even when the knowledge is there and the will to change. But this difficulty has to be faced and overcome by an equal perseverance in the will of the sadhak. It is a steady flame that must burn, as steady as the obstruction is obstinate. Do not therefore be discouraged by the persistence of the obstruction of the ignorance.

The persistence of your own will to conquer with the Mother's force supporting it will come to the end of the resistance.

*

I don't know of any effective outward means of getting rid of it [*inertia*]. Some, in hours when they cannot do sadhana, spend the time in other occupations — reading, writing or working — and do not try at all to concentrate. But I suspect what you need is more strength in the body.

*

It is quite true that physical exercise is very necessary to keep off the tamas. I am glad you have begun it and I trust you will keep it up.

Physical tamas in its roots can be removed only by the descent and the transformation, but physical exercise and a regular activity of the body can always prevent a tamasic condition from prevailing in the body.

*

There should be no yielding to the tamas. In spite of it one should always go on quietly and persistently with the sadhana — otherwise one may be overweighed by the inertia of the physical consciousness from which the tamas comes.

*

The physical always is more tamasic than the rest of the being and does not respond easily. Moreover this is a time of struggle between the higher forces and the resisting forces on the material plane, it is therefore a time when intense attacks on that plane are possible. One has to be on one's guard and keep the true Force always round one as a protecting Power.

*

The adverse forces feel that there is something in you that is discountenanced and restive because of the continuance of the inertia and they hope that by pressing more and more they will create a revolt. What is important for you in these circumstances is to make your faith, surrender and samata absolute. That is as great and essential a progress as to have high experiences, etc.

Physical Fatigue

Fatigue like this in the course of the sadhana may come from various reasons.

(1) It may come from receiving more than the physical is ready to assimilate. The cure is then a quiet rest in conscious immobility receiving the forces but not for any other purpose than the recuperation of the strength and energy.

(2) It may be due to the passivity taking the form of inertia — inertia brings the consciousness down towards the ordinary physical level which is soon fatigued and prone to tamas. The cure here is to get back into the true consciousness and rest there, not in inertia.

(3) It may be due to mere overstrain of the body — not giving it enough sleep or repose. The body is the support of the Yoga, but its energy is not inexhaustible and needs to be husbanded; it can be kept up by drawing on the universal vital Force but that reinforcement too has its limits. A certain moderation is needed even in the eagerness for progress — moderation, not indifference or indolence.

*

Exactly. "The body felt fatigue" — that is what I mean by the habit of tamas. The body cannot bear the continuous experience, it feels it as a strain. That is the case with most sadhaks. But in your case the obstacle seems to develop a great intensity when it comes. I have already told you the means of getting rid of it,[1] but it cannot be done in a day because it is a fixed habit of the nature and a fixed habit takes time to remove. But it can be done in not too long a time provided you don't get disturbed when it comes and deal with it firmly and steadily.

---

[1] *See the letter beginning "The first means" on page 396. — Ed.*

Giddiness

For the giddiness, it may be that in concentration you go partly out of your body; then, if you get up and move before the whole consciousness has come back, there is just such a giddiness as you describe. You can observe in future and see whether it is not this that happens. One has to be careful not to move after deep concentration or trance, till there is the full consciousness in the body.

Restlessness

Yes, this is the time when you have to persist till you are quite settled in the inner consciousness and the persistence of the silence and peace is a sign that it is now possible. When one feels this kind of silence, peace and wideness, one may be sure that it is that of the true being, the real self, penetrating into the mind and vital and perhaps also the physical consciousness (if it is complete). The restlessness of the physical is probably due to the peace and silence having touched the physical but not yet penetrated the material or body consciousness. The old restlessness is there in the body struggling to remain, although it cannot invade either mind or vital or even in a general way the physical consciousness as a whole. If the peace descends there, this restlessness will disappear.

*

This is a form that the resistance in the physical easily and often takes — a restlessness of discomfort in the nervous system. When it is in the legs, it means that it is the most material part of the consciousness that is the seat of the trouble. Since it has come up, it ought to be thrown out for good. Probably this part has become sufficiently conscious to feel the greater pressure when Mother comes down, but not enough to be able to receive and assimilate it, hence the uneasiness and resistance. If so, it should go of itself with a little more opening there.

*

Insist always on the quietude, the peace, the consciousness of the force. Persistently reject the restlessness; it comes always because the physical has the habit of receiving it, accepting it as its own real nature. Always deny it, always reject the unrest; gradually if not immediately, the physical will follow your will and change its habit and its notions.

Habitual Movements and Old Habits

It is obviously because of the past impressions and the habitual movement of consciousness connected with them [*that the old reactions continue*]. In the physical being the power of past impressions is very great, because it is by the process of repeated impressions that consciousness was made to manifest in matter — and also by the habitual reactions of consciousness to these impressions, what the psychologists, I suppose, would call behaviour. According to one school consciousness consists only of these things — but that is the usual habit of stretching one detail of Nature to explain the whole of her.

*

It is really, I think, the physical consciousness that is responsible [*for the return of old movements*]. It is forgetful and obscure and repeats always the old habitual movements even when the mind has abandoned them and the vital is quite willing to abandon them. But when the physical receives the old vibration, the lower vital is affected and responds — otherwise it would be merely a vibration and there would be no danger of its being accepted or affecting the conduct.

*

There is nobody who is free from difficulties, even those who seem the most advanced have them, and all have this obstinacy of the habitual movements in the physical consciousness which recur always in spite of the mind's knowledge and do not want to cease or change. It is only by perseverance in aspiration or will that this difficulty can disappear.

*

The opening of the physical and subconscient always takes a long time as it is a thing of habits and constant repetitions of the old movements, obscure and stiff and not plastic, yielding only little by little. The physical mind can be more easily opened and converted than the rest, but the vital physical and material physical are obstinate. The old things are always recurring there without reason and by force of habit. Much of the vital physical and most of the material are in the subconscience or dependent on it. It needs a strong and sustained action to progress there.

*

It [*getting out of the physical rut*] can only be done by being very quiet and opening oneself continually to the force. The physical needs a very *quiet, persistent* and *patient* action, because it is a thing of inertia and habits. The vehemence of force and struggle which suits the vital, does not act so successfully here. It is a steady opening to the Force, a quiet but unwavering insistence on Faith and the Truth that is to be that is in the end effective.

*

It is not that something is always "wrong" within you but that there is still in the subconscient physical being a part that was accustomed to respond very strongly to the vibrations of these thoughts and feelings and can still respond. Usually you would not allow them to come up at all in thought or feeling form, — it would only manifest as a depression of the body or fatigue — or, if it came, you would get over it at once and the vibrations would sink down and disappear. But in the atmosphere heavily surcharged with this invasion of the ordinary consciousness there is a lessened elasticity in the physical consciousness and they were able to rise. This is an exceedingly common experience. One has to detach oneself from these still weak parts and regard them as if a detail in the machinery that has to be set right. In your case also your nervous (vital physical) being is exceedingly conscious and sensitive and anything wrong in the atmosphere affects it more than it would most of the others.

*

It was certainly not because the Mother was different to you from other days or pushed you to a distance, but because you came rather shut up in that part of your physical being which is still shrinking from the Light. It is this part which was always fundamentally responsible for all your bad passages and painful moments even when the direct difficulty was higher up. Its nature is to cling to the old habitual preyogic consciousness and to shut up doors and windows against the help that is offered and lament in the darkness when it has felt itself hurt. This is a thing that everybody must get rid of who wants to progress. Do not go on identifying yourself with this part and calling it yourself. Get back into your inner being and look at this only as a small though obstinate part of the nature that has to change. For apart from its insistence there is no reason why your way should enter into a desert. It should enter into a wideness of liberation — open to the calm and peace and power and light of a consciousness that is wider than the personal and into which the ego can happily disappear.

*

The physical changes slowly always — its nature is habit — so it is only by constant descents [*of calmness, purity, light and strength*] that gradually its substance gets changed and it becomes accustomed to the higher condition.

*

The obstacle or wall of bondage which you feel is simply that of the habits of the ordinary physical consciousness. It is so with all, — the ordinary vital nature with its ego, desire, passions, disturbances, and the ordinary physical nature with its strong habits and outwardness are the chief obstacles that have to be overcome in the nature. When they fall quiet, then it is easier to enter into the true consciousness and unite with the Mother. But they are not accustomed to quietness and as soon as it is felt they want to come out of it and resume their ordinary movements. But this will go when the inner has sufficiently gained on the outer to dominate it. The inner things will grow and come out more and more as you feel the inner faith growing until they are strong enough to rule the outer conduct. The obstacles you feel, the surging up of old things and repetition of restlessness etc. are due to this strength of habit of the physical nature — it lives by repeating always the same things and the same movements to which it has been accustomed in the past. The inner influence as it comes out will more and more create for it new habits of thought and feeling and action and it will then dwell firmly in these and not in the things of the old nature.

*

The habit in the physical is obstinate and seems unchangeable because it always recurs — even when one thinks it is gone. But it is not really unchangeable; if the physical mind detaches itself, stands separate, refuses to accept it, then the habit in the physical begins to lose its force of repetition. Sometimes it goes slowly, sometimes (but this is less frequent) it stops suddenly and recurs no more.

*

Yes; that [*the idea that things cannot change*] also is the fault of the physical consciousness. It is obsessed by the idea that "what is" must be, — that the habit of things cannot be altered. This inevitability it extends not only to what is but to what it merely thinks of as a fact — it lays itself open inertly to every suggestion or possibility that seems to be justified by the habit of things. It is the main obstacle to the material change.

*

As I have said, the response of the physical mind or vital to these forces is a habit. You get upset as soon as they touch either and lose control over yourself. The concentration in the heart is the way to get rid of them, but there must also be a detachment of the consciousness so that it can stand back from the attack and feel separate from it.

*

The response-giving mechanism is like that [*fixed in its ways*] in everybody. It is not by something shocking but by something enlarging and uplifting that it can get out of its rut of habit.

*

Habits are difficult to overcome. If any have to be got rid of, one must be very persistent and vigilant and not yield or let them have their way. It is only when one does that for a very long time that they go.

*

The physical always finds it difficult to take up a new attitude. It is only by training and discipline that it can be made to do so.

*

I meant [*by "training and discipline" of the physical*] that instead of forgetting it must be trained to remember and fix the right movements of consciousness and right states — by repetition, by enforcing again and again, by teaching it to reject persistently and at once the wrong states and wrong movements.

*

In the purification of the physical nature, more even than in the rest, it is not safe to assume that there will be no more attacks of old forces or habits of the nature — till the thing is actually and unmistakably done. One must remain vigilant till there is the full siddhi. For in the physical, habit, memory, mechanical response have an immense power of survival — therefore a return of old vibrations or formations is always possible. Only when there is the full purification and transformation is there the perfect security.

Mechanical Movements

As for the feeling of being driven, compelled, that is quite usual when it is the physical nature that is being dealt with; there is no need to be upset or think it cannot be got over. The physical is the slave of certain forces which create a habit and drive it through the mechanical force of the habit. So long as the mind gives consent, you do not notice the slavery; but if the mind withdraws its consent, then you feel the servitude, you feel a force pushing you in spite of the mind's will. It is very obstinate and repeats itself till the habit — the inner habit revealing itself in the outward act — is broken. It is like a machine which once set in motion repeats the same movement. You need not be alarmed or distressed; a quiet persistent aspiration will bring you to the point where the habit breaks and you are free.

*

What you describe is what the Gita means by the realisation that all action is done by the Prakriti. You feel it mechanical because you are in the physical consciousness where all is mechanism. On the mental and vital plane one can have the same experience, but of the actions as a play of forces. What is lacking at present to you is the other side of the experience, viz. that of the silent Atman or else of the witness Purusha calm, tranquil, free, pure and undisturbed by the play of the Prakriti. It tries to come and you are on the point of going into it, but the tendency of externalisation is still too strong. This tendency took you when you came down into the physical — for it is the nature of the ordinary physical consciousness to precipitate itself into the action of the external personality. You have to get back the power of the internal consciousness, above as Atman, below as Purusha first witness and then master of the nature.

Externalisation

It is inevitable that in the course of the sadhana all sorts of conditions should come through which one is led towards the fullness of the true consciousness. You are now, as are most, in the physical consciousness and its principal difficulty is externalisation and this covering up of the active experience so that one does not know what is going on inside or feels as if nothing were going on. When that happens, it means that something has come up, some part or layer of the physical, which needs to be worked on and, when that has been done, — it may take longer or shorter, — the conscious active inner experience recommences. The muteness in the mind is not a bad thing in itself, it is a favourable condition for the working. Also what you describe as taking place in the head, must be the working of the Force there, — it sometimes gives the impression of a headache. There must be a working in the physical mind to get rid of some difficulty or else to prepare it better for the admission of what comes from above.

It is necessary to have a great patience — so as to go through these conditions and not get apprehensive or restless — and a confidence that all difficulties will be overcome.

*

The push to externalisation must be rejected always — it is a way the physical consciousness has of slipping out of the condition of concentrated sadhana. To keep in the inner consciousness and work from it on the external being till that also is ready is very necessary when the work of change is being specially directed towards the physical consciousness.

*

As for the going within, the pull of the physical consciousness is always outward and even when experiences are going on and the sadhana in full activity, it is the physical resistance that prevents the sadhak from being all the time in the inner consciousness. This resistance disappears altogether only when one reaches an advanced stage of the sadhana. This resistance is now specially active in the Asram because the force is working on the physical and all that is contrary there has to be met and eliminated. But you have before this several times gone inside and felt the touch of the psychic, so that is bound to resume as soon as the physical difficulty is sufficiently cleared away from the consciousness.

Feelings of Incapacity and Discouragement

The thoughts and feelings expressed in your letter are born of the depression and have no truth in themselves apart from it. Your being here does not in the least take up space that could be occupied by "better" sadhaks. For a good sadhak there will always be a place in one way or another. The incapacity which you discover in yourself is simply the resistance of the habitual external and physical nature, which everyone has and which none, however good a sadhak, has yet been able to transform radically, because it is the last thing to change, and its resistance is acute just now because it is against this that the power of the sadhana is now pressing so that the change may come. When this part presents itself it always tries to appear as something unalterable, incapable of change, impervious to the sadhana. But it is not really so and one must not be deceived by this appearance. As for the fear of madness, it is only a nervous impression which you should throw away. It is not vital weakness that leads to such upsettings — it is an obscurity and weakness in the physical mind accompanied by movements of an exaggerated vital nature (e.g. exaggerated spiritual ambition) which are too strong for the mind to bear. That is not your case. You have had long experience of inner peace, wideness, Ananda, an inner life turned towards the Divine and one who has had that ought not to speak of general incapacity, whatever the difficulties of the external nature, — difficulties common in one form or another to all.

*

I have not the slightest doubt that you can do the sadhana if you cleave to it — not certainly on your own unaided strength, for nobody can do that, but by the will of the psychic being in you aided by the Divine Grace. There is a part in the physical and vital consciousness of every human being that has not the will for it, does not feel the capacity for it, distrusts any hope or promise of a spiritual future and is inert and indifferent to any such thing. At one period in the course of the sadhana this rises up and one feels identified with it. That has happened in you now, but along with an attack of ill health and nervous indisposition which has turned this passage through the obscure physical into a dark and intense trouble. With enough sleep and a quieting of the nerves and return of physical energy that ought to disappear and it would be possible to bring the Light and Consciousness down into this obscure part. An intense concentration bringing struggle is not what is needed, but a very quiet attitude of self-opening. Not any effort of sadhana just now, but the recovery of tranquillity and ease is what is wanted at present to restore the opening of the nature.

*

The feeling of inability is just the thing you have to reject. It is true only of the physical material consciousness and it is true of everybody in the physical consciousness, because that is something very inert and all that it can do is open itself, remain quiet and receive the Influence. But there is no inability in the rest of the being: it can will and reject. If confusion and obscurity come, it is not bound to accept them, — it can open to the true Force and throw them away; it can keep itself open even when the forces of confusion throw themselves upon it. Only the concentration also must be quiet and steady, — not struggling and restless.

*

It is not because you cannot recover the true attitude, but because you admit in part of your mind the false suggestion of your inability that this mixed condition lasts longer than it should. It is part of your physical consciousness that keeps the memory of the old movements and has the habit of admitting them and thinking them inevitable. You must insist with the clearer part of your consciousness on the true Truth, rejecting always these suggestions and feelings, till this obscure part also is open and admits the Light.

*

As to what has happened in your sadhana, it is that you have allowed yourself to fall into a groove of the physical mind and of the external vital nature and got fixed in a persistent or constantly recurrent repetition of the ideas and feelings which they present to you — feelings of settled disappointment and discouragement and pessimism about yourself and your spiritual future, and ideas — or, if you will allow me to call them so, notions — which come to the support of these feelings and sustain them. The result of this is to shut you up against the contact and spiritual influence and help you were once feeling or beginning to feel from us. It also shuts you up against your own deeper self and sterilises your personal effort. An accident of this kind is common enough in the path of spiritual effort, and the first thing to be done to get rid of its effects is to throw away resolutely the persistent ideas and feelings which keep you in the groove. I do not know whether you can return to the former condition, for it is seldom that one can go back to a point in the past; but it is always possible for you to go forward, recovering the force for propulsion of what you then gained and have certainly still within you assimilated in your inner being. If you want to carry on some part of the Yoga by your active efforts and aspiration, there is no reason why you should not find back that capacity; but the first effort to be made is to reject persistently, fully and tenaciously — not for two or three days, but always, so long as they insist or return — these disabling thoughts and feelings which hamstring all hope and faith in you, not to accept them, not to justify them, not to give them by your acquiescence the right to go on harping on the same note always of discouragement, incapacity and failure. The ideas by which you justify them are, I repeat, notions only of the physical mind, not true things — e.g. the notion that you *cannot* understand a given idea (intellectually accepting or not accepting is another matter); for it is perfectly certain that your thinking intelligence is quite trained enough to understand anything that is put before it. It is only the physical mind that is limited even in the most intelligent and opens up pits of stupidity or at least larger or smaller spaces of blank non-understanding in the face of unaccustomed ideas or a new line of possible experience or anything else either alien to the mind's habits or unwelcome to something in the vital parts. I suppose we have all had experience of this incapable element in our nature, and if one fixes oneself in it, it can make even things that would ordinarily be easy for us seem difficult things and things difficult seem impossible. But why should a mind trained to think allow this poorer part of itself to dominate it? So with the other notions. There is nothing anyone else can do in the way of Yoga that you cannot do if you have the fixed will to do it; some things may take a longer time because of past training, habits, mental associations but there is nothing impossible, too difficult, no inherently insuperable obstacle.

*

It [*the thought of leaving the Ashram*] is one of the suggestions of the external physical consciousness that are filling the atmosphere just now. I explain that to you in the answers below.

You used to have dreams on the vital plane also long ago in which you passed through dangerous forests and wildernesses amid perils of land and water and wild beasts etc., but you reached safely under the Mother's protection where you were going. I remember your writing some to me. Also there have been dreams of difficult passages ending in the arrival on the true open way. Only these dreams you are having now indicate the difficulty of the passage through the physical (and no longer through the vital) consciousness — but the common element is that you are under the Mother's protection and reach the way at the end. This is quite natural because what everybody is passing through now are the difficulties of the physical and subconscient nature; but the Mother's protection is the same here as in the past stages of the sadhana.

*

It is the doubt that most or many are raising now in the Asram. "Where am I? Where am I going? Am I really doing the Yoga? It seems to me I am getting nothing. There is no progress anywhere. All is dry and mechanical. What is the use of being here?" These are the thoughts that have been moving about in the atmosphere of the Asram and when you get such thoughts, it means that they are coming to you as suggestions from the atmosphere. If they are in the minds of any of those you move with, it is natural they should try to enter you, but even otherwise they can come to you, just as people catch cold because the germs are in the atmosphere.

Your attitude is all right, but evidently you have allowed your mind to be clouded by the suggestions of which I have spoken above. The feeling of having lost all one had is one of them; the feeling that all is mechanical and uninteresting and it is no use being here is another. Of course they are all false. When one listens to the suggestions, then things begin to *appear* like that. These suggestions are natural to the ignorant physical or body consciousness in human nature, just as suggestions of vital passion and disturbance are natural to the ignorant vital consciousness in human nature. You had vital reactions but you did not allow them to overcome you or make you think yourself unfit for the Yoga, because you relied upon the Mother and did not yield to the contrary vital Force. Here also you will have to have constant reliance on the Mother and reject the suggestions of the physical consciousness in the atmosphere when they come.

Stupidity and Ignorance

Your suggestion that I am telling you things that are untrue in order to encourage you is the usual stupidity of the physical mind — if it were so, it is not you who would be unfit for the Yoga, but myself who would be unfit to be in the search for the Divine Truth anybody's guide. For one can lead through lesser to greater Truth, but not through falsehood to Truth. As for your fitness or unfitness for the Yoga, it is not a question on which your physical mind can be an unerring judge — it judges by the immediate appearance of things and has no knowledge of the laws that govern consciousness or the powers that act in Yoga. In fact the question is not of fitness or unfitness but of the acceptance of Grace. There is no human being whose physical outer consciousness — the part of yourself in which you are now living — is fit for the Yoga. It is by grace and enlightenment from above that it can become capable and for that the necessity is to be persevering and open it to the Light. Everybody when he enters the physical consciousness has the same difficulty and feels as if he were unfit, obscure and nothing done, nothing changed in him since he began the Yoga; he is apt to forget then all that has happened before or to feel as if he had lost it or as if it had all been unreal or untrue.

I suppose that is why you object to my phrase about your having gone so far. I meant that you had had openings in your thinking mind and heart and higher vital and experiences also and had seen very lucidly the condition of your own being and nature and had by that got so far that these parts were ready for the spiritual change — what remains is the physical and outer consciousness which has to be compelled to accept the necessity of change. That is no doubt the most difficult part of the work to be done, but it is also the part which, if once done, makes possible the total change of the being and nature. I therefore said that having gone so far it would be absurd to turn back now and give up because this resists — it always resists in everybody and very obstinately too. That is no reason for giving up the endeavour.

It is this consciousness that has expressed itself in your letter — or the obscure part of it which clings to its old attitude. It does not want to fulfil the sadhana unless it can get by it the things it wanted. It wants the satisfaction of the ego, "self-fulfilment", appreciation, the granting of its desires. It measures the Divine Love by the outward favours showered upon it and looks jealously to see who gets more of these favours than itself, then says that the Divine has no love for it and assigns reasons which are either derogatory to the Divine or, as in your letter, self-depreciatory and a cause for despair. It is not in you alone that this part feels and acts like that, it is in almost everybody. If that were the only thing in you or the others, then indeed there would be no possibility of Yoga. But though it is strong, it is not the whole — there is a psychic being and a mind and heart influenced and enlightened by it which has other feelings and another vision of things and aim in sadhana. These are now covered in you by the upsurge of this part which has to change. It is tamasic and does not want to change, does not want to believe unless it can be done by reassuring the vital ego. But there is nothing new in all that — it is part of human nature and has always been there, hampering and limiting the sadhana. Its existence is no reason for despair — everyone has it and the sadhana has to be done in spite of it, in spite of the mixture it brings till the time comes when it has to be definitely converted or rejected. It is difficult to do it, but perfectly possible. These things I know and realise and it is therefore that I insist on your persevering and encourage you to go on; it is not my statement of the position that is untrue, it is the view of it taken by this obscure part of your being that is unsound and an error.

*

It is the instinctive (not mental) will in the outer being that is blind — the inner mind knows and understands and when it comes out it enlightens the rest so that all is clear. But the outer being readmits the darkness and confusion through a wrong movement of the vital or through an inert acceptance of the obscurity of the ignorant physical consciousness and the knowledge gets darkened over. But it is there and has only to come out again. The physical consciousness is constitutionally ignorant — it may be made to understand, but it goes on forgetting and feeling as if it had never known — till the Force and Light finally get hold of it and then it forgets no more.

Agnosticism

These feelings are the usual attitude of the physical consciousness left to itself towards the Divine — a complete Agnosticism and inability to experience.[2]

---

[2] *The correspondent complained about the difficulty of knowing the Divine and said that he was on the verge of Agnosticism. His letter ends: "But even if I were to know Him, how would it affect the solid material facts of earth?" — Ed.*

The knowledge of the impersonal Divine by itself does not affect the material facts of earth or at least need not. It only produces a subjective change in the being itself and, if it is complete, a new vision and attitude towards all things immaterial or material. But the complete knowledge of the Divine can produce a change in material things, for it sets a Force working which ends by acting even upon these material things that seem to the physical consciousness so absolute, invincible and unchangeable.

Fear of Death

In a certain part of the physical consciousness and in the subconscious there is always the human and animal fear of death and of anything that has to do with death. It is from there that these dreams are rising along with the fear felt by those parts of the nature. These things rise up in order to be rejected and the mind is rejecting them; for all fear must go and there must be in the physical the full confidence in the Divine.

Section Two

Food, Sleep, Dreams and Sex

Chapter One

Food

The Yogic Attitude towards Food

If you want to do Yoga, you must take more and more in all matters, small or great, the Yogic attitude. In our path that attitude is not one of forceful suppression, but of detachment and equality with regard to the objects of desire. Forceful suppression (fasting comes under the head) stands on the same level as free indulgence; in both cases, the desire remains; in the one it is fed by indulgence, in the other it lies latent and exasperated by suppression. It is only when one stands back, separates oneself from the lower vital, refusing to regard its desires and clamours as one's own, and cultivates an entire equality and equanimity in the consciousness with respect to them that the lower vital itself becomes gradually purified and itself also calm and equal. Each wave of desire as it comes must be observed, as quietly and with as much unmoved detachment as you would observe something going on outside you, and must be allowed to pass, rejected from the consciousness, and the true movement, the true consciousness steadily put in its place.

*

About food, tea etc. the aim of Yoga is to have no hankerings, no slavery either to the stomach or the palate. How to get to that point is another matter — it depends often on the individual. With a thing like tea, the strongest and easiest way is to stop it. As to food the best way usually is to take the food given you, practise non-attachment and follow no fancies. That would mean giving up the Sunday indulgence. The rest must be done by an inner change of consciousness and not by external means.

*

It is a mistake to neglect the body and let it waste away; the body is the means of the sadhana and should be maintained in good order. There should be no attachment to it, but no contempt or neglect either of the material part of our nature.

In this Yoga the aim is not only the union with the higher consciousness but the transformation (by its power) of the lower including the physical nature.

It is not necessary to have desire or greed of food in order to eat. The Yogi eats not out of desire, but to maintain the body.

*

That [*disgust for eating*] is rather an excessive feeling. One should eat for maintenance of the body without attaching any other importance, but without repulsion.

*

The vital of most people is of this kind [*too weak to restrain its desires for pleasure*], except in a few who are indifferent to sex or to food desire or to both, by temperament and nature. There is always something in the lower vital which is recalcitrant and takes a pleasure in following its own way and disregarding the higher dictate, and there are always external forces hostile to the Yoga which try to take advantage of its obscurities, revolts and weaknesses. Neither neglect this turn of the nature (food desire) nor make too much of it; it has to be dealt with, purified and mastered but without giving it too much importance. There are two ways of conquering it — one of detachment, learning to regard food as only a physical necessity and the vital satisfaction of the stomach and the palate as a thing of little or no importance; the other is to be able to take without insistence or seeking any food given and to find in it (whether pronounced good or bad by others) the equal *rasa*, not of the food for its own sake, but of the universal Ananda. But the latter comes usually only when one can live in the cosmic consciousness or rise into the Overmind — and for this you are not yet ready. So the first way is the one you should keep in view.

*

Do not trouble your mind about food. Take it in the right quantity (neither too much nor too little), without greed or repulsion, as the means given you by the Mother for the maintenance of the body, in the right spirit, offering it to the Divine in you; then it need not create *tamas*.

*

It is much better to eat the meal in silence or at any rate in quietness.

Attachment to Food

It is the attachment to food, the greed and eagerness for it, making it an unduly important thing in the life, that is contrary to the spirit of Yoga. To be aware that something is pleasant to the palate is not wrong; only one must have no desire nor hankering for it, no exultation in getting it, no displeasure or regret at not getting it. One must be calm and equal, not getting upset or dissatisfied when the food is not tasty or not in abundance — eating the fixed amount that is necessary, not less or more. There should be neither eagerness nor repugnance.

To be always thinking about food and troubling the mind is quite the wrong way of getting rid of the food-desire. Put the food element in the right place in the life, in a small corner, and don't concentrate on it but on other things.

*

The attachment to good food must be given up as also the personal attachment to position and service; but it is not indispensably necessary for that purpose to take to an ascetic diet or to give up all means of action such as money and service. The Yogin has to become *niḥsva* in this sense that he feels that nothing belongs to him but all to the Divine and he must be ready at any time to give up all to the Divine. But there is no meaning in throwing away everything in order to be externally *niḥsva* without any imperative cause.

Greed for Food

The first thing to be attained about eating, is to get rid of the greed of food, the attachment and desire, — to take it only as a need of the body, to think little of it and not to allow it to occupy a big place in the life; also to be satisfied with what you get, not to hanker. At the same time sufficient food should be taken, avoiding either deficiency or excess; an excessive coercion or *nigraha* in this respect (as opposed to reasonable control) often brings a reaction. One should go steadily, but not try to get too much done at once.

*

As for Sannyasis and food, Sannyasis put a compulsion on their desires in this and other matters — they take ascetic food as a principle; but this does not necessarily kill the greed for food, it remains compressed and, if the compulsion or principle is removed, it can come up again stronger than before — for compression without removal often increases the force of these things instead of destroying them.

*

Not to eat as the method of getting rid of the greed of food is the ascetic way. Ours is equanimity and non-attachment.

*

These things [*persistent desires*] still rise in you because they have been for so long prominent difficulties and, as far as the first is concerned, because you gave it much justification from the mind at one time. But if the inner consciousness is growing like that they are sure to go. Only if they rise, don't give them harbourage. Perhaps with regard to the greed for food, your attitude has not been quite correct. Greed for food has to be overcome, but it has not to be given too much thought. The proper attitude to food is a certain equality. Food is for the maintenance of the body and one should take enough for that — what the body needs; if one gives less the body feels the need and hankers; if you give more, then that is indulging the vital. As for particular foods the palate likes, the attitude of the mind and vital should be, "If I get, I take; if I don't get, I shall not mind." One should not think too much of food either to indulge or unduly to repress — that is the best.

*

One does not need to get a hatred for food in order to get rid of the greed for food. On the other hand, to develop dislike for certain things may help to reject them — but that too is not always the cure, for they may remain in spite of the dislike.

*

It is true that the greed of food, the desire of the palate are very strong in a great many if not most of the sadhaks; this is one of the things that they take as natural and seem not at all anxious to get it out of them. I do not think it is active in you; what you felt must have come in from the others, — for very often one feels the things that are in the atmosphere and one must be careful to distinguish that from one's own feeling.

*

As to taking tea or food there [*at a friend's place*], you must always remember that to be governed by these desires is not at all an ideal condition. But if you have the impulse and are not able easily and naturally to reject it, you can take on condition you scrupulously inform the Mother both of the act and of the movement and state of mind accompanying it. Also often the desire may not be yours, but may come on you from outside, imposed on you silently or otherwise by suggestion by the others; you must learn to see when it is like that and then you must reject it. Your aspiration must be for an inner change so that there will be no longer any need to indulge the desires, because they will no longer have a hold on you.

You must learn to watch yourself and know what is the true nature and source of the movements in you and report them carefully — as in fact you had begun to do when you first had the psychic opening and could see the movements in you or many of them at least very clearly.

*

Of course — the vital is insatiable.[1] There are only two things that interfere with it [*greed for food*] — the limitations of the body and the disapprobation of the mind — but the latter is not always there. There is also of course the possibility of the psychic interfering, but to that the vital becomes pervious only at a certain stage. It is therefore the body that is the only check for most people.

*

These complaints about food are of long standing with many — they come from the animal man and will go on so long as the sadhaks identify themselves with the physical animal in them.

Taste

As regards the progress you have made, I do not think you have given us an exaggerated impression of it; it seems to be quite real. It is no part of this Yoga to suppress taste, *rasa* altogether; so, if you found the ice-cream pleasant, that does not by itself invalidate the completeness of your progress. What is to be got rid of is vital desire and attachment, the greed of food, being overjoyed at getting the food you like, sorry and discontented when you do not have it, giving an undue importance to it, etc. If one wants to be a Yogin, it will not do to be like the ordinary man to whom food, sex and gain are nine-tenths of life or even to keep in any of these things the reactions to which vital human nature is prone. Equality is here the test as in so many other matters. If you can take the Ashram food with satisfaction or at least without dissatisfaction, that is already a sign that attachment

---

[1] *The correspondent wrote that the vital being never seems to tire of the enjoyment of food, even though it results in illness, pain and misery for the body.* — Ed.

and predilection are losing their old place in the nature.

*

Taste is no more a guilty thing than sight or hearing. It is the desire that it awakens that has to be thrown away.

It is possible to get rid of taste like Chaitanya, for it is something that depends on the consciousness and so inhibition is possible. In hypnotic experiments it is found that suggestion can make sugar taste bitter or bitter things sweet. Berkeley and physiology are both right. There is a certain usually fixed relation between the consciousness in the palate and the *guṇa* of the food, but the consciousness can alter the relation if it wants or inhibit it altogether. There are Yogis who make themselves insensitive to pain also and that too can be done by hypnosis.

Another method is to find all things good to the taste without attachment to any.

*

No — it [*taste*] is not a bondage, if there is no attachment. Taste is natural and quite permissible so long as one is not the slave of the palate. Certainly, the enjoyment of taste can be offered up. I don't know that there is any fruit of eating in the sense of the phrase in the Gita.

Sensitivity to Smell

This [*reaction of uneasiness after smelling food*] is due to an acute consciousness and sensitiveness of the physical being, especially the vital physical. The sense of being fed by smell has become thereby very acute — the feeding by smell is a well known thing, and there is the Sanskrit proverb, *ghrāṇam ardhabhojanam*, "smell is a half eating". But this by itself would not produce the uneasiness, which must be due to an acute physical sensitiveness to the mass of ordinary human reactions concentrated about the food, greed etc. which fill the atmosphere. It does not look as if more than a very few of the sadhaks were free (even they mainly, not wholly) from these reactions; most seem to accept them as quite normal and proper in a life of Yoga!!

It is good for the physical to be more and more conscious, but it should not be overpowered by the things of which it becomes aware or badly affected or upset by them. A strong equality and mastery and detachment must come in the nerves and body as in the mind, which will enable the physical to know and contact these things without feeling any disturbance; it should know and be conscious and reject and throw away the pressure of the movements in the atmosphere, not merely feel them and suffer.

Hunger

I suppose you have become aware of the principle of hunger in the vital physical. It is not really either by satisfying it or forcibly denying it that it will go — it is by putting a will on it to change and bringing down a higher consciousness that it can change.

*

To suppress hunger like that is not good, it very often creates disorders. I doubt whether fatness or thinness of a healthy kind depends on the amount of food taken — there are people who eat well and remain thin and others who take only one meal a day and remain fat. By underfeeding (taking less than the body really needs) one may get emaciated, but that is not a healthy state. The doctors say it depends mostly on the working of certain glands. Anyhow the important thing is now to get the nervous strength back.

As for the liver also eating little does not help, very often it makes the liver sluggish so that it works less well. What is recommended for liver trouble is to avoid greasy food and much eating of sweets and that is also one way of avoiding fat. But to eat too little is not good — it may be necessary in some stomach or intestinal illness, but not for the ordinary liver trouble.

*

This feeling of not being able to eat and of eating being unnecessary is a sort of suggestion that is coming to several people. It should be rejected and cleared out of the system as it may lead to weakening of the body by taking insufficient food. Often one does not feel weak at first, a vital energy comes which supports the body, but later on the body weakens. This feeling may sometimes come when one is going much inside and there is no insistence on the bodily needs; but it should not be accepted. If it is rejected, it is likely to disappear.

*

When I spoke about the inability to eat being a suggestion, I meant a suggestion to the body consciousness itself, not to your mind. When such suggestions come, they produce physical effects of this kind, instead of the idea of not eating there comes a sort of inability to eat.

*

The absence of hunger and thirst and the eating only for maintenance of the body without any feeling of having eaten is a state that sometimes comes when one is living more and more in the inner being and less in the body.

Quantity of Food

What is necessary is to take enough food and think no more about it, taking it as a means for the maintenance of the physical instrument only. But just as one should not overeat, so one should not diminish unduly — it produces a reaction which defeats the object — for the object is not to allow either the greed for food or the heavy tamas of the physical which is the result of excessive eating to interfere with the concentration on the spiritual experience and progress. If the body is left insufficiently nourished, it will think of food more than otherwise.

*

Too much eating makes the body material and heavy, eating

too little makes it weak and nervous — one has to find the true harmony and balance between the body's need and the food taken.

*

It depends on what you can digest. If you can digest, there is no harm in taking more since you feel hungry. All these things depend upon what is the true need of the body and that may differ in different cases according to the constitution of the body, the amount of work done or exercise taken. It is possible that you have reduced your food too much — so you can try taking more.

*

But it is quite natural. Exercise is always supposed to increase the appetite as the body needs more food to restore the extra expense of energy put out. Normally the more physical work the body has to do the more food it needs. On the other hand mental work requires no increase of food — that has been ascertained scientifically by experiment. Hunger may increase by other causes, but when it coincides with the taking up of play or physical exercise of a strenuous character, that is sufficient to explain it.

*

If the [stomach] pains are strong, you can abstain from work for a day or two till they have subsided. Of course if you feel that you suffer from anything else but liquid food, that settles the question — you can take liquid food only and if you take liquid food only then you will not be strong enough to work. But usually the thought takes a big part in determining these things — the mind has the impression that any solid food will hurt and the body follows — so naturally as a result any solid food does begin to hurt.

*

The mental or vital vigour does not or need not depend on the food — it is the physical that after a time begins to get strained if there is not sufficient nourishment.

*

One can bring down the strength [*from above*], but it is also necessary to see that the body has sufficient food, sleep and rest — absence of these things strains the nerves and if the nerves are strained the body feels fatigue, becomes weakened.

*

It is possible there was a suppression or underfeeding — you were several times even proposing to eat still less and the Mother did not approve. When there is this suppression I have always noticed that there comes for a time a strong eagerness or necessity for eating largely as if the body were taking its compensation for the past want.

*

If these [*practices of self-control*] are done as moral virtues, they need not bring a spiritual state. It is only when they are observed as a spiritual discipline that they help — most of them, at least. A man may eat little and have no spirituality — but if he practises it as a means of self-mastery to get rid of the greed of food, then it helps.

*

It is better to be careful in these matters of food etc., as in the stage through which your sadhana is passing there is a considerable sensitiveness in the vital physical part of the being and it may be easily disturbed by a wrong impact or a wrong movement like overfeeding.

*

When the physical consciousness has been sensitivised, too rich or heavy food becomes offensive to it.

*

It is true that as one reaches an advanced age a diminished diet may become desirable.

Fasting

I have myself fasted first for 10 days and then 23 days just to see what it was like and how far one could live without food, and certain things like that. I found that it was no good. To take with equanimity whatever comes (or does not come) seemed to me more the thing than any violent exercises like that.

*

I think it is not safe to admit any suggestion of not eating — sometimes it opens the door for the non-eating force to take hold of the mind and there is trouble. That comes easily because the inner being of course does not need any food and this non-need is attempted to be thrown by some forces on the body also which is not under the same happy law. It is better to allow the condition [*of peaceful concentration*] to grow in intensity until it can last even through the meal and after. I suppose it is not really the meal that disturbs but the coming out into the outer consciousness which is a little difficult to avoid when one goes to eat; but that can be overcome in time.

*

You must not let that movement [*of reducing food*] go too far. It is one of the dangers of the sadhana, because of the ascetic turn of Yoga in the past that as experiences come the suggestion comes that food or sleep etc. are not necessary and also there may come an inclination in the body not to eat or not to sleep. But if that is accepted the results are often disastrous. It is no more to be accepted than the inertia itself.

*

To make your sadhana depend upon not eating is to make a great mistake. When people fast like that, they get into an abnormal condition and can easily mistake imaginations and delusions for true experiences. Much fasting in the end weakens the nervous system. So you must drop this habit of not eating for days together. For Yoga it is a mistake to eat too much but a mistake also to eat nothing or too little. If you eat too much, you become heavy and tamasic; if you fast or eat too little, you excite the vital energies and finally overexcite them, but at the same time you weaken the body and the nerves; both are bad for sadhana. You should eat regularly a moderate but sufficient amount of food; it is only if there is illness or disturbance of digestion that a low diet or not eating sometimes becomes necessary, but fasting even for the purpose of resting the stomach should not last more than a day.

For your sadhana you have to use, not outward means like this, but quietness, sincere peaceful aspiration, openness to the Mother.

*

It is a fact that by fasting, if the mind and the nerves are solid or the will force dynamic, one can get for a time into a state of inner energy and receptivity which is alluring to the mind and the usual reactions of hunger, weakness, intestinal disturbance, etc. can be wholly avoided. But the body suffers by diminution and there can easily develop in the vital a morbid overstrained condition due to the inrush of more vital energy than the nervous system can assimilate or coordinate. Nervous people should avoid the temptation to fast; it is often accompanied or followed by delusions and a loss of balance. Especially if there is a motive of hunger-strike or that element comes in, as it did in your case, fasting becomes perilous, for it is then an indulgence of a vital movement which may easily become a habit injurious and pernicious to the sadhana. Even if all these reactions are avoided, still there is no sufficient utility in fasting, since the higher energy and receptivity ought to come not by artificial or physical means but by intensity of the consciousness and strong will for the sadhana.

*

I never heard of it [*fasting to get realisation*]; but it is just the way to get the wrong realisation. The nerves get into an excited tense condition (when they do not collapse) and invent realisations or open to a wrong Force. At least that often happens.

*

The idea of giving up food is a wrong inspiration. You can go on with a small quantity of food, but not without food altogether, except for a comparatively short time. Remember what the Gita says, "Yoga is not for one who eats in excess nor for one who abstains from eating altogether." Vital energy is one thing — of that one can draw a great amount without food and often it increases with fasting; but physical substance, without which life loses its support, is of a different order. If at any time it became possible to renew the body without food and that proved necessary for the Yoga, the Mother and I would be the first to do it. So keep to your established diet and do not get impatient with Nature.

*

The transformation to which we aspire is too vast and complex to come at one stroke; it must be allowed to come by stages. The physical change is the last of these stages and is itself a progressive process.

The inner transformation cannot be brought about by physical means either of a positive or a negative nature. On the contrary, the physical change itself can only be brought about by a descent of the greater supramental consciousness into the cells of the body. Till then at least the body and its supporting energies have to be maintained in part by the ordinary means, food, sleep, etc. Food has to be taken in the right spirit, with the right consciousness; sleep has to be gradually transformed into the Yogic repose. A premature and excessive physical austerity (*tapasyā*) may endanger the process of the sadhana by establishing a disturbance and abnormality of the forces in the different parts of the system. A great energy may pour into the mental and vital parts, but the nerves and the body may be overstrained and lose the strength to support the play of these higher energies. This is the reason why an extreme physical austerity is not included here as a substantive part of the sadhana.

There is no harm in fasting from time to time for a day or two or in reducing the food taken to a small but sufficient modicum; but entire abstinence for a long period is not advisable.

Types of Food

I think the importance of sattwic food from the spiritual point of view has been exaggerated. Food is rather a question of hygiene and many of the sanctions and prohibitions laid down in ancient religions had more a hygienic than a spiritual motive. The Gita's definitions seem to point in the same direction — tamasic food, it seems to say, is what is stale or rotten with the virtue gone out of it, rajasic food is that which is too acrid, pungent etc., heats the blood and spoils the health, sattwic food is what is pleasing, healthy etc. It may well be that different kinds of food nourish the action of the different gunas and so indirectly are helpful or harmful apart from their physical action. But that is as far as we can confidently go. What particular eatables are or are not sattwic is another question and more difficult to determine. Spiritually, I should say that the effect of food depends more on the occult atmosphere and influences that come with it than on anything in the food itself. Vegetarianism is another question altogether; it stands, as you say, on a will not to do harm to the more conscious forms of life for the satisfaction of the belly.

As to the question of practising to take all kinds of food with equal rasa, it is not necessary to practise nor does it really come by practice. One has to acquire equality within in the consciousness and as this equality grows one can extend it or apply it to the various fields of the activity of the consciousness.

*

Those who are ready to give up animal food, should certainly do so. The others can do it when they are ready.[2]

*

It is rather certain kinds of food that are supposed to increase it [*sexual desire*] — e.g. meat, onions, chillis etc.

*

It [*the chilli*] is an aphrodisiac — has a strong effect on the sex centre.

*

If it [*taking chillis*] is once only in some months it can't be harmful for the body. For the sadhana what is harmful is taking to satisfy desire, fancy, impulse — it is not the thing in itself.

*

There is no sin at all in eating these things [*onions, potatoes, etc.*]. The only objection to eating much onions is that it is supposed to stimulate not tamoguna but rajas, but there are other foods not forbidden that do that.

*

I think onions can be described as rajaso-tamasic in their character. They are heavy and material and at the same time excitant of certain strong material-vital forces. It is obvious that if one wants to conquer the physical passions and is still very much subject to the body nature and the things that affect it, free indulgence in onions is not advisable. It is only for those who have risen above the body consciousness and mastered it and are not affected by these things that it does not at all matter; for them the use of this or that food or its disuse makes no difference. At the same time I must say that the abstinence from rajasic or tamasic foods does not of itself assure freedom from the things they help to stimulate. Vegetarians, for instance, can be as sensual and excitable as meat-eaters; a man may abstain

---

[2] *This letter was written to someone living outside the Ashram.* — Ed.

from onions and yet be in these respects no better than before. It is a change of consciousness that is effective and this kind of abstention helps that only in so far as it tends to create a less heavy and more refined and plastic physical consciousness for the higher will to act upon. That is something, but it is not all; the change of consciousness can come even in spite of non-abstinence.

Onions are allowed here because the palate of the sadhaks demands something to give a taste to the food. We do not insist on these details, or make an absolutely strict rule, as the stress here is more on the inward change, the outward coming as its result. Only so much is insisted on as is essential for organisation and inner and outer discipline and to point the way to an indispensable self-control. It is pressed on all that the greed of the palate has to be conquered, but it has to be done in the last resort from within, as also the other passions and desires of the lower nature.

*

Betel is anaesthetic, depressive and yet with a certain toxic effect — that is why it is prohibited.

Whatever is done without purpose is a useless and wrong movement.

Eating things from outside is not safe either from the physical or from the spiritual point of view.

Intoxicants

It is the habit in the subconscient material that feels an artificial need created by the past and does not care whether it is harmful or disturbing to the nerves or not. That is the nature of all intoxications (wine, tobacco, cocaine etc.), people go on even after the deleterious effects have shown themselves and even after all real pleasure in it has ceased because of this artificial need (it is not real). The will has to get hold of this subconscient persistence and dissolve it.

*

Smoking is only a morbid craving of physical desire — there is no other reason for people doing it. Smoking is tamasic and prevents control of mind.

*

These intoxicants [*such as bhang*] put one in relation with a vital world in which such things [*as music and song*] exist.

Chapter Two

Sleep

The Yogic Attitude towards Sleep and Food

This is not a Yoga in which physical austerities have to be done for their own sake. Sleep is necessary for the body just as food is. Sufficient sleep must be taken, but not excessive sleep. What sufficient sleep is depends on the need of the body.

*

The loss of sleep must not be there. In this Yoga we insist on regular sleep, rest, food, because then the balance can be kept between the strength of the body and the force of all that comes into it from above. Otherwise the body is not able to keep and hold what comes — there is disturbance and loss of the right poise and balance.

*

The first thing I tell people when they want not to eat or sleep is that no Yoga can be done without sufficient food and sleep (see the Gita on this point). This is not Gandhi's asram or a miracle-shop. Fasting and sleeplessness make the nerves morbid and excited and weaken the brain and lead to delusions and fantasies. The Gita says Yoga is not for one who eats too much or sleeps too much, neither is it for one who does not eat or does not sleep, but if one eats and sleeps suitably — *yuktāhārī yuktanidraḥ* — then one can do it best. It is the same with everything else. How often have I said that excessive retirement was suspect to me and that to do nothing but meditate was a lopsided and therefore unsound sadhana.

*

I must ask you to remember what I told you about sadhana. If you want to do the sadhana here, you must sleep well and eat well. If you try to stop sleeping or eating or unduly diminish sleep and food, you will weaken the body and excite the vital and wrong and excited and exaggerated movements will come into you. Remember this in future.

*

There are stories told of people living without sleep or food — living without sleep has happened, but it came by an abnormal condition in the person which cannot be brought at will. There is no instance of anyone living without food, — none that is to say which is beyond doubt — but that also may be possible — but here also it must depend on some abnormal condition which cannot be brought at will.

The Need of Sleep and Rest

It is not a right method to try to keep awake at night; the suppression of the needed sleep makes the body tamasic and unfit for the necessary concentration during the waking hours. The right way is to transform the sleep and not suppress it, and especially to learn how to become more and more conscious in sleep itself. If that is done, sleep changes into an inner mode of consciousness in which the sadhana can continue as much as in the waking state, and at the same time one is able to enter into other planes of consciousness than the physical and command an immense range of informative and utilisable experience.

*

By not sleeping enough you weaken the forces of the physical consciousness and so the physical basis of the sadhana is less strong than it should be. It gets more open to the forces of inertia.

*

Is that all your sleep [*three-and-a-half hours*]? If so, it is far too little. If you do not sleep enough, the body and the nervous envelope will be weakened and the body and the nervous envelope are the basis of the sadhana.

*

I am glad the peace is coming back at last and I trust it will increase and push out these other things. But how is it, — you have not been taking proper rest? Rest is absolutely necessary for the body and still more for the nervous system; not only for working but for sadhana rest to the body and the nerves is essential. If you allow them to be strained and tired, they will not be able to adapt themselves readily for the required change, all sorts of things, confusion, suggestions etc. are likely to come into a tired nervous system. They too must be strong and at peace.

*

It is the want of sleep itself that brings the symptoms of uneasiness. The action of the Sadhana cannot of itself bring this kind of reaction, it is only if the body gets strained by want of sleep, insufficient food, overwork or nervous excitement that there are these things. It is probably because the nerves are strung in the daytime and you do not relax into ease that it is difficult to sleep.

*

One can assimilate [*spiritual experience*] in sleep also. Remaining awake like that is not good, as in the end it strains the nerves and the system receives wrongly in an excited way or else gets too tired to receive.

*

You should have continuous sleep at night and sufficient — otherwise you will feel sleepy in the day which will be a hindrance to work.

*

Sleep is necessary; this kind of broken rest is not good. It is the consciousness in sleep itself that has to change.

*

Such pressure [*to sleep*] only comes (1) when the body needs sleep, not having had enough or because enough rest is not given, (2) when it wants to recuperate after illness or strong fatigue, (3) when there is a pressure from above which the physical consciousness or part of it replies to by trying to go inside.

*

Take care to rest enough. You must guard against fatigue as it may bring relaxation and tamas. To rest well is not tamas, as some people suppose; it can be done in the right consciousness to maintain the bodily energy — like the *śavāsana* of the strenuous Hathayogin.

*

Both for fevers and for mental trouble sleep is a great help and its absence very undesirable — it is the loss of a curative agency.

The Amount of Sleep Needed

The ordinary period of sleep most people give themselves is 8 hours. In bad health (I am not speaking of acute illness) it can extend to 9. 12 hours is excessive unless one is seriously ill or recovering from illness or else has underslept for a long time and the body is making up arrears of needed sleep.

*

8 hours [*of sleep*] at night is all right, the additional 2 hours is probably necessitated by the bad sleep you were having before. The body recoups itself in this way. That is why it is a mistake to take too little sleep — the body gets strained and has to recoup itself by abnormal sleep afterwards.

*

The normal allowance of sleep is said to be 7 to 8 hours except in advanced age when it is said to be less. If one takes less (5 to 6 for instance) the body accommodates itself somehow, but if the control is taken off it immediately wants to make up for its lost arrears of the normal 8 hours. So often when one has tried to live on too little food, if one relaxes, the body becomes enormously rapacious for food until it has set right the credit and loss account. At least it often happens like that.

*

It must be the want of sleep that keeps your nervous system exposed to weakness — it is a great mistake not to take sufficient sleep. 7 hours is the minimum needed. When one has a very strong nervous system, one can reduce it to 6, sometimes even 5 — but it is rare and ought not to be attempted without necessity.

*

The feeling that you have in the morning proves that you need more sleep, so it is not wise to cut it short to the minimum as that in the end tells on the body. It is better to continue the sleep when you feel sleepy. 7 hours is not too much for sleep.

*

$5\frac{1}{2}$ hours [*of sleep*] is quite insufficient. Six is the absolute minimum, it can go up to seven hours.

*

It is not possible to do at once what you like with the body. If the body is told to sleep only 2 or 3 hours, it may follow if the will is strong enough — but afterwards it may get exceedingly strained and even break down for want of needed rest. The Yogis who minimise their sleep, succeed only after a long tapasya in which they learn how to control the forces of Nature governing the body.

The Real Rest which Restores

In sleep one very commonly passes from consciousness to deeper consciousness in a long succession until one reaches the psychic and rests there or else from higher to higher consciousness until one reaches rest in some silence and peace. The few minutes one passes in this rest are the real sleep which restores — if one does not get it, there is only a half rest. It is when you come near to either of these domains of rest, that you begin to see these higher kind of dreams.

*

A long unbroken sleep is necessary because there are just ten minutes of the whole into which one enters into a true rest — a sort of Sachchidananda immobility of the consciousness — and that it is which really restores the system. The rest of the time is spent first in travelling through various states of consciousness towards that and then coming out of it back towards the waking state. This fact of the ten minutes true rest has been noted by medical men, but of course they know nothing about Sachchidananda!

*

This feeling of having enough sleep [*when one wakes at night*] and after sleeping again of not having had enough is not unusual. It might be inferred that the first sleep is really enough and the second is a tamasic sleep which leaves the body unrested. Some doctors say that there are about ten minutes of rest which are the true sleep and all the rest is only a process of getting into the ten minutes and getting out again — for these ten minutes are difficult to arrive at. Perhaps you get your ten minutes before the first waking. The difficulty is that the length of sleep seems important and that by the habit of less the nerves continually seem to get strained — at least I have seen that with many. If that can be overcome then so much sleep might not be requisite.

*

According to a recent medical theory one passes in sleep through many phases until one arrives at a state in which there is absolute rest and silence — it lasts only for ten minutes, the rest of the time is taken up by travelling to that and travelling back again to the waking state. I suppose the ten minutes sleep can be called *suṣupti* in the Brahman or Brahmaloka, the rest is *svapna* or passage through other worlds (planes or states of conscious existence). It is these ten minutes that restore the energies of the being, and without it sleep is not refreshing.

According to the Mother's experience and knowledge one passes from waking through a succession of states of sleep consciousness which are in fact an entry and passage into so many worlds and arrives at a pure Sachchidananda state of complete rest, light and silence; afterwards one retraces one's way till one reaches the waking physical state. It is this Sachchidananda period that gives sleep all its restorative value. These two accounts, the scientific and the occult-spiritual, are practically identical with each other. But the former is only a recent discovery of what the occult-spiritual knowledge knew long ago.

People's ideas of sound sleep are absolutely erroneous. What they call sound sleep is merely a plunge of the outer consciousness into a complete subconscience. They call that a dreamless sleep; but it is only a state in which the surface sleep consciousness which is a subtle prolongation of the outer still left active in sleep itself is unable to record the dreams and transmit them to the physical mind. As a matter of fact the whole sleep is full of dreams. It is only during the brief time in which one is in the Brahmaloka that the dreams cease.

Getting Good Sleep

The sleep before 12 is supposed to be the best.

*

To sleep without a burdened stomach is obviously more healthy, both psychologically and physically.

*

I don't think the lack of sleep when it comes is due to want of work; for even those who do no work at all, get good sleep. It is something else; but it must be got over.

*

It is restlessness in you which prevents you from keeping still inwardly or outwardly. To sleep well the vital and physical and mind also must learn how to relax themselves and be quiet.

*

Obviously — it [*reading a novel before going to bed*] threw you into a tamasic consciousness and consequently the sleep was heavy in a gross subconsciousness and the fatigue was the result.

*

You should not jump up from sleep. Rise quietly and take a little time. You must give time for the consciousness to come back fully into the body.

Sleep during the Day

Many people can't stand afternoon sleep. But when it is more refreshing, it is because it is lighter than the night sleep — one does not go so deep down to the subconscient.

*

According to the old Ayurvedic shastra "sleep by day impairs the vitality"; but there are conditions in which the rule may not apply. It is however true that these [*sexual*] dreams do easily occur during sleep by day and the dreams themselves come in a state of deep subconscient relaxation, tamasic inertia when the system can be touched by any subconscient suggestion or influence.

Sleep and Sadhana

Sadhana can go on in the dream or sleep state as well as in the waking.

*

Once one is in full sadhana, sleep becomes as much a part of it as waking.

*

If the sleep becomes conscious even for a time, then experience and sadhana of itself can go on in the sleep state and not only in the waking condition.

*

It is usually only if there is much activity of sadhana in the day that it extends also into the sleep state.

*

There is no reason at all why intensity of sadhana should bring insufficient sleep.

*

If you feel the need of sleep you ought to sleep. The pressure of sadhana should not be allowed to become excessive.

*

It [*sleepiness during the day*] may possibly be due to the attempt of the higher consciousness to descend then. It sometimes produces this effect of sleepiness on the body, for the physical attempts to go inside to meet the descending consciousness and if it is not accustomed to enter into one of the higher samadhis on such occasions, the going inside translates itself to the physical as sleep. The exercise may have contributed, of course, by its reaction on the body.

Loss of Consciousness during Sleep

In sleep one easily loses the consciousness of the day, because of the lapse of the physical being into the subconscient. You have to get the power to reestablish it when you wake.

*

Sleep, because of its subconscient basis, usually brings a falling down to a lower level, unless it is a conscious sleep; to make it more and more conscious is the one permanent remedy: but also until that is done, one should always react against this sinking tendency when one wakes and not allow the effect of dull nights to accumulate. But these things need always a settled endeavour and discipline and must take time, sometimes a long time. It will not do to refrain from the effort because immediate results do not appear.

*

It often, even usually happens that after sleep — not the sleep of meditation, but the ordinary sleep — one finds one's consciousness has gone down. It is no use getting distressed by that; one has to remain quiet and call back the higher consciousness.

*

The consciousness in the night almost always descends below the level of what one has gained by sadhana in the waking consciousness — unless there are special experiences of an uplifting character in the time of sleep or unless the Yogic consciousness acquired is so strong in the physical itself as to counteract the pull of the subconscient inertia. In ordinary sleep the consciousness in the body is that of the subconscient physical, which is a diminished consciousness, not awake and alive like the rest of the being. The rest of the being stands back and part of its consciousness goes out into other planes and regions and has experiences which are recorded in dreams such as that you have related. You say you go to very bad places and have experiences like the one you narrate; but that is not a sign, necessarily, of anything wrong in you. It merely means that you go into the vital world, as everybody does, and the vital world is full of such places and such experiences. What you have to do is not so much to avoid at all going there, for it cannot be avoided altogether, but to go with full protection until you get mastery in these regions of supraphysical Nature. That is one reason why you should remember us and open to the Force before sleeping; for the more you get that habit and can do it successfully, the more the protection will be with you.

*

The difficulty of keeping the consciousness at night happens to most — it is because the night is the time of sleep and relaxation and the subconscient comes up. The true consciousness comes at first in the waking state or in meditation, it takes possession of the mental, the vital, the conscious physical, but the subconscious vital and physical remain obscure and this obscurity comes up when there is sleep or an inert relaxation. When the subconscient is enlightened and penetrated by the true consciousness, this disparity disappears. The Pishachic woman that tried to enter [*in a dream*] is the false vital impure Shakti — and the voice that spoke was that of his psychic being. If he keeps his psychic being awake and in front, it will always protect him against these dark forces as it did this time.

*

The sleep you describe in which there is a luminous silence or else the sleep in which there is Ananda in the cells, these are obviously the best states. The other hours, those of which you are unconscious, may be spells of a deep slumber in which you have gone out of the physical into the mental, vital or other planes. You say you were unconscious, but it may simply be that you do not remember what happened; for in coming back there is a sort of turning over of the consciousness, a transition or reversal, in which everything experienced in sleep except perhaps the last happening of all or else one that was very impressive, recedes from the physical awareness and all becomes as if a blank. There is another blank state, a state of inertia, not truly blank, but heavy and unremembering; but that is when one goes deeply and crassly into the subconscient; this subterranean plunge is very undesirable, obscuring, lowering, often fatiguing rather than restful, the reverse of the luminous silence.

*

To get rid of the subconscient in sleep, the proper way is not to diminish sleep, for that only overstrains the body and helps the lower forces to trouble it. The right way is to change gradually (it cannot be done all of a sudden) the character of the sleep.

Conscious Sleep

At night when one sinks into the subconscient after being in a good state of consciousness, we find that state gone and we have to labour to get it back again. On the other hand, if the sleep is of the better kind, one may wake up in a good condition. Of course, it is better to be conscious in sleep, if one can.

*

It is better to go to sleep and make it a discipline to become conscious in your sleep. Sleep may be only a habit, but it is a necessary habit at present and the thing to do is not to suppress, but to transform it into a conscious inner state.

*

You must not try to avoid sleep at night — if you persist in doing that, the bad results may not appear immediately, but the body will get strained and there will be a breakdown which may destroy what you have gained in your sadhana.

If you want to remain conscious at night, train yourself to make your sleep conscious — not to eliminate sleep altogether, but to transform it.

*

Sleep cannot be replaced, but it can be changed; for you can become conscious in sleep. If you are thus conscious, then the night can be utilised for a higher working — provided the *body* gets its due rest; for the object of sleep is the body's rest and the renewal of the vital-physical force. It is a mistake to deny to the body food and sleep, as some from an ascetic idea or impulse want to do — that only wears out the physical support and, although either the Yogic or the vital energy can long keep at work an overstrained or declining physical system, a time comes when this drawing is no longer so easy nor perhaps possible. The body should be given what it needs for its own efficient working. Moderate but sufficient food (without greed or desire), sufficient sleep, but not of the heavy tamasic kind, this should be the rule.

*

To keep yourself awake is not permissible — it depresses the body in the end and excites the brain and leads to an unquiet and unbalanced consciousness. The body needs sufficient rest in order to be able to bear the pressure of sadhana.

You can pray or will before sleeping to be conscious in sleep, and you can get your waking mind full of the Mother. That is the best way. But you must not expect to be able to succeed all at once. First, the sleep-mind must become conscious of what it is doing in sleep; only afterwards can you determine what it is to do there.

*

In the sleep what holds the body is the subconscient — and the subconscient acts according to the already formed present habits or else the impressions left by past thoughts, feelings, memories, activities. If the thought of the Mother and her force and working are fixed in the conscious hours, then it will be easier to bring it into the subconscient.

*

As for asserting one's will in sleep it is simply a matter of accustoming the subconscient to obey the will laid upon it by the waking mind before sleeping. It very often happens for instance that if you fix upon the subconscient your will to wake up at a particular hour in the morning, the subconscient will obey and you wake up automatically at that hour. This can be extended to other matters. Many have found that by putting a will against sexual dreams or emission on the subconscient before sleeping, there comes after a time (it does not always succeed at the beginning) an automatic action causing one to awaken before the dream concludes or before it begins or in some way preventing the thing forbidden from happening. Also one can develop a more conscious sleep in which there is a sort of inner consciousness which can intervene.

*

This [*unconsciousness in sleep*] is quite usual. Consciousness in sleep can only be gradually established with the growth of the true consciousness in the waking state.

*

You cannot expect to be conscious at once in sleep: it takes a long time. If you can be always conscious in waking, then it will be easier to be conscious in sleep.

*

The sleep consciousness can be effectively dealt with only when the waking mind has made a certain amount of progress.

*

All dream or sleep consciousness cannot be converted at once into conscious sadhana. That has to be done progressively. But your power of conscious samadhi must increase before this can be done.

*

That is all right [*if the activity of sadhana goes on at night*]. It shows that the sadhana is becoming continuous and that you are becoming conscious and using a conscious will in sleep as well as in waking. This is a very important step forward in the sadhana.

*

You are more conscious in your sleep than in your waking condition. This is because of the physical consciousness which is not yet sufficiently open; it is only just beginning to open. In your sleep the inner being is active and the psychic there can influence more actively the mind and vital. When the physical consciousness is spiritually awake, you will no longer feel the trouble and obstruction you now have and will be as open in the waking consciousness as in sleep.

Concentration before and after Sleep

The gap made by the night and waking with the ordinary consciousness is the case with everybody almost (of course, the "ordinary" consciousness differs according to the progress); but it is no use waiting to be conscious in sleep; you have to get the habit of getting back the thread of the progress as soon as may be and for that there must be some concentration after rising.

At night, you have to pass into sleep in the concentration — you must be able to concentrate with the eyes closed, lying down and the concentration must deepen into sleep — that is to say, sleep must become a concentrated going inside away from the outer waking state. If you find it necessary to sit for a time you may do so, but afterwards lie down, keeping the concentration till this happens.

*

It [*meditation before sleep*] can certainly have an effect — though not perhaps through the whole sleep — for the sleep passes through many phases or planes and the effect is not likely to survive all these changes of consciousness and domain. It is possible however to get after a time a control and consciousness in the sleep itself. As for the subconscient, it can certainly have an effect, but most when there is a precise and positive will put upon the subconscient in the meditation.

*

You have to start [*becoming conscious in sleep*] by concentrating before you sleep always with a specific will or aspiration. The will or aspiration may take time to reach the subconscient, but if it is sincere, strong and steady, it does reach after a time — so that an automatic consciousness and will are established in the sleep itself which will do what is necessary.

*

You need not meditate at once [*after waking in the morning*] — but for a few minutes take a concentrated attitude calling the Mother's presence for the day.

Hearing Music after Waking

The expression [*of sweet melodious music*] was of the psychic plane — and the music was of that domain. Very often coming out of a conscious sleep like that the inner consciousness (which heard the music) lasts for a few seconds even after waking, before it goes back and is entirely covered by the waking mind. In that case what was heard or seen in sleep would continue for those few seconds after waking.

The Waking Mind and Sleep

It is the waking mind which thinks and wills and controls more or less the life in the waking state. In the sleep that mind is not there and there is no control. It is not the thinking mind that sees dreams etc. and is conscious in a rather incoherent way in sleep. It is usually what is called the subconscient that comes up then. If the waking mind were active in the body, one would not be able to sleep.

*

You are mixing up different things altogether — that is why you cannot understand [*the previous reply*]. I was simply explaining the difference between the ordinary waking consciousness and the ordinary sleep consciousness as they work in men whether sadhaks or not sadhaks — and it has nothing to do with the true self or psychic being. Sleep and waking are determined not by the true self or psychic being, but by the mind's waking condition or activity or its cessation — when it ceases for a time, then it is the subconscious that is there on the surface and there is sleep.

Depression in Sleep

The depression coming on you in sleep must have been due to one of two causes. It might have been the trace left by an unpleasant experience in some disagreeable quarter of the vital world and there are places in plenty of that kind there. It can hardly have been an attack, for that would surely have left a more distinct impression of something having happened, even if there was no actual memory of it; but merely to enter into certain places or meet their inhabitants or enter into contact with their atmosphere can have, unless one is a born fighter and takes an aggressive pleasure in facing and conquering these ordeals, a depressing and exhausting effect. If that is the cause, then it is a question of either avoiding these places, which can be done by an effort of will, once one knows that it is this which happens, or putting around you a special protection against the touch of that atmosphere. The other possible cause is a plunge into a too obscure and subconscient sleep — that has sometimes the effect you describe. In any case, do not allow yourself to be discouraged when these things happen; they are common phenomena one cannot fail to meet with as soon as one begins to penetrate behind the veil and touch the occult causes of the psychological happenings within us. One has to learn the causes, note and face the difficulty and always react — never accept the depression thrown on one, but react as you did the first time. If there are always forces around which are concerned to depress and discourage, there are always forces above and around us which we can draw upon, — draw into ourselves to restore, to fill up again with strength and faith and joy and the power that perseveres and conquers. It is really a habit that one has to get of opening to these helpful forces and either passively receiving them or actively drawing upon them — for one can do either. It is easier if you have the conception of them above and around you and the faith and the will to receive them — for that brings the experience and concrete sense of them and the capacity to receive at need or at will. It is a question of habituating your consciousness to get into touch and keep in touch with these helpful forces — and for that you must accustom yourself to reject the impressions forced on you by the others, depression, self-distrust, repining and all similar disturbance.

As for the actual mastery of a situation by occult powers, it can only come by use and experiment — as one develops strength by exercises or develops a process in the laboratory by finding out through the actual use of a power how it can and ought to be applied to the field in which it operates. It is of no use waiting for the strength before one tries; the strength will come with repeated trials. Neither must you fear failure or be discouraged by failure — for these things do not always succeed at once. These are things one has to learn by personal experiences, how to get into touch with the cosmic forces, how to relate or equate our individual action with theirs, how to become an instrument of the Master Consciousness which we call the Divine.

There is something a little too personal in your attitude — I mean the insistence on personal strength or weakness as the determining factor. After all, for the greatest as for the smallest of us our strength is not our own but given to us for the game that has to be played, the work that we have to do. The strength may be formed in us, but its present formation is not final, — neither formation of power nor formation of weakness. At any moment the formation may change — at any moment one sees, especially under the pressure of Yoga, weakness changing into power, the incapable becoming capable, suddenly or slowly the instrumental consciousness rising to a new stature or developing its latent powers. Above us, within us, around us is the All-Strength and it is that that we have to rely on for our work, our development, our transforming change. If we proceed with the faith in the work, in our instrumentality for the work, in the Power that missions us, then in the very act of trial, of facing and surmounting difficulties and failures, the strength will come and we shall find our capacity to contain as much as we need of the All-Strength of which we grow more and more perfect vessels.

Chapter Three
Dreams

All Sleep Full of Dreams

Again, about the sleep, it is like that because the ordinary state of sleep is an unconscious condition. One has always dreams throughout the night, but the surface being is then unconscious and records only a few of them that come through and even these it records in an incoherent way. Really one is acting or working on one plane or another throughout sleep except for a few minutes. When the inner consciousness grows, then one becomes more and more aware of what is going on, what one is doing and sleep is no longer quite the same thing — for it is more conscious.

*

They [*people who speak of "sound and dreamless sleep"*] simply mean that when they come back, they are not conscious of having dreamed. In the sleep the consciousness goes into other planes and has experiences there and when these are translated perfectly or imperfectly by the physical mind, they are called dreams. All the time of sleep such dreams take place, but sometimes one remembers and at other times does not at all remember. Sometimes also one goes low down into the subconscient and the dreams are there, but so deep down that when one comes up there is not even the consciousness that one had dreamed.

*

All sleep is full of dreams. Why should night or day make any difference?

Different Kinds of Dreams

Everybody has dreams in sleep though all do not remember

them. In these dreams one goes to all kinds of places in all kinds of worlds and sees and does things there or has experience of what happens there. Some of these dreams have importance and a meaning for the sadhana — most have none or very little.

*

These dreams are not all mere dreams, all have not a casual, incoherent or subconscious building. Many are records or transcripts of experiences on the vital plane into which one enters in sleep, some are scenes or events of the subtle physical plane. There one often undergoes happenings or carries on actions that resemble those of the physical life with the same surroundings and the same people, though usually there is in arrangement and feature some or a considerable difference. But it may also be a contact with other surroundings and with other people, not known in the physical life or not belonging at all to the physical world.

In the waking state you are conscious only of a certain limited field and action of your nature. In sleep you can become vividly aware of things beyond this field — a larger mental or vital nature behind the waking state or else a subtler physical or a subconscient nature which contains much that is there in you but not distinguishably active in the waking state. All these obscure tracts have to be cleared or else there can be no change of the Prakriti. You should not allow yourself to be disturbed by the press of vital or subconscient dreams — for these two make up the larger part of dream-experience — but aspire to get rid of these things and of the activities they indicate, to be conscious and reject all but the divine Truth; the more you get that Truth and cling to it in the waking state, rejecting all else, the more all this inferior dream-stuff will get clear.

*

It is the subconscient that is active in ordinary dreams. But in the dreams in which one goes out into other planes of consciousness, mental, vital, subtle physical, it is part of the inner being, inner mental or vital or physical that is usually active.

*

A dream, when it is not from the subconscient, is either symbolic or else an experience of some supraphysical plane or a formation thrown in by some mental or vital or either force or in rare cases an indication of some event actual or probable in the past, present or future.

*

This is an instance of a dream of exact physical prevision. The power to have such dreams is comparatively rare, for ordinarily such previsions come in inner vision but not in sleep. In dreams vital or mental formations often take shape which sometimes fulfil themselves in essence, but not with this accuracy of detail.

It is only a particular class of dreams that do that. Most coherent dreams are either symbolic or indicate things that take place in the mental or vital planes rather than on the physical.

This indicates a power of conscious thought-formation. Thoughts have an effective power — usually by creating an atmosphere or tendencies — thus when one is ill, those around should not have thoughts of gloomy foreboding, grief or fear, for that works against cure. But the capacity of conscious thought-formation is a special power and uncommon. It can be acquired or come of itself by sadhana.

*

All dreams of this kind [*indicating future events*] are very obviously formations such as one often meets on the vital, more rarely on the mental plane. Sometimes they are the formations of your own mind or vital; sometimes they are the formations of other minds with an exact or a modified transcription in yours; sometimes formations come that are made by the non-human forces or beings of these other planes. These things are not true and need not become true in the physical world, but they may still have effects in the physical if they are framed with that purpose or that tendency and, if they are allowed, they may realise their events or their meaning — for they are most often symbolical or schematic — in the inner or the outer life. The proper course with them is simply to observe and understand

and, if they are from a hostile source, reject or destroy them.

There are other dreams that have not the same character but are a representation or transcription of things that actually happen on other planes, in other worlds under other conditions than ours. There are, again, some dreams that are purely symbolic and some that indicate existing movements and propensities in us, whether familiar or undetected by the waking mind, or exploit old memories or else raise up things either passively stored or still active in the subconscient, a mass of various stuff which has to be changed or got rid of as one rises into a higher consciousness. If one learns how to interpret, one can get from dreams much knowledge of the secrets of our nature and of other-nature.

*

Those [*dreams*] which are formed from subconscient impressions arranged at haphazard (subconscient mind, vital or physical) either have no significance or some meaning which is difficult to find and not very much worth knowing even if it is found. Other dreams are either simply happenings of the mental, vital or subtle physical worlds or else belong to the wider mental, vital or subtle physical plane and have a meaning which the figures of the dream are trying to communicate.

*

It often happens that when something is thrown out of the waking consciousness it still occurs in dream. This recurrence is of two kinds. One is when the thing is gone, but the memory and impression of it remains in the subconscient and comes up in dream-form in sleep. These subconscient dream-recurrences are of no importance; they are shadows rather than realities. The other is when dreams come in the vital to test or to show how far in some part of the inner being the old movement remains or is conquered. For in sleep the control of the waking consciousness and will is not there. If then even in spite of that one is conscious in sleep and either does not feel the old movement when the circumstances that formerly caused it are repeated in dream or else soon conquers and throws it out, then it must be understood that there too the victory is won. Your dream which seems to have corresponded with realities was a true experience of this kind; the old movement did come from habit, but at once you became conscious and rejected it. This is an encouraging sign and promises complete removal in a very short time.

*

Subconscient dreams and lower vital dreams are usually incoherent. Higher vital dreams are usually and mental dreams are always coherent.

Subconscient Dreams

When one is in the physical consciousness, then the sleep is apt to be of the subconscious kind, often heavy and unrefreshing, the dreams also of the subconscious kind, incoherent and meaningless or if there is a meaning the dream symbols are so confused and obscure that it is not possible to follow it. It is by bringing the Mother's Light into the subconscient that this can be dispelled and the sleep becomes restful or luminous and conscious.

*

A dream from the subconscious plane has no meaning; it is simply a *khichudi* of impressions and memories left in the subconscient from the past.

*

Dreams of this kind [*in which old vital movements occur*] arise from the subconscient. It is one of the most embarrassing elements of Yogic experience to find how obstinately the subconscient retains what has been settled and done with in the upper layers of the consciousness. But just for that reason these dreams are often a useful indication as they enable us to pursue things to their obscure roots in this underworld and excise them. No, it does not indicate that you are taking in any part of your consciousness your present pursuit of Yoga as a stopgap, but merely that old vital tendencies and activities are still there in that mysterious and obscure subconscient limbo and that their ghosts can rise twittering to the surface when the conscious will is in abeyance. If the dream was trivial, it would seem to show that this ghost was not a strong demon like the militant Norwegian saga *revenants* but a phantom from an unsubstantial Hades.

*

Most people have that kind of dream at night. It is because the thoughts and memories that belong to the past are there always in some part of the being, even if they are not active in the waking state, and they become active at night. That is why one is constantly meeting the people once known, either one goes to the old places and meets them or they come.

*

You seem to be attaching too much importance to dreams. Keep your waking mind and vital free — you can deal afterwards with the dreams which will then be only memories from the subconscient.

Vital Dreams

Most among the sadhaks see many dreams of the vital plane when they sleep. In sleep the being goes out into other worlds and planes and it has to pass through the vital on the way — and as the vital is nearest to the waking consciousness, it is there it most vividly remembers. Probably you see better dreams but do not remember them.

*

In dreams on the vital plane there is always a deviation from the norm of the physical fact — sometimes this is because of the free play in the vital, but at others it is only a fantasy of formation either in the vital itself or in the subconscient mind which transcribes the incidents of the dream and sometimes alters them by contributions of its own.

*

These are dreams of the vital plane — they have probably some reference to something going on in your vital, but these dreams cannot be precisely interpreted unless there is either a clue that is clear on the surface or else you yourself can relate it to something in your experience of which you are aware. The images of the ascent and the coming down of water (consciousness or some other gift from above) are frequent and the general meaning is always the same — but the precise significance here is not clear.

*

Your dreams are of a very familiar kind, both coming often to sadhaks. The first is a sort of formation on the vital plane or a possibility for the future — whether or how it will come about in the physical is a different matter. The other is an excursion into the vital world where there are all the types and forms of things that happen here, each having its own region or province there. One is constantly going into these planes (and others also, mental and psychic and subtle physical as well as vital) and seeing and doing things there. Very often what one does and experiences there is a symbol of things in the nature, tendencies, achievements, difficulties, things hidden within or only half-seen on the surface. This one came clearly to show how far you have travelled from certain elements, tendencies or possibilities that were there in the past. The feeling in the dream was the sign of that progress.

*

A great many people have these dreams [*of flying*]. It is the vital being that goes out in sleep and moves about in the vital worlds and has this sense of floating in the air in its own (vital) body. The waves of a sea having the colour of lightning must have been the atmosphere of some vital province. I have known of some sadhaks, when they go at first out of the body in a more conscious way, thinking they have actually levitated, the vividness of the movement is so intense, but it is simply the vital body going out.

*

Flying during sleep over houses, streets, etc. simply means that the consciousness in the vital sheath has gone out and is moving over places in the vital or subtle physical world (even sometimes the material); it is always in the vital sheath that one flies like that.

The ascending movement is different — in that, it is the consciousness that goes high up to other planes or lands and comes down again to the body.

*

It is a dream of the vital plane. In these dreams the figures of the physical life take another form and meaning and the consciousness that lives and acts among them is not the outer physical consciousness but some inner vital part of the being. The insurrection of the French soldiers is a figure of some disturbance on the vital plane which wants to happen and affect the inner life. The import of the dream is the readiness of the vital inner consciousness to put its reliance on the Mother and take refuge in her against all possible disturbances or perils of the inner life.

*

These dreams are of the vital plane. Those about going home come from a part of the vital which still keeps the memory of the past relations and goes there during the sleep. The dreams about the Mother record meetings with her on the vital plane. For the first you should throw them away when you awake and not let your vital keep their impress. The experiences you had there (of the Mother coming in the heart and telling you) were psychic in character, not of the vital dream kind.

The difficulty you have in sadhana may come from the vital or physical mind becoming active. That often happens after the first experiences of calm and silence. One has to detach oneself from these activities in meditation as a witness and call down the original calm into these parts also. But this may take time. If one can in meditation sufficiently isolate oneself from the surroundings and go inside, the quietude comes more quickly.

*

The dream was of a kind one often has in the vital plane in which one gets into inextricable difficulties till suddenly one finds the way out. Gujerat in the dream was not Gujerat, but only a symbol of one part of the vital world which is opposed to the spiritual life and full of vital powers that come in the way either by fraud or by force. These dreams are indications of certain parts of vital nature (not one's own, but the general vital Nature) which stand in the way of spiritual fulfilment. When one goes there and masters them, then one is free from any intervention of these parts of Nature in the sadhana.

Symbolic Dreams on the Vital Plane

The dreams you describe are very clearly symbolic dreams on the vital plane. These dreams may symbolise anything, forces at play, the underlying structure and tissue of things done or experienced, actual or potential happenings, real or suggested movements or changes in the inner or outer nature.

The timidity of which the apprehension in the dream was an indication, was probably not anything in the conscious mind or higher vital, but something subconscient in the lower vital nature. This part always feels itself small and insignificant and has very easily a fear of being submerged by the greater consciousness — a fear which in some may amount at the first contact to something like a panic alarm or terror.

*

These dreams are quite symbolical of the vital forces that come and attack you. If you face them with courage they are reduced to helplessness. I don't think it is at all your father and brother that you meet — although something of their hostile feelings may be taken advantage of by those forces to take their forms — also they may do it in order to create sympathy in you and prevent you from acting against them. But apart from that the figures of the physical mother and father and relatives are very often symbolical of the physical or the hereditary nature or generally of the ordinary nature in which we are born.

*

Your dream was evidently a symbolic representation of some part of the vital plane (corresponding to a part of human nature also) in which the Mother had made her house (established something of her consciousness). The village represented some formation of human life in which there is outward beauty and harmony as in certain parts of European life, but no touch of the Divine. The jungle represented the surroundings in which this formation has been made — it is made in the midst of a vital nature which is wild and savage and full of dangerous things — the village, the formation is therefore something quite insecure and artificial. That is indeed the nature of much of human civilisation, an artificial construction in the midst of a dangerously unregenerated vital nature, and it can collapse at any moment. The sea is the vital consciousness itself, for water is often a symbol of the vital. The footpath seems to indicate something the Mother wants the sadhaks to build, to form in that part of the vital, but which is not easy to make and only can be made by constant perseverance which will finally prevail against the instability of the vital. Vital dreams of this kind are often very interesting and instructive if one can get the clue to their symbols, but to get the clue is not always easy.

*

The dream you relate in your letter is not of the psychic but of the vital plane — it relates entirely to conflicting movements of the vital consciousness, representing on the one side the attachments of the vital nature, on the other the movement of the higher (inner) vital to get free from them. Dreams like this one on the vital plane have to be observed and understood as indications of what is going on within you, but must not be taken too literally, as they are often symbolic and figurative, and cannot be always accepted as decisive directions for action in the external life. Thus the figure of the Mother taking a meal of rice with rice-water and salt might be a valid symbol — in this case for the

Mother's freedom from all food desire and the necessity of your lower vital attaining to the same freedom; but if you gave it an external and physical application, e.g. that the Mother had actually taken to such a diet and you should do the same, the interpretation would be an obvious mistake. So also the part about the service can only have been enacted on the vital plane to test or to stimulate the vital being's readiness to give up the service, if and when the Mother might demand any such action from you. But to deduce from a vital experience of this kind, however useful for a vital change, that you ought actually to give up service, would be as much a mistake as to take up a diet of rice and salt and rice-water on the strength of that part of the dream.

*

Yes, your feeling about the protection is perfectly true.

The dream about X and going to the Mother was an experience of something that took place on the vital plane. Things happen there that have some connection with the nature and life here, but they happen differently because there it is not the physical beings that meet, but the vital beings of people. One can gather what is the nature of one's own inner vital being — which is often very different from the physical personality that acts in front in the body. By the acting of the consciousness in these dreams the inner parts of the being begin to be more active and have more influence on the outer nature. Your inner vital being seems from the dream experiences that you have related to be very strong, faithful, clear-minded, resolute, able to deal with the hostile forces and their activities in the right way and do the right thing.

The sensation of going somewhere means that part of the consciousness is going into some other plane than the physical. The men you saw and also the vision that came afterwards belonged to these supraphysical worlds. The vision seems to be symbolic of something from above, but of what is not quite clear from the details. Gold is the colour of the Truth that comes from above.

Formations in Vital Dreams

These are dreams of the vital planes. Sometimes they are actual appearances — things that happen on that plane. But sometimes they are merely formations, thoughts or feelings put into shape. Not necessarily your thoughts or feelings, but those of others also or things floating in the atmosphere — or else formations made by the beings of those planes.

*

I said this dream was an actual happening on the vital plane, not a formation. If somebody attacks you in the street, that is not a formation. But if somebody hypnotises you and suggests to you that you are ill — that suggestion is a formation put in by the hypnotiser.

*

Your dream was not a sign of the worldly desire in you, but only a test or ordeal dream such as you have had before. Your absence of response in the dream shows that you have no such inclination towards these things as many have. The whole was only a formation or suggestion of outer forces on the vital plane to see what kind of response, if any, your consciousness would make.

*

These are dreams of the vital plane in which the vital plane takes up the spiritual experience and tries to turn it into forms of ego with a suggestion afterwards of loss of power and of consciousness and a fall. You should attach no importance to these dreams except as an indication of mixture in the sleeping state.

*

It is singular that you should have accepted dreams of this kind as true or allowed them to determine or influence your conduct even in the slightest degree. These dreams are nothing but formations of the obscure lower-vital consciousness; they are made up of its desires, instincts and subconscious memories, all jumbled together to weave an incoherent dream-scene and dream-story and, in this case, used by some vital Desire-Force of that plane to turn you into the instrument of its movement. They have no other value for the Sadhana than to show you vividly what is there in your lower vital nature, whether awake on the surface or lying in wait in the subconscient parts. The only thing to do with them is to turn the Light upon those parts and call on the Divine Power to expunge them from the nature. It is perfectly easy for this Desire-Force or for the subliminal part of the mind to create images of anyone it pleases or to reproduce the voice and make him or her speak or act in any way convenient to it.

*

These are experiences of the vital plane; they have a meaning if one knows how to interpret them. This one indicates the possibility of strong attacks on the vital plane, but at the same time promises protection. These are formations of the vital plane, sometimes things that try to happen but not necessarily effective. One can observe and understand, but not allow them to influence the mind; for often adverse forces try to influence the mind by suggestion through these dream experiences.

*

Your experience of the peace in the body was a very good one. As for the bad dream, it was a hostile formation from the vital world — a suggestion in a dream form intended to upset you. These things should be dismissed — you should say in yourself "It is false — no such thing can happen" and throw it away as you would a wrong suggestion in the waking state.

Unpleasant or Bad Vital Dreams

The experience of the hill and the rose and the sudden cold is one of those dream experiences that one gets on the vital plane, — for there things good and bad, pleasant and unpleasant are very close to each other.

*

Everybody has unpleasant or bad dreams and one can have them very frequently — they mean only that one gets into contact with or passes through the darker parts of the vital world. All of us do that in sleep, for we go out of the material plane and pass through many realms. But there is no reason to be afraid of these things. Have faith in the protection of the Mother and go to sleep with it around you — that is the best way of passing through these regions.

*

These are dreams sent from the vital world. There are three things she must develop with regard to them:
(1) to get the habit of calling the Mother at once in the dream itself;
(2) not to fear — if one does not fear, these other world forces become helpless;
(3) to put no belief in the reality of such formations and regard them only as suggestions put into form, just as one gets a frightful imagination of this or that happening but the reason knows it to be a mere work of imagination and is not moved by it.

*

In sleep one enters into places of the vital world in which there are such dangers [*as the threat of violence*]; but if one goes there in full reliance on the Mother's protection, all dangers either disappear or become ineffective.

*

These dreams come from the vital world, — there is nobody in the Asram who does not have them or else has not had them. You must not get afraid or upset at these things, but look at them with indifference, without fear and passion.

Do not always be thinking of the Hostile Force or believe that everything of this kind is an attack of the Hostile Force. It is simply that in dream you entered into one part of an obscure vital world and saw or heard things there. Even if you are attacked, you have to remain quiet and firm and call in the Mother's Protection and Force.

*

It is evident that X's experience was only what is called a nightmare — an attack in sleep from some force of the vital world, to which he probably opened himself in some way, it may be by answering to the man from the street who carried the worst vital atmosphere around him. The figure of the woman was only a form given by his subconscient mind to this force. These forces are around everywhere, not only in one particular room or house, and if one opens the door to them, they come in wherever you are. It would have no importance but for the nervous reaction of irrational terror indulged in by X. One who wants to do sadhana has no business to indulge in such panics; it is a weakness incompatible with the demands of the Yoga and, if one cannot throw it aside, it is safer not to try the Yoga.

*

Don't allow these bad dreams to trouble you. They are formations meant to disturb the consciousness — if you are troubled and fear they succeed. If you refuse to accept them or, still better, dissolve them, in dream or when you wake, then they can do nothing.

Mental Dreams

There are many kinds of mental dreams, but the main difference [*between mental and vital dreams*] is that the mental are quite clear and coherent, their symbols are well-connected and easily intelligible and the forms also are clear cut and distinct in their significance. The vital are full of a pell mell of scenes, forms and incidents; the significance if any is fluid and depends upon a vital symbolism which it is not always easy for the mind to follow — everything is nearer to ordinary life and its confusions but still more chaotic.

People Seen in Dreams

The people of dream are very often different from the people of actuality. Sometimes it is the real man who comes on another plane — sometimes it is a thought, force etc. that puts on his appearance by some trick of association or other reason.

*

These figures and intimations in dream may be due to three different causes —

(1) Beings whom you meet in the supraphysical world and who interest themselves in you.

(2) Forces of Nature, mind nature or vital nature, that take these human appearances and in a symbolic dream convey to you some formation of the universal Mind or Life. These messages can take the form of intimations or warnings of what is going to happen. The woman must have been such a Force of Nature, for her child and box are evidently symbolic — the child of some creation or formation of hers which she wanted you to accept and keep in your consciousness, the box of some habitual movements which this force also wanted you to harbour. The offer to take care of you was only a way of saying that it wanted to control you. To dismiss all that was the right thing to do.

(3) Constructions of your own mind in the form of dreams so as to convey to you intimations it had received or perceptions of some force of nature which, as in the last dream, it wanted the inner being to reject.

The Waking and Dream States

There is no solid connection [*between the waking and dream states*], but there can be a subtle one. Events of the waking state often influence the dream world, provided they have a sufficient repercussion on the mind or the vital. Formations and activities of the dream planes can project something of themselves or of their influence into the waking physical state, though they seldom reproduce themselves with any exactness there. It is only if the dream consciousness is very highly developed that one can usually see things there that are afterwards confirmed by thoughts, speech or actions of people or events in the physical world.

*

It is a very small number of dreams that can be so explained [*as arising from external causes*][1] and in many cases the explanation is quite arbitrary or cannot be proved. A much larger number of dreams arise from subconscient impressions of the past without any stimulus from outside. These are the dreams from the subconscient which are the bulk of those remembered by people who live in the external mind mostly. There are also the dreams that are renderings of vital movements and tendencies habitual to the nature, personal formations of the vital plane. But when one begins to live within then the dreams are often transcriptions of one's experiences on the vital plane and beyond that there is a large field of symbolic and other dreams which have nothing to do with memory. Of course it has been proved that a very long and circumstantial dream can happen in a second or two, so that objection to Bergson's statement does not stand. But there are also prophetic dreams and many others. Memory holds together the experiences but it is absurd to identify consciousness (even in the restricted European idea of consciousness) with memory. This theory of memory is part of Bergson's fundamental idea that Time is everything. As for *spirituelle*, in Europe mostly no distinction is made between the spiritual and the mental or vital.

Dream-Experiences

Yes, certainly, dream-experiences can have a great value in them and convey truths that are not so easy to get in the waking state.

*

---

[1] *The correspondent, who had just read Henri Bergson's* L'energie spirituelle, *asked whether Bergson is right that many dreams are brought about by external causes. He also noted that Bergson seems to consider all consciousness as memory. Finally he wondered why Bergson used the word* "spirituelle" *in the title of the book since there was hardly anything about* "spirit" *in it. — Ed.*

When you practise Yoga, the consciousness opens and you become aware — especially in sleep — of things, scenes, beings, happenings of other (not physical) worlds and yourself in sleep go there and act there. Very often these things have an importance for the sadhana. So you need not regret seeing all this when you sleep or meditate.

But in no case should you fear. The fact that you were able to destroy the beings that fought with you (these were beings of a hostile vital world) is very good, for it shows that in your vital nature somewhere there is strength and courage. Moreover, using the Mother's name and having her protection, you should fear nothing.

*

They are dreams of the mental and higher vital planes in which things happen with another rhythm than here and freer forms, but some of them are formative of things and events here — not that they are fulfilled exactly like prophecies, but they create forces for fulfilment.

*

The dreams are experiences on the vital plane, actual contacts with myself and the Mother in your inner being, not symbolic though they may have symbolic elements, but expressing relations, influences or mutual workings of our consciousness with yours. The second dream has symbolic elements. The ladder is of course a symbol of an ascent from one stage to another. The snake indicates an energy, sometimes a good one, more often a bad one (vital or hostile). It may be that the energy was quiescent and therefore not alarming, but by touching it to see how it was it awoke and you found it was something not safe to handle. There is no clear indication what this energy was. These dream-experiences do not depend on the waking thoughts as do ordinary subconscient dreams which are dreams only and not experiences. They have a life, a structure, an arrangement and forms and meanings of their own; but they are often connected with the inner condition and experiences or movements of the sadhana. It is not clear whether the flower incident was symbolic or only something that happened on the inner plane. It might have been possible to say if it had been indicated what flower it actually was that you had given.

*

These experiences are normal when the inner consciousness is growing and becoming more and more the natural seat of the being — it is the spontaneous intuitive knowledge of this inner consciousness which is becoming prominent in place of the ordinary reliance of the external mind on sense data and external happenings. It is indeed the being as a whole that becomes conscious — the substance of consciousness that becomes aware of things, not an outer instrumental part.

In the sleep part of the consciousness goes out to other planes of being and sees and experiences things there. It is quite possible for the witness consciousness to follow these happenings which usually transmit themselves in a coherent transcription to the sleeping part of the consciousness — the latter receives them and they appear as clear significant dreams as opposed to the incoherent dreams of the subconscient. Or else the witness consciousness may feel itself there watching the happenings as well as here. This will probably develop after a while.

*

It is the condition of your consciousness I spoke of — the more conscious you become, the more you will be able to have dreams worth having.

Remembering Dreams

Everybody spends the night dreaming — only most of the dreams and even the fact of having dreamed are forgotten. Also most dreams are incoherent. It is only when one becomes more conscious in sleep by sadhana, that the dreams become coherent.

*

When the sleep is more awake, so to say, then one has dreams of all kinds; when there is no such awareness of dreams, it is because the sleep of the body is more deep, — the dreams are there but the body consciousness does not note them or remember that it had them.

*

The consciousness goes into another plane of existence [*during sleep*] and, as the physical consciousness is not connected with or takes no part in the experience there, when it returns, nothing is remembered.

*

The subconscient remains in the body [*during sleep*]. The being really goes out into different planes of consciousness, but its experiences are not kept in the memory, because the recording consciousness is too submerged to carry the record to the waking mind.

*

On coming to the waking consciousness the night experiences are often lost or else fade from the physical memory in a short time, unless they are immediately fixed and recorded before rising.

*

Most people move most in the vital in sleep because it is the nearest to the physical and easiest to remain. One does enter the higher planes but either the transit there is brief or one does not remember. For in returning to the waking consciousness it is again through the lower vital and subtle physical that one passes and as these are the last dreams they are more easily remembered. The other dreams are remembered only if (1) they are strongly impressed on the recording consciousness, (2) one wakes immediately after one of them, (3) one has learned to be conscious in sleep, i.e. follows consciously the passage from plane to plane. Some train themselves to remember by remaining without moving when they wake and following back the thread of the dreams.

*

It [*remembering one's dreams*] depends on the connection between the two states of consciousness at the time of waking. Usually there is a turnover of the consciousness in which the dream state disappears more or less abruptly, effacing the fugitive impression made by the dream events (or rather their transcription) on the physical sheath. If the waking is more composed (less abrupt) or, if the impression is very strong, then the memory remains at least of the last dream. In the last case one may remember the dream for a long time, but usually after getting up the dream memories fade away. Those who want to remember their dreams sometimes make a practice of lying quiet and tracing backwards, recovering the dreams one by one. When the dream state is very light, one can remember more dreams than when it is heavy.

*

There is a change or reversal of the consciousness that takes place [*on waking up*], and the dream-consciousness in disappearing takes away its scenes and experiences with it. This can sometimes be avoided by not coming out abruptly into the waking state or getting up quickly, but remaining quiet for a time to see if the memory remains or comes back. Otherwise the physical memory has to be taught to remember.

Understanding the Meaning of Dreams

Unless they are really significant dreams it is a waste of time [*to study them*].

*

Yes, these are symbolic dreams, but the exact meaning varies with the mind and condition of the one who sees them.

*

That [*dream*] is evidently unlike many others a symbol dream on the vital plane. But it is difficult to interpret these vital symbolic dreams unless they offer their own clue — they are a sort of hieroglyph in their forms. Once one gets the clue some of them can be very significant — others of course are rather trivial.

*

No; all dreams are not true. Even of those which have some truth in them, may have to be interpreted rightly before you can know what is true in them. There are others that are true — they are experiences that you have in other planes or worlds into which you go when you are asleep. As for the bad dreams, you should not allow them to upset you, but reject them as untrue.

*

How do you say that vital dreams have no link or reason? They have their own coherence, only the physical mind cannot always get at the clue by following which the coherence would unroll itself. For that matter the sequences of physical existence are coherent to us only because we are accustomed to it and our reason has made up a meaning out of it. But subject it to the view of a different consciousness and it becomes an incoherent phantasmagoria. That's how the Mayavadin or Schopenhauer would speak of it, the former say deliberately that dream-sequences and life-sequences stand on the same footing, only they have another structure. Each is real and consequent to itself — though neither, they would say, is real or consequent in very truth.

*

The physical mind (or else the subconscient) almost always interferes in dreams and gives its own version. It is only when there is a clear experience on the mental or vital plane that it does not try to intervene.

*

I am not sure that it is advisable to tell these dreams to others — as a rule, the movements of the sadhana should be kept to oneself, because by speaking of them to others there is likely to be a dispersion of their force and perhaps a calling in of other atmospheres by the mental or vital reaction of the people to whom you tell them. It is only to very fit persons that one can safely speak about them. I don't think these dreams could be made into a book because they need a special knowledge to understand them and this knowledge is not common. For yourself you can do it, but perhaps it would be better to wait a little before you do it.

The Meaning of Some Dreams

It is a symbolic dream. The flower-rain is the descent of something from the supramental or else from the higher realms of consciousness — the lake is a formation of it in the consciousness, the steamer symbolises a new movement of the Yoga which Sri Aurobindo is bringing down. The Mother's descent with the diamond light is the sanction of the Supreme Power to the movement, the Peacock being the Bird of Victory.

*

The dreams are very significant and show a great progress in the inner being. The first dream means that to call the Mother is not enough; by that the immediate difficulty is dispelled, but the full victory which will prevent any return of the attack is not won; for that you must cease to be helpless before the attack, you must be able to fight and repel it (of course with the Mother's Force near whether manifest or veiled and supporting you). At present you have got so far that you can sometimes repel it with your safety pin, that is, by a small action supported by the peace behind; but the strength, confidence, courage to leap on the attacking force and drive it out (hands and feet) is not yet there.

In the second dream the servant is the outer physical consciousness while you are your own inner being. The inner being awakes in the darkness of the physical obscurity but is not troubled. It knows and writes the mantra of the Truth and Light and that brings the beginning of the white Light, the highest True Light in the darkness which once begun is sure to increase.

*

The strings you saw me pulling down [*in a dream*] are the lines of consciousness which can connect the personal being with the Divine Truth; they are above out of reach, I am bringing them down into the human mind, life and body. You can see only a part of them because they reach into the heights far above the human mind, and you see only a little of what is brought down because they go into all parts of the Nature down to the subconscient of which the ordinary mind can see very little. That is the meaning of the dream.

*

The meaning of the dream is not very difficult to discover. Our house here represents the higher consciousness in which we live and from which its light must come to you. Between you and it there is what the old books call a lid — represented by the blinds of the windows — created by the mind and the ordinary consciousness. This lid is changed to glass which means that between you and the higher consciousness there is left only a transparent lid (probably the higher mind which is the first stage of the higher consciousness) and through that the light can come to you in your own Adhar. It is a kind of promise or prospect held out to you in answer to your prayer.

*

The three grey-white birds must be your mental, vital and physical consciousness, partly enlightened by the inner Peace etc., therefore white, but still not quite released from the old nature, so grey — the dull movement is due to the obscuration by the old nature. But still they fly towards the right which is the dynamic side in women, the side of action and effectuation and this movement releases into flight the psychic in all its luminousness and purity. That seems to be the significance.

*

The dreams of the lower regions of the consciousness — the lower vital, the physical consciousness or the sheer subconscience — have always or almost always a double character. For there are two parts of the consciousness concerned — one that remains attached to the body but in a passive unsupported subconscient condition not capable of coherent and ordered experience and another that goes out into various planes and worlds of consciousness, has experiences there, moves among their scenes and beings and events, sees symbolic figures, scenes, happenings etc. The experiences of the two mix together often and make a double texture.

The quiescent part is subject during sleep to impressions from outside which it distorts into dream-figures or else, more freely, to impressions arising from the subconscient — sometimes impressions of the day or from the waking environment, sometimes impressions from the past, sometimes things hereditary or even imprecise impressions left from past lives which come up under some obscure or secret impulsion. When one practises Yoga, the more superficial impressions, those which are in a sort accidental or occasional, outside touches, the day's memories etc., do not, after a time, play so active a part as in the sleep of ordinary people; but the others aggrandise their scope and increase. These subconscient emergences are by no means, however obscure or trivial they may seem, always without any use for Yoga. They can indicate things with which the subconscient is burdened and from which it has to be freed, binding memories of the vital and of the cells which have to be dismissed, forms, embedded notions, tendencies, habitual movements which it is no longer good to harbour, seeds of the past which have to be pulled out so that their undesirable fruit may no longer recur. For in the lower obscurer part of our being we are creatures of habit of nature and fixed past formations and complexes — as they are termed by a current Western psychology, — and these things have to be got rid of if we are not to be bound to our past selves, if there is to be a true and complete liberation and transformation of the external being. If one can learn to detect and understand the indications of these dreams when they come up and act upon what they show us to be still there in the obscure bed of our nature, it can be a great help for the successful change of what seems to be the most obscure and trivial and yet the most sticky and intractable part of the nature.

The other, the active part of our consciousness does not remain in the inert and sleeping physical consciousness, but goes out into other planes of existence. For the most part with most people it is some part of the vital, lower or higher, that goes out into the corresponding vital planes, and the experiences it has there are transcribed in the physical consciousness or brought back to it and these transcriptions or these reports are what we call dreams or experiences on the vital plane. The reports, if one may so call them, are the memories of the outgoing part which it brings back to the physical — but it is not easy to retain them in the memory after waking. For there is a crossing of a border, a bridge or a gulf and the turning over of the consciousness, what was put behind by sleep coming in front, what was in front in sleep going behind and in this transition, in this reversing process, the report or memory which can by very vivid and complete is usually lost or only some last experience or a fragment of it lingers and even that is apt to fade away in a very short time. Especially if one wakes abruptly or under pressure or rises immediately without waiting to retain the dream-experience, it is apt to disappear at once and altogether. One can train oneself however to remember one's dreams so that the material is ready to hand for interpretation and use, if they are of a nature to demand interpretation or lend themselves to use. But also, apart from these reports, there is the transcription or translation into the terms of the physical consciousness. For there is a thread that connects the outgoing and the instaying consciousnesses and along this thread messages can be sent either from here to the wandering part, most often for calling it back, but also for other purposes or from the wanderer signalling or transmitting his experiences, as it were, to the body in the measure in which it can receive them. Unfortunately the terms of this transcription are usually supplied by the quiescent and very ill-ordered consciousness that remains in the body, terms belonging to its own normal life and range, and therefore the transcription is often trivial, confused, perplexing, tiresomely null in its terms even when the experience itself is vivid, significant, coherent and full of interest. But as the dream consciousness in sleep develops, the outgoing part can increase its hold, and either manipulate the terms supplied to it from the physical being so as to express directly and vividly or else in significant symbols its own characteristic consciousness and experience or else it can impose its own terms, figures, scenes with more or less modification on the recipient consciousness in the body. In the end the consciousness can become so trained that even for dreams on the vital plane the difference between dreams and visions and experiences disappears or at most one can distinguish between dream-visions and dream-experiences and visions and experiences in a state of willed and perfectly self-conscious concentration. Even the dreams of the lower vital and the subtle physical become entirely vivid, real, coherent, significant and expressive of a truth that one can at once recognise. The dream-experiences of the highest vital, the psychic and the mental or still higher planes have always this character, because when they can get through they impose themselves more than those of the lower vital realms and are less subject to distortion or mixture by the physical subconscience.

In the lower vital dreams, before this development comes, there is usually a mixture or a double texture. This has two disadvantages, first that the scheme used, the terms, the figures are so trivial and uninteresting that one easily misses any significance there can be behind them and, secondly, that the interpretation also becomes often very doubtful or hard to seize. And when as often happens, there is a symbology of the lower vital using the terms of the normal external consciousness, its system which is quite clear and convincing to the lower vital itself, can seem very absurd, incoherent and unintelligible to the physical mind. For the lower vital uses the happenings, scenes, figures, persons of the physical life, but in defiance of the order and logic of the physical world and even without any reference to it, it fits them into a quite different significance-scheme of its own for its own purpose. One has then to seek for a clue in some especially significant figure or detail, and if one cannot find it or cannot catch the clue when it is there, then one remains perplexed or doubtful or simply blank about the meaning of the dream; if it is found, it can often light up all the night and put them into a sufficient coherence.

The last three dreams described by you are of this character. The figures are supplied from the old social life in England, — though the place is not England; in the first, with some attempt at structure, in the others in a more haphazard inconsequent way; but so far as that goes, all seem trivial and unmeaning and, as one might say, not worth dreaming. The strong significant power and purposefulness and quite intelligible symbolism of the higher vital, the psychic or the mental dream-experiences is not there. But still there are in the first dream three *points de repère*, the railway-journey, the meeting with the father and mother, the communion, and these all are suggestive symbols. The railway-journey is *always* in vital dreams a symbol of a journey or progress of the inner being; here it is in the vital consciousness that some movement of progress is under way and it is in the course of it that you get down at a station, that is to say in some particular region of the lower vital where you meet your father and mother. A meeting of this kind by itself might simply be an actual encounter on the vital plane with some contact or interchange there — for in the vital one can meet thus both those who have passed beyond and those who are still in the body. But once the presence of a symbolism is established, it is probable that the father and mother are also part of the symbolism and, as they very often do, represent what might be called the Purusha and Prakriti of that particular kingdom. If it is an actual encounter, it must be with some part of their vital selves which is in sympathy with or representative of this domain, not with the actual persons, not with their whole selves. But the assistant here is clearly not any earthly person, but a being of this world who embodies one of its characteristic forces, the zeal of a dogmatic and ritual religious traditionalism without any deeper spirit or experience behind it; it is with this external ritualism that you clash in the dream, he insisting on the form, you careless of the form and admitting it only as a means for contact with the original spiritual truth behind it. That would justify our taking the whole thing as symbolism, representing a special lower vital world — one which plays a large part in moulding this external human life as it is now. It is a world of social forms, social and domestic feelings, social intercourse; whatever appearance of spiritual life there is, is traditional and formal: this is what you felt in the blessing of your father. The last part of the dream is more obscure — there is evidently a meaning in the luggage and the lost trunk, but the clue is insufficient; if one could catch it, it would probably explain why you got down at all in this province of the lower vital world instead of continuing your journey.

This is a very good example of the nature of these dreams and their indications and that is why I have dealt with it at a greater length than its importance seems to warrant. The other two are of the same world, but the third is ambiguous and in the second the clue is missing. The second, if taken as only an encounter with ordinary beings of the human world met on the vital plane seems merely absurd and trivial; but if the people represent forces or movements of this particular vital province, then some meaning is there — for I have always found that there is something which even the most casual or insignificant dreams of this kind are trying to indicate. If we take the two dreams together, the elderly lady would represent the interest certain beings in this kind of world take in some kind of pseudo-spiritual stuff of the lower occultist kind, e.g. Steiner's anthroposophy — taken by her more as a fad than anything else, a fad which she imposes on her guests. That would explain her wanting to sit in the rain — for the rain is a symbol of a descent from some other consciousness, and it would explain also the remark of the guest who had been in India, that is to say in some hot-air province of this world where the contact with occultist spirituality or pseudo-spirituality could be had more abundantly than here! To the physical mind the working out of the imagery is absurd and illogical, but this kind of dream cares only to get its symbols through and, not addressing itself to the mind, it disregards logical coherence. The whiskey would be the image of the dram drinking which this kind of occultism can be; along with the rain it would be the clue image.

This is how these dreams are built and the question at once arises, what is their utility and why should they with their triviality and incoherent symbolism and the obscurity and pettiness of the world to which they belong take so large a place. The answer is that it is here between the subconscient and the petty lower vital world that there is the hidden basis of a great part of man's ordinary movements, especially the things that are hereditary, customary, imposed by education and surrounding and left strongly entrenched in the subconscious obscurity, even when suppressed and rejected and entirely contradicted by the mind and will and the higher vital: it is the field of the suppressed complexes of the Freudians, it is the basis of the herd mind, it is the support of all that is petty and obscure in the being and of many other undesirable things. In your dreams — even in your lower vital — you are out of sympathy with this world, irritated and ill at ease and yet there is something in the subconscient nature that is tied and constantly going there as soon as the waking mind and will are quiescent. So it is with all, for one has to go there for two reasons, first either to become acquainted with its movements and work them out in the subtle experience till they go out of the system by rejection or to clear them out by a conscious action or else to work upon this world and bring into it a real consciousness and a true Light.

Chapter Four

Sex

The Role of Sex in Nature

Of course, it [*the sexual impulse*] is perfectly natural and all men have it. Nature has put it as part of her functioning for the purpose of procreation, so that the race may continue. In the animals it is used for that purpose, but men have departed from Nature and use it for pleasure mainly — so it has taken hold of them and harasses them at all times.

*

Certainly, Nature gave it [*sexual pleasure*] to encourage her aim of procreation. The proof is that the animal does it only by season and as soon as the procreation is over, drops it. Man having a mind has discovered that he can do it even when there is not the need of Nature — but that is only a proof that Mind perverts the original intention of Nature. It does not prove that Nature created it only to give man a brief and destructive sensual pleasure.

*

The terrestrial sex-movement is a utilisation by Nature of the fundamental physical energy for purposes of procreation. The thrill of which the poets speak, which is accompanied by a very gross excitement, is the lure by which she makes the vital consent to this otherwise unpleasing process — whatever X or others may feel, there are numbers who experience a recoil of disgust after the act and repulsion from the partner in it because of the disgust, though they return to it when the disgust has worn off for the sake of this lure.

*

Conversion [*of the sexual movement*] is one thing and acceptance of the present forms in ordinary human nature is another.

The reason given for indulging the sex-action is not at all imperative. It is only a minority that is called to the strict Yogic life and there will be always plenty of people who will continue the race. Certainly, the Yogi has no contempt or aversion for human nature; he understands it and the place given to each of its activities with a clear and calm regard. Also, if an action can be done with self-control without desire under the direction of a higher consciousness, that is the better way and it can sometimes be followed for the fulfilment of the divine will in things that would not otherwise be undertaken by the Yogin, such as war and the destruction which accompanies war. But a too light resort to such a rule might easily be converted into a pretext for indulging the ordinary human nature.

Sex a Movement of General Nature

All movements are in the mass movements of Nature's cosmic forces — they are movements of universal Nature. The individual receives something of them, a wave or pressure of some cosmic force, and is driven by it; he thinks it is his own, generated in himself separately, but it is not so, it is part of a general movement which works just in the same way in others. Sex, for instance, is a movement of general Nature seeking for its play and it uses this or that one — a man vitally or physically "in love" as it is called with a woman is simply repeating and satisfying the world-movement of sex, if it had not been that woman, it would have been another; he is simply an instrument in Nature's machinery, it is not an independent movement. So it is with anger and other Nature-motives.

*

There is no how to these things — the sex-impulse exists for its own sake and it uses the person as an instrument and hooks him on to another — whenever it can throw the hook, it throws it and once the connection is there holds on for some time at least. This is the physical vital and subtle physical action — for if it is the gross physical that dominates, there is no choice — any woman will serve the fun. The sensation you feel is physical vital + subtle physical, that is why it is so concrete. Naturally these sensations do not stop by enjoyment — they are recurrent and so long as the pressure lasts they continue. It is only by rejection or by the domination of a contrary force that they cease.

*

Naturally, the sex-movement is a force in itself, impersonal and not dependent on any particular object. It fastens on one or another only to give itself body and a field of enjoyment. When it is checked in the vital interchange, it tends to lose its vital character and attacks through its most physical and elemental movement. It is only when it is thrown out from the vital physical and most physical that it is conquered.

*

The sexual sensations do not "become" a principle of the physical consciousness — they are there in the physical nature already — wherever there is conscious life, the sex-force is there. It is physical Nature's main means of reproduction and it is there for that purpose.

*

The sexual impulse is its own reason to itself — it acts for its own satisfaction and does not ask for any reason, for it is instinctive and irrational.

*

The sex exists for its own satisfaction and this or that person is only an excuse or occasion for its action or a channel for awakening its activity. It is from within, by the peace and purity from above coming into that part and holding it, that it must disappear.

*

The sex exists in itself — put a number of sexual men together debarred from all possibility of feminine society — after a time they will begin to satisfy themselves homosexually.

*

Sex-sensation may begin anywhere. As vital love it begins in the vital centre, heart or navel — many romantic boys have this and it starts a love affair (often at the age of 10 or even 8) before they know anything about sex-connection. With others it begins with the nerves or with that and the sex-organ itself. There are others who do not have it. Many girls would not have it at all throughout life if they were not taught and excited by men. Some even then hate it and tolerate only under a sort of social compulsion or for the sake of having children.

*

There is no "delight" in the sex-affair, it is necessarily and can only be a passing excitement and pleasure which finally wears itself out with the wearing out of the body.

*

Yes, it [*the sex-pull*] has become rampant everywhere, especially as men no longer believe in the old moral restraints and nothing else has been substituted.

Sex and Ananda

Sex is a degradation or distortion of the Ananda Force.

*

It is true that the sex-centre and its reactions can be transformed and that an Ananda from above can come down to replace the animal sex-reaction. The sex-impulse is a degradation of this Ananda. But to receive this Ananda before the physical (including the physical vital) consciousness is transformed, can be dangerous; for other and lower things can take advantage and mix in it and that would disturb the whole being and might lead into a wrong road by the impression that these lower things are part of the sadhana and sanctioned from above or simply by the lower elements overpowering the true experience. In the last case the Ananda would cease and the sex-centre be possessed by the lower reactions.

*

The sadhak has to turn away entirely from the invasion of the vital and the physical by the sex-impulse — for, if he does not conquer the sex-impulse, there can be no settling in the body of the divine consciousness and the divine Ananda.

*

The *hlādikā śakti* is the Shakti of the Divine Ananda and Love taking possession of the whole being down to the vital and physical. But it is the Ananda and love of the Divine — the spiritual, it cannot be turned to a human love and vital pleasure. It can have nothing to do with marriage. In your dream it was neither the divine nor the human that came, but a supernormal and supraphysical vital *kāma* and joy — a being from that world intervening in the sleep and trying to take possession of what should be given only to the Divine. That is a particularly dangerous kind of intervention, so I had immediately to put you on your guard against it. It was of the nature of a supraphysical temptation such as the appearance of the Apsaras to the Tapaswis in the stories of the epics and Puranas. The other dreams were dreams of success and fame and were also of the vital plane. You need not be depressed by these ordeals in the subtle worlds; they come to all in one form or another; only you have to learn vigilance and find your way through these lesser planes to the highest, so that it may be the highest that will come down into you. When these trials come, it is a sign that you are advancing, for otherwise the Powers of these worlds, whether lesser gods or Daityas, would not take the trouble to test you.

*

The only truth in that [*the saying that "sexual pleasure and Brahmananda are brothers"*] is that all intense pleasure goes back at its root to Ananda — the pleasure of poetry, music, production of all kinds, battle, victory, adventure too — in that sense only all are brothers of Brahmananda. But the phrase is absolutely inaccurate. We can say that there is a physical Ananda born of Brahmananda which is far higher, finer and more intense than the sexual, but of which the sexual is a coarse and excited degradation — that is all.

Sex and Love

Nature in the material world started with the physical sex-pull for her purpose of procreation and brought in the love on the basis of the sex-pull, so the one has a tendency to wake the other. It is only by a strong discipline or a strong will or a change of consciousness that one can eliminate the pull.

*

It is not that it is not possible to keep the love pure, but the two things [*love and sex-desire*] are so near each other and have been so much twined together in the animal beginnings of the race that it is not easy to keep them altogether separate. In the pure psychic love there is no trace of the sex-desire, but usually the vital affection gets very strongly associated with the psychic which is then mixed though still not sexual; but the vital affection and the vital physical sex-emotion are entirely close to each other, so that at any moment or in any given case one may awake the other. This becomes very strong when the sex-force is strong in an individual as it is in most vitally energetic people. To increase always the force of the psychic, to control the sex-impulse and turn it into the *ojas*, to turn the love towards the Divine are the true remedies for this difficulty. Seminal force not sexually spent can always be turned into *ojas*.

*

When the psychic puts its influence on the vital, the first thing you must be careful to avoid is any least mixture of a wrong vital movement with the psychic movement. Lust is the perversion or degradation which prevents love from establishing its reign; so when there is the movement of psychic love in the heart, lust or vital desire is the one thing that must not be allowed to come in — just as when strength comes down from above, personal ambition and pride have to be kept far away from it; for any mixture of the perversion will corrupt the psychic or spiritual action and prevent a true fulfilment.

*

The movement of self-existent psychic or spiritual love general and without a special object can come, but it must be kept free from all taint of sex — otherwise it cannot endure.

*

What is real love? Get clear of all the sentimental sexual turmoil and go back to the soul, — then there is real love. It is then also you would be able to receive the overwhelming love without getting the lower being into an excitement which might be disastrous.

*

What is this idea that this desire of the heart hungering to love women is not sex-desire? That and the physical lust are both forms of sex-desire.

*

Why hanker [*to meet and talk with women*] when it is a vital desire? It is a form of sex and usually calls up the more physical desire.

*

Oneness with all [*expressed through embracing and kissing*]¹ would then mean satisfying the sex-instinct with all — that would be a rather startling *siddhānta*, though there is something like it in the practice of Tantra of the left hand. But the left-hand Tantriks are more logical than you — for why should oneness,

---

¹ *The correspondent suggested that the "lighter movements" of sex, such as embracing and kissing, seem justified as expressions of one's love for all.* — Ed.

if it is to justify sex-expression, support only the lighter and not the cruder forms of love-expression? But is sex really based on love or sex-love based on sex-instinct? and is sex-instinct an expression of the spiritual feeling of the One in all? Is it not really based on duality, except when it simply seeks satisfaction and pleasure where there is no question of love at all? Is one attracted to a woman by the sense that she is oneself or by the fact that she is somebody else attracting one by some charm or beauty which one wants to enjoy or possess or simply by the fact of the difference from oneself, the fact of her being a female and not a male so that the sex-instinct can find a full field there?

*

Abnormal is a word which you can stick on anything that is not quite common, cheap and ordinary. In that way genius is abnormal, so is spirituality, so is the attempt to live by high ideals. The tendency to physical chastity in women is not abnormal, it is fairly common and includes a very high feminine type.

The mind is the seat of thought and perception, the heart is the seat of love, the vital of desire — but how does that prevent the existence of mental love? As the mind can be invaded by the feelings of the emotional or the vital, so the heart too can be dominated by the mind and moved by mental forces.

There is a vital love, a physical love. It is possible for the vital to desire a woman for various vital reasons without love — in order to satisfy the instinct of domination or possession, in order to draw in the vital forces of a woman so as to feed one's own vital or for the exchange of vital forces, to satisfy vanity, the hunter's instinct of the chase etc. etc.[2] This is often called love, but it is only vital desire, a kind of lust. If however the emotions of the heart are awakened, then it becomes vital love, a mixed affair with any or all of these vital motives strong, but still vital love.

There may too be a physical love, the attraction of beauty,

---

[2] This is from the man's viewpoint — but the woman also has her vital motives.

the physical sex-appeal or anything else of the kind awakening the emotions of the heart. If that does not happen, then the physical need is all and that is sheer lust, nothing more. But physical love is possible.

In the same way there can be a mental love. It arises from the attempt to find one's ideal in another or from some strong mental passion of admiration and wonder or from the mind's seeking for a comrade, a complement and fulfiller of one's nature, a *sahadharmī*, a guide and helper, a leader and master or from a hundred other mental motives. By itself that does not amount to love, though often it is so ardent as to be hardly distinguishable from it and may even push to sacrifice of life, entire self-giving etc. etc. But when it awakes the emotions of the heart, then it may lead to a very powerful love which is yet mental in its root and dominant character. Ordinarily, however, it is the mind and vital together which combine; but this combination can exist along with a disinclination or positive dislike for the physical act and its accompaniments. No doubt if the man presses, the woman is likely to yield, but it is *à contre-coeur*, as they say, against her feelings and her deepest instincts.

It is an ignorant psychology that reduces everything to the sex-motive and the sex-impulse.

*

There are a number of women who can love with the mind, the psychic, the vital (the heart), but they shrink from a touch on the body and even when that goes, the physical act remains abhorrent to them. They may yield, under pressure, but it does not reconcile them to the act which always seems to them animal and degrading. Women know this, but men seem to find it hard to believe it; but it is perfectly true.

Sex and the New European Mystics

The idea of the new European mystics like Lawrence and Middleton Murry etc. is that the indulgence of sex is the appointed way to find the Overself or the Under Self, for that is what it really seems to be! Brunton of course knows better. But if the personal Overself is all that is wanted and not the Divine, then sex and many other things are permissible. One has only to realise that one is not the body, not the life, not the mind, but the Overself and then do whatever the Overself tells you to do.

*

I spoke of the *personal* Overself — meaning the realisation of something in us (the Purusha) that is not the Prakriti, not the movements of mind, vital or physical, but something that is the Thinker, etc. This Purusha can give assent to any movement of nature or withhold it or it can direct the Prakriti what to do or not to do. It can allow it to indulge sex or withhold indulgence. It is usually the mental Purusha (Manomaya Purusha) that one thus realises, but there is also the Pranamaya or vital Purusha. By the word Overself they probably mean this Purusha — they take it as a sort of personal Atman.

Sex-Indulgence and the Integral Yoga

What has this Yoga got to do with sex and sex-contact? I have told you repeatedly that sex has to be got rid of and overcome before there can be siddhi in this Yoga.

*

Any suggestion about Tantric practices must certainly be a trick of the vital. The sex-impulsions can be got rid of without them. They persist only because something still wants to reserve a place for them. So the best answer to the question about the sadhana (What is the place of sex in our sadhana?) is "No place". One must give up the sex-satisfaction and be satisfied with the Divine Love and Ananda.

*

The whole mistake is not to have a clear and unmistakable direction that sex (whether open or masquerading as deep romantic affection) and this Yoga cannot go together. This notion of making sex help the sadhana is one that has been taken hold of by many under one form or another and it has always proved an immense stumbling block to all who indulged it. It ties the being down to the vital and prevents the spiritual liberation which is essential as the basis of the transformation of the nature. Even the higher experiences begin to get coloured with the sexual tinge and falsified in their substance.

*

There is one simple answer to X's falsehood and perversions. In this way of Yoga an absolute mastery of the sex-movements and an entire abstention from the physical (animal) indulgence are first conditions, because this way aims not only at a mental and vital but a physical transformation. A psychic purity is demanded in all the consciousness and there is needed a transformation of all the vital and physical energies which in the absence of these conditions is impossible.

*

The Mother has already told you the truth about this idea. The idea that by fully indulging the sex-hunger it will be finished and disappear for ever is a deceptive pretence held out by the vital to the mind in order to get a sanction for its desire — it has no other raison d'être or truth or justification. If an occasional indulgence keeps the sex-desire simmering, a full indulgence would only sink you in its mire. This hunger like other hungers does not cease by temporary satiation; it renews itself after a temporary abeyance and wants again indulgence. Neither sops nor gorgings are the right treatment for it. It can only go by a radical psychic rejection or a full spiritual opening with the increasing descent of a consciousness that does not want it and has a truer Ananda.

*

I do not know what you mean by harm, but the harm of sex to a sadhak is that it stands as a strong barrier to the realisation and spiritual progress and in that way it harms not only oneself but the person on whom one imposes the sex-touch.

*

It is not a question of fear[3] — it is a question of choosing between the Divine Peace and Ananda and the degraded pleasure of sex, between the Divine and the attraction of women. Food has to be taken to support the body but sex-satisfaction is not a necessity. Even for the rasa of food it can only be harmonised with the spiritual condition if all greed of food and desire of the palate disappears. Intellectual or aesthetic delight can also be an obstacle to the spiritual perfection if there is attachment to it, although it is much nearer to the spiritual than a gross untransformed bodily appetite; in fact in order to become part of the spiritual consciousness the intellectual and aesthetic delight has also to change and become something higher. But all things that have a rasa cannot be kept. There is a rasa in hurting and killing others, the sadistic delight, there is a rasa in torturing oneself, the masochistic delight — modern psychology is full of these two. Merely having a rasa is not a sufficient reason for keeping things as part of the spiritual life.

*

It is possible for anger to be felt as pleasant — there are many people who dislike sweet things — so also there are many, especially women, who dislike the sex-sensation, even hate it.[4]

For the taste, when it exists — some eliminate it by rejection and the calling down of peace and purity into the cells, others by substituting for the lower rasa the higher Ananda — some like the Vaishnavas try to sublimate it by the *madhura bhāva* taking up the sexual rasa from the sex-centre into the heart and turning it there towards the Divine, but the last is a rather risky method.

*

---

[3] *Fear of harm to one's sadhana through indulgence in sex. The correspondent said that he did not wish to live in fear of harm from sex. In all enjoyment, he said, there is some risk of harm, even in eating tasty food.* — Ed.

[4] *The correspondent wrote that the feeling of anger is not pleasant, whereas the taste of sugar and the sex-sensation are pleasant. Is it possible, he asked, to eliminate the liking for sugar or for sex?* — Ed.

It is one of the aims of the Yoga to centralise and harmonise all the parts of the being — not around the ego as is done in ordinary life, but around first the psychic being and then the central being in its station above the head — or else round a nexus of the two. It is the thing that was preparing in you. The consciousness was moving to take its station above the head. But in the meanwhile it has gone down into the physical and the first result has been a relaxation and diffusion which has given an opening to the old movements to recur. When a movement like that happens [*an attraction to women*], there is generally a good reason for it, something that has to be dealt with in the physical consciousness. Instead of getting upset or discouraged, one has to observe from this point of view and see what has to be done.

There is no sense in getting discouraged like this because things recur. They always do. In a transformation such as we have undertaken, movements are not got rid of once for all. They go down from one level of the nature to the other and it is only when one has got them out of the physical and subconscient that one can say "Now that is done." If these recurrences were to be taken as a proof of failure, there are few in the Asram who should not be pronounced as failures. I don't think more than 2 or 3 have got over some sex-trouble; it lasts in one form or another even when people are "advanced" — as they say here. It is because sex is one of the strongest things in man's nature and cannot be overcome till one has got the sex out of the subconscient. Why then consider your case as if it were unique or build on it the idea of personal impossibility or unfitness? It is no use indulging the idea of giving up. You can't give up. So the only thing to do is to recover yourself, look at these things with detachment and push forward to the realisation of the self that was coming.

*

Sex is not a rational force; it is purely irrational, a power of the inferior, animal nature; you cannot therefore be rightly astonished if it acts irrationally without any justification or reason and without any other cause than its own habit and instinct. Moreover, this force as it is now acting in you with regard to X seems to be purely vital physical and physical in its character. It is not supported by your thinking mind or your rational will, these are opposed to its continuance; it has no emotional support, for you are no longer attracted by her or in love with her; the higher vital does not seem to be concerned, for neither beauty nor passion draws or drives you. But at this level of sex none of these things are necessary. The vital physical and physical urge of sex does not ask for beauty or love or emotional gratification or anything else; desire, repetition of vital-physical habit and bodily gratification (most usually, but not necessarily by the sex-act) are its motive forces. To set it in action nothing more is needed. Moreover, by mental and other rejections it has plunged down in the subconscient and is hidden there and rises suddenly from there. It is itself born from the Inconscient as a blind push of its dark force of Nature. It owes no allegiance. It can only be got rid of by a firm and persistent rejection, separation, detachment, not yielding to it by any act, refusing to take joy in it in any part of the being, until it is a dead thing and has no longer any motive or power of existence.

*

It is not meant by "the sacrifice of works" that there should be no choice between different acts, no control over impulse and desire. To regard the sex-act as an offering might easily lead to the sanctification of desire.

*

A married man can get experiences, especially if he is not gross or over-sexy by nature. But if he follows this Yoga, he will have to drop copulation or he will get upsettings.

*

What are these strange ideas? Do you imagine that after the transformation, copulation between man and woman and the desire to copulate will continue as the normal functionings of the life and the body? If so, why should it be forbidden in the sadhana? The injunction would then be not to stop sex-intercourse, but to copulate freely and sublimely and divinely.

Subtle Forms of Sex-Indulgence

Sex (occult) stands on a fair level of equality with ambition etc. from the point of view of danger, only its action is usually less ostensible — i.e. the Hostiles don't put it forward so openly as a thing to be followed after in the spiritual life.

*

This movement [*of vital interchange*] is a wrong and a dangerous one. It is not so much repeating the old game under the garb of Yoga, but, what is worse, turning the Yoga-power itself into the instrument of satisfaction of a vital force. There must be absolute abstention from all vital interchange with others. The warning has often been given that no special or personal relation, even under the colour of a psychic connection or otherwise, must be formed with the women sadhakas. The whole principle of this Yoga is to give oneself entirely to the Divine alone and to nobody and to nothing else, and to bring down into ourselves by union with the Divine Mother Power all the transcendent light, force, wideness, peace, purity, truth-consciousness and Ananda of the supramental Divine. In this Yoga, therefore, there can be no place for vital relations or interchanges with others; any such relation or interchange immediately ties down the soul to the lower consciousness and its lower nature, prevents the true and full union with the Divine and hampers both the ascent to the supramental Truth consciousness and the descent of the supramental Ishwari Shakti. Still worse would it be if this interchange took the form of a sexual relation or a sexual enjoyment, even if kept free from any outward act; therefore these things are absolutely forbidden in the sadhana. It goes without saying that any physical act of the kind is not allowed, but also any subtler form is ruled out. It is only after becoming one with the supramental Divine that we can find our true spiritual relations with others in the Divine; in that higher unity this kind of gross lower vital movement can have no place.

To master the sex-impulse, — to become so much master of the sex-centre that the sexual energy would be drawn upwards, not thrown outwards and wasted — it is so indeed that the force in the seed can be turned into a primal physical energy supporting all the others, *retas* into *ojas*. But no error can be more perilous than to accept the immixture of the sexual desire and some kind of subtle satisfaction of it and look on this as a part of the sadhana. It would be the most effective way to head straight towards spiritual downfall and throw into the atmosphere forces that would block the supramental descent, bringing instead the descent of adverse vital powers to disseminate disturbance and disaster. This deviation must be absolutely thrown away, should it try to occur and expunged from the consciousness, if the Truth is to be brought down and the work is to be done.

It is an error too to imagine that, although the physical sexual action is to be abandoned, yet some inward reproduction of it is part of the transformation of the sex-centre. The action of the animal sex-energy in Nature is a device for a particular purpose in the economy of the material creation in the Ignorance. But the vital excitement that accompanies it makes the most favourable opportunity and vibration in the atmosphere for the inrush of those very vital forces and beings whose whole business is to prevent the descent of the supramental Light. The pleasure attached to it is a degradation and not a true form of the divine Ananda. The true divine Ananda in the physical has a different quality and movement and substance; self-existent in its essence, its manifestation is dependent only on an inner union with the Divine. You have spoken of Divine Love; but Divine Love, when it touches the physical, does not awaken the gross lower vital propensities; indulgence of them would only repel it and make it withdraw again to the heights from which it is already difficult enough to draw it down into the coarseness of the material creation which it alone can transform. Seek the Divine Love through the only gate through which it will consent to enter, the gate of the psychic being, and cast away the lower vital error.

The transformation of the sex-centre and its energy is needed for the physical siddhi; for this energy is the support in the body of all the mental, vital and physical forces of the nature. It has to be changed into a mass and a movement of intimate Light, creative Power, pure Divine Ananda. It is only the bringing down of the supramental Light, Power and Bliss into the centre that can so change it. As to the working afterwards, it is the supramental Truth and the creative vision and will of the Divine Mother that will determine it. But it will be a working of the conscious Truth, not of the Darkness and Ignorance to which sexual desire and enjoyment belong; it will be a power of preservation and free desireless radiation of the life-forces and not of their throwing out and waste. Avoid the imagination that the supramental life will be only a heightened satisfaction of the desires of the vital and the body; nothing can be a greater obstacle to the Truth in its descent than this hope of a glorification of the animal in human nature. Mind wants the supramental state to be a confirmation of its own cherished ideas and preconceptions; the vital wants it to be a glorification of its own desires; the physical wants it to be a rich prolongation of its own comforts and pleasures and habits. If it were to be that, it would be only an exaggerated and highly magnified consummation of the animal and the human nature, not a transition from the human into the Divine.

It is dangerous to think of giving up "all barrier of discrimination and defence against what is trying to descend" upon you. Have you thought what this would mean if what is descending is something not in consonance with the divine Truth, perhaps even adverse? An adverse Power could ask no better condition for getting control over the seeker. It is only the Mother's Force and the divine Truth that one should admit without barriers. And even there one must keep the power of discernment in order to detect anything false that comes masquerading as the Mother's Force and the divine Truth, and keep too the power of rejection that will throw away all mixture.

Keep faith in your spiritual destiny, draw back from error and open more the psychic being to the direct guidance of the

Mother's light and power. If the central will is sincere, each recognition of a mistake can become a stepping stone to a truer movement and a higher progress.

*

I have stated very briefly in my previous letter my position with regard to the sex-impulse and Yoga. I may add here that my conclusion is not founded on any mental opinion or preconceived moral idea, but on probative facts and on observation and experience. I do not deny that so long as one allows a sort of separation between inner experience and outer consciousness, the latter being left as an inferior activity controlled but not transformed, it is quite possible to have spiritual experiences and make progress without any entire cessation of the sex-activity. The mind separates itself from the outer vital (life-parts) and the physical consciousness and lives its own inner life. But only a few can really do this with any completeness and the moment one's experiences extend to the life-plane and the physical, sex can no longer be treated in this way. It can become at any moment a disturbing, upsetting and deforming force. I have observed that to an equal extent with ego (pride, vanity, ambition) and rajasic greeds and desires it is one of the main causes of the spiritual casualties that have taken place in sadhana. The attempt to treat it by detachment without complete excision breaks down; the attempt to sublimate it, favoured by many modern mystics in Europe, is a most rash and perilous experiment. For it is when one mixes up sex and spirituality that there is the greatest havoc. Even the attempt to sublimate it by turning it towards the Divine as in the Vaishnava *madhura bhāva* carries in it a serious danger, as the results of a wrong turn or use in this method so often show. At any rate in this Yoga which seeks not only the essential experience of the Divine but a transformation of the whole being and nature, I have found it an absolute necessity of the sadhana to aim at a complete mastery over the sex-force; otherwise the vital consciousness remains a turbid mixture, the turbidity affecting the purity of the spiritualised mind and seriously hindering the upward turn of the forces of the body. This Yoga demands a full ascension of the whole lower or ordinary consciousness to join the spiritual above it and a full descent of the spiritual (eventually of the supramental) into the mind, life and body to transform it. The total ascent is impossible so long as sex-desire blocks the way; the descent is dangerous so long as sex-desire is powerful in the vital. For at any moment an unexcised or latent sex-desire may be the cause of a mixture which throws back the true descent and uses the energy acquired for other purposes or turns all the action of the consciousness towards wrong experience, turbid and delusive. One must therefore clear this obstacle out of the way; otherwise there is either no safety or no free movement towards finality in the sadhana.

The contrary opinion of which you speak may be due to the idea that sex is a natural part of the human vital-physical whole, a necessity like food and sleep, and that its total inhibition may lead to unbalancing and to serious disorders. It is a fact that sex suppressed in outward action but indulged in other ways may lead to disorders of the system and brain troubles. That is the root of the medical theory which discourages sexual abstinence. But I have observed that these things happen only when there is either secret indulgence of a perverse kind replacing the normal sexual activity or else an indulgence of it in a kind of subtle vital way by imagination or by an invisible vital interchange of an occult kind, — I do not think harm ever occurs when there is a true spiritual effort at mastery and abstinence. It is now held by many medical men in Europe that sexual abstinence, *if it is genuine*, is beneficial; for the element in the *retas* which serves the sexual act is then changed into its other element which feeds the energies of the system, mental, vital and physical — and that justifies the Indian idea of Brahmacharya, the transformation of *retas* into *ojas* and the raising of its energies upward so that they change into a spiritual force.

As for the method of mastery, it cannot be done by physical abstinence alone — it proceeds by a process of combined detachment and rejection. The consciousness stands back from the sex-impulse, feels it as not its own, as something alien thrown on it by Nature-force to which it refuses assent or identification

— each time a certain movement of rejection throws it more and more outward. The mind remains unaffected; after a time the vital being which is the chief support withdraws from it in the same way, finally the physical consciousness no longer supports it. This process continues until even the subconscient can no longer rouse it up in dream and no farther movement comes from the outer Nature-force to rekindle this lower fire. This is the course when the sex-propensity sticks obstinately; but there are some who can eliminate it decisively by a swift radical dropping away from the nature. That however is more rare.

It has to be said that the total elimination of the sex-impulse is one of the most difficult things in sadhana and one must be prepared for it to take time. But its total disappearance has been achieved and a practical liberation crossed only by occasional dream-movements from the subconscient is fairly common.

*

I have not said [*in the preceding letter*] that the sex-impulse has not been mastered in other Yogas. I have said that it is difficult to be free from it entirely and that the attempt at sublimation as in the Vaishnava sadhana has its dangers. That is evidenced by all one knows of what has frequently and even largely happened among the Vaishnavas. Transcendence and transformation are different matters. There are three kinds or stages of transformation contemplated in this sadhana, the psychic transformation, the spiritual and the supramental. The first two have been done in their own way in other Yogas; the last is a new endeavour. A transformation sufficient for spiritual realisation is attainable by the two former; a transformation sufficient for the divinisation of human life is, in my view, not possible except by a supramental change.

Transformation of the Sex-Energy: The Theory of Brahmacharya

The sex-energy utilised by Nature for the purpose of reproduction is in its real nature a fundamental energy of life. It can be used not for the heightening but for a certain intensification of the vital emotional life; it can be controlled and diverted from the sex-purpose and used for aesthetic and artistic or other creation and productiveness, or preserved for heightening of the intellectual or other energies. Entirely controlled it can be turned into a force of spiritual energy also. This was well known in ancient India and was described as the conversion of *retas* into *ojas* by Brahmacharya. Sex-energy misused turns to disorder and disintegration of the life-energy and its powers.

*

That is correct.[5] The whole theory of Brahmacharya is based upon that by the Yogis. If it were not so, there would be no need of Brahmacharya for producing *tejas* and *ojas*.

It is not a question of vigour and energy *per se*, but of the physical support — in that physical support the *ojas* produced by Brahmacharya counts greatly. The transformation of *retas* into *ojas* is a transformation of physical substance into a physical (necessarily producing also a vital-physical) energy. The spiritual energy by itself can only drive the body, like the vital and mental, but in driving it it would exhaust it if it has not a physical support. (I speak of course of the ordinary spiritual energy, not of the supramental to be which will have not only to transmute *retas* into *ojas* but *ojas* into something still more sublimated.)

*

The sex-impulse is certainly the greatest force in the vital plane; if it can be sublimated and turned upwards *ojas* is created which is a great help to the attainment of higher consciousness. But mere restraint is not sufficient.

*

Doctors advise marriage because they think satisfaction of the sexual instinct is necessary for the health and repression causes

---

[5] *The correspondent wrote: "Is it not said that the sexual fluid, if prevented from being spent away, becomes transformed into* tejas *and* ojas?" — Ed.

disturbances in the system. This is true only when there is no true giving up of the sexual indulgence, but only a change in the way of indulging it. Nowadays a new theory has come up which confirms the Indian theory of Brahmacharya, viz. that by continence *retas* can be changed into *ojas* and the vigour and power of the being enormously increase.

*

It [*inhibition of the sex-impulse*] would not be permanently effective in itself, because the seed would always be there unless removed by a transformation of the sex-impulse; but the inhibition can help towards this transformation. It is now being recognised in Europe by the doctors — who used formerly to say that sex was to be inhibited at the risk of complications in the body, that on the contrary there is part of the seminal force that is used for health, strength, youth etc. (turned into *ojas*, as the Yogins say), another that serves for sex purposes; if a man is perfectly chaste, the latter turns more and more into the former. Only of course the external inhibition does not help this change, if the mind indulges in sex-thought or the vital or body in the unsatisfied sex-desire or sex-sensation. But if all these are stopped then the inhibition is useful.

*

You mean the doctors.[6] But even all doctors do not agree on that; there are many (I have read their opinions) who say that sex-satisfaction is not an absolute necessity and sex-abstinence can be physically very beneficial and is so — of course under proper conditions. As for scientists the product of the sex glands is considered by them (at least so I have read) as a great support and feeder of the general energies. It has even been considered that sex force has a great part to play in the production of poetry, art etc. and in the action of genius generally. Finally, it is a doctor who has discovered that the sex-fluid consists of two parts, one meant for sex-purposes, the other as a basis of general energy,

---

[6] *The correspondent wrote, "Some scientists say that sex is an absolute physiological necessity." — Ed.*

and if the sex-action is not indulged, the first element tends to be turned into the second (*retas* into *ojas*, as the Yogis had already discovered). Theories? So are the statements or inferences of the opposite side — one theory is as good as another. Anyhow I don't think that the atrophy of the sex-glands by abstinence can be supported by general experience. X's contention [*that the sex-glands of those who practise Brahmacharya may atrophy*] is however logical if we take not individual results but the course of evolution and suppose that this evolution will follow the line of the old one, for the useless organs are supposed to disappear or deteriorate. But will the supramental evolution follow the same course as the old one or develop new adaptations of its own making? — that is the uncertain element.

*

You have not understood [*what was said in the preceding letter*]. I was answering the statement that scientists don't attach any value to sex-gland product and think it is only of use for an external purpose. Many scientists on the contrary consider it a base of productive energy; among other things it plays a part in artistic and poetic production. Not that artists and poets are anchorites and Brahmacharis but that they have a powerful sex-gland activity, part of which goes to creative and part to (effectual or ineffectual) procreative action. On the latest theory + Yoga theory, the procreative part would be *retas*, the creative part the basis of *ojas*. Now supposing the artist or poet to conserve his *retas* and turn it into *ojas*, the result would be an increased power of creative productivity. Q.E.D., sir! Logic, sir!

*

The most recent discovery about the sex is that the liquid is composed of two elements — one is used for sexual purposes, the other supplies all kinds of higher energies, vital, mental and, I would add, spiritual. It was formerly supposed by the doctors that the sex-liquid had to be spent in order to relieve its excess from time to time, otherwise there would be bad results. It is now found that that is not necessary — if the sex is controlled both in act and thought, there is an automatic *diminution* of the amount of liquid used for sex and a corresponding increase of the other element available for higher energies. In other words, the old knowledge of the Vedic and Vedantic Yogis and Rishis about becoming *urdhwaretaḥ*, viz. that by control one can turn *retas* into *ojas* and use it for higher energies vital, mental and spiritual is amply justified by this discovery. The use made naturally depends upon a man's occupations and interests. The athlete etc. would use it for physical strength and its work, the poet and artist for creation, others for study or mental work of different kinds, the Yogi for the increase and use of spiritual energy.

*

If it [*turning the seminal energy into* ojas] is to be done by a process, it will have to be by Tapasya (self-control of mind, speech, act) and a drawing upward of the seminal energy through the Will. But it can be better done by the descent of the Force and its working on the sex-centre and consequent transformation, as with all other things in this Yoga.

Mastery of the Sex-Impulse through Detachment

As to the sexual impulse. Regard it not as something sinful and horrible and attractive at the same time, but as a mistake and wrong movement of the lower nature. Reject it entirely, not by struggling with it, but by drawing back from it, detaching yourself and refusing your consent; look at it as something not your own, but imposed on you by a force of Nature outside you. Refuse all consent to the imposition. If anything in your vital consents, insist on that part of you withdrawing its consent. Call in the Divine Force to help you in your withdrawal and refusal. If you can do this quietly and resolutely and patiently, in the end your inner will will prevail against the habit of the outer Nature.

*

To be conscious [*of the sexual movement*] is the first step, but by itself it is not enough; there must come an automatic force of rejection which the moment desire and passion arise throws it off so that it ebbs back from the mind or vital or wherever it touches. This comes either by a strong will of rejection becoming habitual in its action on the consciousness, or by the detached inner being developing an automatic dynamic strength in itself so that it is not only not touched, but refuses these things by an active purifying power or, finally, by the full emergence of the psychic and its government of the mind, vital and body. The last is the most rapid and easy way. Till then these things recur. But probably in yourself there is still some sense of the old idea of sin or fault which makes you feel troubled. You must take it as an adjustment of the nature that is going on in which old movements which you no longer accept as yours return from force of habit and get a habitual response from some part of the being. But if that part of the being can be made to reject it, then the response begins to fade away. You must not allow yourself or your mind to feel troubled by the returns; for that only weakens the power of resistance. There should be calm dissociation of yourself from these things; then the detached inner being will become more easily dynamic and able to reject them from the vital nature.

*

The trouble of the sex-impulse is bound to dwindle away if you are in earnest about getting rid of it. The difficulty is that part of your nature (especially, the lower vital and the subconscient which is active in sleep) keeps the memory and attachment to these movements, and you do not open these parts and make them accept the Mother's Light and Force to purify them. If you did that and, instead of lamenting and getting troubled and clinging to the idea that you cannot get rid of these things, insisted quietly with a calm faith and patient resolution on their disappearance, separating yourself from them, refusing to accept them or at all regard them as part of yourself, they would after a time lose their force and dwindle.

*

The small tendencies, rajasic vital, which you enumerate are of minor importance. They have to be removed in this sense that attachment to these things has to be given up; the vital part of the being must be prepared to consent to their absence with quietude and indifference, taking them only if they are given freely by the Divine without demand or claim or clinging, but there is nothing very grave about them otherwise.

The one serious matter is the sex-tendency. That must be overcome. But it will be more easily overcome if instead of being upset by its presence you detach the inner being from it, rise up above it and view it as a weakness of the lower nature. If you can detach yourself from it with a complete indifference in the inner being, it will seem more and more something alien to yourself, put upon you by the outer forces of Nature. Then it will be easier to remove.

*

There is something in that. Too much importance given [*to sex troubles*], too much tension does sometimes make the struggle worse. To dissociate quietly and to reject steadily without being moved by the recurrence is the best way — if one knows how to do the trick.

*

As for the other point, the right attitude is neither to worry always about the sex-weakness and be obsessed by its importance so as to be in constant struggle and depression over it, nor to be too careless so as to allow it to grow. It is perhaps the most difficult of all to get rid of entirely; one has to recognise quietly its importance and its difficulty and go quietly and steadily about the control of it. If some reactions of a slight character remain, it is not a thing to get disturbed about — only it must not be permitted to increase so as to disturb the sadhana or get too strong for the restraining will of the mental and higher vital being.

*

It is best not to pay too much attention to this [*sex-*]movement, but to let it drop off quietly by lack of support and assent from the mind and the higher vital.

*

To think too much of sex, even for suppressing it, makes it worse.

You have to open more to positive experience. To spend all the time struggling with the lower vital is a very slow method.

*

Detachment is the first step. If you can detach yourself from the sex suggestions even when having them as you say, then they do not matter so much as the tamas, inertia etc. which interfere with your sadhana. They can wait for their final removal hereafter.

*

It is true that the removal of the sex-impulse in all its forms and, generally, of the vital woman-complex is a great liberation which opens up to the Divine considerable regions of the being which otherwise tend to remain shut up. These things are a degradation of the source in the being from which bhakti, divine love and adoration arise. But the complex has deep roots in human nature and one must not be disappointed if it takes time to pull them up. A resolute detachment rejecting them as foreign elements, refusing to accept any inner association with them as well as outer indulgence even of the slightest kind is the best way to wear out their hold upon the nature.

*

Pranayama and other physical practices like asana do not necessarily root out sexual desire — sometimes by increasing enormously the vital force in the body they can even exaggerate in a rather startling way the force too of the sexual tendency, which, being at the base of the physical life, is always difficult to conquer. The one thing to do is to separate oneself from these movements, to find one's inner self and live in it; these movements will not then any longer appear as belonging to oneself but as surface impositions of the outer Prakriti upon the inner self or Purusha. They can then be more easily discarded or brought to nothing.

Mastery through a Change in the Consciousness

Hurting the flesh is no remedy for the sex-impulse, though it may be a temporary diversion. It is the vital and mostly the vital-physical that takes the sense-perception as pleasant or otherwise. If by the real Being you mean the silent Atman, that does not identify itself [*with the sex-sensation*], but is felt as standing aloof. If you mean the Purusha, the sensation is a movement of Prakriti and the Purusha can stand back from it and reject it or identify and accept it.

Reduction of diet has not usually a permanent effect; it may give a greater sense of physical or vital-physical purity, lighten the system and reduce certain kinds of tamas. But the sex-impulse can very well accommodate itself to a reduced diet. It is not by physical means but by a change in the consciousness that these things can be surmounted.

*

It is only if the whole consciousness is awake and aware of its concealed movements that such [*sexual*] reactions can be avoided. It does not mean that you are worse than others, but that in all men the sexual element is there, active or dormant, indulged or suppressed. It can only be overcome by a spiritual awakening in *all* parts of the nature.

Mastery through the Force of Purity

There is a force of purity, not the purity of the moralist, but an essential purity of spirit, in the very substance of the being. When that comes, then sex-waves either cannot approach or they pass without imparting any impulse, without touching anywhere.

*

The desires of the heart and the body which stand in the way of Brahmacharya give a glow to the vital and emotive nature and prevent it from being dry and shut to feeling. To keep the heart warm and open, not dried up or closed, and at the same time attain to spiritual purity the best way is to turn it towards that which is eternal, pure and ever true, behind and beyond these earthly emotions — the ever-living Love, Bliss and Beauty.

*

If it [peace] is established *all through*, then it brings purity and the purity throws off the sexual suggestions.

Mastery through the Working of the Higher Consciousness and Force

It is always difficult to get rid of sex when it has had a strong hold on the system. It needs probably more than a mental will, — a stronger Force from above, to get rid of it altogether.

*

X seems in his letter to want only a liberation from sexual thoughts and desires by an intervention of another's will; but this is not how it should be done. Those who practise this Yoga can escape from it by a rejection of sexual suggestions aided by the influence of the Divine Power which acts through the Mother, but it is not instantaneous, except in the case of those who have a complete receptivity and an absolute faith. Usually it takes a steady tapasya to get rid of a lifelong habit.

*

What seems to be best is that the movement of rising above should be completed and if you can feel there the wideness, peace, calm, silence of the Self and that can come down into the body through all the centres and there can be the working of the Force in that condition of the physical being, then the vital-physical difficulty can be faced. The effort to do it by personal tapasya can carry one to a certain point, it can throw out sex etc., but for most it does not prevent all coming back by attack — unless the force of tapasya is so great and continuous that these forces get no chance. But the elimination of these things can only come, I think, by the descent of the higher consciousness — bringing with it the self-existent calm and wideness, the higher force and the Ananda occupying all down to the cells of the body. It is quite certain that these three together in the body can leave no room for sex — even if sex came, it would at once get so transmuted that it would be sex no longer.

*

It is the physical centre — sex is only one of its movements. Naturally, if the sex is active (instead of giving place to Beauty and Ananda) and if the lower movements are active, it forms an obstacle to the establishment of the higher consciousness. But the higher can descend, if there is at all an opening, even before the lower movements have definitely gone — it has then to complete the work of displacing them.

*

It [*the sex-impulse*] can be got rid of only when a higher consciousness comes down permanently into the vital.

*

I don't think it [*sex*] is *always* feeble in its going, sometimes it gets a singular intensity just before it goes — but it exhausts itself, tires and sinks, pressed out by the pressure from above. It depends of course on the nature. Sometimes it goes out like a snuffed candle, sometimes dwindles away, sometimes expires in a last flame. There is no rule applicable to everybody.

Rejection of the Sex-Impulse from the Various Parts of the Being

The sex-impulse is the chief difficulty in your way and, if that were got rid of, it would make the ground clear for the sadhana in you to take a much fuller course. If it persists, it is because some part of your being still clings to it and your mind and will have remained divided and found some kind of half-justification for the continuance. The first thing is for the mind and also the higher vital to withdraw their consent altogether; if that is done, it becomes only a mechanical return from outside on the physical and finally only an active memory which will disappear when it is able to find no welcome in any part of the nature.

*

The sex-trouble is serious only so long as it can get the consent of the mind and the vital will. If it is driven from the mind, that is, if the mind refuses its consent, but the vital part responds to it, it comes as a large wave of vital desire and tries to sweep the mind away by force along with it. If it is driven also from the higher vital, from the heart and the dynamic possessive life force, it takes refuge in the lower vital and comes in the shape of smaller suggestions and urges there. Driven from the lower vital level, it goes down into the obscure inertly repetitive physical and comes as sensations in the sex-centre and a mechanical response to suggestion. Driven from there too, it goes down into the subconscient and comes up as dreams or night-emissions even without dreams. But to wherever it recedes, it tries still for a time from that base or refuge to trouble and recapture the assent of the higher parts — until the victory is complete and it is driven even out of the surrounding or environmental consciousness which is the extension of ourselves into the general or universal Nature.

*

Is it that the body does not accept the sex-thoughts and desires? If so, you are entitled to reject it as something external to you or at most existing only in the subconscient. For it is only what something in us accepts, supports, takes pleasure in, or still mechanically responds to, that can still be called ours. If there is nothing of that, it belongs to general Nature but not to us. Of course it returns and tries to take possession of its lost territory, but that is a foreign invasion. The rule of these things is that they have to be extruded outside the individual consciousness. Rejected by the mind and higher vital, they still try to hold on to the lower vital and physical. Rejected from the lower vital, they still hold the body by a physical desire. Rejected from the body, they retire into the environmental consciousness (sometimes the subconscient also, rising in dreams) — I mean by the environmental a sort of surrounding atmosphere which we carry about with us and by which we communicate with the universal forces — and try to invade from there. Rejected from there, they become in the end too weak to be more than external suggestions till that too ends — and they are finished and non-existent.

*

There are two places into which it [*the suggestion of sex*] can retire — the subconscient vital below or the environmental consciousness around. When it returns it surges up from below, if it is the former, or approaches and invades from outside, if it is the latter.

*

It [*the pleasure of sex*] is the reason why the vital sex-difficulty is the hardest to get rid of — even those who have sincerely given up the more physical form are liable to the vital form of the impulse. But it is harmful because it allows a subtle infiltration of the forces that stand in the way of the sadhana. One must get rid of them if the vital is to become entirely pure and able to contain the divine love and Ananda.

*

Of course [*the vital is connected with the play of sex*]. It is the vital that gives it its intensity and power to hold the consciousness.

*

It is the entire inner rejection of the sex-pulls and vital pulls that is necessary, a rejection by the whole lower vital itself — the outer rejection can only be effective if this inner rejection comes to reinforce it. Usually people adopt the outer rejection because otherwise (if these things are indulged) the inner rejection is not likely to come since the vital trend is always being confirmed by the outer action — but if the outer is rejected, then the conflict is confined to the internal desire and fought out there. Naturally an outer renunciation by itself does not liberate.

*

There are people outside the Asram even who have got free from the sex without seclusion — even sleeping in the same bed with the wife. I know one at least who did it without any higher experience. The work of these people is ordinary service or professional work, but that did not prevent their having the sex-struggle nor did it help them to get rid of it. The thing came after a prolonged struggle because they were determined to be rid of it and at a certain stage they got a touch which made the determination absolutely effective. Possibly they were sattwic, but that did not prevent their having strong sex-impulses and a hard and prolonged struggle.

I meant by cutting off [*the sex-impulse*] a determined rejection of the inward as well as the outward movement whenever it comes. Something in the nature accepts and lets itself go helplessly and something in the mind allows it to do so. The mind does not seem to believe in its power to say No definitely to inward movements as it would to an outer contact — and yet the Purusha is there and can put its definite No, maintaining it till the Prakriti has to submit — or else till the confirming touch from above makes its determination perfectly effective.

*

Sex is your main difficulty — it is in fact the only very serious one and it is so because it is always behind and you have sometimes pushed it back, but never cut with it entirely. It is the physical vital that is weak and when the thing comes, becomes pliant to it in spite of the mental will's resistance. But even so; if the mental will made itself real and strong, these crises would be met and overcome, or at least pass without leading to indulgence in one form or another. The other possibility is the settled descent of the higher consciousness into the physical being. It is in these two ways that liberation from sex is possible.

*

The sexual urge is something that tries to take complete hold and leave no room for inhibition or control. It has a power of temporary possession which no other passion or life-impulse has to the same degree, more even than anger which comes second to it. That is why it is so difficult to get rid of it — because even when the mind or higher vital refuses, the vital physical feels this possessive force and has an ingrained tendency to be passive to its urge.

*

In the vital physical the "[sex-]response" lingers long after the mind and higher vital have turned from it. I have seen that in men who were mentally and emotionally quite sincere. A few get rid of it easily, but these are a small minority. But there must be no justification on the "what harm" basis — that is an attempt of the lower vital to get the mind and higher vital to adhere. There is always room for harm so long as the sex-response is not eliminated in *both*, not in you only.

*

It is the crude vital-physical that returns upon you in this way [*sexual suggestions*] — and these returns must be the cause of all the feeling of illness, weakness, tamas that you get. A purification of this part by the descent of the higher consciousness into it is a very great necessity for your sadhana.

*

Sex is strongly connected with the physical centre, but also with the lower vital — it is the lower vital that gives it most of its intensity and excitement. It can be disconnected from the lower vital and then it becomes a purely physical movement of a mechanical kind which has no great force except for the more animal natures. If the physical centre also is freed, then the sex-impulse ceases.

*

It [*sexual desire*] is the habitual mechanical response to the sex-force in the physical nature. It gets this intensity in spite of the mind's rejection because something in the vital physical (nervous) being still remembers and responds to the suggestion of the craving and the pleasure. If the nervous being can be got to reject it then it becomes a purely physical wave without mental assent or vital desire — that is the last stage after which it can be thrown out of even the environmental Nature through which the suggestion or denial of the general sex-force comes to the individual being.

*

These difficulties [*of human relationship*] in one form or another are felt by all — but they take a stronger form when the root is sexual. The obstinacy with which they return is due to the obscurity of the physical which always responds to an old habit of the nature (even when the mind has rejected it) and it is this obscurity and subjection to habit that the adverse vital forces take advantage of to repeat the trouble.

*

It is of course the physical that is at once responsive in the most material way to sex-suggestion. What you are doing [*rejecting the sex-movement*] is right. As you are controlling it in the waking state, it comes out at night. That too has to be got rid of.

*

That is usual — the subconscient acts of itself on its own store of impressions or habitual past movements. When one drives sex from the mind and conscious vital and physical it remains in the subconscient and rises from there in sleep.

Sex and the Subconscient

The sex-sensation came from the subconscient. When it is unable to manifest in the waking consciousness, it comes up from the subconscient in sleep. The mind must not allow itself to be disturbed — it will go out with the rest.

*

There is no reason for you to be depressed or discouraged. The defects of the nature of which you speak are habits of the lower vital and the external being; if you recognise them fully and frankly and detect them and reject whenever they act or try to act upon you, they will in time disappear. The sexual desires show that the subconscient still retains the old impressions, movements and impulses; make the conscious parts of the being entirely free and aspire and will for the higher consciousness to come fully into the subconscient so that even in sleep and dream something in you may be aware and on guard and reject these things when they try to take form at that time.

*

I do not suppose the sex-touch came at all from them personally; at most some contact with the outside world and its consciousness might have touched the subconscient. But the real reason for these upsurgings of old movements is the subconscient itself where the old things remain in seed and can sprout up after long cessation or interruption. To be completely secure against all possibility of their return one must have established the higher consciousness in all the being down to the subconscient. But meanwhile these returns can be used as a test of the progress made. If for instance the sex-thought rises into the mind, but cannot remain there, that means the mind is substantially free; if the sex-desire comes into the vital and falls away without taking a hold, it is the same for the vital. The last question is for the body where it can come as a physical urge or sensation. If it can hold none of these there is no refuge left for it except the subconscient from which it can try to rise, especially in dreams, or the environmental consciousness from which it can try to come as a wave invading the being.

*

If you can exclude sex from the waking thought and consciousness, the survival in sleep will not be so important. It will mean that the sex has sunk down from the conscious mind, vital, physical being into the subconscious; from there it comes up in sleep. But if it has no support from the conscious being, it may be active for a time but its activity will afterwards diminish, become more and more rare till it is eliminated. This may take time, shorter or longer, but in the end the elimination is bound to come.

*

If the waking state is freed from indulgence whether mental or physical in sex-thoughts, sex-impulses, sex-action, then the subconscient can be better dealt with; till then what is indulged by the mind in the waking state or else is suppressed but not yet entirely rejected can always lurk in the subconscient and rise from it in sleep. Turn away the conscious mind and vital from the sex-impulse *entirely*, that is the first step.

*

Naturally, if you read about these [*sexual*] things [*in novels*] they enter the mind and pass into the subconscious where they leave their impression. If the consciousness is not free from the sexual impulse, this impression can rise up from the subconscient and work in the mind.

*

The sex-impulse is deeply rooted in the subconscient and it is difficult to get rid of it. Only the full transformation of the physical consciousness can do that — except for a few who are not strongly bound by it.

Tamasic Inertia and the Sex-Impulse

When there is the dullness — tamas of any kind — it is much easier for the sex-force to act.

*

Inactivity is an atmosphere in which sex easily rises.

*

A state of tamasic inertia of the mind and body is always favourable to the sex-urge by the sex-impulse. What I meant was that there is something (not the whole) of your lower vital and physical that can respond to the sex-impulse. There may be another part that has already the aspiration — but when the condition favourable to the sex-invasion comes, then the aspiration is quiescent or not strong enough and the other elements allow the sex-force to come in.

*

The exercise has probably helped [*the body*] both by engaging the vital energies of the body and by giving it strength and tone. Sex always increases when the vital physical is indolent, unoccupied or without tone.

*

It is the most dangerous moment for sex things when just after waking one remains lying in bed; one should either go to sleep again, if there is time, or else fix the mind on wholesome things.

*

There is no condition more dangerous for the sex-imagination to come than this lying in bed in a half-awake or else a relaxed inert condition unoccupied by any activity or any experience.

Sex-Thoughts and Imaginations

That [*indulgence in sex-thoughts*] is just the thing that ought not to be done. It would be merely a gratuitous increasing of the difficulties. For the spiritual endeavour is part of your nature and, if it is difficult to get rid of the sex-impulse, you would find it still more difficult to do without the spiritual life in you. Sex is the one difficulty in its way that is hardest to get rid of, because it sticks and returns, but one has to be more persistent than the difficulty — there is no other way.

*

By giving up contact [*with women*] it [*sexual desire*] can be reduced to two forms — dream and imagination. Dream is not of much importance unless it affects the waking mind which it need not at all do; it can besides be discouraged and, if not fed, fades out in the end. Imaginations can only be got rid of by a tapasya of the will not allowing them to run their course, but breaking them off as soon as they begin. They come most easily when lying in bed after waking from sleep in a tamasic condition. One has to break them off either by shaking off the tamas or by emptying the mind and going to sleep again. At other times one ought to be able to stop it by turning the mind elsewhere.

*

To let the memory or imagination dwell on things that excite the sex-desire is unhealthy for the sadhana and an obstacle to the development of the Yogic consciousness. Discourage these imaginations and memories when they come.

*

That [*support of the sex-sensation by the imagination*] is the difficulty. The imagination means a consent of the physical or else the vital mind. Otherwise the [*sex-*]sensation is often only due to physical causes and, if not supported by this automatic assent of a part of the mind, would before long diminish in its habit of recurrence.

*

Care must be taken that the sexual or erotic imagination does not take hold of the consciousness representing itself as spiritual truth.

Sexual Difficulties among Men

In most men the sexual is the strongest of all the impulses of Nature.

*

The vital needs something to hook itself on to, but for a sadhak women are obviously the wrong things for it to hook itself on to — it must get hold of the right peg.

*

If it [*the vital*] admires all beautiful things, not women only, without desire — then there would be no harm [*in admiring women*]. But specially applied to women, it is a relic of the "sex-appeal".

*

It [*the sense of one's own vital charm and power of attraction*] is the usual vanity of the lower vital — it is very common. Any man can have an attraction for any woman, and vice versa, when the sex-forces are active, but that attraction is not his, it is the pull of the sex-force.

Sex-Dreams and Emissions

There are two kinds of these [*sex-*]dreams, one kind which are things happening on the vital plane, another kind which is made up of impressions and impulses coming up from the subconscient, not actual happenings. Dreams in which emission takes place are usually of the second kind — but not always; for sometimes they come through the touch of vital beings or forces in the vital plane or through a meeting of one's own sexual thought-forms with those of another there.

*

Apart from the total rejection of sex-thoughts and imaginations and actions, which ends by acting in the subconscient also, I don't know any remedy for sex-dreams except the putting of a force as concrete as possible on the sex-centre and organ prohibiting this urge and its result, put when about to sleep and renewed each time one wakes and goes to sleep again. But this all cannot manage to use, for they employ a mental will instead of a concrete force (the mental will can be effective, but is not always so). This method, besides, only acts for the time, it inhibits but except in rare cases does not permanently cure; it does not get rid of the sex-impressions in the subconscient, and of course it means thinking of the sex-affair though only negatively.

I have heard it said that even very advanced Yogis get the dreams at least once in six months, — I don't know how far it is true or what the Yogis themselves say about it. But the sex-impressions in the heart can be got rid of long before the end of life, and even the seed state in the subconscient which comes up in dreams, though sticky enough, is not quite so irremovable as all that.

Anyway, the dream kind is not so much to trouble about, unless it is frequent — it is the waking state that must be rigorously cleared out. Sometimes, if that is done, there is automatic extension of the habit of rejection to the subconscient, so that when the dream is coming there is an automatic prohibition that stops it. Under a regime like that I think the sex-pressure would become, if not non-existent, yet permanently quiescent in its seed state and so practically *non est*.

*

Night-dreams are involuntary upsurgings of the sex-impressions from the subconscient; most men when they are not indulging in the sex-act have it from time to time though it varies in period from a week, a fortnight, a month to three or four months or even less. To have it more frequently indicates either indulgence in sex-imaginations which stimulate the sex-centre or else a nervous weakness in that part due to past indulgence. Some have benefited by putting a will on the body before going to sleep at night that these dreams should not happen — though it may not succeed at the beginning, it tells in most cases after a time by fixing a certain inhibitory force on the subconscient from which these dreams arise. As to children indulging, that is not hereditary, but a thing taught by bad company and these children are sometimes spoiled in this way at a very early age.

*

When the waking consciousness has renounced the indulgence of the sexual desires and impulses, these take refuge in the subconscient as impressions, memories, suppressed desires and come up in sleep as dreams and involuntary sleep emissions. If the waking consciousness is not itself clear, if, that is to say, though there is no physical indulgence, yet there are imaginations in the mind or desires in the vital or the body, then these dreams and emissions can be frequent. Even if the waking consciousness is clear, the subconscient emergences can still come for a time, but in time they diminish. Some are able to get rid of this by putting a strong prohibiting will or force on the subconscient or on the sex-centre before going to sleep, but this does not succeed with everyone. The main thing is to get the increasing force of brahmacharya in the waking consciousness, complete expulsion of sex-thoughts, speech, physical craving or impulse — the subconscient remnants will either die out or be cleared out afterwards when one is able to bring the higher consciousness down here.

*

In order that the dream emissions may diminish or cease, it is necessary first to have complete brahmacharya, *kāyamanovākyena* — not only to banish sexuality from the bodily action, but also sexual impulses from the vital and body consciousness and sexual thoughts and imaginations from the mind and speech — and not talk or like to talk about sexual things. The dreams arise from the subconscient where all impressions and instincts are stored up and any of these things stimulates the subconscient and increases its store which can well up in dreams. If one makes the waking consciousness entirely pure, then by putting a will or force on the subconscient (especially before going to sleep) one can after a time eliminate the sex-dreams and emissions.

*

It is obviously an attack which falls upon your nervous system through the subconscient. It comes in sleep because in the waking consciousness you are more on your guard and able to react against attacks. Usually this kind of dream and discharge come when the physical consciousness is in a tamasic condition through fatigue or strain or any other cause, in a heavy sleep or under a stress of inertia.

The first thing to do is to reject the after consequences as you have done this time — for you say you do not feel any weakness, but rather as if nothing had happened. It is not at all inevitable that one should feel weakness after a dream of this kind and a discharge; it is only by a habitual association in the physical mind that these forces can bring these reactions of nervous weakness.

As for preventing the discharge, it can be done by becoming more conscious in sleep. You were conscious of all that happened, but you must besides develop the power of a conscious will which sees what is going to happen and interferes to prevent it, either by waking in time or by stopping the dream or prohibiting the discharge. All this is perfectly possible, it is a matter of habit and a little persistence.

It is also often found very effective to put a will or force upon the body consciousness before going to sleep that it should not happen — especially when you feel the predisposing condition of heaviness or inertia, it should be done. This will is not always immediately successful, but after a time the subconscient gets the habit of responding to the will or force thus laid upon it and the trouble dwindles and finally disappears altogether.

*

As for the discharges, that is less dangerous; most who live unmarried have them from time to time. Only, if they occur too often, they are depressing to the vital force. Certainly, they must be stopped; but do not have exaggerated ideas on the matter. To stop them, the first necessity is to discourage sexual imaginations in the waking state. Even if that is totally done, the discharge may still continue at night, because the subconscient keeps the memory and the habit. To stop it, you have to have a strong will before sleeping that it should not happen; also, if you can learn how to do it, direct a strong force on the sexual centre before going to sleep to inhibit this kind of accident. After a time this method usually succeeds.

Physical Causes of Sex-Dreams and Emissions

This [*problem of emission*] is a quite usual phenomenon when one stops sexual activity and rejects it in the conscious mind and vital. It takes refuge in the subconscient where the mind has no direct control and comes up in the form of dreams causing emission. That lasts so long as the subconscient itself is not cleared. This can sometimes be done by putting a strong will or, if possible, a concrete current of Force on the sex-centre before sleeping against this thing happening. The success is not always immediate, but if effectively done it tends first to reduce frequency and finally stop it.

These things (accumulation of urine, hot stimulating food etc.) are all predisposing or auxiliary causes or can be so. There is often as described a rhythm in this subconscient urge — it happens at a particular time in the month or else after a fixed period of time (week, fortnight, month, six months).

*

The first thing necessary in such matters [*sex-dreams and emissions*] is to be perfectly calm and refuse to be upset by these difficulties. If they rise one must take it that they do so in order to be worked out. If there is nothing in the waking consciousness to encourage the sex-difficulty, then these dreams or discharges without dream can only be a rising up of old dormant impressions in the subconscient. Such risings often take place when the

Force is working in the subconscient to clear it. It is also just possible that the discharges may be due, especially where there are no dreams, to purely material causes, e.g. the pressure of undischarged urine or faecal matter on the bladder. But in any case the thing is not to be disturbed and to put a force or will on the sex-centre or sex-organ for these things to cease. This can be done just before sleeping — usually after a time if done regularly, it has an effect. A calm general pressure of Will or Force on the physical subconscient is to be put. The subconscient may be often obstinate in its continual persistence, but it can and does accommodate itself quickly or slowly to the will of the conscious being.

*

The pressure from the kidneys or the intestines causing dream of sex-tendency or imagination is the last and most physical form — it often remains when the others have gone. The body dull and the mind half awake is indeed what gives it its opportunity. But if it is only for a few minutes and leaves no after effect, then the tendency ought to disappear after a time.

*

Your dreams were mostly on the vital physical plane. There if there is any physical contact of a sexual or other kind that acts strongly on the sexual centre or on a sensory contact, it may even without raising any lust produce an emission by a mechanical blind and inconscient action of a purely physical (not even vital physical) kind. It is only when the sex-centre has become very strong that this becomes impossible.

Worry, Depression and Sex-Dreams and Emissions

People get too much worried about these [*sex-*]dreams which are only mechanical movements of the subconscient physical. If the conscious vital is cleared, they will after some time, with a little concentration, dwindle away.

*

It is a mistake to make so much of emissions — everybody has them. The subconscient has its own movement and the want of control there is a thing one can get rid of only when there is the full light down there. At most one can deal with this special factor by putting a will into the subconscient (in the sex-centre or the organ itself) for prohibition, so that even in the subconscient during sleep there may be something that reacts. Many have been able to diminish and almost get rid of the recurrence by this means, but others have succeeded less well. In one case there was a recurrence every fortnight and that stood in spite of the will. As for the waking difficulty do not make too much of it. Press on with the positive side of the sadhana towards realisation — these things will fade and disappear when the higher consciousness is down in the sex-centre. Meanwhile it has first to be controlled and got rid of as much as possible.

*

There is no reason to be depressed to this extent or to have these imaginations about failure in the Yoga. It is not at all a sign that you are unfit for the Yoga. It simply means that the sexual impulse rejected by the conscious parts has taken refuge in the subconscient, somewhere probably in the lower vital physical and the most physical consciousness where there are some regions not yet open to the aspiration and the light. The persistence in sleep of things rejected in the waking consciousness is a quite common occurrence in the course of the sadhana.

The remedy is (1) to get the higher consciousness, its light and the workings of its power down into the obscurer parts of the nature, (2) to become progressively more conscious in sleep, with an inner consciousness which is aware of the working of the sadhana in sleep as in waking, (3) to bring to bear the waking will and aspiration on the body in sleep.

One way to do the last is to make a strong and conscious suggestion to the body, before sleeping, that the thing should not happen; the more concrete and physical the suggestion can be made and the more directly on the sexual centre, the better. The effect may not be quite immediate at first or invariable; but usually this kind of suggestion, if you know how to make it, prevails in the end; even when it does not prevent the dream, it very often awakes the consciousness within in time to prevent untoward consequences.

It is a mistake to allow yourself to be depressed in the sadhana even by repeated failures. One must be calm, persistent and more obstinate than the resistance.

*

It is all nervous. If you did not get depressed and despondent and create a weakness by the depression, the discharges would do no harm. All get them except those who indulge and so get out the sex-fluid or those who have a strong Yogic or other control over their sleep. That control has to be got, but the first thing is to get rid of this reaction of despondency and weakness which is quite unnecessary.

*

There is no inevitable necessity for a dream emission making the body weak — it is probably the past sanskar that makes it have such strong results.

Masturbation

The theory of masturbation as a physiological necessity is a most extraordinary idea. It weakens the nervous force and nervous balance, — as is natural since it is an artificial and wholly uncompensated waste of the energy — and it disorganises the sex-centre. Those who indulge in it inordinately may even upset their nervous balance altogether and bring about neurasthenia or worse. It is not by disorganisation of the sex-centre and sex-functioning that one should avoid the consequences of the sex-action, but by control of the sex itself so that it may be turned into higher forms of Energy.

It is perfectly possible to check the habit. There are any number of people who have had it for years and yet been able to stop it.

*

The habit you speak of is exceedingly harmful and dangerous; it wastes the energy that should be preserved for the sadhana; it tends to weaken the mind, dislocate the consciousness, exhaust the nervous power, diminish the life-force, create inertia and impotence in the body. The excitations etc. that accompany it build up nothing; their tendency is to disintegrate. Often the result of this habit is to destroy the health and bring in undermining illnesses — it always does so when there is unrestrained indulgence.

There is only one thing to do for those on whom it comes — to break off the habit entirely, uncompromisingly and for ever and *never to touch the sex-centre.*

*

Necessarily, you must give up the perverse habit which is one of the main causes of your despondency, vital weakness etc. There is nothing that has more power to derange and weaken the system. If not only in your mind but in your vital also you had made the resolution to give it up, it would have disappeared long ago.

*

There is one way by which it is possible for you to get rid of the perverse habit: to establish a strong mental control and so get rid of the wrong movement. It is not true that it is unconquerable; on the contrary, the fact that you were able to interrupt it for some time shows that you can conquer it. It returned because these things are a movement of certain universal life-forces that, once allowed a habitual wrong response in the individual system, tend to continue in that form and, even if evicted, try always to recur. Your mind has rejected them, but something in your vital nature — the part that responds directly to the universal life-forces — still takes pleasure and has preserved the capacity and desire of the wrong response. A resolute and persistent effort of will can enforce in the end the rejection of the desire and finally even of any mechanical habit of the movement upon this part of the nature also. Only you must not be discouraged by relapses;

your will must be more persevering than the habit and persist till there is a complete conquest.

*

It is of course true that the nerves get upset by the habit of masturbation (frequently done daily or continued for a long time) apart from other untoward results. In Hathayoga and Rajayoga to carry on sex along with the Yoga is extremely dangerous. But it is not safe (physically) with any Yoga, unless the practice of Yoga is only nominal or unless the mind and nerves are made of iron. The spiritual unsafeness is of course always there.

*

Any intervention, however imperative, cannot be effective without the cooperation and assent of the being. If you continue to entertain and justify with your mind such [*sexual*] movements as you described and gave expression to, if you go on doing physical violence to yourself and adopting it as a means of sadhana or admitting as a part of sadhana the method of revolt or other Asuric errors, how do you expect to have the will and needed discrimination? You have first to throw out these things which have been shown to you to be false and from a hostile source. It is because the mind justified or excused them, that the will became weak to dismiss them. You have to dismiss these errors altogether, if you want to do this Yoga in which they have no place at all.

On the other hand, if you are unable to control these movements and dismiss them in spite of your mind refusing them, that means a weak condition of the nerves in which the remedy I proposed is the only one. I meant by change of air not only a change of climate, but of place, surroundings and atmosphere — to remain for a time where there will not be any pressure. You speak of the danger of not being able to come back or of losing the sadhana, but to allow these things to go farther is much more dangerous to the sadhana and, if they increase or continue, you will not be able to remain here.

As for the secretiveness you spoke of, it is one main reason of your going astray — for it has made you shut yourself up in your own wrong movement. If you have got yourself into an imprisoning circle, the first thing you have to do is to get out of it — secretiveness must be renounced altogether.

*

If you cannot stop the masturbation, I think you are right in going [*from the Ashram*], as to continue might have serious consequences for the nervous system. It is better in that case to live the ordinary life and let the sex-instinct have its natural outlet so long as it is so irresistible. It is not necessary to wait for training somebody to do the work. Mother appreciates very much all the work you have done and we had hoped the earnest spiritual effort you have made would prevail over this tendency. But it would not be wise to insist too much against the obstinately strong indication that the vital nature needs a relief. Wherever you are, the Mother's blessings and mine will be with you and you will receive from us all the inner help we can give you.

Sexual Difficulties among Women

There is no universal rule. Women can be as sexual as men or more. But there are numbers of women who dislike sex and there are very few men. One Sukhdev in a million, but many Dianas and Pallas Athenes. The virgin is really a feminine conception; men are repelled by the idea of eternal virginity. Many women would remain without any wakening of the sexual instinct if men did not thrust it on them and that cannot be said of many, perhaps of any man! But there is another side to the picture. Women are perhaps less physically sexual than men on the whole, — but what about vital sexuality? the instinct of possessing and being possessed etc. etc.?

*

If there were not the sex-push in her, how could that [*feeling of unpleasant warmth*] be? The sex-push is not merely the impulse to the act, as she perhaps thinks, as the push to envelop and occupy the man and to possess and be possessed. That is so especially with women, the sex-act being very often less attractive to them than to men; but of course always, if the vital physical reaches a certain point, the physical sex-movement tends to follow.

*

She may not have the sex-feeling towards you, but there is a certain kind of vital push, throwing out of tentacles — I don't know exactly how to express it — the secret object of which in Nature is to attract the man, to draw his attention and fix it on the woman, hook and draw him in a less or greater degree. The intention may not be at all conscious in the woman's mind, that is to say, it may not be clear or even present to her mind, — it may be merely instinctive or subconscious. There need be no physical sexual intention, only the vital in spontaneous movement. All women of a strongly vital temperament (and X is that) have it — some more, some less. There may be no specific sex-impulse in it, but it will still raise the sex-idea in the man. X naturally has no psychological knowledge and these things are too subtle for her to perceive or realise. She may easily think she is acting in a perfectly innocent and natural way and not at all know this activity of the Nature push in her.

*

A smile or any movement, appearance or action of the woman can be the starting point for these vibrations. I don't suppose it is anything inherent in the smile itself, but all these things have been the habitual means by which sex has been excited in man (*hāvabhāva*) and the woman uses them, often unconsciously and by mere habit when coming into contact with man, whether she has or has not any intention of pleasing or moving the man, it still comes up as an instinctive movement. X is of the type of woman who has this instinctive movement to please the male. But even when the woman smiles quite casually and without even the habitual instinctive movement, still there may be the vibration on the man's side owing to the habit of response in him to feminine attractions. These things are almost mechanical in their starting. As I wrote before it is the automatic answer of the physical or vital mind (imagination etc.) that prolongs it and makes it effective. Otherwise the vibrations would die away after a time.

*

Dress has always been used by woman as an aid to her "sex-appeal" as it is now called and man has always been susceptible to it; women also often find dress in man a cause of attraction (e.g. soldier's uniform). There are also particular tastes in dress — that a sari of a particular colour should attract is quite normal. The attraction works on the sense and the vital, while it is the mind that dislikes the psychological defects and gets cooled down by their exposure; but this repulsion of the mind cannot last as against the stronger vital attraction.

*

It is of course the universal sex-force that acts, but certain people are more full of it than others, have the sex-appeal as they now say in Europe. This sex-appeal is exercised especially by women even without any conscious intention of putting it on a particular person. Consciously they may turn it on a particular person, but it may exercise itself on many others whom they do not wish particularly to capture. All women have not the sex-appeal, but some force of sex-pull there is in most. There is of course a similar pull in men for women.

*

The sex-pull is that of a general force, which uses the individual for its purpose and it takes advantage of any proximity of the other sex to work in. The remedy lies in oneself — in immediate detachment (standing apart, not accepting as one's own) and rejecting it.

*

It is certainly naive to think that because a girl is simple, i.e. instinctive and impulsive and non-mental in her movements, she can be relied upon to be an asexual friend. Some women can be, but it is usually those who have a clear mental consciousness and strong will of self-control or else those who are incapable of a passion for more than one person in their life and you are lucky enough not to be that person.

*

Tell X on behalf of myself and the Mother that she must not allow herself to be crushed by the burden of the past. All she has to do is to turn her back on this past of sexual weakness, for which she was not herself primarily responsible, and to consecrate herself entirely to the Divine. If she so consecrates herself, the past will be wiped out and a new life begin for her. This is the true atonement and the only one asked from her.

*

Write to X that this case of Y and Z is perfectly clear. The girl [Z] is moved by sexual desire and its impulse of vital interchange; not being satisfied in her married life, she seeks the satisfaction from others. All these pleas about affection etc. are the usual tricks with which women (and men too) cover their approach to the vital and sexual interchange. Sometimes they use the trick knowingly, sometimes they try to deceive themselves also with it — or in some cases they actually believe in it, the vital covering up the mind and deluding it. It does not matter which it is, — the actual fact behind the cover and the final outcome are the same. Even sadhaks when moved by the sexual force are deceived by their vital or try to deceive themselves, alleging spiritual affinities, psychic ties or anything else that can justify their lapse; if they yield they can go far out of the way.

For Y it is a test, — difficult for him because he is at an age when the sexual element is awake but there is not sufficient experience for a true understanding of its workings and not sufficient maturity of mind to make up for want of experience. If he yields to the girl's pressure, he is likely to lose his sadhana, perhaps for a long time — if he is led too far it might even be a decisive fall. If he wants the spiritual life, he must be on his guard and draw back entirely from this movement.

Social Contact and Sex

In an Asram or other religious institution men and women are not usually allowed to live together. Where they do, as among the Vaishnavas, these difficulties [*of sex*] invariably arise. The difficulty lies in the enormous place given to sex in the lower Nature. But there is no reason if one fixes oneself firmly in the spiritual consciousness why one should not speak and act between men and women without the least reference to sex.

*

You can have right relations with women only when you can forget that they are women and meet them as human beings — when you can forget sex in your feeling and action towards them.

*

All that [*mental excitement when a man meets a woman*] happens because the vital is conscious of sex in the approach and immediately assumes the "man to woman" attitude. To get rid of that, one must be able to look on the woman and feel to her as to a human being only. That is difficult and needs a certain training; for even if the mind is able to take the position, the vital is unreliable and one has to be on guard that it does not suddenly or surreptitiously get in into the relation with its partiality for the sex-interchange.

*

Of course one must be able to come in contact with women without feeling or thinking about sex; but to seek contact and test is not the way, it can too easily turn the other side when the mastery is not complete. The facing and conquering must be an inner process — the Tantrik outer method is not indicated.

It [*renunciation of contact with women*] has been prescribed not only in your case, but to all who drag the sex-idea into their relations with women in the Yoga. External as well as internal renunciation of the sex-relation vital or physical has been made the rule. The idea of internal detachment and external indulgence has been found always to be a cover under which the vital continues its operations. For you the continuance would be dangerous both spiritually and for the body.

*

It usually happens that when actual indulgence of the vital is given up (external exchange, touch or contact), imagination still goes on. But if this can be overcome, then the whole thing is overcome. External indulgence on the other hand keeps the activity alive. This is the raison d'être of the external avoidance. If anything can be got rid of without the necessity of avoidance, so much the better.

*

Both methods [*giving up contact with women and keeping it*] have their disadvantage. If one allows the opportunities, the sex-movement continues — if one suppresses only, then the movement goes back into imaginations. If it is only imaginations then there is less harm, for in the end the imaginations can be got rid of, but if the imaginations precipitate into some material act, then nothing is gained.

*

The mental acceptance of X's philosophy about sex was the mistake. It may be true that ordinarily mixing with women removes shyness etc., — though it is not always so, for many people are sex-timid by nature — but that is a means for ordinary life, not Yoga, and in ordinary life marriage is the direct means for getting rid of sex-uneasiness; marriage or else having love affairs with women and satisfying the sex. But that is not the proper means for an Asram and Yoga. In Yoga the proper means is to train the mind and vital to meet women without thought of sex, to look on them as sadhaks and human beings only, not as objects of sexual possession and enjoyment.

*

Strength and purity in the lower vital and wideness in the heart are the best condition for meeting others, especially women, and if that could always be there sex could hardly have a look in.

Touch and Sex

The association [*of touch*] with sex is vital-physical — otherwise there need be no connection between the expression of affection by touch and the sex-feeling. Except in unusual cases, when the mother and son or brother and sister embrace, they do not have the sex-feeling. It is a sort of habitual conversion operated in the passage from the emotional to the physical and, being a habit only, though a strong one, can be changed.

*

It [*touch*] is vital-physical. All sex movement has a vital element in it, but the mere vital movement is not directly interested in touching or the sex act. It is interested more in the play of the emotions, domination and subjection, quarrels, reconciliations, the interchange of vital forces etc. It is the vital-physical consciousness that gives so much importance to the touch, embrace, sex act etc.

*

In ordinary society people touch each other more or less freely according to the manners of the society. That is quite a different matter because there the sex-impulse is allowed within certain more or less wide or narrow limits and even the secret indulgence is common, although people try to avoid discovery. In Bengal when there is purdah, touching between men and women is confined to the family, in Europe there is not much restriction so long as there is no excessive familiarity or indecency; but in Europe sex is now practically free. Here all sex-indulgence inner or outer is considered undesirable as an obstacle to the sadhana — as it very evidently is. For that reason any excessive familiarity of touch between men and women has to be avoided, anything also in the nature of caressing, as it creates or tends to create sex-tendency or even the strong sex-impulse. Casual touching has to be avoided also if it actually creates the sex-impulse. These are commonsense rules if the premiss is granted that sex has not to have any indulgence.

*

It is surprising you should not see that these things [*kisses and caresses*] belong to the vital sex-movement, even if there is no physical sex-act. If one wants to live in the unreformed vital plane, one can indulge them — but it is certainly unyogic.

*

The difficulty about the kisses and embraces is that they are the expression of a vital love which is not based on the psychic or spiritual or at least does not keep to that basis, so that when it touches the body, it awakens the reactions of the ordinary body love. The ordinary vital and the ordinary body love are intimately connected with sex — and for sex procreative intention is not at all necessary.

*

Avoidance of touch is best so long as there is the sex-response to touch on either side. At a higher stage, it is indifferent to touch or not to touch. What it will be in the supramental culmination, let the supramental decide.

Touch may be neutral or it may imply interchange of forces. When the interchange is that of spiritual or spiritualised forces, then it has its meaning and it is that that will justify it in the supramental realisation. But till then, it is better to be circumspect.

Celibacy

Celibacy means first "not marrying" — it can be extended to not having sexual (physical) relations with any woman, though that is not its proper meaning. It is not equivalent to Brahmacharya. Brahmacharya is not binding in *bhaktimārga* or *karmayoga,* but it is necessary for ascetic *jñānayoga* as well as for Raja and Hatha yogas. It is also not demanded from Grihastha yogis. In this Yoga the position is that one must overcome sex, otherwise there can be no transformation of the lower vital and physical nature; all physical sexual connection should cease, otherwise one exposes oneself to serious dangers. The sex-push must also be overcome but it is not a fact that there can be no sadhana or no experience before it is entirely overcome, only without that conquest one cannot go to the end and it must be clearly recognised as one of the more serious obstacles and indulgence of it as a cause of considerable disturbance.

*

Celibacy is one thing and freedom from sex-pushes is another. These have to be conquered and got rid of, but if freedom from them were made a test of fitness to go on, I wonder how many could be declared fit for my Yoga. The will to conquer must be there, but the elimination of the sex-impulse is one of the most difficult things for human nature and, if it takes time, that is only natural.

*

If it is like that [*a natural control of sexual excitement*] then it is the power of self-control, automatic and therefore belonging to the inner being that is coming — the genuine thing. Of course to be complete the sexual passion and the thoughts that encourage it should disappear also. The idea about impotence [*being caused by celibacy*] is rather irrational — impotence comes from overindulgence or wrong indulgence (certain perverse habits); it does not come from self-control. Self-control means only a diversion to other powers, because the controlled sex-power becomes a force for the life-energies, the powers of the mind and the more and more potent workings of the spiritual consciousness.

*

Why impose one rule of Brahmacharya to an advanced age on all men or the age of 25 on all women? Everybody is not intended to be a Brahmachari. Men and women belong to every stage of development and need different kinds of experience suitable for their stage in order to grow and advance farther.

Marriage

It is not helpful to abandon the ordinary life before the being is ready for the full spiritual life. To do so means to precipitate a struggle between the different elements and exasperate it to a point of intensity which the nature is not ready to bear. The vital elements in you have partly to be met by the discipline and experience of life, while keeping the spiritual aim in view and trying to govern life by it progressively in the spirit of Karmayoga.

It is for this reason that we gave our approval to your marriage.

*

If she consents to marry, that would be the best. All these vital disturbances proceed from suppressed sex-instinct, suppressed but not rejected and overcome. A mental acceptance or enthusiasm for the sadhana is not a sufficient guarantee nor a sufficient ground for calling people, especially young people, to begin it. Afterwards these vital instincts rise up and there is nothing sufficient to balance or prevail against them, only mental ideas which do not prevail against the instinct but on the other hand also stand in the way of their natural social means of satisfaction. If she marries now and gets experience of the human vital life, then hereafter there may be a chance of her mental aspiration for sadhana turning into the real thing.

*

As to the question of marriage in general, we do not consider it advisable for one who desires to come to the spiritual life. Marriage means usually any amount of trouble, heavy burdens, a bondage to the worldly life and great difficulties in the way of single-minded spiritual endeavour. Its only natural purpose would be, if the sexual trend was impossible to conquer, to give it a restricted and controlled satisfaction. I do not see in what way it could help you to keep the mind under control and subjugation; a restless mind can only be quieted from within.

*

It is not right once you have turned to the Divine, to allow despondency of any kind to take hold of you. Whatever the difficulties and troubles, you must keep this confidence that by relying on the Divine, the Divine will take you through. Now I answer the questions you put to me in your letter.

1. If to follow the spiritual path is your resolve, marriage and family life can only come across it. Marriage would be the right thing only if the sexual push was so strong that there was no hope of overcoming it except by a controlled and rational indulgence for some time during which it could be slowly brought under subjection to the will. But you say its hold on you is diminishing, so that does not seem indispensable.

2. As for leaving all and coming away from there that must be only when there is a clear and settled decision within you. To do so on an impulse would be to feel all the pull of old things after you come here and entail severe disturbance and struggle in the sadhana. When the other things fall away or are cut away from you then it can be done. Persist in your aspiration, insist on your vital to have faith and be more quiet. It will come.

*

You are right in feeling that the protection and grace are always there and that all has been for the best. In your wife's condition, the best was that she should change her body and she has been able to do so in the state of mind which would give her the happiest conditions both after death and for a renewal hereafter of the spiritual development for which she had begun to aspire. It is good also that you have been able to keep your poise and the freedom of your spirit in this occurrence.

Again, you are entirely right in your resolution not to marry again; to do so would be in any case to invite serious and probably insuperable difficulties in your following the path of Yoga, and, as in this path of Yoga it is necessary to put away sexual desire, marriage would be not only meaningless but an absolute contradiction of your spiritual life. You can expect full support and protection from us in your resolve and, if you keep a sincere will and resolution in this matter, you may be sure that the Divine Grace will not fail you.

The Relationship of Man and Woman

These are ideas of the vital plane[7] where the strong demand subservience from those who are not physically or otherwise so strong. The spiritual truth is quite other than these things.

Skin Diseases and Sex

Yes, of course, skin diseases have much to do with sexual desires — not of course always, but often.

*

I suppose it [*pimples on the face*] is often the result of suppressed sexuality — suppressed in act but still internally active. These things do not act in the same way with all, with some it may act on the blood, with some it may not or else not in the same form. Moreover I do not suppose that sex is the only cause of pimples on the face — there are other things also that can give that.

---

[7] *The correspondent asked whether there was any "basic truth" in these two ideas: first, that in a relationship the woman should surrender to the man, and second, that a man has a right to be attracted to several women at a time, whereas a woman should be devoted to one man alone. — Ed.*

Section Three

Illness, Doctors and Medicines

Chapter One
Illness and Health

Illness and Yoga

Whatever it may be — the power of the illness to prevent the sadhana ought not to exist. The Yogic consciousness and its activities must be there whether there is health or illness.

*

You ought not to allow the physical illnesses to interfere with your sadhana or affect your mind — these illnesses are nothing compared with what many others have had to pass through — you have some constipation, headaches, rheumatic pains, that ought not to be so difficult to bear. You have to separate yourself from the body consciousness and not allow yourself to be overpowered by it.

*

Physical sufferings are due to attacks of the forces of the Ignorance. But if one knows how to do it, one can make them a means of purification. There are however better and less difficult means of purification.

*

Illness must not be accepted as a means of transformation; it rather indicates certain difficulties encountered by the force of transformation especially in the vital and the body. But it is not necessary that these difficulties should be allowed to take this obscure form of illness. All illness should be rejected and all suggestions of illness; the Force should be called in to cure by the assent to health and the refusal of assent to the suggestions that bring or prolong its opposite.

*

All illnesses are obviously due to the imperfect nature of the body and the physical nature. The body can be immune only when it is open to the higher consciousness and the latter can descend into it. Till then what he writes is the remedy — if he can also call in the force to throw out the illness, that is the most powerful help possible.

*

It is only by the conquest of the material nature that illness can cease altogether to come.

*

I do not think X's trance has anything to do with her ill health; I have never known the habit of trances of that kind to have any such result, only the violent breaking of a trance might have a bad result though it would not necessarily produce a disaster. But there is the possibility that if the conscious being goes out of the body in an absolutely complete trance, the thread which connects it with the body might be broken or else cut by some adverse force and it would not be able to return into the physical frame. Apart from any such fatal possibility there might be a shock which might produce a temporary disorder or even some kind of lesion; as a rule, however, a shock would be the only consequence.

The general question is a different matter. There is a sort of traditional belief in many minds that the practice of Yoga is inimical to the health of the body and tends to have a bad effect of one kind or another and even finally leads to a premature or an early dropping of the body. Ramakrishna seems to have held the view, if we can judge from his remarks about the connection between Keshav Sen's progress in spirituality and the illness which undermined him, that one was the result and the desirable result of the other, a liberation and release from life in this world, mukti. That may or may not be; but I find it difficult to believe that illness and deterioration of the body is the natural and general result of the practice of Yoga or that that practice is the cause of an inevitable breakdown of health or of the final illnesses which bring about their departure from the body. On what ground are we to suppose or how can it be proved that while non-Yogis suffer from ill health and die because of the disorders of Nature, Yogis die of their Yoga? Unless a direct connection between their death and their practice of Yoga can be proved — and this could be proved with certainty only in particular cases and even then not with an absolute certainty — there is no sufficient reason to believe in such a difference. It is more rational to conclude that both Yogis and non-Yogis fall ill and die from natural causes and by the same dispensation of Nature; one might even advance the view, since they have the Yoga Shakti at their disposal if they choose to use it, that the Yogi falls ill and dies not because of but in spite of his Yoga. At any rate, I don't believe that Ramakrishna (or any other Yogi) fell ill because of his trances; there is nothing to show that he ever suffered in that way after a trance. I think it is said somewhere or he himself said that the cancer in his throat of which he died came by his swallowing the sins of his disciples and those who approached him: that again may or may not be, but it will be his own peculiar case. It is no doubt possible to draw the illnesses of others upon oneself and even to do it deliberately; the instance of the Greek king Antigonus and his son Dimitrius is a famous historical case in point. Yogis also do this sometimes; or else adverse forces may throw illnesses upon the Yogi, using those round him as a door or a passage or the ill wishes of people as an instrumental force. But all these are special circumstances connected, no doubt, with his practice of Yoga; but they do not establish the general proposition as an absolute rule. A tendency such as X's to desire or welcome or accept death as a release could have a force because of her advanced spiritual consciousness which it would not have in ordinary people.

On the other side there can be an opposite use and result of the Yogic consciousness: illness can be repelled from one's own body or cured, even chronic or deep-seated illnesses and long-established constitutional defects remedied or expelled and even a predestined death delayed for a long period. Narayan Jyotishi, a Calcutta astrologer, who predicted, not knowing then who I was, in the days before my name was politically known, my struggle with Mlechchha enemies and afterwards the three cases against me and my three acquittals, predicted also that though death was prefixed for me in my horoscope at the age of 63, I would prolong my life by Yogic power for a very long period and arrive at a full old age. In fact I have got rid by Yogic pressure of a number of chronic maladies that had got settled in my body, reduced others to a vanishing minimum, brought about steadily progressing diminution of two that remained and on the last produced a considerable effect. But none of these instances either on the favourable or unfavourable side can be made into a rule; there is no validity in the tendency of human reason to transform the relativity of these things into an absolute.

Finally I may say of X's trances that they are the usual *savikalpa* kind opening to all kinds of experiences, but the large abiding realisations in Yoga do not usually come in trance but by a persistent waking sadhana. The same may be said of the removal of attachments; some may be got rid of sometimes by an experience in trance, but more usually it must be done by persistent endeavour in waking sadhana.

Illness Not the Result of the Force

Illness does not rise up by the descent of the Force, nor hereditary taint nor madness. They come up of themselves, as in X's case who never had even the smallest grain of a descent of a Force anywhere. It is only after he went off his centre, that we are putting Force (not as a descent, but as an agent) to keep him as straight and as sound as possible.

*

A descent [*of the force*] cannot possibly produce nausea and vomiting etc. There can, if one pulls down too much force, be produced a headache or giddiness; both of these go if one keeps quiet a little, ceases pulling and assimilates. A descent cannot produce blood pressure, madness or apoplexy or heart failure or any other illness.

*

A heat is sometimes created in the body by the pressure of a Force of tapas because there are things that resist in the vital or in the body habit or in the brain-mind — the cause of the heat is therefore not the Force itself but the resistance. As soon as the system is cleared there is no sense of heat any longer. But this heat is clearly distinguishable from illness.

*

Whatever force is sent is for cure. Increase of illness or physical suffering is not the result of the force.

The Lower Nature, the Hostile Forces and Illness

Attacks of illness are attacks of the lower nature or of adverse forces taking advantage of some weakness, opening or response in the nature, — like all other things that come and have got to be thrown away, they come from outside. If one can feel them so coming and get the strength and the habit to throw them away before they can enter the body, then one can remain free from illness. Even when the attack seems to rise from within, that means only that it has not been detected before it entered the subconscient; once in the subconscient, the force that brought it rouses it from there sooner or later and it invades the system. When you feel it just after it has entered, it is because though it came direct and not through the subconscient, yet you could not detect it while it was still outside. Very often it arrives like that, frontally or more often tangentially from the side, direct, forcing its way through the subtle vital envelope which is our main armour of defence, but it can be stopped there in the envelope itself before it penetrates the material body. Then one may feel some effect, e.g. feverishness or a tendency to cold, but there is not the full invasion of the malady. If it can be stopped earlier or if the vital envelope of itself resists and remains strong, vigorous and intact, then there is no illness; the attack produces no physical effect and leaves no traces.

*

Illness is always an attack of contrary forces in Nature — but not always of what are specially called the Hostile Forces or intended to frustrate aspiration. A desire is an ordinary force of the lower Nature, though it may be used by the Hostile Forces.

*

Hostile [*source of illness*] here means hostile to the Yoga. An illness which comes in the ordinary course as the result of physical causes — even though adverse universal forces are the first cause — is an ordinary illness. One brought by the forces hostile to Yoga to upset the system and prevent or disturb progress — without any adequate physical reason — is a hostile attack. It may have the appearance of a cold or any other illness, but to the eye which sees the action of forces and not only the outward symptoms or results, the difference is clear.

*

These are waves of the hostile force which come trying whom they can touch. When you feel an attack of this kind, you must realise that this comes on you from outside and touches some weak point in you, and you have to remain as quiet as you can, reject it and open yourself. I judge from what you have written that it was the physical and vital-physical consciousness that it made restless and inclined to revolt and it did not take the whole of your consciousness. If you can keep it localised like that when it comes and remain quiet in mind and heart and reject it, then it will not be so difficult to throw it out. The peace and force must be called down into this vital-physical (nervous) part and the whole body until you feel the atmosphere and force pervading you and in you always in all the body and not only upon or around you. If you still find a difficulty, it is because of the past habit of reaction in the nervous being and a certain weakness there; but persevere, do not consent to the invasion of the old forces. The habit will lessen and disappear and the true Force occupying the body will remove the weakness.

*

It is a hostile pressure that is organising a habit in the body of recurrence at a fixed time or times. This habit of fixed recurrence gives a great force for any illness to persist, as the body consciousness expects the recurrence and the expectation helps it to come.

*

It is this expectation in the mind [*that an attack of obscurity will come at a fixed time*] that helps most to maintain the rhythm of the attack. If it could be got rid of, the rhythm also could be broken.

*

According to all statements the deaths in early age are much less in Europe and men live longer on the whole. But certain diseases have greatly increased in spite of the advance in hygiene — influenza, T.B. and venereals. There are also new diseases coming in that hardly existed before. That seems obviously the work of the Hostiles.

The Suggestion of Illness

The feeling of illness is at first only a suggestion; it becomes a reality because your physical consciousness accepts it. It is like a wrong suggestion in the mind; if the mind accepts it, it becomes clouded and confused and has to struggle back into harmony and clearness. It is so with the body consciousness and illness. You must not accept but reject it with your physical mind and so help the body consciousness to throw off the suggestion. If necessary, make a counter-suggestion, "No, I shall be well; I am and shall be all right." And in any case call in the Mother's Force to throw out the suggestion and the illness it is bringing.

*

By suggestion [*of illness*] I do not mean merely thoughts or words. When the hypnotist says, "Sleep", it is a suggestion; but when he says nothing but only puts his silent will to convey sleep or makes movements of his hands over the face, that also is a suggestion.

When a force is thrown on you or a vibration of illness, it carries to the body this suggestion. A wave comes in the body — with a certain vibration in it, the body remembers "cold" or feels the vibrations of a cold and begins to cough or sneeze or to feel chill — the suggestion comes to the mind in the form, "I am weak, I don't feel well, I am catching a cold."

*

A suggestion is not one's own thought or feeling, but a thought or feeling that comes from outside, from others, from the general atmosphere or from external Nature, — if it is received, it sticks and acts on the being and is taken to be one's own thought or feeling. If it is recognised as a suggestion, then it can be more easily got rid of. This feeling of doubt and self-distrust and hopelessness about oneself is a thing moving about in the atmosphere and trying to enter into people and be accepted; I want you to reject it, for its presence not only produces trouble and distress but stands in the way of restoration of health and return to the inner activity of the sadhana.

*

The suggestion of weakness comes to the subconscient part of the body consciousness and therefore the mind is most often unaware of it. If the body itself were truly conscious, then the suggestions could be detected in time and thrown off before they took effect. Also the rejection by the central consciousness would be supported by a conscious rejection in the body and act more immediately and promptly.

*

All these suggestions that came to you were of course part of the attack on the physical consciousness, — the attack on the body is used to raise these ideas and the ideas are used to make it more difficult for the body to recover. At a certain stage attacks fall heavily on the body because the opposing forces find it more difficult than before to upset the mind or vital directly, so they fall on the physical in the hope that that will do the trick, the physical being more vulnerable. But the sensibility of the body to attacks is no proof of incapacity, just as a finer sensibility of the mind or vital to attacks was no proof — it can in due time be overcome. As for the feelings about the Mother and that her love is only given for a return in work or to those who can do sadhana well, that is the usual senseless idea of the vital-physical mind and has no value.

There is nothing wrong in taking care of the body in regard to health and, if the liver has gone wrong, the instinct to refuse too sweet or greasy or heavy foods is a right instinct. Mother has no objection to your abstaining while the illness is there nor has she insisted on your taking *dal*. Her objection is only to what people often do, getting ideas about this or that food and abstaining even when there is no acute illness. During an acute state of bad liver, abstinence is often necessary. Only one must not create by wrong ideas a nervous incapacity of the stomach or a chronic nervous dyspepsia. She had no other meaning.

I hope you will be all right soon. If the body does not right itself, you must keep me informed from time to time.

*

There is a general suggestion in the air about catching dengue or influenza. It is this suggestion that is enabling the adverse forces to bring about symptoms of this kind and spread the complaints; if one rejects both the suggestions and the symptoms, then these things will not materialise.

*

That is how illnesses try to come from one person to another — they attack, by a suggestion like this or otherwise, the nervous being and try to come in. Even if the illness is not contagious, this often happens, but it comes more easily in contagious illnesses.

The suggestion or touch has to be thrown off at once.

There is a sort of protection round the body which we call the nervous envelope — if this remains strong and refuses entrance to the illness force, then one can remain well even in the midst of plague or other epidemics — if the envelope is pierced or weak, then illness can come in.

What you felt attacked was not really the physical body, but this nervous envelope and the nervous body (*prāṇakoṣa*) of which it is an extension or cover.

*

A body is not a cloth — nor is a sick body a torn cloth. A body weak or sick can renew itself, recover its vitality — that happens to thousands of people. A cloth has not a renewable vitality. It is only if one is old beyond fifty-five or sixty that the renewal becomes difficult — even then health and strength can be kept or recovered enough to keep the body in a good condition.

I do not also quite catch what you mean about the inner being. If you mean by the *vikās* the development of the sadhana, to recover health and strength is very necessary for that. The body is an instrument for the sadhana no less than the mind and vital, and it should be kept in a good condition as far as possible. Not to care for the body, thinking it is of no importance compared with the inner state, is not the rule of this Yoga.

*

It is a pity that X could not write all this time. Formerly when she wrote often she used to get better after writing. It is also a pity that she has been told by the doctors that she is not going to live; even if it is true, such a thing should not be told unless in case of necessity (which does not exist in her case) for it takes away much of the power of resistance and diminishes what chances of cure and survival there were. X's physical destiny has always been against her but this is a thing that can be cancelled if one can have sufficient faith and inner strength and openness and receive the spiritual force.

*

These auto-suggestions [*of being restored to good health*] — it is really faith in a mental form — act both on the subliminal and the subconscient. In the subliminal they set in action the powers of the inner being, its occult power to make thought, will or simple conscious force effective on the body — in the subconscient they silence or block the suggestions of death and illness (expressed or unexpressed) that prevent the return of health. They help also to combat the same things (adverse suggestions) in the mind, vital, body consciousness. Where all this is completely done or with some completeness, the effects can be very remarkable.

*

In much the same way as Coué's suggestion system cured most of his patients, [*so an ordinary doctor would cure his patients,*] only by a physical instead of a mental means. The body consciousness responds to the suggestion or the medicine and one gets cured for the time being or it doesn't respond and there is no cure. How is it that the same medicine for the same illness succeeds with one man and not with another or succeeds at one time with a man and afterwards doesn't succeed at all? Absolute cure of an illness so that it cannot return again depends on clearing the mind, the vital and the body consciousness and the subconscient of the psychological response to the force bringing the illness. Sometimes this is done by a sort of order from above (when the consciousness is ready, but it cannot always be done like that). The complete immunity from all illness for which our Yoga tries can only come by a total and permanent enlightenment of the below from above resulting in the removal of the psychological roots of ill health — it cannot be done otherwise.

Curative Auto-Suggestion: The Coué Method

It is the final discovery that one makes that in this world everything depends upon consciousness and its movements, even the things that seem not to do so. In these matters of illness, vital trouble etc., that resolves itself into suggestion (hostile) and auto-suggestion. Coué, though he did not know these things, had the brilliant intuition of adopting the contrary method of curative auto-suggestion and giving it a thorough and systematic application. Here it does not succeed so well because the anti-Coué spirit is very strong in many, the habit of entertaining hostile suggestions or this openness to them. Yet in Yoga also faith and right auto-suggestion are of great use until the point comes when no suggestion is necessary because the Truth-consciousness acts automatically and produces its natural results.

*

The suggestions that create illness or unhealthy conditions of the physical being come usually through the subconscient — for a great part of the physical being, the most material part, is subconscient, i.e. to say, it has an obscure consciousness of its own but so obscure and shut up in itself that the mind does not know its movements or what is going on there. But all the same it is a consciousness and can receive suggestions from Forces outside, just as the mind and vital do. If it were not so, there would not be any possibility of opening it to the Force and the Force curing it; for without this consciousness in it it would not be able to respond. In Europe and America there are many people now who recognise this fact and treat their illnesses by making conscious mental suggestions to the body which counteract the obscure secret suggestions of illness in the subconscient. There was a famous Doctor in France who cured thousands of people by making them persistently put such counter-suggestions upon the body. That proves that illness has not a purely material cause, but is due to a disturbance of the secret consciousness in the body.

To bear quietly and in silence does help to release from the reaction of grief, if one makes the vital quiet; but it should be at the same time surrendered to the Mother. For the Mother to know from within is not enough; there must be this laying before her and giving up to her so that the reaction may disappear.

*

It is certainly better not to dwell on the difficulties or give them too much voice, because, our experience shows us, to do so helps to make them return like a recurring decimal. The Coué formula is too crude and simple to be entirely true in principle, but it has a great practical force, and behind it there is a very great truth in a world and a consciousness governed by the Overmind Maya: it is this, that what we affirm strongly gets power to persist in the consciousness and experience and calls circumstances to its support, what we deny and reject and refuse to support by the power of the Word, tends, after a time and some resistance, to lose force in the consciousness and the circumstances and movements that support it tend also to recur less often and finally disappear. It is fundamentally the principle of the mantra. On that ground I approve of your resolution not to give any more the *avalambana* of the written word to these things. A constant affirmation from within on the other side — of that which is to be realised — brings always in the end a response from above.

*

These things [*cures by faith-healing and psychotherapy*] are a matter of evidence and the evidence for Coué's success is overwhelming. There have also been many great healers (*guérisseurs*) all over the world whose successes are well-attested. Faith-healing and psychotherapy are also facts.

Faith, Confidence and Cure

Most of them [*illnesses*] can be got rid of almost at once by faith and calling in the force. Those that are chronic are more difficult, but they too can be got rid of by the same means if persistently used.

*

You have only to admit that the mind and vital can influence the body — then no difficulty is left. In this action of mind and vital on the body faith and hope have an immense importance. I do not at all mean that they are omnipotent or infallibly effective

—that is not so. But they assist the action of any force that can be applied, even of an apparently purely material force like medicine. In fact however there is no such thing as a purely material force, but the action may be purely material when it is a question of material objects. But in things that have life or mind and life one cannot isolate the material operation like that. There is always a play of other forces mixed with it in the reception at least and for the most part in the inception and direction also.

*

Remain quiet, within, concentrated only on receiving strength and health, confident that we are with you all the time, and you will soon be all right.

Parts of the Being and Illness

Your description makes it clear that the obstruction in the throat is not physical, it is the obstruction of a formation of obscure force in the physical mind, — for the throat is the centre of the physical mind. In your other parts of the mental there is not any opposition, but here in the physical mind there is probably a habitual form of old external ideas which are rejected but something of them remains. It is this that translates itself in the obstruction and pain. It is a mechanical difficulty which we must try to remove.

*

It is neither the vital nor the body that contains these illnesses — it is a force from outside that creates them and the nervous being (physical vital) and the body respond from habit or inability to throw it away. It is always better not to say, "I will now have no more illness", it attracts the attention of these malevolent powers and they immediately want to prove that they can still disturb the body. Simply when they come, reject them.

*

The nervous (vital-physical) being supports the body — if it is calm and strong and solid, then the body is well supported and can withstand illness and weakness or, if illness comes, it will bear and more easily get rid of it. If the nervous being is weak, then it is the opposite. If the nervous being is not merely weak, but nervous and unstable, over-sensitive, vehement or excitable, then there is much fluctuation, restlessness, exaltation and depression in the being — there may even be a wrongly acute creative imagination which brings in disorders into the body that are nervous and not physical — there is no physical illness of the heart but there are pains and palpitations, nothing physically wrong with stomach and intestines and yet there is inability to digest — nervous dyspepsia; pains are created in different parts of the body and so on — sometimes there is hysteria.

These conditions are not always native to the body — they are often created by troubles in the life, some disturbing illness or other reasons — but often it is due to some hereditary cause or otherwise native to the system. Women tend to get like this sometimes if there is disorder of the menstruation.

When there is this tendency of the nervous being, it is imperative to get down peace and strength into the nervous being and not allow it to upset the body or the general system.

*

Always the same rigid mind that turns everything into a statement of miraculous absoluteness! It is my experience and the Mother's that all illnesses pass through the nervous or vital-physical sheath of the subtle consciousness and subtle body before they enter the physical. If one is conscious of the subtle body or with the subtle consciousness, one *can* stop an illness on its way and prevent it from entering the physical body. But it may have come without one's noticing, or when one is asleep or through the subconscient, or in a sudden rush when one is off one's guard; then there is nothing to do but to fight it out from a hold already gained on the body. Let us suppose however that I am always on guard, always conscious, even in sleep — that does not mean that I am immunised in my very nature from all illness. It only means a power of self-defence against it when it tries to come. Self-defence by these inner means may become so strong that the body becomes practically immune as many Yogis are. Still this "practically" does not mean "absolutely" for all time. The absolute immunity can only come with the supramental change. For below the supramental it is the result of an action of a Force among many forces and can be disturbed by a disruption of the equilibrium established — in the supramental it is a law of the nature; in a supramentalised body immunity from illness would be automatic, inherent in its new nature.

There is a difference between Yogic Force on the mental and inferior planes and Supramental Nature. What is acquired and held by the Yoga Force in the mind and body consciousness is in the supramental inherent and exists not by achievement but by nature — it is self-existent and absolute.

*

What I meant was that the body consciousness through old habit of consciousness admits the force of illness and goes through the experiences which are associated with it — e.g. congestion of phlegm in the chest and feeling of suffocation or difficulty of breathing etc. To get rid of that one must awaken a will and consciousness in the body itself that refuses to allow these things to impose themselves upon it. But to get that, still more to get it completely is difficult. One step towards it is to get the inner consciousness separate from the body — to feel that it is not you who are ill but it is only something taking place in the body and not affecting your consciousness. It is then possible to see this separate body consciousness, what it feels, what are its reactions to things, how it works. One can then act on it to change its consciousness and reactions.

*

I am glad to know the disturbance was expelled last night. Now the receptivity in the body consciousness has to be kept so that it may not at all return or, if it tries, may immediately be expelled. You must always try to keep the quietude, not allow depressing or disturbing thoughts or feelings to enter you or take hold of your mind or your speech — there is no true reason after one has gained the inner quietness and wideness why that should be allowed to lapse and these things enter. And if the mind keeps its quietude and receptivity to higher forces only, it can then easily pass on that quietude and receptivity to the body consciousness and even to the material cells of the body.

*

As the body consciousness becomes more open to the Force (it is always the most difficult and the last to open up entirely), this frequent stress of illness will diminish and disappear.

*

As for the question about the illness, perfection in the physical plane is indeed part of the ideal of the Yoga, but it is the last item and, so long as the fundamental change has not been made in the material consciousness to which the body belongs, one may have a certain perfection on other planes without having immunity in the body.

Accepting and Enjoying Illness

Your theory of illness is rather a perilous creed — for illness is a thing to be eliminated, not accepted or enjoyed. There *is* something in the being that enjoys illness, it is possible even to turn the pains of illness like any other pain into a form of pleasure; for pain and pleasure are both of them degradations of an original Ananda and can be reduced into the terms of each other or else sublimated into their original principle of Ananda. It is true also that one must be able to bear illness with calm, equanimity, endurance, even recognition of it, since it has come, as something that had to be passed through in the course of experience. But to accept and enjoy it means to help it to last and that will not do; for illness is a deformation of the physical nature just as lust, anger, jealousy etc. are deformations of the vital nature and error and prejudice and indulgence of falsehood are deformations of the mental nature. All these things have to be eliminated and rejection is the first condition of their disappearance while acceptance has a contrary effect altogether.

*

If one has faith and is open to the Force, illnesses can of course be removed in that way. What I objected to was the acceptance of illness and taking pleasure in it; that is admissible in Yogas which do not aim at transformation of the physical consciousness, but not here.

*

By will [*to get rid of illness*] I meant this that there is something in the body that accepts the illness and has certain reactions that make this acceptance effective — so there must always be a contrary will in the conscious parts of the being to get rid of this most physical acceptance.

*

All that is quite wrong.[1] Illness is a wrong movement of the body and is no more to be cherished than a wrong movement of the mind or vital. Pain and illness have to be borne with calm, detachment and equanimity, but not cherished — the sooner one gets rid of them the better.

*

It is always wrong to wish for illness. Fever is not a purifying action; it is the sign of an attack on the body and a fight and resistance to the attack. Illness in the body is like impurity in the vital, a thing undesirable and to be rejected. It may happen that in throwing out the illness (the attacking force) one throws out also something within, some impurity which helped it to come, but that is the result of a Force working within and not

---

[1] *The correspondent wrote: "Some sadhaks hold the theory that illness is a thing to be cherished. It comes to us from the Divine who wants to test our faith by it. Illness makes us remember the Divine more often than otherwise. Therefore one should not even ask the Mother to throw it away from us. How do you regard this?" — Ed.*

of the illness. It is quite possible that an illness or attack can be transferred in this way from one to another and indeed it very commonly happens; but it does not follow that it happened in this instance.

*

It was the mind that did not want it [*illness*]; this vital when left to itself often invites illness, it finds it dramatic — thinks it makes it interesting to others, likes to indulge the tamas, etc. etc.

*

That [*weakness of the body*] also is tamas. If you threw off the strain of the idea of weakness, the strength would come back. But there is always something in the vital physical which is pleased with becoming more weak and ill so that it can feel and lament its tragic case.

*

If this [*stomach acidity and colic*] is his only illness, there is absolutely no reason why it should not be cured, if he keeps proper habits and diet and above all the right attitude. I expect that the reason why the illness has such a hold and strong effect on him, is in the imagination and the nerves, more than anything else. There is something there that expects the illness, accepts it when it comes and gives it free play. He must learn to keep calm and quiet in the mind and vital being, to refuse to regard the illness and the tendency to it in the body as something normal to it, regarding it rather as something imposed from outside, and he must believe firmly that it must and will go. If he can keep this attitude and open to the true force, the mind and nervous being once strengthened, the illness and weakness will disappear.

Depression and Illness

It is not anything physical but a vital depression (in some part of the vital, not the whole) that prevents the body from recovering its elasticity. There was some part of the vital that was resisting a radical change and even, unknown to your mind, trying to go on as it was under cover of the change in the rest of your being. This has now, owing to this last affair, received a blow and got depressed and, when the vital is depressed like that, it affects the body. You say rightly that it is part of a change or turn that is taking place. But these effects of inertia and weakness need not continue; as soon as this vital part acquiesces gladly in the turn or change, the elasticity and energy will return.

*

It is good that you reject the sense of illness and allow no depression. Let there be no apprehension in the physical consciousness; with faith make it open to the Force.

*

The seeds of these old illnesses remain in the subconscient after they are cured. So when the subconscient is being worked, an adverse push bringing a general depression may make them sprout up; but they can be counteracted by the Force if you are vigilant and persistent in your sadhana and not remain to trouble.

Fear and Illness

If you have fear or apprehension of illness in your vital, that is the first thing to be thrown away, as it helps the illnesses to come in.

*

People taking the utmost precautions catch an illness, while often those who take no precautions escape. One has to take reasonable care if there is some immediate and definite cause of apprehension, but that is all.

*

What is the difficulty [*in understanding how the subtle forces of illness attack the body using bacilli and viruses for their purpose*]? You are like the scientists who say or used to say that there is no such thing as mind or thought independent of the physical brain. Mind and thought are only names for brain quiverings. Or that there is no such thing as vital Force because all the movements of life depend upon chemicals, glands and what not. These things and the germs also are only a minor physical instrumentation for something supraphysical.

They [*the forces of illness*] first weaken or break through the nervous envelope, the aura. If that is strong and whole, a thousand million germs will not be able to do anything to you. The envelope pierced, they attack the subconscient mind in the body, sometimes also the vital mind or mind proper — prepare the illness by fear or thought of illness. The doctors themselves said that in influenza or cholera in the Far East 90 per cent got ill through fear. Nothing to take away the resistance like fear. But still the subconscient is the main thing.

If the contrary Force is strong in the body, one can move in the midst of plague and cholera and never get contaminated. Plague too, rats dying all around, people passing into Hades. I have seen that myself in Baroda.

*

I have gone through the report of the Doctor and it seems to be clear from it — he says so himself — that there is nothing serious the matter and no danger. If there is some dilation of the heart, it was so slight that it was difficult to detect it and all else in it is healthy and normal.

Whatever is wrong in the system can easily be set right — but the first thing necessary is that you should dismiss this fear which hampers the action of the Force and opposes the cure. It is also necessary that you should now abstain finally not only from alcohol and wine, but from sex and smoking. Healthy conditions of living are necessary to help the Force to undo what has been done in the past and restore the full strength and normality of the body.

Fix in yourself the calm and courage of the sadhak. Fear nothing, open yourself, reject the weaknesses that remain — then the progress that had begun here will complete itself and the body also become an abiding place of the true consciousness and force.

Inertia and Illness

The human body has always been in the habit of answering to whatever forces chose to lay hands on it and illness is the price it pays for its inertia and ignorance. It has to learn to answer to the one Force alone, but that is not easy for it to learn.

*

It is a weakness and inertia in the physical nature which makes it undergo and acquiesce in the attacks of illness, instead of refusing and repelling them. That is the character of the material physical in all. It can only be remedied by the Force and Consciousness from above occupying the whole physical being.

*

There seem to be two elements in the physical difficulty that is weighing on you. The first is the liver trouble which weakens and must weaken still more if it leads you to diminish your food below what the body needs for maintaining sufficient strength to react — also probably the nervous tendency to insomnia with its consequences. The second is an inertia of the lower vital and physical consciousness which prevents it from throwing off the lassitude, from reacting against the attacks and from opening steadily to the Force which would remove these things. All that is due to the breakdown of the poise that you had for so long, the vital trouble that caused it and the reaction of the lower vital to the insistence on throwing out the causes of the trouble. This reaction seems to have been a listlessness at losing the things to which it was still holding — such a reaction always brings the inertia of the physical consciousness, while the right reaction in the lower vital brings on the contrary a sense of peace, release, quietude which definitely opens the lowest physical parts to the higher consciousness and force. If you can get over this and get back the old poise, then all these things can be made to disappear.

X was of course right from the medical point of view in recommending exercise — both for the liver and as a tonic to the body it is helpful. So some walking may be advisable. Care should be taken of the body certainly, the care that is needed for its good condition, rest, sleep, proper food, sufficient exercise; what is not good is too much preoccupation with it, anxiety, despondency in illness etc., for these things only favour the prolongation of ill-health or weakness. For such things as the liver attacks treatment can always be taken when necessary.

But it is always the right inner poise, quietude inward and outward, faith, the opening of the body consciousness to the Mother and her Force that are the true means of recovery — other things can only be minor aids and devices.

Anger and Illness

What has caused all the trouble for X is his insistence on his ego, its ideas, claims, desires, intentions and his aggressiveness in expressing them so that he quarrels with everybody. This quarrelsomeness opens him to all sorts of forces of the vital plane and their attacks. It is also the cause of the damage done to the liver and organs of digestion — for anger and quarrelsomeness always tend to spoil the liver and through it the stomach and intestines. As his quarrelsomeness is colossal, so also is the damage done to liver and digestion extreme. He must get rid of his egoism, quarrelsomeness and bad feelings towards others, if he wants to recover his health and his sadhana.

Work and Illness

I do not know why working with X must make good health impossible, unless you mean that there is too much work imposed on you, — but then the work can be lessened. In fact a complete rest and relief from the work can be arranged at present and for the future we can see afterwards. If you mean that working according to somebody else's ideas makes or keeps you ill, I do not see why it should be so. 999 people out of every 1000 do that — only a few are able to carry out their own ideas and even they have to a large extent to suit their ideas to those of other people in the actual execution of their work. If you mean that to have to work under discipline, doing things in what you consider not the best way, makes you nervous, discouraged and ill, that is a pity. It would be so much better if you could leave the responsibility of the way of doing things to the Mother and do cheerfully what you have to do. However, if you cannot bring yourself to that attitude, some other way will have to be found hereafter. But at the present, if that is the case, to take rest as a relief would seem the only way.

*

It is no use stopping work because of rheumatism (unless it is of the kind that disables one from working), — it only makes things worse.

Sleep and Illness

Yes. If you don't sleep enough the physical system becomes more open to these attacks [*of illness*]. If it is kept in good condition, then usually it repels them automatically and one does not notice even that there has been an attack.

*

I said that when the body is in good condition it automatically repels any attack of illness which is in the air without the mind even having to notice that there is an attack. If the attack is automatically repelled what is the need of dealing with it?

Pain

Pain is caused because the physical consciousness in the Ignorance is too limited to bear the touches that come upon it. Otherwise, to cosmic consciousness in its state of complete knowledge and complete experience, all touches come as Ananda.

*

Yes — all pain can become Ananda — pain is only the perversion of what in the original Consciousness would be Ananda.

*

Pain can be turned into Ananda, but I don't think that there is a special stage for that.

*

Peace in the cells first, then consolidated force [*is the secret of being able to bear heat and cold*]. Pain and discomfort come from a physical consciousness not forceful enough to determine its own reaction to things.

*

The healing of the nervous pain in the stomach does not depend on more or less eating — often these pains come when one does not eat enough, not only when one eats too much — so it is not by eating less you can cure it.

These pains are a part of the pressure of the old nature on the body; that is why we consider it can only be healed by the Peace and Power bringing a new movement of the physical nature there. In the stage of the struggle between the two natures, the peace does not always remain, but it will remain longer and longer as you get the habit of opening constantly to it.

*

The pains in the body come from the same source as the trouble in the vital nature; both are attacks from the same outside Force that wants to mislead or, when it cannot mislead, to trouble and disturb you. When once you can get rid of the vital invasion and prevent its recurrence, it will be easier to get rid too of the physical trouble whose origin is nervous (vital-physical); although its symptoms seem to be those of a physical illness, it is really an attack on the nervous part and a weakening of it for the time that gives you these pains.

Remain always quiet and persist in opening yourself. The Force that releases you from the vital trouble, can also remove the disturbance in the nervous part and the physical body.

*

The physical pain is obviously due to attacks — any physical cause being only a means for the action of the attack. I have often seen that when the mind and consciousness have rejected the attacks, the contrary forces fall on some weak point in the body hoping that by pain or illness they will depress the consciousness and so make it less strong to resist and reject them. We must see whether this recurrence of the pain cannot be quietly pushed out altogether.

*

It is a great gain if you feel no depression when the attack on the body comes.

The pain itself is, from your description, evidently nervous and, if you develop openness in the more physical layers of the being, then the action of the Force can always remove it or you will yourself be able to use the Force to push it away. It is a matter of getting the habit of opening in the body consciousness.

The consciousness or unconsciousness, as you have seen in the matter of the French studies, is dependent on the condition. It is not that you are unconscious, but that the physical being is prone to the tamasic condition (the condition of inertia) and then it becomes either inactive or obscure, stupid and unconscious; when the tamas goes away the condition becomes bright and what was difficult before becomes natural and easy. The whole thing is to get the physical out of its habit of falling back into tamas or inertia, and that can be done by opening and accustoming it to the action of the Force. When the action of the Force becomes constant, then there will be no more tamas.

*

You had opened your consciousness, so the pain disappeared. If it came back during sleep, it must have been because you lost touch and fell back into the ordinary consciousness. That often happens.

*

Pains of that kind must be due to some resistance or obstruction to the force on the body — it is not the pressure that creates them.

*

All these pains are a sign that you have put too great and sudden a strain on your physical system. The mind and vital were ready, but the body could not follow. You will have to diminish your work until you recover from the pains and fatigue. You may remember that I suggested to you to do only part of the sweeping work; it was for this reason that I was not sure that the physical system was ready. Now you should follow that — do only part of the work and ask X to arrange for the rest. See whether with this diminution and taking rest during the spare time the pain and the fatigue of the body disappear. If it does, then we can see what is best to do.

*

That is what they [*pains*] do at first; when one drives them out of one place, they go to another. It is better than their fixing in any place.

Separation and Detachment from Pain

The body [*experiences physical pain*], naturally — but the body transmits it to the vital and mental. With the ordinary consciousness the vital gets disturbed and afflicted and its forces diminished, the mind identifies and is upset. The mind has to remain unmoved, the vital unaffected, and the body has to learn to take it with equality so that the higher Force may work.

The Self is never affected by any kind of pain. The psychic takes it quietly and offers it to the Divine for what is necessary to be done.

*

You must arrive at a complete separation of your consciousness from these feelings of the body and its acceptance of illness and from that separated consciousness act upon the body. It is only so that these things can be got rid of or at least neutralised.

*

If it [*the consciousness*] is separate, it should not suffer from them [*pains*]. Even for the pains, the body may suffer but the consciousness should not feel itself suffering or overpowered.

*

I suppose there are only two ways [*to prevent the lowering effect of pain*]: (1) to think of something else if you can manage it, (2) to be able to detach yourself from the body consciousness, so that the body alone feels the pain, the mind and the vital are not affected.

*

It is a detachment of even the physical mind from the pain that makes one able to go on as if nothing were there, but this detachment of the physical mind is not easy to acquire.

*

It is by an attack on your physical consciousness that the old forces are bringing back the wrong condition. As you got the power before to stand back from the vital movement and localise it, while the rest of your consciousness observed and was not overpowered, so you must learn to stand back from the physical pain or uneasiness and localise it. If you can do that and do it completely, the pain or uneasiness itself will be more easily and quietly removed and you will not be overpowered like this with the sense of weakness. You can see that the Force has the power to take away the pains; but you allow yourself to be nervously overcome and therefore it is difficult for it to act with a continuous result. What was done at that time in the vital, must be done in the physical also. It is the only way to get free from the attacks.

*

The main difficulty seems to be that you are too subject to an excitement of the nerves — it is only by bringing quietude and calm into the whole being that a steady progress in the sadhana can be assured.

The first thing to be done in order to recover is to stop

yielding to the attack of the nerves — the more you yield and identify yourself with these ideas and feelings, the more they increase. You have to draw back and find back something in you that is not affected by pains and depressions, then from there you can get rid of the pains and depressions.

Chapter Two
Doctors and Medicines

Cure by Yogic Force and by Medicines

To heal [*illness*] by the true force is obviously the best — provided the body is amenable. It has a consciousness of its own which must be fully enlightened before it gives a full response.

*

Yes, if the faith and opening are there, medicines are not indispensable.

*

To separate yourself from the thing and call in the Mother's force to cure it [*is the Yogic method*] — or else to use your own will force with faith in the power to heal, having the support of the Mother's force behind you. If you cannot use either of these methods then you must rely on the action of the medicine.

*

Yogic force is all right when one is in a Yogic condition and when it acts. But when it does not, medicine is handy.

*

All ill-health is due to some inertia or weakness or to some resistance or wrong movement there [*in the vital*], only it has sometimes a more physical and sometimes a more psychological character. Medicines can counteract the physical results.

*

Medicines are a *pis aller* that have to be used when something in the consciousness does not respond or responds superficially to the Force. Very often it is some part of the material consciousness that is unreceptive — at other times it is the subconscient which stands in the way even when the whole waking mind, life, physical consent to the liberating influence. If the subconscient also answers, then even a slight touch of the Force can not only cure the particular illness but make that form or kind of illness practically impossible hereafter.

*

As for the illness itself, we understood from what you wrote that it was only a cold and not a serious illness. In such a case one can take medicines from the Dispensary to hasten the cure or one relies on the Force and opens oneself to the Mother, rejecting the suggestions of illness, putting oneself on the side of the helping forces. You had sufficient experience of sadhana to know that and we did not think it necessary to write what we supposed to be in your knowledge.

*

Try to keep yourself open to our Force in the body, that is the main thing. If the nerves (physical) are quieted, the illness itself will be less intense in its symptoms and can be more easily got over.

*

As for curing you by the Force, the main obstacle is your own vital movements. All this egoistic insistence on your own ideas, claims, preferences — assertion of your own righteousness as against the wickedness of others, complaints, quarrels, disputes, rancours against those around you and the reactions they cause — have had this effect on your liver and stomach and nerves. If you give up all that and live quietly and at peace with others, thinking less of yourself and others and more of the Divine, it would make things much easier and help to restore your health. Quietness of the mind in facing your illness is also necessary — agitation stops the action of the Force.

*

Certainly, one can act from within on an illness and cure it. Only it is not always easy as there is much resistance in Matter, a resistance of inertia. An untiring persistence is necessary; at first one may fail altogether or the symptoms increase, but gradually the control of the body or of a particular illness becomes stronger. Again, to cure an occasional attack of illness by inner means is comparatively easy, to make the body immune from it in future is more difficult. A chronic malady is harder to deal with, more reluctant to disappear entirely than an occasional disturbance of the body. So long as the control of the body is imperfect, there are all these and other imperfections and difficulties in the use of the inner force.

If you can succeed by the inner action in preventing increase, even that is something; you have then by *abhyāsa* to strengthen the power till it becomes able to cure. Note that so long as the power is not entirely there, some aid of physical means need not be altogether rejected.

*

Illness marks some imperfection or weakness or else opening to adverse touches in the physical nature and is often connected also with some obscurity or disharmony in the lower vital or the physical mind or elsewhere.

It is very good if one can get rid of illness entirely by faith and Yoga-power or the influx of the Divine Force. But very often this is not altogether possible, because the whole nature is not open or able to respond to the Force. The mind may have faith and respond, but the lower vital and the body may not follow. Or if the mind and vital are ready, the body may not respond, or may respond only partially, because it has the habit of replying to the forces which produce a particular illness and habit is a very obstinate force in the material part of the nature. In such cases the use of the physical means can be resorted to, — not as the main means, but as a help or material support to the action of the Force. Not strong and violent remedies, but those that are beneficial without disturbing the body.

The Role of Doctors

If the whole being is open to the force, then only outward means have not to be taken or used very little. But till then Doctors and their ways of treating things cannot be dispensed with altogether.

*

I have got X's report. I gather from it that there is general nervous weakness. I shall write to ask him if this is correct and what treatment he proposes to give. As for medical treatment it is sometimes a necessity. If one can cure by the Force as you have often done, it is the best — but if for some reason the body is not able to respond to the Force (e.g. owing to doubt, lassitude or discouragement or for inability to react against the disease), then the aid of medical treatment becomes necessary. It is not that the Force ceases to act and leaves all to the medicines, — it will continue to act through the consciousness but take the support of the treatment so as to act directly on the resistance in the body, which responds more readily to physical means in its ordinary consciousness.

*

You refuse to speak to the Doctor and on the other hand your body is not yet able to receive the Forces in such a way as to cure it. When the body is not able to receive the Forces *unaided*, it is then that we send the Doctor and work through him — but here your mind comes in and refuses. So both means are stopped.

*

Where the illness becomes pronounced and chronic in the body, it is necessary often to call in the aid of physical treatment and that is then used as a support of the Force. X in his treatment does not rely on medicines alone, but uses them as an instrumentation for the Mother's force.

*

You are very much behind the times. Do you not know that even many doctors now admit and write it publicly that medicines are an element but only one and that the psychological element counts as much and even more? I have heard that from doctors often and read it over reputable medical signatures. And among the psychological elements, they say, one of the most important is the doctor's optimism and self-confidence, (his faith, what? it is only another word for the same thing) and the confidence, hope, helpful mental atmosphere he can inspire in or around his patient. I have seen it stated categorically that a doctor who can do that is far more successful than one who knows Medicine better but cannot.

*

Miracles can be done, but there is no reason why they should be all instantaneous, whether from Gods or doctors.

Medical Systems

Of course injections are all the fashion; for everything it is "inject, inject and again inject". Medicine has gone through three stages in modern times — first (at the beginning in Molière's days) it was "bleed and douche", then "drug and diet", now it is "serum and injection". Praise the Lord! not for the illnesses, but for the doctors. However each of these formulas has a part truth behind it — with its advantages and disadvantages. As all religions and philosophies point to the Supreme but each in a different direction, so all medical fashions are ways to health — though they don't always reach it.

*

Medicine is not exactly science. It is theory + experimental fumbling + luck.

*

The theory [*of allopathic medicine*] is imposing, but when it comes to application, there is too much fumbling and guesswork for it to rank as an exact science. There are many scientists (and others) who grunt when they hear medicine called a science. Anatomy and physiology, of course, are sciences.

*

There are plenty of allopathic doctors who consider homeopathy, Nature-Cure, Ayurveda and everything else that is not orthodox "medical science" to be quackery. Why should not homeopaths etc. return the compliment?

*

I have put down a few comments to throw cold water on all this blazing hot allopathism. But all these furious disputes seem to me now of little use. I have seen the working of both systems [*allopathy and homeopathy*] and of others and I cannot believe in the sole truth of any. The ones damnable in the orthodox view, entirely contradicting it, have their own truth and succeed — also both the orthodox and heterodox fail. A theory is only a constructed idea-script which represents an imperfect human observation of a line of processes that Nature follows or can follow; another theory is a different idea-script of other processes that also she follows or can follow. Allopathy, homeopathy, naturopathy, osteopathy, Kaviraji, hakimi have all caught hold of Nature and subjected her to certain processes; each has its successes and failures. Let each do its own work in its own way. I do not see any need for fights and recriminations. For me all are only outward means and what really works are unseen forces behind; as they act, the outer means succeed or fail — if one can make the process a right channel for the right force, then the process gets its full utility — that is all.

*

Tumour, syphilis etc. are specialities, but what I have found in my psycho-physical experience is that most disorders of the body are connected, though they go by families, — but there is also connection between the families. If one can strike at their psycho-physical root, one can cure even without knowing the pathological whole of the matter and working through the symptoms is a possibility. Some medicines invented by demi-mystics have the power. What I am now considering is whether homeopathy has any psycho-physical basis. Was the founder a demi-mystic? I don't understand otherwise certain peculiarities of the way X's medicines act.

*

Of course [*X consults his homeopathy books in choosing medicines*]. He learned homeopathic medicine in America and his ideas of homeopathy are the American ideas. But how does his knowledge prevent intuition? Even an allopathic doctor has often to intuit what medicine he should give or what mixture — and it is those who intuit best that succeed best. All is not done by sole rule of book or sole rule of thumb even in orthodox Science.

The Right Use of Medicines

X wrote two or three days ago that you were not regular in taking his medicine and in that case he could not be responsible (if the treatment was not strictly followed to the end) if the cure was imperfect or if afterwards there was a relapse which might be irremediable. Dr. Y told the Mother that he was amazed at the improvement in your case. He had not believed such a thing was possible, but he had seen with his own eyes and now knew that it was. It would be a pity if such a result were not carried out to full success because of carelessness in following the treatment. I would recommend you to give it a full chance.

*

I did not mean that it [*cure through the Force*] cannot be done without medicines. But if it is to be done with the aid of medicines, then the right medicine is helpful, the wrong one obviously brings in a danger.

*

It is not enough for a medicine to be a specific [*for it to be helpful*]. Certain drugs have other effects or possible effects which can be ignored by the physician who only wants to cure his case, but cannot be in a whole-view of the system and its reactions. The unfavourable reactions of quinine are admitted by medical opinion itself and doctors in Europe have been long searching for a substitute for quinine.

*

There are some remedies which cure the disease temporarily but are bad for the system like quinine — others which suit some people but harm others, others which have a good effect one way, but a bad one in another way. That is why Mother does not like them to be used indiscriminately. Some she disapproves of altogether, e.g. quinine. She also disapproves of the excessive use of purgatives.

*

It is hardly possible to give a list of drugs [*not to be prescribed for persons practising Yoga*], but the general rule is that very strong or violent medicines should be avoided as much as possible — for Yoga increases the sensitivity of the vital and physical reactions and drugs tend to produce stronger or other effects than with ordinary persons.

*

The morphia stuns locally or otherwise the consciousness and its reaction to the subconscient pressure and so suspends the pain or deadens it. Even that it does not always do — X took five morphine injections in succession without even diminishing his liver inflammation pains. What became of the power of the drug over the subconscient in that case? The resistance was too strong just as the resistance of Y's subconscient to the Force.

*

Injection should be taken only if indispensable. Medical treatment can be resorted to if the illness is or has become of a chronic kind.

Chapter Three

Specific Illnesses, Ailments and Other Physical Problems

Cancer

I do not know why the doctors speak of cancer as inevitable. There are so many people who carry gall-stones in the bladder for so many years without any development of cancer. It is evident that it is a dangerous illness, not easily curable — but we cannot say positively either that she will not survive. There is no such thing as an incurable illness in reality — for what the doctors call such is only an illness for which they have not yet been able to discover a physical remedy. X has one force on her side, her faith and her will to survive for the sadhana; on the other side is a kind of destiny of the body which is strong but not absolutely insurmountable. Her faith must be left intact — and we must send force to help her. That is all that we can say at present. If she can by her faith draw down and open to such a force as will counteract the adverse physical forces in her body, then she will survive.

*

Of course it [*cancer*] can [*be cured by Yoga*], but on condition of faith or openness or both. Even a mental suggestion can cure cancer — with luck, of course, as is shown by the case of the woman operated on unsuccessfully for cancer, but the doctors lied and told her it had succeeded. Result, cancer symptoms all ceased and she died many years afterwards of another illness altogether.

Tuberculosis

T.B. is the result of a strong psychic-vital depression. Sex cannot directly cause T.B. though it may be a factor in bringing about a fall of the vital forces and a withdrawal of the psychic supporting forces leading to T.B. The lack of vitality which easily comes as a result of modern civilisation is therefore a very strong contributing cause. Moderns have not the solid nervous system and the natural (as opposed to the artificial and morbid) zest of life that their ancestors had. But I don't know about the soldiers — the hideous trench war with all its ghastly circumstances and surroundings was, I imagine, far more difficult to bear than the open air marching and fighting of the Napoleonic times.

Fever

Fever is of course more often than not a struggle of the body to fight out impurities that have got in, but sometimes the remedy is as bad if not worse than the disease. It is the same with the mind difficulties — an illness sometimes results in a throwing out of some impurities but it can also do more harm than good.

Influenza

The first thing to do is to keep throughout a perfect equanimity and not to allow thoughts of disturbed anxiety or depression to enter you. It is quite natural after this severe attack of influenza that there should be weakness and some fluctuations in the progress to recovery. What you have to do is to remain calm and confident and not worry or be restless — be perfectly quiet and prepared to rest as long as rest is needed. There is nothing to be anxious about; rest, and the health and strength will come.

Head Cold

What you describe [*a "loaded" head with sluggish thinking and mechanical thoughts*] happens very usually during a cold in the head, as ordinarily one depends upon the brain cells for the transmission of the mental thought. When the mind is not so dependent on the brain cells, then their obscuration by the cold does not interfere with clear seeing and thinking and one is not thrown back in the mechanical mind.

Weak Vision

Finally about your eyes. The wearing of glasses does inevitably confirm any weakness in the eyes, so we would not recommend you to resort to them for a strain which can surely be remedied in other ways.

*

It is better to take the sun-treatment (for the eyes) if you give up your spectacles. It is not a treatment in the ordinary sense, as there are no medicines, but a use of certain natural forces and physical observations to correct the impaired mechanism of the eye.

*

You will have to be careful about your eyes. Reading by night (too much) is inadvisable. There are two suggestions of the sun-treatment man which I have found to be not without foundation. First, one should blink freely in looking at things or reading and not fix the eyes or stare. Second, palming gives a very useful rest — palming means keeping the hands crossed over the closed eyes (without pressing on the eyes) so as to shut out all light.

Glaucoma

We cannot take the responsibility of advising against operation. Glaucoma is supposed to bring inevitable blindness — there is no known successful medical treatment — the operation is considered the only chance of avoiding the natural result of the illness. So they must be left free to undergo it if there is no way out.

Stammering

I don't think stammering has anything to do with insufficient lung-power nor is it usually caused by malformation of the vocal organ — it is commonly a nervous (physico-nervous) impediment and is perfectly curable. I can't say that I know of any especial device for it — people have used various kinds of devices to get over it, but behind them all will-power and a patient discipline of the utterance are indispensable.

Menstrual Problems

The attack you had on the body must, from the description, have been a crisis of the circulation due to the period you are passing through, the turning of the age when the menstruation is preparing to cease but has not yet ceased altogether. It is a very uncomfortable period because of the irregularities and these things can happen — they cease when this period of life is over. Some pass through it very easily with only the irregularities of the flow and an occasional trouble of this kind; others have more difficulty. If there is then no sexual movement in the nature or none of any intensity, then things go more smoothly.

Constipation

Constipation is not determined by food; it is due to an inertia in the physical — get off the inertia and the constipation goes.

Sciatica

Sciatica is something more than nervous — it affects the movement of the muscles through the nerves. It can be got rid of at once, however, if you can manage to direct the Force on it.

*

There is no outer means. Sciatica is a thing which yields only to inner concentrated force or else it goes away of itself and comes of itself. Outer means at best can only be palliatives.

*

If you cannot get rid of the sciatica by inner means, the medical remedy (not for curing it, but for keeping free as long as possible) is not to fatigue yourself. It comes for periods which may last for weeks, then suddenly goes. If you remain quiet physically and are not too active, it may not come for a long time. But that of course means an inactive life, physically incapable. It is what I meant by eternising the sciatica — and the inertia also.

*

The inertia is there because there was always in your outer being a great force of tamas and it is this that is being used by the resistance. There was also a deficiency of steady will-power in the outer mind which makes it more difficult for the Force to come down than for the Knowledge. When you are entirely open the Force can act on the sciatica and it lessens or disappears, but with the consciousness blocked by the inertia these difficulties come in the way.

*

If you can cure by withdrawing [*from work*] so much the better. The sciatica has often tried to fall on the Mother and on myself — we have always found that it cannot resist the Force quietly and persistently applied. Other illnesses can resist, but sciatica being entirely tamasic cannot. The application of Force does not yet, probably, come natural to you, so it brings a sense of struggle not of quiet domination, hence the restlessness etc.

Growing Taller

It is rather difficult to grow taller when once the period of growth is over. It may come in the period of material transformation at the end of the Yoga — but that is far off and I don't think there are any means by which it can be done otherwise.

Bearing the Heat

Dry heat is supposed to be less bad for the general health than damp heat. There is however usually less need of food and therefore less appetite. From the point of view of Yoga if one can keep a certain quiet in the material body, "peace in the cells", the heat is easier to bear.

Section Four

The Subconscient and the Inconscient and the Process of Yoga

Chapter One

The Subconscient and the Integral Yoga

The Change of the Subconscient

The change of the subconscient is most important for our Yoga — for without it there can only be an incomplete personal experience without the change we seek for being established in the very roots of the being here and consequently in the earth-consciousness.

*

No man is perfect; the vital is there and the ego is there to prevent it. It is only when there is the total transformation of the external and the internal being down to the very subconscient, that perfection is possible. Till then imperfection will remain as our common heritage.

*

So long as there is not the Supramental change down to the subconscient complete and final the lower nature has always a hold on some part of the being.

*

The Yoga cannot be done in a minute. Some essential changes are made rapidly, but even these have to be worked out and confirmed in the detail of action. What you speak of [*a sudden change in the subconscient*], only the Supramental could do if it acted directly or some force fully supported by the Supramental, but that occurs rarely.

The Subconscient, the Inner Being and the Outer Being

In our Yoga we mean by the subconscient that quite submerged part of our being in which there is no wakingly conscious and coherent thought, will or feeling or organised reaction, but which yet receives obscurely the impressions of all things and stores them up in itself and from it too all sorts of stimuli, of persistent habitual movements, crudely repeated or disguised in strange forms can surge up into dream or into the waking nature. For if these impressions rise up most in dream in an incoherent and disorganised manner, they can also and do rise up into our waking consciousness as a mechanical repetition of old thoughts, old mental, vital and physical habits or an obscure stimulus to sensations, actions, emotions which do not originate in or from our conscious thought or will and are even often opposed to its perceptions, choice or dictates. In the subconscient there is an obscure mind full of obstinate sanskaras, impressions, associations, fixed notions, habitual reactions formed by our past, an obscure vital full of the seeds of habitual desires, sensations and nervous reactions, a most obscure material which governs much that has to do with the condition of the body. It is largely responsible for our illnesses; chronic or repeated illnesses are indeed mainly due to the subconscient and its obstinate memory and habit of repetition of whatever has impressed itself upon the body consciousness. But this subconscient must be clearly distinguished from the subliminal parts of our being such as the inner or subtle physical consciousness, the inner vital or inner mental; for these are not at all obscure or incoherent or ill-organised, but only veiled from our surface consciousness. Our surface constantly receives something, inner touches, communications or influences, from these sources but does not know for the most part whence they come.

*

The subconscient is below the waking physical consciousness — it is an automatic, obscure, incoherent, half-unconscious realm into which light and awareness can with difficulty come. The inner vital and physical are quite different — they have a larger, plastic, subtler, freer and richer consciousness than the surface vital and physical, much more open to the Truth and in direct touch with the universal.

*

The inner being does not depend on the subconscient, but the outer has depended on it for thousands of lives — that is why the outer being and physical consciousness's habit of response to the subconscient can be a formidable obstacle to the progress of the sadhana and is so with most. It keeps up the repetition of the old movements, is always pulling down the consciousness and opposing the continuity of the ascent and bringing the old nature or else the tamas (non-illumination and non-activity) across the descent. It is only if you live wholly and dynamically in the inner being and feel the outer as a quite superficial thing that you can get rid of the obstruction or minimise it until the transformation of the outer being can be made complete.

*

It [*a condition of obscurity*] is most probably something that has come from outside and covered. This happens at this stage when the working is in the physical and subconscient — for that is the nature of these parts, to live in the external with the inner being covered up by a sort of natural veil of obscurity. Therefore when one makes the opening through this veil, it has a tendency to come back. When that happens, one has to remain undisturbed and call down the Force and Light from above to remove the obstacle. This must be done till the opening is permanent and complete and no covering is possible.

The Subconscient and the Physical Being

The subconscient difficulty is *the* difficulty now[1] — because the

---

[1] *This letter was written in April 1935.* — Ed.

whole struggle in the general sadhana is now there. It is in the subconscient, no longer in the vital or conscious physical that the resistance is all massed together.

*

There is a close connection between the subconscient and the physical and lower vital parts; so long as the subconscient is not cleared, the seed you speak of remains.

*

The material [*consciousness*] is for the most part subconscient — it depends upon the subtler parts for its waking consciousness.

*

The subconscient material plane is a field that still opposes the entrance of the Divine Light.

*

Until they [*the material and subconscient parts of the being*] aspire or at least assent fully to the aspiration and will of the higher being, there can be no lasting change in them.

*

It [*the reason the physical can help to remove inertia*] is because, the subconscient being just below the physical, the enlightened physical can act on it directly and completely in a way in which mind and vital cannot and by this direct action can help to liberate the mind and vital also.

*

Yes, what you write is correct. When the physical consciousness has to be changed, it is of course essential to work on the subconscient, as it has a great influence on the physical which is very dependent on it.

The loss of consciousness comes naturally at first when the subconscient is being worked upon. You have to be careful that it does not become habitual. If you react with a will for the change of this tendency (no struggle is needed) it will pass in time.

*

It is not a fact that formless things [*such as vague subconscient impressions*] can have no power — all that is necessary is that they should have a force in them. The subconscient influences the body because all in the body has developed out of the subconscient and all in itself still is only half conscious and much of its action can be called subconscious. It is therefore much more easily influenced by the subconscious than by the conscious mind and conscious will or even the vital mind and vital will except in those things in which a conscious mental or vital control has been established and the subconscious itself has accepted it. If it were not so, man's control of his actions and physical states would be complete, there would be no illness or, if there were, it could be immediately cured by mental action. But it is not so. For that reason the higher consciousness has to be brought down, the body and the subconscient enlightened by it and accustomed to obey its control.

*

It is good. Emptiness and silence of the consciousness prepare the being to live within, with the outer consciousness only as a means of communication and action on the physical world instead of living in the external only.

As there is a superconscient (something above our present consciousness) above the head from which the higher consciousness comes down into the body, so there is also a subconscient (something below our consciousness) below the feet. Matter is under the control of this power, because it is that out of which it has been created — that is why matter seems to us to be quite unconscious. The material body is very much under the influence of this power for the same reason; it is why we are not conscious of what is going on in the body, for the most part. The outer consciousness goes down into this subconscient when we are asleep, and so it becomes unaware of what is going on in us when we are asleep except for a few dreams. Many of these dreams rise up from the subconscient and are made up of old memories, impressions etc. put together in an incoherent way. For the subconscient receives impressions of all we do or experience in our lives and keeps these impressions in it, sending up often fragments of them in sleep. It is a very important part of the being, but we can do nothing much with it by the conscious will. It is the higher Force working in us that in its natural course will open the subconscient to itself and bring down into it its control and light.

*

It is in the Yogic consciousness that one feels the seat of the subconscient below the feet, but the influence of the subconscious is not confined there — it is spread in the body. In the waking state it is overpowered by the conscious thinking mind and vital and conscious physical mind, but in the sleep state it comes on the surface.

Habits and the Subconscient

The subconscient is a thing of habits and memories and repeats persistently or whenever it can old suppressed reactions, reflexes, mental, vital or physical responses. It must be trained by a still more persistent insistence of the higher parts of the being to give up its old responses and take on the new and true ones.

*

The subconscient is the support of habitual action — it can support good habits as well as bad.

*

The exterior consciousness can be invaded by what rises up from the subconscient or comes in from outside and owing to a renewed vibration of the past habit can respond — but that does not mean that the will of the vital or of the physical mind is for these things. If there was anything in them normally on the side of sex or violence, then you could say the impurities were there. But if it were so, there would be more than these attacks, there would be a daily struggle with anger and desire.

If one had to wait for an absolute purity free from all possibility of these attacks before beginning to realise the Divine, nobody would ever be able to realise. It is as the realisation progresses, that the fundamental transformation takes place.

The Environmental Consciousness and the Subconscient

These cravings and desires are old habits of the physical which came to it from the universal Nature and which it accepted and took as part of itself and its life. When these things are rejected by the waking consciousness they try to take refuge in the subconscient or else in what may be called the environmental consciousness and from there they press upon the consciousness trying to recover their hold or simply to recur for a time. If they are in the subconscient they come up most usually in dreams, but they may also surge up into the waking consciousness. If they come from the environment they take the form of thought-suggestions or impulses or a vague restless or disturbing pressure. It is probably this environmental pressure that you feel. When the body is full of the new consciousness, Peace and Power at the same time, then this outward pressure is felt but can no longer disturb and finally it recedes to a distance (no longer pressing immediately on the physical mind or body) and either gradually or rapidly disappears.

By environmental consciousness I mean something that each man carries around him, outside his body, even when he is not aware of it, — by which he is in touch with others and with the universal forces. It is through this that the thoughts, feelings etc. of others pass to enter into one — it is through this also that waves of the universal force — desire, sex, etc. — come in and take possession of the mind, vital or body.

*

When these things [*base feelings such as jealousy*] are rejected and disappear for a time, some part of them may go out into the environmental consciousness and from there they can return in a wave from the general Nature. If one is conscious, one can even feel them coming in. The rejection of such returns is an important part of the purification and it is not complete till this power of returning is no longer there. But also it may be that some part is not so much rejected as suppressed by mental control, then it sinks into the subconscient and when the subconscient is active (as in dream or in a passive state of the mind) or else when the subconscient itself is brought up for purification, then it may rise up even with much violence. There especially the sense that one has to begin all again and nothing has been done may come upon the sadhak. But it is not so really. One has to be firm and not get upset but this time detach firmly and completely so as to uproot completely from the nature.

*

What is taking place, the subsiding of the surge of subconscient thoughts and movements, and their pressure on the mind, is just what ought to take place. It is not a suppression or pulling back into the subconscient, it is an expulsion from the conscious self into which it has arisen. It is true that something more may rise from the subconscient, but it will be what is still left there. What is now rejected, if it goes anywhere and is not abolished, will go not into the subconscient but into the surrounding consciousness which one carries around him — once there it no longer belongs to oneself in any way and if it tries to return it will be as foreign matter which one has not to accept or allow any longer. These are the two last stages of rejection by which one gets rid of the old things of the nature, they go down into the subconscient and have to be got rid of from there or they go out into the environmental consciousness and are no longer ours.

The idea that one should let what rises from the subconscient go on repeating itself till it is exhausted is not the right idea. For that would needlessly prolong the troubled condition and might be harmful. When these things rise they have to be observed and then thrown out, not kept.

The Rising Up of Things from the Subconscient

The human like the animal mind lives largely in impressions rising up from the subconscient.

*

What must have happened was that as the physical consciousness is now being worked upon, all the past impressions (which usually remain in the subconscious and rise up from time to time and meanwhile influence the thought and action and feelings without being noticed) rose up in a mass and threw themselves on the consciousness. This usually happens in order that the sadhak may see and reject them and get liberated entirely (in the subconscious as well as the conscious parts) from his physical past. That is why you felt afterwards the sense of release. The throat is the centre of the externalising mind (physical mind).

*

I do not think you have gone back — probably what has been happening to many if not most in the Asram (especially those who have done some serious sadhana) is happening to you. It is the rising of old habitual thoughts, feelings, impulses in a confused way from the subconscient in a mechanical repetition. The subconscient is the basis of the ordinary physical nature and the light has to come into it also. Moreover even if the progress gained has been covered over by these things, what is once gained is not lost; it always reemerges after obscuration and one can get back into it. Ideas of discouragement should always be rejected.

*

What is happening just now [*the rising of confused, depressing thoughts*] is that there is a great uprush of the subconscient in which are the seeds or the strong remnants of the habitual difficulties of the nature. But its character is a confusion and obscurity without order or clear mental or other arrangement — it is a confused depression, discouragement, inability to progress

— a feeling of what are we doing? why are we here? how can we go on? will anything ever be attained? and along with it old difficulties recurring in a confused and random but often violent and distressing fashion.

You cannot "begin" again; it would be too difficult a thing in this confusion. You have to get back to the point at which you deviated. If you can get back to the Peace that was coming and with it aspire to the freedom and wideness of the Purusha consciousness forming a *point d'appui* of detachment and separation from all this confusion of the subconscient Prakriti, then you will have a firm ground to stand upon and proceed. But for that you must make your choice firmly and refuse to be upset at every moment and diverted from it.

*

But in reality these things [*old movements of the lower nature*] are not sufficient reasons for getting sad and depressed. It is quite normal for difficulties to come back like that and it is not a proof that no progress has been made. The recurrence (after one has thought one has conquered) is not unaccountable. I have explained in my writings what happens. When a habitual movement long embedded in the nature is cast out, it takes refuge in some less enlightened part of the nature, and when cast out of the rest of the nature, it takes refuge in the subconscient and from there surges up when you least expect it or comes up in dreams or sudden inconscient movements or it goes out and remains in wait in the environmental being through which the universal Nature works, and attacks from there as a force from outside trying to recover its kingdom by a suggestion or repetition of old movements. One has to stand fast till the power of return fades away. These returns or attacks must be regarded not as parts of oneself, but as invasions — and rejected without allowing any depression or discouragement. If the mind does not sanction them, if the vital refuses to welcome them, if the physical remains steady and refuses to obey the physical urge, then the recurrence of the thought, the vital impulse, the physical feeling will begin to lose

The Subconscient and the Integral Yoga 605

its last holds and finally they will be too feeble to cause any trouble.

*

You do not realise how much of the ordinary natural being lives in the subconscient physical. It is there that habitual movements, mental and vital, are stored and from there they come up into the waking mind. Driven out of the upper consciousness, it is in this cavern of the Panis that they take refuge. No longer allowed to emerge freely in the waking state, they come up in sleep as dreams. It is only when they are cleared out of the subconscient, their very seeds killed by the enlightening of these hidden layers, that they cease for good. As your consciousness deepens inwardly and the higher light comes down into those inferior covered parts, the things that now recur in this way will disappear.

*

What you describe seems to be in its nature an uncontrolled rushing up of the subconscient taking the form of a mechanical recurrence of old thoughts, interests or desires with which the physical mind is usually occupied. If that were all, the only thing would be to reject them, detach yourself and let them pass till they quieted down. But I gather from what you write that there is an attack, an obscure force using these recurrences to invade and harass the mind and body. It would be helpful if you could give an exact description of the main character of the thoughts that come, what things and ideas they are concerned with etc. But in any case the one thing to do is to open yourself to the Mother's force by aspiration, thought of the Mother or any other way and let it drive out the attack. We shall send Force continually till this is done. It will be better to let us know every three days or so how you go on, for that will help to make the action of the Force more precise.

*

These thoughts that attack in sleep or in the state between sleep and waking do not belong to any part of your conscious being, but come either from the subconscient or from the surrounding atmosphere through the subconscient. If they are thoughts you had in the past and have thrown out from you, then what rises must be impressions left by them in the subconscient — for all things thought, felt or experienced leave such impressions which can rise from there in sleep. Or the thoughts can have gone out from you into the environmental consciousness, that is, an atmosphere of consciousness which we carry around us and through which we are connected with universal Nature and from there they may be trying to return upon you. As it is difficult for them to succeed in the waking state, they take advantage of the absence of conscious control in sleep and appear there. If it is something new and not yours, then it can be neither of these, but an attack of some outside Force.

It is to be hoped that as you have rejected them, they will not come again, but if they do, then you must put a conscious will before going to sleep that they should not come. A suggestion of that kind on the subconscient is often successful, if not at once, after a time; for the subconscient learns to obey the will put upon it in the waking state.

*

The dream you had was really a rising up of past formations or impressions from the subconscient. All that we do, feel or experience in life leaves an impression, a sort of essential memory of itself in the subconscient and this can come up in dreams even long after those feelings, movements or experiences have ceased in the conscious being, — still more when they have been recent and are only now or lately thrown away from the mind or vital. Thus long after one has ceased to think of old acquaintances or relatives dreams about them go on coming up from this source. So too when sex or anger no longer troubles the conscious vital, dreams of sex or dreams of anger and strife can still rise. It is only when the subconscient is cleared that they cease; meanwhile they are of not much importance (provided one understands what they are and is not affected) so long as the old movements are not allowed to recur or remain in the waking state.

*

It [*variation in the intensity of past memories*] is always so with the impressions left in the subconscient physical. One day they come as pale and distant things, with no life in them, another they seem to get a certain force. It depends on whether they are caught up by a current of force from the universal or rise up of themselves with no force except what is left in them from the past.

*

All these movements simply mean that a certain part of the nature, full of habitual emotional movements, had been lying suppressed but not definitely dealt with and has now come up with as much force as possible, taking advantage of the descent of the consciousness from the peace and Ananda. It is an old habitual movement of the egoistic vital that is repeating itself. You had pushed it down into the subconscient and away to the outskirts of your nature, but not cleared the nature of it entirely. It is not surprising that it has pushed back the inner self and its experiences for the time being; if it had not done that, it could not last for a moment. But that is no reason why you should talk as if it were a hopeless downfall; it is not that, though it is a serious stumble. You have to recognise it for what it is and get out of the wave and throw it away from you. Steady yourself and look straight at what has happened without overstressing its importance; it will then pass away sooner.

*

As for the mood that came on you, it comes up from the subconscient, where things of the old nature sink when they are rejected. When moods come up like that, you have to remain quiet and call the Mother till it is gone. After a time this power of mechanical repetition without reason from the subconscient gets worn out and disappears — then these moods come no more.

*

All that [*sense of grief and sorrow*] is probably things that rise from the subconscient — or perhaps the subconscient itself is being worked upon to arrive at a state of light and peace. It sometimes enters into a happy condition, sometimes into a neutral one, sometimes it raises up a causeless sorrow. The movements of the subconscient take place even without reason, of themselves, owing to the inherent habit in Nature, that is why the grief is without discoverable cause. It is only because it is in the subconscient that you cannot locate it. When the grief comes, you must dissociate yourself from it and reject it, not taking it as your own, until it ceases to come and call down the Mother's peace and Ananda in its place.

*

Yes, surely it is present [*vanity in the subconscient*]. All normal reactions and characteristics are there in the subconscient, and even remain there after they have been rejected from the conscious nature and can return from it in the conscious nature.

*

Certainly, the subconscient has many more fears in it than those admitted or acknowledged by the waking consciousness.

*

The dark wells of the subconscient are deep and until they are altogether cleared some gushing up of the old sources is always possible.

Dealing with the Subconscient

As for the subconscient that is best dealt with when the opening of the consciousness to what comes down from above is complete. Then one becomes aware of the subconscient as a separate domain and can bring down into it the silence and all else that comes from above.

*

The subconscient can be entirely dealt with only when the other parts are sufficiently open and changed — but meanwhile it can feel the pressure of the change in the mind and vital.

*

The conscious parts have to be prepared first — impossible to deal successfully with the subconscient till then, except in points and details. Just as the musician has first to learn the right principle and execution of his music with his mind and vital (aesthetic) perception and will — and teach his fingers to execute it — afterwards the subconscient in his fingers will learn its work and do the right thing of itself — e.g. touching the right keys without his eyes having to follow.

*

These [*vital and physical weaknesses*] are symptoms and feelings that can easily come in the period when the subconscient is being dealt with — tamas, age, decay, illness, death, weakness, inertia, the mechanical play (as if the inevitable round of a machine) of the lower vital have their seeds in the subconscient and when the subconscient rises up in its native power, these threaten to rise with them. Never consent to the attack or allow the faith and the will to go down before them. Affirm always the higher Truth against them and call down the Power and Light into the cells, into the whole body and plunge them into the subphysical below the body so that the very roots of the subconscient may get illuminated and change. It is only by doing this that realisation in the body will become possible.

*

It [*insincerity in the vital*] can only be dangerous if the waking mind accepts it. All the same, so long as it remains in the subconscient, it keeps a seed of possibility — so it must be got out altogether.

*

Just as one can concentrate the thought on an object or the vision on a point, so one can concentrate will on a particular part or point of the body and give an order to the consciousness there. That order reaches the subconscient.

Dealing with Memories from the Subconscient

It is most probably from the subconscient [*that the past memories come*]. When these memories arise, they should be treated on the basis that they have arisen in order to be dissolved and dismissed, so that by their persistent dissolution one may not be tied by the impressions in the subconscient to the past (that is the machinery of Karma) but free for the spirit's unbound future.

The best is when you can get the true knowledge about it, why it happened and what purpose it served; then it goes easily.

*

Reject them [*past memories*] from their roots with the idea that they have come up in order to be abolished from the subconscient. It may take a little time to get rid of some memories which are persistent and recurrent, but usually this process has an effect of clearance after a time.

*

If you do not pay attention, they [*past memories*] fall into the background and become a mechanical action which it is more easy to get rid of.

*

This review of the past is a very good sign, for it usually comes when there is a preparation of the physical consciousness and subconscient for change. One has not to regret the stumbles of the past but look with a quiet eye and understand, for all came — the stumbles included — as part of the necessary experience by which the being learns and advances through error to the Light and through the imperfections of Nature towards the divine perfection.

Clearing or Emptying the Subconscient

There is always a great deal to do in the subconscient, but if you specially feel it [*the need to clear the subconscient*], it must be that the time for clearing it has come. If the other parts keep open and responsive, this should not give too much trouble.

*

It is only if the mind is silent that the subconscient can be empty. What has to be done is to get all the old ignorant unyogic stuff out of the subconscient.

*

If the subconscient is emptied, it would mean that you have got beyond the ordinary consciousness and the subconscient itself is prepared to be an instrument of the Truth.

Illumining the Subconscient

The subconscient is a dark and ignorant region, so that it is natural that the obscurer movements of the Nature should have more power there. It is so indeed with all the lower parts of the nature from the lower vital downwards. But it does send up good things also though more rarely. It has in the course of the sadhana to be illumined and made a support of the higher consciousness in the physical nature instead of a basis of the instinctive lower movements.

*

The work [*going on in the subconscient*] is of a general nature, not individual, but necessarily everyone here is to some extent affected by it.[2] If consciousness and light is not brought into the subconscient, then there can be no change. For it is in the subconscient that there are the seeds of all the old lower vital instincts and movements and however much they may be cleared in the

---

[2] *This letter was written in November 1937. — Ed.*

lower vital itself, they may sprout up again from below. Also the subconscient is the secret basis of the bodily consciousness. The subconscient must admit into itself the higher consciousness and the Truth light.

*

[*First effects of the Light penetrating and changing the subconscient:*]
    1. The subconscient begins to show more easily what is in it.
    2. Things rising from there come to the awareness of the mind before they can touch or affect the consciousness.
    3. The subconscient becomes less the refuge of the ignorant and obscure movements and more an automatic response of the material to the higher consciousness.
    4. It gives less covert and less passage to the suggestions of the hostile forces.
    5. It is more easy to be conscious in sleep and to have higher forms of dream experience. Hostile dreams — e.g. sex-suggestions can be met and stopped in the dream itself and any result like emission prevented.
    6. A waking will put on the dream state before sleeping becomes more and more effective.

*

The subconscient is to be penetrated by the light and made a sort of bedrock of truth, a store of right impressions, right physical responses to the Truth. Strictly speaking, it will not be subconscient at all, but a sort of bank of true values held ready for use.

Psycho-analysis and the Integral Yoga

Your practice of psycho-analysis was a mistake. It has, for the time at least, made the work of purification more complicated, not easier. The psycho-analysis of Freud is the last thing that one should associate with Yoga. It takes up a certain part, the darkest, the most perilous, the unhealthiest part of the nature, the lower vital subconscious layer, isolates some of its most morbid phenomena and attributes to it and them an action out of all proportion to its true role in the nature. Modern psychology is an infant science, at once rash, fumbling and crude. As in all infant sciences, the universal habit of the human mind — to take a partial or local truth, generalise it unduly and try to explain a whole field of Nature in its narrow terms — runs riot here. Moreover, the exaggeration of the importance of suppressed sexual complexes is a dangerous falsehood and it can have a nasty influence and tend to make the mind and vital more and not less fundamentally impure than before.

It is true that the subliminal in man is the largest part of his nature and has in it the secret of the unseen dynamisms which explain his surface activities. But the lower vital subconscious which is all that this psycho-analysis of Freud seems to know — and even of that it knows only a few ill-lit corners, — is no more than a restricted and very inferior portion of the subliminal whole. The subliminal self stands behind and supports the whole superficial man; it has in it a larger and more efficient mind behind the surface mind, a larger and more powerful vital behind the surface vital, a subtler and freer physical consciousness behind the surface bodily existence. And above them it opens to higher superconscient as well as below them to lower subconscient ranges. If one wishes to purify and transform the nature, it is the power of these higher ranges to which one must open and raise to them and change by them both the subliminal and the surface being. Even this should be done with care, not prematurely or rashly, following a higher guidance, keeping always the right attitude; for otherwise the force that is drawn down may be too strong for an obscure and weak frame of nature. But to begin by opening up the lower subconscious, risking to raise up all that is foul or obscure in it, is to go out of one's way to invite trouble. First, one should make the higher mind and vital strong and firm and full of light and peace from above; afterwards one can open up or even dive into the subconscious with more safety and some chance of a rapid and successful change.

The system of getting rid of things by *anubhava* can also be a dangerous one; for on this way one can easily become more entangled instead of arriving at freedom. This method has behind it two well-known psychological motives. One, the motive of purposeful exhaustion, is valid only in some cases, especially when some natural tendency has too strong a hold or too strong a drive in it to be got rid of by *vicāra* or by the process of rejection and the substitution of the true movement in its place; when that happens in excess, the sadhaka has sometimes even to go back to the ordinary action of the ordinary life, get the true experience of it with a new mind and will behind and then return to the spiritual life with the obstacle eliminated or else ready for elimination. But this method of purposive indulgence is always dangerous, though sometimes inevitable. It succeeds only when there is a very strong will in the being towards realisation; for then indulgence brings a strong dissatisfaction and reaction, *vairāgya*, and the will towards perfection can be carried down into the recalcitrant part of the nature.

The other motive for *anubhava* is of a more general applicability; for in order to reject anything from the being one has first to become conscious of it, to have the clear inner experience of its action and to discover its actual place in the workings of the nature. One can then work upon it to eliminate it, if it is an entirely wrong movement, or to transform it if it is only the degradation of a higher and true movement. It is this or something like it that is attempted crudely and improperly with a rudimentary and insufficient knowledge in the system of psychoanalysis. The process of raising up the lower movements into the full light of consciousness in order to know and deal with them is inevitable; for there can be no complete change without it. But it can truly succeed only when a higher light and force are sufficiently at work to overcome, sooner or later, the force of the tendency that is held up for change. Many, under the pretext of *anubhava*, not only raise up the adverse movement, but support it with their consent instead of rejecting it, find justifications for continuing or repeating it and so go on playing with it, indulging its return, eternising it; afterwards when they want to get rid of

The Subconscient and the Integral Yoga

it, it has got such a hold that they find themselves helpless in its clutch and only a terrible struggle or an intervention of divine grace can liberate them. Some do this out of a vital twist or perversity, others out of sheer ignorance; but in Yoga, as in life, ignorance is not accepted by Nature as a justifying excuse. This danger is there in all improper dealings with the ignorant parts of the nature; but none is more ignorant, more perilous, more unreasoning and obstinate in recurrence than the lower vital subconscious and its movements. To raise it up prematurely or improperly for *anubhava* is to risk suffusing the conscious parts also with its dark and dirty stuff and thus poisoning the whole vital and even the mental nature. Always therefore one should begin by a positive, not a negative experience, by bringing down something of the divine nature, calm, light, equanimity, purity, divine strength into the parts of the conscious being that have to be changed; only when that has been sufficiently done and there is a firm positive basis, is it safe to raise up the concealed subconscious adverse elements in order to destroy and eliminate them by the strength of the divine calm, light, force and knowledge. Even so, there will be enough of the lower stuff rising up of itself to give you as much of the *anubhava* as you will need for getting rid of the obstacles; but then they can be dealt with with much less danger and under a higher internal guidance.

*

I find it difficult to take these psycho-analysts at all seriously when they try to scrutinise spiritual experience by the flicker of their torch-lights, — yet perhaps one ought to, for half-knowledge is a very powerful thing and can be a great obstacle to the coming in front of the true Truth. This new psychology looks to me very much like children learning some summary and not very adequate alphabet, exulting in putting their a-b-c-d of the subconscient and the mysterious underground super-ego together and imagining that their first book of obscure beginnings (c-a-t=cat, t-r-e-e=tree) is the very heart of the real knowledge. They look from down up and explain the higher lights by the lower obscurities; but the foundation of these things is above and not below, *upari budhna eṣām*. The superconscient, not the subconscient, is the true fountain of things. The significance of the lotus is not to be found by analysing the secrets of the mud from which it grows here; its secret is to be found in the heavenly archetype of the lotus that blooms for ever in the Light above. The self-chosen field of these psychologists is besides poor and dark and limited; you must know the whole before you can know the part and the highest before you can truly understand the lowest. That is the province of a greater psychology awaiting its hour before which these poor gropings will disappear and come to nothing.

Chapter Two

The Inconscient and the Integral Yoga

The Descent of the Sadhana into the Inconscient

There is another cause of the general inability to change which at present afflicts the sadhak.[1] It is because the sadhana, as a general fact, has now and for a long time past come down to the Inconscient; the pressure, the call is to change in that part of the nature which depends directly on the Inconscient, the fixed habits, the automatic movements, the mechanical repetitions of the nature, the involuntary reactions to life, all that seems to belong to the fixed character of a man. This has to be done if there is to be any chance of a total spiritual change. The Force (generally and not individually) is working to make that possible, its pressure is for that, — for, on the other levels, the change has already been made possible (not, mind you, assured to everybody). But to open the Inconscient to the light is a Herculean task; change on the other levels is much easier. As yet this work has only begun and it is not surprising that there seems to be no change in things or people. It will come in time, but not in a hurry.

As for experiences, they are all right but the trouble is that they do not seem to change the nature, they only enrich the consciousness — even the realisation, on the mind level, of the Brahman seems to leave the nature almost where it was, except for a few. That is why we insist on the psychic transformation as the first necessity — for that does change the nature — and its chief instrument is bhakti, surrender etc.

*

---

[1] *This letter was written in April 1944, the one that follows it in June 1944. The final letter in the group was written in April 1947. — Ed.*

The sunlit path can only be followed if the psychic is constantly or usually in front or if one has a natural spirit of faith and surrender or a face turned habitually towards the sun or psychic predisposition (e.g. a faith in one's spiritual destiny) or if he has acquired the psychic turn. That does not mean that the sunlit man has no difficulties; he may have many, but he regards them cheerfully as "all in the day's work". If he gets bad beatings, he is capable of saying, "Well, that was a queer go, but the Divine is evidently in a queer mood and if that is his way of doing things, it must be the right one; I am surely a still queerer fellow myself and that, I suppose, was the only means of putting me right." But everybody can't be of that turn, and surrender which would put everything right is, as you say, difficult to do completely. That is why we do not insist on total surrender at once, but are satisfied with a little to begin with, the rest to grow as it can.

I have explained to you why so many people (not by any means all) are in this gloomy condition, dull and despondent. It is the tamas, the inertia of the Inconscient, that has got hold of them. But also it is the small physical vital which takes only an interest in the small and trivial things of the ordinary daily and social life and nothing else. When formerly the sadhana was going on on higher levels (mind, higher vital etc.), there was plenty of vigour and verve and interest in the details of the Asram work and life as well as in an inner life; the physical vital was carried in the stream. But for many this has dropped; they live in the unsatisfied vital physical and find everything desperately dull, gloomy and without interest or issue. In their inner life the tamas from the Inconscient has created a block or a bottleneck and they do not find any way out. If one can keep the right condition and attitude, a strong interest in work or a strong interest in sadhana, then this becomes quiescent. That is the malady. Its remedy is to keep the right condition and to bring gradually or, if one can, swiftly the light of the higher aspiration into this part of the being also, so that whatever the conditions of the environment, it may keep also the right poise. Then the sunlit path should be less impossible.

*

The extreme acuteness of your difficulties is due to the Yoga having come down against the bedrock of Inconscience which is the fundamental basis of all resistance in the individual and in the world to the victory of the Spirit and the Divine Work that is leading toward that victory. The difficulties themselves are general in the Asram as well as in the outside world. Doubt, discouragement, diminution or loss of faith, waning of the vital enthusiasm for the ideal, perplexity and a baffling of the hope for the future are the common features of the difficulty. In the world outside there are much worse symptoms such as the general increase of cynicism, a refusal to believe in anything at all, a decrease of honesty, an immense corruption, a preoccupation with food, money, comfort, pleasure to the exclusion of higher things and a general expectation of worse and worse things awaiting the world. All that, however acute, is a temporary phenomenon for which those who know anything about the workings of the world-energy and the workings of the Spirit were prepared. I myself foresaw that this worst would come, the darkness of night before the dawn; therefore I am not discouraged. I know what is preparing behind the darkness and can see and feel the first signs of its coming. Those who seek for the Divine have to stand firm and persist in their seeking; after a time, the darkness will fade and begin to disappear and the Light will come.

Part Four

Difficulties in the Practice
of the Integral Yoga

Section One

Difficulties of the Path

Chapter One
The Difficulties of Yoga

Difficulties and the Aim of Life

It is the lesson of life that always in this world everything fails a man — only the Divine does not fail him, if he turns entirely to the Divine. It is not because there is something bad in you that blows fall on you, — blows fall on all human beings because they are full of desire for things that cannot last and they lose them or, even if they get, it brings disappointment and cannot satisfy them. To turn to the Divine is the only truth in life.

*

As for the blows, well, are they always given by the Yoga — is it not sometimes the sadhak of the Yoga who gives blows to himself? There are plenty of blows too in ordinary life according to my experience. Blows are the order of existence, and of Yoga; our nature or the nature of things brings them upon us until we learn to present to them a back which they cannot touch.

*

The ordinary life naturally has its mental, vital and physical pleasures, but it is of a superficial character and there is no firm foundation of the consciousness anywhere — all is at the mercy of the play of forces. In Yoga there is the period of struggle and difficulty in which the difficulty and suffering can be acute and the period of the foundation in the true consciousness after which there is no serious disturbance of the peace and freedom leading to the state of realisation in all the being in which grief etc. are impossible.

*

All X's troubles are due partly to past Karma in another life, partly to his nature which is unable to harmonise with his surroundings or to master them by strong will and clear understanding or to face them with calm poise and balance. Life is for experience and growth and until one has learned one's lesson things go on happening that are the result of one's imperfect balance with Nature or inner imperfections. All that happens is for the best is true only if we see with the cosmic view that takes in past and future development which is aided by ill fortune, as well as good fortune, by danger, death, suffering and calamity, as well as by happiness, success and victory. It is not true if it means that only things happen which are fortunate or obviously good for the person in the human sense.

*

What you describe is a nature divided against itself by a mind which has corrupted its action through a wrong use of its powers and a physical weakened by indulgence of vital desire.

Introspection is good only when it is used as a means for changing the nature so as to bring it into accordance with a higher ideal steadily held before you. The present nature of man is egoistic in motive, full of falsehoods created by the Ignorance into which he is born and which the mind and life accept in order to follow their ego's aims and desires. By introspection one comes to see that, but by itself that can only create distrust of oneself, loss of motive to action, cynicism and weakness. One must have the faith and aspiration towards a higher consciousness which one has to build up in place of this lower nature, then the introspection and the knowledge of the defects of the nature it gives become useful, as it helps one to see what has to be changed while the higher ideal gives what has to take the place of the old movements and the old nature.

But all that is not easy to do unless you resolve to give an aim to your life and erect the higher ideal towards which you have to grow. Just as the mind can destroy the force of life and its balance, so it can do that also, it can help to restore the power on a new basis and acquire a new and greater force and true balance. But for that you must have the will to do it. To create the will the mind must press for faith and vision and discourage their opposites.

What you have written has some power of thought and style and vision though of a mixed character. There is no harm in writing these things when they of themselves come; it may help the inner element of aspiration to grow in you.

Difficulties and the Integral Yoga

This Yoga is certainly difficult, but is any Yoga really easy? You speak of the lure of liberation into the extracosmic Absolute, but how many who set out on the path of Nirvana attain to it in this life or without a long, strenuous and difficult endeavour? Which of the paths has not to pass through the dry desert in order to reach the promised land? Even the path of Bhakti which is said to be the easiest is full of the lamentations of the bhaktas complaining that they call but the Beloved eludes their grasp, the place of meeting is prepared but even now Krishna does not come. Even if there is the joy of a brief glimpse or the passion of *milana*, it is followed by long periods of *viraha*. It is a mistake to think that any path of Yoga is facile, that any is a royal road or short cut to the Divine, or that like a system of "French made easy" or "French without tears", so there can be a system of "Yoga made easy" or "Yoga without tears". A few great souls prepared by past lives or otherwise lifted beyond the ordinary spiritual capacity may attain realisation more swiftly; some may have uplifting experiences at an early stage, but for most the *siddhi* of the path, whatever it is, must be the end of a long, difficult and persevering endeavour. One cannot have the crown of spiritual victory without the struggle or reach the heights without the ascent and its labour. Of all it can be said, "Difficult is that road, hard to tread like the edge of a razor."

You find the path dry precisely because you have not yet touched the fringe of it. But all paths have their dry periods and for most though not for all it is at the beginning. There is a long stage of preparation necessary in order to arrive at the inner psychological condition in which the doors of experience can open and one can walk from vista to vista — though even then new gates may present themselves and refuse to open until all is ready. This period can be dry and desert-like unless one has the ardour of self-introspection and self-conquest and finds every step of the effort and struggle interesting or unless one has or gets that secret of trust and self-giving which sees the hand of the Divine in every step of the path and even in the difficulty the grace or the guidance. The description of Yoga as "bitter like poison in the beginning" because of the difficulty and struggle "but in the end sweet as nectar" because of the joy of realisation, the peace of liberation or the divine Ananda and the frequent description by sadhaks and bhaktas of the periods of dryness shows sufficiently that it is no unique peculiarity of this Yoga. All the old disciplines recognised this and it is why the Gita says that Yoga should be practised patiently and steadily with a heart that refuses to be overcome by despondency. It is a recommendation applicable to this path but also to the way of the Gita and to the hard "razor" path of the Vedanta, and to every other. It is quite natural that the higher the Ananda to come down, the more difficult may be the beginning, the drier the deserts that have to be crossed on the way.

Certainly, the supramental manifestation does not bring peace, purity, force, power of knowledge only; these give the necessary conditions for the final realisation, are part of it, but Love, Beauty and Ananda are the essence of its fulfilment. And although the supreme Ananda comes with the supreme fulfilment, there is no real reason why there should not be the love and Ananda and beauty of the way also. Some have found that even at an early stage before there was any other experience. But the secret of it is in the heart, not the mind — the heart that opens its inner door and through it the radiance of the soul looks out in a blaze of trust and self-giving. Before that inner fire the debates of the mind and its difficulties wither away and the path however long or arduous becomes a sunlit road not only towards but through love and Ananda.

Nevertheless, even if that does not come at first, one can arrive at it by a patient perseverance — the psychic change is indeed the indispensable preliminary of any approach to the supramental path and this change has for its very core the blossoming of the inner love, joy, bhakti. Some may find a mental opening first and the mental opening may bring peace, light, a beginning of knowledge first, but this opening from above is incomplete unless it is followed by an opening inward of the heart. To suppose that the Yoga is dry and joyless because the struggles of your mind and vital have made your first approach to it dry is a misunderstanding and an error. The hidden springs of sweetness will reveal themselves if you persevere, even if now they are guarded by the dragons of doubt and unsatisfied longing. Grumble, if your nature compels you to it, but persevere.

*

The only thing to do with such depressing thoughts is not to indulge them, to send them away at once. Vital difficulties are the common lot of every human being and of every sadhak — they are to be met with a quiet determination and confidence in the Divine Grace.

*

It needs either a calm resolute will governing the whole being or a very great *samatā* to have a quite smooth transformation. If they are there, then there are no revolts though there may be difficulties, no attacks, only a conscious dealing with the defects of the nature, no falls but only setting right of wrong steps or movements.

*

These obstacles can only be got rid of gradually by persistent sadhana. The alternation of dark and bright states is normal and inevitable.

*

The headache if it comes is only a result of the body not being accustomed to the pressure or else to some resistance there. The difficulties of course rise up, but it is not always in the beginning. Sometimes the first effect is such that one feels as if there were no difficulties, — they rise afterwards when the exultation wanes and the normal consciousness has a chance to assert itself against the flood of power or light from above. There is a resistance that has to be fought out or worked out — fought out if the nature is unsteady or resists violently, worked out if the will is steady and the nature moderate in its reactions. On the other hand if there has been a long preparation and the resistances of the nature have been already largely dealt with by the psychic or by the enlightened mental will, then there are no primary or later aggravations but a steady and quiet pulsing of the change, the remaining difficulties falling away of themselves as the new consciousness develops, or else there may be no difficulties at all, only a necessary readjustment and change.

*

If X has allowed any fall in her consciousness and action which retards her sadhana and is not yet able wholly to overcome her weakness, that is no reason why you should allow *her* difficulty to overcome *your* faith and endeavour. There is no natural connection between the two and no reason why there should be — it is only your mind that is making one. Each sadhak has his own separate sadhana, his own difficulties, his own way to follow. His sadhana is between him and the Divine; no one else has a part in it. Nor is there any reason why, even if one falls or fails, the other should torment himself for that, lose his faith and abandon his way. X's struggle, whatever its nature or limits, is her own and concerns herself and the Mother. It is not yours and ought not to touch or concern you at all; if you allow it to touch and shake you because she happens to be your sister, you bring in an unnecessary difficulty to add to your own and hamper your own progress. Keep to your own path, concentrate on your own obstacles to overcome them. As for her, you can at most pray to the Divine Power to help her and leave it there.

*

Yoga has always its difficulties, whatever Yoga it be. Moreover it acts in a different way on different seekers. Some have to overcome the difficulties of their nature first before they get any experiences to speak of, others get a splendid beginning and all the difficulties afterwards, others go on for a long time having alternate risings to the top of the wave and then a descent into the gulfs and so on till the vital difficulty is worked out — that is the case with X; others have a smooth path which does not mean that they have no difficulties — they have plenty, but they do not care a straw for them, because they feel sure that the Divine will help them to the goal, or that he is with them even when they do not feel him — their faith makes them imperturbable. What Y feels is true — there are certain signs by which one can know it. As for Z he never tried to do Yoga, so he is not a case in point at all — if he had wanted he might have done something, but except at the beginning he did not want it in the least.

For yourself it seems to me that the consciousness is growing towards the point at which there can be the decisive change upwards and inwards, decisive and effective, and there is no cause for depression — for that change is the one thing needful.

*

The difficulties that remain, although not identical, are similar in their cause and their fundamental nature to those you have either largely or completely overcome, and they can be conquered in the same way; it is a question of time and of acquiescence within yourself in the pressure from the Divine which makes man change.

Human nature and the character of the individual are a formation that has arisen in and out of the inconscience of the material world and can never get entirely free from the pressure of that Inconscience. As consciousness grows in the being born into this material world, it takes the form of an Ignorance slowly admitting or striving with difficulty after knowledge and human nature is made of that Ignorance and the character of the individual is made from the elements of the Ignorance. It is largely mechanistic like everything else in material Nature and there is almost invariably a resistance and, more often than not, a strong and stubborn resistance to any change demanded from it. The character is made up of habits and it clings to them, is disposed to think them the very law of its being and it is a hard job to get it to change at all except under a strong pressure of circumstances. Especially in the physical parts, the body, the physical mind, the physical life movements, there is this resistance; the tamasic element in Nature is powerful there, what the Gita describes as *aprakāśa*, absence of light, and *apravṛtti*, a tendency to inertia, inactivity, unwillingness to make an effort and, as a result, even when the effort is made, a constant readiness to doubt, to despond and despair, to give up, renounce the aim and the endeavour, collapse.

Fortunately, there is also in human nature a sattwic element which turns towards light and a rajasic or kinetic element which desires and needs to act and can be made to desire not only change but constant progress. But these too, owing to the limitations of human ignorance and the obstructions of the fundamental inconscience, suffer from pettiness and division and can resist as well as assist the spiritual endeavour. The spiritual change which Yoga demands from human nature and individual character is, therefore, full of difficulties, one may almost say that it is the most difficult of all human aspirations and efforts. In so far as it can get the sattwic and the rajasic (kinetic) elements to assist it, its path is made easier but even the sattwic element can resist by attachment to old ideas, to preconceived notions, to mental preferences and partial judgments, to opinions and reasonings which come in the way of higher truth and to which it is attached: the kinetic element resists by its egoism, its passions, desires and strong attachments, its vanity and self-esteem, its constant habit of demand and many other obstacles. The resistance of the vital has a more violent character than the others and it brings to the aid of the others its own violence and passion and that is a source of all the acute difficulty, revolt, upheavals and disorders which mar the course of the Yoga. The Divine is there, but He does not ignore the conditions, the laws, the circumstances of Nature; it is under these conditions that He does all His work, His work in the world and in man and consequently also in the sadhak, the aspirant, even in the God-knower and God-lover; even the saint and the sage continue to have difficulties and to be limited by their human nature. A complete liberation and a complete perfection or the complete possession of the Divine and possession by the Divine is possible but it does not usually happen by an easy miracle or a series of miracles. The miracle can and does happen but only when there is the full call and complete self-giving of the soul and the entire widest opening of the nature.

Still, if the call of the soul is there, although not yet full, however great and obstinate the difficulties, there can be no final and irretrievable failure; even when the thread is broken it is taken up again and reunited and carried to its end. There is a working in the nature itself in response to the inner need which, however slowly, brings about the result. But a certain inner consent is needed; the progress that you have marked in yourself is due to the fact that there was this consent in the soul and also in part of the nature; the change was insisted on by the mind and desired by part of the vital; the resistance in part of the mind and part of the vital made it slow and difficult but could not prevent it. The strong development you have observed in your powers with its proof in the response of others is due to the same reason; part of your being consented to it, wanted and needed it as a self-fulfilment of the nature and the soul wanted it as a means of service to the Divine; the rest was due to the pressure of the Divine force and my pressure. As for the distaste, the lack of interest etc. all this is temporary and belongs only to a part of you. In so far as it comes from a kind of *vairāgya*, it may have helped you in overcoming some of your attachments, but it is defective in so far as the element of *tamas* and *apravṛtti* is there; it is not so fundamental as to resist the victorious drive of the pressure of the Divine Force.

You ask what I want you to do. What I want is that you should persist and give more and more that assent in you which brought about the progress you have made so that here too the resistance may diminish and eventually disappear.

And you must now get rid of an exaggerated insistence

on the use of reason and the correctness of your individual reasoning and its right to decide in all matters. The reason has its place especially with regard to certain physical things and general worldly questions — though even there it is a very fallible judge — or in the formation of metaphysical conclusions and generalisations; but its claim to be the decisive authority in matters of Yoga or in spiritual things is untenable. The activities of the outward intellect there lead only to the formation of personal opinions, not to the discovery of Truth. It has always been understood in India that the reason and its logic or its judgment cannot give you the realisation of spiritual truths but can only assist in an intellectual presentation of ideas; realisation comes by intuition and inner experience. Reason and intellectuality cannot make you see the Divine, it is the soul that sees. Mind and the other instruments can only share in the vision when it is imparted to them by the soul and welcome and rejoice in it. But also the mind may prevent it or at least stand long in the way of the realisation or the vision. For its prepossessions, preconceived opinions and mental preferences may build a wall of arguments against the spiritual truth that has to be realised and refuse to accept it if it presents itself in a form which does not conform to its own previous ideas: so also it may prevent one from recognising the Divine if the Divine presents himself in a form for which the intellect is not prepared or which in any detail runs counter to its prejudgments and prejudices. One can depend on one's reason in other matters provided the mind tries to be open and impartial and free from undue passion and is prepared to concede that it is not always right and may err; but it is not safe to depend on it alone in matters which escape its jurisdiction, especially in spiritual realisation and in matters of Yoga which belong to a different order of knowledge.

*

The Divine may be difficult, but his difficulties can be overcome if one keeps at him.

Why Difficulties Come

No, it is not a test. The difficulties come because the mind, vital and physical or some part is open to the movements which bring the difficulties.

*

The difficulties are there in vital and physical nature because they are full of obscurity, falsehood, inertia and ignorance. They have to be got rid of by opening the vital and physical wholly to the power of the psychic and the power of the Truth from above.

*

It is quite true that falsehood reigns in this world; that is the reason why these difficulties manifest. But you have not to allow yourself to be shaken. You must remain calm and strong and go straight, using the power of Truth and the Divine Force supporting you to overcome the difficulties and set straight what has been made crooked by the falsehood.

*

All who enter the spiritual path have to face the difficulties and ordeals of the path, those which rise from their own nature and those which come in from outside. The difficulties in the nature always rise again and again till you overcome them; they must be faced with both strength and patience. But the vital part is prone to depression when ordeals and difficulties rise. This is not peculiar to you, but comes to all sadhaks — it does not imply an unfitness for the sadhana or justify hopelessness. But you must train yourself to overcome this reaction of depression, calling in the Mother's force to aid you.

All who cleave to the path steadfastly can be sure of their spiritual destiny. If anyone fails to reach it, it can only be for one of two reasons, either because they leave the path or because for some lure of ambition, vanity, desire etc. they go astray from the sincere dependence on the Divine.

*

The Power does not descend with the object of raising up the lower forces, but in the way it has to work at present, that uprising comes in as a reaction to the working. What is needed is the establishment of the calm and wide consciousness at the base of the whole Nature so that when the lower nature appears, it will not be as an attack or struggle but as if a Master of forces were there seeing the defects of the present machinery and doing step by step what is necessary to remedy and change it.

*

It [*progress, then struggle*] is the usual course of the process by which the change of consciousness is effected. The lower Forces seldom yield the ground without a protracted and often repeated struggle. What is gained can be covered over, but it is never lost.

*

If you go down into your lower parts or ranges of nature, you must be always careful to keep a vigilant connection with the higher already regenerated levels of the consciousness and to bring down the Light and Purity through them into these nether still unregenerated regions. If there is not this vigilance, one gets absorbed in the unregenerated movement of the inferior layers and there is obscuration and trouble.

The safest way is to remain in the higher part of the consciousness and put a pressure from it on the lower to change. It can be done in this way, only you must get the knack and the habit of it. If you achieve the power to do that, it makes the progress much easier, smoother and less painful.

*

There are higher forces and the lower — the latter have to be worked out by contact with the higher and in the working out sometimes they rise, sometimes disappear till they are done with. It is not necessarily due to some mistake or fault that they rise.

*

I am not aware of any case in which the lower forces did not rise up. If such a case occurred, I fancy it would be the first in human history.

*

All the difficulties are bound to vanish in time under the action of the Force. They rise, because if they did not rise the action would not be complete, for all has to be faced and worked out, in order that nothing may be left to rise up hereafter. The psychic being itself can throw the light by which the full consciousness will come and nothing remain in the darkness.

Chapter Two
The Difficulties of Human Nature

Obstacles of Human Nature

There are only three fundamental obstacles that can stand in the way:
(1) Absence of faith or insufficient faith.
(2) Egoism — the mind clinging to its own ideas, the vital preferring its own desires to a true surrender, the physical adhering to its own habits.
(3) Some inertia or fundamental resistance in the consciousness, not willing to change because it is too much of an effort or because it does not want to believe in its own capacity or the power of the Divine — or for some other more subconscient reason.

You have to see for yourself which of these it is.

*

These obstacles are usual in the first stages of the sadhana. They are due to the nature being not yet sufficiently receptive. You should find out where the obstacle is, in the mind or the vital, and try to widen the consciousness there, call in more purity and peace and in that purity and peace offer that part of your being sincerely and wholly to the Divine Power.

*

In one form or another the resistance of the mind and the Prana seeking to be independent and fulfil ego under the plea of spiritual realisation is a frequent obstacle in the Yoga.

*

The main difficulty in the sadhana consists in the movements of the lower nature, ideas of the mind, desires and attractions of the vital, habits of the body consciousness that stand in the way of the growth of the higher consciousness — there are other difficulties, but these make the bulk of the opposition.

*

Each part of the nature wants to go on with its old movements and refuses, so far as it can, to admit a radical change and progress, because that would subject it to something higher than itself and deprive it of its sovereignty in its own field, its separate empire. It is this that makes transformation so long and difficult a process.

Mind gets dulled because at its lower basis is the physical mind with its principle of tamas or inertia — for in matter inertia is the fundamental principle. A constant or long continuity of higher experiences produces in this part of the mind a sense of exhaustion or reaction of unease or dullness. Trance or *samādhi* is a way of escape — the body is made quiet, the physical mind is in a state of torpor, the inner consciousness is left free to go on with its experiences. The disadvantage is that trance becomes indispensable and the problem of the waking consciousness is not solved; it remains imperfect.

The Dual Nature of the Human Being

There are usually in the human being two different tendencies in two parts of the being, one psychic or mental supported by the psychic which seeks the better way and higher things, the other whose main seat is in the vital part of the being which is full of the life-instincts and life-desires, which is attached to or turns towards the things of the lower nature and is subject to the passions, anger, sex etc. If the higher part is dominant, then the lower is kept under control and does not give much trouble. But often the latter is supported by outer forces and powers of the lower Nature in the universe and sometimes these intrude and give the coarse part of the being a separate personality and independence of its own. This may be the explanation of the dream of the ugly monster and of the resistance of this other personality. If it be so, then this must be regarded not as part of oneself but as a foreign element to the true being. It is only by a persistent choice of the dictates of the higher and a persistent rejection of the other that the latter loses ground and finally recedes. This should be met as calmly as possible without allowing the mind to be troubled by any fall or failure — with a quiet constant vigilance and resolute will.

*

The difficulty is that in everyone there are two people (to say the least) — one in the outer vital and physical clinging to the past self and trying to get or retain the consent of the mind and the inner being, the other which is the soul asking for a new birth. That which has spoken in you and made the prayer is the psychic being expressing itself through the aid of the mind and the higher vital, and it is this which should always arise in you through prayer and through turning to the Mother and give you the right idea and the right impulse.

It is true that if you refuse always the action suggested by the old Adam, it will be a great step forward. The struggle is then transferred to the psychological plane, where it will be much easier to fight the matter out. I do not deny that there will be difficulty for some time; but if there is the control of action, the control of thought and feeling is bound to come. If there is yielding, on the contrary, a fresh lease is given to the old self.

*

The reason why you have these alternating moods is because there are two different elements in you. On one side there is trying to develop in you your psychic being which, when it awakes, gives you the sense of closeness or union with the Mother and the feeling of Ananda; on the other, there is your old vital nature, restless and full of desires and, because of this restlessness and desire, unhappy. It is this old vital nature, which you were accepting and indulging, that made you go wrong and stood in the way of your progress. It is when the desire and restlessness of the vital are rejected that the psychic in you comes forward and then the vital itself changes and feels full of the joy and the nearness. When the old unhappy and restless vital comes up again, you feel yourself unfit, without pleasure in anything. What you have to do when this returns is not to accept it, to call in the Mother's nearness again and let the psychic being grow in you. If you do that persistently, rejecting restlessness and desire, the vital part of you will change and become fit for the sadhana.

*

I have explained to you that there is a division between your internal and external being — as it is in the case of most people. Your inner being wants and has always wanted the Truth and the Divine — when the peace and power are felt it comes forward and you feel it as yourself and understand things and grow in knowledge and happiness and true feeling. The external nature is being changed by the influence of the inner being, but what is pushed out returns constantly from old habit — and then you feel this old nature as if it were yourself. This external nature has been like that of almost all human beings, like that of most of the sadhaks here, selfish and full of desires and wanting its own desires, not the Truth and the Divine. When it returns like this and covers you up, all these old ideas and feelings which are always the same take hold of you and try to push you to despair — for it is an enemy force that pushes them back into you. The difficulty is that your physical consciousness does not yet know how to reject this when it comes. The inner being rejects it, but as the physical consciousness lets it in, the inner being is pushed back for the time being. You must absolutely learn not to allow this thing to come in, not to indulge and support it when it comes. It is a falsehood and cannot be anything else, and by falsehood I mean not only contrary to the sadhana and contrary to the Divine truth, but contrary to the truth of your own inner being and of your soul's aspiration and your heart's desire. How can such a thing be true? it exists but that does not make it the truth of your being. It is the soul, the inner being that is the true self in everyone. It is that you must know to be your self and reject this as a false thing imposed on you by the lower ignorant Nature.

*

You must remember that your being is not one simple whole, all of one kind, of one piece, but complex, made up of many things. There are the inner parts of the being which are easily conscious of the Truth and Divine, — when these come forward, then all is well. There is the external being which is full of past ignorance and defect and weakness, but has begun to change. It is not yet sufficiently changed or changed in all its parts. When any part that is partly changed opens strongly to the peace and force, then all the rest become either quite quiet or not very active and you are aware of the peace and force and at ease or else aware only vaguely of confusion etc. somewhere. But when something ignorant comes up from below or is a little prominent (or else some old movement of consciousness that was thrown out returns and clouds you), then you feel the peace, the force as something alien to you or non-existent or outside you or at a distance. If you keep the quiet persistently, then this instability will begin to decrease, the Mother's Force will get in everywhere and, though there will still be much to do, there will be a firm foundation for what has to be done.

*

It is different parts of the being that have these different movements. It is, as you say, something in you, something in the vital that has the "insincerity" or the attraction to the wrong confused condition; but this you should not regard as yourself, but as part of the old nature which has to be transformed. So it is something in the physical that has the obscurity and the unconsciousness; but this too you should not look at as yourself, but as something formed in the exterior nature which has to be changed and will be changed. The real "you" is the inner being, the soul, the psychic being, that which calls the peace and the quiet and the working of the force.

*

It is not necessary to put so many questions and get their separate answers. All your ten questions resolve themselves into one. In every human being there are two parts, the psychic with so much of the thinking mind and higher (emotional, larger dynamic) vital that is open to the psychic and cleaves to the soul's aims and admits the higher experiences and on the other hand the lower vital and the physical or external being (external mind and vital included) which are attached to the ignorant personality and nature and do not want to change. It is the conflict between these two that makes all the difficulty of the sadhana. All the difficulties you enumerate arise from that and nothing else. It is only by curing the duality that one can overcome them. That happens when one is able to live within, aware of one's inner being, identified with it and to regard the rest as not oneself, as a creation of ignorant Nature from which one has separated oneself and which has to disappear and, secondly, when by opening oneself constantly to the Divine Light and Force and the Mother's presence a dynamic action of sadhana is constantly maintained which steadily pushes out the movements of the ignorance and substitutes even in the lower vital and physical being the movements of the inner and higher nature. There is then no struggle any longer, but an automatic growth of the divine elements and fading out of the undivine. The devotion of the heart and the increasing activity of the psychic being, which is best helped by devotion and self-giving, are the most powerful means for arriving at this condition.

*

Everyone whose psychic being calls him to the spiritual path has a capacity for that path and can arrive at the goal if or as soon as he develops a single-pointed will towards that alone. But also every sadhak is faced with two elements in him, the inner being which wants the Divine and the sadhana and the outer mainly vital and physical being which does not want them but remains attached to the things of the ordinary life. The mind is sometimes led by one, sometimes by the other. One of the most important things he has to do, therefore, is to decide fundamentally the quarrel between these two parts and to persuade or compel by psychic aspiration, by steadiness of the mind's thought and will, by the choice of the higher vital in his emotional being the opposing elements to be first quiescent and then consenting. So long as he is not able to do that his progress must be either very slow or fluctuating and chequered as the aspiration in him cannot have a continuous action or a continuous result. Besides so long as this is so, there are likely to be periodical revolts of the vital, repining at the slow progress, despairing, desponding, declaring the Adhar unfit; calls from the old life will come; circumstances will be attracted which seem to justify it, suggestions will come from men and unseen powers pressing the sadhak away from the sadhana and pointing backward to the former life. And yet in that life he is not likely to get any real satisfaction.

Your circumstances are not different from those of others in the beginning and for a long time afterwards. You have come away from the family life, but something in your vital has still kept a habit of response and it is that that is being used to pull you away. This is aided by the impatience of the vital because there is no rapid spiritual progress or continuous good condition — things which even the greatest sadhaks take time to acquire. Circumstances combine to assist the pull — things like X's illness or your husband's appeals which when he soothes and flatters and prays and promises instead of being offensive succeed in mollifying you and creating a condition of less effective defence. And there is the vital Nature and its powers suggesting this and that, that you are not fit, that there is no aspiration, that the Mother and Sri Aurobindo do not help, are displeased, do not care, and it is best to go home.

All that most sadhaks have gone through and come out of it and left the old bonds behind them. There is no reason why you should not do so too. Our help is there always, it is not given at one time and withheld at another, nor given to some and denied to others. It is there for all who make the effort and have the will to arrive. But you have to be steady in your will and not be taken in and deceived by the suggestions from outside or those that come in the shapes of your own adverse thoughts and depressions — you have to fight these and surmount them. It may take a shorter or longer time according to your energy

The Difficulties of Human Nature

in combating and overcoming them. But everybody has to make that effort of mastery and overcome the old vital nature.

As for your going over there, you have to look at yourself and see clearly what is wanting to take you there. The plea from inability to do the sadhana has no value whatever. It is merely a plea put forward by the opposing elements in the vital and strengthened by the suggestion of adverse forces. If you say that you find your attachment to husband and son or others is so strong that your soul and your aspiration can do nothing against it and home is the real place for you, then of course your departure is inevitable — but such a statement can hardly in your case be accepted as true. Or if you say that still the pull is so great that you think it better to go for a time and test yourself and exhaust it, then that might just be true for a time, if the vital has risen up strongly; and we would not say no, as we did not say no when you wanted to go and nurse X. But even in that case it would be wiser for you to examine it seriously and not make a decision on the strength of a condition which could pass otherwise. Your husband's letters have no value for us; he has always written like that whenever he saw any hope of your coming away from here; at other times he has a very different tone.

I have put the whole thing before you at length. For us the straight course is always to keep on one's way, whatever the difficulties, until one has got mastery and the way becomes smoother. But at bottom the decision must be left with the sadhak himself — one can press for the right choice but one cannot command that he should make it.

*

I don't think it can be said that you have no personality. Coordination and harmonisation of parts is absent in many; it is a thing that has to be attained to or built up. Moreover at a certain stage in sadhana there is almost always a disparity or opposition between the parts that are already turned towards the Truth and are capable of experience and others that are not and pull one down to a lower level. The opposition is not equally acute in all cases, but in one degree or another it is almost universal. Coordination and organisation can be satisfactorily done only when this is overcome. Till then oscillations are inevitable. As for violence, violence of action has been confined to a few only, but what about violence of speech and the quarrels that take place in the Asram? These are not difficulties that ought to prevent you from looking beyond them to the ultimate spiritual issue out of this flux of contending forces of Nature.

*

Aspiration and will to change are not so very far from each other, and if one has either, it is usually enough for going through, — provided of course it maintains itself. The opposition in certain parts of the being exists in every sadhak and can be very obstinate. Sincerity comes by having first the constant central aspiration or will, next, the honesty to see and avow the refusal in parts of the being, finally, the intention of seeing it through even there, however difficult it may be. You have admitted certain things changed in you, so you can no longer pretend that you have made no progress at all.

The peculiarity you note is pretty universal — it is one part of the being which believes and speaks the right and beautiful things; it is another which doubts and says just the opposite. I get communications for instance from X in which for several pages he writes wise and perfect things about the sadhana — suddenly without transition he drops into his physical mind and peevishly and complainingly says — well, things ignorant and quite incompatible with all that wisdom. X is not insincere when he does that — he is simply giving voice to two parts of his nature. Nobody can understand himself or human nature if he does not perceive the multipersonality of the human being. To get all parts into harmony, that is the difficult thing.

As for the lack of response, — well, can't you see that you are in the ancient tradition? Read the "lives of the saints" — you will find them all (perhaps not all, but at least so many) shouting like you that there was no response, no response and getting into frightful tumults, agonies and desperations — until the response came. Many people here who can't say they have had no experiences, do just the same — so it does not depend on experiences. I don't advise this procedure to anybody — mind you. I only want to say that the feeling of never having had a response does not mean that there never will be a response and that fits of despair at having arrived nowhere do not mean that one will never arrive.

*

The thing is that it is unavoidable in the course of the sadhana that some parts of the being should be less open, less advanced, as yet less aware of the Peace and Force, less intimate to them than others. These parts have to be worked upon, and changed, but this can be done smoothly only if you are detached from them, able to regard them as not your very self, even though a part of the nature you have to change. Then when they appear with their defects, you will not be upset, not carried away by their movements, lost to the sense of the Peace and Force; you will be able to work on them (or rather let the Force work) as one would on a machine that has to be repaired or a work that has defects and has to be done better this time. If you identify yourself with these parts, then it is very troublesome. The work will still be done, the change made, but with delay, with bad upsettings, in a painful and not in a smooth way. That is why we always tell people to be calm and detached and look upon these things not as their true selves but as an outer part that has to be worked upon quietly until it is what it should be.

The Good and the Evil Persona

Every man has a double nature except those who are born (not unborn) Asuras, Rakshasas or Pishachas and even they have a psychic being concealed somewhere by virtue of their latent humanity. But a double being (or a double nature in the special sense) refers to those who have two sharply contrasted parts of their being without as yet such a linking control over them. Sometimes they are all for the heights and then they are quite all right — sometimes all for the abysses and then they care nothing for the heights, even sneer or rail at them and give full rein to the lower man. Or they substitute for the heights a smoky volcano summit in the abyss. These are extreme examples, but others while they do not go so far, yet are now one thing, now just the opposite. If they can convert the lower fellow or discover the central being in themselves, then a true harmonious whole can be created.

*

There are always two sides to every human being. In Western occultism they call them the good and the evil Persona (personality). X has a strong personality and a formed, forceful and independent vital. It is a kind of character with great possibilities in it, but not liked by most people because they prefer girls to be soft, butterlike and docile and full of gushing affection and "sweetness". Such characters, if badly used by life, may develop great vital difficulties. Y and Z probably see only this side; the other side is too unusual for them to appreciate.

*

What you say about the "Evil Persona" interests me greatly as it answers to my consistent experience that a person greatly endowed for the work has, always or almost always — perhaps one ought not to make a too rigid universal rule about these things — a being attached to him, sometimes appearing like a part of him, which is just the contradiction of the thing he centrally represents in the work to be done. Or, if it is not there at first, not bound to his personality, a force of this kind enters into his environment as soon as he begins his movement to realise. Its business seems to be to oppose, to create stumblings and wrong conditions, in a word, to set before him the whole problem of the work he has started to do. It would seem as if the problem could not, in the occult economy of things, be solved otherwise than by the predestined instrument making the difficulty his own. That would explain many things that seem very disconcerting on the surface.

*

The Difficulties of Human Nature 649

Yes, the solution is certainly the Divine Grace — it comes of itself, intervening suddenly or with an increasing force when all is ready. Meanwhile it is there behind all the struggles, and "the unconquerable aspiration for the light" of which you speak is the outward sign that it will intervene. As for the two natures, it is only one form of the perpetual duality in human nature from which nobody escapes, so universal that many systems recognise it as a standing feature to be taken account of in their discipline, the two Personae, one bright, one dark, in every human being. If that were not there, Yoga would be an easy walk-over and there would be no struggle. But its presence is not any reason for thinking that there is unfitness; the obstinacy of the worldly element is also not a reason, for it is always obstinate — in its very nature. It is like the Germans in their trenches, falling back and digging themselves in for a new mass attack, every time they are baffled. But for all that, if the bright persona is equally determined not to be satisfied without the crown of light, if it is strong enough to make the being unable to rest content in lesser things, then that is the sign that the being is called, one of the elect in spite of outward appearances and its own doubts and despairs — who has them not, not even a Christ or a Buddha is without them — and that the inner spirit *will surely win* in the end. There is no cause for any apprehension on that score.

*

There are two or three things that I think it necessary to say to you about your spiritual life and your difficulties.

First, I should like you to get rid of the idea that that which causes the difficulties is so much a part of your self that a true inner life is impossible to you. The inner life is always possible if there is present in the nature, however much covered over by other things, a divine possibility through which the soul can manifest itself and build up its own true form in the mind and life, — a portion of the Divine. In you this divine possibility exists in a marked and exceptional degree. There is in you an inner being of spontaneous light, intuitive vision, harmony and creative beauty which has shown itself unmistakably every time it has been able to throw off the clouds that gather in your vital nature. It is this that the Mother has always tried to make grow in you and bring it to the front. When one has that in oneself, there is no ground for despair, no just reason for any talk of impossibility. If you could once firmly accept this as your true self, (as indeed it is, for the inner being is your true self and the external, to which the cause of the difficulties belongs, is always something acquired and impermanent and can be changed,) and if you could make its development your settled and persistent aim in life, then the path would be clear and your spiritual future not only a strong possibility but a certitude.

It very often happens that when there is an exceptional power like this in the nature, there is found in the exterior being some contrary element which opens it to a quite opposite influence. It is this that makes the endeavour after a spiritual life so often a difficult struggle: but the existence of this kind of contradiction even in an intense form does not make that life impossible. Doubt, struggle, efforts and failures, lapses, alternations of happy and unhappy or good and bad conditions, states of light and states of darkness are the common lot of human beings. They are not created by Yoga or by the effort after perfection; only in Yoga one becomes conscious of their movements and their causes instead of feeling them blindly, and in the end one makes one's way out of them into a clearer and happier consciousness. The ordinary life remains to the last a series of troubles and struggles, but the sadhak of the Yoga comes out of the trouble and struggle to a ground of fundamental serenity which superficial disturbances may still touch but cannot destroy, and, finally, all disturbance ceases altogether.

Even the experience which so alarms you, of states of consciousness in which you say and do things contrary to your true will, is not a reason for despair. It is a common experience in one form or another of all who try to rise above their ordinary nature. Not only those who practise Yoga, but religious men and even those who seek only a moral control and self-improvement are confronted with this difficulty. And here again it is not the Yoga or the effort after perfection that creates this condition;

there are contradictory elements in human nature and in every human being through which he is made to act in a way which his better mind disapproves. This happens to everybody, to the most ordinary men in the most ordinary life. It only becomes marked and obvious to our minds when we try to rise above our ordinary external selves, because then we can see that it is the lower elements which are being made to revolt consciously against the higher will. There then seems to be for a time a division in the nature, because the true being and all that supports it stand back and separate from these lower elements. At one time the true being occupies the field of the nature, at another the lower nature used by some contrary Force pushes it back and seizes the ground, — and this we now see, while formerly the thing happened but the nature of the happening was not clear to us. If there is the firm will to progress, this division is overpassed and in the unified nature, unified around that will, there may be other difficulties, but this kind of discord and struggle will disappear. I have written so much on this point because I think you have been given the wrong idea that it is the Yoga which creates this struggle and also that this contradiction or division in the nature is the sign of an unfitness or impossibility to go through to the end. Both ideas are quite incorrect and things will be easier if you cast them out of your consciousness altogether.

But it is true that in your case as in others this contradiction has been given a special and very discomforting kind of intensity by a hereditary weakness of the nervous parts which has always shown itself in you by fits of despondency, gloom, unrest and self-tormenting darkness and spoiled for you the savour of life. Your mistake is to think that this is something to which you are bound and from which you cannot escape, a fate which makes a spiritual change of your nature impossible. I have seen other families afflicted by this kind of hereditary nervous weakness accompanying very often exceptional gifts of intelligence or artistic capacity or spiritual possibilities. One or two may have succumbed to it, like X, but others, sometimes after a period of acute disturbance, overcame the perturbations caused by this weakness; either it disappeared or it took some minor and innocuous form which did not interfere with the development of the life and its capacities. Why then despair of yourself or fix without any true cause the conviction that you cannot change and this thing will always be there? This despondency, this adverse conviction is the real danger for you; it prevents you from making a quiet and settled resolution and a permanent effective effort; because of it the return of this darker condition makes you quickly yield and allow the adverse external Force which uses this defect to play and do its will with you. It is this false idea that makes more than half the trouble.

There is no true reason why you should not overcome this defect of your external being as many others have done. It is only a part of your vital nature that is affected, even though it often overclouds the rest; the other parts of your being can be easily made the fit instruments of the divine possibility of which I have spoken. Especially, you have a clear and fine intelligence which, when rightly used, becomes a ready instrument of the light and can be of great use to you in overcoming this vital weakness. And this divine possibility, this truth of your inner being, if you accept it, can of itself make certain your liberation and the change of your external nature.

Accept this divine possibility in you; have faith in your inner being and its spiritual destiny. Make its development as a portion of the Divine your aim in life, — for a great and serious aim in life is a most powerful help towards getting rid of this kind of disturbing or disabling nervous weakness; it gives firmness, balance, a strong support to the whole being and a powerful reason for the will to act. Accept too the help we can give you, not shutting yourself against it by disbelief, despair or unfounded revolt. At present you cannot prevail because you have not fixed in yourself a faith, an aim, a settled confidence; the black mood has been able to cloud your whole consciousness. But if you have fixed this faith in you and can cling to it, then the cloud will not be able to fix itself for any long period, the inner being will be able to come to your help. And even the better self will be able to remain on the surface, keep you open to the light and maintain the inner ground for the soul even if the outer is partly clouded or troubled. When that happens, the victory will have been won and the entire elimination of the vital weakness will be only a matter of a little perseverance.

Outward Circumstances and Personal Defects

That [*proneness to anger*] is the real reason for all these things happening to X. When there is something in the nature that has to be got over, it is always drawing on itself incidents that put it to the test till the sadhak has overcome and is free. At least it is a thing that often happens especially if the person is making a sincere effort to overcome. One does not always know whether it is the hostiles who are trying to break the resolution or putting it to the test (for they claim the right to do it) or whether it is, let us say, the gods who are doing it so as to press and hasten the progress or insisting on the reality and thoroughness of the change aspired after. Perhaps it helps most when one can take it from the latter standpoint.

*

You are quite right — that is the way you must take it, that here is an opportunity given to you for overcoming this stumbling block in the nature. When one does sadhana, it is constantly seen that so long as there is an important defect somewhere, circumstances so happen that the occasion comes for the defect to rise until it is thrown out of the being. If one can take the coming of these circumstances clairvoyantly as a call and an opportunity for conquering the defect, then one can progress very quickly.

On the other point, it is very good that you have taken the right attitude and perception with regard to the criticism of others; but this must be extended to their wrong actions also, if there are any. For if their defects flow from their nature, the common human nature of all, their actions flow from the same source, and it is enough to see and understand — the same rule must apply to both these things.

*

Outward difficulties are really nothing — it is the inward that are difficult to get rid of, because something in the nature gives consent to them — or at least is accustomed to suffer and tolerate them.

Chapter Three
Imperfections and Periods of Arrest

Imperfections and Progress towards Perfection

Human nature is always full of impurities and imperfections and of itself cannot reach the Divine. It is by the descent of the higher consciousness from above that all that can change; but you must not expect the change to take place in a few days.

*

It is not my working, but your moods that are queer. You get something[1] no reasonable being would expect under the ordinary laws of Nature and then you fancy you haven't got it and wail because everything is not absolutely, continuously, faultlessly, increasingly, illimitably miraculous through and through and always and for ever. In no sadhana that I know of does absolute sustained perfection in everything come with a rush and stay celestially perfect for ever more. If it were so there would be no need for sadhana — one would only have to gaze at heaven a little and grow wings and fly into the spheres, a triumphant godhead.

*

As I have a few minutes, I may comment on your today's letter so as to get that out of the way. I must say your arguments about X and Y made me smile. When on earth were politeness and good society manners considered as a part or a test of spiritual experience or true Yogic siddhi? It is no more a test than the capacity of dancing well or dressing nicely. Just as there are many very good and kind men who are boorish and rude in their manners, so there may be very spiritual men (I mean those who

---

[1] *Sri Aurobindo sent the disciple a spiritual force which enabled him to write a very good poem.* — Ed.

have deep spiritual experiences) who have no grasp over physical life or action (many intellectuals too are like that) and are not at all careful about their manners. I suppose I myself am accused of rude and arrogant behaviour because I refuse to see people, do not answer letters, and a host of other misdemeanours. I have heard of a famous recluse who threw stones at anybody coming to his retreat because he did not want disciples and found no other way of warding off the flood of candidates. I at least would hesitate to pronounce that such people had no spiritual life or experience. Certainly, I prefer that sadhaks should be reasonably considerate towards each other, but that is for the sake of collective life and harmony, not as a siddhi of the Yoga or an indispensable sign of inner experience.

As for the other matter how can the *écarts* of the sadhaks here, none of whom have reached perfection or anywhere near it, be a proof that spiritual experience is null or worthless? You write as if the moment one had any kind of spiritual experience or realisation, one must at once become a perfect person without defects or weaknesses. That is to make a demand which it is impossible to satisfy and it is to ignore the fact that spiritual life is a growth and not a sudden and inexplicable miracle. No sadhak can be judged as if he were already a siddha Yogi, least of all those who have only travelled a quarter or less of a very long path as is the case with most of us who are here. Even great Yogis do not claim perfection and you cannot say that because they are not absolutely perfect, therefore their spirituality is false or of no use to the world. There are besides all kinds of spiritual men, some who are content with spiritual experience and do not seek after an outward perfection or progress, some who are saints, others who do not seek after sainthood, others who are content to live in the cosmic consciousness in touch or union with the All but allowing all kinds of forces to play through them, e.g., as in the typical description of the Paramhansa. The ideal I put before our Yoga is one thing, but it does not bind all spiritual life and endeavour. The spiritual life is not a thing that can be formulated in a rigid definition or bound by a fixed mental rule; it is a vast field of evolution, an immense kingdom potentially larger than the other kingdoms below it with a hundred provinces, a thousand types, stages, forms, paths, variations of the spiritual ideal, degrees of spiritual achievement. It is from the basis of this truth which I shall try to explain in subsequent letters that things regarding spirituality and its seekers must be judged, if they are to be judged with knowledge. Let me do that first and afterwards if I am able to give some idea of it, which is not easy, particular questions can be more soluble.

P.S. All these things I say, must not be applied to the personal cases you mention which are only an occasion for saying them. The one thing that applies to them is that they are sadhaks, not siddhas, raw still, not ripe.

*

I am glad to have got your second letter in which the psychic being in you expresses itself with such fullness. It would have been impossible for me to go on with my explanations of the case for spirituality if the exposition of it, carrying as it must do many things contrary to your own mental views, were to upset or hurt you. I have no intention of doing that and have always avoided it except that sometimes I had to express an unpalatable view of things rather plainly in answer to your own insistence. If I write about these questions from the Yogic point of view, even though on a logical basis, there is bound to be much that is in conflict with your own settled and perhaps cherished opinions, e.g. about "miracles", persons, the limits of judgment by sense data etc. I have avoided as much as possible writing about these subjects because I would have to propound things that cannot be understood except by reference to other data than those of the physical senses or of reason founded on these alone. I might have to speak of laws and forces not recognised by physical reason or science. In my public writings and my writings to sadhaks I have not dwelt on these because they go out of the range of ordinary knowledge and the understanding founded on it. These things are known to some, but they do not usually speak about it, while the public views of such of them as are known are either credulous or incredulous, but in both cases without experience or knowledge. So if the views founded on them are likely to upset, shock or bewilder, the better way is silence.

I should like, however, to clear up first some misunderstandings in your letter about what I had written:

(1) What I wrote about politeness had nothing to do with X or the quarrel with Y — I referred to that as an *écart* and I said that such lapses on the part of sadhaks who were far from being siddha Yogis could not be advanced as a disproof of spiritual experience or of its value. My remark was not at all meant as justification of loss of self-control in an argument and getting angry and excited if crossed in one's views. It was merely a refusal to accept that as an argument against spirituality in general — spiritual experience, as I said, does not immediately lead to perfection and you cannot expect it to do so. Equality and self-control are most necessary to Yoga, but also *most difficult*, one has to strive slowly after them; they are not, at least in their completeness, easily attainable. The whole being has to be pervaded by calm and peace; the nerves and cells of the body have to be full of calm and peace. Until then what one has to strive to attain is an inner calm in the inner being which remains even when the outer is disturbed by invasions of grief, unease or anger. The Yogi arrives first at a sort of division in his being in which the inner Purusha fixed and calm looks at the perturbations of the outer man as one looks at the passions of an unreasonable child; that once fixed, he can proceed afterwards to control the outer man also. Whether he can easily control the actions depends on the temperament of his outer man, whether it is vehement, emotional and passionate or comparatively sedate and quiet. But a complete control of the outer man needs a long and arduous tapasya. It cannot be expected and even the assured inner calm cannot be expected of those who are still in a very early stage of the journey, who are still sadhaks and not Yogis.

(2) I said that as regards both cases, Z and X, my remarks must be taken as limited to this proposition that you cannot expect from the raw what you can expect from the ripe, that is from the siddha Yogi.

(3) But even from the siddha Yogi you cannot always expect

a perfect perfection; there are many who do not even care for the perfection of the outer nature, yet they have spiritual experience, even spiritual realisation and the unperfected outer nature cannot be held as a disproof of their realisation or experience. If you so regard it, you have to rule out of court the greater number of Yogis of the past and the Rishis of the old time also.

(4) I said that the ideal of my Yoga is different, but I cannot bind by it other spiritual men and their achievements or discipline. My own ideal is transformation of the outer nature, perfection as perfect as it can be. But it is impossible to say that those who have not achieved it or did not care to achieve it had no spirituality or that their spirituality was of no value. Beautiful conduct — not politeness which is an outer thing, however valuable, — but beauty founded upon a spiritual realisation of unity and harmony projected into life, is certainly part of the perfect perfection. But all that I regard as the ideal, the thing to be attained in the fullness of the siddhi. I do not expect perfect perfection from those who are on the way and as yet far from the goal. If they have it, it is delightful; but if they do not have it, I cannot deduce from that that they have no spiritual experiences or that these experiences are of no value.

You yourself speak of the Baradi Brahmachari. Because of his habits of speech, it is surely impossible to deny greatness as a spiritual man to this remarkable ascetic admired by Ramakrishna and revered by Vivekananda. Even Ramakrishna himself had habits of speech about which Vivekananda in a letter to his gurubhais rates them for translating these portions as it would make a very bad impression on his English readers. But would these English readers have been justified in denouncing Ramakrishna on that account as an unspiritual man or spirituality as therefore without value?

This was my reasoning and, so stated in a clearer way, I hope, you will not find it either irrational or offensive. I wanted to clear this because, if you remain under the impression that I am saying outrageous things, it will be difficult to go farther.

I want to show that spiritual seeking and achievement are

not one limited thing that can be clearly defined in a single mental formula and reduced to a single rule or set of rules but a kingdom like the mental kingdom with all sorts of stages, lines, variations, provinces, types of spiritual men, and it is only by so understanding it that one can understand it truly, either in its past or in its future or put in their place the spiritual men of the past and the present or relate the different ideals, stages etc. thrown up in the spiritual evolution of the human being.

*

I reply to your letter as Mother is still too much occupied to write.

What was in her view at the time was what is called in the psychology of Indian Yoga a "sattwic" perfection, perfection in the form of the qualities and actions such as would satisfy a mental idealism and be very visible and appreciable to others. This often generates a kind of pride and self-righteousness, a "sattwic" egoism, which makes the consciousness rigid and not flexible and plastic to the Divine Will. The true spiritual perfection is not so much of form; it is of the very substance of the consciousness and, as it consists at its base in an entire harmony with the Divine Consciousness and a free and plastic self-adaptation at each moment to the Divine Will, its forms and the forms of its action are not so easily visible or appreciable. The word "righteous" does not apply to its movements — they are simply right because they are in unison with the Divine.

Obviously real imperfections are not to be indulged — to take that as a principle would be dangerous; the "apparent" imperfections are those which might appear so to an outward view only. A "righteous" anger might easily be part of that self-righteousness which the Mother had in view, and to be identified with the movement of anger righteous or otherwise is spiritually undesirable. But a movement of the kind meant may seem to an outward view identical with the movements of imperfection in the nature, yet be quite the right one in the sense of rightness which I have indicated above. It is not a question of any particular action or attitude to be taken but of the consciousness within giving a free and supple expression to the Divine Will acting through it.

*

The existence of imperfections, even many and serious imperfections, cannot be a *permanent* bar to progress in the Yoga. (I do not speak of a recovery of the former opening, for, according to my experience, what comes after a period of obstruction or struggle is usually a new and wider opening, some larger consciousness and an advance on what had been gained before and seems — but only seems — to be lost for the moment.) The only bar that can be permanent — but need not be, for this too can change — is insincerity, and this does not exist in you. If imperfections were a bar, then no man could succeed in Yoga; for all are imperfect, and I am not sure, from what I have seen, that it is not those who have the greatest power for Yoga who have too, very often, or have had the greatest imperfections. You know, I suppose, the comment of Socrates on his own character; that could be said by many great Yogins of their own initial human nature. Also, self-expression in some form of art does not preclude serious imperfections and, of itself, does not cure them. Here again my experience is that men of this kind have great qualities, but also great faults and defects as a weight in the other balance. In Yoga the one thing that counts in the end is sincerity and with it the patience to persist in the path — many even without this patience go through, for — again I speak from personal experience, — in spite of revolt, impatience, depression, despondency, fatigue, temporary loss of faith, a force greater than one's outer self, the force of the Spirit, the drive of the soul's need, pushes them through the cloud and the mist to the goal before them. Imperfections can be stumbling blocks and give one a bad fall for the moment, but not a permanent bar. Obscurations due to some resistance in the nature can be more serious causes of delay, but they too do not last for ever.

The length of your period of dullness is also no sufficient reason for losing belief in your capacity or your spiritual destiny. I can look back to periods not of two but of many months of blank suspension of all experience or progress. I believe that alternations of bright and dark periods are almost a universal experience of Yogins, and the exceptions are very rare. If one enquires into the reasons of this phenomenon, — very unpleasant to our impatient human nature, — it will be found, I think, that they are in the main two. The first is that the human consciousness either cannot bear a constant descent of the Light or Power or Ananda, or cannot at once receive and absorb it; it needs periods of assimilation, but this assimilation goes on behind the veil of the surface consciousness; the experience or the realisation that has descended retires behind that veil and leaves this outer or surface consciousness to lie fallow and become ready for a new descent. In the more developed stages of the Yoga these dark or dull periods become shorter, less trying as well as uplifted by the sense of the greater consciousness which, though not acting for immediate progress, yet remains and sustains the outer nature. The second cause is some resistance, something in the human nature that has not felt the former descents, is not ready, is perhaps unwilling to change, — often it is some strong habitual formation of the mind or the vital or some temporary inertia of the physical consciousness and not exactly a part of the nature — and this, whether showing or concealing itself, thrusts up the obstacle. If one can detect the cause in oneself, acknowledge it, see its workings and call down the Power for its removal, then the periods of obscurity can be greatly shortened and their acuity becomes less. But in any case the Divine Power is working always behind and one day, perhaps when one least expects it, the obstacle breaks, the clouds vanish and there is again the light and the sunshine. The best thing in these cases is, if one can manage it, not to fret, not to despond, but to insist quietly and keep oneself open, spread to the Light and waiting in faith for it to come: that, I have found, shortens these ordeals. Afterwards, when the obstacle disappears, one finds that a great progress has been made and that the consciousness is far more capable of receiving and retaining than before. There is a return for all the trials and ordeals of the spiritual life.

I write all this to show you that there is nothing peculiar to you in this untoward experience, nothing that would warrant you in thinking yourself less called and fit than others for the Yoga, nothing that would justify you in taking the hand from the plough, even though you find long bits of hard soil that resist and need much labour. The opening you had is sufficient proof that you are meant for the Path; for it is a sure sign of the dawns that are to come hereafter.

Periods of Difficulty and Arrest

These periods of difficulty inevitably come — none is without them, for the lower nature is there in all. What you have to do is to keep the firmness of which you speak and persevere till the Divine Power and your will together have dealt with what rises from below. Why do you regard what rises and shows itself (*hīnatā, kṣudratā, āsakti, lobha*) as if it were peculiar to yourself? They are part of the very substance of the lower vital of the human being and there is no one who is without them. So their presence does not at all mean that you cannot reach the Mother. When the mind and soul have chosen the goal, the rest is bound to follow; only as they are more obscure, the resistance there is more blind and obstinate. But even in your vital there is now fixed the will to attain, it is only a lower part there that has had the habit of responding to these things and therefore when a wave comes, it does not know how to avoid and is swallowed up for a time. It can be for a time only, because these things are no longer really yours, since the central being and the greater part of the nature no longer desire them. You have only to go on firmly and the time will come when the waves no longer rise.

*

The real reason of the difficulty and the constant alternation is the struggle between the veiled true being within and the outer nature, especially the lower vital full of desires and the physical mind full of obscurity and ignorance. This struggle is inevitable in human nature and no sadhak escapes it; everyone has to deal with that obscurity and resistance and its obstinacy and constant recurrence; for the lower nature is not only persistent in its repetitions and returns, but even when it is on the point of changing, the general Powers of that plane in universal Nature try to keep up the resistance by bringing back the old movements at each step in order to prevent the progress from being confirmed for good and made final. It is true therefore that a constant sadhana persistent and unceasing is necessary if one wants to go quickly — though even otherwise one will arrive if the soul within has the call, for the soul will persist and after each obscuration or stumble will bring back the light and drive one on on the path till it feels that it is at last secure of a smooth and easy march to the goal.

*

A difficulty comes or an arrest in some movement which you have begun or have been carrying on for some time. How is it to be dealt with? — for such arrests are inevitably frequent enough, not only for you, but for everyone who is a seeker; one might almost say that every step forward is followed by an arrest — at least, that is a very common, if not a universal experience. It is to be dealt with by becoming always more quiet, more firm in the will to go through, by opening oneself more and more so that any obstructing non-receptivity in the nature may diminish or disappear, by an affirmation of faith even in the midst of the obscurity, faith in the presence of a Power that is working behind the cloud and the veil, in the guidance of the Guru, by an observation of oneself to find any cause of the arrest, not in a spirit of depression or discouragement but with the will to find out and remove it. This is the only right attitude and, if one is persistent in taking it, the periods of arrest are not abolished, — for that cannot be at this stage, — but greatly shortened and lightened in their incidence. Sometimes these arrests are periods, long or short, of assimilation or unseen preparation, their appearance of sterile immobility is deceptive: in that case, with the right attitude, one can after a time, by opening, by observation, by accumulated experience, begin to feel, to get some inkling of what is being prepared or done. Sometimes it is a period of true obstruction in which the Power at work has to deal with the obstacles in the way, obstacles in oneself, obstacles of the opposing cosmic forces or any other or of all together, and this kind of arrest may be long or short according to the magnitude or obstinacy or complexity of the impediments that are met. But here too the right attitude can alleviate or shorten and, if persistently taken, help to a more radical removal of the difficulties and greatly diminish the necessity of complete arrests hereafter.

On the contrary, an attitude of depression or unfaith in the help or the guidance or in the certitude of the victory of the guiding Power, a shutting up of yourself in the sense of the difficulties impedes the recovery, prolongs the difficulties, helps the obstructions to recur with force instead of progressively diminishing in their incidence. It is an attitude whose persistence or recurrence you must resolutely throw aside if you want to get over the obstruction which you feel so much — which the depressed attitude only makes, while it lasts, more acute.

*

You should realise that these periods of clouding are not due to any special incapacity or perversity in you — even the best sadhaks have them. It is the difficulty of the human nature in getting transformed. This difficulty sometimes takes the form of a bad will in the vital somewhere or a tendency in the physical to cling to old mistakes and old habits or to shrink from the trouble of transformation — but in these respects you have made a great progress. What is there, is the mechanical habit of the lower nature in general — mechanical, not voluntary — to repeat the old movements to which it has been or was quite recently accustomed when any strong wave of them comes in from the surrounding universal Nature. This creates a kind of recurrence of relapse into the states which the spiritual progress is pushing out and it is not easy to get rid of this recurrence altogether. The one thing when they come is not to get distressed or upset, to realise what it is and to remain very quiet calling for the Mother's Force to push it away. In this way the habit of these recurrences diminishes, the strength and intensity also, and on the other side one is able to recall the true consciousness and the true force, the bright, happy, peaceful, open condition more and more easily and quicker. One can then proceed on an assured basis to a more and more positive progress.

*

Do not allow these ideas [*of unfitness*] to gain on you or even to occupy your mind. It is not by their merit or their effort or the capacity they show that men advance in the spiritual path, but by their opening to the divine help and grace. For that you must have the confidence that whatever your own weakness, the grace will not fail you. Difficulties may come, dry and barren moments or even periods may come, but they will be passed over and overcome. It is this idea and feeling that you must cherish and encourage and make to grow in you. Then it will be easier for you to advance.

*

I do not think there is any sadhak however advanced who has the full consciousness all the time. These changes come and one cannot help it because there is something of the ordinary consciousness that is still left and it comes up to be dealt with. One has to understand this and not get upset — for getting upset only delays the process. If the true consciousness were constant in its fullness, the sadhana would be finished and there would be the siddhi. That cannot come at once.

Chapter Four
Resistances, Sufferings and Falls

Resistances in Sadhana

There are always these resistances in sadhana; it is because the world is full of forces that don't want men to find the Divine. Even the Rishis of old times used always to be obstructed and disturbed until they conquered desire, anger and all else and became full of the Divine.

*

The resistance is not always an intentional one. It is the resistance of the nature, the mind's personal ideas and preferences, the vital's desires, attachments, depressions, revolts, egoistic insistences on its own ways and freedom to follow its inclinations and fancies, the physical's tamas, want of faith, inertia. These things are parts of human nature. The Force comes to change them, but if the sadhak accepts these things, justifies them, or simply allows them to hold his consciousness without reacting, then their resistance which is always there can last a long time.

*

Your proposed remedy would be no remedy at all. One has to go forward not backward to some old starting point.

It is a wrong idea to get disgusted with doing the right thing because you cannot do it absolutely now. It has to be done by a progressive movement. In everyone there is something that resists, until the ignorant parts of the being are transformed. That is no reason for giving up. It is sufficient if there is something behind that feels and can respond even if it is very much covered by the obscure external nature. It is that in you which feels the Force above the head and the atmosphere of quietness, and it is through that that it will be done whatever the amount of the external resistance.

*

What you feel coming across the meditation is a resistance in the subconscient material throwing up a thing like the cold or a nervous unrest or a causeless uneasiness. They must of course be dismissed. When this part opens to the pressure from above, then these things are felt no more.

*

To break and rebuild is often necessary for the change; but once the fundamental consciousness has come there is no reason why it should be done with trouble and disturbance — it can be done quietly. It is the resistance of the lower parts that brings in trouble and disturbance.

*

There is no invariable rule of such suffering. It is not the soul that suffers; the Self is calm and equal to all things and the only sorrow of the psychic being is the sorrow of the resistance of Nature to the Divine Will or the resistance of things and people to the call of the True, the Good and the Beautiful. What is affected by suffering is the vital nature and the body. When the soul draws towards the Divine, there may be a resistance in the mind and the common form of that is denial and doubt — which may create mental and vital suffering. There may again be a resistance in the vital nature whose principal character is desire and the attachment to the objects of desire, and if in this field there is conflict between the soul and the vital nature, between the Divine Attraction and the pull of the Ignorance, then obviously there may be much suffering of the mind and vital parts. The physical consciousness also may offer a resistance which is usually that of a fundamental inertia, an obscurity in the very stuff of the physical, an incomprehension, an inability to respond to the higher consciousness, a habit of helplessly responding to the lower mechanically, even when it does not want to do so; both vital and physical suffering may be the consequence. There is moreover the resistance of the Universal Nature which does not want the being to escape from the Ignorance into the Light. This may take the form of a vehement insistence on the continuation of the old movements, waves of them thrown on the mind and vital and body so that old ideas, impulses, desires, feelings, responses continue even after they are thrown out and rejected, and can return like an invading army from outside, until the whole nature, given to the Divine, refuses to admit them. This is the subjective form of the universal resistance, but it may also take an objective form — opposition, calumny, attacks, persecution, misfortunes of many kinds, adverse conditions and circumstances, pain, illness, assaults from men or forces. There too the possibility of suffering is evident. There are two ways to meet all that — first that of the Self, calm, equality, a spirit, a will, a mind, a vital, a physical consciousness that remain resolutely turned towards the Divine and unshaken by all suggestion of doubt, desire, attachment, depression, sorrow, pain, inertia. This is possible when the inner being awakens, when one becomes conscious of the Self, of the inner mind, the inner vital, the inner physical, for that can more easily attune itself to the divine Will, and then there is a division in the being as if there were two beings, one within, calm, strong, equal, unperturbed, a channel of the Divine Consciousness and Force, one without, still encroached on by the lower Nature; but then the disturbances of the latter become something superficial which are no more than an outer ripple, — until these under the inner pressure fade and sink away and the outer being too remains calm, concentrated, unattackable. There is also the way of the psychic, — when the psychic being comes out in its inherent power, its consecration, adoration, love of the Divine, self-giving, surrender and imposes these on the mind, vital and physical consciousness and compels them to turn all their movements Godward. If the psychic is strong and master throughout, then there is no or little subjective suffering and the objective cannot affect either the soul or the other parts of the consciousness — the way is sunlit and a great joy and sweetness are the note of the whole sadhana. As for the outer attacks and adverse circumstances, that depends on the action of the Force transforming the relations of the being with the outer Nature; as the victory of the Force proceeds, they will be eliminated; but however long they last, they cannot impede the sadhana, for then even adverse things and happenings become a means for its advance and for the growth of the spirit.

Pain and Suffering

The sufferings and distress which come to people are part of their karma, part of the experience the being has to go through on its way through life after life till it is ready for spiritual change. In the life of the sadhak all vicissitudes are part of the path and, if he is a sadhak, he will recognise them as such though he may not understand their full meaning till afterwards — good and bad fortune, outward happiness and suffering are to be taken with an unshaken equality and trust in the Divine Wisdom till one has attained a position in which, united with the Divine Will, one can dominate them.

*

Suffering is not inflicted as a punishment for sin or for hostility — that is a wrong idea. Suffering comes like pleasure and good fortune as an inevitable part of life in the ignorance. The dualities of pleasure and pain, joy and grief, good fortune and ill fortune are the inevitable results of the ignorance which separates us from our true consciousness and from the Divine. Only by coming back to it can we get rid of suffering. Karma from the past lives exists, much of what happens is due to it, but not all. For we can mend our karma by our own consciousness and efforts. But the suffering is simply a natural consequence of past errors, not a punishment, just as a burn is the natural consequence of playing with fire. It is part of the experience by which the soul through its instruments learns and grows until it is ready to turn to the Divine.

*

Sometimes pain and suffering are means by which the soul is awakened and pushed forward to the Divine. That is the experience on which X constantly dwells as he has suffered much in his life — but all do not find it like that.

*

The idealist's question is why should there be pain at all, even if it is counterweighed by the fundamental pleasure of existence. The real crux is why should inadequacy, limit and suffering come across this natural pleasure of life. It does not mean that life is initially miserable in its very nature.

*

Life as it is is certainly full of mishap and suffering and looks like an inconsequence of Nature that has no eventual significance. But even if one does not find the concealed significance, yet if one can live in the higher calm, one can pass through it without being immersed in its bitternesses or its engulfing turmoils. That you have seen for yourself. I certainly hope that you will arrive at stability and security in that higher calm and with it the security of life cannot fail to come.

The divine support will always be there if you hold on to it and our direct help cannot but be yours when you ask and call for it. You have only to hold on to your effort in spite of what seeks to shake you. Then certainly you will reach the height to which you aspire. I do not see why it should not be in the end the highest height — but that we will leave for the future to decide. To have solid calmness is in itself something fundamental and sufficient.

*

There is no need of suffering. Refuse it when it comes.

*

There is no reason why suffering should be indispensable for making progress. You bring the suffering on yourself by the wrong ideas of the mind and by the revolts of the vital. The Mother's grace and love are there, but the mind refuses to recognise it. If there is confidence, if the mind and vital consent to surrender and have full faith and reliance, then there may be difficulties but there is no suffering.

There are people who think that the proper way of progress is through revolt, but this is a mistake. Conditions of light followed by darker conditions come to everyone, but to revolt because there is delay and difficulty does not help. One has to go on in the confidence that in spite of all delays and difficulties, if one is faithful, then in the end, the goal will be reached and one will attain to the Divine.

*

I cannot say that I follow very well the logic of your doubts. How does a brilliant scholar being clapped into prison invalidate the hope of the Yoga? There are many dismal spectacles in the world, but that is after all the very reason why Yoga has to be done. If the world were all happy and beautiful and ideal, who would want to change it or find it necessary to bring down a higher consciousness into earthly Mind and Matter? Your other argument is that the work of the Yoga itself is difficult, not easy, not a happy canter to the goal. Of course it is, because the world and human nature are what they are. I never said it was easy or that there were not obstinate difficulties in the way of the endeavour. Again I do not understand your point about raising up a new race by writing trivial letters. Of course not — nor by writing important letters either; even if I were to spend my time writing fine poems it would not build up a new race. Each activity is important in its own place — an electron or a molecule or a grain may be small things in themselves, but in their place they are indispensable to the building up of a world, — it cannot be made up only of mountains and sunsets and streamings of the aurora borealis — though these have their place there. All depends on the force behind these things and the purpose in their action — and that is known to the Cosmic Spirit which is at work, — and it works, I may add, not by the mind or according to human standards but by a greater consciousness which, starting from an electron, can build up a world and, using a "tangle of ganglia", can make them the base here for the works of the Mind and Spirit in Matter, produce a Ramakrishna, or a Napoleon, or a Shakespeare. Is the life of a great poet, either, made up only of magnificent and important things? How many "trivial" things had to be dealt with and done before there could be produced a *King Lear* or a *Hamlet*! Again, according to your own reasoning, would not people be justified in mocking at your pother — so they would call it, I do not — about metre and scansion and how many ways a syllable can be read? Why, they might say, is X wasting his time in trivial prosaic things like this when he might have been spending it in producing a beautiful lyric or fine music? But the worker knows and respects the material with which he must work and he knows why he is busy with "trifles" and small details and what is their place in the fullness of his labour.

As for faith, you write as if I had never had a doubt or any difficulty. I have had worse than any human mind can think of. It is not because I have ignored difficulties, but because I have seen them more clearly, experienced them on a larger scale than anyone living now or before me that, having faced and measured them, I am sure of the results of my work. Even if I still saw the chance that it might come to nothing (which is impossible), I would go on unperturbed, because I would still have done to the best of my power the work that I had to do and what is so done always counts in the economy of the universe. But why should I feel that all this may come to nothing when I see each step and where it is leading and every week and day — once it was every year and month and hereafter it will be every day and hour — brings me so much nearer to my goal? In the way that one treads with the greater Light above, even every difficulty gives its help and has its value and the Night itself carries in it the burden of the light that has to be.

As for your own case, it comes to this that experiences come and stop, there are constant ups and downs, in times of recoil and depression no advance at all seems to have been made, there is as yet no certitude. So it was with me also, so it is with everyone, not with you alone. The way to the heights is always like that up to a certain point, but the ups and downs, the difficulties and obstacles are no proof that it is a chimera to aspire to the summits.

*

What you said to X is indeed very true, especially the phrase, "However feeble the clay, the flower is in the bud and it will blossom." That is true not only of individuals, but of the earth as a whole — Earth is a feeble clay for the spiritual planting, but all that is sown in it buds eventually and the bud once there will blossom.

La Rochefoucauld's saying ["*We are always strong enough to bear the sufferings of others*"] is true in general, but not quite true. There are some who can bear their own sufferings much better than they can bear the sufferings of others, while the Yogi can bear the whole world's suffering in himself and yet not falter.

*

The attitude you express in your letter is quite the right one — whatever sufferings come on the path, are not too high a price for the victory that has to be won and, if they are taken in the right spirit, they become even a means towards the victory.

Dangers, Falls and Failures

I have never said that Yoga or that this Yoga is a safe and easy path. What I say is that anyone who has the will to go through can go through. For the rest, if you aim high, there is always the danger of a steep fall if you misconduct your aeroplane. But the danger is for those who allow themselves to entertain a double being, aiming high but also indulging their lower outlook and hankerings. What else can you expect when people do that? You must become single-minded, then the difficulties of the mind and vital will be overcome. Otherwise those who oscillate between their heights and their abysses, will always be in danger till they have become single-minded. That applies to the "advanced" as well as to the beginner. These are facts of nature — I can't pretend for anybody's comfort that they are otherwise. But there is the fact also that nobody need keep himself in this danger. One-mindedness (*ekaniṣṭhā*), surrender to the Divine, faith, true love for the Divine, complete sincerity in the will, spiritual humility (real, not formal) — there are so many things that can be a safeguard against any chance of eventual downfall. Slips, stumbles, difficulties, upsettings everyone has; one can't be insured against these things, but if one has the safeguards, they are transitory, help the nature to learn and are followed by a better progress.

*

Men like X and Y are not likely to pretend to have experiences they do not have. Z's fall after his one year's rapid progress had obvious reasons in his character which do not exist in theirs. But apart from that the fall of a sadhak from Yoga proves nothing against the truth of spiritual experience. It is well known to all Yogis that a fall is possible and the Gita speaks of it more than once. But how does the fall prove that spiritual experience is not true and genuine? The fall of a man from a great height does not prove that he never reached a great height. The experiences of Y have been those of many others before him and will be those of many others who do not yet have them; I fail to see why the fact of people having them or their intensity or the joy and confidence they give should make them suspect as untrue.

*

A man who has risen high *can* fall low, especially if his experiences are only through the spiritual mind and the vital and physical remain as they were. But it is an absurdity to say that he is *sure* to fall low.

*

I have not said that to reach the overmind is impossible; I have only said that it is difficult. Difficulty is not a reason why the things should not be done.

It is not easy for a physical being to reach the highest truth because his consciousness is something ignorant that has emerged out of the material inconscience and is very much tied to and hampered by the obscurity of its origin — in addition to the mental and vital difficulties of ego and desire. Yoga itself is not easy; if it were so, it would be a multitude and not only a few that would be practising it.

*

There is no reason to have a vague doubt about one's own future founded upon no other ground than the failure of others. That is what X and Y are always doing, and it is a great disturber of their progress. Why not instead, if one is to go by others, gather hope from the example of those who are satisfied and progressing? It is true however that these do not show their success as the others do their failure. However, that apart, failure comes by very positive errors and not by the absence of an invariable and unflagging aspiration or effort. The effort demanded of the sadhak is that of aspiration, rejection and surrender. If these three are done, the rest is to come of itself by the grace of the Mother and the working of her force in you. But of the three the most important is surrender of which the first necessary form is trust and confidence and patience in difficulty. There is no rule that trust and confidence can only remain if aspiration is there. On the contrary when even aspiration is not there because of the pressure of inertia, trust and confidence and patience can remain. If trust and patience fail when aspiration is quiescent, that would mean that the sadhak is relying solely on his own effort — it would mean, "Oh my aspiration has failed, so there is no hope for me. My aspiration fails so what can Mother do?" On the contrary, the sadhak should feel, "Never mind, my aspiration will come back again. Meanwhile I know that the Mother is with me even when I do not feel her; she will carry me through even the darkest period." That is the fully right attitude you must have. To those who have it depression could do nothing; even if it comes, it has to return baffled. That is not tamasic surrender. Tamasic surrender is when one says, "I won't do anything; let Mother do everything. Aspiration, rejection, surrender even are not necessary. Let her do all that in me." There is a great difference between the two attitudes. One is that of the shirker who won't do anything, the other is that of the sadhak who does his best but even when he is reduced to quiescence for a time and things seem adverse, keeps always his trust in the Mother's force and presence behind all and by that trust baffles the opposition force and calls back the activity of the sadhana.

Section Two

Overcoming the Difficulties of Yoga

Chapter One

The Right Attitude towards Difficulties

The Sunlit Path and the Path of Darkness

I don't believe much in this Divine Darkness. It is a Christian idea. For us the Divine is Peace, Purity, Wideness, Light, Ananda.

*

I spoke of strange ideas in connection with what you said about peace and cheerfulness being obstacles in the Yoga because they are incompatible with an ardent longing for realisation. Peace was the very first thing that the Yogins and seekers of old asked for and it was a quiet and silent mind — and that always brings peace — that they declared to be the best condition for realising the Divine. A cheerful and sunlit heart is the fit vessel for the Ananda and who shall say that Ananda or what prepares it is an obstacle to the divine union? As for despondency, it is surely a terrible burden to carry on the way. One has to pass through it sometimes, like Christian of *The Pilgrim's Progress* through the Slough of Despond, but its constant reiteration cannot be anything but an obstacle. The Gita specially says, "Practise the Yoga with an undespondent heart", *anirviṇṇacetasā*.

I know perfectly well that pain and suffering and struggle and excesses of despair are natural — though not inevitable — on the way, — not because they are helps, but because they are imposed on us by the darkness of this human nature out of which we have to struggle into the Light....

The dark path is there and there are many who make like the Christians a gospel of spiritual suffering; many hold it to be the unavoidable price of victory. It may be so under certain circumstances, as it has been in so many lives at least at the beginning, or one may choose to make it so. But then the price has to be paid with resignation, fortitude or a tenacious resilience. I admit that if borne in that way the attacks of the Dark Forces or the ordeals they impose have a meaning. After each victory gained over them, there is then a sensible advance; often they seem to show us the difficulties in ourselves which we have to overcome and to say, "Here you must conquer us and here." But all the same it is a too dark and difficult way which nobody should follow on whom the necessity does not lie.

In any case one thing can never help and that is to despond always and say, "I am unfit; I am not meant for the Yoga." And worse still are these perilous mental formations such as you are always accepting that you must fare like X (one whose difficulty of exaggerated ambition was quite different from yours) and that you have only six years etc. These are clear formations of the Dark Forces seeking not only to sterilise your aspiration but to lead you away and so prevent your sharing in the fruit of the victory hereafter. I do not know what Krishnaprem has said but his injunction, if you have rightly understood it, is one that cannot stand as valid, since so many have done Yoga relying on tapasya or anything else but not confident of any Divine Grace. It is not that, but the soul's demand for a higher Truth or a higher life that is indispensable. Where that is, the Divine Grace whether believed in or not, will intervene. If you believe, that hastens and facilitates things; if you cannot yet believe, still the soul's aspiration will justify itself with whatever difficulty and struggle.

*

I am extremely glad to know that the worst of the attack has passed; I hope the after-effects will quickly disappear. You had stood out so well for two months and repelled all incipient movements of the kind, that the sudden violence of this one was not expected — especially as the last darshan had gone off well. But when they get a chance these forces take it.

I quite agree with you in not relishing the idea of another attack of this nature. I am myself, I suppose, more a hero by necessity than by choice — I do not love storms and battles —

at least on the subtle plane. The sunlit way may be an illusion, though I do not think it is — for I have seen people treading it for years; but a way with only natural or even only moderate fits of rough weather, a way without typhoons surely is possible — there are so many examples. *Durgam pathastat* may be generally true and certainly the path of laya or nirvana is difficult in the extreme to most (although in my case I walked into nirvana without intending it or rather nirvana walked casually into me not so far from the beginning of my Yogic career without asking my leave). But the path *need* not be cut by periodical violent storms, though that it *is* so for a great many is an obvious fact. But even for these, if they stick to it, I find that after a certain point the storms diminish in force, frequency, duration. That is why I insisted so much on your sticking — for if you stick, the turning-point is bound to come. I have seen some astonishing instances here recently of this typhonic periodicity beginning to fade out after years and years of violent recurrence.

These things are not part of the normal difficulties, however acute, of the nature but especial formations — tornadoes which start (usually from a particular point, sometimes varying) and go whirling round in the same circle always till it is finished. In your case the crucial point, whatever may have been the outward starting-point if any, is the idea or feeling of frustration in the sadhana; once that takes hold of the mind, all the rest follows. That again is why I have been putting all sorts of suggestions before you for getting rid of this idea — not because my suggestions, however useful and true if they can be followed, are binding laws of Yoga, but because if followed they can wipe out this point of danger. A formation like this is very often the result of something in past lives — the Mother has so seen it in yours — which prolongs a karmic sanskara (as the Buddhists would say) and tries to repeat itself once again. To dissolve it ought to be possible if one sees it for what it is and is resolved to get rid of it — never allowing any mental justification of it, however logical, right and plausible the justification may seem to be — always replying to all the mind's arguments or the vital's feelings in favour of it, like Cato to the debaters, *"Delenda est*

Carthago" — "Carthage must be destroyed", Carthage in this case being the formation and its nefarious circle.

Anyway the closing idea in your letter is the right one. "The Divine is worth ferreting out even if oceans of gloom have to be crossed." If you could confront the formation always with that firm resolution, it should bring victory. In the Mother's vision Kali did express a wish to interfere and break the thing — I don't know how she proposes to do it — by giving you the strength you pray for or by breaking the head of the unwelcome lodger or visitor. I hope she will soon do it.

*

A possibility in the soul or in the inner being generally remains always a possibility — at the worst, its fulfilment can be postponed, but even that only if the possessor of the possibility gives up or breaks away from the true spiritual path without probability of early return — because he is in chase of the magnified and distorted shadow of his own ego or for some other distortion of the nature produced by a wrong egoistic misuse of the Yoga. A mere appearance of inability or obstruction of progress in the outer being, a covering of the inner by the outer, even if it lasts for years, has no probative value, because that happens to a great number, perhaps to the majority of aspirants to Yoga. The reason is that they take somehow the way of raising up all the difficulties in their nature almost at the beginning and tunnelling through the mass instead of the alternative way of going ahead, slowly or swiftly, and trusting to time, Yoga and the Force Divine to clear out of them in the proper season what has to be eliminated. It is not of their own deliberate choice that they do it, something in their nature drives them. There are many here who have had or still have that long covering of the inner by the outer or separation of the inner from the outer consciousness. You yourself took that way in spite of our expostulations to you advising you to take the sunlit road, and you have not yet got out of the habit. But that does not mean that you won't get out of the tunnel and when you do you will find your inner being waiting for you on the other side — in the sun and not in the shadow. I don't think I am more patient than a guru ought to be. Anyone who is a guru at all ought to be patient, first because he knows the difficulty of human nature and, secondly, because he knows how the Yoga force works, in so many contrary ways, open or subterranean, slow or swift, volcanic or coralline, — passing even from one to the other — and he does not use the surface reason but the eye of inner knowledge and Yogic experience.

*

There is no contradiction between my former statements about the sunlit path and what I have said about the difficult and unpleasant passages which the Yoga has to pass through in its normal development in the way of human nature. The sunlit path can be followed by those who are able to practise surrender, first a central surrender and afterwards a more complete self-giving in all the parts of the being. If they can achieve and preserve the attitude of the central surrender, if they can rely wholly on the Divine and accept cheerfully whatever comes to them from the Divine, then their path becomes sunlit and may even be straightforward and easy. They will not escape all difficulties, no seeker can, but they will be able to meet them without pain and despondency, — as indeed the Gita recommends that Yoga should be practised, *anirviṇṇacetasā*, — trusting in the inner guidance and perceiving it more and more or else in the outer guidance of the Guru. It can also be followed even when one feels no light and no guidance if there is or if one can acquire a bright settled faith and happy bhakti or has the nature of the spiritual optimist and the firm belief or feeling that all that is done by the Divine is done for the best even when we cannot understand his action. But all have not this nature, most are very far from it, and the complete or even the central surrender is not easy to get and to keep it always is hard enough for our human nature. When these things are not there, the liberty of the soul is not attained and we have instead to undergo the law or fulfil a hard and difficult discipline.

That law is imposed on us by the Ignorance which is the

nature of all our parts; our physical being is obviously a mass of ignorance, the vital is full of ignorant desires and passions, the mind is also an instrument of Ignorance struggling towards some kind of imperfect and mostly inferior and external knowledge. The path of the seeker proceeds through this ignorance; for a long time he can find no light of solid experience or realisation, only the hopes and ideas and beliefs of the mind which do not give the true spiritual seeing; or he gets glimpses of light or periods of light but the light often goes out and the luminous periods are followed by frequent or long periods of darkness. There are constant fluctuations, persistent disappointments, innumerable falls and failures. No path of Yoga is really easy or free from these difficulties or fluctuations; the way of bhakti is supposed to be the easiest, but still we find constant complaints that one is always seeking but never finding and even at the best there is a constant ebb and tide, *milana* and *viraha*, joy and weeping, ecstasy and despair. If one has the faith or in the absence of faith the will to go through, one passes on and enters into the joy and light of the divine realisation. If one gets some habit of true surrender, then all this is not necessary; one can enter into the sunlit way. Or if one can get some touch of what is called pure bhakti, *śuddhā bhakti*, then whatever happens that is enough; the way becomes easy, or if it does not, still this is a sufficient start to support us to the end without the sufferings and falls that happen so often to the ignorant seeker.

In all Yoga there are three essential objects to be attained by the seeker: union or abiding contact with the Divine, liberation of the soul or the Self, the Spirit, and a certain change of the consciousness, the spiritual change. It is this change, which is necessary for reaching the other two objects, necessary at least to a certain degree, that is the cause of most of the struggles and difficulties; for it is not easy to accomplish it; a change of the mind, a change of the heart, a change of the habits of the will is called for and is obstinately resisted by our ignorant nature. In this Yoga a complete transformation of the nature is aimed at because that is necessary for the complete union and the complete liberation not only of the soul and the spirit but of the nature itself. It is also a Yoga of works and of the integral divine life; for that the integral transformation of nature is evidently necessary; the union with the Divine has to carry with it a full entrance into the divine consciousness and the divine nature; there must be not only *sāyujya* or *sālokya* but *sādṛśya* or, as it is called in the Gita, *sādharmya*. The full Yoga, Purna Yoga, means a fourfold path, a Yoga of knowledge for the mind, a Yoga of bhakti for the heart, a Yoga of works for the will and a Yoga of perfection for the whole nature. But, ordinarily, if one can follow wholeheartedly any one of these lines, one arrives at the result of all the four. For instance, by bhakti one becomes close to the Divine, becomes intensely aware of Him and arrives at knowledge, for the Divine is the Truth and the Reality; by knowing Him, says the Upanishads, one comes to know all. By bhakti also the will is led into the road of the works of love and the service of the Divine and the government of the nature and its acts by the Divine, and that is Karmayoga. By bhakti also comes spiritual change of the consciousness and the action of the nature which is the first step towards its transformation. So it is with all the other lines of the fourfold path.

But it may be that there are many obstacles in the being to the domination of the mind and heart and will by bhakti and the consequent contact with the Divine. The too great activity of the intellectual mind and its attachment to its own pride of ideas, its prejudices, its fixed notions and its ignorant reason may shut the doors to the inner light and prevent the full tide of bhakti from flooding everything; it may also cling to a surface mental activity and refuse to go inside and allow the psychic vision and the feelings of the inner heart to become its guides, though it is by this vision and this feeling that bhakti grows and conquers. So too the passions and desires of the vital being and its ego may block the way and prevent the self-giving of the mind and heart to the Divine. The inertia, ignorance and inconscience of one's physical consciousness, its attachment to fixed habits of thought and feeling and action, its persistence in the old grooves may come badly in the way of the needed change. In such circumstances the Divine may have to bide his time; but if there is real hunger in the heart, all that cannot prevent the final realisation; still, it may have to wait till the obstructions are removed or at least so much cleared out as to admit an unimpeded working of the Divine Power on the surface nature. Till then, there may be periods of inner ease and some light in the mind, periods also of the feeling of bhakti or of peace, periods of the joy of self-consecration in works and service; for these will take long to stay permanently and there will be much struggle and unrest and suffering. In the end the Divine's working will appear and one will be able to live in his presence.

I have described the difficulties of Yoga at their worst, as they may hamper and afflict even those predestined to the realisation but as often there is an alternation or a mixture of the light and the darkness, initial attainment perhaps and heavy subsequent difficulties, progress and attacks and retardations, strong movements forward and a floundering in the bogs of the Ignorance. Even great realisations may come and high splendours of light and spiritual experience and yet the goal is not attained; for in the phrase of the Rig Veda, "As one climbs from peak to peak there is made clear the much that is still to be done." But there is always something that either carries us on or forces us on. This may take the shape of something conscious in front, the shape of a mastering spiritual idea, indestructible aspiration or fixed faith which may seem sometimes entirely veiled or even destroyed in periods of darkness or violent upheaval, but always they reappear when the storm has passed or the blackness of night has thinned, and reassert their influence. But also it may be something in the very essence of the being deeper than any idea or will in the mind, deeper and more permanent than the heart's aspiration but hidden from one's own observation. One who is moved to Yoga by some curiosity of the mind or even by its desire for knowledge can turn aside from the path from disappointment or any other cause; still more can those who take it up from some inner ambition or vital desire turn away through revolt or frustration or the despondency of frequent check and failure. But if this deeper thing is there, then one cannot permanently leave the path of spiritual endeavour: one may decide to leave the path but is not allowed from within to do it or one may leave but is obliged to return to it by the secret spiritual need within him.

All these things are common to every path of Yoga; they are the normal difficulties, fluctuations and struggles which come across the path of spiritual effort. But in this Yoga there is an order or succession of the workings of the secret Force which may vary greatly in its circumstances in each sadhak, but still maintains its general line. Our evolution has brought the being up out of inconscient Matter into the Ignorance of mind, life and body tempered by an imperfect knowledge and is trying to lead us into the light of the Spirit, to lift us into that light and to bring the light down into us, into body and life as well as mind and heart and to fill with it all that we are. This and its consequences, of which the greatest is the union with the Divine and life in the divine consciousness, is the meaning of the integral transformation. Mind is our present topmost faculty; it is through the thinking mind and the heart with the soul, the psychic being behind them that we have to grow into the Spirit, for what the Force first tries to bring about is to fix the mind in the right central idea, faith or mental attitude and the right aspiration and poise of the heart and to make these sufficiently strong and firm to last in spite of other things in the mind and heart which are other than or in conflict with them. Along with this it brings whatever experiences, realisations or descent or growth of knowledge the mind of the individual is ready for at the time or as much of it, however small, as is necessary for its further progress: sometimes these realisations and experiences are very great and abundant, sometimes few and small or negligible; in some there seems to be in this first stage nothing much of these things or nothing decisive — the Force seems to concentrate on a preparation of the mind only. In many cases the sadhana seems to begin and proceed with experiences in the vital; but in reality this can hardly take place without some mental preparation, even if it is nothing more than a turning of the mind or some kind of opening which makes the vital experiences possible. In any case, to begin with the vital is a hazardous affair; the difficulties there are more numerous and more violent than on the mental plane and the pitfalls are innumerable. The access to the soul, the psychic being, is less easy because it is covered up with a thick veil of ego, passion and desire. One is apt to be swallowed up in a maze of vital experiences, not always reliable, the temptation of small siddhis, the appeal of the powers of darkness to the ego. One has to struggle through these densities to the psychic being behind and bring it forward; then only can the sadhana on the vital plane be safe.

However that may be, the descent of the sadhana, of the action of the Force into the vital plane of our being becomes after some time necessary. The Force does not make a wholesale change of the mental being and nature, still less an integral transformation before it takes this step: if that could be done, the rest of the sadhana would be comparatively secure and easy. But the vital is there and always pressing on the mind and heart, disturbing and endangering the sadhana and it cannot be left to itself for too long. The ego and desires of the vital, its disturbances and upheavals have to be dealt with and if not at once expelled, at least dominated and prepared for a gradual if not a rapid modification, change, illumination. This can only be done on the vital plane itself by descending to that level. The vital ego itself must become conscious of its own defects and willing to get rid of them; it must decide to throw away its vanities, ambitions, lusts and longings, its rancours and revolts and all the rest of the impure stuff and unclean movements within it. This is the time of the greatest difficulties, revolts and dangers. The vital ego hates being opposed in its desires, resents disappointment, is furious against wounds to its pride and vanity; it does not like the process of purification and it may very well declare Satyagraha against it, refuse to cooperate, justify its own demands and inclinations, offer passive resistance of many kinds, withdraw the vital support which is necessary both to the life and the sadhana and try to withdraw the being from the path of spiritual endeavour. All this has to be faced and overcome, for the temple of the being has to be swept clean if the Lord of our being is to take his place and receive our worship there.

*

I know that this is a time of trouble for you and everybody. It is so for the whole world; confusion, trouble, disorder and upset everywhere is the general state of things. The better things that are to come are preparing or growing under a veil and the worse are prominent everywhere. The one thing is to hold on and to hold out till the hour of light has come.

*

I am afraid I can hold out but cold comfort for the present at least to those of your correspondents who are lamenting the present state of things. Things *are* bad, are growing worse and may at any time grow worst or worse than worst if that is possible — and anything however paradoxical seems possible in the present perturbed world. The best thing for them is to realise that all this was necessary because certain possibilities had to emerge and be got rid of if a new and better world was at all to come into being; it would not have done to postpone them for a later time. It is as in Yoga where things active or latent in the being have to be put into action in the light so that they may be grappled with and thrown out or to emerge from latency in the depths for the same purificatory purpose. Also they can remember the adage that night is darkest before dawn and that the coming of dawn is inevitable. But they must remember too that the new world whose coming we envisage is not to be made of the same texture as the old and different only in pattern and that it must come by other means, from within and not from without — so the best way is not to be too much preoccupied with the lamentable things that are happening outside, but themselves to grow within so that they may be ready for the new world whatever form it may take.

Optimism and Pessimism

You are quite right in taking an optimistic and not a pessimistic attitude in the sadhana — progressive sadhana is enormously helped by an assured faith and confidence. Such a confidence helps to realise, for it is dynamic and tends to fulfil itself.

*

As for the sceptics — well, optimism even unjustified is still justifiable because it gives a chance and a force for getting things done, while pessimism even with all the grounds that appearances can give to it, is simply a clog and a "No going" affair. The right thing is to go ahead and get done all that can be, if possible all that ought to be, but at least do so much that all that ought will feel bound to come along on the heels of my doing. That is the prophets and the gospel.

Treating Difficulties as Opportunities

The attitude you have taken is the right one. It is this feeling and attitude which help you to overcome so rapidly the attacks that sometimes fall upon you and throw you out of the right consciousness. As you say, difficulties so taken become opportunities; the difficulty faced in the right spirit and conquered, one finds that an obstacle has disappeared, a fresh step forward has been taken. To question, to resist in some part of the being increases trouble and difficulties — that was why an unquestioning acceptance, an unfailing obedience to the directions of the Guru was laid down as indispensable in the old Indian Yogas — it was demanded not for the sake of the Guru, but for the sake of the disciple.

*

This kind of acute struggle comes very often to a sadhak when he wants to make a complete and decisive progress instead of the slow elimination which is the usual course of nature; the strong urge upward is resisted by a vehement pull-back from below.

The Right Attitude towards Difficulties

But the advantage is that when one persists and conquers, much has been gained by the struggle and in that part of the being that resists a decisive advantage. Persevere therefore and do not grieve for occasional waverings or stumbles which can easily happen in so arduous a combat. It should always be the rule for the sadhak not to linger over such things but to pick oneself up again and go resolutely forward. Our help, our force, our blessings will be with you always aiding each step till the final victory.

*

Why get excited over these small things or let them disturb you? If you remain quiet, things will go much better and, if there is any difficulty, you are more likely to find out a way in a quiet mind open to the Peace and Power. That is the secret of going on, not to allow things and happenings, not even real mistakes, to upset you, but to remain very quiet, confiding in the Power to lead you and set things more and more right. If one does that, then things do get actually more and more right and even the difficulties and mistakes become means for learning and steps towards progress.

*

Do not allow yourself to be worried or upset by small things. Look at things from an inner point of view and try to get the benefit of all that happens. If you make a mistake, don't get distressed because you made a mistake — rather profit by it to see the reason so as to get the right movement in future. This you can do only if you look at it quietly from the inner being without sorrow or disturbance.

*

Of course, one must not make a mistake for the purpose of bringing it out or accept the mistake once made, — but if it comes, one has to take advantage of it to change.

*

An occurrence like that should always be taken as an opportunity of self-conquest. Put your pride and dignity in that — in not being mastered by the passions, but their master.

*

It is indeed true that when one conquers a difficulty or goes forward, it creates a right current in the atmosphere. Moreover each time one gets an opening, it becomes more possible to make it permanent.

*

It is true that if one has the true basis, then after every attack one finds oneself farther advanced in progress.

*

Yes, a great progress should only spur one on to a greater progress beside which the first will appear as nothing.

*

Yes, that is so. Each victory gained over oneself means new strength to gain more victories.

The Certitude of Victory

You must make grow in you the peace that is born of the certitude of victory.

*

If these things [*anger, desire etc.*] had disappeared already, there would be the victory already. What I mean [*by "the certitude of victory"*] is the certitude of the eventual victory which is a matter of faith and an inner reliance upon the Divine. The peace born of this certitude carries one through all persistence or return of difficulties.

*

Whatever resistance there is in the outer being will go, only it takes time. It is always best to take one's foundation on that certitude and remain quiet and steadfast with it in mind even when one cannot react actively against the difficulty. For the quiet passive resistance will make it pass sooner, — even if one is disturbed and anxious.

Even when one cannot call in actively the Mother's Force, one must keep the reliance that it will come.

*

Do not let the difficulties you feel or meet from outside overcome or depress you. Keep this one thing in your mind that to come to the Divine is your spiritual destiny and since you have been here and been accepted by us that can be taken as the seal upon it. If it takes a little longer time than you could wish for it to materialise, this should not make you think of it otherwise — for these difficulties and external obstacles and incertitudes always come to the seeker. Neither the difficulties in yourself or the obstacles presented by life are as insurmountable as they seem to your physical mind when they are pressing upon it. Remember also that although here the conditions would be more favourable, yet even at a distance the grace and help can be there with you. Only fix yourself on the goal, make the inner choice once for all firmly and completely; it is there in your soul, fix it in your mind also. Once there, fixed and unalterable, it will prevail over the difficulties of your own vital nature and the physical world's opposition, misunderstanding or reluctance.

*

The reaching is already assured, as it cannot but be when a sincere and abiding aspiration is supported by a sincere and abiding endeavour. With that and the Grace supporting, all difficulties can be and surely will be overcome.

*

The victory is always sure — even when there is difficulty, never doubt that the victory will be there.

Chapter Two

Steps towards Overcoming Difficulties

Ways of Dealing with Difficulties

This sadhana is a Yoga of transformation of the human consciousness into the divine consciousness. The sadhaks who come here are human beings with all the human weaknesses, but with a possibility of the transformation and an aspiration for it. For getting rid of their human weaknesses — such as lust, greed, vanity, pride, falsehood — they must become conscious of them, must always reject them, must call in the Mother's presence, the divine Consciousness, the divine Force to help them in rejecting their defects and to transform them. If they do that, then all that is necessary for the change will be done.

*

When the old movements or suggestions or voices come, —
   (1) Reject them always — do not listen, take no interest.
   (2) If they persist, do not believe what they say or allow them to influence you — know that they are voices or movements of a false, confused and inferior consciousness. You have seen what the real Truth is and how great it is.
   (3) Concentrate on something else, as firmly as possible.
   (4) Aspire steadily for contact with the Mother's Light and Force.

*

This is the right attitude, to have faith and not mind the difficulties. Difficulties — and serious ones — there cannot fail to be in the path of Yoga, because it is not easy to change all at once the ignorant human consciousness and make it a spiritual consciousness open to the Divine. But with faith one need not mind the difficulties; the Divine Force is there and will overcome them.

*

Whatever is difficult can indeed be made easy by truth in the heart and sincerity and faith in the endeavour, even what is impossible can become possible. It is often found too that after some amount of practice and faithful endeavour, there comes an intervention from within and what might have taken long is decisively and quickly done.

Your prayer will surely be answered, for it is to that you are moving.

Facing Circumstances

You should not be so dependent on outward things; it is this attitude that makes you give so excessive an importance to circumstances. I do not say that circumstances cannot help or hinder — but they are circumstances, not the fundamental thing which is in ourselves, and their help or their hindrance ought not to be of primary importance. In Yoga, as in every great or serious human effort, there is always bound to be an abundance of adverse interventions and unfavourable circumstances which have to be overcome. To give them too great an importance increases their importance and their power to multiply themselves, gives them, as it were, confidence in themselves and the habit of coming. To face them with equanimity — if one cannot manage a cheerful persistence against them of confident and resolute will — diminishes on the contrary their importance and effect and in the end, though not at once, gets rid of their persistence and recurrence. It is therefore a principle in Yoga to recognise the determining power of what is within us — for that is the deeper truth — to set that right and establish the inward strength as against the power of outward circumstances. The strength is there — even in the weakest; one has to find it, to unveil it and to keep it in front throughout the journey and the battle.

*

It was inevitable that there should be difficulties once your husband has turned back from his favourable attitude. But as we told you the only way to face and overcome them is to remain firm with a confidence in the Divine that beyond all difficulties lies the realisation and to proceed either boldly or silently on your way in spite of all that people may do or say and in spite of all troubles and trials that may come in the course of the life or in the course of the sadhana. If one keeps this position the difficulties will either diminish or disappear or if for any reason they become acute for a while, will collapse after a time.

You are not at any time out of our minds. We are there with you in your difficulties and troubles — remain calm and assured and you will feel the inner help. Do not yield to depression for depression only gives the opposition and difficulties a hold upon you; call quietly and persistently for strength and the strength will come.

*

That is the inconvenience of going away from a difficulty, — it runs after one, — or rather one carries it with oneself, for the difficulty is truly inside, not outside. Outside circumstances only give it the occasion to manifest itself and so long as the inner difficulty is not conquered, the circumstances will always crop up one way or another.

*

As for his difficulties and troubles, there is little hope of his overcoming them if he does not realise that they come from within him and not from outside. It is the weakness of his vital nature, the inefficient helplessness of his nervous being always weeping and complaining and lamenting instead of facing life and overcoming its difficulties, it is the sentimental lachrymose attitude it takes that keeps his troubles unsolved and alive. This is a temperament which the gods will not help because they know that help is useless, for it will either not be received or will be spilled and wasted; and all that is rajasic and Asuric in the world despises and tramples upon this kind of nature. If he had learned a calm strength and quiet courage without weakness and without fuss and violence, founded on confidence in the help he could always have received from here and on openness to the Mother's force, things would have been favourably settled by this time. But he cannot take advantage of any help given him because his vital nature cherishes its weakness and is always indulging and rhetorically expressing it instead of throwing it away with contempt as a thing unworthy of manhood and unfit for a sadhaka. It is only if he so rejects it that he can receive strength from us and stand in life or progress in the sadhana.

*

It is also well that you have reconciled yourself with the place [Sylhet, Bengal] and have the feeling of strength to deal with the situation there. A certain power of adaptation and harmonisation of the surroundings is necessary — you had it very strongly and were therefore successful wherever you went. The recoil from Sylhet made you nervous and depressed and spoiled for a time the action of this power in you. Now with your new attitude I hope it will return and bring the solution of all your difficulties.

We send you our blessings. Keep yourself always open to the Power from above and to our help from here and remain firm and strong against all difficulties that may yet remain either in the outer life or the sadhana. On these conditions victory is always sure.

*

When the soul is meant to go forward and there is an external weakness like that, circumstances do come like that to help the external being against itself — which means that there must be a truly sincere aspiration behind; otherwise it does not happen.

Recognising One's Weaknesses

To recognise, as you have done, a fault in the nature does not indeed remove it altogether at once, but it is a great step towards it. It does not remove it at once because of the force of habit in the nature, but still to be conscious and have the will to remove it helps to weaken its force and assists the Mother's working very greatly.

*

To recognise one's weaknesses and false movements and draw back from them is the way towards liberation.

Not to judge anyone but oneself until one can see things from a calm mind and a calm vital is an excellent rule. Also, do not allow your mind to form hasty impressions on the strength of some outward appearance, nor your vital to act upon them.

There is a place in the inner being where one can always remain calm and from there look with poise and judgment on the perturbations of the surface consciousness and act upon it to change it. If you can learn to live in that calm of the inner being, you will have found your stable basis.

*

If the imperfection is there, one has to see it. The thing to be done is to live in the true self and from there see the imperfection and change it.

*

You must remain always aware of the self and the obscure nature must not be felt as the self but as an instrument which has to be put into tune with the self.

*

You have to be conscious of the wrong movements, but not preoccupied with them only.

*

The defects should be noticed and rejected, but the concentration should be positive — on what you are to be, i.e., on the development of the new consciousness rather than on this negative side.

*

It is necessary to observe and know the wrong movements in you; for they are the source of your trouble and have to be persistently rejected if you are to be free.

But do not be always thinking of your defects and wrong movements. Concentrate more upon what you are to be, on the ideal, with the faith that, since it is the goal before you, it must and will come.

To be always observing faults and wrong movements brings depression and discourages the faith. Turn your eyes more to the coming Light and less to any immediate darkness. Faith, cheerfulness, confidence in the ultimate victory are the things that help, — they make the progress easier and swifter.

Make more of the good experiences that come to you; one experience of the kind is more important than the lapses and failures. When it ceases, do not repine or allow yourself to be discouraged, but be quiet within and aspire for its renewal in a stronger form leading to still deeper and fuller experience.

Aspire always, but with more quietude, opening yourself to the Divine simply and wholly.

*

While the recognition of the Divine Power and the attunement of one's own nature to it cannot be done without the recognition of the imperfections in that nature, yet it is a wrong attitude to put too much stress either on them or on the difficulties they create, or to distrust the Divine working because of the difficulties one experiences, or to lay too continual an emphasis on the dark side of things. To do this increases the force of the difficulties, gives a greater right of continuance to the imperfections. I do not insist on a Couéistic optimism — although excessive optimism is more helpful than excessive pessimism; that (Couéism) tends to cover up difficulties and there is besides always a measure to be observed in things. But there is no danger of your covering them up and deluding yourself with too bright an outlook, quite the contrary; you always lay stress too much on the shadows and by so doing thicken them and obstruct your outlets of escape into the Light. Faith, more faith! Faith in your possibilities, faith in the Power that is at work behind the veil, faith in the work that is to be done and the offered guidance.

There cannot be any high endeavour, least of all in the spiritual field, which does not raise or encounter grave obstacles of a very persistent character. These are both internal and external, and, although in the large they are fundamentally the same for all, there may be a great difference in the distribution of their stress or the outward form they take. But the one real difficulty is the attunement of the nature with the working of the Divine Light and Power. Get that solved and the others will either disappear or take a subordinate place; and even with those difficulties that are of a more general character, more lasting because they are inherent in the work of transformation, they will not weigh so heavily because the sense of the supporting Force and a greater power to follow its movement will be there.

*

Of course consciousness grows as the opening increases and one result of consciousness is to be able to see in oneself — but not to see the weaknesses only, to see the whole play of forces. Only in the right consciousness one does not regard the weaknesses even in a too personal way so as to get discouraged. One has to see them as the play of nature, mental nature, vital nature, physical nature, common to all human beings — to see them so and remain calm and detached, calling in the Mother's force and light for transformation of this defective play into the true nature — not getting impatient if it is not done at once, but going on steadily and giving time for the change. The full change indeed cannot come till all is ready for the descent of a greater, calmer, larger consciousness from above and that is only possible when the ordinary consciousness has been made thoroughly ready for it.

The intense love and bhakti does not come at once. It comes as the power of the psychic grows more and more in the being. But to aspire for it is right and the sincere aspiration is sure to fulfil itself. Always seek to progress in quietude, happiness and confidence, that is the most helpful attitude. Do not listen to contrary suggestions from outside.

Stating One's Difficulties

There is no reason why you should stop writing letters — it is only one kind of letter that is in question and that is not a very good means of contact; you yourself felt the reaction was not favourable. I asked you to write because your need of unburdening the perilous matter in you was very great at the time and, although it did not relieve you at once, it kept me exactly informed of the turns of the fight and helped me to put a certain pressure on the attacking forces at a critical moment. But I do not believe any of these necessities now exists. It is rather a discouragement from within yourself of the source of these movements that is now the need; but putting them into words would tend, as I have said, to give them more body and substance.

It is an undoubted fact proved by hundreds of instances that for many the exact statement of their difficulties to us is the best and often, though not always, an immediate, even an instantaneous means of release. This has often been seen by sadhaks not only here, but far away, and not only for inner difficulties, but for illness and outer pressure of unfavourable circumstances. But for that a certain attitude is necessary — either a strong faith in the mind and vital or a habit of reception and response in the inner being. Where this habit has been established, I have seen it to be almost unfailingly effective, even when the faith was uncertain or the outer expression in the mind vague, ignorant or in its form mistaken or inaccurate. Moreover, this method succeeds most when the writer can write as a witness of his own movements and state them with an exact and almost impartial precision as a phenomenon of his nature or the movement of a force affecting him from which he seeks release. On the other hand if in writing his vital gets seized by the thing he is writing of, and takes up the pen for him, — expressing and often supporting doubt, revolt, depression, despair, it becomes a very different matter. Even here sometimes the expression acts as a purge; but also the statement of the condition may lend energy to the attack at least for the moment and may seem to enhance and prolong it, exhausting it by its own violence perhaps for the time and so bringing in the end a relief, but at a heavy cost of upheaval and turmoil — and at the risk of the recurring decimal movement, because the release has come by temporary exhaustion of the attacking force, not by rejection and purification through the intervention of the Divine Force with the unquestioning assent and support of the sadhak. There has been a confused fight, an intervention in a hurly-burly, not a clear alignment of forces — and the intervention of the helping force is not felt in the confusion and the whirl. This is what used to happen in your crises; the vital in you was deeply affected and began supporting and expressing the reasonings of the attacking force — in place of a clear observation and expression of the difficulty by the vigilant mind laying the state of things in the Light for the higher Light and Force to act upon it, there was a vehement statement of the case for the Opposition. Many sadhaks (even "advanced") had made a habit of this kind of expression of their difficulties and some still do it; they cannot even yet understand that it is not the way. At one time it was a sort of gospel in the Asram that this was the thing to be done, — I don't know on what ground, for it was never part of my teaching about the Yoga, — but experience has shown that it does not work; it lands one in the recurring decimal notation, an unending round of struggle. It is quite different from the movement of self-opening that succeeds, (here too not necessarily in a moment, but still sensibly and progressively) and of which those are thinking who insist on everything being opened to the Guru so that the help may be more effectively there.

It is inevitable that doubts and difficulties should arise in so arduous an undertaking as the transformation of the normal nature of man into the spiritual nature, the replacement of his system of externalised values and surface experience into profounder inner values and experience. But the doubts and difficulties cannot be overcome by giving them their full force;

it can be rather done by learning to stand back from them and to refuse to be carried away; then there is a chance of the still small voice from within getting itself heard and pushing out these louder clamorous voices and movements from outside. It is the light from within that you have to make room for; the light of the outer mind is quite insufficient for the discovery of the inner values or to judge the truth of spiritual experience.

Detaching Oneself from Difficulties

Not to be touched or disturbed by the difficulties, to feel separate from them is the first step towards freedom.

*

If you cannot do anything else, you must at least remain detached — there is always a part of the being that can remain detached and go on persisting, calling down the Force from above.

*

When vital difficulties assail a sadhak, he has not to identify his consciousness with them, but to stand back and remaining quiet in the observing part of his being call down persistently the Divine Force. The help will then come through this steady and silent part of the being.

*

Knowledge in the mind is not sufficient by itself to prevent it [obscurity] so long as the whole consciousness is not liberated. What can be done is for the inner being to be always detached and separate so that it does not feel obscured by the obscurity or attacked by the attack and is able to see and deal with it as something of the surface. Your difficulty is that you are constantly identifying yourself with the outer parts and feel yourself submerged by the attacks on them.

*

Do not yield to the Tamas; the more you yield, the more it will stick.

For all these things, the way is detachment, to stand back; separate yourself from the desire, observe it, refuse sanction and put a quiet and persistent will for it to cease, calling on the Mother's force at the same time to dissolve and eliminate the greed, desire, attachment, obscurity and inertia. If sincerely, persistently and rightly done, it will succeed in the end, even though it may take time.

*

These things rise because either they are there in the conscious part of the being as habits of the nature or they are there lying concealed and able to rise at any moment or they are suggestions from the general or universal Nature outside to which the personal being makes a response. In any case they rise in order that they may be met and cast out and finally rejected so that they may trouble the nature no longer. The amount of trouble they give depends on the way they are met. The first principle is to detach oneself from them, not to identify, not to admit them any longer as part of one's real nature but to look on them as things imposed to which one says, "This is not I or mine — this is a thing I reject altogether." One begins to feel a part of the being inside which is not identified, which remains firm and says, "This may give trouble on the surface, but it shall not touch me." If this separate being within can be felt, then half the trouble is over — provided there is a will there not only to separate but to get rid of the imperfection from the surface nature also.

*

The difficulties of the character persist so long as one yields to them in action when they rise. One has to make a strict rule not to act according to the impulses of anger, ego or whatever the weakness may be that one wants to get rid of, or if one does act in the heat of the moment, not to justify or persist in the action. If one does that, after a time the difficulty abates or is confined purely to a subjective movement which one can observe, detach oneself from and combat.

*

Do not allow yourself to be shaken or troubled by these things [*demands made by others*]. The one thing to do always is to remain firm in your aspiration to the Divine and to face with equanimity and detachment all difficulties and all oppositions. For those who wish to lead the spiritual life, the Divine must always come first, everything else must be secondary.

Keep yourself detached and look at these things from the calm inner vision of one who is inwardly dedicated to the Divine.

*

Well, that is right. The difficulty of the difficulties is self-created, a knot of the Ignorance; when a certain inner perception loosens the knot, the worst of the difficulty is over.

Rejecting Wrong Movements

It is simply a steady and quiet rejection [*of the lower forces*] that is needed and a quiet and steady calling down of the true Force. All this emotional excitability must be quieted down; it is that that makes the vital open itself to these forces. If it were not so, all the defects of the nature could be quietly observed and quietly mended.

*

If one part of you keeps its quietude — the inner being — then the rest can be dealt with. So not to allow the vital to be upset and the disturbance cover up the inner self, that is the most important thing. Keep up the rejection always.

*

It would be easier [*to get rid of wrong movements*] when you bring down a settled peace and equanimity into that part of the being. There will then be more of an automatic rejection of such movements and less need of tapasya.

*

If you accept your weakness which means accepting the thing itself — some part of your nature accepts it and to that you yield — then what is the use of our telling you what to do? That part of your vital will always be able to say, "I was too weak to carry it out." The only way out of it is for you to cease to be weak, to dismiss this sentimental and sensuous part of you, to call down strength to replace its weakness and to do it with a settled and serious purpose. If we cannot get you who have had some foundation in the sadhana to overcome this element in you, how do you expect us to get X to do it who says he has no firm foundation but is still floating?

*

It is always their [*the lower forces'*] endeavour to rise up and get the sanction of the mind and higher vital — or if they cannot do that, to cover them up so that the lower nature may act in its ordinary way without being pressed by the higher consciousness to change. The first thing necessary for the sadhak is not to give any consent of his mind or higher vital and to keep them from being covered. If that can be done, then it becomes possible to push the lower forces out of the lower vital and body and not allow them to return. It is the Mother's Force which you feel — for all the higher forces are hers.

Chapter Three

Vigilance, Resolution, Will and the Divine Help

The Need of Vigilance

One is always open [*to the surrounding atmosphere*] so long as there is not the final change. If things do not come in it is because the consciousness is vigilant or the psychic in front; but the least want of vigilance or relaxation can allow something to enter.

*

It [*the experience of liberation*] is likely to be fundamental and definite. But in these matters, even after the liberation one has to remain vigilant — for often these things go out and remain at a far distance waiting to see if under any circumstances, in any condition they can make a rush and recover their kingdom. If there has been an entire purification down to the depths and nothing is there to open the gate, then they cannot do it. But it is only after one has been a long time free that one can say, "Now it is all right for ever."

*

As for your inner attitude, it must remain the same. Not to be excited or drawn outwards by these "incidents" of the outward life or by the coming in of new elements is the rule; they must come in like waves into an untroubled sea and mix in it and become themselves untroubled and serene.

Your present attitude and condition is all that it should be, — only you must remain vigilant always. For when the condition is good, the lower movements have a habit of subsiding and become quiescent, hiding as it were, — or they go out of the nature and remain at a distance. But if they see that the sadhak is losing his vigilance, then they slowly begin to rise or draw near, most often unseen, and when he is quite off his guard, surge up suddenly or make a sudden irruption. This continues until the whole nature, mental, vital, physical down to the very subconscient is enlightened, conscious, full of the Divine. Till that happens, one must always remain watchful in a sleepless vigilance.

*

It is perhaps that the attitude you took of going on with the calm within and slowly changing what had to be changed, postponing certain things for the future, — though not a wrong attitude in itself, — made you somewhat lax, allowing things to play on the surface (desires etc.), which should have been kept in check. This relaxation may have opened the way for the old movements to rise through this part which was not yet ready to change at all and the hostile forces finding you off your guard took the opportunity to push the attack home. They are always vigilant for an opportunity and there must be a sufficient vigilance on the sadhak's side to refuse it to them. It is also possible that as the Force descending in the general atmosphere has carried in it some pressure on the consciousness of the sadhaks to be more ready, more awake, less engrossed in the movements of the ordinary nature than they are now, it fell upon this part and the resistance in it, which was mostly passive for a long time, became suddenly active under the pressure.

*

There is no reason for despondency; when one has progressed as far as you did, that is, so far as to feel and maintain the calm and have so much of the psychic discrimination and the psychic feeling, one has no right to despair of one's spiritual future. You could not yet carry out the discrimination into an entire psychic change, because a large part of the outer physical consciousness still took some pleasure in old movements and therefore their roots remained alive in the subconscient. When you were off your guard the whole thing rose up and there was a temporary and violent lapse. But this does not mean that the nature is not changeable. Only the calm inner conscious poise, the psychic discrimination and above all a will to change, stronger and steadier than before, must be so established that no uprising or invasion will be able to cloud even partly the discrimination or suspend the will. You saw the truth but this part of the old nature which rose up did not want to acknowledge — it wanted its play and imposed that on you. This time you must insist on a complete truthfulness in the whole being which will refuse to accept any denial of what the psychic discrimination sees or any affirmation or consent anywhere to what it disapproves, spiritual humility and the removal of self-righteousness, self-justification and the wish to impose yourself, the tendency to judge others etc. All these defects you know are in you; to cast them out may take time, but if the will to be true to the inner self in all ways is strong and persistent and vigilant and always calls in the Mother's force, it can be done sooner than now seems possible.

*

That is all right [*not to worry about the recurrence of thought-movements*] — provided there is detachment and refusal of consent. One ought not to worry, but also one ought not to be negligent, i.e., one ought not to give the consent of the will or of the reason to these movements. For all consent prolongs their action or their recurrence. If they do not go when rejected by the mind and will, it is because of the habitual response in the less conscious parts of the nature. These have to become conscious by receiving the Light and Force until finally they refuse response to the calls of the lower nature.

*

This is quite right. If you keep this condition [*of trust and devotion*], not allowing it to be entirely obscured or long clouded, you can move rapidly towards a new birth of your nature and the foundation of your life and all your thoughts and acts and movements in your true being, the psychic being. Never consent to the ideas, suggestions, feelings that bring back the cloud, the confusion and the revolt. It is the consent that makes them strong to recur. Refuse the consent and they will be obliged to retire either immediately or after a time.

Remain fixed in the sunlight of the true consciousness — for only there is happiness and peace. They do not depend upon outside happenings, but on this alone.

The Need of Resolution

There is no reason why you should abandon hope of success in the Yoga. The state of depression which you now feel is temporary and it comes even upon the strongest sadhaks at one time or another or even often recurs. The only thing needed is to hold firm with the awakened part of the being, to reject all contrary suggestions and wait, opening yourself as much as you can to the true Power, till the crisis or change of which this depression is a stage, is completed. The suggestions which come to your mind telling you that you are not fit and that you must go back to the ordinary life, are false tamasic promptings from a hostile source. Ideas of this kind must always be rejected as inventions of the lower nature; even if they are founded on appearances which seem convincing to the ignorant mind, they are false, because they exaggerate a passing movement and represent it as the decisive and definite truth. There is only one truth in you on which you have to lay constant hold, the truth of your divine possibilities and the call of the higher Light to your nature. If you hold to that always or, even if you are momentarily shaken from your hold, return constantly to it, it will justify itself in the end in spite of all difficulties and obstacles and stumblings. All in you that resists will disappear in time with the progressive unfolding of your spiritual nature.

The disabilities of your past character and mind and vital habits need not discourage you. Some of them are, no doubt, serious — especially the animal sexuality of the vital parts and the support which the mind has given to it; but others have had to face obstacles as serious in themselves and have surmounted them in the purifying and liberating process of the Yoga. It may not be easy to get rid of them altogether and it may take time; but if you persist and refuse all justification and all possibility of return to these things, you are bound in the end to conquer.

When you came, the psychic call in you was true and sincere, but in your external nature the response was confused and mixed with foreign elements of a lower kind. What has sunk in you is not the pure psychic urge, even if that is temporarily veiled, but a vital flame that was not entirely pure. It is because these foreign elements have been discouraged, that the vital nature in you feels despondent and refuses its support to the belief of the mind and to the psychic call. This often happens in the process of purification; what is needed is the conversion and surrender of the vital part. It must learn to demand only the highest Truth and to forego all insistence on the satisfaction of its inferior impulses and desires. It is this adhesion of the vital being that brings the full satisfaction and joy of the whole nature in the spiritual life. When that is there, it will be impossible even to think of returning to the ordinary existence. Meanwhile the mental will and the psychic aspiration must be your support; if you insist, the vital will finally yield and be converted and surrender.

Fix upon your mind and heart the resolution to live for the Divine Truth and for that alone; reject all that is contrary and incompatible with it and turn away from all lower desires; aspire to open yourself to the Divine Power and to no other. Do this in all sincerity and the present and living help you need will not fail you.

*

The resolution, to be a real resolution, must be there always, fixed. If it is dependent on an urge, not self-dependent, it can also be knocked down by inertia.

The Need of Aspiration

It is good. When the external consciousness covers the inner being, then it is by a calm and patient aspiration — without restlessness or disturbance — that the inner state must be called back until the external consciousness itself gets so habituated to the true condition that it is no longer willing to respond to anything else.

*

I have told you that if you feel quietness somewhere in your consciousness, even if a part is not quiet, that is sufficient to lean on and get the Force to act through it. The quietness is quite as much a fact as the outer confusion. You have to accept it, to stress it, to aspire to keep and increase it — to reject the confusion.

What "reason" do you need to aspire for peace, purity, freedom from the lower nature, light, strength, Ananda, divine love, divine service? These are things good in themselves and the highest possible aim of human endeavour.

*

If not a will, you have a wish in you or an aspiration; the word does not matter, the thing is there. If it gets clouded over, it is not the less there. There are the two things — the inner being with its aspiration, the physical and material with its obscurity and depressions. If you lay stress on the former instead of constantly denying its presence, that would make the progress easy; by laying stress on the outer obscurity and affirming that always and always thinking of it, you help it to last and delay the progress. Even so, if the inner aspiration is there, it must in the end conquer.

*

Yes, but it is an absence of the one-pointed aspiration more than of strength of will — they [*certain sadhaks*] left because some desire or other got hold of them which was incompatible with the steadfast single-minded aspiration to the Divine Realisation.

If Buddha had the will only after tapasya, how was it that he left everything without hesitation in the search for Truth and never once looked back, regretted nor had any struggle? The only difficulty was how to find the Truth, his single will to find it never faltered; the intensity of his tapasya itself would have been impossible without that strength of will. People less strong than Buddha may have to develop it by endeavour. Those who cannot do that have to find their strength in their reliance on the Divine Mother.

The Need of Will

There must be a fixed will for the spiritual life — that alone can overcome all obstacles.

*

To be conscious is the first step towards overcoming [*lower movements*] — but for the overcoming strength is necessary and also detachment and the will to overcome.

*

There must first be the will to change firmly conceived and held — then to open the consciousness to the Force and let it work with the inner assent to its working. When there is the psychic opening, then even the things most obstinate in the nature can change.

*

Obviously what the Mother told you was the fact — but such missing of opportunities should not discourage, the recognition of it must be a spur to do better in future. Human nature is weak and is always missing the divine opportunities; but if the spirit is willing, the weakness of the nature is obliged eventually to yield to its will. Renew that will always, so that failure as well as success may become an opportunity and an incentive for farther progress.

*

Develop the will — the will grows by a steady use, like the muscles, and grows strong.

*

The only way to do it [*develop the true will-power*] is (1) to become aware of a conscious Force behind that uses the mind etc. (2) to learn by practice to direct that Force towards its object. I do not suppose you will find it easy to do either of these things at once — one must first learn to live more deeply in the inner consciousness than you have done hitherto.

*

I suppose it must be [*weakness of the will*] because you have not been in the habit of using the will to compel the other parts of the nature — so when you want it done, they refuse to obey a control to which they are not accustomed and it also has not any habitual hold upon them.

The will is a part of the consciousness and ought to be in human beings the chief agent in controlling the activities of the nature.

*

If there is a constant use of the will the rest of the being learns however slowly to obey the will and then the actions become in conformity with the will and not with the vital impulses and desires. As for the rest (the feelings and desires etc. themselves) if they are not indulged in action or imagination and not supported by the will, if they are merely looked at and rejected when they come, then after some struggle they begin to lose their force and dwindle away.

*

There is no process [*for using the will*]. The will acts of itself when the mind and vital agree as in the case of a desire. If the desire is not satisfied, it goes on hammering, trying to get it, insisting on it, repeating the demand, making use of this person or that person, this device or that device, getting the mind to support it with reasons, representing it as a need that must be satisfied etc. etc. till the desire is satisfied. All that is the evidence of a will in action. When you have to use the will for the sadhana, you have not the same persistence, the mind finds reasons for not going on with the effort, as soon as the difficulty becomes strong it is dropped, there is no continuity, no keeping of the will fixed on its object.

*

There can be no persistence or insistence without will.

*

By development it [*the will*] becomes fit to merge into the Mother's will. A will that is not strong is a great hindrance to sadhana.

*

It is of course a fluctuation of the mental will that often prevents a knowledge gained from being put into steady practice. If the will is not strong enough, then the greater Will behind which is the will of the Mother, her conscious Force in which knowledge and will are united, must be called in to strengthen and support it. Very often, however, even if the will as well as the knowledge are there, the habit of the vital nature brings in the old reactions. This can only be overcome by a steady undiscouraged aspiration which will bring out more and more of the psychic and its true movements to push out and displace the wrong ones. The gradual and steady replacement of the old ignorant consciousness and its movements by the true psychic and spiritual consciousness is the nature of the transformation that is to be accomplished in the Yoga. But that takes time, it cannot be done easily or at once. Therefore one should not mind or be discouraged if meanwhile one finds the old movements recurring in spite of one's knowledge. Only one should try to keep more and more separate from them, so that even if they recur the consent of the being to them shall no longer be there.

*

It depends[1] — if the consciousness is developed only on the side

---

[1] *The correspondent asked whether the consciousness merely warns a person not to do something or whether it also has the power to prevent him from doing it.* — Ed.

of knowledge, it will warn only. If on the side of will or power, it will help to effectuate.

*

The will can make itself work — it is in its own nature a force or energy.

*

The energy which dictates the action or prevents a wrong action is the Will.

*

Peace is not a necessary precondition for the action of the will. When the being is troubled, it is often the business of the will to impose quiet on it.

*

There is no such thing as an inert passive will. Will is dynamic in its nature. Even if it does not struggle or endeavour its very presence is dynamic and acts dynamically on the resistance. What you are speaking of is a passive wish = I would like it to be like that, I want it to be like that. That is not will.

*

It [*a will without much energy*] simply means that your will is weak and not a true will. Queer kind of will! Perhaps it is like a motor car that won't go and you have to push from behind.

*

It is not the right kind of will-power then [*if it increases fatigue*] — probably they use some fighting or effortful will-power instead of the quiet but strong will that calls down the higher consciousness and force.

*

Will is will whether it is calm or restless, whether it acts in a Yogic or unyogic way, for a Yogic or an unyogic object. Do you think Napoleon and Caesar had no will or that they were Yogis? You have strange ideas about things. You might just as well say that memory is memory only when it remembers the Divine and it is not memory when it remembers other things.

Lack of Will

Why cannot you see that this condition is not a true consciousness, but only a clouding of the truth, a clouding which you can always get rid of if you firmly choose to do so? What you express here is not a lack of understanding, but a lack of will — and this lack of will is not your own, but is forced upon you by a lower consciousness which overpowers you and forces you to reverse all the true values of feeling and knowledge. Your being does want to be free and at peace and happy in the light — it is this Falsehood seizing hold of your external mind that makes you want to be more dark and miserable and revolted and hate yourself and not to live. Such feelings, such a perverted will is entirely opposed to the normal feelings of the nature and cannot be "true" and right. There is nobody who asks you to pretend — what we ask you is to reject false perversions and wrong feelings and ignorance and not to go on supporting them as they want you to do. It is not courage and nobility to accept these things as the law of your nature, nor is it meanness and cowardice to aspire to a higher Truth and try to act according to it and make that the law of your nature.

*

In the indolence of the will which does not want to make a sustained effort for a long period [*lies the difficulty*]. It is like a person who moves slightly half a leg for a second and then wonders why he is not already a hundred miles away at the goal after making such a gigantic effort.

*

That [*the idea that one lacks will-power*] is the suggestion that has been enforced on you by the physical inertia. It has covered up your will and persuaded you that there is no will left and no possibility of any will.

*

One can always use the will. The idea that you cannot is only a suggestion of the inertia.

Will and the Divine Force or Power

There are always two elements in spiritual success — one's own steady will and endeavour and the Power that in one way or another helps and gives the result of the endeavour.

*

The Force produces no definite and lasting fruit unless there is the will and the resolution to achieve in the sadhak.

*

The higher action does not preclude a use of the will — will is an element of the higher action.

*

These things [*the removal of vital demand and ego*] cannot be done in that way [*by a direct higher action*]. For transformation to be genuine, the difficulty has to be rejected by all the parts of the being. The Force can only help or enable them to do that, but it cannot replace this necessary action by a summary process. Your mind and inner being must impart their will to the whole.

*

Yes. So long as there is not a constant action of the Force from above or else of a deeper Will from within, the mental will is necessary.

*

You had written, "I need not bother about it — if peace is needed it will bring itself." Certainly the main stress should be on the

Force, but the active assent of the sadhak is needed; in certain things his will also may be needed as an instrument of the Force.

*

It is true that the Force can work effectively without any effort on your part. It is not the effort, it is the assent of the being that it needs for its work.

*

The Power can do everything, change everything and will do that but it can do it perfectly and easily and permanently only when your own will mental, vital and physical has been put on the side of the Truth. If you side with the vital ignorance and want to fight against your own spiritual change, it means a painful and difficult struggle before the work is done. That is why I insist on quietude at the very least and patient confidence with it, as far as you can — so that there may be a quiet and steady progress, not a painful and tormented movement full of relapse and struggle.

*

Hardly anyone is strong enough to overcome by his own unaided aspiration and will the forces of the lower nature; even those who do it get only a certain kind of control, but not a complete mastery. Will and aspiration are needed to bring down the aid of the Divine Force and to keep the being on its side in its dealings with the lower powers. The Divine Force fulfilling the spiritual will and the heart's psychic aspiration can alone bring about the conquest.

*

There is only one way if you cannot exert your will — it is to call the Force; even to call only with the mind or the mental word is better than being entirely passive and submitted to the attack, — for although it may not succeed instantaneously, the mental call even ends by bringing the Force and opening up the consciousness again. For everything depends upon that. In the externalised consciousness obscurity and suffering can always be there; the more the internalised consciousness reigns, the more these things are pushed back and out and with the full internalised consciousness they cannot remain — if they come, it is as outside touches unable to lodge themselves in the being.

*

The Force can bring forward and use the will.

Personal Effort and the Divine Force or Power

If there is no personal effort, if the sadhak is too indolent and tamasic to try, why should the Grace act?

*

All that [*thinking one's efforts are useless*] is the physical mind refusing to take the trouble of the labour and struggle necessary for the spiritual achievement. It wants to get the highest, but desires a smooth course all the way. "Who the devil is going to face so much trouble for getting the Divine?" — that is the underlying feeling. The difficulty with the thoughts is a difficulty every Yogi has gone through — so is the phenomenon of a little result after some days of effort. It is only when one has cleared the field and ploughed and sown and watched over it that big harvests can be hoped for.

*

Of course — personal effort without the supporting Force can do only a little, slowly, with much labour.

*

One can either use effort [*to remove difficulties*], and then one must be patient and persevering, or one can rely on the Divine with a constant will and aspiration. But then the reliance has to be a true one, not insisting on immediate fruit.

*

The only truth in your other experience — which, you say, seems at the time so true to you, — is that it is hopeless for you or anyone to get out of the inferior consciousness by your or his unaided effort. That is why when you sink into this inferior consciousness, everything seems hopeless to you, because you lose hold for a time of the true consciousness. But the suggestion is untrue, because you have an opening to the Divine and are not bound to remain in the inferior consciousness.

When you are in the true consciousness, then you see that everything can be done, even if at present only a slight beginning has been made; but a beginning is enough, once the Force, the Power is there. For the truth is that it can do everything and only time and the soul's aspiration are needed for the entire change and the soul's fulfilment.

*

It does not matter what defects you may have in your nature. The one thing that matters is your keeping yourself open to the Force. Nobody can transform himself by his own unaided efforts; it is only the Divine Force that can transform him. If you keep yourself open, all the rest will be done for you.

*

As I have told you it is no longer useful to think of right understanding and wrong movements and get upset when they are felt to be not there or imperfect. Nobody can change himself — even the strongest sadhaks here recognise that. Their effort is to let the Peace, Force, Light, Ananda of the Mother come in, to let that grow — for that will change them, they know. So long as it is not there, has not yet touched, is not growing, they struggle with the mind and vital, because they cannot help doing so and it is necessary for preparing the consciousness a little to admit the Peace and Force. But once these have touched, the only thing to do is to lay all the stress on that, trust to it, surrender and give oneself to it — for the straight road is found and the true power and consciousness have been experienced.

Letting the Force Work

The way in which the pains went shows you how to deal with the whole nature, — for it is the same with the mental and vital as with the physical causes of ill-ease and disturbance. To remain quiet within, to hold on to the faith and experience that to be quiet and open and let the Force work is the one way. Naturally, to be wholly conscious is not possible yet, but to feel it, to open, to let it work, to observe its result, that is the first thing. It is the beginning of consciousness and the way to complete consciousness.

The Divine Help

Help is given in whatever way is necessary or possible. It is not limited to Force, Light, Knowledge.

*

Certainly, all the help possible will be given. As for the method, there are always the two ways possible — one to overcome the difficulty in its own field, the other to develop the inner realisation until it grows so strong that the roots you speak of have no longer any soil to hold by and come out easily by a spontaneous psychic change.

*

Cling to the help always, — when you cannot feel, call for it and remain quiet till you feel it again. It is only the covering you spoke of that comes between you and the sense of its presence — for it is always there.

*

It [*the need to call for help*] diminishes as one gets higher and higher or rather fuller and fuller, being replaced more and more by the automatic action of the Force.

The Divine Protection

The grace and protection are always with you. When in any

inner or outer difficulty or trouble do not allow it to oppress you; take refuge with the Divine Force that protects.

If you do that always with faith and sincerity, you will find something opening in you which will always remain calm and peaceful in spite of all superficial disturbances.

*

Yes, the Divine's Protection is surely with you, since it sustains you through all. The untoward physical happenings are transient and will certainly pass away leaving full room for a greater state.

*

One should not expect too much from the Divine Protection for, constituted as we are and the world is, the Divine Protection has to act within limits. Of course miracles happen, but we have no claim to it.

Chapter Four
Time and Change of the Nature

Time Needed for Change

The change of the nature cannot take place in a few days. It is a constant progressive movement.

*

The change of the lower consciousness (vital and physical) is a big work and takes a long time and much action of the higher forces to accomplish. Nobody has ever done it in a short time.

*

That is nonsense — no one can get free from the lower nature in such a short time [*eight or nine months*]. It takes years for even the greatest Yogis — it is the work of a life-time.

*

As I have constantly told you, you cannot expect all to be enlightened at once. Even the greatest Yogis can only proceed by stages and it is only at the end that the whole nature shares the true consciousness which they first establish in the heart or behind it or in the head or above it. It descends or expands slowly conquering each layer of the being one after the other, but each step takes time.

*

All comes in its time. One has to go on quietly and steadily increasing the higher consciousness till it takes possession of the vital and physical parts.

*

I want you to be open and in contact with the Peace and Presence and Force. All else will come if that is there and then one need not be troubled by the time it takes in the *péripéties* of the sadhana.

*

It is no doubt the pressure of the psychic in you which you express in the letter. That is how the psychic being wants it to be. But it is a mistake to accept any suggestion of self-distrust or incapacity on the ground that it is not like that yet or is not always like that. These things always take time; even after they have begun, they always take time. It is impossible to expect from the mixed and confused nature of the human being that it should be constantly in a state of ardent aspiration, perfect faith and love or full and constant openness to the Divine Force. There is the mental with its limited knowledge and its hesitations, there is the vital with its desires, unwillingnesses and its struggles; there is the physical with its obscurity, slowness and inertia. Even to clear the field sufficiently for a beginning of experience is usually a very long labour. But afterwards if the peace begins or any other right condition, it comes and stays for a time — then what is left of the lower nature surges up on some excuse or with no excuse and veils the condition. Peace and opening may come so strongly that it seems all difficulties are gone and can never return — but that is only an indication, a promise. It shows that it will be so when the peace and opening are irrevocably settled in all the nature. For that what is needed is perseverance — to go on without discouragement, recognising that the process of the nature and the action of the Mother's force is working through the difficulty even and will do all that is needed. Our incapacity does not matter — there is no human being who is not in his parts of nature incapable — but the Divine Force also is there. If one puts one's trust in that, incapacity will be changed into capacity. Difficulty and struggle themselves then become a means towards the achievement.

*

I repeat what I wrote in the morning that the one thing to be seen is whether there is the true yearning for the Divine or, to put it more strongly, whether that is the one thing that really matters to the being. If there is that, then all other considerations become minor or irrelevant: what is happening in the world or how others react to the search for the Divine or how long the search takes. One must be prepared to give one's whole lifetime and one's whole self to that and count all well spent for the one only and supreme object. When the Divine is a necessity of the being, what is the use of mental questionings as to whether He exists or what He is like, kind or cruel, slow or swift in response, easy to reach or hard to discover? He appears all or any of these things to different seekers, but to all He is the one necessity of their existence. If one finds Him quickly, so much the better; if it takes long, still one has to go on seeking till one finds. One may have hard moments of anguish or despair because the human vital is weak, but still one goes on because the soul insists. But there is no logic in the position that because my need of the Divine is entire and even in six years I have not got Him, therefore the proper thing to do is to despair and give up. The logical position is, my need for the Divine is entire, so I must go on till I find Him, however long it may take, whether one year or six or twelve; for if my need is entire and persists always, I cannot fail to arrive. That is the position that is taken by the spiritual seeker and it is the true and natural one. It is no use saying that you are unfit and cannot take it; you have to come to it, if your need is true and entire.

The misery of the world or the activity of the Asuras is also irrelevant. Nobody has ever contended that this is a happy and perfect world, nobody in India at least, or the best possible world or put that forth as a proof of the Divine Existence. It is known that it is a world of death, ignorance, suffering and that its pleasures are not enduring. The spiritual seeker takes that not as a disproof of the Divine Existence, but as a greater spur for seeking and finding it out. He may seek it as a means of escape from life and entry into Nirvana or moksha or Goloka, Brahmaloka or Vaikuntha; he may seek the divine Self and its peace or Ananda behind existence and if he attains to that and is satisfied with it he can move through the world untouched by its vicissitudes and troubles; or he may seek it, as I have done, for the base of a greater and happier life to be brought now or hereafter into the world-existence. But whatever be the aim, the actual state of the world is no argument at all against the seeking for the Divine or the truth of Yoga. Also the accidents of the search, that A is dead and will attain only in another body or B is ill or C misbehaves are side matters altogether. It makes no difference to one's own entire need of the Divine and the necessity of persevering in one's seeking till one finds and reaches.

My words about the great secret of sadhana[1] simply pointed out that that was the most effective way if one could get the things done by the Power behind, did not rule out mental effort so long as one could not do that. Ramakrishna's way of putting it was the image of the baby monkey and baby cat; I have only said the same thing in other words; both are permissible methods, only one is more easily effective. Any method sincerely and persistently followed can end by bringing the opening. You yourself chose the method of prayer and japa because you believed in that, and I acquiesced because it does prepare something in the consciousness and, if done with persistent faith and bhakti, it can open all the doors. Another method is concentration and aspiration in the heart which opens the inner emotional being. Another is the concentration in the head of which I spoke which opens the inner mind or opens the passage through the Brahmarandhra to the higher consciousness. These things are no fantastic invention of mine which one can dismiss as a new-fangled and untested absurdity; they are recognised methods which have succeeded in thousands of cases and here also there are plenty who have found their effect. But whatever method is used will not bring its effect at once; it must be done persistently, simply, directly till it succeeds. If it is done with a mind of doubt or watching it as an experiment to see if it succeeds or if it is continually crossed by a spirit of hasty despondency saying constantly, "You see it is all useless," then it ought to be obvious that the opening will be

---

[1] *"That is a great secret of sadhana, to know how to get things done by the Power behind or above instead of doing all by the mind's effort."* Letters on Yoga — II, *volume 29 of* THE COMPLETE WORKS OF SRI AUROBINDO, *p. 215.*

very difficult, because there is that clogging it every time there is a pressure or a push to open. That is why I wanted you to get rid of these two things and have harped on that so much, because I know by my own experience and that of others how strongly they can stand in the way of what you seek. For you are not the only one who have been troubled by these two obstacles; most have had to struggle against them. If one can get rid of them in their central action, the survival of their activity in the circumference does not so much matter; for then the opening becomes possible, both to make and to keep and the rest can follow.

The six years of which you speak have been spent by you mainly in struggling with sex and doubt and vital difficulties — many take more than that time about it. What I have been wanting you to do now is to get the right positive attitude within at the centre free from these things. Its basis must be what I have said, "I want the Divine and the Divine only; since I want and need, I shall surely arrive, however long it takes, and till I do, I shall persist and endure with patience and courage." I do not mean by that that you should have no activity but prayer and concentration; few can do that; but whatever is done should be done in that spirit.

Freedom from the Past

Do not let the things of the past trouble you. Leave them behind and prepare yourself for a new being.

*

To be no longer bound by the past or by surface formations is always a great step in advance.

*

There is no need to give up entirely what you had in the past. Spiritual truths are not warring enemies — they are parts of a single truth and complete each other. It is only the mind that turns them into disputants and wants one to bar out another. That is the weakness of making something in the past the standard by which you judge the present — the mind takes advantage of its own limitations to declare that the two are incompatible. But it is not so in reality — between two truths of the Divine there is always a reconciliation when to the limiting mind they seem opposites; as one is realised after the other, their unity appears, it is not necessary to deny the past experience in order to go forward to the new realisation.

This will before long become apparent to you if you do not allow the mind to stand in the way of the heart's permanent opening. Let the doors of the heart swing open freely — allow yourself to enter into the stream without making any mental conditions before you plunge in; the stream itself will carry you to your goal.

*

So long as you have not learned the lesson the past had to teach you, it comes back on you. Notice carefully what kind of remembrances come, you will see that they are connected with some psychological movements in you that have to be got rid of. But you must be prepared to recognise all that was not right in you and is still not corrected, not allow any vanity or self-righteousness to cloud your vision.

*

The past actions do count so long as the man does not change.

*

It is not a question of pardon or punishment. The past can be effaced, but only if it is sincerely rejected from within and repaired and atoned for by a change which gets rid of the movements that caused it. A merely external submission, punishment or pardon are of no use. Otherwise the past prolongs itself into the present and the future. To get rid of the self-justifying mind and the mixture of motives in the vital is what would prevent that and give the psychic being a chance.

*

The past can be abolished — on condition that nothing of it is allowed to continue in the present.

*

You ask how you can repair the wrong you seem to have done. Admitting that it is as you say, it seems to me that the reparation lies precisely in this, in making yourself a vessel for the Divine Truth and the Divine Love. And the first steps towards that are a complete self-consecration and self-purification, a complete opening of oneself to the Divine, rejecting all in oneself that can stand in the way of the fulfilment. In the spiritual life there is no other reparation for any mistake, none that is wholly effective. At the beginning one should not ask for any other fruit or results than this internal growth and change — for otherwise one lays oneself open to severe disappointments. Only when one is free, can one free others and in Yoga it is out of the inner victory that there comes the outer conquest.

The Past and the Future

One cannot go back to the past, one has always to go in the future.

*

The past has not to be kept, — one has to go into the future realisation. All that is necessary in the past for the future will be taken up and given a new form.

*

It is always preferable to have one's face turned towards the future than towards the past.

*

Yes — one should always have one's look turned forwards to the future — retrospection is seldom healthy as it turns one towards a past consciousness.

*

Take with you the peace and quietude and joy and keep it by remembering always the Divine.

If the thoughts about the past and the future come merely as memories and imaginations, they are of no use and you should quietly turn away your mind from them back to the Divine and to the Yoga. If they are anything to the purpose, then refer them to the Divine, put them in the light of the Truth, so that you may have the truth about them or the right decision or formation for the future, if any decision is needed.

There is no harm in the tears of which you speak, — they come from the soul, the psychic being, and are a help and not a hindrance.

Chapter Five
Dealing with Depression and Despondency

Despondency over Difficulties

Mistakes are always possible, so long as any part of the mental (even the subconscient part of it) is not thoroughly transformed. There is no need to be disturbed by that.

*

Whatever you see, don't get disturbed or depressed. If one sees a defect, one must look at it with the utmost quietude and call down more force and light to get rid of it.

*

When some weakness comes up you should take it as an opportunity to know what is still to be done and call down the strength into that part. Despondency is not the right way to meet it.

*

Let the peace and self-giving increase till it takes hold also of the parts in which there are imperfections and gets rid of them. As for the imperfections, it is right not to be troubled by them — only one has to be conscious of them and have the steady and quiet will that they should go.

*

There was no true cause for the trouble. You have allowed it to come into you from outside. There are always forces moving about in the atmosphere trying to disturb the sadhana and the progress. You must be careful not to allow them to invade you with their suggestions whether of depression, despondency, discontent or of anger or desire or of any ego-movement, for it is these things that they try to raise. When they come, instead of remaining in this way and trying to find an external cause for them, recognise them and reject at once.

*

When a habit of these moods (depression or revolt) has been formed, they cannot be got rid of at once. There are three ways of doing it — (1) to strengthen your own will, so that nothing can come or stay as *it* likes but only as *you* like; (2) to think of something else, plunge the mind in some healthy activity; (3) to turn to the Mother and call in her force. One can do any of these or all, but even in doing them, it will take a little time to get rid of the habit.

*

There are two golden rules. (1) Never be depressed or upset by difficulties or stumbles. (2) Press always quietly forward, then however long it seems to take, always progress will be made and one day you will be surprised to find yourself near the goal. It is like the curves followed by the train in the ascent of the mountain — they circle round but always nearer and nearer to the goal.

*

The experience is correct.[1] Everything is prepared above, then worked out through the inner being till the results are accomplished and perfected in the outer personality. Therefore the sadhak ought not to allow himself to be alarmed, upset or grieved or made despondent by any apparent difficulties of the moment. He must know that all has been prepared above and calmly and confidently watch and assist its working out here.

*

There is no need for sadness. Everyone has his difficulties and

---

[1] *In this experience the correspondent rose up into the infinite sky and saw the Mother, who, having prepared things on a higher plane, sent down her Force to work out the results on the planes below.* — Ed.

it is a mistake to desire the state of another. One must follow the movement of one's own heart and self and psychic without looking elsewhere.

*

The egoism, desires, faults of the nature are in everybody very much the same. But once one begins to be conscious of them and has the will to be free, then one has only to keep that will and there will be no real danger. For when one begins to be conscious in the way you have begun and something from within raises up all that was hidden, it means that the Mother's grace is on your nature and her force is working and your inner being is aiding the Mother's force to get rid of all these things. So you must not be sorrowful or discouraged or fear anything, but look steadily at all that comes out and have the will that it should go completely and for ever. With the Mother's force working and the psychic being supporting the force, all can be done and all will surely be done. This purification is made just in order that no trouble may occur in the future such as happened to some because they were not purified — in order that the higher consciousness may come into a purified nature and the inner transformation securely take place. Go on therefore with faith and courage putting your reliance on the Mother.

*

These questionings and depressions are very foolish movements of the mind. If you were not open to the Grace, you would not have had these descents or experiences and there would have been no such progress as you have made. You have not to put such questions but to take it as a settled fact, and with full faith in the Mother and her working in you go on with your sadhana. Whatever difficulties there may be, will be solved in time by the natural progress of the sadhana.

*

What you write is no doubt true and it is necessary to see it so as to be able to comprehend and grasp the true attitude necessary for the sadhana. But, as I have said, one must not be distressed or depressed by perceiving the weaknesses inherent in human nature and the difficulty of getting them out. The difficulty is natural, for they have been there for thousands of lives and are the very nature of man's vital and mental ignorance. It is not surprising that they should have a power to stick and take time to disappear. But there is a true being and a true consciousness that is there in us hidden by these surface formations of nature and which can shake them off once it emerges. By taking the right attitude of selfless devotion within and persisting in it in spite of the surface nature's troublesome self-repetitions one enables this inner being and consciousness to emerge and with the Mother's Force working in it deliver the being from all return of the movements of the old nature.

*

Why do you indulge in these exaggerated feelings of remorse and despair when these things come up from the subconscient? They do not help and make it more, not less difficult to eliminate what comes. Such returns of an old nature that is long expelled from the conscious parts of the being always happen in sadhana. It does not at all mean that the nature is unchangeable. Try to recover the inner quietude, draw back from these movements and look at them calmly, reducing them to their true proportions. Your true nature is that in which you have peace and ananda and the love of the Divine. This other is only a fringe of the outer personality which in spite of these returns is destined to drop away as the true being extends and increases.

*

To be miserable may remind you of the defects of your external nature, but I do not see how it is going to cure them. I am not asking you to be frivolously happy, but to be quiet and quietly confident, rejecting these old movements, but for the rest trusting not in a restless self-torturing personal effort but to the Divine Force to change the external nature.

*

As to your going away for a time in order to get rid of your difficulty with X, a difficulty can never be overcome by your running away from it. And if you cannot overcome it with the direct and immediate help we can give you and have always been giving you and the support of our presence, I do not see how you are going to do it at a distance and without our immediate help and presence.

It seems to me that all this comes from your having taken a wrong way with yourself in meeting the consequences of your stumble. It is not by tormenting yourself with remorse and harassing thoughts and sleepless nights that you can overcome. It is by looking straight at yourself, very quietly, with a quiet and firm resolution and then going on cheerfully and bravely in full confidence and reliance, trusting in the grace, serenely and vigilantly, anchoring yourself on your psychic being, calling down more and more of the love and Ananda, turning more and more exclusively to the Mother. That is the true way — and there is no other.

*

There is no reason to be so much cut down or despair of your progress. Evidently you have had a surging up of the old movements, but that can always happen so long as there is not an entire change of the old nature both in the conscious and subconscient parts. Something came up that made you get out of poise and stray into a past round of feelings. The one thing to do is to quiet yourself and get back into the true consciousness and poise. Always keep within and do things without involving yourself in them, then nothing adverse will happen or, if it does, no serious reaction will come.

The idea of leaving for any reason is of course absurd and out of the question. Eight years is a very short time for transformation. Most people spend as much as that or more to get conscious of their defects and acquire the serious will to change — and after that it takes a long time to get the will turned into full and final accomplishment. Each time one stumbles, one has to get back onto the right footing and go on with fresh resolution; by doing that the full change comes.

Dwelling on One's Weaknesses or Difficulties

Of course it is necessary to see one's own weaknesses, but it is not good to dwell too much upon them, — it only brings sadness and restlessness and despondency. Fix your mind rather on what you want to be, for that concentration brings the power to become it — it is the best way also to get rid of the defects and weaknesses; for it is when something strong and positive fills the nature that it changes and its defects begin to disappear.

*

Mistakes of action and thought and feeling naturally bring these outward reactions [*of regret and sorrow*]; they are an obstinate part of human nature, but one has to outgrow them steadily. If they recur, one must not get upset and brood over them; the aim must be to keep quiet and recover as quickly as possible — so that the Force can at once resume its work and not be held suspended by the mind's preoccupation with mistakes and stumbles.

*

Difficulties and perplexities can never be got rid of by the mind brooding on them and trying in that way to get out of them; this habit of the mind only makes them recur without a solution and keeps up by brooding the persistent tangle. It is from something above and outside the perplexities that the solution must come. The difficulty of the physical mind — not the true thinking intelligence — is that it does not want to believe in this larger consciousness outside itself because it is not aware of it; and it remains shut like a box in itself, not admitting the light that is all round it and pressing to get in. It is a subtle law of the action of consciousness that if you stress difficulties — you have to observe them, of course, but not stress them, they will quite sufficiently do that for themselves — the difficulties tend to stick or even increase; on the contrary, if you put your whole stress on faith and aspiration and concentrate steadily on what you aspire to, that will sooner or later tend towards realisation. It is this change of stress, a change in the poise and attitude of the mind, that will be the more helpful process.

As for details, the method of the mind concentrating on details and trying to put them right is a slow and tardy one; it has to be done, but as a subordinate process, not the chief one. If it succeeds at all, it is because after some period of struggle and stress, something is released and there is an opening and the larger consciousness of which I speak gets through and produces some general result. But the progress is much more rapid if one can make the opening the main thing and keep the dealing with details as something resultant and subordinate. When there is this opening, some essential (therefore general) progress can be made and, as you yourself say, "express and translate itself into details". The mind is always trying to handle details and construct out of them some general result; but what is above mind and even the best powers of the higher ranges of mind tend rather to bring about some *essential* change and make it or let it express itself, translate itself in the necessary details.

I may add, however, that one can feel the essential change without its expressing itself in details; e.g., one can feel a wide silent peace or a state of freedom and joy and rest silent and secure in it without needing to translate it into sundry details in order to feel the progress made.

It is not a theory but a constant experience and very tangible when it comes that there is above us, above the consciousness in the physical body, a great supporting extension as it were of peace, light, power, joy — that we can become aware of it, and bring it down into the physical consciousness and that that, at first for a time, afterwards more frequently and for a longer time, in the end for good, can remain and change the whole basis of our daily consciousness. Even before we are aware of it above, we can suddenly feel it coming down and entering into us. The need is to have an aspiration towards it, make the mind quiet so that what we call the opening is rendered possible. A quieted mind (not necessarily motionless or silent, though it is good if one can have that at will) and a persistent aspiration in the heart are the two main keys of the Yoga. Activity of the mind is a much slower process and does not by itself lead to these decisive results. It is the difference between a straight road and an approach through constant circles, spirals or meanders.

*

In your dealing with your difficulties and the wrong movements that assail you, you are probably making the mistake of identifying yourself with them too much and regarding them as part of your own nature. You should rather draw back from them, detach and dissociate yourself from them, regard them as movements of the universal lower imperfect and impure nature, forces that enter into you and try to make you their instrument for their self-expression. By so detaching and dissociating yourself it will be more possible for you to discover and to live more and more in a part of yourself, your inner or your psychic being, which is not attacked or troubled by these movements, finds them foreign to itself and automatically refuses assent to them and feels itself always turned to or in contact with the Divine Forces and the higher planes of consciousness. Find that part of your being and live in it; to be able to do so is the true foundation of the Yoga.

By so standing back it will be easier also for you to find a quiet poise in yourself, behind the surface struggle, from which you can more effectively call in our help to deliver you. The Divine presence, calm, peace, purity, force, light, joy, wideness are above, waiting to descend in you. Find this quietude behind and your mind also will become quieter and through the quiet mind you can call down the descent first of the purity and peace and then of the Divine Force. If you can feel this peace and purity descending into you, you can then call it down again and again till it begins to settle; you will feel too the Force working in you to change the movements and transform the consciousness. In this working you will be aware of the presence and power of the Mother. Once that is done, all the rest will be a question of time and of the progressive evolution in you of your true and divine nature.

*

The statement[2] is a general one and like all general statements subject to qualification according to circumstances. What I meant was to discourage what some do which is to be always dwelling on their difficulties and shortcomings only, for that makes them turn for ever like squirrels in a cage always in the same circle of difficulties without the least breaking of light through the clouds. The sentence would be more accurate or generally applicable if it were written "dwell too much" or "dwell solely". Naturally, without rejection nothing can be done. And in hard periods or moments concentration on the difficulties is inevitable. Also in the early stages one has often to do a great amount of clearance work so that the road can be followed at all.

*

It [*the descent of the sadhana from the mind into the vital*] came by being preoccupied too much with the difficulties of the nature. It is always better to dwell on the good side of things in yourself — I do not mean in an egoistic way, but with faith and cheerful confidence, calling down the positive experience of which the nature is already capable so that a constant positive growth can help in the rejection of all that has to be rejected. But in fact one gets often projected into the vital difficulties at an early stage and then instead of going from the mind into the psychic (through the heart) one has to go through the disturbed vital.

*

It [*retracing one's steps from the vital into the psychic*] can be done, if you refuse to be preoccupied with the idea of your difficulties and concentrate on really helpful and positive things. Be more cheerful and confident. Sex and Doubt and Co. are there,

---

[2] *A statement of Sri Aurobindo which the correspondent wrongly quoted as follows: "It is a mistake to dwell on the lower nature and its obstacles, which is the negative side of the Sadhana.... The positive side of experience of the descent is the more important thing." In transcribing this statement, the correspondent left out two words: Sri Aurobindo wrote "dwell too much", not simply "dwell". — Ed.*

no doubt, but the Divine is there also inside you. Open your eyes and look and look till the veil is rent and you see Him or Her!

*

You are not asked to do anything that you are incapable of; it is something that you have done already and of which, therefore, you are capable — you are not asked to change your nature by your own effort but only to stand back from these ideas and thoughts, refuse to indulge them and remain quiet within and allow the Force you have repeatedly felt to change you. To repeat constantly, "I am weak, I am unfit, I am bad" will lead you nowhere.

Raising Up Difficulties

As to the obstacles, you should not do anything to call them up or increase their intensity or take pleasure in them. If they come of themselves, you have to surrender your being to the Mother and call in the Light and the psychic being to remove them.

*

The method you speak of is, I understand, that of raising up the difficulties in order to know and exhaust or destroy them. It is inevitable once one enters into Yoga that the difficulties should rise up and they go on rising up so long as anything of them is left in the system at all. It may be thought then that it is better to raise them oneself in a mass so as to get the thing done once for all. But though this may succeed in some cases, it is not even in the mental and vital a safe or certain method. Exhaustion, of course, is impossible; the things that create the difficulties are cosmic forces, forces of the cosmic Ignorance, and cannot be exhausted. People talk of their getting exhausted because after a time they lose strength and dwindle, but that is only by force of the constant rejection by the Purusha and by force of a divine intervention aiding this rejection and dissolving or destroying the difficulty each time it shows its face. Even so, the idea of getting rid of difficulties in a lump seldom works; something remains and returns until suddenly there comes a divine intervention which is final or else a change of consciousness which makes the return of the difficulty impossible. Still, in the mental and vital it can be done.

In the physical it is much more dangerous, because here it is the physical adhar itself that is attacked and a too great mass of physical difficulties may destroy or disable or permanently injure. The only thing to do here is to get the physical consciousness (down to the most material parts) open to the Power, then to make it accustomed to respond and obey and to each physical difficulty as it arises, apply or call in the divine Power to throw out the attacking force. The physical nature is a thing of habits; it is out of habit that it responds to the forces of illness; one has to get into it the contrary habit of responding to the Divine Force only. This of course so long as a highest consciousness does not descend to which illness is impossible.

*

It is the old habit of the outer consciousness from which it refuses to be delivered. Until this will to repeat the old movements is thrown away, the Force works but under difficulties and behind instead of taking up the frontal consciousness as it would if the assent of the external nature were there. There is also the old persistent habit of raising up and stressing the difficulties instead of rejecting them — the wrong idea that accepting, approving and insisting on their presence is the only way of getting rid of them. I have told you that that is not the way and only prolongs the struggle.

Struggling with Difficulties

There can be no doubt that you can go through — everyone has these struggles; what is needed to pass through is sincerity and perseverance.

There is no use in inviting these struggles, as many do, or even in accepting them when they come for the sake of fighting them out, for they always repeat themselves. When they cannot

Dealing with Depression and Despondency

be avoided then they must be faced — one cannot be altogether without them, especially in the earlier part of the Yoga; but if you can quietly evade them, that is already an advance. To become quiet and quietly to call back the true psychic state until it becomes normal and either eliminates or minimises the struggle, that is the best way to progress.

*

It is better [*in dealing with the hostile forces*] to proceed by a quiet rejection and growth in consciousness — and not invite battle — though, if a struggle is forced on you, you must meet it with calm and courage.

*

No objection — it is a very good thing to keep working in the higher consciousness. It is more effective than struggling all the time down below with the lower forces.

*

There is no objection to doing the sadhana, but it must be done quietly without this constant struggle and disquietude — not minding if it takes time, not getting into a constant rhythm of struggling against difficulties. That is my point.

*

One must get a knack of remaining quiet and bringing into the quietude the play of the Presence, Force, Light, etc. which is the action of the Sadhana. A struggling effort brings only a minimum result at the price of much confusion and disorder.

*

From your last letter it is clear that it is not your own will that pushes you to go but something that has taken hold of your mind, a clutch of some Force which is using old movements of the outward mind and vital to drive the action. All the more reason to reject this action as contrary to the soul's and heart's true feeling. The pride that says, "I am one of those who can break but will not bend", is a poor thing and conceals the fact that one is bending before forces and impulses that are ignorant and obscure. Its result is, as you yourself have seen at the end of your letter, that one bends to the lower forces of nature but refuses to bend to the Divine.

If sadhana is a struggle between the higher will and the old forces of nature bringing suffering and inner torment, we do not want you to do that kind of sadhana. That is not the spirit of our Yoga. What we want you to do is to recover your quietude and go on in that. To have the basis of quietude and allow the Divine Force to work in you firmly and quietly is always the best method — it is not necessary to proceed through a big personal effort, disturbance and struggle. Come back to this — open yourself once more, as you did before — then you could get back sleep or health in a day or two and were growing inwardly without excessive trouble — and let the Mother's Power and Grace lead you.

I shall do all to help you and pull you out, but that which has closed itself in you must open for the help to work quickly as it did before. Otherwise too it can pull you out, but if there is this strong obstruction that has to be undone, time is needed. A central change of attitude in your mind would, I believe, make all the difference — it has done so before.

*

He can continue his endeavour and let us know if there is any result. The difficulties that have risen in him are quite normal and a natural reaction to the effort he is making. It is usual for these resistances to rise up, for they have to manifest themselves in order that they may be dealt with and thrown out. If he perseveres, that should happen sooner or later. But it is best not to struggle with the resistances but to stand back from them, observe as a witness, reject these movements and call on the Divine Power to remove them. Surrender of the nature is not an easy thing and may take a long time; surrender of the self, if one can do it, is easier and once that is done, that of the nature will come about sooner or later. But for that it is necessary to detach oneself from the action of the Prakriti and see oneself as separate.

That is why I asked whether he had any (major) realisation from his previous sadhana. To observe the movements as a witness without being discouraged or disturbed is the best way to effect the necessary detachment and separation. This also would help to increase the receptivity to any aid that may be given to him and to bring about the reliance, *nirbhara*.

If he turns to us, we will of course give him whatever help he can just now consciously or subconsciously receive.

The Absurdity of Suicide

Suicide is an absurd solution; he is quite mistaken in thinking that it will give him peace. He will only carry his difficulties with him, enter into a more miserable condition of existence beyond and bring them back to another life on earth. The only remedy is to shake off these morbid ideas and face life with a clear will for some definite work to be done as the life's aim and with a quiet and active courage.

*

That is absurd! Dropping the body because of a difficulty does not enable one to come back with a better body. One comes back with the same difficulty to solve.

People do not come here in order to throw off the body. If everybody here dropped his body because of acute difficulties, three quarters of the Asram would be dead by this time.

*

That is not right. Throwing away the life does not improve the chances for the next time. It is in this life and body that one must get things done.

*

Sadhana has to be done in the body, it cannot be done by the soul without the body. When the body drops, the soul goes wandering in other worlds — and finally it comes back to another life and another body. Then all the difficulties it had not solved meet it again in the new life. So what is the use of leaving the body?

Moreover if one throws away the body wilfully, one suffers much in the other worlds, and when one is born again, it is in worse, not in better conditions.

The only sensible thing is to face the difficulties in this life and this body and conquer them.

*

Death is not a way to succeed in sadhana. If you die in that way [*suicide*], you will only have the same difficulties again with probably less favourable circumstances.

The way to succeed in sadhana is to refuse to be discouraged, to aspire simply and sincerely so that the Mother's force may work in you and bring down what is above. No man ever succeeded in this sadhana by his own merit. To become open and plastic to the Mother is the one thing needed.

*

Despair is absurd and talking of suicide quite out of place. However a man may stumble, the Divine Grace will be there so long as he aspires for it and in the end lead him through.

*

If she remains firm and calm and keeps an unshaken faith in the Divine Power, that will carry her through every trial. Suicide is no solution; it only injures the life of the soul and the problems and difficulties one tries to evade by it seize one again in another form in another life.

*

It [*an impulse to commit suicide*] can come from two sources. (1) An old impression in the subconscient, usually from a past suicide in the family or surroundings. (2) An invasion from one of those around you. Many sadhaks have this suggestion and in some it takes the form of a periodic attack. One must never allow the suggestion to stick or in the least entertain it, otherwise it may fasten in the subconscient and give trouble.

*

Dealing with Depression and Despondency

It [*the thought of committing suicide*] seems to me an excessive reaction considering that all that is in question is some habitual movements of the external being which do not affect the inner realisation. These external habits have to be changed, but you can do it quietly without allowing their presence to throw you into despondency and despair. It is best done by detaching yourself from them and calling in the Mother's Force to act there and spread the deeper realisation into the outward parts. Your reasoning about violently getting rid of the body in order to get a better one hereafter is entirely wrong. For when one throws away the present life in that way instead of facing its difficulties one not only gets into blacker difficulties after death but in the next life all becomes not better but worse — an inferior embodiment with all the former difficulty from which you fled renewed with less favourable circumstances. There is no way out there. Instead of indulging such feelings, you should put them away from you and turn to the Mother's Grace which has not failed and which is not going to fail you for strength and succour. Recover your balance and develop the psychic progress you were already making so rapidly up to now.

*

Suicide is the worst way that anyone could take to get out of a spiritual difficulty. It only increases and prolongs the difficulty; for it continues it after death, the struggle, the suffering in an exaggerated form and it has to be faced again in another life. The dissolution of the physical elements into Nature would leave the mind and vital as they are, with all their problems present and unsolved. Surely you are not so ignorant as to think that you will cease to be merely by leaving the body?

When the Mother said that by doing that you would bring trouble to the Asram, it is not merely the entry of the police into the Asram, the inquiry and the immediate local scandal that she meant. It would bring a general discredit on the Asram, the Yoga, myself and my work, arm all the numerous enemies here and outside against me, shake the whole Asram and create a terrible example and perhaps make the fulfilment of my work impossible for some years together. Nothing written by you could prevent that from happening — for it would be the natural, logical and inevitable result and it is what the hostile Influences intend when they put this suggestion into your mind or the mind of others. I write plainly because you must realise what would be the natural consequences of doing what is suggested to you by these Powers in your fits of irrational despair.

In view of what it would mean for yourself and for me and the Divine Work, I ask you to give me your promise never again to yield to this suggestion or contemplate seriously its fulfilment.

I have promised you that, if you keep on, the transformation shall take place and it is not an idle promise that I have made. If once you threw off this Influence, the one that gives you fits like this, the transformation would not only be certain but swift and easy. But in any case, if you keep on aspiring for transformation and not for escape, as you wrote today, the transformation is bound to come.

P. S. I have written in the last paragraph above what I wanted to say in brief. I ask you to react more decisively against the old influence of vital darkness and confusion — to decide firmly not to let it prevail ever again to this extent. It is not even transformation, but a chance that is needed for the true being that is in you, the being of love and radiance and harmony to come out from the clouds in a lasting way. Once it can do that, all trouble would be over.

*

I must remind you of your promise not to yield to sorrow and despair and to face your difficulties with fortitude and patience. Suicide is not only a weak and unmanly evasion, but it is worse than useless since the same misery continues after death intensified in the consciousness which can think of nothing else and one has to come back to earth and face the same difficulties under worse conditions. The Gita has never said that suicide can under any circumstances lead to Nirvana; the death spoken of is a natural or a Yogic death with the mind concentrated with faith and absorption in the Divine. I am sure that Ramakrishna also never meant such a thing as that anyone dying under any circumstances would have his last wish satisfied. There is no escape by that kind of exit. I do not know either how you can say that you love me and at the same time deliberately decide to deal such a blow to me as your suicide would be. I do not speak of X and others to whom you have still some obligations and what it would mean for them. It is also strange that you should think *I* could be willing to receive your property or any money offered at such a price or ask Y to aid in such an arrangement. You must have been very much clouded by your fit of despair not to see that. All that apart, I must press on you not to allow these dark attacks with their morbid suggestions to carry you away. If you have the true yearning for the Divine, as you have undoubtedly in your soul, it is not by yielding to vital weakness that you will show it but by persisting, whatever the time and the difficulties, till it is achieved. You have promised to do that and I again recall you to your promise. Nirvana itself cannot be so achieved, but only by rising above all other desires and attachments until one has the supreme liberation and peace. Ramana Maharshi himself would tell you that and I suppose you can believe him if you cannot believe me.

It is difficult for me to say anything else since you have told me that no words of mine have any truth or value and that all my experiences also are subjective delusions without any truth or value. I suppose all spiritual or inner experiences can be denounced as merely subjective and delusive. But to the spiritual seeker even the smallest inner experience is a thing of value. I stand for the Truth I hold in me and I would still stand for it even if it had no chance whatever of outward fulfilment in this life. I should go on with it even if all here abandoned and repudiated me and denounced it to the world as a delusion and a folly. I have never disguised from myself the difficulties of what I have undertaken, it is not difficulties or the threat of failure that can deter me.

I hope however that you will get over this attack and see things one day as all the past seekers of the Divine have seen it, viz. that what one seeks is so precious and such a supreme thing that a whole lifetime of effort however arduous or painful is not by any means too much to give to it. I say nothing else since you say that words of encouragement from me can have no value for you. But this at least is a thing that is true and that others whose spiritual experience and greatness cannot be disputed would tell you.

If you have the love for me you speak of — I will say nothing of mine for you, since you do not seem to believe much in it — you will listen to what I say and renew and carry out your promise to go through with your quest to the end with patience and courage.

*

To characterise suicide as a willed withdrawal from life is the most astounding statement that would not bear a moment's scrutiny. Suicide is accompanied in most cases by a morbid feeling of disappointment with life, a violent revolt against what is considered the imposition of an unjust providence or an adverse malignant fate. It has nothing of the sense of freedom behind it, no knowledge of the play of forces behind the exterior life, no means of mastering them or using them as stepping-stones to a higher freedom, a greater destiny. The calm poise of the soul, the peace that surpasseth understanding are not his. He is moved by dark forces who hold him completely in their grip. The sense of freedom of which he vaunts is the conjuring trick of the black magician by which he is deluded and dragged to a greater degradation. That is why it is said in the Upanishads that those who slay themselves enter into blind worlds of darkness. A violent exit by suicide is an act of excessive egoism, not of freedom.

The true freedom is found in unity with God and in the abiding sense of immortality, when the soul has risen above the bondage of his lower nature, and from the spirit heights of his being can survey his actions seated in a calm, untouched, unmoved by happenings in Time.

*

Suicide is never the right thing to do, but its psychic consequences can be mitigated by the spirit in which it is done or if some feeling of sacrifice or self-offering enters into it as in the case of the Sati. It is always possible to help departed souls in their passage if one has the necessary psychic feeling towards them and the psychic force to make it effective. Contact can also be maintained so long as this passage does not carry them beyond the borders of the communication possible or into the region of psychic sleep or trance in which they remain within themselves and prepare their new birth in future.

The experiences related are of a high character and show an advanced state of the consciousness. The overhead station especially is not common and is usually attained only after a considerable psychic and spiritual growth. It is always possible indeed to ascend and descend in the consciousness reaching very high in planes above the head but usually one does not stay there.

There are always two things possible for the spiritual seeker, remain among others and then they can act, as she puts it, as a ferment, the other to congregate together and even to form a separate body for a common sadhana or for a common work or both as in this Ashram. Which is to be done depends on the urge of the spirit within or on a call from above.

*

Well, that [*the quietude of death*] is not the right kind of quietude. The peace of Nirvana would have some meaning in it, but death into the quietness of exhausted Prakriti is no release at all.

*

The real rest[3] is in the inner life founded in peace and silence and absence of desire. There is no other rest — for without that the machine goes on whether one is interested in it or not. The inner mukti is the only remedy.

---

[3] *The correspondent expressed a desire for "the long rest that is one's due after death".* — Ed.

Section Three

The Opposition of the Hostile Forces

Chapter One

The Hostile Forces and the Difficulties of Yoga

The Existence of the Hostile Forces

Whenever anything has to be done, there are always forces that want to interfere. I suppose they want to show that smooth walking and the "wide unbarred and thornless path" belong only to the Vedic Ritam satyam brihat and we must get up there — if we can.

*

What occult secret? It is a fact always known to all Yogis and occultists since the beginning of time, in Europe and Africa as in India, that wherever Yoga or Yajna is done, there the hostile forces gather together to stop it by any means. It is known that there is a lower nature and a higher spiritual nature — it is known that they pull different ways and the lower is strongest at first and the higher afterwards. It is known that the hostile forces take advantage of the movements of the lower nature and try to spoil through them, smash or retard the siddhi. It has been said as long ago as the Upanishads, "Hard is this path to tread, sharp like a razor's edge"; it was said later by Christ, "Hard is the way and narrow the gate by which one enters into the kingdom of heaven" and also "Many are called, few chosen" — because of these difficulties. But it has also always been known that those who are sincere and faithful in heart and remain so and those who rely on the Divine will arrive in spite of all difficulties, stumbles or falls.

*

Yes, certainly [*there are hostile forces active in the outside world*]. Men are being constantly invaded by the hostiles and there are great numbers of men who are partly or entirely under their influence. Some are possessed by them, others (a few) are incarnations of hostile beings. At the present moment they are very active all over the earth. Of course in the outside world there is no consciousness such as is developed in Yoga, by which they can either become aware of or consciously repel the attacks — the struggle in them between the psychic and the hostile force goes on mostly behind the veil or so far as it is on the surface is not understood by the mind.

*

Yes, of course, there is always a fight between the forces of Light and Darkness.

In sadhana it becomes concentrated and conscious to us.

As for the hostile beings, they are always in battle with each other; but they make common cause against the Truth and Light.

The Function of the Hostile Forces

The hostile forces have a certain self-chosen function: it is to test the condition of the individual, of the work, of the earth itself and their readiness for the spiritual descent and fulfilment. At every step of the journey, they are there attacking furiously, criticising, suggesting, imposing despondency or inciting to revolt, raising unbelief, amassing difficulties. No doubt, they put a very exaggerated interpretation on the rights given them by their function, making mountains even out of what seems to us a mole-hill. A little trifling false step or mistake and they appear on the road and clap a whole Himalaya as a barrier across it. But this opposition has been permitted from of old not merely as a test or ordeal, but as a compulsion on us to seek a greater strength, a more perfect self-knowledge, an intenser purity and force of aspiration, a faith that nothing can crush, a more powerful descent of the Divine Grace.

*

The purpose they [*the hostile forces*] serve *in the world* is to

The Hostile Forces and the Difficulties of Yoga

give a full chance to the possibilities of the Inconscience and Ignorance — for this world was meant to be a working out of these possibilities with the supramental harmonisation as its eventual outcome. The life, the work developing here in the Asram has to deal with the world problem and had therefore to meet, it could not avoid, the conflict with the working of the hostile Powers in the human being.

*

The hostile forces make it their function to attack and disturb the sadhaks, but if there were no wrong movement and no imperfection and weakness, they would not be disturbed.

*

It happens so with everybody [*that the external nature responds to lower vibrations*] so long as there is not the positive siddhi of transformation by which it becomes contrary to the very nature of the instrument to respond to these vibrations — because they have become foreign to it. Till then all depends on the vigilance of the consciousness and its will. The repetition of the response does not increase the difficulty — it only retards the clearing out of the invading forces.

*

Whatever point the adverse forces choose for attack, however small it may seem to the external human mind, becomes a crucial point and to yield it up may be to yield to them one of the keys of the fortress. Even if it is a small postern door, it is enough for them if they can enter.

Nothing is really small and unimportant in the Great Path. Especially when the struggle has come down to the physical level, these distinctions cease to have any value; for there "small" things have a not easily calculable index value and are of great importance. On that level to lose a small post may be to make certain the loss of the big battle.

All have had to pass through the ordeal and test through which you are passing. We would have avoided it for you if it had been possible, but since it has come we look to you to persist and conquer. Patience, quiet endurance, calm resolution to go through to the end and triumph, these are the qualities now required of you — the less spectacular but more substantial of the warrior virtues.

Also perspicacity and vigilance. Do not shut your eyes to the difficulty in you or turn away from it, but also let it not discourage you. Victory is certain if we persevere and what price of difficulty and endeavour can be too great for such a conquest?

*

Hostile forces attack every sadhak; some are conscious, others are not. Their object is either to influence the person or to use him or to spoil the sadhana or the work or any other motive of the kind. Their object is not to test — but their attack may be used by the guiding Power as a test.

*

Your description [*of recent tests in sadhana*] is too vague. From what you write it may just as well be the reaction that frequently follows an experience; the adverse Force coming in with a contrary movement. Tests come sometimes from the hostile forces, sometimes in the course of Nature. I suppose they must be necessary, since they always come in sadhana.

*

The method of the Divine Manifestation is through calm and harmony, not through a catastrophic upheaval. The latter is the sign of a struggle, generally of conflicting vital forces, but at any rate a struggle on the inferior plane.

You think too much of adverse forces. That kind of preoccupation causes much unnecessary struggle. Fix your mind on the positive side — open to the Mother's power, concentrate on her protection, call for light, calm and peace and purity and growth into the divine consciousness and knowledge.

This idea of tests also is not a healthy idea and ought not

to be pushed too far. Tests are applied not by the Divine but by the forces of the lower planes — mental, vital, physical — and allowed by the Divine because that is part of the soul's training and helps it to know itself, its powers and the limitations it has to outgrow. The Mother is not testing you at every moment, but rather helping you at every moment to rise beyond the necessity of tests and difficulties which belong to the inferior consciousness. To be always conscious of that help will be your best safeguard against all attacks whether of adverse powers or of your own lower nature.

Testing Oneself against the Hostile Forces

If one knows how to profit by experience, even the Hostile Forces and their attacks can be useful — although of course that does not mean that the attacks should be invited. What they do is to press with all their force upon some weak point of our nature and if we are vigilant, we can see and throw away that weakness. Only the attack method of these Forces is too violent and upheaving and endangers the good things in one also, faith and peace etc. — so one has to be careful to keep these against all attacks.

*

There is no use of testing [*one's capacity*] at all — whatever test is needed, comes of itself in the ordinary way in the very use of the capacity and in the very steps of the progress — no other is needed. Beyond that the tests that come are from the hostile forces — but their way of testing is to take advantage of any point of weakness and push with all their force at that point to break down the sadhana or else to hurl all the adverse forces on the consciousness while it is still in process of transition and not yet mature so as to shatter all that has been done. It is not a true test but mere destruction replacing the constructive method. By unnecessary "testing" one dangerously invites this hostile pressure and raises up things which one has to banish. To be conscious is necessary, but quiet self-examination is sufficient for that — raising up difficulties under plan of testing is quite the wrong method.

The Divine Force and the Adverse Force

Do you not know the story of the Elephant Brahman? All is Brahman, but in action you have to treat the elephant as the Elephant Brahman and the Asura as the Asura Brahman and neither as merely Brahman pure and simple. One has either to avoid the Rakshasa or overcome him; otherwise the Rakshasa may eat up the man, all Brahman though both be. The Brahman realisation is an inner static realisation, until one has become the dynamic instrument of the Divine Consciousness and Force — then the problem of the elephant and the Rakshasa won't arise, for the Divine Consciousness will know and the Divine Force will execute what is to be done in each case. There is no need to have *vaira* inside, but to be friendly with the Rakshasa is not prudent, as the Rakshasa is impervious to that kind of thing — he will take advantage of it to farther his own purpose.

*

Your description of the "Golden One" was the description of an Asura — how can that be the Divine? — "efficiently cruel" etc. etc. And, taken in that way, submission to such a Power so conceived would justify a yielding to anything coming with sufficient force from the lower Nature on the ground that it is *He* who is making you do it.

There is a right and discriminating use of the Vedantic Knowledge that all is One and there is a wrong and undiscriminating use. The latter is more dangerous than complete ignorance. Especially at this moment sadhaks must be on their guard against the subtle intrusion of this error (the undiscriminating acceptance of all as coming from the Divine) — for more than one has fallen a victim to it and got badly hurt.

*

Your statement about the Shakti. The mere intensity of the force does not show that it is a bad power; the Divine Force often works with a great intensity. Everything depends on the nature of the force and its working; what does it do, what seems to be its purpose? If it works to purify or open the system, or brings with it light or peace or prepares the change of the thoughts, ideas, feelings, character in the sense of a turning towards a higher consciousness, then it is the right force. If it is dark or obscure, or perturbs the being with rajasic or egoistic suggestions or excites the lower nature, then it is an adverse Force.

The Forces of the Lower Nature and the Hostile Forces

There are [at work in the world] the higher forces of the Divine Nature — the forces of Light, Truth, divine Power, Peace, Ananda — there are the forces of the lower nature which belong either to a lower truth or to ignorance and error — there are also the hostile forces whose whole aim is to maintain the reign of Darkness, Falsehood, Death and Suffering as the law of life.

*

The lower nature is ignorant and undivine, not in itself hostile but shut to the Light and Truth. The hostile forces are anti-divine, not merely undivine; they make use of the lower nature, pervert it, fill it with distorted movements and by that means influence man and even try to enter and possess or at least entirely control him.

Free yourself from all exaggerated self-depreciation and the habit of getting depressed by the sense of sin, difficulty or failure. These feelings do not really help, on the contrary, they are an immense obstacle and hamper the progress. They belong to the religious, not to the Yogic mentality. The Yogin should look on all the defects of the nature as movements of the lower prakriti common to all and reject them calmly, firmly and persistently with full confidence in the Divine Power — without weakness or depression or negligence and without excitement, impatience or violence.

*

No, [*the vital ego is*] certainly not [*a hostile power*] — it is part of the ordinary human nature, everybody has it. It has to be purified and transformed, the ego being replaced by the true vital being of which it is a distorted shadow. The forces of the lower nature are often rebellious and resist transformation out of attachment to the familiar movements of the Ignorance, desire, vanity, pride, lust, self-will etc., but they are not in their nature hostile. The hostile Forces are those whose very raison d'être is revolt against the Divine, against the Light and Truth and enmity to the Divine Work.

*

Normal human defects are one thing — they are the working of the lower nature of the Ignorance. The action of the hostile forces is a special intervention creating violent inner conflicts, abnormal depressions, thoughts and impulses of a kind which can be easily recognised as suggestions, e.g. leaving the Asram, abandoning the Yoga, revolt against the Divine, suggestions of calamity and catastrophe apparently irresistible, irrational impulses and so on. It is a different order from the usual human weaknesses.

*

The defects of the nature are nothing, they can be dealt with progressively. It is these outward attacks, these suggestions and throwing in of wrong forces to which the sadhak must shut himself altogether.

*

To have weaknesses of the lower nature is one thing — to call in the hostile forces is quite another. Whoever does the latter, takes his risk. He is going towards the opposite camp — for the marks of the hostile Force are contempt of the Divine, revolt and hatred against the Mother, disbelief in the Yoga, assertion of ego against the Divine Being, preference of falsehood to Truth, seeking after false gods and rejection of the Eternal.

*

The Hostile Forces and the Difficulties of Yoga

There are some who are never touched by the hostile forces.

The normal resistance of the lower Nature in human beings and the action of the Hostiles are two quite different things. The former is natural and occurs in everybody; the latter is an intervention from the non-human world. But this intervention can come in two forms. (1) They use and press on the lower Nature forces making them resist where they would otherwise be quiescent, making the resistance strong or violent where it would be otherwise slight or moderate, exaggerating its violence when it is violent. There is besides a malignant cleverness, a conscious plan and combination when the Hostiles act on these forces which is not evident in the normal resistance of the forces. (2) They sometimes invade with their own forces. When this happens there is often a temporary possession or at least an irresistible influence which makes the thoughts, feelings, actions of the person abnormal — a black clouding of the brain, a whirl in the vital, all acts as if the person could not help himself and were driven by an overmastering force. On the other hand instead of a possession there may be only a strong influence; there the symptoms are less marked, but it is easy for anyone acquainted with the ways of these forces to see what has happened. Finally it may be only an attack, not possession or influence; the person then is separate, is not overcome, resists.

*

It is difficult to observe the difference between the action of the hostile Force and the pressure of the lower Nature because it is the latter that the Force takes hold of for its purpose. But there is in the Force a suggestive character, a conscious arrangement of the attack so as to upset or destroy the sadhana which there is not in the ordinary movement of the lower Nature — for that only comes to satisfy itself and then ceases. In your case the tactical use of a suggestion, the sudden rush clouding the knowledge, the rhythmic character of the periodic return, the attempt to bring despondency and hopelessness and push to departure — all these are clear signs of the hostile attack. People like X and Y who are moving forward in a leisurely way, are not usually subjected to the hostile pressure. One with an intense and sensitive vital nature is more open; also those who have some vital proclivity in a very developed or exaggerated form e.g. pride, ambition, jealousy, sexuality etc. A complete surrender from the beginning does protect — suggestions may come, but they have no power to develop into a crisis.

*

There is a natural movement of the ordinary human nature in the material consciousness which takes time to get rid of. Of course we call them forces of the lower nature but one must not regard them as hostile, but only ordinary. They have to be changed but it usually takes time and it can be done quietly. One must be more occupied with the positive side of the sadhana than with them. If one is always thinking of them as hostile things, getting disturbed when they come, considering as hostile possessions, then it is not good.

The things that are really hostile are few and must be distinguished from the ordinary movements of the nature. The first must be repelled, the second dealt with quietly and without getting troubled or discouraged by their appearance.

*

They [*certain lower forces*] are not hostile forces, they are simply the forces of the ordinary Nature. The hostile forces are those which try to pervert everything and are in revolt against the Divine and opposed to the Yoga.

*

The forces of the Ignorance are a perversion of the earth-nature and the adverse Powers make use of them. They do not give up their control of men without a struggle.

*

There is a pressure on the forces of the lower nature to change — through that the pressure is felt by the hostiles; but whether they change or are destroyed seems to be left very much to them to choose.

Vital Resistance, Physical Inertia and the Hostile Forces

There are almost always some parts of the being that are either unwilling or feel an incapacity for the effort demanded of them. It is the psychic and the mind and the higher vital usually that join together for the Yoga — for if these three do not join, it is difficult to do any Yoga at all beyond getting a few experiences from time to time. But in the lower vital there is almost always something recalcitrant and there is much of the physical that is too obscure. If the sadhak were left to himself this could be remedied without much difficulty, but it is here that the hostility in the universal (lower) forces comes in — they want to keep their reign over the being. The result is an exacerbation of the resistance of the lower vital and an exaggeration of the obstruction (inertia, passive resistance) in the physical which then admit these suggestions of self-destruction, depression or despair.

*

It is more the lack of sleep that is responsible [*for the physical weakness*], I think; also the excess of struggle which the constant pressure of the vital disturbances and the physical tamas bring in and by that weaken the nerves.

Like the vital disturbance the physical inertia with all its symptoms is an attack of the hostile forces intended to cut short and prevent the higher opening. The ideas that arise to justify it are of no value — it is not true that physical work is of an inferior value to mental culture, it is the arrogance of the intellect that makes the claim. All work done for the Divine is equally divine, manual labour done for the Divine is more divine than mental culture done for one's own development, fame or mental satisfaction.

This inertia, numbness, pain should be thrown off with the same resolution as the vital disturbances. The only peculiarity of it in your case is the persistent violence of the attack as in the case of the vital — otherwise it is what others get also; but each time they reject, call on the Mother and get free, after a little time if the attack is violent, at once if it is of a lesser character.

If there is temporary physical inability, one can take rest, but solely for the purpose of recovering the physical energy. The idea of giving up physical work for mental self-development is a creation of the mental ego.

*

The inertia gives room and power for the hostile forces to act.

The Hostile Forces and Universal Forces

No, they [*the hostile forces*] do not create universal forces; they are themselves moved by them and move them.

The Hostile Forces and the Spiritual Consciousness

From the higher mind upwards, all is free from the action of the hostile forces. For they [*the higher planes*] all belong to the spiritual consciousness though with varying degrees of light and power and completeness.

Chapter Two
Attacks by the Hostile Forces

Attacks Not Uncommon

I do not see how I could say that you were not fit for this Yoga when you had and still get the experiences that are characteristic of the Yoga. The obstacles in the consciousness and the attacks are no proof that a man is not fit for Yoga. There is no one practising Yoga who does not get them. Even those who have become great siddha Yogis had them during their time of sadhana.

There is not only yourself or X who have been touched, but others have been violently affected. The attack has been extremely serious this time — as these attacks always are at the moment when something is about to be effected in the individual or the general consciousness.

*

There are always hostile forces that try to stop or break the experience. If they come in, it is a sign that there is something in the being, vital or physical, that either responds or is too inert to oppose.

*

The hostile forces do not need a cause for attacking — they attack whenever and whoever they can. What one has to see is that nothing responds or admits them.

*

There is always this critical hostile voice in everybody's nature, questioning, reasoning, denying the experience itself, suggesting doubt of oneself and doubt of the Divine. One has to recognise it as the voice of the Adversary trying to prevent the progress and refuse credence to it altogether.

*

It is not a fact that the Rajayogin or others are not attacked by environmental forces. Whether moksha or transformation be the aim, all are attacked — because the vital forces want neither liberation nor transformation. Only the Yogins speak of it in general terms as Rakshasi Maya or the attacks of *kāma, krodha, lobha*, — they don't trace these things to their sources or watch how they come in — but the thing itself is known to all.

*

Naturally, the hostile forces are always on the watch to rob what they can of the things received by the sadhak — not that they profit by them, but they prevent them from being used to build up the divine in life.

Attacks Often Follow a Progress

It often happens like that. When a progress has been made (here it is the opening of the inner vision) the hostiles attack in a fury. You must be especially on your guard when you are making a progress — so as to check the attack before it can get in.

*

It is a fact that the lower forces always attack when they see that a sadhak is making too much progress for their taste. But they can do nothing against a clear and steady will and a faithful perseverance.

*

A progress made often stirs the adverse forces to activity, they want to diminish its effect as much as possible. When you get a decisive experience of this kind, you should remain concentrated and assimilate it — avoiding self-dispersion and all externalising of the consciousness.

*

It is very often after a good experience or a decisive progress that the beings of the vital world try to attack and threaten.

The being who took the form of X was one of these. They have always the hope that they can turn back the sadhak from his path by attacks and menaces.

*

About the attacks and the action of the cosmic forces — these attacks very ordinarily become violent when the progress is becoming rapid and on the way to be definite — especially if they find they cannot carry out an effective aggression into the inner being, they try to shake by outside assaults. One must take it as a trial of strength, a call for gathering all one's capacities of calm and openness to the Light and Power so as to make oneself an instrument for the victory of the Divine over the undivine, of the Light over the darkness in the world tangle. It is in this spirit that you must face these difficulties till the higher things are so confirmed in you that these forces can attack no longer.

*

There is always a struggle going on between the forces of Light and the opposing forces — when there is a true movement and progress the latter try to throw a wrong movement across to stop or delay the progress. Sometimes they do this by raising up old movements in yourself that have still the power to recur; sometimes they use movements or thoughts in the atmosphere, things said by others to disturb the consciousness. When a settled peace and working of the Power and self-giving of the being can be fixed in the physical, then there comes a secure basis — there are no more fluctuations of this kind, though superficial difficulties may continue.

*

That is right [*to remain confident, cheerful and hopeful*]. The rest is the remnant of the attack — such an attack, sudden and violent, as sometimes, indeed often comes when one is making full progress to the straight and open way. It cannot permanently deflect the progress and, when it disappears, there is usually a chance of going on more firmly and swiftly towards the goal.

That is what we must do now.

*

Krishnaprem's letter is admirable from start to finish and every sentence hits the truth with great point and force. He has evidently an accurate knowledge both of the psychological and the occult forces that act in Yoga; all he says is in agreement with my own experience and I concur. His account of the rationale of your present difficulties is quite correct and no other explanation is needed — except what I was writing in my unfinished letter about the descent of the sadhana into the plane of the physical consciousness and that does not disaccord with but only completes what he says. He is quite right in saying that the heaviness of these attacks was due to the fact that you had taken up the sadhana in earnest and were approaching, as one might say, the gates of the Kingdom of Light. That always makes these forces rage and they strain every nerve and use or create every opportunity to turn the sadhak back or, if possible, drive him out of the path altogether by their suggestions, their violent influences and their exploitation of all kinds of incidents that always crop up more and more when these conditions prevail, so that he may not reach the gates. I have written to you more than once alluding to these forces, but I did not press the point because I saw that like most people whose minds have been rationalised by a modern European education you were not inclined to believe in or at least to attach any importance to this knowledge. People nowadays seek the explanation for everything in their ignorant reason, their surface experience and in outside happenings. They do not see the hidden forces and inner causes which were well-known and visualised in the traditional Indian and Yogic knowledge. Of course, these forces find their *point d'appui* in the sadhak himself, in the ignorant parts of his consciousness and its assent to their suggestions and influences; otherwise they could not act or at least could not act with any success. In your case the chief *points d'appui* have been the extreme sensitiveness of the lower vital ego and now also the physical consciousness with all its fixed or standing opinions, prejudices, prejudgments, habitual reactions, personal preferences, clinging to old ideas and associations, its obstinate doubts and its maintaining these things as a wall of obstruction and opposition to the larger light. This activity of the physical mind is what people call intellect and reason, although it is only the turning of a machine in a circle of mental habits and is very different from the true and free reason, the higher Buddhi which is capable of enlightenment and still more from the higher spiritual light or that insight and tact of the psychic consciousness which sees at once what is true and right and distinguishes it from what is wrong and false. This insight you had very constantly whenever you were in a good condition and especially whenever Bhakti became strong in you. When the sadhak comes down into the physical consciousness, leaving the mental and higher vital ranges on which he had first turned towards the Divine, these opposite things become very strong and sticky and, as one's more helpful states and experiences draw back behind the veil and one can hardly realise that one ever had them, it becomes difficult to get out of this condition. The only thing then, as Krishnaprem has told you and I also have insisted, is to stick it out. If once one can get and keep the resolution to refuse to accept the suggestions of these forces, however plausible they may seem, then either quickly or gradually this condition can diminish and will be overpassed and cease. To give up Yoga is no solution; you could not successfully do it as both Krishnaprem and I have told you and as your own mind tells you when it is clear. A temporary absence from the Asram for relief from the struggle is a different matter. I do not think, however, that residence in the Ramana Asram would be eventually helpful except for bringing back some peace of mind; Ramana Maharshi is a great Yogi and his realisation very high on its own line; but it does not seem to me that it is a line which you could successfully follow as you certainly can follow the path of Bhakti if you stick to it, and there might then be the danger of your falling between two stools, losing your own path and not being able to follow the path of another nature.

*

The main obstacle in your sadhana has been a weak part in the vital which does not know how to bear suffering or disappointment or delay or temporary failure. When these things come, it winces away from them, revolts, cries out, makes a scene within, calls in despondency, despair, unbelief, darkness of the mind, denial — begins to think of abandonment of the effort or death as the only way out of its trouble. It is the very opposite of that equanimity, fortitude, self-mastery which is always recommended as the proper attitude of the Yogi. This has been seized upon by the forces adverse to the sadhana with their usual cleverness to prevent you from making the steady and finally decisive progress which would put all the trouble behind you. Their method is very simple. You make the effort and get perhaps some of these experiences which are not decisive but which if continued and followed up may lead to something decisive or at least you begin to have that peace, poise and hopefulness which are the favourable condition for progress — provided they can be kept steady. Immediately they give a blow to that part of the vital — or arrange things so that it shall get a blow or what it thinks to be a blow and sets it in motion with its round of sadness, suffering, outcry and despair. It clouds the mind with its sorrow and then gets that clouded mind to find justifications for its attitude — it has established a fixed formation, a certain round of ideas, arguments, feelings which it always repeats like a mechanism that once set in motion goes its round till it stops or something intervenes to stop it. This justification by the mind gives it strength to assert itself and remain or, when thrown back, to recur. For if these reasonings were not there, you would at once see the situation and disengage yourself from it or at any rate would perceive that such a course of feeling and conduct is not worthy of you and draw back from it at its very inception. But as it is you have to spend days getting out of the phase and getting back into your normal self. Then when you are back to your right walk and stature they wait a little and strike again and the whole thing repeats itself with a mechanical regularity. It takes time, steadfast endeavour, long continued aspiration and a calm perseverance to get anywhere in Yoga; that time you do not give yourself because of these recurrent swingings away from the right attitude. It is not vanity or intellectual questioning that is the real obstacle — they are only impedimenta, — but they could well be overcome or one could pass beyond in spite of them if this part of the vital were not there or were not so strong to intervene. If I have many times urged upon you equanimity, steadfast patience, cheerfulness or whatever is contrary to this spirit, it is because I wanted you to recover your true inner vital self and get rid of this intruder. If you give it rein, it is extremely difficult to get on to anywhere. It must go, — its going is much more urgently required than the going of the intellectual doubt.

How you got to this condition is another matter. When you came it was not apparent and for a long time did not manifest itself. When Mother first saw you in the verandah of the old house she said, "That is a man with a large and strong vital" and it was true, nor do I think it has at all gone, but you have pushed it to the back and it turns up only when you are in good condition. The other, this small vital which is taking so much space now, must have been there but latent, perhaps because you had had a strong and successful life and it had no occasion to be active. But at a certain moment here it began to be impatient for immediate results, to fret at the amount of tapasya or effort to control its habits and indulgences and the absence of immediate return for the trouble. At a later stage it has tried to justify and prolong itself by appealing to your penchant for the Vaishnava attitude. But the emotional outbreaks of the Vaishnava — or such impulses as Vivekananda's *prāyopaveśana* — spring from a tremendous one-minded, one-hearted passion for the Divine or for the goal which tries to throw itself headlong forward at any cost. It was another part of your vital that would have liked to take that attitude, but this smaller part prevented it and brought in a confusion and a mixture which was rather used by the adverse forces to turn you away from belief in or hope of the goal. This confusion of mind and vital you must get rid of — you must call in the true reason and the higher vital to cast out these movements. A higher reason must refuse to listen to its self-justifications and tell it that nothing, however plausible, can justify these motives in a sadhak; your higher vital must refuse to accept them, telling it, "I do not want these alien things; I do not recognise them as part of myself or my nature."

Positive and Negative Means of Attack

The hostiles when they cannot break the Yoga by positive means, by positive temptations or vital outbreaks, are quite willing to do it negatively; first by depression, then by refusal at once of ordinary life and of sadhana.

Attacks through Suggestions

Indirect attacks are not of this kind, a violent rush and covering by hostile forces — they are done through covert suggestions, half-truth, half-falsehood, attempts to represent the falsehood in the garb of the Divine Truth or to mix the lower consciousness cleverly with the higher. Their attempt is to mislead by guile rather than to conquer by force.

*

When the vital forces or beings throw an influence, they give it certain forms of thought-action and put them in the minds and vital of people so that they feel, think, act, speak in a particular way. Whoever opens to the influence acts according to this formation, perhaps with variations due to his own vital temperament.

*

Always refuse your assent to these forces and their suggestions and movements — that is the one imperative rule. It is not that you cannot understand the Truth, you understand the Truth perfectly well — but once you begin listening they confuse your mind, cover up the understanding and then torment you with their false suggestions. Always remain quiet, always open to the help of the Force, always call for the peace.

*

Do not allow these suggestions to prevail. Each time these powers attack, if you hold them at bay, you gain an added force for progress. They attack and suggest to you a wrong understanding in the hope that, if you accept, their power to return on you will last a little longer. Do not allow them to prevail for however short a time.

*

I do not see what reasons can be so subtle as to justify or even appear to justify something that opposes and tries to destroy the sadhana. Whatever stands in the way of spiritual progress, must be a falsehood whatever reasons it gives in its own favour. The best thing is not to listen to its reasons.

*

There is no issue out in such persistence in a wrong mood and a false attitude. It is the old foolish idea that the ignorance is the truth for you because you are still ignorant in your external consciousness and that if the divine Light and Truth are not perfectly established in the ignorance, then the Light and Truth are false and the ignorance is the only truth and that to believe in the Truth and the Divine is a pretence. Nothing can be more irrational than these arguments of the dark Forces to which your external vital so foolishly lends its adherence. The Truth remains the Truth in spite of all denial and it is to that you will have to give your assent and allegiance, not to confusion and darkness.

*

But when the suggestions come, surely it is possible to know from their very character what they are and that itself shows that they must come from wrong vital Forces. The only thing is that they must be at once rejected and the entry into your own mind and vital refused to them — i.e. they must not be accepted or allowed to influence. Very few have the direct occult perception of the Forces behind the suggestion — at least until the cosmic consciousness fully opens, for then direct perception becomes more easily possible, — but the mental understanding can be used with good effect.

*

Vital forces can attack the mind and do. Many receive suggestions from them through the brain, so it is quite possible that it may be felt as coming in through the head from above. That does not mean that it came from regions above the mind (higher Mind, intuition or Overmind). Correct reasoning means no more than coherent argument from a certain standpoint and does not validate a fit of anger or indicate for it a non-adverse source.

*

It [*a vibration of anger which entered the body from behind the shoulder blades*] must have been an indication of the source and location of the suggestion or influence. Either thoughts or vibrations or some pressure of wrong force can be felt being thrown or sent in a very concrete way when the consciousness is open. When it is not, they come in without being noticed, only the result is felt.

*

There has been progress in all these parts [*of the being*], but they seem to be subject still to a response to the suggestions of the hostile forces. Everybody gets these suggestions, but they ought not to be allowed to enter inside, especially in the heart, or to be accepted by the vital. Evidently, they enter through the physical mind (from the throat upwards means that) and affect the surface vital and emotional being. You must get the power to reject them from there by a constant and steady denial and refusal of their suggestions. So long as anything in you says "yes" or accepts, there is always the possibility of a return.

*

These [*thoughts of unfitness for Yoga*] are the usual suggestions that come when there is the attack of the hostile forces. You should know that they have no value and reject. The spiritual perfection, the full transformation of the nature is not a thing that can come without long and steady endeavour. Movements like these have many refuges in different parts of the being and it is not till they are driven out of all and out of the environmental consciousness that one can be free from their recurrence. One must learn to be inflexible, fixed in one's aim and not discouraged by the recurring difficulties of the nature, for they have been long ingrained in the vital and physical of the human being and they are also in the play of the universal forces — so if it takes long to get them out, as it does even with the best sadhaks, that is no proof that one is not fit for the sadhana. Reject all that and go on steadily — aim always at getting more of the higher consciousness down, that is the cure for all these things.

*

What is there in you is the capacity for response to these suggestions [*of unfitness for Yoga*] that still remains owing to the stamp of the past habit on the physical, especially the subconscient physical. I have explained to you what happens — that these things when rejected by the mind and vital descend into the subconscient or else go out into the environmental consciousness and from there they can return when pushed by the hostile forces. It is in these two ways that the hostiles try to recover their hold. But the rising from the subconscient is not so important except for its long persistence — it comes up in dream or it is, in the waking consciousness, fragmentary. But when it comes from the environmental consciousness then it can be a strong attack and it is evidently that which is taking place now.

I think what lends force to these attacks and tends to upset you, is a feeling of impatience somewhere that things are not going forward, progress of a definite kind is not being made and that these things are not done with already for ever. A period of apparent halt is not necessarily an adverse thing, it can be a preparation for a fresh progress of a more decisive character — that often happens in the sadhana — but you have to keep vigilantly the advance gained in spite of attacks. The next progress ought to be the descent of the full spiritual calm and peace from above — an opening of the consciousness into wideness. Till it comes, keep yourself firm and do not allow these attacks to shake your basis.

*

They [*hostile attacks on the outer being*] are felt as suggestions, or a touch on the surface mind, vital, physical or as movements in the atmosphere (the personal or the general environmental consciousness) — but for the inner being it is like gusts or storms outside. If they penetrate by chance into the house, they are immediately ejected and the doors and windows banged on them — there is nothing that accepts or tolerates them inside.

Attacks through Others

All these difficulties [*in dealing with others*] should be faced in a more quiet and less egoistic spirit.

This Yoga is a spiritual battle; its very attempt raises all sorts of adverse forces and one must be ready to face difficulties, sufferings, reverses of all sorts in a calm unflinching spirit.

The difficulties that come are ordeals and tests and if one meets them in the right spirit, one comes out stronger and spiritually purer and greater.

No misfortune can come, the adverse forces cannot touch or be victorious unless there is some defect in oneself, some impurity, weakness or at the very least ignorance. One should then seek out this weakness in oneself and correct it.

When there is an attack from the human instruments of adverse forces, one should try to overcome it not in a spirit of personal hatred or anger or wounded egoism, but with a calm spirit of strength and equanimity and a call to the Divine Force to act. Success or failure lies with the Divine.

In dealing with others there is a way of speaking and doing which gives most offence and opens one most to misunderstanding and there is also a way which is quiet and firm but conciliatory to those who can be conciliated — all who are not absolutely of bad will. It is better to use the latter than the former. No weakness, no arrogance or violence, this should be the spirit.

*

The attack of illness after seeing the woman is very evidently the result of an adverse Force leaping upon you. There are men and women who are the vehicles of these adverse Forces and if you come in contact with them when you are off your guard and have a movement (in this case a sexual movement) which gives them an opportunity for a grip, then some adverse Force can leap upon you and hold, and the attack takes either the form of a mental unsettling, a moral disturbance (loss of character etc.), a vital upheaval or nervous breakdown or, as in this case, a physical illness. These things are well known to all who are acquainted with the working of occult forces and the details in the letter are quite unmistakable signs; such attacks are always happening to people, but most are unconscious and feel only the results but not the movements that attended the attack or their causes. When the consciousness has opened by Yoga one becomes aware and it is easy to fix the source of the attack and its nature. The illness can only be cured for good by the throwing out or the departure of the force that causes it; a certain quiet will has to be exercised or else a calling in of the Yoga-force or the Divine Sanction for the removal; there should be no struggle but a very tranquil pressure. The greater the faith, the easier it is for the action to be successful.

*

Yes, it was an attack — the hostile forces often take the form of this or that person so as to get through the physical associations a more concrete grip on the physical consciousness.

Chapter Three
Dealing with Hostile Attacks

Fear of Attacks

Yes, the adverse forces take advantage of any perturbation of that kind [*mental anxiety and fear when something bad happens*] — for it opens as it were a passage to their action. Fear is the one thing that one must never feel in face of them, for it makes them bold and aggressive. Moreover fear, as you justly say, calls the thing feared — it must therefore be thrown out altogether.

*

If you are afraid of the hostile forces when they try to come, you expose yourself to their power.

Thinking Too Much about Attacks

The worst thing for sadhana is to get into a morbid condition, always thinking of "lower forces, attacks" etc. If the sadhana has stopped for a time, then let it stop, remain quiet, do ordinary things, rest when rest is needed — wait till the physical consciousness is ready. My own sadhana when it was far more advanced than yours used to stop for half a year together. I did not make a fuss about it, but remained quiet till the empty or dull period was over.

*

How can you have peace and quiet when you are always thinking of "lower forces" and "attacks" and "possessions" etc.? If you can look at things naturally and quietly, then only you can have quiet and peace.

*

Dealing with Hostile Attacks

Do not think too much of the hostile Force. The only thing you have to do with it is to dismiss it and even the suggestion of it when it comes.

*

It is quite true. To talk of one's experiences to others tends to diminish the power of the experience. Also to think too much of the hostile Powers is to bring in their atmosphere. One has to recognise them when they come and repel them, but to think much about them, to fear, to be expecting or looking out for them is a mistake.

*

It is so that they [*hostile suggestions*] must be regarded — without interest, with indifference. That removes the necessity for constant struggle which is itself a form of interest, and it is as discouraging and more to these suggestions.

*

It is better not to trouble about the hostile forces. Keep your aspiration strong and sincere and call in the Divine in each thing and at each moment for support and in all that you feel keep yourself open to us. That is the easiest way to the Divine. If you begin to concern yourself about the hostile forces, you will only make the path more difficult.

*

Write to X that if he indulges these ideas about hostile beings etc., it will be a serious hindrance to his sadhana. It only puts him and others around him in undesirably close relations with the adverse vital world and its forces. These beings can have no "important part" to play in the life and sadhana. The only part they can play is to attack and interfere with the sadhana. When that happens, their suggestions and approaches have to be rejected, at once and summarily, and the power of the Mother called on to clear the nature or the atmosphere. But they must not be dwelt upon by the mind or any kind of relation admitted or any imaginations about themselves that they suggest entertained or encouraged.

Discouragement about Attacks

These attacks should not discourage you. There are always moments — so long as there is not the complete basis in the physical when old movements seem to revive. But so long as it is only a rush of an outside force churning up the subconscient and it does not last, it does not at all mean that the progress is not there. We have to deal with all the complexity of the human consciousness in its hidden parts as well as on its surface — and there are layers on layers of the consciousness in which something may lurk of the old reactions, but each conquest makes the control stronger and brings the full purification nearer.

*

You need not be upset about the matter; it is sufficient if you note movements like these and are vigilant that they should find no ground in you again. The cause is probably to be found in the contact with the outside world renewing some possibilities of the old Adam in you. When there is some lowering or diminution of the consciousness or some impairing of it at one place or another, the Adversary — or the Censor — who is always on the watch presses with all his might wherever there is a weak point lying covered from your own view, and suddenly a wrong movement leaps up with unexpected force. Become conscious and cast out the possibility of its renewal, that is all that is to be done.

*

It is certainly the force hostile to the Yoga and the divine realisation upon earth that is acting upon you at the present moment. It is the force (one force and not many) which is here in the Asram and has been going about from one to another. With some as with X, Y and Z it has succeeded; others have cast it from them and have been able to liberate the light of their soul; open in that light to the nearness and constant presence of the Mother, feel her working in them and move forward in a constant spiritual progress. Some are still struggling, but in spite of the bitterness of the struggle have been able to keep faithfully to the divine call that brought them here.

That it is the same hostile force would be shown, even if its presence were not for us visible and palpable, by the fact that the suggestions it makes to the minds of its victims are always the same. Its one master sign is always this impulse to get away from the Asram, away from myself and the Mother, out of this atmosphere, and *at once*. For the force does not want to give time for reflection, for resistance, for the saving Power to be felt and act. Its other signs are doubt; tamasic depression; an exaggerated sense of impurity and unfitness; the idea that the Mother is remote, does not care for one, is not giving what she ought to give, is not divine, with other similar suggestions accompanied by an inability to feel her presence or her help; a feeling that the Yoga is not possible or is not going to be done in this life; the desire to go away and do something in the ordinary world — the thing itself suggested varying according to the personal mind. If it were not this one invariable hostile force acting, there would not be this exact similarity in all the cases. In each case it is the same obscurities thrown on the intelligence, the same subconscious movements of the vital brought to the surface, the same irrational impulses pushing to the same action, — departure, renunciation of the soul's truth, refusal of the Divine Love and the Divine Call.

It is the vital crisis, the test, the ordeal for you as for others — a test and ordeal which we would willingly spare to those who are with us but which they call on themselves by persistence in some wrong line of movement or some falsification of the inner attitude. If you reject entirely the falsehood that this force casts upon the sadhaka, if you remain faithful to the Light that called you here, you conquer and, even if serious difficulties still remain, the final victory is sure and the divine triumph of the soul over the Ignorance and the darkness.

The opportunity for these forces is given when the sadhaka descends in the inevitable course of the sadhana from the mental or higher vital plane to the physical consciousness. Always this is accompanied by a fading of the first deep experiences and a descent to the neutral obscure inertia which is the bedrock of the unredeemed physical nature. It is there that the Light, the Power, the Ananda of the Divine has to descend and transform everything, driving away for ever all obscurity and all inertia and establishing the radiant Energy, the perfect Light and the unchanging Bliss. There and not in the mind or the higher vital is all the difficulty, but there too must be the victory and the foundation of the new world. I do not wish to disguise from you the difficulty of this great and tremendous change or the possibility that you may have a long and hard work before you; but are you really unwilling to face it and take your share in the great work? Will you reject the greatness of this endeavour to follow a mad irrational impulse towards some more exciting work of the hour or the moment for which you have no true call in any part of your nature?

There is no true reason for despondency; in nothing that has passed in you or which you have written do I find any good ground for it. The difficulties you experience are nothing to those that others have felt and yet conquered them, others who were not stronger than you. All that has happened is that by this descent into the physical consciousness, the ordinary external human nature has come to the front with its elementary imperfections and subconscient unsatisfied impulses and it is to these that the contrary force is appealing. The mind and the higher vital have put away from them the ideas and illusions which gave them a sanction and an illusion of legitimacy and even nobility in their satisfaction. But the root of them, their inherent irrational push for satisfaction, has not yet gone — this for instance is the reason for the sexual movements which you have recently felt in sleep or in waking. This was inevitable. All that is needed is for your psychic being to come forward and open you to the direct and real and constant inner contact of myself and the Mother. Hitherto your soul has expressed itself through the mind and its ideals and admirations or through the vital and its higher joys and aspirations; but that is not sufficient to conquer the physical difficulty and enlighten and transform Matter. It is your soul in itself, your psychic being that must come in front, awaken entirely and make the fundamental change. The psychic being will not need the support of intellectual ideas or outer signs and helps. It is that alone that can give you the direct feeling of the Divine, the constant nearness, the inner support and aid. You will not then feel the Mother remote or have any farther doubt about the realisation; for the mind thinks and the vital craves, but the soul feels and knows the Divine.

Cast away from you these movements of doubt, depression and the rest which are no part of your true and higher nature. Reject these suggestions of inability, unfitness and all these irrational movements of an alien force. Remain faithful to the Light of your soul even when it is hidden by clouds. My help and the Mother's will be there working behind even in the moments when you cannot feel it. The one need for you and for all is to be, even in the darkness of the powers of obscurity of the physical consciousness, stubbornly faithful to your soul and to the remembrance of the Divine Call.

Be faithful and you will conquer.

Rejection of Attacks

They [*the vital forces*] come because they were freely permitted in the past — so they want to renew and continue their action. An entire rejection and a complete turning to the Divine are the way to meet them.

*

It is sufficient if you can keep in touch with the Force and reject any strong attack of the confusion. The rest will be done by the Force itself — for no one is really strong enough to change himself, it is the Divine Force called down that does it.

*

This kind of attack is always possible. What one has to have is an inner condition which at once throws them off and a faith in the Mother's power and name which is quite sufficient to dissolve these Rakshasi Maya formations.

*

This state which tries to come upon you and seize is not part of your true self, but a foreign influence. To yield to it and to express it would therefore be not sincerity, but the expression of something false to your true being, something that will grow more and more foreign to you as you progress. Always reject it, when it comes, even if you feel strongly its touch; open in your mind and soul to the Mother, keep your will and faith and you will find it receding. Even if it returns obstinately, be equally and more obstinate against it, firm in rejection — that will discourage and wear it out and finally it will grow weak, a shadow of itself and disappear.

Be true to your true self always — that is the real sincerity. Persist and conquer.

*

You ought to realise that these things [*negative thoughts and feelings*] are attacks which come on you from an adverse Force to which your nature was responsive because of vital desire and the vital ego — what you call selfishness. When it comes, you have to realise that it is an attack and refuse instead of accepting it — and in order to be able to do that you must always discourage desire and selfishness in you and all that comes from them such as jealousy, claim, anger etc. It is no use alleging that there are good reasons for their rising — even if all the alleged reasons were true, they would not justify your indulging them, for in a sadhak nothing can justify that. There is no need to understand — for there is only one thing that it is necessary to understand — that, reason or no reason, desire, selfishness, jealousy, demand, anger have no place in the spiritual life.

If you keep to what you have resolved, then all will be right — and the right knowledge will come not from the mind and its reasonings but from the soul and its true vision of things.

*

You must throw this black poison [*of dissatisfaction and revolt*] out of you at once instead of dallying with it and giving it expression as if it were your own feelings and as if such an attitude could ever be justifiable. It is that weakness in the vital which enables them [*the hostile forces*] to keep up their attack. Instead of allowing the weakness, revive your will and aspiration and love and let them throw out this egoistic darkness.

*

All these things, feelings, suggestions etc. [*depression, wanting to die*], are the workings of an adverse Force which wants to break up the Asram, upset or drive away the workers and prevent the Truth and Light which are descending from having any fruition. There is no truth behind it, it is a Force of the Devil or Falsehood — there is no rational ground for the feelings of despair it suggests, but it throws itself with fury on the mind and vital and tries to possess them, ousting the Truth and the Divine Presence. Even the strongest have felt its attacks. You must understand what it is and, the moment it comes, oppose it with a resolute No. For the more the Truth descends, the more furious this adverse Force becomes. It is making desperate attacks and putting out all its force in the hope of snatching the victory before the full Truth can come down. Remain firm, understand what it is and give it no admission — to reject it, to drive it out of his atmosphere is the greatest help any sadhak can give to the Mother.

*

All naturally in these difficulties has its original roots in the vital and its expectations of all kinds. When one wants to get rid of them, the vital resists and is unwilling to part with them, but this by itself would not be anything more than a work of change, adjustment, rearrangement which might take time but not cause serious conflicts and upheavals. For once the mind and inner will are settled to be rid of these movements, the will of the higher vital would also come into line and the rest which is more obstinate against change because it is a thing of habitual movements, supported on the subconscient and not governed by reason or knowledge, would yet be unable to resist permanently or vehemently the pressure from the higher will of the being. Its force of resistance would diminish and the habitual reactions wear out or fall away. But the prolongation of the difficulty and its acuteness come from the fact that there are Forces in Nature, not personal or individual but universal, which live upon these movements and through them have long controlled the individual nature. These do not want to lose their rule and so when these movements are thrown out, they throw them back on the sadhak in strong waves or with great violence. Or they create in the vital a great depression, discouragement, despair — that is their favourite weapon — because it is losing its former field of desires and has not yet in any continuity something that would replace it, the assured continuous psychic or spiritual condition or experience. To prevent that is the whole effort of these Forces. So they create these upheavals and the vital admits them because of its old habit of response to the lower Forces. At the same time they put in suggestions to the mind so as to make it also accept the disturbance, discouragement and depression. That is what I meant by saying that these are attacks from outside and must be rejected. If they cannot be rejected altogether, yet one must try to keep a part of the mind conscious which will refuse to admit the suggestions or share in the depression and trouble, — which will say firmly, "I know what this is and I know that it will pass and I shall resume my way to the goal which nothing can prevent me from reaching, since my soul's will is and will always be for that." You have to reach the point where you can do that always; then the power of the Forces to disturb will begin to diminish and fall away. Our Force is there with you and will not fail to support and strengthen you. The suggestion that we are indifferent is obviously nothing but a suggestion, intended to help and fortify the depression. As such you should regard it and not accept it as true or as your own thought; for it could not possibly be true. Your success in reaching peace and light is as much our concern as yours and even more so.

*

In your letter you write that you are very tired, restlessness and tamas prevail in the physical, there is a constant struggle more or less intense between the psychic being and the physical nature. Now this was exactly your condition in the last months when you were here. Then you wanted to go because the pressure was too great, because the struggle with the restless and tamasic physical nature and the Asuric influence was too hard and continuous, because you felt very tired and needed to go away for a rest, for respite, to recover.

How then can you come back in the same condition? The pressure will be still greater than before, the struggle constant; you are likely to be still more tired and depressed than you were. And it will be harder for you to bear because the personal position will entirely be changed. You will have no special place, no authority delegated, no work entrusted to you; you will not be near the Mother but at a distance among the others. The Asuric nature in you which had become an intolerable hindrance to the work and dangerous to yourself and to others will be given no kind of indulgence. It is clear that you would find the conditions unbearable unless you had undergone in the meantime a fundamental change. Therefore you must not ask to come here until you have acquired a stable quiet and peace both within you and in your external atmosphere.

Wherever you are, we shall always be near to your psychic being and ready to help it to conquer. As things are with you now, that help is likely to act better at a distance than when you were near and were at every moment repelling it by your wrong inner movements and reactions and your wrong speech and acts. But to profit by our help you will have to do what you have never yet really done, at least in your external being. You will have in your physical nature itself resolutely to turn from the Asura and his ways and refuse to indulge him on any pretext in any thought, feeling, speech or action which would help him still to possess your instruments and determine or influence your attitude and your acts. To become quiet and quietly and simply to maintain this persistent and patient rejection with our help, without rajasic struggle, sincerely and in fact and in every detail, not merely in wish and idea, is what you need to do. To be divided, to aspire in one part of your being and to indulge and justify and cherish the wrong movements with another part can lead to nothing but endless struggle and fatigue. Only by this turn and change will the struggle and fatigue pass away and purity come.

*

Either to reject by dynamic means[1] or to remain unaffected and let it pass are the two usual ways of dealing with these attacks.

Detachment

Yes, the difficulty is always that something in the nature gives a hold to the attack. It either still indulges it and likes it or even, if wanting to be free, is too accustomed to receive and respond to the old feelings, thoughts, suggestions and does not yet know how *not* to respond. The first thing is for the mental being to stand back, refuse to accept, say "This is no longer mine." Then, even if the vital feeling responds to the attack, one part of the nature can be free and observe and discourage it. The next thing is for this free part to impose the same will of detachment on the vital so that after a time this also when the attack comes feels that it is something foreign, not its own, — as if a stranger had come into the room and was trying to impose his ideas or his will on the inmates. After that it becomes more easy to get rid of it altogether. Of course, there is the Mother's Force working, but this kind of assent from the mind and vital makes the result quick and easy — otherwise it takes time and more labour and struggle.

Dissolution

You can dissolve a thought formation which is made of subtle mental stuff — why not then a mental Asura? There are Asuras

---

[1] *In his letter the correspondent mentioned "a dynamic will and aspiration". — Ed.*

who are *predominantly* mental — who live in the false Idea and can even be vitally ascetic and appear to men as great Tapaswis. All the same there is a stern and violent vital as the effective instrument of their nature.

Steadiness and Persistence

The one thing wrong [*when attacked by hostile forces*] would be to allow yourself to be overcome by them. If you remain steady in yourself, you can repel the attack or else it will exhaust itself and pass. In such circumstances you have to be like a cliff attacked by a stormy sea but never submerged by it.

*

Very glad to know that you are able to keep up your wicket so well. These bodyline attacks are always a nasty trick of the retiring hostiles and they go on with it as long as they just can, for they are unrelenting and obstinate even in defeat; but one has only to be as stiff to them as possible and their action will get more and more tired until it stops altogether.

*

They [*the hostile forces*] hope by persistence to tire you out or to get in by sheer obstinacy — or at least to delay the realisation by their attacks. That is always their method. If they can shake the faith, the peace and *samatā*, they think themselves richly recompensed.

Peace and Purity

If you can feel even in these attacks that part in you in which there is constant Peace even amidst the pains and darkness, and if you can keep it always, that is an immense gain. The something in you which does not always feel it, which remains half way, undecided, must also now take the step of complete surrender. It is only a part of your physical mind that does not understand, that receives back the old ideas — that must be converted. It does not matter about the weakness and incapacities — when the full peace and Power is there in the physical, they will be removed. The new birth in you is certain to come — the first touch of it is already there in the awakened psychic — the rest cannot fail to come.

*

Vital purity is very necessary, but it is not easy to make it immune from attack unless the wideness is there along with a solid *spiritual* purity and peace descending in the wideness. Of course, wideness *by itself* is not sufficient.

Faith and Surrender

If the faith and surrender are complete in all parts of the being then there can be no attack. If there is a strong central faith and surrender at all times, then there can be attacks but the attacks will have no chance of success.

*

There are no sadhaks who are never attacked by wrong forces — but if one has a complete faith and self-consecration, one can throw off the attack without too much difficulty.

*

It is those who are of a highly sattwic nature, especially if strongly surrendered to the Mother, who escape the invasion or attacks of the hostile Forces on the mind and vital. That does not mean that they escape the difficulties of the lower human nature or of the sadhana, but these are not complicated by the effective support given to them by the hostiles. It is not that there is no point in them that might be pressed upon by the hostiles but in actual fact they cannot get at these points because of the build of the nature which is fortified against them owing to the large proportion of *prakāśa* and *sukha* which the sattwic brings with it. But otherwise there is an internal clarity, a balance, a happy composition in the being reflecting sunlight easily, less amenable to the touch of cloud and tempest, which gives no handle to the hostile forces. The nature refuses to be violently agitated or darkened or upset. At most it is the body that the hostiles can attack and there too because the nervous being is calm and it is only through the most material that it can be done.

Psychic Openness

The experience you write of in today's letter shows clearly the only way of safety against these attacks, to get back to the close and happy connection, the psychic openness to the Mother which has been so long the foundation of your sadhana and the cause of the great progress you were making.

Do not listen to the clamour of the adverse vital Force which has been attacking you, its reasonings or its wrong emotional suggestions — it only wants you to fall from happiness, to suffer and to descend into a lower consciousness and lose your progress.

Get back into the true spirit of love and closeness, surrender and confidence and Ananda and remain there — then in due time all problems and difficulties will solve themselves as the light and power of the Truth descend into the still weak and obscure parts of the nature.

*

If the attacks of the hostile forces have been made less strong by concentrating in the heart (or if they have become less frequent) then you must continue that concentration until you are able to join the head and the heart, the psychic and the higher consciousness. It all depends on that. The psychic must be strong enough to compel the vital and physical to give themselves to the Divine — or the higher consciousness must so descend and occupy everything that the old movements can only at most move on the surface without being able to enter in or touch the inner calm — or the two together, psychic and higher consciousness, must occupy the whole being. These are the three ways in which the Yoga moves. If the concentration in the heart, which means the awakening of the psychic, is most effective against the attacks, then it is that you must follow.

*

There are two things that make it impossible for them [*the hostile forces*] to succeed even temporarily in any attack on the mind or the vital — first, an entire love, devotion and confidence that nothing can shake, secondly, a calm and equality in the vital as well as in the mind which has become the fundamental character of the inner nature. Suggestions then may still come, things go wrong outside, but the being remains invulnerable. Either of these two things is sufficient in itself — and in proportion as they grow, even the existence of the hostile forces becomes less and less of a phenomenon of the inner life — though they may still be there in the outer atmosphere.

Reliance on the Power or Force

About the contact with the world and the hostile forces, that is of course always one of the sadhak's chief difficulties, but to transform the world and the hostile powers is too big a task and the personal transformation cannot wait for it. What has to be done is to come to live in the Power that these things, these disturbing elements cannot penetrate, or, if they penetrate, cannot disturb, and to be so purified and strengthened by it that there is in oneself no response to anything hostile. If there is a protecting envelopment, an inner purifying descent and, as a result, a settling of the higher consciousness in the inner being and finally, its substitution even in the most external outwardly active parts in place of the old ignorant consciousness, then the world and the hostile forces will no longer matter — for one's own soul at least; for there is a larger work not personal in which of course they will have to be dealt with; but that need not be a main preoccupation at the present stage.

*

Yes, the Power with its help and inner working is always there with you and always will be. In the strongest attacks and darkest hours it was covered up and hidden, but it was never absent or withdrawn and never will be.

*

Evil forces can always attack in moments of unconsciousness or half-consciousness or through the subconscient or external physical — so long as all is not supramentally transformed. Only if the force is there, they can at once be pushed back.

Reliance on the Mother

Attacks are always going about and it is a period when they have fallen on many. But with a strong faith founded in the Mother and a whole-hearted aspiration, no attack can leave any lasting result.

*

When there is an attack or obstruction the call or the thinking of the Mother may not succeed at once; even the will to get rid of the attack or obstruction may not succeed at once, but one must persevere till the result comes and if one perseveres the result is bound to come.

One sees the negative side only during the attack, because the first thing the attack or obstruction does is to try to cloud the mind's intelligence. If it cannot do that, it is difficult for it to prevail altogether for the time being. For if the mind remains alert and clings to the truth, then the attack can only upheave the vital and, though this may be painful enough, yet the right attitude of the mind acts as a corrective and makes it easier to recover the balance and the true condition of the vital comes back more quickly. If the vital keeps its balance, then the attack touches the physical consciousness only with its suggestions and is much more superficial or even it can do no more than create a temporary restlessness, uneasiness or ill-health in the body — the rest of the consciousness remaining unaffected. It is therefore very important to accustom oneself to keep the right mental attitude even in the midst of an attack, however strong it is. To keep faith is the best help for that — the faith that the Divine is there always and I shall pass to Him through whatever trials. That helps to look at other things also in the true light.

By tamasic ego is meant the ego of weakness, self-depreciation, despondency, unbelief. The rajasic ego is puffed up with pride and self-esteem or stubbornly asserts itself at every step or else wherever it can; the tamasic ego on the contrary is always feeling, "I am weak, I am miserable, I have no capacity, I am not loved or chosen by the Divine, I am so bad and incapable — what can the Divine do for me?" or else, "I am specially chosen out for misfortune and suffering, all are preferred to me, all are progressing, I only am left behind, all abandons me, I have nothing before me but flight, death or disaster" etc., etc., or something or all of these things mixed together. Sometimes the rajasic and tamasic ahankar mix together and subtly support each other. In both cases it is the "I" that is making a row about itself and clouding the true vision. The true spiritual or psychic vision is this, "Whatever I may be, my soul is a child of the Divine and must reach the Divine sooner or later. I am imperfect but seek after the perfection of the Divine in me and that not I but the Divine Grace will bring about; if I keep to that, the Divine Grace itself will do all." The "I" has to take its proper place here as a small portion and instrument of the Divine, something that is nothing without the Divine but with the Grace can be everything that the Divine wishes it to be.

The Mother's help is always there but you are not conscious of it except when the psychic is active and the consciousness not clouded. The coming of suggestions is not a proof that the help is not there. Suggestions come to all, even to the greatest sadhaks or to the Avatars — as they came to Christ or Buddha. Obstacles are there — they are part of Nature and they have to be overcome. What has to be attained is not to accept the suggestions, not to admit them as the truth or as one's own thoughts, to see them for what they are and keep oneself separate. Obstacles have to be looked at as something wrong in the machinery of human nature which has to be changed — they should not be regarded as sins or wrongdoings which make one despair of oneself and of the sadhana.

*

You ask whether the adverse Force is stronger than the Divine Force. The implication is that a man has no responsibility for his action and whatever he does or however he errs and falls in consequence, the Divine Force is to blame. It may be so, but in that case there is no need or utility in doing sadhana. One has only to sit still and let the adverse Force or the Divine Force do what they like! According to that theory the Devil was quite right in telling Christ, "Cast thyself down from this mountain and let His angels come and upbear thee" and Christ was quite wrong in rejecting the suggestion and saying, "It is written 'Thou shalt not tempt (put to a test) the Lord thy God.'" He ought to have jumped and if he got smashed, it would only have proved that the adverse forces were greater than the Divine Force!

If an adverse Force comes, one has not to accept and welcome its suggestions, but to turn to the Mother and refuse to turn away from her. Whether one can open or not, one has to be loyal and faithful. Loyalty and fidelity are not qualities for which one has to do Yoga; they are very simple things which any man or woman who aspires to the Truth ought to be able to accomplish.

It is what everybody should realise. It is the psychic fidelity that brings the power to stand against the Asuras and enables the Protection to work.

Chapter Four
Accidents, Possession, Madness

Accidents

There is no such thing as a mere accident. There is some — perhaps a very slight — unconsciousness in the physical and it is taken advantage of by these small beings of the vital physical plane — who are more mischievous than consciously hostile.

*

It is not a bad shakti that gets inside you and from there does these things — it is small forces from outside that amuse themselves by creating small accidents of that kind, taking advantage of some inattention or forgetfulness etc.

*

You are right about the accidents. It is chiefly the physical mind's unconsciousness that makes these accidents or interventions of mischievous forces easy.

*

It has often been seen that when an accident takes place at a particular spot, there is a tendency for some time for other accidents to happen there. It was so with a place near Villianur some years ago. There is the same tendency with suicides at a particular place. It is a sort of powerful formation that remains there with or without a vital being (spirit) in charge of the formation.

*

It sometimes happens that by a carefully formed formation like this and through the instrumentality of a third person whose movements they control, the hostile forces get through the conscious guard and bring about an accident like this.[1] It is through

---

[1] *The correspondent was cycling down the road when an approaching cyclist collided with him; he fell to the ground and injured his legs.* — Ed.

the subconscient that they manage to do it, for the subconscient has not yet either the mass of force descended from above which could have repelled the arriving cycle and turned its movement away or the instinctive sureness which would have felt beforehand what the cyclist was going to do and done just the thing to avoid it. However when the protection is there such accidents even when grave in character are usually reduced to something minor in their results.

*

That is right. These accidents happen only to disturb you. You must not allow yourself to be disturbed.

Yes — it is because they [*the hostile forces*] know that Peace is the basis and if that is there in full, all the rest will come. So they want anyhow to prevent it.

Possession by Vital Forces

It is one thing to see things and quite another to let them enter into you. One has to experience many things, to see and observe, to bring them into the field of the consciousness and know what they are. But there is no reason why you should allow them to enter into you and possess you. It is only the Divine or what comes from the Divine that can be admitted to enter you.

To say that all light is good is as if you said that all water is good — or even that all clear or transparent water is good: it would not be true. One must see what is the nature of the light or where it comes from or what is in it, before one can say that it is the true Light. False lights exist and misleading lustres, lower lights too that belong to the being's inferior reaches. One must therefore be on one's guard and distinguish; the true discrimination has to come by growth of the psychic feeling and a purified mind and experience.

*

The first attempt of the possessing entity is to separate the person from his psychic, and it is that that creates the struggle. All depends on the extent and persistence of the possession — how much of the being it occupies and whether it is constant or not.

*

That is very interesting — for it agrees with the Mother's constant insistence that to feel sympathy or any emotion of the weak philanthropic kind with those possessed by vital forces is most dangerous as it may bring an attack upon oneself which may take any form. One must do what is to be done but abstain from all such weakness.

Neurasthenia

It is not, certainly, your own vital that engenders these movements, but its revolts seem to have made it subject to the suggestions of a hostile force from outside. If the suggestions had been confined to mental thoughts, that would have been normal, but it seems to have taken power enough to hold your mind and to push you to action. That means either an acute state of neurasthenia due to some wrong movements (the sexual habit you speak of, if you have been indulging, that would explain it) or a vital inability to bear the pressure of a spiritual struggle. The Asuric idea of self-destruction or of a solution through violence on yourself is entirely false and a suggestion of the hostile force, as are too the imaginations against the Mother. If the neurasthenic condition has gone so far or if there is so acute a vital inability to bear the pressure of your inner struggle, the one immediate remedy would be a rest and relief from the struggle. A change of air and surroundings, the restoration of contact with ordinary life and the cessation of a constant preoccupation with your difficulties would seem to be urgent and imperative. An appeasement of the nervous system is needed and, at the moment, this seems to be the only way. I am not suggesting a permanent departure or giving up of the spiritual endeavour. It is quiet and repose that you need, a temporary relief and release from the inner struggle. It is better to do this than to go on in the condition you describe in your letter. Consider what I have written and reply to me in the morning, so that something may be immediately decided; for the sooner you get the relief you need from these suggestions and their nervous pressure, the better.

*

Neurasthenia in the sense it is now given is not nervous debility — that is an antiquated definition. Nervous debility is a special thing, an illness of the physical nervous; — neurasthenia proper is a weakness of the vital nervous. One may be as strong as a bull and hardy as an evergreen, yet have neurasthenia. Its mark is depression, gloom, reiteration of melancholy slogans, broodings on darkness, death, despair. The bull indulges in a sorrowful lowing; the evergreen moans, "Sunshine? sunshine? it is a fable — there is only cloud, mist, rain and tears!" That's neurasthenia! Of course there are other and more exaggerated forms, but those are not in question. One can get rid of this kind, if the will is determined to do so.

*

If you want to get back your faith and keep it, you must first quiet your mind and make it open and obedient to the Mother's force. If you have an excited mind at the mercy of every influence and impulse, you will remain a field of conflicting and contrary forces and cannot progress. You will begin to listen to your own ignorance instead of the Mother's knowledge and your faith will naturally disappear and you will get into a wrong condition and a wrong attitude.

Your ailment is evidently in its foundation an illness of the nerves, not an ordinary physical disease. These maladies are a creation of the pressure of hostile forces; they increase if anything in you assents to them and accepts, and the more the mind gives value to them and dwells on them, the more they grow. The only way is to remain quiet, dissociate yourself and refuse to accept it or make much of it, allow the calm and strength that the Mother has been putting around you to enter your mind and permeate your nervous system. To do otherwise is to place yourself on the side of the hostile forces that are afflicting you. The cure may take time because your nervous system has been long subjected to these influences and, when they are evicted, they return with violence to re-establish their hold. But if you can acquire and keep patience and fortitude and the right consciousness and right attitude with regard to these things, the hold they have will progressively disappear.

There are defects in your vital nature which stand in the way of a settled spiritual progress: but they can be eliminated if, dropping all exaggerated ideas of "sin" and unfitness, you look quietly at them and recognise and reject them. Tranquillise in yourself all over-eager demands and desires, all excitement and exaggeration of opposite feelings and impulses; seek first intensity of devotion but also calm strength, purity and peace. Allow a quiet and steady will to progress to be settled in you; learn the habit of a silent, persistent and thorough assimilation of what the Mother puts into you. This is the sound way to advance.

Hysteria

The attacks you speak of can come anywhere. It is an attack of the nervous centres and on the nervous being by contrary vital forces. The fact that it was not allowing you to come here and that it began to go when you steeped yourself in the atmosphere and ideas of *The Yoga and Its Objects* is significant of its origin. As for the other symptoms they were amassing to a height of the restlessness of the nervous being and are quite familiar in such cases. The desire to run away somewhere is a very usual symptom. Hysteria is also an attack by similar forces; but it is only one form; the attack need not take the appearance of any illness. The Doctors usually consider it as a type of what they call neurasthenia, nerve-weakness; but that simply locates the thing without explaining its real nature and cause. In both cases, here and there, it was an attempt to come across your spiritual life by creating a disability and state of disturbance in the vital-physical part of the being. Anyhow the fact that you could not go from here and that the whole thing could be removed by us at once as soon as you opened somewhere by this feeling of sorrow at going shows that the spiritual life is stronger deep within you, even when covered over, than the opposite forces at their height. That is the main thing.

*

In these cases of hysteria usually nothing is gained by humouring or indulgence — firmness generally pays better, because most often there is something there that wants to be interesting and get sympathy and have a fuss made over the person. As for cure, that is a different matter, the subjective cause has to be got rid of and it is not easy.

Epilepsy

It is epilepsy. I had surmised from the beginning — the first attack and fall; but the acute condition must have been developed by the shock of the fall on the head — otherwise it might have taken a longer time to develop.

Epilepsy is itself a sign of vital attack, even if there is a physical cause for it — the attacking force not being able to disturb the mental and vital (proper) falls on the body and uses some physical cause (latent or growing) for the base of its action. For everything manifested in the physical must have a physical support or means for its expression.

*

I don't think — I know it is so [*that epilepsy and insanity are due to the influence of evil spirits*]. Epilepsy however is not possession — it is an attack or at most a temporary seizure. Insanity always indicates possession. The hereditary conditions create a predisposition. It is not possible for a vital Force or Being to invade or take possession unless there are doors open for it to enter. The door may be a vital consent or affinity or a physical defect in the being.

Madness

Insanity is always due to a vital attack, or rather possession although there is often a physical reason as well. Hysteria is due to a pressure from the vital world and there may be momentary possessions also. The same thing cannot be said of ordinary delirium, the cause of which is physical only — except in so far as all illness is an attack of lower forces of Nature, but these lower forces are not vital beings or what we call specifically hostile forces. They are simply performing their role in nature and of course there may be and probably is a being of some kind presiding over each kind of illness — in Bengal they give a special name to some of them and worship them as goddesses to avert the visitation. But as I say these are really Forces, not vital hostiles.

As for the interest of vital beings in possessing men — beings of the vital world are not constituted like men — they take a delight in struggle and suffering and disorder — it is their natural atmosphere. They want besides to get the taste of the physical world without being under the obligation of taking on birth and developing the psychic being and evolving towards the Divine. They wish to remain what they are and yet amuse themselves with the physical world and physical body.

*

Loss of balance produces disorder in the consciousness and the adverse forces use that loss of balance for attacking and wholly upsetting the system and doing their work. That is why people become hysterical or mad or filled with the desire to die or go away.

*

More easily [*a loss of balance*] occurs in the women than in the men but in some of the latter also. What produces the loss of balance is an inability to control the vital movements by the reason and an instability of the vital itself so that it sways from one feeling to another, one impulse to another without harmony or order.

*

Loss of mental balance is due to exaggerated ego, exaggerated sex, acceptance of a hostile force etc.

*

I may observe that X does not seem to me to be mad — there is no sign of a dislocation of the thinking mind due to lesion or accident or illness. What there is is a fixed idea and what is called *folie de persécution*, but that is not due to insanity — people have it who have otherwise an acute and perfectly well-ordered intelligence. X from his photograph appears to have had a mediumistic element in him and to have by some ill-chance entered into contact with powers of the vital plane which were able to put their suggestions in him — in that part of the consciousness which we call the vital mind — so that he is unable to ascertain things in their proper light and is tormented by the suggestions that have driven their furrows there in the form of habitual ideas that tyrannise over him and which he is unable to embrace or refuse. Unfortunately this is a malady of the consciousness, which it is very difficult to cure because the patient himself gives no assistance, as he clings to his fixed idea and even when the influence is taken away, calls it back upon him. Certainly he could be told from here that he is not mad and is not cursed of God — but that of itself might not be sufficient to cure him.

*

Usually there is some predisposition [*to madness*] behind, hereditary, natal (due to some circumstances of birth) or founded in insufficient nervous balance. Often there is in the vital excessive ambition, lust or some other violent Ripu. But these though they might distort or break the sadhana by opening it to undesirable Forces could not bring madness (megalomania, erotic mania, or what is called religious mania) — only if there is some taint or want of nervous balance. Anxiety or excessive stress of meditation would not bring it either except by acting upon some such predisposing weakness. In some cases possession by beings of the vital worlds without any such predisposing cause may be possible, but that will be more easily curable. There are however cases of people who break down their nervous balance by wrong practices — there the madness has nothing really to do with the sadhana.

*

It is quite impossible for the descent of the Divine Grace to produce nausea and nervousness and a general disturbance like that — to think so is self-contradictory and foolish. Sometimes when one has pulled or strained, there is a headache or sensation as if of headache or if one pulls down too much force, then there may be a giddiness but one has only to remain quiet and that sets itself right by an assimilation of what has come down or otherwise. There is never any adverse or troublesome after-consequence. What seems to have happened is that X's finding the Force he had called down much more than what he was accustomed to, got nervous and went from nervousness into a panic — with the result of an upsetting of his stomach and circulation. If it is not that, then it must have been an attack of illness which he associated with the descent, but the attack seems to be of a nervous character. Probably if he had had the experience of this increased descent some time ago, he would not have been frightened and nothing would have happened, but the madness of Y following on the death of Z has created a panic and at the least thing each person thinks he is going to go mad or die. As nothing upsets the organism more than fear, they create by this general atmosphere of panic danger where there was none.

The idea that Y was sent mad by a descent of Divine Force is an absurdity and an irrational superstition. People go mad because they have a physical predisposition due either to heredity (as in the case of Y and A) or to some kind of organic cause or secret illness, like syphilis gone to the head or colon bacillus similarly misdirected or brain lesion or other material cause, the action being often brought up by some psychological factor (ambition turning to megalomania, hypochondria, melancholia etc.) or on the contrary itself bringing these to the surface. All that happens in ordinary life and not only in Yoga; the same causes work here. The one thing is that there may be an invasion of an alien Force bringing about the upsetting, but it is not the Divine Force, it is a vital Force that invades. The Divine Force cannot by its descent be the cause of madness any more than it can be of apoplexy or any other physical illness. If there is no predisposition one may have all kinds of attacks from vital or other forces or from one's own movements of the lower nature, as violent as possible, but there will be no madness.

*

As to X's collapse, I did not intend to say anything about it just now, — for mental discussion of causes and consequences is not of much help at this juncture. I must say however that it is not the push for union with the Divine nor is it the Divine Force that leads to madness — it is the way in which people themselves act with regard to their claim for these things. To be more precise, I have never known a case of collapse in Yoga — as opposed to mere difficulty or negative failure, — a case of dramatic disaster in which there was not one of three causes, or more than one of the three at work. First, some sexual aberration — I am not speaking of mere sexuality which can be very strong in the nature without leading to collapse — or an attempt to sexualise spiritual experience on an animal or gross material basis; second, an exaggerated ambition, pride or vanity trying to seize on spiritual force or experience and turn it to one's own glorification — ending in megalomania; third, an unbalanced vital and a weak nervous system apt to follow its own imaginations and unruled impulses without any true mental will or strong vital will to steady or restrain it, and so at the mercy of the imaginations and suggestions of the adverse vital world when carried over the border into the intermediate zone of which I spoke in a recent message.[2] All the cases of collapse in this Asram have been due to these three causes — to the first two mostly. Only three or

---

[2] *This message is reproduced in* Letters on Yoga — III, *volume 30 of* THE COMPLETE WORKS OF SRI AUROBINDO, *pp. 296–303.* — Ed.

four of them have ended in madness — and in these the sexual aberration was invariably present; usually a violent fall from the Way is the consequence. X's is no exception to the rule. It is not because she pushed for union with the Divine that she went mad, but because she misused what came down for a mystic sexuality and the satisfaction of megalomaniac pride, in spite of my repeated and insistent warnings. For the moment that is all the light I can give on the matter — naturally I generalise and avoid details.

*

Those who fall into insanity have lost the true touch and got into the wrong contact. It is due either to some impurity and unspiritual desire with which the seeker enters into the way or some insincerity, egoism and false attitude or to some weakness in the brain or nervous system which cannot bear the Power it has called down into it.

The safest way is to follow the guidance of someone who has himself attained to mastery in the path. Only that guidance should be implicitly and sincerely followed; one's own mind and its ideas and fancies must not be allowed to interfere. It goes without saying that it must be a true guidance, not the leading of a tyro or an impostor.

*

I am not aware that anyone who has made a true surrender [*to his Guru*], loses his balance. Those who allow ego to come in naturally may, whether they follow a Guru as most Yogis have done, or try to go on their own individual strength.

Note on the Texts

Note on the Texts

LETTERS ON YOGA — IV, the last of four volumes, contains letters in which Sri Aurobindo speaks about the transformation of human nature that is attempted in the practice of his system of Yoga. The letters have been arranged in four parts dealing with these broad subject areas:

1. Sadhana on the Level of the Mind
2. Sadhana on the Level of the Vital
3. Sadhana on the Physical, Subconscient and Inconscient Levels
4. Difficulties in the Practice of the Integral Yoga

The letters in this volume have been selected from the extensive correspondence Sri Aurobindo carried on with his disciples and others between 1927 and 1950. Letters from this corpus appear in seven volumes of THE COMPLETE WORKS OF SRI AUROBINDO: *Letters on Poetry and Art* (Volume 27), *Letters on Yoga* (Volumes 28–31), *The Mother with Letters on the Mother* (Volume 32), and *Letters on Himself and the Ashram* (Volume 35). The titles of these works specify the nature of the letters included in the volumes, but there is some overlap. For example, a number of letters in the present volume are also published in *Letters on Himself and the Ashram*. Another volume, *Autobiographical Notes and Other Writings of Historical Interest* (Volume 36), contains letters written by Sri Aurobindo before 1927, as well as some written after that date, mainly to persons living outside the Ashram.

The Writing of the Letters

Between 1927 and 1950, Sri Aurobindo replied to hundreds of correspondents in tens of thousands of letters, some of them many pages in length, others only a few words long. Most of his replies, however, were sent to just a few dozen disciples, almost all of them resident members of his Ashram; of these disciples, about a dozen received more than half the replies. Sri Aurobindo wrote most of these letters between 1931 and 1937, the prime period of his correspondence. Letters before and after this period were written on a more restricted scale and confined to a few persons for special reasons.

Disciples in the Ashram wrote to Sri Aurobindo on loose sheets or sent him the notebooks in which they kept diaries as a record of their spiritual endeavour and as a means of communicating with him. These notebooks and loose sheets reached Sri Aurobindo via an internal "post" once or twice a day. Letters from outside which his secretary thought he might like to see were sent at the same time. Correspondents wrote in English if they knew the language well enough, but a good number wrote in Bengali, Gujarati, Hindi or French, all of which Sri Aurobindo read fluently, or in other languages that were translated into English for him. The disciples usually addressed their letters to the Mother, since Sri Aurobindo had asked them to do so, but most assumed that he would answer them. He generally replied in the notebook or on the sheets sent by the correspondent, writing beneath the correspondent's remarks or in the margin or between the lines; sometimes, however, he wrote his reply on a separate sheet of paper. In some cases he had his secretary prepare a typed copy of his letter, which he revised before it was sent. For correspondents living outside the Ashram, Sri Aurobindo sometimes addressed his reply not to the correspondent but to his secretary, who quoted, paraphrased or translated the reply and signed the letter himself. In these indirect replies, Sri Aurobindo often referred to himself in the third person.

While going through Sri Aurobindo's letters, the reader should keep in mind that each letter was written to a specific person at a specific time, in specific circumstances and for a specific purpose. The subjects taken up arose in regard to the needs of the person. Sri Aurobindo varied the style and tone of his replies according to his relationship with the correspondent; to those with whom he was close, he sometimes employed humour, irony and even sarcasm.

Although written to specific recipients, these letters contain much of general interest, which justifies their inclusion in a volume destined for the general public. For the reasons mentioned above, however, the advice in them does not always apply equally to everyone. Aware of this, Sri Aurobindo himself made some cautionary remarks about the proper use of his letters:

> I should like to say, in passing, that it is not always safe to apply practically to oneself what has been written for another. Each sadhak is a case by himself and one cannot always or often take a mental rule and apply it rigidly to all who are practising the Yoga.
>
> The tendency to take what I lay down for one and apply it without discrimination to another is responsible for much misunderstanding. A general statement, too, true in itself, cannot be applied to everyone alike or applied now and immediately without consideration of condition or circumstance or person or time.
>
> It is not a fact that all I write is meant equally for everybody. That assumes that everybody is alike and there is no difference between sadhak and sadhak. If it were so everybody would advance alike and have the same experiences and take the same time to progress by the same steps and stages. It is not so at all.[1]

The Typing and Revision of the Letters

Most of the shorter items in this volume, and many of the longer ones, were not typed or revised during Sri Aurobindo's lifetime and are reproduced here directly from his handwritten manuscripts. A good number of the letters, however, as mentioned above, were typed for Sri Aurobindo and revised by him before sending. Other letters were typed by the recipients for their own use or for circulation within the Ashram. At first, circulation of the letters was restricted to members of the Ashram and others whom Sri Aurobindo had accepted as disciples. When these letters were circulated, personal references were removed. Persons mentioned by Sri Aurobindo were indicated by their initials or

---

[1] First and third passages: *Letters on Himself and the Ashram*, volume 35 of THE COMPLETE WORKS OF SRI AUROBINDO, pp. 473 and 475. Second passage: *The Mother with Letters on the Mother*, volume 32, p. 349.

by the letters X, Y, Z, etc. Copies of these typed letters were kept by Sri Aurobindo's secretary and sometimes presented to Sri Aurobindo for revision before publication. These typed copies sometimes contained errors, most of which were corrected by him while revising.

Sri Aurobindo's revision sometimes amounted merely to making minor changes here and there, sometimes to a complete rewriting of the letter. He generally removed personal references if this had not already been done by the typist. When necessary, he also rewrote the openings or other parts of the replies in order to free them from dependence on the correspondent's question. As a result, some of these letters have an impersonal tone and read more like brief essays than personal communications.

The Publication of the Letters

Around 1933, Sri Aurobindo's secretary Nolini Kanta Gupta began to compile selections from the growing body of letters in order to publish them. During Sri Aurobindo's lifetime, four small books of letters were published: *The Riddle of This World* (1933), *Lights on Yoga* (1935), *Bases of Yoga* (1936) and *More Lights on Yoga* (1948). Sri Aurobindo revised the typescripts of most of the letters in these books. During this revision, he continued the process of removing personal references. A letter he wrote in August 1937 alludes to his approach to the revision:

> I had no idea of the book being published as a collection of personal letters — if that were done, they would have to be published whole as such without a word of alteration. I understood the book was meant like the others [*i.e., like Bases of Yoga, etc.*] where only what was helpful for an understanding of things Yogic was kept with necessary alterations and modifications.... With that idea I have been not only omitting but recasting and adding freely. Otherwise as a book it would be too scrappy and random for public interest. In the other books things too personal were omitted — it seems to me the same rule must hold here — except very sparingly where unavoidable.

A number of letters not included in the four books mentioned above were published in the mid and late 1940s in several journals associated with the Ashram: *Sri Aurobindo Circle*, *Sri Aurobindo Mandir Annual*, *The Advent* and *Mother India*. Many letters in these journals were revised by Sri Aurobindo before publication.

By the mid-1940s a significant body of letters had been collected, typed and revised. In 1945 plans were made, with Sri Aurobindo's approval, to publish a collection of his letters. The work of compiling and editing these letters was done under his guidance. At that time, many typed or printed copies of letters, some revised, some not, were presented to Sri Aurobindo for approval or revision. The resulting material was arranged and published in a four-volume series entitled *Letters of Sri Aurobindo*. Series One appeared in 1947, Series Two and Three in 1949 and Series Four in 1951. The first, second and fourth series contained letters on Yoga, the third letters on poetry and literature. In 1958, most of these letters on Yoga, along with many additional ones, were published under the titles *On Yoga II: Tome One* and *On Yoga II: Tome Two*, as Volumes VI and VII of the Sri Aurobindo International University Centre collection. The first tome, with further additions, was reissued in 1969. In 1970 a new edition of the letters was published under the title *Letters on Yoga*; this edition contained many new letters not included in *On Yoga II*. The three volumes of the enlarged edition constituted volumes 22, 23 and 24 of the Sri Aurobindo Birth Centenary Library.

The present edition, also titled *Letters on Yoga*, incorporates most of the Centenary Library letters, but also contains a large number of letters that have come to light in the four decades between the two editions. One source of new letters is the correspondences of several disciples which were published in books after the Centenary Library edition had been issued. Govindbhai Patel's correspondence was published in 1974 in a book entitled *My Pilgrimage to the Spirit*; an enlarged edition appeared in 1977. Nagin Doshi's correspondence, *Guidance from Sri Aurobindo: Letters to a Young Disciple*, was brought out in three volumes in 1974, 1976 and 1987. *Nirodbaran's Correspondence with Sri Aurobindo* came out in two volumes in 1983 and 1984. Sahana Devi's correspondence came out in 1985 in a book entitled *At the Feet of Sri Aurobindo and the Mother*. Prithwi Singh's correspondence came out in 1988 as *Sri Aurobindo and the Mother to Prithwi Singh*. Dilip Kumar Roy's correspondence was issued in four volumes in 2003, 2005, 2007 and 2011 under the title *Sri Aurobindo to Dilip*. A second source of new material is individual letters and small collections of letters published in Ashram journals and elsewhere after the Centenary Library had been issued. A third source is letters transcribed from manuscripts or from early typed copies. Many unpublished letters were discovered while reviewing correspondences long held by the Ashram; some of these had never been assessed to find letters for publication; others had been assessed, but relatively few letters were selected at the time. Additional letters were received by the Ashram upon the passing away of disciples. From the three sources mentioned above, many letters have been found that are worthy of publication. The present edition contains about one-third more letters than appear in the Centenary Library.

The Selection, Arrangement and Editing of the Letters

In compiling the present edition, all known manuscripts, typed copies or photographic copies of manuscripts and printed texts of letters were checked. From these sources, letters that seemed to be of general interest were selected. Electronic texts of the letters were then made and carefully checked at least twice against the handwritten, typed, photocopied, and printed versions of the texts.

The selected letters have been arranged according to subject and placed in the four volumes of the present edition. Each volume is divided and subdivided into parts, sections, chapters and groups with descriptive headings; each group, the lowest unit of division, contains one or more letters devoted to the specific subject of the group.

The present volume consists of 2147 separate items, an "item" being defined as what is published between one heading or asterisk and another heading or asterisk. Many items correspond exactly to individual letters; a good number, however, contain only part of the individual letters; a small number consist of two or more letters (or parts of them) that were joined together by early typists or editors and then revised in that form by Sri Aurobindo.

Whenever possible, the letters are reproduced to their full extent.

In some cases, however, portions of the letters have been omitted because they are not of general interest. A number of letters, for example, begin with personal remarks by Sri Aurobindo unrelated to the more substantial remarks which follow; these personal openings have often been removed. In some letters, Sri Aurobindo marked the transition from one part of a letter to another with a phrase such as "As to"; these transitional phrases have often been retained and stand at the beginning of abbreviated letters — that is, letters in which the first part of the letter has been omitted or placed elsewhere.

A number of letters, or portions of them, have been published in more than one volume of THE COMPLETE WORKS OF SRI AUROBINDO. Most of this doubling of letters occurs between *Letters on Yoga* and *Letters on Himself and the Ashram*. The form of these letters is not always the same in both places. In *Letters on Himself and the Ashram*, the manuscript version of a given letter has often been used because it contains Sri Aurobindo's remarks on himself or the Mother or members of the Ashram. These personal remarks, as noted above, were usually removed by Sri Aurobindo when he revised the letter for publication as a letter on Yoga. This revised form of the letter has generally been reproduced in *Letters on Yoga*. Thus, a number of letters are available both in their original form and their revised form.

As in previous collections of Sri Aurobindo's letters, the names of Ashram members and others have often been replaced by the letters X, Y, Z, etc. In any given letter, X stands for the first name replaced, Y for the second, Z for the third, A for the fourth, and so on. An X in a given letter has no necessary relation to an X in another letter. Names of Ashram members to whom Sri Aurobindo referred not as sadhaks but as holders of a certain position — notably Nolini Kanta Gupta in his position as Sri Aurobindo's secretary — are given in full. Sometimes the names of people who played a role in the history of the period are also given.

In his letters Sri Aurobindo sometimes wrote Sanskrit words in the devanagari script; these words have been transliterated into roman script in this edition. Words in Bengali script have likewise been transliterated. This policy is in accord with the practice followed in Sri Aurobindo's lifetime.

The reader may note that Sri Aurobindo almost always spelled the word "Asram" without an "h" in his manuscripts. Around 1945, due to failing eyesight, he began dictating most of his writings to his amanuensis Nirodbaran; Nirodbaran sometimes spelled the word without an "h", sometimes with one. In the present edition, the word is always spelled as it occurs in the manuscripts, both those of Sri Aurobindo and of Nirodbaran. In headings and other editorial matter, the spelling "Ashram" has been used, since this is now the official spelling of the Sri Aurobindo Ashram.

Index

INDEX

A

Abhiman (*abhimāna*), 245, 248
Abstention, from particular foods in the absence of acute illness, 557
Accidents, 800–1
Activity, mental, *see* Mind, active; Mind, activity of
Adverse force(s),
  and the Divine Force, 762–63
Affection(s),
  and friendship, 294–98
  is psychic in its nature, 284
  tamasic, rajasic, sattwic, 296
Agitation,
  stops the action of the Force, 579
Agnosticism, 414–15
Ahankara, 225, 231, *see also* Ego; Egoism; Egocentricity
Allopathy, 582–83
All-strength,
  must be relied on, 454
Aloofness, 325–26
Alternation, of good and bad vital conditions, 148–49
Ambition, 239
Amour-propre, 152–53, 243
Analysis, 25–26
Ananda,
  and the lower vital, 165–68
  should not be let out in speech / action or turned into outward vital joy, 134
  true, 121
Anger, 348–49
  comes from outside, 271–74
  and illness, 571
  nature of, 267–71
  opens the door to hostile forces, 267
  and the psychic, 274
  righteous, 660
    and hostile powers, 276
Animals,
  have much intelligence, 15–16
Anthroposophy, 483

Anubhava, 614–15
Anutāp, 188
Apsaras, and the Tapaswis, 489
Arrest, periods of, 664–65
Asana,
  of the old Rishis, 197–98
Ascent, of the Being, 387
Ashram (Sri Aurobindo Ashram),
  leaving the Ashram, 411, 738
  of very imperfect sadhaks, 288
Aspiration,
  in the lower vital, 168–69
  need of, 713–15
  and will to change, 646
Asura, 762
  dissolution of, 792–93
Attachment, 233
  to food, 421
  freedom from, 254
  overcoming, 316–17
Attacks,
  by hostile forces, *see* Attacks by hostile forces
  vital, followed by clearance of the inner atmosphere, 132
Attacks by hostile forces,
  and detachment, 792
  discouragement about, 784–87
  and faith and surrender, 794–95
  fear of, 782
  not uncommon, 769–70
  often follow a progress, 770–76
  and peace and purity, 793–94
  by positive and negative means, 776
  and psychic openness, 795–96
  rejection of, 787–92
  and reliance on the Mother, 797–99
  and reliance on the Power or Force, 796–97
  steadiness and persistence in dealing with, 793
  thinking too much about, 782–84
  through others, 780–81
  through suggestions, 776–80

Attitude,
　right, 220
　sentimental lachrymose, 698
Aura, 569
Auto-suggestion, 559–61

B

Baby monkey and baby cat, 729
Being,
　ascent of, 387
　nervous, *see* Nervous being
Bergson, Henri, 471*(fn)*
Betel, 435
Bilwamangal, 202
Body consciousness, 379
Body (the), 379–81
　care for, 381
　forgetfulness of, 383
　only an incident in the progress of the soul, 379
　sense of being the receptacle of a higher consciousness, 379
　weakness of, 381–83
Brahmacharya, 526
　theory of, 504–8
Brooding, 350, 384
Brunton, Paul, 494
Buddha, 714–15
Buddhism, Japanese, 202

C

Calm(ness),
　in the lower vital, 169
　and true perceptions, 7
　Cf. Peace; Quiet; Silence
Cancer, 586
Celibacy, 542–43
Chaitanya, 425
Change, time needed for, 726–30
Chat,
　about others, 82
　for chat's sake, 81
Cheerfulness, 173–74, 194
Chilli, 434
Christianity,
　idea of Divine Darkness, 681
Circumstances, 644
　created by what we have within us, 255
　facing, 697–99
　outward, and personal defects, 653–54

Civilisation, nature of, 464
Clashes, 347–50
Classification, and science, 16
Cold (head cold), 587–88
Collapse in Yoga, three causes of, 809
Common sense, 74
Comparison with others, 244
Concentration,
　before and after sleep, 450–51
　and physical illness, 34
Concern for others, 320–21
Conditions, external, often imposed at first as a kind of ordeal, 124
Consciousness,
　body consciousness, 379
　dispersion of, 81–82
　Divine, *see* Divine Consciousness
　Earth-consciousness, 222
　environmental, *see* Environmental consciousness
　higher, *see* Higher consciousness
　material, 378, 598
　physical, *see* Physical consciousness
Consecration, vital, 113
Constipation, 589
Contact with others, 337–38
Contentment, and happiness, 175–76
Control,
　mental, temporary diminution of, 124
　spiritual, replacing mental tapasya, 384
Conversion, of the vital, 110–11
Cooperation,
　with the Divine Power, 32
Copulation (love-making), 336, 498–99
Coué, Émile, 559–61
Creation, supramental, 161–62
Criticism, 87–88, 351–52
　benefiting from, 352–53
Crow parliament, 16
Cruelty, 276
Cure,
　by faith and confidence, 561–62
　by Yogic force and by medicines, 578–80

D

Danger, of a steep fall, 674–75
Dark Forces, 682
Darkness,
　of night before dawn, 619
　periods of, 32

Index

Das, C.R., 17
Death, fear of, 415
Debate, 16
Deceptiveness, of the vital, 104–5
Defect(s),
  cardinal, 150
  personal, and outward circumstances, 653–54
Demand, 258–60
Dependence, overcoming, 315–16
Depression, 183–206
  of another person, effect of, 186
  dealing with, 186–88
  and the gospel of sorrow, 189–206
  and illness, 567–68
  often comes from outside, 185–86
  in sleep, 452–54
Descent, of the sadhana into the Inconscient, 617–19
Desire,
  for food, two ways of conquering, 420
  getting rid of, 260–64
  nature of, 251–56
  and need, 257–58
  and suppression, 264–66
Despair / despondency, 206–9
  nothing more futile, 201
  over difficulties, 734–38
Detachment,
  inner, and outer withdrawal, 338–39
Development, mental, 59–60, 61
Difficulties,
  and the aim of life, 625–27
  despondency over, 734–38
  detaching oneself from, 705–7
  do not always rise up in the beginning, 629–30
  dwelling on one's, 739–43
  and the Integral Yoga, 627–34
  mental, *see* Mental difficulties
  no proof of incompetence, 130
  as opportunities, 212, 692–94
  pain and suffering, 670–74
  periods of difficulty and arrest, 663–66
  raising up, 743–44
  the real difficulty, 388–89
  stating one's, 703–5
  struggling with, 744–47
  ways of dealing with, 696–97
  why they come, 635–37
Discipline,
  meaning of, 107

of the vital, 107–9
Discouragement, 182–83, 408–12
Dislike or disgust for others, 346–47
Disobedience, 153
Dispersion,
  through contact with others, 323–25
Dissatisfaction,
  feelings of, 222–23
  vital, 138–40
Dissection, 25–26
Dissimulation, 153–54
Dissolution,
  of a mental Asura, 792–93
Disturbance, vital, 140–41
Divine (the),
  complete knowledge of can change material things, 415
  his difficulties can be overcome, 634
  knows better than we can know, 5
  and the laws of this world, 32
Divine Consciousness,
  and knowledge, 49
  and the mind, 5
Divine Force (Power),
  and the Adverse Force, 762–63
  often works with a great intensity, 763
  and personal effort, 722–23
  and the will, 720
Divine Help, 724
Divine Protection, 724–25
Divine Will,
  being an instrument of, 142
Doctors, role of, 581–82
Dreams, 411
  all sleep full of, 455
  different kinds of, 455–59
  double character / texture of, 479–84
  of flying, 461–62
  and knowledge of the secrets of our nature and of other-nature, 458
  meaning of some dreams, 477–84
  meeting attacks in, 477
  memory of, 480–81
  mental, 469
  people seen in, 470
  of physical relatives, 463
  of prevision, 457
  railway journey, 482
  remembering, 473–75
  snake, 472
  subconscious, 459–60
  symbolic, on the vital plane, 463–65

telling others, 476
as tests, 458, 489
understanding the meaning of, 475–77
vital, 460–63
   formations in, 466–67
   unpleasant or bad, 467–69
See also Dream ...
Dream-experiences, 471–73
Dream state, and waking state, 470–71
Dress, as aid to "sex-appeal", 536
Dryness, vital, 134–36
Duty, 291–92

E

Earth-consciousness, 222
Education, in India, 71
Effort, personal,
   and the Divine Force or Power, 722–23
Ego, 217–43 *passim*
   in different parts of the being, 221
   getting rid of, 232–38 *passim*
   magnified, 231
   tamasic and rajasic, 225–28, 798
   vital, 222–25
   See also Ahankara; Egoism;
      Egocentricity; Selfishness
Egocentricity, 228–30, *see also* Ego
Egoism, 218, 225
   getting rid of, 232, 234
   of the instrument, 230–32
   See also Ego
Einstein, Albert, 15
Elephant Brahman, 762
Emissions,
   and sex-dreams, 529–31
Emotional man,
   and intellectual man, 18–19
Envelope,
   nervous, *see* Nervous envelope
Environmental consciousness,
   and hostile attacks, 779
   meaning of, 516, 606
   and the subconscient, 601–2
Epilepsy, 805
Equality, cultivating, 312–13
Evil persona, 648
Expansiveness, vital, 326–28
Expression,
   and language, 76–77
   power of, 76–79
   spoken and written, 77
   verbal, 76
Externalisation, 406–7

F

Faith, and cure of illness, 561–62
Falls and failures, 674–77
Falsity of speech, 153–54
Family ties, 291–92
Fasting, 430–33
Fatigue, physical, 399
Fault-finding, 351–52
Fear,
   of attacks by hostile forces, 782
   of death, 415
   and illness, 568–69
   and Yoga, 278–80
Feeling,
   of being driven or compelled, 405
   of dissatisfaction, 222–23
   of incapacity, 408–12
   wounded, 247–50
Feet, must be sure of their ground before the head can hope to kiss the skies, 213
Fever, 587
Fiasco, no sanction to a new edition of the old, 150–51
Fitness / unfitness,
   for (this) Yoga, 108, 412
   not a question of fitness but of acceptance of the Grace, 412
Food,
   attachment to, 421
   fasting, 430–33
   greed for, 422–24
   hunger, 426–27
   intoxicants, 435–36
   quantity of, 427–30
   taste, 424–25
   types of, 433–35
   yogic attitude towards, 419–21, 437–38
Force (the),
   divine, *see* Divine Force (Power)
   letting it work, 724
Forces,
   dark, 682
   helpful, opening to, 453
   vital, *see* Vital forces
Ford, Henry, 15
Forgetfulness of the body, 383
Freedom, from the past, 730–32

Freud, Sigmund, 612–13
Friendship and affection, 294–98

G

Germs (bacilli, viruses), 568–69
Giddiness, 400
  can be produced by pulling down too much force, 552, 808
Gita (the Bhagavad Gita), 32, 201, 277, 406, 632, 687
  (paraphrased) quotations from, 367, 432, 437, 628, 681, 685
Glaucoma, 588
Goodwill, cultivating, 312–13
Gospel of sorrow, 189–206
Gossip, 88–89, 352
Greed, for food, 422–24
Greek (the), and the Roman, 210
Growing taller, 590
Guru, 692, 704
  must be patient, 685

H

Habits,
  old, 401–5
  and the subconscient, 600–1
Happiness, and contentment, 175–76
Hatred, 346
Headache(s), 144, 629, 808
  from pulling down too much force, 552
  impression of, 407
Heart, has intuitions as well, 7
Heat, bearing, 590–91
Help,
  Divine, 724
  helping others, 317–20
  receiving from others, 320
Helplessness,
  idea of, 388, 390
Henry IV of France, 280
Higher consciousness,
  and the vital, 116–20
Homeopathy, 583–84
Homo intellectualis, 18
Homo psychicus, 18
Hostile forces,
  attacks by, *see* Attacks by hostile forces
  existence of, 757–58
  and the forces of the lower nature, 763–66

function of, 758–61
  and illness, 553–55
  and spiritual consciousness, 768
  testing oneself against, 761–62
  and universal forces, 768
Human being,
  dual nature of, 639–47
  multipersonality of, 646
  See also Humanity, Man
Human mind,
  not really conscious of itself, 351
Human nature, obstacles of, 638–39
Humanity,
  has made little progress in the last three thousand years, 101
  See also Human being; Man
Humour, 174
Hunger, 426–27
Hunger-strike, 431
Hypocrisy, 92
Hysteria, 804–5

I

Idea, and what lies behind, 47–48
Identification, with the part that has to undergo change, 366
Ignorance, and knowledge, 48–49
Illness, 385
  accepting and enjoying, 565–67
  and anger, 571
  and concentration, 34
  and curative auto-suggestion, 559–61
  and depression, 567–68
  faith, confidence, and cure, 561–62
  and fear, 568–69
  immunity from, 559, 564
  and inertia, 570–71
  and lower nature and hostile forces, 553–55
  not the result of the Force, 552–53
  and parts of the being, 562–65
  recurrence at fixed times, 555
  and sleep, 572
  suggestion of, 555–59
  taking precautions, 568
  and work, 571–72
  and Yoga, 549–52
  See also specific illnesses (Cancer *etc.*) and other physical problems (Constipation *etc.*)
Imaginations, 21–22

Immunity (from illness), 559, 564
Imperfections, and progress towards perfection, 655–63
Impotence, 542
Inability, plea of, 370
Incapacity, feeling of, 408–12
Inconscient (the),
　descent of the sadhana into, 617–19
Indecision, 213–14
India, education in, 71
Indifference, to what others say, 313–15
Indiscipline, 153
Indulgence, purposive, 614
Inertia, 391–95
　dealing with, 395–97
　difficulty of eliminating, 397–99
　and illness, 570–71
　physical,
　　and the hostile forces, 767–68
　tamasic, and the sex-impulse, 522
　See also Tamas
Influenza, 587
Ingratitude, 250
Injections, 582
Inner life,
　and outer speech, 80–81
Insanity, 805, see also Madness
Inspiration, and the mind, 7
Instability, 213–14
Instrument, of the Divine Will, 142
Integral Yoga,
　decisive ordeal of, 150–56
　does not approve of sorrow and suffering, 177
　the main difficulty in, 158
　not for our own sake but for the sake of the Divine, 161–62
　and psycho-analysis, 612–16
　See also Yoga; cf. Sadhana
Intellect,
　and intelligence, 15–17
　and knowledge, 14
　limitations of, 11–14
　needs an inner light as much as the vital, 13
　and the pure reason, 14–15
　to be transformed into higher mind, 11
　See also Intelligence; Mind; Reason
Intellectual man,
　and emotional man, 18–19
Intelligence, 15–16
　of animals, 15
　a quality of the mind, 70
　See also Intellect; Mind; Reason
Interchange, vital, 328–34
Interest in outward things, 31, 59
Intoxicants, 435–36
Intuition,
　and the mind, 6–7
　and the vital, 120
Irrationality of the vital, 103
Isolation (being too much shut up in oneself), 84

J

Jealousy, 244–47
Joy, and sorrow, 177

K

Karma,
　from past lives, 670, 683
　machinery of, 610
Knowledge,
　book knowledge, 70
　and the Divine Consciousness, 49
　has a marvellous healing power, 212
　and ignorance, 48–49
　and the intellect, 14
　mental,
　　of little use, 49
　　and knowledge from above, 49–50
　　and mental questions, 50–52
　　and mental silence, 54–56
　　and the psychic, 53–54
　　and thought, 48
Krishnaprem, 204, 682, 772–73

L

Languages, study of, 71–72
Lawrence, D.H., 493
Laws of this world, and the Divine, 32
Laxity, 214
Lele, Vishnu Bhaskar, 44
Lesson of life, 625
Letter writing, and vital interchange, 334
Liberation, of the vital, 111
Life,
　always has a meaning so long as it is turned towards the Divine, 188
　inner, see Inner life
Life-force, 106, 116–18

Living within, meaning of, 167
Logic,
  least common-sense-like thing, 74
  study of, 74
Loneliness, 310–11
Lotus, significance not to be found in the mud but in the heavenly archetype, 616
Love,
  between human beings, 284
  dynamic versus static, 305
  for others and for the Divine, 290–91
  mental, vital and physical, 492–93
  psychic in its nature, 284
  universal, and personal relations, 304–6
  vital, 298–302
    and psychic, 301–2
  what men call by that name, 265
Lower nature,
  forces of, and the hostile forces, 763–66
  and illness, 553–55
  and the mind, 9–10
Lower vital,
  and Ananda, 165–68
  aspiration and offering in, 168–69
  avoiding premature engagement with, 164–65
  not reasonable, 156–57
  peace and calm in, 169
  rejecting wrong movements of, 158–64
  resistance of, 157–58
Lust, 490–91
Lying, 91

M

Madness, 806–10, see also Insanity
Madura bhāva, 496, 502
Man,
  intellectual and emotional, 18–19
  made up of different personalities, 27
  See also Human being; Humanity
Marriage, 310, 543–45
Masturbation, 531–34
Mauna, 92–94
Maya, overmind, see Overmind Maya
Mayavada, 476
Medical systems, 582–84
Medicines,
  cure by, 578–80
  right use of, 584–85

Melancholy, 180–81
Memory(ies), 70–71
  of dreams, 480–81
  from the subconscient, dealing with, 610
Menstrual problems, 589
Mental silence,
  and knowledge, 54–56
  makes possible strongest and freest action, 55–56
Mental difficulties,
  confusion, 22–23
  hastiness, 23–24
  opposing points of view, 25
  slowness, 24–25
  worry, 23
Mental training, meaning of, 69
Mental work, and sadhana,
  not easy to do at the same time, 47
Middleton Murry, John, 493
Mind,
  active, an obstacle which can become a great force, 6
  activity of, 20–21
  and Divine Consciousness, 5
  human, see Human mind
  and inspiration, 7
  and intuition, 6–7
  intuitivised, and perception, 7
  and the Light or the Force which comes from beyond mind, 20
  and the lower nature, 9–10
  mental development, 59–60, 61
  mind-energy, 40
  outer, 11, see also Intellect
  perverts the original intention of nature, 485, cf. Sex
  physical, see Physical mind
  and the psychic, 7–9
  a rigid instrument, 5
  and supermind, 5–6
  and the vital, 123–27
  waking, see Waking mind
  See also Intellect; Intelligence; Reason; cf. Mental . . .
Mistakes, 188, 206, 502, 693
  reparation for, 732
Mixing, with others, 325–26
Morphia, 585
The Mother,
  Her reasons and motives do not belong to the ordinary consciousness, 224

misunderstanding or misreporting Her statements, 198
wish for more physical nearness to or contact with, 122
Mothering others, 321–22
Movements,
  habitual, 401–5
  mechanical, 405–6
  vital, see Vital movements
  wrong, see Wrong movements
Mukti, 234
Music, hearing after waking, 452

N

Nature,
  human, see Human nature
  physical,
    exists by constant repetition, 361
Need, and desire, 257–58
Nervous being, 139, 519, 554, 562, 804
  unstable, over-sensitive or excitable, 563
Nervous envelope, 83, 335, 438–39, 558, 569
Nervous weakness, hereditary, 651
Neurasthenia, 802–4
New world,
  must come from within, 691
Night,
  darkest before the dawn, 364, 691
Nightmares,
  reaction of terror incompatible with the demands of the Yoga, 469
Nigraha, 266
Nirvana,
  Sri Aurobindo's experience of, 683
Non-cooperation, vital, 138–39

O

Obscuration / obscurity, 390–91
Obstruction, 389–91
Offering, in the lower vital, 168–69
Ojas, 490
  and *retas*, 500, 503, 505
Onions, 434–35
Opinion,
  only the Divine's matters, 89
Optimism, and pessimism, 692
Ordeal, 365
  decisive, of this Yoga, 150–56

Others,
  concern for, 320–21
  dispersion through contact with, 323–25
  drawing of vital forces by, 335–37
  helping, 317–20
  imposition of pet ideas on, 5
  limiting contacts with, 337–38
  meeting or mixing with, 249, 325–26
  mothering, 321–22
  receiving help from, 320
  sympathy for, 321
  talking or thinking about, 334–35
  true unity with, 283, 285
  working with, 322–23
Overmind Maya, and power of affirmation or rejection, 561
Overself, personal, 494
Overstraining, 382

P

Pain, 572–77
  and cosmic consciousness, 572
  nervous, 573
  separation and detachment from, 575–77
  and suffering and sorrow, 177–80
  See also Suffering
Passion for reading or study,
  a force that wants to satisfy itself, 62
Passivity, wrong kind of, 393–94
Past (the),
  freedom from, 730–32
  and the future, 732–33
Path of Yoga, "hard to tread like the edge of a razor", 627
Peace,
  in the lower vital, 169
  Cf. Calm
Perfection, imperfections and progress towards, 655–63
Periods,
  of rest and assimilation, 374
Persona,
  the good and the evil, 647–53
Personal relations,
  and universal love, 304–6
  in Yoga, 302–4
Pessimism, and optimism, 692
Philosophy,
  of the early Greeks, 73

study of, 73–74
Physical (the),
  bringing realisation into, 366–67
  coming down into, 363–66
  mental and vital, 375–77
  and the mind, 383–84
  need to transform, 359–63
  and the psychic, 385–87
  use of violence to change it, 371
  and the vital, 127–28
  vital, see Vital physical; cf. Vital, and the physical
  and the vital, 384
  See also Physical …
Physical being,
  and the subconscient, 597–600
Physical consciousness, 372–74
  constitutionally ignorant, 414
  stupid and obscure, 369
Physical mind,
  activity of, 30–33
  and the brain, 35
  and the lower vital, 37–38
  obscurity of, 34–35
  and peace and silence, 39
  and the psychic, 38
  unsteadiness of, 33–34
Poetry, and sadhana, 78–79
Points of view, opposing, 25
Politeness, and Yogic siddhi, 655
Possession, by vital forces, 801–2
Power,
  of affirmation or rejection in a world governed by the Overmind Maya, 561
  divine, see Divine Force (Power)
  there is only one at work, 349
Praise and blame, 352–53
Pranayama, and sex, 511–12
Pravṛtti, and apravṛtti, 395
Pride, 241–43
Progress,
  comes by ever new waves of an inner Power, 193
  one's own, should be neither over-estimated nor underestimated, 184
Protection, Divine, 724–25
Psychic being (the Psychic),
  and knowledge, 53–54
  and the mind, 7–9
  and the vital, 120–22
  See also Soul; Weeping, psychic

Psycho-analysis,
  and the Integral Yoga, 612–16
Psychology, modern, 613
Pulling, 192
Purification, of the vital, 107

Q

Quarrels, 347–50
  and egoism, 348
Questioning,
  of spiritual experience, 37
Quiet (ude/ness), 27–29, 370, 714, cf. Calm; Silence
Quinine, 585

R

Rain, and tamas, 395
Ramakrishna, 19, 192, 276, 550–51, 659, 729, 750–51
Ramana Maharshi, 203, 209, 751
Rasa, 420
  sexual, 496
Reactions, vital, 129–30
Reading,
  and detachment, 64–65
  of novels or newspapers, 65–68
  and sadhana, 60–64
Reason,
  and the Divine, 634
  pure, and the intellect, 14–15
  See also Intellect; Intelligence; Mind
Recurrence,
  of illness at fixed times, 555
Rejection,
  of wrong movements, 707–8
  of the lower vital, 158–64
  of wrong vital movements, 143–45
Relations with others,
  between men and women in Yoga, 306–10, 545
  family ties, 291–92
  friendship and affection, 294–98
  helping and receiving help, 317–20
  old, 293–94
  in ordinary life, 344–45
  parents and children, 293
  "partner" versus companion, 309
  in yoga, 283–90, 302–4
Religions, 102
Remorse, 188

Repentance, 188
Resistance,
  of the lower vital, 157–58
  physical, whole base of denial of the Divine, 360
  subjective and objective, 668–70
  vital, 136–38
  and the hostile forces, 767–68
Resolution, need of, 712–13
Rest,
  need of, 438–40
  which restores, 441–43
Restlessness, 400–1
  vital, 132–34
Retas, and *ojas*, 500, 503, 505
Retirement,
  dangers of complete, 337, 341–44
  qualified utility for sadhana, 339–41
Return, of vital movements after rejection, 145–48
Review, of the past, 610
Revolt, of the vital, 141–42
Rig Veda, 688
Right (the),
  the dynamic side in women, 478
Rising up of things,
  from the subconscient, 603–8
Roman (the),
  and the Greek, 210
Royal road to the Divine, 627
Rudra power, 271
Russell, Bertrand, 17

S

Sadhak,
  "advanced", 223
  each has his own separate sadhana, 630
Sadhana,
  descending into the vital, 123, 124
  each sadhak has his own, 630
  great secret of, 729
  meaning of, 78
  no better mental foundation for, 195
  physical, 367–71
  and poetry, 78–79
  and reading, 60–64
  resistances in, 667–70
  and sleep, 444–45
  and study, 69
  and writing, 77–78
  Cf. Integral Yoga; Yoga

Sadness,
  vital, and psychic sorrow, 378
Sati, 753
Schopenhauer, Arthur, 476
Sciatica, 589–90
Science,
  and classification, 16
  study of, 75
Self, subliminal, 613
Self-control, psychic, 87
Self-esteem, 242
Self-giving, a change from ego-centricity to God-centricity, 229
Selfishness, 238–39
Self-justification, 154
Self-observation, and mastery over the inner universe, 26
Self-respect, 243
Self-vision, true, 26
Sensitivity / Sensitiveness, 210–13
  to small and outward things, 368
  to smell, 425–26
Sentimentalism, 210
Seriousness, 174–75
Sex,
  and Ananda, 488–90
  and disorders of the system, 503
  harm of, 495–96
  "lighter movements", 491–92
  and love, 490–93
  mastery of,
    through a change in consciousness, 512
    through the force of purity, 512–13
    through the working of the higher consciousness / force, 513–14
  masturbation, 531–34
  mixing spirituality with, 500, 502
  a movement of general nature, 486–88
  and the new European mystics, 493–94
  not always feeble in its going, 514
  and pranayama, 511–12
  role of in nature, 485–86
  sexual difficulties, *see* Sexual difficulties
  and skin diseases, 545
  and social contact, 538–40
  and the subconscient, 520–21
  thoughts and imaginations, 522–24
  and touch, 540–41
  See also Sex-...; Sexual...; Sexuality
Sex-dreams,
  and emissions, 524–31

physical causes of, 528–29
and worry and depression, 529–31
Sex-energy,
  transformation of, 504–8
Sex-impulse,
  mastery of, through detachment, 508–12
  rejection from the various parts of the being, 514–19
  and tamasic inertia, 522
Sex-indulgence,
  and the Integral Yoga, 494–99
  subtle forms of, 499–504
Sex-vampirism, 336
Sexual difficulties,
  among men, 524–31
  among women, 534–38
Sexuality, vital, 534
Shaw, George Bernard, 17
Shiva, 287
Shyness, 213
Silence,
  keeping, 92–94
  mental, *see* Mental silence
  Cf. Calm; Quiet
Silliness, 25
Sincerity, vital, 113
Skin diseases, and sex, 545
Sleep,
  all full of dreams, 455
  amount needed, 440–41
  asserting one's will in, 449
  changed into an inner mode of consciousness, 438
  concentration before and after, 450–51
  conscious, 448–50
  a curative agency, 440
  depression in, 452–54
  during the day, 444
  getting good sleep, 443–44
  going into the vital world during, 446
  hearing music after waking, 452
  and illness, 572
  loss of consciousness during, 445–47
  need of, 438–40
  one is acting on one plane or another throughout, 455
  and sadhana, 444–45
  two accounts of: scientific and occult-spiritual, 443
  and the waking mind, 452
  yogic attitude towards, 437–38

Slough of Despond, 201, 681
Smell, sensitivity to, 425–26
Smoking, 436
Sorrow,
  gospel of, 189–206
  and joy, 177
  and pain and suffering, 177–80
Soul,
  "complementary", 310
  evolution of, 379
  human, cannot be dealt with by a set of mental rules, 249
  See also Psychic being
Spectator-actor-manager, 26
Speech,
  control of, 85–87, 94–95
  outer, and the inner life, 80–81
  in the past has worked as an expression of the vital, 88
  useless, unnecessary or light, 36, 83–85
Spinoza, 190
Spirit,
  and the vital, 116
Spiritual achievement, cannot be defined in a mental formula, 659–60
Spiritual downfall, most effective way to head towards, 500
Spiritual experience,
  must be accepted as it is, 37
  questioning of, 37
Sri Aurobindo,
  arrests in his sadhana, 782
  in a dream experience, 478
  experiences and realisations, 44–45, 205, 430, 683
  had doubts worse than any human mind can think of, 673
  has passed through most of the difficulties of the sadhak, 196
  more a hero by necessity than by choice, 682
  on his public writings and his writings to sadhaks, 657–58
  and the predictions of a Calcutta astrologer, 551–52
  works of,
    Essays on the Gita, 277
    Savitri, 205
    The Synthesis of Yoga, 232
Stammering, 588–89
Steiner, Rudolf, 483
Straining or tension, 191–93

Struggles,
  not indispensable to progress, 173
Study,
  of languages, 71–72
  of logic, 74
  and mental development, 69–71
  of philosophy, 73–74
  and sadhana, 69
  of science, 75
Stumbles, of the past, should not be regretted, 610
Stupidity, 412–14
Subconscient (the),
  change of, 595
  clearing or emptying, 611
  dealing with, 608–10
  and environmental consciousness, 601–2
  and habits, 600–1
  illumining, 611–12
  and the inner and the outer being, 596–97
  and the physical being, 597–600
  rising up of things from, 603–8
Subliminal self, 613
Suffering,
  and pain and sorrow, 177–80
  spiritual, gospel of, 681
  See also Pain
Suggestions,
  of being an instrument to help someone else on the path, 236
  as means of attack by hostile forces, 776–80
  vital, 130–32
Suicide, 206
  absurdity of, 747–53
Sunlit path / road, 192, 618, 628
  and the path of gloom or darkness, 173, 681–91
Sun-treatment (for eyes), 588
Superconscient (the),
  the true foundation of things, 616
Superiority, 243–44
Supermind, and mind, 5–6
Suppression,
  of desire, 264–66
  on the same level as indulgence, 419
Surrender, of the vital, 109–10
Swadharma, 244
Sympathy, for others, 321

T

Tagore, Rabindranath, 17
Talking,
  about others, 334–35
  and dispersion of consciousness, 81–82
  and fatigue, 82–83
  and vital interchange, 333–34
Tamas,
  dealing with, 396
  difficulty of eliminating, 398
  See also Inertia
Taste, of food, 424–25
Temperament,
  one which the gods will not help, 698
Tension or straining, 191–93
Theory, an idea-script representing an imperfect human observation, 583
Thinking, about others, 334–35
Thought(s),
  come from outside, 40–43, 44
  control of, 43–47
  have an effective power, 457
  and knowledge, 48
  thought substance, 40
  and words, 47
Time, needed for change, 726–30
Training, mental, 69
Trance (*samādhi*), 639
  and ill health, 550
Transformation,
  of the sex-centre and its energy, 501
Troubles, help to prepare the victory of the soul, 269–70
True vital, emergence of, 111–13
Truth,
  each plane of consciousness has its own standard of, 90
  speaking, 86, 89–92
Tuberculosis, 586–87

U

Understanding,
  and the true or higher light, 52–53
  two kinds: by the intellect and in the consciousness, 53
Unity with others, true, 283, 285
Upanishads, most commentaries written out of the reasoning or speculating intellect, 73

V

Vairagya (*vairāgya*), 27, 286, 288, 614
Vaishnava movement, 305
Vaishnava sadhana, 192
Vampirism, 335–36
Vanity, 240
Veil between inner and outer consciousness, lifting of, 386
Vexation,
  by defects of others *etc.*, 36
Vicāra, 614
Victory,
  certitude of, 694–95
Vigilance, 86, 279–80
  need of, 709–12
Vindictiveness, 276
Violence, 276–77
  use of to change the physical, 371
Vision (eyesight), weakness of, 588
Vital (the),
  conversion of, 110–11
  deceptiveness of, 104–5
  discipline of, 107–9
  dissatisfaction of, 138–40
  disturbance of, 140–41
  dryness of, 134–36
  good instrument but bad master, 105–7
  and the higher consciousness, 116–20
  the higher vital movement, 111
  insatiable, 424
  and intuition, 120
  irrationality of, 103
  liberation of, 111
  living in, 101–3
  lower, *see* Lower vital
  and the mind, 123–27
  movements of, *see* Vital movements
  needs the opposites of joy and peace, 168
  non-cooperation of, 138–39
  peace and quiet in, 114–15
  and the physical, 127–28
  and the psychic, 120–22
  purification of, 107
  revolt of, 141–42
  sadhana descending into, 123, 124
  and the spirit, 116
  surrender of, 109–10
  true, *see* True vital
  vital love, 298–302
  See also Vital . . .

Vital comedy and drama, 200
Vital conditions,
  alternation of good and bad, 148–49
Vital forces,
  drawing of by others, 335–37
  possession by, 801–2
Vital movements,
  apparent increase when trying to control them, 125
  rejection of, 143–45
  return after rejection, 145–48
  wrong, 143–45
    of the lower vital, 158–64
Vital physical, small desires of, 256–57
Vital plane, experiences of, 121
Vivekananda, 659, 775
Voices, 42

W

Waking mind, and sleep, 452
Waking state, and dream state, 470–71
Waves, mental or vital, 337
Weakness(es),
  of the body, 381–84
  dwelling on one's, 739–43
  recognizing one's, 699–703
Weeping, psychic, 179
Wells, H.G., 17
Will,
  divine, *see* Divine Will
  and the Divine Force or Power, 720–22
  lack of, 719–20
  need of, 715–19
  weakness of, 393
Withdrawal, outer,
  and inner detachment, 338–39
Witness-control, 26
Woman-complex,
  vital, removal of, 511
Work,
  and illness, 571–72
  mental, 47
  right attitude in, 109
  working with others, 322–23
World, new, 691
Wounded feeling, 247–50
Writing, and sadhana, 77–78
Wrong movements, 129
  of the lower vital, 158–64
  rejection of, 707–8
  of the vital, 143–45

Y

Yoga,
  and fear, 278–80
  bitter like poison in the beginning, sweet as nectar in the end, 628
  drawing others to, 325
  and illness, 549–52
  integral, *see* Integral Yoga
  a spiritual battle, 780
  three causes of collapse in, 809
  "Yoga without tears", 627
  See also Integral Yoga; Yogi; Yogic ...; *cf.* Sadhana

Yogi, can bear the whole world's suffering in himself, 674
Yogic attitude,
  towards food/sleep, 419–21, 437–38
Yogic concentration, three forms of, 20
Yogic control,
  can come in one of two ways, 46
Yogic force, cure by, 578–80
Yogic thought, 9